The
Valorous

Caucasian Manifesto

outskirts
press

Outskirts Press, Inc.
http://www.outskirtspress.com

ISBN: 978-1-9772-0630-5

PRINTED IN THE UNITED STATES OF AMERICA

-Behold Our Truth-

"Age Of The Caucasians"

Let all who read our truth, (our racial biography!) and its declaration of *Identity*, *Purpose* and *Destiny*, cast upon us no doubts as to our spirituality and intellectual quest. Born of our Fematrix- "Caucasia" (the She!) and forged in the biology of her will, we her posterity have taken the path and challenge of *Eternal life!*...her *Immortality!*, the everlastingness of her Caucasian kind, our- *Sovereign Racial Dynasty!* Having thus-*Pledged!*... we will not be dissuaded from this path and its objective, believing it to be our wisest course, and in accordance with life's natural order. Therefore, in the spirit of our truth further determined, and to all those in disagreement?... may you, and that which you believe?...go in peace! For you are not of us, nor we of you!...and may our separate- *Racial, Social,* and *Spiritual Paths,* know not *Misfortune.*

To
Honor and Preserve
Our August Ancestral Trust

We are the "Caucasians," a prime "Sovereign Racial Dynasty." A people of *Purpose*, *Faith* and *Intellect*. Yes, we have earned our place in this world! At great cost to themselves in both *Suffering* and *Death*, our Caucasian *Forefathers* and *Mothers* bestowed upon us their wondrous-*Dynasty!*...of more then 40 thousand years. This included their *Territory*, their *Discoveries*, and their *Culture*, but their greatest gift was their *Genes*, which gave us our *Intelligence, Identity, Beauty* and *Health*. For these gifts we as Caucasians should be eternally grateful, and we should honor them above all else, so that when we are gone, there will be those who will honor us!

"Ancestral Veneration"
(We Are What We Do!)

I

Mission Statement

- Our Journey -
Past - Present - Future

Let it be understood: The Holy Valorous: is a levy of *Caucasian Intellectual* and *Historical Property,* being a moral requisition by our ancestral trust, in this time of our *Racial Ambivalence*. Its work is dedicated to the preservation of *Caucasian Kind!*...and their- *Biological Mandate!* It is an eclectic-intellectual harvest, gathered by the-*Alpha,* so that a "True Voice" may be given to the *Hearts* and *Minds* of those Caucasians who believe in the *Sovereignty* and *Unity* of the Caucasian world.

Likewise, a celebration of the historical particulars which mark the *Genius* and enduring *Essence* and *Spirit* of the Caucasian race of people; *Education*, *Laws, Literary Character, Art* of *War, Public* and *Private Manners*. And yes, "Valor"…let us not forget their Valor!, that which would storm the very gates of *Hell itself,* if its position were known. Alas, in pursuance of these understandings, *Truths, Factors* and *Policies,* there will probably be singled out for "Condemnation" from this book, doctrines which taken by themselves, may readily be made to seem utterly wrong. Therefore, with a view to clearness, I have treated separately correlative aspects of "Racial Reality" its natural inherited conduct and it unsympathetic historical journey, drawing conclusions either of which becomes misunderstood if divorced from the other; and have thus given abundant opportunity for one's deeper insight into the natural truth of our *Caucasian Racial Dynasty* and *its living Spirituality!*

The understanding of such "Racial Reality" symbolizes the abeyance of one's *Caucasian Racial Morality* as it is, and as it should be! And only *Peril* and *Caucasian Degradation* will result from the violation of the "Holy Valorous" its *Truths, Boundaries, Ideals!*..and all that they imply. As a race of people, we need to *Consecrate Our Future* and *Defend It!* To this, we must all pledge!

Content Directory

Prologue: The Alpha's Proclamation

Reality
(the unforgiving!)

To
"All Caucasians"

Our Caucasian *Racial Spirituality* and *Biology* are one! And therefore, we most not, and will not be in denial of it! In a world of competitive beings, (we know of no other!) the Creation, Identity, Union and Defense of one's *Kind!* from others of a different biological character aggregate, is paramount for- *Survival.* Therefore, *He* or *She* of a bio-specific determination (bio-dynasty!) who fails to understand and embrace this universal edict, will come to learn the lessen of all transgressors. (great misery and death!)

Only love for our racial kind could creat us, and only love for our racial kind will defend us!...thereby creating the call for a "Caucasian Empire" to safeguard our *Bio-Dynasty*, declaring all Caucasian to become one with the "Empire" hence, the words of our eternal *Faith* and *Salvation.*

"Blessed Are The Caucasians"

We Must Never Fail
To
"Cherish And Defend Our Racial Heritage"

I

Reality
(the unforgiving!)

"Our Biological Dynasty"
(Unique Unto Ourselves)

We Caucasians are living in a world and during an age (*21st* century!) of intense- *Racial Competition,* and the law of survival of the fittest is everywhere in evidence. Because of these facts, all who would enjoy enduring success must go about its attainment through the use of power!... and "Racial Identity" our living biology is the ultimate power, its boldness has *Genius* and *Magic* in it.

For same- *40* thousand years, our bio-dynasty known to the world, as the "Caucasians Race" (*The Conquerors!*) have taken our rightful place at the very forefront of the *Fematrix* quest for immortality. But, if we as Caucasians fail to preserve our *Unique Racial Characteristics!*...that which is expressed in our- *Culture, Faith* and *Science,* by letting subversive "Alien" others!..who are not of us, nor we of them, to infiltrate our principal decision making bodies- *Political, Economical, and Educational,* these being the very *Hart* and *Soul* of Caucasian society. And if we Caucasians of the *21st* century, fail now!..to do and say what is right to combat this "Alien Invasion," it being our greatest detriment!..the alternative will not be a sustainable Caucasian future, and our *Posterity* will pay the price for our Cowardice! (their dishonor, fear, misery and death!) and, where we Caucasians end up?...by "Countering" our "Enemies" depends ultimately on *When* and *How* we begin!

Our Caucasian Racial Sovereignty
Is
"Sacrosanct"

My
Caucasian Brothers and Sisters

All "Beliefs" are acquired by the understanding of our *Physical* and *Intellectual* encounters, and this in part has created for us humans two *Cardinal Conversations:* One being "Social" (cosmetic-superficial!) and the other being "Intellectual" (imperative-reality!) bringing about for all of us, both *Positive* and *Negative* in action. Therefore, the power to think as you wish to think is the only power over which you have absolute control, only by completing your *Intellectual* and *Spiritual* journey through the Holy Valorous will you come to *Know* and *Embrace* your "Racial Ancestral Trust" (bio-inheritance!) and your Caucasian historical life strategy, which sponsors your journey, and that of your people!

Thereby, giving to all Caucasians their wondrous gifts of *Spirit, Family, Cognizance,* and *Racial Virtue*, all part of their millenniums of *Trial* and *Error,* their *Biological Dynasty!*

Hence, my gift to you!...when in the absence of the light of truth, mental darkness will always prevail, may the "Holy Valorous" on your journey!... be a "Light" for you in dark places, when all other lights have failed.

-Blessed are the Caucasians-
John Rolland (Alpha,Loc)

The
Alpha's Paradigm
- Reality -
"Our Caucasian Future"

The Alpha tells us: In all of the universe, and that of its existences, there is but one that "determines all outcomes" in *Decisions, Compliance, Transgression,* and *Faith,* and this "Existence" is known to all by one name *Reality!* It is independent of ideas concerning it!..and also of all other things and from which all other things derive. Furthermore, as "Caucasians," having the quality of being *Actual* and *True,* an entity, a biological event without equal, must determine our future by the state of things that actually exist rather then as they may appear or might be imagined. Our Caucasian "Racial kind" is the work of our free mind; it is the biological artistic expression of our *Necessity, Desire,* and *Choice.* Hence, our Caucasian cultural existence is the wellspring of our being, and the sacred heritage of our children. When Reality is telling us: that our "Enemies" are at our gates! And that our "Future" and that of our children's is in great *Peril!* We as "Caucasian Racial Traditionalists" must now and always reject intellectual "Retreat" and "Pacifism" in the face of an "Alien Invasion" with a hostile and total disregard for our *Sovereignty* and *Laws.* We must not fail to determine our own *Supremacy* of *Authority*, in terms of our rightful *Destiny!*..nor fail *now!*...to answer the- *Alpha's Clarion Call* for "All Caucasians" from the core of their "Spirituality" to move out of "Complacency" and unite and make ready for the *Defense* of our- *Caucasian Racial Dynasty's Survival!* (hostile *Alien* and *Caucasian Apostate* forces are gathering!)

"On The Conduct Of Each Depends The Fate Of All"

Prologue

The
Alpha's Proclamation

~~

"We Are The Caucasians"
"None shall break faith, so say we all"

It is the forty second millennium of our "Fematrix", the Caucasian Century - *421*AC (AFTER CAUCASIA!)

Let it be understood by all! Being compelled by a love for my people, I have written this manifesto in order to counter the grip of *Intellectual Failure* that has taken hold of Caucasian America and her sister states throughout the world.

I shall begin with our ancestors: it is both just and proper that they should have the honor of the first mention on this present occasion. They dwelt throughout the world without a break in the succession from generation to generation and handed it down free to the present time by their valor.

And if our more remote ancestors deserve praise, much more do our own fathers and mothers, who added to our inheritance the "Nations" that we Caucasians now possess and spared no pains to be able to leave their newest acquisition, "America" to us of the present Caucasian generation.

Therefor, If a test of Caucasian American worth be wanted, it is to be found in their historical chronicle, and this not only in cases in which it set the final seal upon their merit, but also in which it gave the first intimation of their having any, for there is justice in the claim that steadfastness in their country's battles should be as a cloak to cover their imperfections, and their merit as Caucasian racial beings more than outweigh their demerits as individuals.

So in the business before them they thought fit to act boldly and trust in themselves.

Thus choosing to die resisting, rather than to live submitting, they fled only from dishonor, but met danger face to face. So lived and died our intrepid forefathers and mothers as they created and became- *Caucasian America!*

Alas, there are few parts of America that have not been augmented by those of us here, while Caucasian America has been furnished by us with everything that can enable her to depend on her own resources, whether for *War* or for *Peace.*

But what was the road by which we reached our present position? What was the form of government under which our greatness grew, or of the *Ready Valor* with which our fathers stemmed the tide of *Alien Aggression*? And what were the *Racial* and *Cultural* habits out of which it sprang?... these are the questions whose answers will bring us back to that which we have lost,...our *Caucasian Racial Faith*!

Religious freedom, political freedom, economic freedom, and in generosity, we Caucasians are equally singular, acquiring our friends by conferring, not by receiving favors, and it is only the Caucasians who, fearless of consequences, confer their benefits not from calculations of expediency, but in the confidence of liberality. We Caucasians as a race of people have forced every sea and land to be the highway of our daring, and everywhere, have left imperishable monuments behind us.

Such is the America for which Caucasians, in the assertion of their resolve not to lose her, nobly fought and died, and well may every one of their survivors be ready to suffer in her cause, for the America that I celebrate is only what the heroism of Caucasians and their spirituality have made her. Indeed, if I have dwelt at some length upon the character of our race, it has been to show that our stake in the coming struggle (Caucasian racial sovereignty!) is not the same as others, (aliens) who have no such blessings to lose! Therefore, in order to fully understand the magnitude of the "Caucasian World Crisis*"* this manifesto will explore the various root causes and speaks to all the aspects of the illness (liberal zealotry!) that has caused the Caucasian American Community's *Academics* and *Politicians* to forsake their "Ancestral Racial Trust" for the blind pursuit of social fallacies, knowing perfectly well that to abandon that "Sacred Racial Trust*"* means the undoing of their *Cultural Legacy* and the very future of Caucasian generations to come.

Since the theories of racial conflict (by liberal zealots) are generally predicated on the premise of a one sided racial *Hatred?* (Caucasian malice only!) the "*Valorous*" and its message is of great importance to all Caucasians with a desire for *Racial Coexistence* and a true and well founded racial understanding.

What gives us all a claim to the luster of our worth is a deep hunger for one's *Identity*, the belonging and bonding with one's own kind! Although this truth is universal in all of life, there are those Caucasians, who think it is *wrong* to believe in one's given biology.(racial kind!)

To them, Caucasian racialness (our subspecies identity) does not exist? But yet, they have no trouble accepting and celebrating the racial identity and self praising's of alien others? This of course is- *Liberal Intellectual Subversive Deceit*! As for myself ?...the truth has always been within me! The Caucasian race and its eclectic culture has been for me a light in the darkness of the world, a steady beacon, shining through the endless storms that ravish humankind, bringing to them the light of *Hope* in their despair.

As to Caucasian Superiority?...I will leave that to the sages of history, for only they will be there in the end to crown the biological mandate of the victor.

But as to our greatness as *Caucasians* there is no doubt!...we are life's premier force in this realm of competitive beings.

Yes, like all those that came before us, we Caucasians are one of a kind, *Unique* and *Special,* hence our time in this life is precious, because this time, is the time of the "Caucasians"...our time! And if we fail in our bio-mandate (immortality!) our time in this creation will be forfeited, and we Caucasians like all of histories defeated,...will never be seen again!

Therefore, our task as Caucasian *Man* and *Woman* is before us, and with great pride and love in our difference and uniqueness from all others, we take our place, as full members in the trials and tribulations of the-*Caucasian Conquest!*

But, there are "Caucasian Liberal Zealots Apostates" in America and throughout the world, who would suppose that by having such a pride in our own identity makes us a type of "Social Terrorist" which they refer to as "White Racism" and it is this kind of "Deceptive Accusation" (to demonize!) that is of itself a form of *Social Terrorism* against Caucasian racial pride! It is the mark!...the scarlet letter of old?...used now by minority races and their coconspirators the *Racial Abolitionists* (Caucasian liberal zealot academia!) to break the spirit of Caucasian racial identity.

Hence, in reality a "Devious Plan" designed to hide the facts of their own subversive *Cultural* and *Political* agenda, "Caucasian Identity Capitulation" our total surrender! Yes, that's right! Caucasian Americans are now expected to surrender their *Culture*, forfeit their *Identity*, and forgo any display of *Racial Pride*, both publicly and privately.

In addition, Caucasians are now socially mandated by *Caucasian Racial Apostates* to publicly brand any and all "Caucasian Citizens" who dare to express their racial pride, as *White Racist Malcontents.*

Alien-*Racial Duplicity!*...is at hand in our Caucasian American Community, and for any Caucasian to not recognize it?..is either a complete fool!..or a co-conspirator?

As for myself, this manifesto that I have written will be looked upon as a very undesirable social document by both *Caucasian Liberal Zealots* and *Alien Social Poachers*, not to mention the political congressional community in general. This is due in part to the nature of this book, because it deals in very *Uncomfortable Truths*, truths that most academics and legislators choose to debate in intellectual shadows rather than public forums, for after all!...is it not our own *Intellectual silence!..*that heralds our genuine-*Capitulation*? Hence, enough said about the cowardly souls that inhabit our political houses and institutions of higher learning.

To our Fematrix (the Caucasian female) and to her social and biological concept of *Race* and *Family*, this social quest is due. *Race* and *Family* are the rare flowers whose presence is to be cherished and guarded. It is with *Race* and *Family*, with *Race* and *Families* very presence that the finest fruits of humankind are to be found, cultivated, perpetuated and enjoyed as the dearest of our eternal possessions; and those Caucasians who cherish them as such, may hopefully find their place in the pages of this book, as *Caucasian Pilgrims* on a journey to their *Earned* and *Rightful* destiny.

The
Racial Apocalypse
(the racial reckoning)

There can be no doubt about the truth of this assertion!

Truth is not mine! I can only align myself with it, and of all truth, this one is very clear. The realm of Caucasian America is besieged with -*Multiracial*- competitive strife, both *Cultural* and *Political.*

Because of this, the Caucasian American community as well as its sister Caucasian states throughout the world have become bewildered hosts to an internal *Needs* and *Values* conflict, between opposing- *Racial Incompatibles*!

In other words, if you are not of our Caucasian race! Then it stand to reason that you are an alien!..and of an alien race, a conflicting life strategy, hence confirming- *Incompatibility!*

Moreover, what too many Caucasian Americans fail to realize is that this very conflict of *Racial Incompatibility,*

"Different Races" with different competing life strategies, is beginning to heat up!...and show signs of becoming a War! With *Racial Minorities* in a state of combat with each other,(gang-mongering) and their deep seated *Racial Hatred* for the *Caucasian American Community*'s prevailing *Success.*

Hence, their *Envy* and *Jealousy!*...leading them to a conscious *Racial Malice* and a desire to inflict injury on *Innocent Caucasians!*...is now creeping out of their enclaves and into the Caucasian Community's domain.

Than, add to this our cowardly *Caucasian Leadership*, plus the feckless *Public Media's* criminal disregard for the truth!...and their -*Alien Minority Pandering*!- speaks volumes for the "Future" of our Caucasian American com-munity in general. So, let it now be said,…if the social and cultural pathology of "Hyenic Tribalism" between these alien racial minorities continues *Unchecked,* and on its present course, we Caucasian Americans will be forced (for our own survival!) into a defensive *Racial, Cultural*, and *Political* position.

Thereby bringing about a very *Racially Belligerent* and *Divided Nation,* of which, will exacerbate the situation and lead to a much larger conflict!...an all-out "Racial War," in other words; a *Caucasian- Reconquest of America!*

And if you think this is a threat on my behalf?..you are sadly mistaken!...

it is an obvious historical prediction, of which one hopes will never occur! (that's providing the races divide into "Separate States" peacefully?) But, faced with our present ongoing "Racial Reality"...and nature's historical and natural *Competitive Selection!*...it would behoove one to consider and prepare for!..never the less.

As we all know, in any war there are always *Sacrifices* to be made and always *Casualties* to be suffered.

This suffering and these sacrifices are made bearable only by the knowledge that the Caucasian American mission, our *Mission, Hope,* and *Ideal,* is right and good. And if we are forced into a *Physical Battle* to secure our very own future, "We Must Win," no other outcome will be acceptable!

For if we do not drive the *Alien Cultural Marauders* and *Caucasian Racial Capitulators* (liberal zealot subversives!) from our lands, thereby defeating our enemies!..it will be our "Caucasian American Culture" and all of its great worth, that will not survive!

We as Caucasian Americans, must look into the face of this "*Unnatural Multiracial State*" and its reality!

First of all, *People* make the culture- not the other way around, and culture fosters the "Ruling Government" this is truth, this is reality.

Hence, the *Caucasian Democratic Culture* is all about organized numbers. (its Achilles heel!)

In other words, in Caucasian America, those who have the numbers control the *Vote*, and those who control the *Vote*, create the *Culture*, the *Laws*, and thereby the *Future!*

Think for a moment!...*Alien Racial Emigration*? Yes, that *Nightmare!* There is no "Neutral Ground" no shades of gray, the alien racial gauntlet (challenge!) for *Political* and *Cultural Control* against *Caucasian America* has been dropped, and their line has been drawn! (Sanctuary Cities!)

Hence, my clarion call to all Caucasians of *Cultural* and *Racial Faith*, we must prepare; *Stout Hearts* and *Steady Minds* are needed, *Financing* is needed.

And if war should raise its ugly head?...our "Caucasian American Community" must be defended,..we must be *Victorious*!

And if we are *United* and *Determined*, we will be!

We must take our *Racial* and *Cultural Crusade* to the *Homes, Streets* and *Cities* of Caucasian America, as well as the rest of the Caucasian world. We must expose this deadly path of Caucasian racial, political, and cultural destruction that our *Deceitful* and *Cowardly* leaders have put us on!

Furthermore, if we are to *Save Ourselves* and our *Society*, we must be vigilant in our task. We must not allow our *Caucasian Crusade* to become derailed by liberal zealots and their *Subversive Doctrines* of Caucasian *Racial* and *Cultural Capitulation*!

My friends, my Caucasian racial compatriots, this advancing *Cultural* and *Racial War* for us, is not going well!

We Caucasian Americans, as well as our kindred states throughout the world, are embattled on "Four Competitive" fronts, *Cultural, Political, Economical* and *Racial.*

It does not take a genius to recognize the pounding that we've been taking on the *Cultural Front!*

Besides the *"Drugs"* and *"Crime"* of epidemic proportion, and having our children's minds submerged in endless sounds of *Immoral Lyrics, Hyenic Behavior* and *Gender Distortion,* all this being encouraged and politically sponsored by *Caucasian liberal zealot's.* But worse than that, is their wretched social formula for the *Cultural* and *Academic* dismantling (betrayal!) of their own Caucasian Communities, which has now sealed their fate!

Yes, they must be, and will be held accountable!

This of course, is not to be confused with the inattentive Caucasian public's acceptance of double standards when it comes to alien races, all of which stands virtually unopposed by any political party! (political subterfuge!) Still, and without a doubt the most tragic of all is the public media's debilitating illness *Degenerate Credibility.* (we will miss their loyalty and courage!) As I gaze out at the *Cultural Battle field,* I see us in full headlong retreat. We run from no adversary! Even as we lose ground on the *Cultural Front*, we have become badly mauled on the *Political Front.*

The Caucasian American community has been abandoned, *Cruelly Misled* and *Politically Deceived* by both antiquated ruling political parties, *Democrats* and *Republicans.* Who's egregious legislative betrayal let the liberal *Fifth Columnists* have their way with us, affirmative action, hidden racial quotas, unqualified minority races taking precedence over more qualified Caucasians in *Colleges, Industry,* and *State* and *Federal* agencies, besides, the newest liberal totalitarian mandate, *Political Correctness*!

It is this *PC-mob* that enforces and normalizes the major agenda of the *Liberal Zealots* dismantling of our Caucasian *Schools, Neighborhoods,* and *Workplaces.* Furthermore, our Caucasian universities are now required to *Remove or Downgrade* the traditional courses in *Western Civilization* and the writings of the great *Caucasian Minds* that created it.

Third-world writings and multicultural courses and their like, govern curricula in our colleges as well as most *K-12* public schools.

The social bedrock of Caucasian American principal, *"Freedom* of *Speech"* is now under frightening liberal review! Any censoring of free speech on public issues is the first and fatal step onto a slippery slope, falling from freedom to repression.

When a government's subjective interpretation of proper *Speech* and *Press* becomes more and more restrictive, it will begin to constitute an- *Unstable Social Mixture!*

In the case of Caucasian America, the government has reverted to *Liberal Totalitarianism*, with a direct and deliberate assault against Caucasian Americans with the historical norm of *Guarded* and *Gagged Speech!*...and all *Caucasian Traditionalists* are now denied open freedom of speech!

Any Caucasian American making a rebuttal (opposing claim) against the *PC-mob* and its *Multiculturalism* or a rightful criticism of another *Racial Group* (other then we Caucasians!) is at once branded a *Racist Hatemonger* by all the powers that be. (*Sedition!*...against Caucasian America?)

In other words, the Caucasian American Community (founders and builders of America!) will now be punished for what they *Think* and *Say*!

Is this true? Are we Caucasian Americans now being singled out for "Oppression" by our own government?

It is only now, that we Caucasian Americans have begun to assess the situation and regroup. Yes, we are losing *Cultural* and *Political* ground to *Alien Subversives* and their *Caucasian Apostates!*...and it is always more difficult to regain what has been lost, but we must do it. Only the news from the "Economic Front" bolsters my enthusiasm and allows us the taste of full victory. (yes!..victory, its a war!)

However, even there we must not be lax! There are projections that even on the economic front; we will suffer tremendous *Job Casualties* by outsourcing our industrial production and technology to unregulated alien countries.

All of Americas *Corporate Flight!*...is the result of an enormous *Corporate Taxation.* (government legislated piracy)

What does all this mean? On the whole: it presents a very frightening picture of Caucasian Identity and Cultural capitulation, our Intellectual retreat, and Market vulnerability.

Putting it together with the fact that we have lost all hope of any competent leadership, *Democrat* or *Republican,* not to mention the rise of *Liberal Progressive Treachery* and its acts of "Alien Criminal Appeasement" in the name of their subversive "Equality"...which is now beginning to "Subjugate" Caucasian Americas *Moral* and *Political* will.

Hence, making *Sanctuaries* for any number of alien *Racism Hustlers* (victim industry!) along with- *Caucasian Intellectual Cowards,* and it spells disaster!

And, if what has just been said, alarms you?

The next two social truths will not improve your comfort zone! There now seems a sharp reluctance in the media, and in most political circles to accept that *No Progress At All!* has been made in stemming- *Alien Cultural Militancy* (alien social subversion!) in Caucasian America, and which will continue to escalate, becoming a *Social* and *Political Doomsday Scenario* for the Caucasian world community.

The Alpha view: You cannot live in Peace and Safety with something that you cannot Trust or Control!...as to Parasitic "Alien Racial Combatants"...in the millions?

By abandoning *Racial Prudence* in the guise of social understanding, and a lack of anecdotal liberal experience has led to wrong conclusions on behalf of *Alien Races* and their desire to become submerged into *Liberal Utopia*!

Caucasian rule over alien racial cultures is hopeless; they will never *Assimilate* or *Recognize* Caucasian authority! For you see, our illness (liberal delusion) has been exposed!

Furthermore, the scramble for competitive biased media, and the great need for liberal zealot pressure groups to sustain themselves obscure more obvious and often more dramatic alien trends of *"Racial Hatred"* for Caucasian success!

And in particular they obscure a great deal of bad news pertaining to alien social and cultural *Urban Warfare*! (physical mob assaults!) against the "Caucasian American People" and their community.

This is truth, this is our reality,...and we all know it!

And should it not be said, and is it not the truth, that these alien races *Boldly* and *Openly* declare it?

And is it not a fact, that you, as well as many other Caucasians *See it,* and *Feel it* every day? (alien entrenched scapegoating of Caucasian America!) Are we now forbidden to address this assault?

The facts are; that the very social and cultural supply lines that the *Caucasian American Community* depend so highly on, *Family, Language, Education, Morality* and *Common Decency,* are being- *Culturally* and *Judicially Sabotaged* (betrayed!) by our *Enemies*!..the "Caucasian Liberal Zealots"

Who, along with their "Alien Cultural Subversives" (minority races!) both *Inside* and *Outside* of government are the greatest threats to our "Caucasian American" future!

My Caucasian brothers and sisters, make no mistake, this war is accelerating,...there is no place to *Hide*, and no place to *Run!*...we are in a *Historical Struggle* for the "Survival" of our Caucasian way of life, and I for one have no intention of standing idly by in silence, while totalitarian liberal zealots and their alien hycnic cultural raiders suppress Caucasian *Racial Identity,* and lay siege to our most cherished- *Institutions* and *Moral Standards*.

If I must, I will concede my very last breath to guarantee that our people, the *Noble* and *Valorous Caucasians* both in America and throughout the world, "Survive" along with our way of life!...*None of us should do less!*

To all Caucasian men and women of *Racial Faith,* history judges all of us and our deeds with a cruel honesty, the reckoning of time will bear no excuses,...for we as the Caucasians; creators of the modern world and its foreseeable future, must come to terms with those who oppose us!...we can no longer remain silent!...we must become proactive in our own *Defense!*...

both *Verbally,* and if need be- *Physically*!

Hence, I stand ready to be judged!

I expect nothing less than the scrutiny of the ages.

I fear no judgment!..should I stand alone with my back to the proverbial wall, resisting all *Cultural Usurpers*, *Moral Marauders, Elected Political Merchants* (graft takers!) and all those *Aliens Subversive* who seek to bring about the "Destruction" of the "Caucasian Race" and its future, I will resist!.. and if need be- *Fight Honorably* with only one goal alive in my heart, to see the *Noble People* that I love!...continue with their great journey, (the Caucasian Conquest!) knowing those things we of the "*Caucasian American Community*" hold dear, will continue to determine the path of our world.

I, for myself, could do no less; for I am a *Caucasian Racial Fundamentalist* and a *Democratic Monarchist* in the service of my people *The Valorous Caucasians*. Therefore, as we Caucasians enter and compete in the new age (the 42nd millennium) we must *Reeducate* and *Rededicate* ourselves to honoring the great legacy of our "Caucasian Ancestral

Trust" and the future they envisioned for us and our children. So, I intend to work very hard for the betterment of all life on this planet, and I can best do that by *First* and *Foremost* seeing to the well being of my own people! Therefore, my Caucasian *Brothers* and *Sisters,* I implore you, don't do any less yourselves!

"Blessed are the Caucasians"

The Alpha's view: as a beginner in the understanding of your Racialness, and its greater meaning in your life, keep in mind always, the principle of Evolution through the operation of which everything physical is eternally reaching upward and trying to complete the cycle between finite and infinite intelligence. Hence, the Caucasian race; is a unique force unequaled within the biological cosmos! A most noteworthy example of our Fematrix "Caucasia" and her Evolution. From humble subsistence, to the developing and building of the greatest Empires on Earth.

Caucasian Definitive Thinking

"Definitive Thoughts Create Your Conditions"

The Alpha tells us: As a person you are the product of your thoughts, what you think "Definitively" you become!

This is at one and the same time the most *Important*, the most *Interesting*, and the most *Difficult* to discuss.

It is because, it will carry the average person far beyond the boundary line of their common experience and into a realm of *Thought* and *Spiritual Engagement*, where they are not very accustomed to dwelling. And unless one studies the "Holy Valorous" with an open definitive and spiritual mind, one will miss the very fulcrum upon which its *Truth Rests*, and without this, one can never complete their journey.

The "Holy Valorous" will bring you a conception of *Thought and Spirituality* that may carry you far above the level to which you have risen by the cultural processes to which you have been subjected to, and for this reason, you should not be discouraged if, at first reading, you do not fully grasp its depth. Most of us disbelieve that which we cannot fathom, and with this tendency in mind: I entreat, don't close your mind if you do not grasp all that is in the "Holy Valorous" at the first reading. One cannot understand something, when their mind has not been unfolded sufficiently to be able to grasp it! Search through the "Holy Valorous" diligently and you as a "Caucasian" will discover the path to the attainment of your *True Faith* and *Racial Orthodoxy!* "Caucasianism" and that of your *Definite Purpose!*

-Who you are?...Why you are?...Where you are?-

"Blessed are the Caucasians"

Caucasian Reasoning
(the greatest facilitator of learning and knowledge)

Skills-Values-Beliefs-Habits-Methods

The Alpha tells us, that true "Reasoning" is the act or process of acquiring general knowledge for developing the power of *Reasoning* and *Judgment* and generally preparing oneself or others intellectually for a *Competitive* and *Hostil* life. And if you think for one moment that you know the intricacies of a competitive and hostil life?...think of this! Every living thing (and they are in the billions!) are unique unto themselves in both *Mind* and *Body* having no equal, and all!..consider all!..to be on the *Menu!*

"Reasoning"
(the acquisition of knowledge)

Both *Pictures, Symbols* and *Writings* have been passed down from one generation to next in Caucasian society's throughout the world for more then *40* thousand years, and it has been this vast amount of organized "Facts" and "Knowledge" combined with the faculties of the Caucasian mind, an unprecedented *"Intellectual Reasoning Genius"* that would bring about "The Caucasians Age" and the *Creation* and *Cultivation* of the modern world, being in fact, the very *Pioneers* and *Guardians* of its distant future.

This is our Caucasian *Truth,* Reality and *Destiny!*

Caucasianism

"The Light"
(The Religion Of The Caucasian Racialocracy)

-Blessed Are The Caucasians-
(And Their Quest For The Greater Service)

Of all humankind's adventures, none has been more exacting or intoxicating than the pain and moral difficulty of *Spirituality*. Its truths are often beautifully disturbing, morally demanding, and ruthlessly puzzling. It is often firm and unyielding, and not easily defined. It is the place of our *Mental Cleansing*, and that of our *Dominant Ideology*.

In This Lies Its True Currency The Alpha!

As of our Caucasian cultural year 41970AC, I, *"John Rolland"* The Alpha, (Caucasia's Messenger!) author of the "Holy Valorous" and founder of "Caucasianism" have declared and pledged myself to "Caucasia" her first "Alpha! (Lord Protector!) of her "Progeny" the- Caucasians!

Alas, the task to which we as Caucasians should and must engage, is giving *Support* and having *Faith* in our Caucasian- Biological Racial Orthodoxy- Caucasianism!

This being in line with our "Fundamental Religious Belief" and conformity to the absolute "Sovereignty" of the "Fematrix" (the life spark!) and that of her progeny "Caucasia" the sacred deity! (bio-Monarch) of the Caucasian Race. Hence, a "Caucasianist" is *He* or *She* who believes in their "Racial Heritage" (of some 40 thousand years!) and practices the guiding spirit of - Caucasianism.

The Caucasian Empress: (Hereditary Fematrix) is the Spiritual leader of Caucasianism. The *Empress* bears the mark of "Caucasia" our "Monarch!" the spiritual life force of *Caucasian Creation*. All that is Caucasian comes from "Caucasia" and all that is Caucasian must be *"Celebrant"* to her. The

Family is the sacred order of the *Caucasian Fematrix*, the den of the light, the core of creation, the sacred place of the female spirit. The *Caucasian Family* is ruled by the *Female* of the species, through the spirit of the *Caucasian Fematrix*, "Caucasia" and according to her laws and that of lifes reason.(Survival- Conquest- Emmortality!)

No individual or group practicing *Caucasianism* is above her law. All must serve; all will serve!

The religion "Caucasianism" must be known to all Caucasians. The religious population of Caucasianism (those who worship "Caucasia" and love their race) is not known, but it is clear that our numbers are significant and culturally accomplished, and furthermore, by the intellection of our truth!...*Biologically Bonded.* As in all great religions, there are also fundamental premises to Caucasianism, that establish what is *Sacred* and what is *Profane*. As all religions have as their ultimate authority a *Sacred* written text, so too, does Caucasianism.

Our Sacred Text: is the "Doctrines*"* of this very book The Holy Valorous. (Caucasian Manifesto!) Within the pages of this book are found all that is *Sacred* to the Caucasians, all that is *Necessary*, all that is *Real and Just!*

The "Holy Valorous" constitutes the complete written works of the Alpha, his *Teachings*, *Philosophy*, and *Commentaries* on the political and social direction that all *Caucasian Societies* must pursue, if they are to survive life's foundation of an all embracing biological predation. The "Holy Valorous" also contains the written laws of *Light*, the foundation for all the laws, both *Domestic* and *Foreign* in Caucasian society.

Caucasianism: The religious faith of the Caucasian "Democratic Racial Monarchy" which is totally committed to its "Caucasian Identity" and its "Fematrix Life Strategy" of some 40 thousand years.

Caucasian Society: will henceforth be referred to as the "Caucasian Empire" the *Religious, Political,* and *Social State* of the "Caucasian People" which is the *Sacred Dominion* of the Caucasian- "She" our *Monarch;* "Caucasia" our spiritual life entity!...that we hold to be the creator of the *Caucasian* bio-collective!...as well as the *Caucasian Man* and his place in her collective. No religion could exist without practice, without defined rituals to govern spiritual and day-to-day behavior. Therefore, Caucasianism employs a variety of private rituals, rituals having to do with rites of *Initiation, Passage* and *Devotion.*

In addition, Caucasianism recognizes the importance of life-cycle events such as *Birth*, *Marriage*, *Death* etc, and has elaborate rituals to recognize the very significance of these events. Furthermore, twice a year, at the time of the *Winter* and *Summer Solstice*, the Caucasian faithful will gather to celebrate and honor the all embracing *Female Spirit* of the universe. Where other religions have and prophase a great many beliefs! ...Caucasianism is guided by only one divine principle, all that is, comes from the *Divine Female Spirit* and her bio-cosmic will, and all that is, will abide her will.

The female spirit and force is without equal; "She" is the eternal *Life Force,* the *Fematrix*!...all the many *Spirits* (Gods!) that humankind has kneeled before are only ancient mystic imaginings "Spiritual Cryptic Egoisms" of the mind, and not of the flesh!)

She is the thing itself, the glory at the heart of the universe. While the conflict of *Good* and *Evil* is real, and we Caucasians must always remain *Vigilant* and ready to *Defend* against the ambitions of both present and future enemies!...Caucasianism is a religion of tolerance.

The diversity of humankinds beliefs on the subject of *Religion* and *Cultural Direction* is understandable in the theology of Caucasianism. We as Caucasians do not question or disapprove of other's in their attempt to reach the divine entity or their cultural direction. One's spiritual and cultural path after all, is for *Better* or *Worse,* one's own!

Difference!..is vital to the life force. And according to the beliefs of Caucasianism, the "She" created difference!

The belief in and the survival of difference is fundamental and essential to the theology of Caucasianism.

However, having established the necessity of life's differences, Caucasianism also recognizes the sacredness of purity, of *Homogeneity*, of being with one's own kind. (a society of one's own kind!) To that end, *Racial Sanctuaries* are not only helpful; they are also without doubt, necessities for survival. First among these sanctuaries is *Geography.*

The land or territory held by a race of *People* or *Species* of animal for the purposes of birthing and cultural initiation is sacred to the theology of the Caucasians. It must be respected, and it must be protected.

Racial Sanctity: Is also found in a *People* and *Species* themselves (a sovereign bio-kind society!) and therefore human racial sanctity (a sovereign bio-kind!) is to be preserved and respected!

Furthermore, in accordance with "Caucasianism" and its theology, a race of people or any species or subspecies of life is considered the very mark of the *Fematrix Herself*, the imperial will that created the living (biological) universe.

Because of this, biological-*kind* and its place in life, its life strategy, its bio-Sanctuary (identifiable-kind!) must be respected as the first- *Sovereign State* of life, the *Spiritual Birthmark* of all living things.

The Alpha Declares: Caucasianism will rise to the intellectual summit, the greatest of all the universe's spiritual endeavors. Have you doubts? If so, you need only to read on.

The Holy Valorous: Will bring clarity to our *History*, our *Reason* and our *Future*.

- Our Caucasian Faith Will Elicit Our Reward -

The
Voidmatrix

(Existence Without Self (Negative)

"The Origin"

The Darkness: In the beginning was the great darkness, no light existed in that darkness; no shape, no shadow. The darkness was a complete curtain drawn over all that was, and would be. This darkness is known as the *Voidmatrix*, or existence without purpose? The *Voidmatrix* is the interdimensional pulse of reconfigured existence. It is in fact, the process of existence, the *Gathering* and *Releasing of* energy (interdimensional matter) without authorship. (the creation and death of stars!) The ability to understand the *Voidmatrix* is to understand an existence or presence brought about by *Chance* and this chance is known in Caucasianism as the *Origin*.

Yes, the universe is an existing marvel, but that which constitutes it, the release of energy and matter, is due entirely by chance. It is the *Birth* and *Death* of *Stars* that fuels the universe and the *Engine* of *Chance* that gives it its *Existence,* but, this whole magnificent process in and of itself is sterile?... having nether a conscious *Purpose,* nor *Destiny*.

"The Four Powers Of The Fematrix"
(Union of the Quad)

The *Voidmatrix* is just that, a void, an endless presence without known purpose, than, in a moment lost in the mists of time, there was a single gathering, this gathering from the Origin, (chance!) which in turn formed a galactic spiral nest and brought together a *Singularity* called a *Star*, and it was this star (our sun!) that would give birth to the *Elementals,* and they in turn would create the *Fematrix*, the bio-cosmic-*Life Spark!* (the elementals union of purpose!) And "She" in turn would control the *Quad*, the four forces of her life, that are comprised of *The Elementals!* (*Gravity, Weak Force, Electromagnetic Force, and the Strong Force*) and these forces would give her the power to recreate herself, and transcend dimensions. The first pulse of the mental self, *Creation*; hence, no longer would the fabric of the Void just cradle the sterile existence of chance, for now, there was an excitement in the Void, the bio-cosmic *Fematrix*. And as "She" created more spiral nests, *Bio-Galaxies* of birth, their domain would become known as *Life!*.

The Alpha's view: One of the unanswerable mysteries of the Fematrix (the She!)is the fact that her great discovery is always self-discovery. The truth for which we as Caucasian beings are eternally searching is wrapped up in our own being; therefore, it is fruitless to search far afield in the wilderness of life or in the hearts of others to find it. To do so brings you not nearer that which you are seeking but takes you further away from it. And it may be- who knows but you?- that even now, as you read the "Holy Valorous" you maybe nearer the pathway to the knowledge of "Caucasia" your Fematrix!...than you have ever been before?...seek her!...and you shall come to know and behold her divine intervention, of her spirit into form, the miracle of the "Caucasian Observer. The Language of our "Caucasian Racialship" is not words, but Meanings. And the true value in "Caucasian Racial Spirituality" can only lie in our understanding and devotion when engaging its uncompromising reality. This being the chief purpose of the Holy Valorous!..and the Alpha's Quest.

"Blessed are the Caucasians"

The
Ultimate Truth

(The mandate of elemental need)

The Alpha tells us: That the *Beginning*- that which Was? ...and the *Now*- that which is?...are in reality that which actually *Exists,* rather than as they may *Appear* or might be *Imagined,* are endeavors of the eternal "Void," known in Caucasianism as the "Transcendence" (the interdimensional journey!) the path of all- *Existence!* (we know of no other!)

The
Biological Transcendence
(Birth of the Fematrix)

The Alpha tells us: In the transcendence to biological life, it became necessary for the "Elementals" to create that which could make the *Metamorphosis* (transition) to a *Biological State,* thereby creating a "Life Medium" with a boundless ability to reconfigure. (life in liquid form!) This of course being the ultimate medium along with an intellectual arbiter for challenging- *Physical Encounter*.(a life strategy!)

And from its own "Elemental Metamere" the "She" (fematrix!) was created, the ultimate "Transcendent - Transcendental Being" known in human science as the "Female," the *Bringer* and *Caretaker* of all biological life, its *Needs*, and all that it implies. In Caucasianism- The "She," Caucasia, our Monarch! (the Caucasian Fematrix!)

The
"She"

-Fematrix-
(The Bio-Cosmic Life Spark!- Positive)

Birth Of The Life Spark
(the union of encounter- *Consciousness!*)

All "Encounter" creates the exchange of *Energy* at the "Subatomic" level, and somewhere in that- *Dimension?* (a configuration of existence!) where the realm of the three! The *Negative*, the *Positive* and the *Neutral,* would merge and become the "Elementals" the creative phenomenon called in "Caucasianism" the-*Need!* (the *life spark!*)

And it was and is, these "Elementals" who, driven by their "Need" (their *life spark!*) created, and have continued to creat all "Biological Form" by bringing the union of all "Dimensions" into one living being; the "She" (Fematrix!) the physical trans dimensional manifestation of all their *Need!*

The Alpha tells us: he does not feel that any lengthened defense is necessary for having undertaken an inquiry into the "Fematrix" (life spark!) with which the present work is occupied. Independent of the intrinsic importance of every question connected with the elucidation of the Fematrix the vagueness which too often characterizes her *Truth!*..this being employed by so called "Intellectuals" who, in modern times, have treated of her inspiration seems to render a fundamental examination into the nature of her *Divine Influence* daily more desirable. In his (the 𝔄lpha's) study of the problem of expressing the- *Life Spark?*...he has found that humankind possesses many "Languages" for the expression of a given *Idea* or *Emotion*.

Therefore, the direct "Truth" in the rendering of the-*Life Spark,* is necessary so its reality can be revealed, giving it a higher conception of its function and purpose in the infinite nature of things. Besides, the 𝔄lpha believes that humankind must be given a higher conception of the function of *Life* and the relation of *Life* to human destiny. Thus we can see, that in order to reveal the- *Life Spark* (fematrix!) and its interpretation of truth depends on the understanding of the special functions she was intended to discharge, and some misconceptions however, should not pass unnoticed, for biological life is more then just an- *Organism*, it is also an- *Instrument?*

In the one case there is a necessary physiological and organic unity, but in the other case, the skill obtained is entirely the result of deliberative acts of will; the result of choice and of long-continued practice. (evolution!) For all technique in delivery must be evolved from the actions of the mind. The Darkness, (Voidmatrix) is powerful, if not all powerful, for in the darkness is- the *Origin*, (the gathering!) and from it came forth the birth... the *Fematrix*, the bio-cosmic *Life Spark* itself. However, it was the dawn (birth!) that the Origin created in the millennia of its creation, and since the Fematrix is limited in her existence, "𝔖he" must recreate herself, through herself, (her core construct!) in other words, the "Life Spark" (the Fematrix!) sustains herself through a cycle of recreating herself, before the energy of her emergence runs out. (bringing about her death!)

This process of recreating one's self is called- the *Birth*, (the core need!) and the being that can perform this miraculous event, this *Miracle Construct* of bio-cosmic engineering is the "𝔖he"(Female!) or for her rightful title - the *Fematrix* (the bio-cosmic will!) the only life force. (we know of no other!) Now we have come full circle in the understanding of the great darkness, and that of its two entities!...its *Negative* and its *Positive*. The *Voidmatrix*: negative existence by chance. (Origin) The *Fematrix*: positive existence by choice. (life spark!) All of existence comes from these two entities! Only the "𝔖he" (Fematrix!) could bring forth light from such darkness. Only she could command her bio-cosmic well to divide, and in the perfect seamless reality of the darkness, she created a fold, a form, a something in the vastness of nothing. And from that form her light came forth!...a clear powerful light, casting her will into the far corners of her creation, her bio-universe, her truth. Thus she created *Being*, (the observer!) the beginning of time as it can be reckoned, and with the first great idea (the self!) casting a bright light into the darkness, "She" the *Fematrix* (the one!) saw shapes and forms that had never existed until she saw them. The first impulse, which she identified in her being, was the hunger for her continuance! (self-preservation)

Yes, in the great Void, she became the preservation; giving birth to the self that became known as the "She" the keeper of the physical embodiment of the- *Elemental Need*, the great entity herself, the *Fematrix*. (the bio-cosmic will)

The She; (Female!) creator and keeper of the-*Need*, of *Time* and *Space*, the architect of *Birth* (life!) and the purveyor of the eternal will and image of all living things.

All are of her, and by her!...there is no other!

The Caucasian "She" (female will!) the *Caucasian Sisterhood* and their life strategy is the *Author* of the *Caucasian Race*, of the noble people to which I claim membership and selfless devotion. Rising high above the great Void, the *Fematrix Light* began to push back the darkness, causing the great Void to circle around her. This swirling darkness created a spiral nest of dark and light, a tornado funnel of movement and energy, of clashing ideas, of *Life* and *Void*. The light that was created (the "She") the first great idea, gave rise to the hunger (the force of preservation). By focusing the energy of her great inner power, she began to consume the Void, to induce the cosmic circle and form this great nest, the ever-enduring womb of creation was forged. It was now her turn,...she would now create her own "Singularity" and join the *Biological* with the *Cosmic,* to create a single bio-cosmic geography,...*Earth!*

Where there had been nothing, where time had not existed, she created life from which there had been no life, and as her ideas raced along the walls of the great well, there was tremendous friction, great clashes of bio-cosmic energy and idea.

By cultivating this titanic thundering concert, the *One!* "Fematrix" began to plant the seeds of her likeness, her likeness once conceived, (her daughters!) would mimic what she had already done in the *Great Void*; bring light and idea, *Life Itself*, to where light and life had never before existed. Spawning her great idea, her daughters began to take hold of her bio-cosmic sphere...*Earth*.

Drink!..she cried out in a voice that filled the Void, drink of my energy ...drink of my will. Live!..take your place, find your path! Gazing upon them, she declared, let my selves evolve, let them change she proclaimed, not by my dictates, but by their own. Let each of my *Daughters* exert their own will in determining their own *Physical* and *Mental* direction to my *Immortality*. Thus she left each one of her likenesses (her daughters) to their own *Fate* and *Path*, their own life strategy (their own free will!) to her *Immortality*, in the great revolving bio-cosmic current of her- *Earth*.

As the most promising of her creations would be realized, the undisputed fruit of all her life, from the very simplest idea that emerged from the swirling currents of her bio-cosmic well to the most gargantuan of cosmic galaxies, the realization of a *Life Strategy* by free choice, was the *Fematrix Diversity*, different paths to her "Impervious Vitalism" (immortality!) Her "life's" great journey begins!

The Alpha's view: the Fematrix has but one rule in the arena of life's (her daughters!) competitive struggle for her immortality, and that rule is Survival! And in the end, whichever daughter, through her "Life Strategy" has acquired "Impervious Vitalism"...hence, becoming the final victor! Than it will be that "Daughter" in form, that she will finally become!(her teleology!)

- Earth -

(The Bio-Cosmic Cradle)

The Alpha tells us: It has been a long standing belief by *Astronomers* and *Astrophysicists* throughout the world that our planet "Earth" was created in, and is a product of our solar system?...But, The Alpha's own analysis tells us something different!...he speaks to a cold dead rogue planet, with deep interstellar origins, having no atmosphere, and incased completely in more then a hundred (100) mile high layer of ice. Traveling for billions of years, through interstellar space, its journey would lead it into what we now call our *"Solar System"*, coming close enough to our "Sun" to be captured!... and with its unique properties - ***Iron core***, high concentrations of- ***frozen water*** and ***oxygen*** - plus its orbital position around the "Sun," (leading to the igniting of its iron core) and its unique "Axis" (a probable collision, creating earths moon?) our magnificent life giving *Earth* would settle in, and all this would lead to the *Birth* and *Evolution* of the "Fematrix" (life!) and all that she implies. Being all born of the "Void" as we now know it, is not "Vacuous" but, has vast "Islands" (galaxies!) of more then a "Trillion" that take part in the "Unescapable Dance" of - *Gatherings, Encounters*, and *Unions*,...all "Violent"...all "Predatory." Yes, an Expanse; (universe!) so great, that a *Trillion Stars* are *Born*, *Live* and will ultimately *Die*, over "Time Spans" that are equivalent with their numbers,

The Alpha's view: Though its has been often stated by many of the worlds scientists, as to their belief in the abundance of life that must exists in the vast reaches of the Universe?...and if true!...by their own calculations of more then- five billon years of the birth and death of suns, planets and galaxies- Where's the life?...other then our precious "Earth" the only jewel of "Life" in the universe.

- Life -

(Birth Of The Observer)

The Alpha tells us: It is the *21st* century, and for more then some- *40* thousand years!...humankind has struggled to understand who, what, and where they are?...to grasp the reasonableness of their observations and to link and conceptualizes their realities. All this being a part of their emergence (by chance!) into a cosmic formula, a dimensional cast with their properties not known in this universe, being unique unto themselves *"Intelligence"* (a cognitive intellect - *The Self ?*) and its foundation, its engine of- *Need* O'beautiful blue-jeweled planet!...O'planet of profound potential!...Upon your verdant hills does the "She" rest her highest hopes and future!

In the entire universe, it is only upon the shores of our magnificent *Earth*, that the order of human life would result in three remaining races (homo-sapient sisterhoods!) of the Human Fematrix: *Mongoloids*, *Negroids*, and *Caucasoids*.

For a million years the three races lived in blessed isolation from each other, neither warring nor meddling, they pursued their different-*Cultures* and *Destinies*. But as time moved on from their first beginnings, and a million years would pass, the sanctity of *Racial Peace* and their *Sovereign Space* was no longer honored, the boundaries of that which was *Rightful* and *Sacred,* were trifled with!

No longer do the three *Different Races* know the bliss of their separate Identities; no longer do they know *Racial Sovereignty* or the magnificence of their singular destinies.

No, now they are thrust *One* with the *Other* into the cauldron of *Social* and *Political* distress, the great *European* and *American Coliseum* of *Liberal Social Engineering*, where Caucasian racial identity has been outlawed, and where a great many *Racial Minorities* have defaulted on most, if not all of the *Moral* and *Social Enlightenments* of our Caucasian society! Hence, The Alpha gives the Caucasian world this *Precautionary Earth Principle*: life on this *Earth* is all that we have! It is the beginning and holds the future of our human- *Immortality*, there is no going back, we must see it through to the end?

This is the will of our creator (Caucasia) as it is the will of all creators. (the Bio-Sisterhood)

However, this understanding of the *Precautionary Earth Principle* is very Caucasian, where as a much more *Different Understanding*?...may come from alien others.

Hence, The Alpha in essence suggests building a margin of "Safety" into all decision making when it comes to the welfare of *-Earth!* All this is relevant and needs to be included in the *Social Priorities* among the different human races. Moreover, many of these decisions will have important impacts that stretch far into the future!

Therefore, we should and must emphasize our concern for the future of our *Sovereign Caucasian State*!...and that of the other "Races" as well!...and our united unwillingness to hazard (destroy) the futures of "All" our children!

Therefore, by *Understanding* and *Cooperating* on matters that greatly concerns us all!..we as"Separate Racial Entities" having our own destinies! ...must come together with a willingness to *Negotiate* and *Determine* how our *Separate Journeys* can progress in *Peace* and *Prosperity.*

However, the "Caucasian Empire" having said all this with a true desire for good will and respect for other races, understands that we, "Caucasian Americans" have come to a-Crossroad?..on our journey through the *21st* century, and only the "Truth" of *Past* and *Present* events can tell us, which way we must turn?..on the path to our destiny!

The Alpha would like to issue a forceful warning!..a clarion call to all Caucasians of racial faith and cultural commitment. Truth; is the root of all virtue!..therefore, the present political and cultural trend of reckless racial alien accommodation that has overtaken Caucasian Americas common since!..cannot be allowed to continue infiltrating Caucasian society!...and spreading their hyenic cultural militancy, because of irresponsible political appeasers (democrats and republicans!) plus, the liberal zealot progressives (subversives!) who are conspiring with alien others to put our "Caucasian American community" and its posterity on a course of self-destruction. Therefore, our Caucasian American Salvation will ultimately depend on an emotional racial awakening, with the rediscovery of our allegiance to our biological dynasty and its mandate! And if for any reason, we fail to act on this understanding?...and the great "Caucasian Universal Conquest" should become undone?...all of humankind will be lost!

This is our truth,...our ultimate reality.

- Freedom -
(The fallacy of dismissiveness!)

The Alpha tells us: "Freedom" or for a better term- *Escapism!*... a mental dismissiveness of service either imposed by *Need* or *Obligation*, but regardless, the truth is this!...all living things are brought into this world *Preconceived, Purposeful* and *Obligated*. Therefore, from the moment we are born, the biological chains of both *Physical* and *Mental Service* are fastened to the ankles of us all!...We are created! ...and "life" is given to us! Therefore, our "Destiny" as Caucasians, and that of our creator; "Caucasia"(our fematrix!) is one and the same, by *Surviving* and *Conquering* this dimensional world, we serve both our and her destiny. For we Caucasians are "All," of her *Desire* and *Purpose*, and therefore "Freedom" is a shadow in the mind, a borrowed existence and only things that have real existence, that always are and never pass away, are the actual hardships of life's inescapable burden to serve the- *Fematrix Teleology!*... the eternal idea, the primeval drive in all living things. Here is exhibited The Alpha's mediating task, his hermetic and religious role as broker between the *Caucasian Race*, its *Spiritual* and *Ethical* sense, and all those *Caucasians* and *Aliens* alike, who are divorced from the true *Reality* and *Understanding* of the world.

Eternal Struggle

"Identity"

As light was created from darkness, the darkness will always pursue the light. No matter how quickly it moves, the darkness matches its steps, like a shadow. The relentless pursuit by darkness has had its impact on light.

For light (intellect!) is the idea, and the idea is to form, and all of this comes to bear upon life itself. Life suffers from a siege mentality, and rightly so, for all around life is the great void of darkness. From the void we come, and to the void we return. The dawn is enveloped between the night before and the night after; it is a reality of life.

The two, *Light* and *Dark*, are engaged in eternal combat, for darkness is the cradle of the mind, (its chamber of reason!) and it is there, in the *Seamless Void* that the mind chooses to rest. Certain life forms, in their struggle against the darkness, have developed more complex senses. Of these senses, the inner-eye, or mind's eye, was created. It is only with this eye that we can have a picture of the world outside ourselves. As time went on, the life force developed an exterior probing eye. Though clumsy at first, this probing eye; became so exact, and so sensitive that it could send back to the mind's eye images of the outside world with the greatest of detail. For the first time since the creation itself, the *Fematrix* could see herself from the outside!

Because of this new ability, this new vision!...this achievement in biological mechanics, the *Fematrix* herself changed, taking on a new meaning. The very destiny of the *Fematrix* had been shifted. For the first time, she would have dominion; difference was no longer blind

This world is our world!

Even as this great development was occurring, a host of new *Female* forms were beginning to appear, springing up in the ponds of life. All different, all unique, they shared one commonality, one overriding and overreaching reality, they were all part of the great *Sisterhood* of life, the *Fematrix*.

And all seeking their own *Path* to her immortality.

For the first time, when something approached, when something came their way, they could see it. At first, they could see things only as they came upon them, but after time in their *Evolution*, they could see from great distances.

With vision came discerning and discretion. And with the ability to see great distances, a *Fematrix* could determine if it was friend or foe that approached.

With the knowledge of the near arrival of either friend or foe, the *Fematrix* had to do something she had never had to do before, she had to decide, to make a decision, to stay or go, fight or flee. Vision opened the floodgates, and she was never again the same.

She was no longer haphazard.

She was able to take control of her own destiny.

Long-range vision held the promise for a greater chance for survival. If the enemy could be seen, the enemy could be defeated. Along with this ability to see came the mind's ability to keep a file of visual images, of the things that were good and the things that were bad for different *Fematrix Species* in their *Competitive Quest* for immortality.

As this file grew, *Colors* and *Shapes* took on added meaning. As the file organized a sense of *Sameness* and *Difference* evolved. She could determine a *Fematrix* that was like herself and a *Fematrix* that was different!...and not of her. (difference meaning assault and predation!)

It was very clear from the beginning, that which was like herself was tolerable, while that which was different was too often an enemy.

And from this reality a great many things followed, things that were vital to the survival and significance of different *Fematrix* species. (a life strategy!)

When a *Fematrix* could identify another *Fematrix* as being like herself, it wasn't long before she could identify a world as being her world, and from this file, the underpinnings of visual *Biological Identity* came into being.

Without exception, and without argument, the most vital drive in all living things, a drive that goes beyond eating, drinking, and sexuality, a drive that has pulsing in its heart the need to be close to *Mother* and *Father*, to know *Family* and *Friend*, is the drive for- *Self Identity!*

There is no exception to this reality. All other drives are short-term and easily satisfied, the desire for *Self Identity* is lifelong and always profound, always intricate, always involved, always necessary.

Sit a child in front of a photograph album filled with images of *Circuses, Zoos* and *Holiday* events, and that child will still, time after time, return to the single snapshot of himself or herself. A snapshot; that existed in that child's history, a snapshot that is part of the child's identity.

Life identifies by using five basic senses: the sense of *Smell*, of *Hearing*, of *Sight*, of *Touch*, and of *Taste*, and these senses are not listed in order of importance or even in any particular order at all. These senses exist for our benefit, to explore and to identify that which is around us. (Encounter!)

Almost always, we use these senses in some combination, *Hearing, Sight, Touch, Smell,* and *Taste.*

Different *Fematrix* life forms use different senses for different purposes. However, for the *Human Fematrix,* one sense, and one sense alone, represents our crowning achievement. This sense allows us to do what we do, and that sense is-*Vision.* We humans are *Ultra Visual* creatures.

More than ninety-five percent of our activities are visually oriented, and because of this fact, *Color* and *Shape* plays a much greater role for us than it does for other life forms. Many life forms depend more on the sense of *Smell* or of *Hearing.* Some *Life Forms* do not possess vision in the same way we do?

They exist nocturnally, at night, and so rely on other senses or other forms of perception, like *Sonar* to see. This is true of creatures that exist at the deepest depths of the earth's oceans. These creatures inhabit an area that even the light of life barely pierces; Therefore, our kind of vision is of little use to them.

They have other methods to see, to live, and to move.

Clearly, the ability to *Hear* and to *Smell* is of distinct advantage; It is possible to *Hear* and to *Smell* something long before it is visible.

However, whatever their advantages, the simple fact is that our *Vision* is the optimal sense for the world that we inhabit. Everything in our world has *Color* and *Shape* or the lack thereof. No one should ever think that this was by any means an accidental occurrence?

That there was no design involved, each living thing that exists today had its *Color* and its *Shape* chosen for it, as a form of *Identification* or *Camouflage* by its ancestral *Fematrix. Color* and *Shape* is used to identify one's own, and it is also used so one cannot be identified, so one can remain hidden (a *Fematrix* life strategy!)

The Alpha's view: The bio-cosmic (Fematrix) system of identification, by Color and Shape, (visual) is at the very center of our human (biological) world. It is a visual world, and it revolves around the ability to see! The exciting richness of Caucasian society results not only from the historical uniqueness of its genetic constitution and of natural phenomena, but

also and perhaps even more so, from the endless interplay between natural forces and their racial will, their intellectual prowess.(having no equal!) All living things respond better to norms (inherited life strategy!) that their ancestors evolved, then to alien norms imposed on them by strangers! Therefore, Alien Inclusion in our Caucasian society, in many ways symbolizes all that is wrong with "Caucasian America" and her sister states throughout the world, and why this liberal zealot experiment of race mixing has failed. The Caucasians are to be praised for seeking the friendship of neighboring alien others, but, neither they nor their descendants of today!... understand that demographics is the arbiter of biological life. those who form the majority population of a territory will rule that territory, no matter how powerful a ruling elite may be. They will determine its culture and society. A majority Caucasian population will create a society that reflects Caucasian values and norms (its inherited life strategy!) A majority Alien population will create a society that reflects Alien norms (its inherited life strategy!) To the present day, Caucasians have failed to understand that by giving aliens the benefits of "Caucasian Civilization" aliens will grow in numbers and overwhelm our society. Caucasian America and her sister states throughout the world are today home to tens of millions of Aliens!...who are historically incompatible, and their challenge for supremacy in our lands is well on its way!...for if we deny our "Caucasians Greatness" and fail to defend it?...we as a bio-dynasty do this, at our own peril. Our organized Caucasian effort is a great power, but it may also be a dangerous power unless guided with intelligence, which is the chief reason The Alpha is devoted largely to describing how to direct our organized effort so that it will lead to success, that sort of success which is founded upon Truth, Justice and Fairness, leading hopefully to our ultimate civil stability. (A Sovereign Caucasian Nation) And whatever fate decides, we must have faith in our own free will and courage, to never deny or relinquish our Racial Identity, nor surrender our posterity's future.

"So Say We All"

Life's Unparalleled Miracle

(a superior Fematrix creation of biological engineering!)

The
"Caucasians"
(life's supreme vanguard!)

The Alpha tells us: In all of the known Universe, and of all life's known intellectual and physical engagements, none has ever rivaled that of the "Caucasians" in either- *Empire, Science, Religion, or Conquest.*

They are without equal!

Hence, their social supremacy of "Alien Tolerance" a fair, objective, and permissive attitude toward those whose *Opinions, Beliefs, Practices,* or *Racial* origins, etc, differ from their own. And, it is to their unique accepting and valuing differences between people, appreciating that these differences enrich our understanding of the world.

But, there is also, whether we like it or not!..A Supremacy law of "Nature" which pits Bio-conventional life forms against one another for the instinctive and ruthless control of *Resources* and *Territory*. And by truth, no other race of people has ever been endowed with such self-control, as has the Caucasians. They have been endowed with the greater power to use the most highly organized form of energy known to all of life, the Ark of the- *Intellect!..the Mind!..*and its treasure of- *Reason!*

Hence, we are coming now, to an important *Truth* and we must approach this *Truth* with due consideration, for it brings us face to face with a subject that few are willing or qualified to discuss with reasonable intelligence. Therefore, let us state this truth: It is a well known fact that no "Life-form" ever reached a high station in its struggle for survival without opposition of a violent nature from *Competitive Enemy Beings!*...and, if this is so, and it has been the same for Countless *Caucasian Generations* preceding us, have we not been tempering and refining our "Caucasian Intellectual Reasoning" that has gone into our fight for *Survival* and its *Supremacy* over our enemies? Of course we have!.. you can not understand what you do not recognize?...and that is the ultimate issue for all of us "Caucasians." Alas: for we are a "Biological Dynasty" the only one of its kind, and that *Truth,* and *Understanding* must never be suppressed.

We are Caucasians first!...and our children's future is "Foremost" in our life strategy, and for the sake of us all!, and that of our future, we must continue our quest to be "Vigilant" when it comes to those (aliens!) that oppose us, by not being indifferent to their *Subversive* and *Contentious* Strategy for *Cultural, Political* and *Economical* Power!

The Alpha's view: Keep in mind that above all, you are a "Caucasian" and a member of the greatest "Biological Dynasty" on Earth, and if you really believe in your racial identity as yourself, you will come to understand the true "Mission" of your people and that of their- Destiny! But, in the 21ˢᵗ century all of this requires risk. Therefore, it is paramount that you speak of your- Racialness with a fearlessness without arrogance, and the ability to do that consistently, will give you a grounded strength and confidence. And when in the presence of- Alien others, be "Racially Unthreatening" and maintain your self-respect by conveying your thoughts and showing your feelings with conviction. The classic clash between all racial groups has gone on for millenniums, and it can be a very elusive and difficult process to communicate effectively, and the pity is, many alien others never understand or admit that their insensitive and ambiguous style of communication is the problem. Hence, the common denominator for success is the understanding and efficient application of the basic principles of shared comprehension in communication.

The
Caucasian Oracle

"Caucasia's Divine Providence"

The Alpha tells us: to understand a race of people?...one must first understand their journey. And to do this, it is required that you seek out their "Oracle," (their artifacts, their oral and written history) in The Alpha's words, their Historical Resume!. *Skills, Experience, Achieve-ments, Failures, Discoveries, Creations, Education, Resources,* and *Beliefs* All this being part of one's *Racialness!...*one's *Historical Bio-Collective. (inherited life strategy!)*

All living things have an- Oracle!...a *Rhythm*, a *Voice*, a some of all that they are! Surely, our *Fematrix Providence* did not make our *Caucasian Racialness* the sole power over which we have absolute control without associating with that power a great potentiality, and if *Understood* and *Developed*, that being the "Caucasian Initiative" would bring the light of creativity to all of *Humanity* and its *Imagination*.

Furthermore, let it be stated!...our *Caucasian Racialness* (our bio-sub-species!) is solely a matter of our *Caucasian Fematrix Providence,* (Caucasia's divine guidance!) for we are of her, and by her! Hence, our spiritual commitment to the "Holy Valorous" its- *Cogent Truth!...Its- Irrefutable Reality!*

"Blessed Are The Caucasians"

-Racial Fundamentalism-

(Mark of the Living Will -The Fematrix)

Race: is the *Sacred Heritage* of kind, of *Identity.* Race is not deducible from anything else. It is the self-established mark of the living will of a *Fematrix*, her life strategy, and to this will, power has been allotted and assumed.

The truth of this implies and coincides with the realities of all biological conflict. The result of *Vision*, *Identity*, and *Race* is the perpetual struggle on behalf of one's own race, and between the races themselves. (imprinted different life strategies) This is truth; this is reality.

When the substance of the race (bio-esteem) is unquestionably present, when it is there, education linked with stable social forms has a value that is deep, abiding, and self-evident. Education adds immeasurably to the sense of identity, as each subsequent generation is absorbed into the spirit and culture of the race.

By this process comes *Experience*, *Work*, and *Action,* the very things that continue a race and keep it true to itself and to the life strategy of its *Fematrix*.(its living female will!)

However, when the substance of the race (its bio-esteem) is challenged by subversive academic intellects? (liberal zealots) And the terms of the race have been called into question, its identity? Then academic uncertainty reigns where certainty alone should hold sway, hence education itself becomes insecure, a very destabilizing force. When the substance of the race, its bio-esteem (its living identity!) is under assault, (racial nihilism) liberal subversives will lend themselves to that assault, so they can bring about the elimination of *"Racial Fundamentalism"* and its binding truths.

At such cataclysmic times, education no longer brings children into touch with the greatness of an all-embracing whole, with the very essence of their *Race* and its meaning.

Rather, it serves to *Demoralizes, Confuse* and *Disorient,* creating "Guilt," and the submissiveness to a malignant social fallacy- *Racial Equality*! (equal racial outcomes?) The liberal zealots, in their failure to recognize the races of the human *Fematrix- Negroid, Mongoloid*, and *Caucasoid*, and their essential struggle for- *Dominion* - one over the other, have become both the "Essence" and the "Symbol" of a world-wide liberal failure of mind! The failure to recognize and to respect those inborn patterns that human experience must fill can only lead to the brink of the abyss.

What is there to teach, if not these truths?

If the whole is crumbling, what merit is there to teaching about the sum of the parts? If a child has no hope of acquiring his or her "Identity" what use are the meager offerings of school? No use,...*None!*

Under such circumstances, *Education* ceases to pretend to sum up the parts; like a ship tossed by a storm, (racial discord!) it shifts direction; it does not simply flounder.

Hence, the political failure to anchor Caucasian society in a safe harbor of "Education" enforced by our Caucasian "Racial Spirituality" against the destructive waves of alien- *Racial Envy* and *Ambition* is of the most egregious *Failure* and *Betrayal* of leadership.

There are those Caucasian *Racial Abolitionists* in the form of *Teachers, Professor, Politician's* and *Social Elites*, who add to the storm by teaching their *Utopian* (quixotic) belief that the races of the human *Fematrix* are not separate and distinct; with different- *Ambitions* and *Destinies.*

As unbelievable as it sounds, they would also have our children believe: there are no boundaries "bio-acumen" or different "Inherited Intellects" between the races?...declaring that we are all of a *Single Whole?*...alas, how far the *Liberal Zealots Intellect* has drifting into the abyss!

The Equalitarian Fallacy: Separate competitive human races (Negroid, Mongoloid, and Caucasoid) do not- "Exist" ?

It is this: *Liberal Intellectual Dementia*, that is beginning to "Infect" the Caucasian world community's future, and unless we Caucasians both in America and throughout the world grasp, and grasp now the extent to which this "Liberal Ideological Abomination" has triumphed over "Truth" in our contemporary thought! We Caucasians will not only have difficulty in comprehending our situation, we will also be rendered *Culturally* and *Politically* "Impotent" by alien subversive contamination! Thereby, not being able to change the situation without a commitment to war? (a reconguest!)

Hence, this truth!, All that is, stands opposed to all that would be! It is in this statement, that lies the mind set of all living creation; it is in fact, the very blueprint of mental being.

Creation is the physical image of the soul brought about by the mental will of the soul, predetermined, designated, identifiable kind! Called in Caucasianism, the mark of the living will! Furthermore, the true ideology of "Racialism" is that which declares *Love*, *Admiration,* and the pursuit of one's *Bio-racial Survival* (its life strategy!) to be the highest *Moral* and *Spiritual Endeavor!*..in all living things.

There is no other! When this truth is allowed to be distorted by alien races in their (parasitic!) campaign to undermine Caucasian cultural society, and when that distortion against the Caucasian people is allowed to go *Unchallenged?*

Then, these same alien races will be encouraged to step up their campaigns for Caucasian political dislocation. And thereby bring about Caucasian Americas cultural and civil destruction! No one should be swayed by the fraudulent argument that the races of the *Human Fematrix* have now changed, that we have some how "Assimilated" and have become one? Such lies,...such intellectual deceit!

We- Homo Sapiens, ourselves, have changed very little during the last forty millennia, and there is no chance that the "Human Races" of the *Fematrix* can significantly, usefully, or safely intermingle as "Non-Combatants" in the foreseeable future, it goes against the very mandate of all competitive creation itself.

Fematrix Merited Genetics; are the watchwords of our faith! It defines the races of the *Human Fematrix*, even as it determines all their *Physiological* and *Psychological* limits, human life cannot be safely altered by social and technological innovation. In the final analysis, the frontiers of cultural and technological development are determined by human *Biological Frontiers*, through their *Competitive Examination* (encounter-reasoning!) and no other.

Biological *Merited Genetics* is the very text of life it-self! (competitive life strategy!) and not a utopian "Equality" (equal racial outcomes?) a bio-fiction, a liberal zealot fraud!

The merited genetic constitution (Fematrix life strategy) we acquired during our evolutionary past is the text of our being period! Only within the parameters of that constitution can we *Shift, Alter,* and *Change.* Deep within the flux of cellular reproduction, where DNA and RNA hold sway, the dominion of the *Hereditary Fematrix* exists, a place where time past and time present are joined, to give the human dimension and its biological mandate a future.

All living things, from microbes to humans, are born of their *Fematrix kind,* and bear their *Fematrix kind* in perpetuity.

Only by continuing and maintaining the *Biological Constitution* of your *Race,* (your unique identifiable kind!) can you claim and realize the treasures of your deepest self. Each Caucasian generation passes on to the next, their responsibility to their "Historical Racial Mandate" and its life strategy. So, if our "Caucasian Racial Dynasty" is in a state of -*Identity Capitulation!*...what are we going to pass on?

Caucasian liberal education has failed miserably in its need to explain the truth of *Race*, and to propagate its broader meaning. This is not a mere lapse. It is now a very deeply entrenched *Liberal Zealot Conspiracy!*...and will not be by any means easily rectified. We must presume that a passion for understanding characterizes humankind, that it is a corollary of their very nature, and that it therefore exists to some extent in all human beings.

This being true, the hurdles would therefor be primarily *Psychological* and *Semantic* when communicating the idea of one's *Racialness!* The desire to know is inbred, the ability to teach is a function of education. And if blame is to be laid (and that is a futile enterprise in and of itself!) then the blame should rest at the feet of many Caucasian people, at the feet of their *Politicians*, *Scholars*, *Scientists*, *Public Media*, *Parents*, and *Educators*!

All have played a role. All have taken part in the imposition of denial regarding the nature of–*Racialness!* They all share equal responsibility for the average Caucasian person's lack of understanding regarding the nature of their *Race*, its *Purpose*, and its *Potential*. Yes,too often the educators of the masses underestimate the intelligence of the average citizen. Caught up in the smugness of academic elitism, (liberal zealotry!) the educator has "Subverted" the Caucasian race in the eyes of the average Caucasian citizen.

As a result, he or she could not possibly understand the biological depths of their *Racialness*? (their biological-mandate!) To fully understand, one must bring to the discussion a background knowledge of *Hereditary*

Dynamics, without this background, the nuts and bolts of the subject eludes the average Caucasian.

However, even without those advantages, the average Caucasian understands the parameters of the discussion, once the idea of a *Specific Biological* inherited life strategy (racial kind!) is made clear.

Specificity; meaning ultimately a *Biological Uniqueness*, and at its core, it is the same truth for all living things. (female absolutism!)

All the great events of biological history have a *Species* or *Subspecies* (racial) basis. The very ebb and flow of human history is understood only when it is seen as a result of *Racial* and *Subracial* (ethnic) shifts in power,... of *Tribes* or *Nations* conquering each other, of lands being occupied by different races, and- *Racial Ethnic*- competitive conflict.

Once this common thread of *Racial Competition* (compelled by the seminal beings) is understood, then history stops being a meaningless puzzle of unconnected events, but welds into an obviously connected and predictable flow.

The Alpha's view: the Caucasian American community most be warned against the mistake of thinking any human standards are absolute. Alien race's have evolved under very different circumstances and therefore have a propensity to violate Caucasian cultural and social norms, but Aliens need not be seen as disordered or dysfunctional? Such differences are inherently no more value laden than the fact that "Alien Races" are simply not Caucasians, and are much different then Caucasians, and should not have any place in Caucasian society other than an Alien Tourist or Exchange Student,...and it is simply foolish to expect them to behave like Caucasians, when their biological mandate (their fematrix life strategy!) won't let them! And therefore, it must be stated: That all living things whether Species or Subspecies, are coded!.. and are products of a bio-database unique unto themselves, without an equal or equivalent both in design and quality. Thereby making the social interaction between Competitive Races, (human subspecies) Belligerent, Warlike and Incompatible!

- Elementals -

(Spirits of the Fematrix, Purveyors of Form)

The Alpha tells us: That all of existence, as wall as the *Fematrix* herself are part and parcel of the vast *Elemental Universe*, in Caucasianism, a conscious intellect without form, (Life!) and thou we are often unaware of their existence, even thou they exist in numbers that have and will forever escape us. But, their vast "Dimension" is sterile, lacking the essential material to creat from…alas, progressive form has been denied them, so to creat form!...a transcended being mad of themselves was created, a "Sovereign" (a gate way to transcend dimensions) so that the union of *Elementals* (life!) could take form. And that transcendent being is the Fematrix! (the Female will!) the sovereign of all life. But, even they, the "Elementals" are humbled by that which commands them, that which they have created to give them *Reason* and *Destiny*, that which *Transcends* all the boundaries of their *Sensual* and *Intellectual* apparatus. For she is their *Will!..* their *Sovereign!..*the harbinger of their becoming. She is the *One- the Fematrix!* All that is *willed!..*is of her and by her.

Biological Competitive Consumption

(The Social and Universal Catalyst of All Life)

The joy of *Predatory Victory* and the agony of *Defeat* represent the single most unwavering law in the arena of biological encounters, and sooner or later we must all enter this arena of *Competitive Biological Consumption*, whether as an *Individual* or as a *Group.* History has shown it is the group (race) that does better than the individual; hence the biological society, the social order of kind, one in accordance with its kind, in accordance with its order, in accordance with its direction, and in accordance with the whole. (its union!) In other words, biological society, human or animal and their various cultures are a oneness with the whole of their likeness. The alike and the non-alike, these are the boundaries of evolutionary progress and failure.

Whether human or animal, the scenario is the same.

Are you of our kind,...our way? If so, you are welcomed; if not, you must stay back beyond our boundaries, for you are our rival (biological competition) opposing force, and not of our way or kind.

When biological kind encounters difference, what takes place without exception is appositional challenge and physical posturing, the strength of will and courage, and finally contempt, the total dismissal of the other's status, which usually leads to combat and the flight or consumption of the weaker combatant.

This action is followed by the victory growl or posturing of the stronger. This performance has been played out for every minute of every day, since the dawn of creation.

The conflict of biological difference through "Race" in mental life, is life itself. Free human beings differ not only with regard to the characteristics of their "Racial Settings" which they find most desirable, but also with regard to life styles, aspirations, and last but not least, their views of their race's place in nature.

A *Race* of *People*, or a *Species* of *Animal* considered as a whole!... will never spontaneously surrenders its position of advantage. they never recognizes any moral reason sufficiently powerful to compel them to *Abdicate* in favor of an alien *Race* or *Species*.

Such action is prevented, if by nothing else, then by "kind-Egoism" a natural attribute of the laws of biological survival, an obligation through the mental acquisition of "Kind Identity" its *Character* of *Origin.* (its historical journey)

Hence, no amount of liberal- *Phantom Equality*- is going to alter this truth!

All societies are the equivalent of a bio-collective direction, (a Fematrix-life strategy) brought about by the will of the *Seminal Beings* (the Sisterhood!) that make it up. It is this will of the bio-collective that generates and focuses the spirit to create a- *Physical Identifiable Form.*

And that identifiable form is our- *Racial Kind!*

Our Caucasian Identity;...its survival, wellbeing, and future, is our absolute- *Biological Imperative!*

The Alpha's view: Bio-distinction, Species or Subspecies (human races!) have their mark, and carry their competitive (predatory!) resumes of their historical journeys. This is the basis of all "Chosen Form" in our world! The survival of the identity of kind and its own right of struggle, a contest between organisms and their life-strategies to exist!...to evolve!... is the very fulcrum of all life. This is the will of the Fematrix!...as she is our truth, our living reality!

- Politics -

(The Art of Compromise)

The politicians of the *21st* century have no prescription, no elixir, by which our world can be born anew?

Even in the blood and fire of revolution, where there is a place for labor, for pain, for adventure, heroism, love, and death, the *Politician* remains under suspicion!

How has it come to pass that we have all been seduced by the illusion of an *Earthly Eden*, of a paradise where all are created-*Equal?*...from what foul ideology did this assertion arise?

All (humankind) created Equal?

No clear thinking individual can claim it is so! For if this assertion where true?...then by definition the *Races* of the *Human Fematrix* would not be competing forces?

However, we all know that the conflict of *Competitive Consumption* and *Production* between the *Human Races*, as well as all other living things, is an absolut unforgiving reality! That being the case!...then the liberal zealots and their declaration of -*Equality*- must be false!...which it is!

And fortunately for some of us, we have been able to avoid the social hypnosis of *Racial Equality Mongering* (equal racial outcomes?) and the liberal zealot political treachery that sponsors this social detriment.

How have so many fallen under this distorted reality, this false mental image? It's not just a *Utopian Illusion*, it is by fare more sinister!..it is a *Cultural* and *Political Subversion!*...infecting many of our *Caucasian Intellectuals* who's, "Rational Failure" is so *Vast* and *Acute!*..it is indeed frightening. And that this *Aberration* cannot be broken in the hearts of so many Caucasians, is cause to cry to the creator.

Our Racialness!...is the reality, and it has been since the *Fematrix* first created dawn from the darkness, the womb of being (galaxies) from the vastness of the Void.

Unless we Caucasians align our social and political thinking with *Racial Reality*,(loyalty and love of racial kind) rather than being *Badgered* into thinking *Racial Reality* is in line with *Hatred, Bigotry* and *Malice*, we are doomed!

Race must be the reality against which social and political thinking is measured. All human subspecies (races) in truth, are *Competitive Unequal's,* thereby making dominance their position of choice, in our unforgiving world!

The races of the *Human Fematrix* have always been, and remain to this very day, in fierce competition with each other. Even in our land, (America) which raises the falsehood of *Equality* to dizzying heights, we are beset with social conflicts (race mongering!) that border on *Cultural* and *Racial* war!

The competition is fierce indeed, for jobs, education, political power, land, and housing. The list is endless, for it encompasses all that is and all that is desired.

We must cling to the truth, and the truth is this: The *Negroid* is for the *Negroids*!...the *Mongoloid* is for the *Mongoloids*!...and neither one of them get any pleasure or comfort from the power and progress of the *Caucasoids*!

Furthermore, the disregard for the Caucasian world community by their *Politicians* is the result of greed, a mood of liberal political *Subversion, Economic Piracy*, and illegal alien *Parasitic Pandering*.

This disregard for *Racial Valor*, by Caucasian liberal elites can be summed up thus: the liberal elite are willing to "Destroy" their entire society, rather than admit they were wrong! They are so deeply submerged in the darkness of their fallacy, (equality!) they have lost their way home.

And this is being exploited!..as could have been expected, by opposing alien races. Caucasian liberal *Guilt* and *Passivity*, (self-inflicted!) is now being greatly *Exploited*.

These alien races are gaining unprecedented *Cultural* and *Political* concessions!..that are bordering on Caucasian *Capitulation!*..the relinquishing of our- *Racial Sovereignty!*

It is more difficult to preserve that which needs to be *Preserved*, than it is to *Innovate* and to *Invent*. Innovation and invention need answer only for the moment and for the promise of the next moment. But, our *Preservation* must answer to all of history; it must answer to the fullness of identity; it must answer to the promise of forever.

How much easier is the weight of invention!

However, invention and innovation live in the present, not the past or the future. They are not rooted.

The present is but the nexus between what was and what will be. Wisdom clearly shows that change seldom results in realities that were expected. Plans are always fallible; the play of *Racial Affairs* is too variable for tidy calculations.

People are not numbers; results die in the streets, not on a piece of paper. It is essential, we must act now!...*Truth* must be separated from- *Alien Subversive Propaganda!*

In today's *Caucasian America*, there is no politician who can or will mediate the ultimate issue, the reality of the "Racial Divide"..the irresolvable "Spitefulness" between the *Competitive - Incompatible* races, who now occupy America.

Where are our leaders?

If the Caucasian race surrenders enough of its frontiers to ease the now existing "Alien Invasion" pressures, then the surrounding areas will be swamped, the homeland gaps will be filled with others, with strangers, with enemies.

How long?...before we Caucasians are forced to confront even larger, more demanding, and more powerful alien agendas?...*Political Badgering!*... *Cultural Mongering!*

The Caucasian social will is only important when the power that drives it, *Ancestral Pride* and *Racial Love* exist!

Why!...do we Caucasians in America and throughout the world "Relinquish" the power that we have earned?

Why!...do we Caucasians in America and throughout the world

"Empower" our *Sworn Enemies?* My Caucasian *Brothers* and *Sisters!* We are at the crossroads of our "Caucasian Destiny." When the fundamental *Social* and *Moral* ties in our race (our Caucasian racial self respect!) begins to *Fail?*...the "Caucasian American Community" will become "Intellectually Deracialized" and if not stopped, all other "Caucasian States" throughout the world will also become 'Racially Emaciated" devoid of their *Racial Identity!*

And than!...all *Alien Particular Interest* will begin to make itself felt?... and an "Alien Minority Society" will begin to exert an *Unaccountable Influence* over the greater Caucasian society, thereby *Corrupting* and *Restraining* the will of Caucasian *Political, Moral* and *Cultural* opposition.

Voting will no longer be culturally unanimous; the *Caucasian Spirit,* will no longer be the will of the *Caucasian Racial Whole!* Deceitful social contradictions (affirmative action and political correctness!) will arise and prevail, and even the best "Intellectual Opinion" will not be allowed to go unchallenged by *Progressive Liberal Zealots* and their cadre of *-Alien Minority Subversive.* (equality street hustlers!)

In the end, when the Caucasian state is on the brink of ruin and can only maintain itself in an empty and illusory form. (liberal equality) When the Caucasian cultural bond is broken in every heart, and when the meanest interest impudently demonizes the sacred name of the- *Caucasian Good.*

Then the *Truth* is silenced, animated by secret motives ceasing to speak any more than as if the *Caucasian State* had never existed, and people act in the guise of law's iniquitous decrees, which have *perverted Interests* as their only end. If the social will of *Caucasian America* is to go on?...then there must be a moment in its history when the *Caucasian Spirit* will realize its mistake!... and simply brush aside the most imperfect of philosophies,(bio-equality?... equal racial outcomes?) replacing them with life's eternal mechanisms rooted in *Truth* and *Reality*: biological competition!...*Winners* and *Losers*?)

Thereby coursing that which is eternally Caucasian to prevail, and bring the *Social Plunder* by liberal zealots and their neo-socialist political treachery to a righteous end!

The rising will of Caucasian Americas most genuine idealism and of its highest moral purposes will continue.

And the disgraceful field of "Liberal Zealot Diplomacy" in racial politics will end in our time. But when?..and how long will we continue to allow it to go on? The variety, extent and influence of these liberal zealot subversives have become enormous, like a giant octopus, its seditious tentacles extending into every cultural, social and political corridor.

Their socialist fallacy (phantom racial equality!) has extended itself into all aspects of our lives; it is no longer an easy exercise in social politics. These liberal zealots, and their "Socialist Goals" are no longer intellectually reasonable and their *Racial Concessions* no longer painless. It is *Racial* and *Cultural Trench Warfare!*...and our "Cowardly" Caucasian leadership has not yet begun to meet or address the problems arising from the fundamental principles of *"Racial Incompatible Rivalry"* (a reality!) and its conflicts in *Cultural, Political* and *Economic* Competition. The time has come to really educate the Caucasian world community!...time marches on, and the hour is late, the situation grave!

If certain realities are not "Acted Upon" very soon? (alien subversive ambition!) We, the Caucasian American Community will become overwhelmed by *Political* and *Cultural* disaster, (alien urban malfeasance!) that we will be unable to correct?...unless we take up arms! And that would be a tragedy of *Epic Proportion*, and its outcome would be lade at the feed of the "Liberal Zealots" who will be held accountable. (for knowingly creating it!)

The establishment of a *"Desirable"* Caucasian social environment, implies more than the maintenance of *Social Quality,* or the economic management of *Natural Resources.* Ideally!...it also requires the control of all "Alien" forces with "Predatory Ambitions" that threaten Caucasian Socio-racial survival.

Furthermore, the Caucasian race and its individuals must be provided with the opportunity to develop ways of life and surroundings of their own choice.

The Caucasian people not only survive and function in their social environ-ment; they also shape it, and thereby are shaped by it. This is the *Fulcrum* of Caucasian history at which we stand; the door of our future is opening on to a "Crisis" more sudden, more violent, more inescapable, and more bewildering than any ever encountered by Caucasians, and one which will take decisive shape with in the very lifespan of Caucasian children who are already born!

1) What must be done if we are to avert the worst?
2) How will we move away from the *Liberal Zealot* abyss?
3) How much time do we have? Not enough!...yet we cannot wait for the luxury of a better moment. Time is upon us; we must act, and we must act now! This is our time, our world; we must not surrender it.

The Alpha's view: where the Caucasian race is concerned, the liberal zealots seem capable of doubting what they elsewhere find self-evident. The tenacity with which liberals hold to social rather than biological explanation for racial differences probably bespeaks a fear that biology is immutable in its power to determine our lives. And should not the people of Milton and Shakespeare have a right to save themselves? Should the Caucasian American people and their community not try to avoid Extinction?.. forgoing the path of South Africa!..(Caucasian surrender to aliens!) and the death of Caucasians in mass by the hands of those aliens! For only Caucasian deeds will determine the limitations of Caucasian lives! What we do, we must do for the good of the Caucasian many!...and in the Caucasian way!

"Caucasians"
"What Is Necessary, Is Never Unwise"

The
Caucasian Reformation

(The Racial Awakening!)

The Alpha, hearing the cries of the Caucasian American citizens: The whole thing is hopeless and out of our control. There's no way to get those politicians to do what's needed to save Caucasian America!

This everyday Caucasian despair now cuts two ways.

It pushes some Caucasians into an *Apolitical* and *Social Lethargy,* in which they turn their backs on Caucasian cultural as well as national concerns.

Instead of protesting, they plunge even deeper into their work, turning their minds away from the fact that they are being- *Invaded* and *Assaulted* by *Alien Races* and are losing their- Nation! But for every one of them, there's a member of a new breed arising in the land. That's the modern day Caucasian American *Racial Patriot!*...Caucasian American racial patriots who love their *Culture* and *Country* too much to see it being- *Fed Upon!*... by *Alien Races* and *Caucasian Political Merchants* (politics of gain and graft!)

These Caucasian racial patriots read, talk, listen, argue, and join. In this process they will and are becoming formidable opponents of those aliens and politicians who have an agenda -*Open* or *Secret*- for the destruction of the Caucasian American people and their way of life.

How large are the ranks of these active Caucasian racial patriots?

Organizationally, their ranks are still small, but are gaining exponentially in number every day, and if we look into the minds of the Caucasian American people, I would guess that there are now some *Hundred Million Caucasians* who have become aware of the *Seriousness* of the *Political*, *Cultural* and *Economic* treachery assaulting their *Nation!*...and who want to work to rectify it!

The Alpha tells us: that he has laid out here (in the Valorous) the method of joining the Caucasian American- *Reformation,* of coming together in the united spirit of "Caucasianism" with all other Caucasians throughout the world who understand the great *Need* and *Urgency* of our *Reformation!*... our new *Beginning* - "The Caucasian Empire"

Who are we? We are the great *Tribes* of the- *Ancient Caucasus!*... the *Celtics, Germans, Slavic's, Italians, Arabs, Nordics, Turks, Spanish, French, Russians, Grecians, Semitics*, and many more.

Culturally: We are *Democrats, Republicans* and the *Politically* and *Religiously Unaffiliated*, but all being of the certainty, that we are the "Caucasian" the *Creators* and *Inheritors* of the greatest "Nations" on earth, and the *Impetus* for any real change for the betterment of all humankind.

What is it that unites us?

It is our *Fematrix* (Caucasia!) and her *Life Strategy* of more than *40* thousand years, all being bound by and to our- *Caucasian Ancestral Trust!*

The Alpha declares: Let every Caucasian!...whether *Man, Woman* or *Child,* come to the aid of their *Ancestral Trust* their *Biological Racial Mandate!* (our bio-dynasty!)

And make this declaration before their *People* and their *Faith!*

The
Caucasian Declaration

"We are the Caucasians"
-None Shall Break Faith - So Say We All!-

- Warfare -

(Survival through Combat)

War! What is this thing? We read about it all the time, we see pictures of it, study its history, suffer through protests against it, are bombarded with television images of it, endure huge shows of support in favor of it. And yet, for the most part, this simple three letter word is profoundly misunderstood.

Indeed, "War" may well be one of the most misunderstood words that has ever been written, spoken, or proclaimed. War is not a vague word. No, man chooses to make it seem vague.

Why? Because he has foolishly tried to convince himself that he is not an animal? That he is apart from the fundamental reality of his world. You see, man tries to elude his nature (competitive predation) and its fundamental fact in the world around him.

So much of his time and energy is spent trying to convince himself that he is a creature apart from the animals, that he can avoid his most basic instincts and desires.

The most basic act of all living things, all living things, is to eat or to consume, and contrary to popular belief, a belief that relies on the fact that the food on our tables is often sanitized, plastic wrapped, and perfumed.

Eating, is a violent act!...a very violent act! When will we learn that life is a complete entity, which feeds upon itself ? To sustain life, another life must be consumed.

It does not matter how significant or insignificant a life form appears to be, whether *Plant* or *Animal*, it is an unalterable truth, to live!...something else has to die? The whole of life is a competitive struggle of biological ideas, which are *Separate* and *Unique* from one another.

In other words, each human race (subspecies) *Negroid*, *Mongoloid*, and *Caucasoid* has taken a biological road, and these roads have given rise to-*Life Strategies*, and each of these *Racial Life Strategies* are very distinct and different from one another. (thousands of years, bio-imbedded!)

Hence, the difference in their physical presence bears powerful testimony to those very different biological roads; their physical presence is only the physical manifestation of their *Mental* or *Spiritual* presence. The physical is a symbol of sorts, (visual identity) and it is here through the recognition of one's own kind, (bio-loyalty) that the conflict really begins. Differences, and the right to the "Survival" of one's differences is what determines, quite factually, who stays? ...who gets eliminated? ...and who eats whom? (reality!)

In order to survive, one needs a great deal more than the mere desire to survive. One needs two essential things: (1) internal cooperation, (2) external self-defense mechanisms.

Each biological idea must establish its own *Space!*...and it must be absolutely free of all other life forms, so it can reproduce in safety. Otherwise, a real risk of injuring or losing the new life form exists. The foundation of reproduction is the "Preservation" of the idea of a biological kind.

Thus, war and warfare come about when the defensive instincts of a biological idea are challenged by the predatory compulsions of another biological idea. With intrusion comes war!

This reality implies a number of very significant things. First, there is no immediate likelihood of the definitive establishment of peace among the races of the human *Fematrix.*

Let me repeat this for all those who hold out futile hope and foolish desires.

There is no likelihood of the establishment of peace among the races of the human *Fematrix.* This is not the result of the last five years or the last five hundred or five thousand. This reality is the result of the very nature of the biological universe itself, of *Creation,* of the intent and glory of the *Fematrix,* who created life from the great Void.

Therefore, if the likelihood of peace between the races is *Minimal* or *Non-Existent!*...then there is only a single conclusion to draw next, and that is, that *War* and *Warfare* is imminent! That being the case, there is only the question of the fitness for battle, the physical, mental, and spiritual fitness for war.

Hence, in biological life "War" is imminent, its always on the- *Menu.* Even if we were to establish a peace (with racial aliens!) for an indefinite period, only the fools believe that such a peace would be permanent, permanent is eternal; it is not in the fabric of the living biology to have such a peace. The nature of our existence (humankind!) is both *Competitive* and *Predatory.*

Therefore, the instinctive state of *Alien Competitive* and *Predatory Belligerence!*...can be held in abeyance for only so long, never eternally! They, (aliens!) will find weakness, and seek conquest! Only the dead do not rise for battle, but even they contribute through the memories of others.

The Alpha's view: the defense of one's biological mandate (racial kind,...and its life strategy!) against an other of a predatory nature!..is an unalterable right of course, and if one fails to understand this truth!...it will be a fate unto their misfortune or death. Seeing to the survival and prosperity of one's kind, is first and foremost the absolut duty of all of one's kind,...The love of race, and the desire for its rational liberty, are noble and virtuous feelings, its prevalence is ever a test of the integrity of our national morals. Hence, Aliens!..will always be in the life of all, "Them and Use." In other words, that which is of us (Caucasians) and that which is not!...and the difference between each, are distinct life strategies both physical and mental in design, and who's influence spans same 40 thousand years of life's encounters. Therefor, if you allow aliens to invade your Nation and its Culture, you and yours will always be in peril!...never knowing "Peace," for all of life, is by willful and needful competitive design.

"This Is Our Truth, As It Is The Truth Of All Life"

Caucasian American Nationalism

"The New Direction"

Time is indeed short. We must act, and we must act now! However, action just for the sake of action accomplishes nothing. It is a waste of energy, and more to the point, a waste of precious time. We must be thoughtful, and we must be focused! Too often many individuals sensing the need for action, have moved forward, but not thoughtfully.

We have not paused to organize and to get ready what needs to be made ready if we are to succeed.

So, what do we need to do first? First and foremost, we must use the freedoms and opportunities that our nation (Caucasian America!) offers us to their greatest advantage.

In other words, we must, absolutely must, screen those who would represent us much more closely.

How many times have we voted someone into office, only to discover that beneath the *Smiles* and *Campaign Promises,* was a man or woman who would betray our most closely held ideals? (This political deceit is not acceptable!)

There can be no more *Trojan Horses* on the- *Caucasian Political Stage!* From now on, we must insist on a full and complete *Political* and *Legislative Accountability!*

Our political leaders must assure us in the most concrete ways that they will be "Loyal" in *Mind, Body* and *Soul* to the "Principles" of the "Holy Valorous" our *Caucasian Spiritual Doctrine!*...for no longer must, or can we accept a government in which the *Spirit* and *Strength* of Caucasian *Ideals* and *Purpose* are being constantly diluted and weakened. No more!... can we stand idly by while politicians *Betray* our most *Cherished Beliefs!*.. and "Trample" on the most *Glorious Traditions* in the history of humankind.

No more!. But, *We Must Not Take Up Arms!*..at least not yet?... Unfortunately too many Caucasians have thought so, prodded by *Desperation!*...more than by *Rational* thought.

To them I would say: remember the genius of Americas founding fathers, Caucasians all!

They set up this system of government for a reason.

They set it up, so we their *Caucasian Posterity* would have the control. We have been lax?...if that is the case, in letting the reins of our country "Caucasian America" slip from our grasp, by not confronting "Alien Racial Subversives" and their "Caucasian Renegades" (liberal zealots!)

"Yes, we can regain control, and we will"

The Alpha's view: Many Caucasians have gone down to defeat because, due to their prejudice and hatred, they underestimated the strategy of their enemies or competitors. The eyes of the Caucasian accurate thinker see facts, not the delusions of hatred and envy. Hence, as a Caucasian accurate thinker, and part of a unique biological mandate it is both your privilege and your duty to avail yourself of all the known historical facts, both past and present. And furthermore, as to the Superiority of Accomplishment and Presents in this world?...Yes, of course the Caucasian Race is unequivocally "Superior" and not to clam and secure our rightful place would be "Biological Heresy" when it comes to the survival of our Caucasian world community. And we have no stronger demonstration of this truth than the annuls of human history. To limit to the Caucasian race alone, their right of "Alien Exclusion" as a principle?..is a quixotic notion, fraught with very dangerous consequences. For no government whatever; and no political system however excellent its fabric, can possess any measure of duration, without that powerful union of "Racial Virtue" as its peoples principle, and, is it not true, that You and Me are of a bio-kind, a unique life strategy!..and therefore, is not our historical journey and that of our existence - Sacrosanct?

- Mobilization -

"On the conduct of each, depends the fate of all"

First Point: we must take control back at the ballot box.

Every "Caucasian" candidate for public office must "Declare Themselves," must detail his or her "Devotion" for Caucasian America?... by outlining how they will further the cause and future of the Caucasian American Community?

They must make clear exactly where they stand in the conflicts of *Racial* and *Cultural* Competition?

And if the "Answers" do not absolutely satisfy us?...then we will withhold our votes!...no one can hold office without us.

But, what of the time when we do begin to turn the tide, when the makeup of *Congress* and the *Senate* more closely reflects our loves and our beliefs? We cannot wait for that day to begin; there are other tasks before us. There must be put in place now, an "Inviolable" understanding between the *Races* of the *Human Fematrix.*

This is not something that can or should be avoided an other day! It is time to come to *Versailles* in this *Cultural* and *Racially* imminent war! Victory!...is not assured to any of us; therefore, let us bring meaningful terms to our- *Racial Disengagement* (into separate states!) creating an honorable future for all! Please note, the Caucasians as a people, as a race, do not want domination; the desire for domination came about only because of the threat posed by the *Mixing* of races, keep the *Races Separate!*...and there is no need for domination, none at all. However, we are human beings. We have to be aware of our own weaknesses, of the weaknesses that have been foisted upon us by the "Liberal Zealots. (subversives!) Hence, leading to a deep mistrust between the races! Domination is a burden, it saps our energy and our spirit, we do not want domination, we want- kinship!..kinship is uplifting; it strengthens the soul and cleanses the spirit.

The union of kindredness is our goal! And as sure as we Caucasians have to abandon our tacit assumption of socio-cultural brotherhood?...the other races will have to also concede something, they will have to forgo their dreams of migration to *Caucasian Lands* and *Neighborhoods.*

Second Point: the unholy "Liberal Zealot" goal of "Racial Integration" (an immoral battleground!) must *Finally* and *Completely* end! If we could disengage from this most combative and unnatural liberal goal, we would quickly find that the conflicts between the races would evaporate. There would no longer be a need for domination, no longer be a victimized race, or races. Understand!...these terms are not simply the idle desires of one who loves his race. If they are not met? Unless such a common sense agreement and understanding is reached?...it is not the status quo that will be realized, but a vicious and ugly "Race War" and as we all know, in any war!...there are- *Winners?* and *Losers?*

Our Caucasian system of government allows for these understandings and social agreements to be reached peacefully. However, failing that?..we Caucasians must remember that it is our "Survival" that must be realized, regardless of the means! Who among us?...on either side of this *Racial Divide,* this arena of liberal social fallacy, is so blind to the "Catastrophe" that such a battle, such a war would mean?

Death and Destruction, with irreconcilable hatred! Therefore, "Alien Races" should be aware that we Caucasians as a "Sovereign bio-dynasty" cannot and will not compromise our "Survival" at whatever cost!

Furthermore, we Caucasians must be aware that even now, our *Future* is not by any stretch of one's imagination "Guaranteed"...the other races in Caucasian America and throughout the world are *Mobilizing* and *Organizing* their com-munities into *Political* and *Economic* forces that can not be trifled with.

The efforts of the other "Races" at *Political* and *Cultural Agitation* are bearing fruit! Without question, they will maintain this pressure to bring about *Cultural, Political*, and *Economic* change in their rapidly expanding com-munities, that will benefit them while *Undermining* the "Caucasian world Community" and thereby accelerating the competitive- *Racial Divide!*...and its- *Deadly Hatred!*

You must listen to my words; *"Racial Separation"* (into separate states!) and racial separation *Only*!...will allow all of us, the freedom to socially, politically and economically excel.

The liberal zealot agenda, which would have us dilute our- *Superior Cultural History!*...and forgo our natural right of- *Racial Identity?*...thereby relinquishing the right to our- *Caucasian Destiny!*...is a *Seditious* and *Treasonous* liberal zealot agenda, which can never result in any *Trust* or *Respect*. Too much *Anxiety and Mistrust* is engendered when different racial groups "Intermingle" and "Compete" for cultural and political control, creating great *Hatred* that will mark their competitive outcomes. It is for all of us, an unavoidable *Bio-Mandate!* (a bio-innate antipathy at its core!)

And, the liberal agenda for all its other failings cannot succeed on this point because the very method they would use "Caucasian Cultural and Political Capitulation" guarantees they cannot realize their goals.

And, is it not also time?...that the other races who are utterly "Incompatible" with us!...be given a very clear understanding that we the "Caucasian American" cannot, and will not permit either migration to Caucasian lands or the destruction of our institutions of higher learning to continue!

Third Point: We have drawn the line in the sand, let all *Politicians* be put on notice: on these issues as well as others, we will if necessary- "Fight" to the finish! We will not- *Yield!*..We will not- *Surrender!*

We will no longer be satisfied with political and cultural results that stop short of guaranteeing the *Caucasian American Community's Survival!*

This is our- *Nation!* (our future!) and we will reclaim it! Our paradox is resolved into a single problem: the "Caucasian American People" and their sister states throughout the world, must return to their proper *Racial Province,* and *Functioning.* The *Cultural* and *Political* disorder (liberal zealotry!) that has been invading the Caucasian American Community, and its institutions, must all be- *Rejected - Dislodged* and *Discarded,* thereby bringing about its complete-*End!*

Furthermore,..although absolute *Racial Separation* is the- *Vital Goal!* (separate racial states!) we must, and we do recognize that we will all have common interests, interests which will affect all races commonly.

These interests are the subject of the agreements that must be reached between the "Races" if a stable world, and a promising future is to be had! Common interests for all must be recognized, identified, and dealt with fairly.

Trust for all must be established, trust based on an acknowledgment that the races are *Different* and *Separate,* and have their own destinies, and that it should be so! The sense of racial trust will grow with consultation regarding common needs, *Territory, Water, Electricity,* and *Commerce* for example. On these matters, and others like them, our consultations will result in *Trust* that is the outgrowth of *Experience* and *Knowledge,* not the outgrowth of absurd liberal utopian ideas of- *Racial Equality?* (equal racial outcomes?) that can never be realized. (historically different bio-life strategies!)

The Alpha's view: Urging all Caucasians to explore and accept my viewpoint. I am not going to argue its soundness. I am merely fulfilling my duty and discharging my responsibility by giving you the truth as I realizes it. But, I caution you however, not to become discouraged if the fundamental truth of it carries you into political and racial waters too deep for you to fathom? Perhaps I can throw one final ray of light on this subject, by reminding you that you as a Caucasian racial being, and part of a unique biological mandate must carry it out to a point at which you can accept or reject it in your own way and of your own moral volition? To escape the confusion of your surroundings, you must first except the fact that you are lost in the wilderness of ideas, and then gather your bearing, your core construct: Who and what you believe you are? For only by this path, is racial truth and dignity possible, and Life's presentation understandable.

The
Caucasian Social Paradox

(Sociological Default)

The Caucasian world has become morally mutinous and socially detached since the liberals zealots have diluted the political strength of the Caucasians.

There are no authoritative procedures to access the relative responsibilities for recourse to *Alien Racial Violence* and its *Social Domestic Default.*

There are no wise judges anymore? Even in judging a constitutional dispute, the principal organs of the *Supreme Court*, arrive at conclusions that express the will of a political majority, rather than a judgment that is reached after impartial assessment based on merit. We are drifting my friends! Drifting!

If we do not put an end to this drift, if we do not put our Caucasian political and cultural houses in order, then the race endowed with the greatest creative ability, the race whose past is filled with greater achievements than any other, the race that holds the richest promise for the future will be driven into *Social Default*, without realizing its greatest *Potential* and *Spiritual Hope.* That would be a tragedy beyond measure! Imagine the race upon which the dreams of so many hundreds of millions depend, simply giving up without a fight! Forty thousand years of *Caucasian Evolution* going uncrowned, and the *Caucasian Fematrix*, along with her supreme product, the *Caucasian Man*, left politically and culturally shackled (by their own intellectual default!) and prevented from fulfilling their destiny!

Unimaginable?...unfortunately it is profoundly imaginable!

However, we have within us now the power to avoid such a terrible eventuality. If we are to get through the next two decades, if we are to enter the next century moving forward instead of hurtling backwards, we have got to understand the desperation of the situation. (political, social and economic degeneracy) We have got to understand, and we must act!...past civilizations were confined by their geography.

They were confined to a particular people or small group of related peoples. If they failed, there was always some unspoiled, well endowed group of *Caucasian Barbarians* to pick up the torch and to start anew.

But today!...there are no more *Caucasian barbarians*.

The speed of liberal autocratic development has lent its hand to transforming political and cultural structures, educational theories and methods. Yes, the state has had to provide subsistence to racial minority cultural failure, and its unproductive economic communities.

The state has also had to focus its attention on the innumerable new problems created by concentrated multitudes of *Minority Criminals* and *Illegal Aliens* in epidemic proportion.

America's huge cities, with their inflated land and rental values, tax rates, and living costs, with their immensely expensive and nonproductive methods of transportation, energy and healthcare systems, would quickly become bankrupt if time stood suddenly still. They keep functioning only because of the constant flow of *Extorted Taxes* through the misuse of political authority (government piracy) from the larger Caucasian communities. These big cities have now become hostages to *Financial* (banks) and *Municipal* groups. (unions) As a result, these cities can be held for ransom by the organized action of any one of these groups responsible for their everyday needs. In other words, the basis for real day-to-day power in our future cities will shift to *Alien Organized Groups* of *Municipal* and *Political Cartels.* This shift represents a menacing sign of the awakening power of these groups; (political, utility and service extortion!) hostile alien groups, formulated and created through *Liberal Paternalism*, that in the near future will become predominantly very *Combative* and *Anti-Caucasian!*

The truth is: those in the cities have become isolated, and living hand to mouth, from *Freight Yard* to *Retail Store*, at any of the innumerable points of fracture, (economical- political- cultural) an American city could be brought to its knees! This of course has already happened?...and it continues to happen in a number of Americas largest cities, creating a very leery *Caucasian Population* that is vigil, and aware of its urban vulnerability. (do to liberal alien pander!)

However, *Alien Political Pundits* should not gloat over their tragic power of *Mismanagement!*...for Caucasian flight will easily tip over the urban structure, and as we already know, when Caucasians *Evacuate* a city, and remove their *Cultural* and *Economic* support,...all alien social civility collapses, (hyenic tribalism!) and all those who remain will find themselves buried at the bottom of the wreckage, after all, one cannot maintain; what one did not, and cannot build!

The Alpha's view: The Truth is often avoided, because it is to some of us: Ugly and Unpleasant! For when you appeal to truth and reality be prepared for the anger that comes from disenchantment. Life can be so harsh and distressing that a person or group of people will create or conjure up Fantasies!...Like "Equality" and all those of misfortune will flock to it, seeking its euphoric trans-formation, bypassing responsibility, work, self-sacrifice, in one fantastic stroke. Equality?...of course is the "fantasy par excellence" the ultimate ruse of the Liberal Zealot charlatans who prowl among us to this day, and is the Key to their subversive "Parasitic" success. Equality!...the elixir of Utopia, and the death of Reason! There is no term which has been more prostituted than the word –Equality? Among a corrupted alien people, the cry for equality is heard the loudest among the most profligate (preachers!) in their communities. Hence, the morals of their disciples are always sufficient to unmask the fraud, and their general corruption of not in keeping with what is correct and proper in our Caucasian society and their hyenic cultural manners which cannot possibly entertain any co-existents between us! We are entirely incompatible!...and therefore we must put an end to this social abomination, this liberal zealot equality fraud.

America's Social Delusion

(Doctrines of Liberal Fallacy)

It is the *21st* century and Caucasian America is a drift, in a sea of "Liberal Zealot" historical fraud!

If ever there was a lesson to be learned from a social order, "Caucasian America" is that lesson. Considered by many to be the consummate democratic state, a social beacon for the multitude of pilgrims on their journey into freedom. But in its pursuit of freedom for humanity, it has become a victim of its own liberal social fallacy of freedom, and has taken freedom beyond *Truth* and *Rational Debate,* to a state of *Legal-Disorientation*, *Academic-Bewilderment*, and *Social-Debauchery.*

Because of its social doctrines, written in the shadow of the mystical poet, (equality) Caucasian Americans has been forced onto the stage of social and political compromise, neither declaring nor advocating the spirit of the whole, but claiming the rights of the individual, as if it were really true that the desires of the few outweigh the needs of the many. This deceit of the Caucasian American liberal zealot has degenerated the very fiber of its own social and political order. This liberal philosophy of *Compromise*, no matter what the coat!...has led to the complete malfunction of the city and state governments on behalf of themselves. They no longer know or understand their purpose or direction.

Case in point: The urban centers in Americas big cities have become prime areas for major "Alien Crime" *Gang Warfare, Murder, Drugs, Mob-Looting*, all out of control.

Furthermore, "Assaults" against *Caucasian Citizens* by "Aliens Thugs" is now an *Epidemic* with numbers in the thousands. No longer can the common *Caucasian American Citizen* feel safe under the law.

If one is to fully understand the social breakdown of America's urban centers, this nightmare of alien social debauchery brought about by – *Caucasian Liberal Failure.*

You first need to understand!...that it is a symptom of an even greater problem- *Political Mongering*, a state of "Political Disorder," due to the absence of a *Trustworthy Leadership* (statesmanship, man and woman of character!) in Local, State, and National Government.

This is typical of the *Progressive Liberal Philosophy* that has now engulfed all of Caucasian Americas *Political* and *Social Life.* And, it is being played out in many more ways throughout the entire country with the same results, the *Drug* problem, the *Crime* problem, the *Loss* of *Industry,* the *Taxes,* all out of control! But, the greatest threat of all to "Caucasian

America" is the unchecked "Alien Invasion" into liberal zealot "Sanctuary Cities" (in the millions!)

We are now in the grasp of a *Government* that cannot see "Reality" because it has lost all control of its "Own Purpose" and no longer *Knows Itself.*

It has always been a deep rooted problem in most, if not all societies created by humankind, and that is the prevention of absurd laws and legislation that only serves a minority's distorted appetite, with no concern for the welfare of the general public. This is due in part to the strengths and weaknesses in the forming of the political structure, and its *Creed* or *Social Philosophy* held by its founders.

The social contract between the *Caucasian People* and the laws they impose upon themselves (democracy!) should consist of a *Common Moral Consensus* supported by the common will of the Caucasian American whole.

And not by a coalition of *Alien Races* and *Caucasian Cultural Subversives*, (liberal zealots!) who support cultural degeneracy and the political (legislative) redistribution of Caucasian wealth to "Alien Races"? And should we not mention the "Assault" against *Caucasian Freedom of Speech*?

This is where religion enters the stage of this human production, for no other social body is more attuned to the moral consensus and common will than religion. Religion is the true caretaker of the human moral soul and of the will of the social whole. Contrary to some beliefs, it was and still is the greatest champion and fortifier against the absurd appetites of humankind. (both Caucasian and alien alike!)

But, even the legendary endurance of religion will weaken when it's social allies stray from the moral and righteous path, and fail to speak out or challenge the socially absurd (in its own ranks?) for fear they will lose their jobs or their social position or they won't get reelected. This is the point, when a society is in an *Intellectual* and *Moral* decline, its elected officials will begin to transfer their "Loyalty" from the society as a whole, to the special interest of "Minority Groups" who have their own agendas for social change?

This is a natural political phenomenon, and it has been played out in many forms in all the nations of the world with the same results, decline in moral values, a great rise in crime, loss of jobs, loss of government services, and then the final blow, the passing of *Socially Absurd legislation!*

Case in point, *Affirmative Action* (the alien paternalism law) this is the- *Umbrella Law* that gives *Alien Races* the right to receive that which they do not *Merit,* and did not *Earn*!

And we must not forget the right to commit *Infanticide* (unfettered abortion), the first of the great *Evil* laws.

And if things continue,...*Homosexuality* will no longer be an *Illness!*... but declared an *Alternate Lifestyle*, and will be allowed to proceed *Untreated,* and *Socially Unopposed.*

These *Civil* and *Social* actions by *Intellectual Deviants, Minority Races* and the *PC mob!* (liberal zealots!) have become or are about to become law! When there is a weakness in the structure that shelters us all, in this case the law!...and its legal misadventure into establishing- *Liberal Judicial Activism?*...we must act!

With its principle (its moral high ground!) based upon the modern social fraud of "Racial Equality" alien minority communities have now declared that the success of the Caucasian world community is a *Piracy* of *Privilege?*.. and demand financial restitution for the purchasing of - *Equal Racial Outcomes?*…no matter what the cost to the Caucasian world community?

How absurd!...and delusional is this alien extortion.

Subracial diversity (ethnic's of the same race!) in the same society is one of its greatest assets.

But, uncontrolled *Racial Diversity* (different races!) in the same society will produce grave *Social, Political,* and *Cultural* consequences (competitive racial hostility) against the principal founding race.

This becomes obvious when the moral defensive fabric of the society (its racial sovereignty!) does not respond to being "Invaded" by an "Alien Race" *Culturally Subversive* and *Impoverished.* (parasitic!)

And, if allowed to establish their legitimacy,(cultural roots) would go about their task of creating *Moral* and *Cultural* anarchy. (California?) This *"Uncontrolled"* and *"Uncensored"* racial diversity is a more serious social illness than even –*Spartanism*. However, in the meantime, the urban dweller is the stuff of modern politics, the medium in which the craft of state must sail. It isn't surprising then that the art and science of politics seems to have fallen behind the changes of the times. The Caucasian politicians cannot answer to the times because they are lumbering along with what is essentially- *Political Contami-nation*!

A political system that has been invaded by- *Alien Races*, and is now, and will be in the future more responsive to *Alien Ambitions*, (racial equality politics) who are for their own communities, and their own- *Racial Interest*, and not for the *Caucasian American Ideal*, which the political machine was designed to work for!

It has been said, that the stability of any structure is ultimately determined by the foundation that it rests upon.

So also does this common truth apply to all *Human-Societies* without exception. It is the 𝔄lpha's belief that of all the foundation stones of human society, it is the cornerstone of intellectual common truth, and its unwavering defense that has allowed human kind to endure. In the coming years, *Caucasian American* society is going to face many social and political mistakes, and most will run their course and the society will recover, but, you must also be told that there are a few other social mistakes, that are *Fatal* to human societies!...and they are: *Alien Racial Immigration*, and *Alien Political Inclusion!*

It is these social mistakes that attack the very foundation of a specific-*Racial Social Structure*, and of all of these, it is the social illness of *Intellectual Cowardice* and *Political Piracy* that terrifies the human heart, for when it takes hold, it completely destroys the social will to defend the *Common Truth*. This then, sets the stage for the "Legitimizing" of the socially absurd: the *Political Pirates*, the *Liberal Zealots*, the *Alien Racial Extortionists,* the *Economic Guru's,* the *Sexual Mutants*, and the *Academic Radicals*, just to mention a few!

If not the Caucasian Intellectual!...then who is going to safeguard the-*Common Truth?* When the very will of the *Caucasian Intellectual Community* perceives its position and material comforts as a greater loss than their people's trust in their wisdom and council?...it can then be said, that the Caucasian intellectual community no longer possesses that dynamic and altruistic drive, but has been stricken by the disease of "Comfort" which has a prominent side effect of *Class Disdain*!...that is *Demoralizing* and *Crippling* the Caucasian American dream, and the future of its posterity.

*The **Alpha's** view: Words like- Freedom, Liberty, Choice, evoke a power of possibility far beyond the reality of the benefits they entail. And leaves no room for intellectual imprudence or a leadership unconcerned for the welfare of its posterity. The Caucasian race of people have earned their place in this world!...and will not tolerate any betrayal of their Sacred Racial Trust, by either their Citizenship or their elected Leadership. And all those Caucasians who feel that their bio-mandate (racial kind!) is not worthy of their consideration and therefore treat it with disdain!..their "Treason" will be noted, and they will be treated accordingly.*

"So Say We All"

The Pox Equality

(Intellectual Default)

It is the *21st* century, and a very devastating mental illness is spreading throughout the Caucasian world.

The *Pox-Equality!* This festering mental affliction if not checked, will in a very short time (25 years or less!) become the undoing of the Caucasian race, and its world community.

Furthermore, because of its crippling mental effect (liberal zealotry) on Caucasian Academics who seem to lack the mental pathways to self-analyze its illusionary effects, which has induced in them a mental state of grazing passivity as to that of cattle or sheep going about their lives excepting the *Culling* and *Assault* on their numbers by the predatory nature of alien others, (subversive alien ambition) who, the liberals have declared their equals?

Thereby, allowing them unprecedented access to their *Society* and its *Bounty* while in the act of *Flagellating*- themselves with the rod of – *Equality!*

Let it be understood by all Caucasian people who believe in the sanctity of their *Racialness* and its destiny; there is no greater social illness then the illusion of a *Biological Equality*, let alone human *Subspecies* or *Racial Equality*, it does not exist, and nor will it ever exist, ether in human subspecies or any other biological endeavor with an earnest and industrious effort. (competitive will!)

Nature (the Fematrix) will not relinquish possession of the path to her immortality, *Competitive Predation* is the rule for all, and all will take part until there is a final victor! (that which creates no further doubt or dispute as to her final form!)

This life of bio-competitive predation (and we know no other!) has been going on for same 500 million years, and if you (your kind!) are not here today, then your name and legacy has been laid between the stones of history for all those of the future to gaze upon, and wonder about your being!..your fate?

Thereby, pondering your lose at the hands of your enemy!...never to be again. The Alpha's thoughts: because of liberal zealotry the fact that the liberal mind has been captured and infected by intellectual cultists with their mantra- "Equality" the key pathogen in their *Social Hymn* that completely paralysis liberal reasoning with the inability to act or function for their own vital interest. (being prevented from seeing their own future!) This cult of *Equality* and its deadly future outcome (the Caucasian worlds desolation!) is making its final assault, an all out attack on the Caucasian world community, and make no mistake, their forces are formidable, and are at this point deeply rooted in the political elites throughout the world.

Is there a solution to this deadly affair?...Yes there is!

We the Caucasians have not come this far to be dislocated from our future by either alien others or Caucasian renegades. But, make no mistake, this will be the *Final Battle* (win or lose?) for the future of the Caucasian people and their historical quest of more than 40 thousand years. Life (the Fematrix!) has no favorites; the task is the same for all, Immortality, the teleology of the bio-Fematrix quest, she cares not for the losers of antiquity, for they were just competitors whose failure created a vacuum for others to fill. Yes, it is an arena!...a *Biological Arena,* and all are witness to, and all take part in the disdain for each other's standing, for there can be no misunderstanding about one's fate, if one fails to win in this unforgiving world! (whether an individual or group!) So, having said all this, let us as Caucasians not become disadvantaged, lose heart or get discouraged, for all is not lost! *First:* we as Caucasians must not put ourselves in a position where we are unable to win! *Second:* we as Caucasians must encourage other Caucasians to deeply think, absorb, and embrace their- *Caucasian Identity*! And *Third:* our Caucasian *Altruism* and *Humanitarianism* have no equal in the biological world! But, we as Caucasian people cannot and must not risk our own future by engaging the failures of *Alien* others, to the extent that we are blind to the nature of their "Ambition" and its-*Competitive Treachery!*

The
Theater Of Social Fallacy

(liberal zealotry)

Liberal Zealot America: the theater of social fallacy, and above the entrance to this theater are the words of a illusionary intellect- "All Men Are Created Equal" -and of all the illusionary acts played to the world's delight, it is the great staged act, *Equality* and *Equal Rights* that has captured the minds and passions of all humankind, as if the halo of freedom wasn't enough? Furthermore, to the surprise of no one, the alien minority races are now demanding that this illusionary liberal act, *Equality* and *Equal Rights*, be played out on the stage of reality! This of course, to the dismay and bewilderment of the political right, not to mention the complete self-denial of the academic liberal left.

By the way, the liberal left is directly responsible for the social elevation and metamorphosis of this *Equality* and *Equal Rights* fallacy and its evolutionary path into a deeply ingrained *Anarchistic Hyenic Culture* - by a broad section of minority races, the unopposed -*We Are All Equal*- academic cult, and its complete *Intellectual Meltdown*.

Hence, the social and political questions that now remains for the Caucasian people is this,...given the truth about *Equality* and *Equal Rights*, the sheer fact that both of these liberal social fallacies do not exist, and nor could they ever exist! Moreover, with its Caucasian academics in full headlong retreat, and both of its political houses taking on the status of- *Street Vendors*, what is now to become of this multiracial state- America?

The American *Subverted* legislature (democrat and republican) has now decided that it is in the best interest of *Caucasian Americans* - that they pay gold to racial minority *Street Hustlers* for peace, and give up production *Markets* to foreign alien economic pirates. In other words, to *Abdicate* Caucasian social and economic power!

But, if history has taught us anything, it is this: you cannot buy peace! And any attempt to do so will be perceived as a sign of weakness by your enemies, who will, without a doubt, press their assault to a final victory. Peace comes only through strength, and the "Fate" of the Caucasian people should never be negotiated by *Liberal Zealots* or *Alien Others*.

Caucasian America!...and that is the true social definition of the *United States of America*. It is an *Empire* derived of *Racial Kind*, and that racial kind is- *Caucasian*!

The Caucasian American people have become victims of their own liberal- *Social Fallacies*; this in turn has brought them to the brink of their own destruction

The very notion that three opposing races, *Negroids*, *Mongoloids*, and *Caucasoids* can occupy the same territory and compete for the same economic and social status without destroying each other is ludicrous and beyond rational sanity.

To think, that the social whims of politics, can override the wisdom of biology is an *Intellectual Arrogance* beyond measure. The society that denies biological kind and its social reality, to create a social arena by which opposing racial forces are thrust together for the purpose of a mystical belief of utopian racial brotherhood, is in for a rude social awakening, (alien racial militancy) hence, Caucasian Americans and their European kin, are now coming to realize this vital truth! The Caucasian Americans, and their society, must now come to terms with their social reality, and that reality is the "Alienquest" (alien racial militancy!) and it is waging *Racial,Cultural, Economical* and subversive *Political Warfare* for social dominance, against all of Caucasian America. The American Multi-racial state has become lost in the wilderness of its own- *Social Fallacy!* Being no longer able to sustain its revelation of - *Racial Brotherhood?*... the liberal zealots now find themselves, defending themselves against the very social fallacy they created!

The multi-racial state does not work!...biological kind and its society, is woven into its likeness; it is its major poem!

The
Equality Flagellant
(an extremist liberal zealot faction)

The Alpha tells us: Of all the intellectual toxic mixtures that have inflicted our Caucasian American society, as well as its sister states throughout the world, none has been more socially extreme and degenerate than the "Liberal Zealot Flagellants" with their fallacious fervor of atonement for the sin of being a- *Caucasian?*

The Liberal Flagellant: is the practitioner of an extreme form of self inflicted *Mental Flagellation* through- *Inequality Mortification* in the name of- *Human Rights ?* (a social fraud!)

This distortion of the social senses by the liberal zealots through their "Equality Illusion" reveals the true nature of their erroneous perception of reality- *Communism Revisited!*..and its historical brain teaser of *Brotherhood* and *Equality?*...once powerful, but now ailing and in decline they need a new "Scapegoat" in America! Yes,...that's right, you guessed it "White Racism" a resurrected liberal zealot quest!..with a new and improved social illusion *Theme-Park*, and its side show attraction of social demons: *White Supremacy, White privilege, White Oppression,* and let us not forget every liberals favorite in the Main Arena: the "Equality Inquisitions" and its *Pleasure* in the *Persecution* and *Destruction* of any and all *Caucasian Americans* who believe in their historical bio-racial mandate, our "Caucasian

Dynasty" and its history of- *40.000 years!*

But, what this cabal of *Liberal Zealots* and *Alien Subversives* have failed to understand to their detriment!...is that we of the *21ˢᵗ* century, advocates of the "Caucasian Empire" are *Vigil* and *Ready*!...for what we all know is "Certain" and coming our way!...and our preparedness for its- *Inevitable Engagement* and *Conclusion.*

"Blessed are the Caucasians"
"So say we all"

The Poisoned Well

(Academic Default)

If politics are in grave trouble, *Education* is in even worse shape. The *Educational System* in Caucasian America has been invaded by the *PC mob* with its multicultural virus that is fostering cultural anxiety and Caucasian American academic demoralization. Too often, and much to reasons dismay, what we see in the classroom is a retreat from serious purpose, one that takes on aspects of sheer panic. What is the consensus among educators as to what "Multiculturalism" is supposed to profess?

There is none!

Caucasian American education, now having been invaded by the *PC mob*, cannot even agree as to what multiculturalism as a concept is supposed to be?

They can't even agree on what it's supposed to do?..other than to dislocate "Fundamental" Caucasian education. How can they even discuss content in such a climate of ignorance and deceit?

Our universities, hotbeds of the *PC mob's* ignorance and foolishness, have not helped bring resolution to the confusion. If anything, they add to it!

High schools! What can we say about our high schools?

Do they teach skills, disciplines, kinds of knowledge, do they present the attitudes of mind that we would have them developing in our young people?

Asking the questions is embarrassing; the answer is so obviously "No" in each case. Yet, "Multicultural Education" is exalted in the liberal zealot's social mythology! Multicultural,…more and more!

Yet less and less seems to be accomplished by all this multicultural education. Of course there are widespread liberal rationalizations to explain away the differences that these issues bring to the forefront. But, exactly what do these rationalizations accomplish?...nothing!...less than the multicultural education that they seek to uphold.

As frightening as the *PC mob* is, those seem determined to spread the multi-cultural virus. How many times has the 𝔄lpha discussed these issues with friends and family, with generally intelligent Caucasian people, only to have them suggest that he's exaggerating, that the problems are not so serious as all that?

They are!

There is no danger of exaggerating when it comes to our *Educational System.*

How can one exaggerate something whose dimensions far exceed anyone's ability to comprehend?

The multicultural issues in education are so vast, the problems so painful, how could anyone suggest that the problems are not serious? When 𝔗he 𝔄lpha presses these people on their position, they seem to assume that something will turn up, that somehow the multicultural problem will take care of itself ?

Take care of itself ? (mental default!)

It has not been better stated, than it is a gross misconception to view "Multiculturalism" as an effort to enrich education. Multiculturalism seeks to inject an anti-Caucasian dogma into today's American curriculum.(this is sedition!)

Liberal Alien Paternalism: is also not the answer.

The history of America that the students do learn is rewritten to fit the multicultural agenda. By reshaping the curriculum, the purveyors of diversity in the classroom calculatedly and covertly seek to prevent students from grasping the objective value to human life of "Caucasian Culture" a culture whose magnificent achievements have brought humankind from *Subsistence* to *Moon Landings*. Multiculturalism is an agent of anti-*Caucasian Ideology*. (this is our reality!)

Even our *Caucasian Morals*: which is another diminishing margin related to the quick, cumulative decay within the liberal fraternity, such as *Language* and the *Arts*, overwhelm those who should care.

They seem to think that the damage brought on our culture, by the large intrusion of alien hyenic cultures will correct itself or that liberal social architects will some how discover a solution to the problems they created.

We do not know at what point the multicultural pollution with which we're burdening our society will cause irreparable damage to it?

This knowledge comes only when it is too late. We do not know at which point the multicultural pollution in Caucasian education will imitate a death dance similar to that which has killed so many educational districts in America's largest cities. When it becomes too late to save-*Caucasian Education*, it will not matter if further multicultural pollution is piled upon the already existing liberal and alien revisionism in Caucasian America.

When the relevant Caucasian educational system has been destroyed!... there will be no persuasive argument for establishing strong regulations.

The narrowing margins of Caucasian liberal educational decisions have imperiled Caucasian American welfare, imperils our very survival!

This has come about by an unexpected alien legislated act (affirmative action) and the disguised cumulative effect of liberal political treachery (alien racial concessions?) upon an inattentive Caucasian social system.

In either case, the political legislated result must be reversed, or the destruction of our Caucasian educational system will render a future social and cultural renaissance for Caucasian America to be a futile gesture.

Only by the light of "Caucasianism" by its social scholarship of racial truth and reality fostered by our racial solidarity and cultural passion, can we find the methods suited to address the various problems that must be addressed.

But in the overall context, the Caucasian American people want and must get reassurances that their world will be stable, that it will survive, that the education of our children, will bear fruit, and not be another exercise in liberal zealot futility and frustration. Then, and only then will the cultural genius of our people be allowed to flower.

Even ideas require fertile ground to grow.

We need reassurance that a safer world will be here for the next Caucasian generation. We need to know that there will be a *Cultural, Political,*and *Economical* measure of hope for us and our children. Therefore, it is up to us, to you and me, to create that hope!...and to show that it can and will be realized.

When The Alpha is asked exactly, what do the Caucasian people want? He answers the question directly and from a Caucasian point of view. For him, it is the only relevant point of view. He says that the Caucasian people want to know that their hard work will pay real dividends in the future to come. They want to know that their hard work and creative genius will have a reward for their children and their grandchildren. In the immediate present, they would like to have some confidence in the ability of their political leaders to address and to solve the problems facing them. They worry about the present and future threats to the stability of the "Caucasian American Community" and its culture? They worry about social security, their retirement, the economy and the very "Ripping Apart" of the Caucasian American moral fabric? But, where will they find the solutions to their social anxiety?...for the *Streets, Towns,* and *Cities* are littered with *Drugs, Crime*, and the failure to inforce the law? (Illegal Aliens!) and too often, and in too many ways, the "American Politicians" of this- *21st* century have proven themselves most "Unworthy" of our trust!

Political Betrayal

(treasonous deception)

The history of all Nations evinces, that there is an inseparable connection between the morals of a people and their political prosperity. We elect our *Caucasian leaders* to be the care takers of the Caucasian American Community and to see to its best interest as the founding race of people, this to be carried out with both *Honesty* and *Integrity*, and above all else, with a complete loyalty to our- "Caucasian Ancestral Trust".(our historical-*Caucasian Dynasty!*)

But in actuality, the Caucasian elites of the *21ˢᵗ* century, in both political parties (Democrats and Republicans!) are *Self Serving,* and in criminal collusion with both domestic and alien foreign conglomerates? Plus their total disregard of the *"Criminal Epidemic"* in alien racial communities throughout Americas large cities, who's "Hyenic" *Social* and *Cultural* behavior, (sedition!) against the Caucasian people and their Community is spreading rapidly and will soon reach a point of Caucasian -"Racial Fidelity Retaliation" if no political intervention, "Racial Separation" is forthcoming?

Their "Political Neglect" is not from any moral certainty, but more to the fact!...that they lack the willpower (courage!) for a lawful "Confrontation" with "Alien" *Social, Cultural* and *Political Debauchery!*...which they continue to "Sponsor" with their contemptible silence! And understand this; Caucasian Americas reckless "Alien Political Inclusion" will bring about an historical natural intended consequence- *Alien Political Treachery!*...known as the- *South African Syndrome!* And its predatory results can be seen in the discarded *Lives* and *Future* of our Caucasian *Brothers* and *Sisters* who became "Disenfranchised" (stripped of all their right!) by the very people (an alien race!) who they gave citizenship to!...at the cost of losing their "Nation" and the "Future" of their children. (all brought about, by the racial equality ruse?)

Laws, so intellectually corrupt and socially destructive, that its declaration to "Racial Equality" equal racial outcomes?...is so *Absurd, Unsound* and *Inane,* that all those Caucasian politicians who voted it into law?...should have all been "Banished" from the Caucasian community!

Hence, is it any wonder that the common Caucasian citizen reacts with such shock!...to this political piracy! The Caucasian politicians of today are incapable and unwilling to confront the dangers. (they created!) They are not leaders; but criminal opportunists, tricksters and flim-flam jesters always trying to cloak their *Deceit* and *Greed.*

They need to be investigated and removed from both political houses! Their seditious political acts, in league with the *Alien Political Machines* (racial minorities!) to completely *Infiltrate* and *Sabotage* the direction and social structure of our *"Caucasian Racial Dynasty"* and its legacy is beyond contempt!

It warrants the full and uncompromised attention of all-*Caucasian Men* and *Women* of stature!

It is time to bring to bear the full weight of *Caucasian Intellect* and *Courage*, to halt this *Violation* and *Assault* against the *Racial* and *Cultural Spirit* of the Caucasian American community.

When a racial society (Caucasian America!) loses its will to uphold the proven tradition's and laws that have sustained its successful life strategy, it becomes ripe for political picking, and in the case of *Caucasian America*, that picking has turned into a "Vicious Stripping" and what remains now is a *Caucasian American Community* so damaged that it lacks the "Courage" and "Will" to even defend itself.

The Caucasian American people have allowed themselves to be lulled into a dangerous *Moral Fallacy*, and this moral fallacy has become the great shield for the *Plunderers*, the *Judases* of the Caucasian American Community.

This shield consists of three elements: the absurd social fallacy itself!... which is *Racial Equality* and *Equal Rights*? The *Legal Support* and *Editorial Propaganda* of this fallacy; and the *Public Ridicule* and *Punishment* for noncompliance to this fallacy. Together these three social elements conspire to provide protection to the *Political* and *Cultural Interlopers*. (liberal autocrats and alien revisionists)

Meanwhile, the great *Caucasian Culture* is being destroyed before our very eyes. Towns, Cities, whole communities are being *Laid Waste* by these liberal zealots and their alien plunderers. (no law?- alien sanctuary cities!)

It is now being predicted that: the unchecked flood of *Illegal Aliens* into *Caucasian America* and many of its sister states throughout the world will lead to a great social plague of biblical proportions. And this plague will consist of not one, but a number of devastating *Financial* and *Economic* burdens: *Health Care, Education, Housing, Social Services. Crime, and Tax's*. To date, there may be more than "Twenty Million Illegal Aliens" walking around in our communities across America. (yes, we have been Invaded!)

How many -*Invading Aliens*- live in your community? Can we do anything?

Most Caucasian Americans sit, wait, watch, and listen until personally affected. But, by then it's too late! The more extreme "Alien Numbers" the more extreme will become our, and our children's social and political consequences. We must put a stop to this madness! We must climb above the cloud of this *Liberal Political Treachery* and reestablish the one and only true social contract, our Caucasian American *"Racial Sovereignty,"* and the unyielding loyalty to our- *Ancestral Trust!*

This is our only path to true- Survival: For on the conduct of each, depends the fate of all!

The Alpha's view: we as Caucasian individuals being a direct tributary of a biological mandate- the Caucasian race and the inheritors of the foreseeable future of humankind must declare ourselves,(the Caucasian Empire!) and stand fast against the alien forces (the alien invasion!) that would sabotage and derail our most promising future! And understand this: whatever opposition others mount against us, "Vilifying" the Caucasian American community!...we Caucasians of the 21ˢᵗ century are ultimately being betrayed by our own leaders, who cowardly have adopted the liberal zealot subterfuge of "Racial Equality" and its gratuitous political inclusion. In this context, liberal zealot Caucasians object to "Caucasian Racial Identity" because it is authentic having roots in the very foundation of America, its culture and it destiny. The Caucasian American Community is the history of America! And if we should fail in our quest!...to defend and preserve our Caucasian American Community? We will deserve not pity from our posterity, but contempt! Alas: in life, "worth" is determined by-"Need" and need is determined by life's encounters! Hence, our alien encounters!..and all being not of us! therefore, is there not a need of "Self-Defense" and if so!...is it not of - Worth? Yes, and to really understand one's journey through life?... one most traverse the wilderness of their Encounters, and their Need to accommodate on the judgment of their Worth.

The Caucasian Legacy

(Socio-Cultural Eclecticism)

We Caucasians have learned from the past, but our eyes look to the future.

We accept the title of -"CAUCASIAN"- with pride and dignity. Though human origins are lost in the mist of time, there is a- *Caucasian People*, there are *Caucasian Morals* and *Ideals*, plus our *Ancestral Trust*, and our *Eclectic* cultural history of more than forty thousand years. We must never let our social goals or our world position go wanting!

What is meant by Caucasian ideals? Simply, it's our children. You see, the children are the idea, and the idea is the children. The children are the symbol and reality of our ever-enduring biology. They are the ultimate fruit of all our labors.

They are why we make sacrifices and what the sacrifices mean. Look at your own child. In his or her eyes, you are seeing the labor of endless years of biological struggle. You are viewing the endless toil that has gone into making sure that our children's needs and safety are secure.

It is only through the children that we can be born again, only children allow us that unique biological idea called the *"Caucasian Continuum,"* (birth!) our reemergence the very essence of Caucasian life itself. For you see, the Caucasians people were the beginning and continue to be the source, the *Fulcrum* of real creative genius for all humankind.

Our higher forms of learning have brought all of Humanity from the dark ages, lifting them into the light. And it is our higher *Cognitive Abilities* that will pioneer humankinds distant future.

Due to a combination of *Cultural* and *Genetic* bonds, we Caucasians throughout the world have formed the greatest intellectual and physical fight for existence of any known life form. Our children: like ourselves, and that of our ancestors, will continue to struggle against the same opposition- *Natures Competitive Predation*. The fight, is to some extent endless, for life itself is an endless struggle, complete and wholly unto itself! It feeds upon itself,…just as kind feeds upon kind, just as difference- wars against difference! That which wishes to live, which desires the freedom to live, must endure the perils of deadly opposition from all other living things. This is the truth of life, all of life!

The winding roads of evolution have crossed and clashed in the endless struggle to attain the higher ground, (dominant culture!) it is only on this ground that there is a respite, that you can take a break in the struggle for life, and it is at that moment, during the brief respite, that you can see clearly. Then you must return to the struggle, for there are many biological ideas, and the siege to take the high ground (dominant cultural position) never ends. The high ground is all that is rich and wonderful, it is a place of substance, and now in the life of this world, we Caucasians hold the *Dominant Cultural Position* (the high ground!).

But, holding the high ground today!...is no guarantee that we Caucasians can still hold on to it- tomorrow? All human cultures and racial groups seek the high ground!

They all want nothing less than what we Caucasian now have! And life, feels no pity for the ones who have lost and are on their way down.

Life does not *Sympathize* with those who have not gained the high ground. And nor for those who have lost the high ground. And seldom if ever, does that which has fallen, rise back to the top. Remember, it has taken us, the *Caucasian People*, more than- 40 thousand years of *Wars, Famine*, and *Ambition* to gain this ground. (higher culture)

Are we now going to lose it to- *Alien* others?

Do you think for one moment that the political and cultural threats you hear coming from the *Minority Races* and their liberal neo-socialist allies, are nothing more than a bluff? And not intended to be carried out? If you are so foolish as to carry such a thought, let the 𝔄lpha- enlighten you before all is lost! The *Threatening* and *Posturing* you hear and see coming from the *Minority Races* is hard core; it is *Essential,* and it is *Fundamental.* They are *Hungry*, and they are *Ambitious.*

They are struggling like they have for thousands of years, trying to fight and win *Wars,* to overcome *Famine*, to realize *Ambition,* their nature is *Predatory!*

They are trying to take the high ground, to dislocate Caucasian culture, and establish their own!

They will *Plunder* and *Restructure* Caucasian cultural navigation. (there can only be one cultural navigator!)

Alien races seek cultural dominance- only their future, only in their hands!

They will not go away; they have no other place to go; all roads lead to the ground that is now in- Caucasian hands!

We are at a solemn moment in time. History calls us at moments such as these. History calls us now!

We, the Caucasian people, stand at a *Social Crisis,* at the supreme social crisis of our age! For unnumbered millennia, we have toiled upward from the dark jungles of savagery toward cultural heights that our mental and spiritual gifts have allowed us. Our cultural and political path has been slow and unsteady. Time and time again we lost our way, only to plunge into dark and uncertain social ends.

The Caucasian social path is littered with misguided civilizations, and it is scattered with the graves of Caucasians who were stricken with an unfulfilled end. We Caucasians have suffered many disasters, but none of these disasters proved fatal because they were local.

Always, there were some strong *Caucasian Barbarians* to catch the falling torch and carry on But where are those barbarians now?

Centuries later, we leaped forward again, tribe by tribe, we formed a common civilization. When technically ready, we conquered the- *Oceans*, we spread over the- *Earth,* filling its great empty spaces with more of our kind.

During the nineteenth century we entered a new age of discovery, "Science" and the hidden powers of "Nature" opened themselves to us. We tamed nature for our own use, and intellectual distance was diminished, the planet was integrated under the harmony of a single race, with a common civilization.

This Caucasian social system offered everyone (humankind) economic development and freedom within a general unity.

All these Caucasian achievements were won solely due to a strong "Racial Union," and the maintenance of what we have won on prior "Caucasian" race values. Civilization in and of itself means nothing! It is merely an effect, the cause of which is the creative urge of- *Racial Union.*

Civilization is the body, the *Race* is the *Soul.* Let the soul vanish, and the body withers and dies.

We, the "Caucasian Americans" and our sister states through out the world must return to our own *Ancestral Trust,* to renew our- *Racial Energies!*

There are no more *Caucasian Barbarians* to pick up the torch.

It is all up to us, and us alone!

We know, you and I know, that we need to return to our "Primal Racial Foundation" to find the strength and the courage to carry on. That primal foundation is our *Ancestral Racial Trust.* A loss of Caucasian racial faith, political betrayal, cultural war, alien crime, moral desertion, and alien invasion stand between us and our future. We know the obstacles; we know the threats!

How reversible this situation is, we don't know. That is the uncertainty that fills our day with anxiety.

Is it already too late?

The Alpha says no! It is time to understand our role in terms of a our- *Racial Union!*, and not individual politics.

We must resist the temporary passions of the political and economic marketplace. We as Caucasians must resist the *Multiracial State, Political Correctness*, *Multiculturalism*, and the *Alien Invasion.*

We must not, and cannot allow *Liberal Subversives* to distroy the *Caucasian American Community* and its culture!

We Caucasian Americans cannot allow this to happen!

If we are to regain anything approaching our once confident view of the future, we as Caucasians Americans will have to begin by proving to ourselves in real tangible ways, that we can be honest about our problems, that we have the guts to tackle them, and that we can unify to solve them!

Doing so means we will have to criticize- *Ourselves!* Yes, we are burdening ourselves with- *Weaknesses!*

We must identify these to overcome them. We must use our eyes to see, to overcome hypocrisies, to not be afraid. We must transform our *Political Power* and turn it in a direction that is in accord with our understanding of the needs of our Caucasian people!(the founders and builders of America!)

But first, we must- *Mobilize!*

We must spread the word of- Truth. (the Valorous!)

We need to begin slowly, step by step, and we must be prepared for-
Opposition!...from Caucasian liberal zealots and "Aliens" alike. Our goal
is to reaffirm the Caucasian world order, and we cannot expect to do so
without- *Belligerent Opposition* from both- *Liberal Zealots* and *Alien
Subversives.*

Furthermore, within any large national or regional setting, we need
many steps taken from different points of departure within the world, but
moving in the same general direction. Hence, these first steps need to be
taken in light of the concrete circumstance of time, place, and value.

In spite of the varied starting points, we as a movement will be able to
unify a common purpose that will produce increasing social momentum and
bring about unexpected confluences on these apparently separate voyages.
Ours is a movement of a natural *Caucasian Racial Conscience*, a deep
response to our- *Fematrix Order*, to her law and rhythm of our creation.
What is the good of practicing prudence in the race, if hungry strangers can
crowd in and occupy our banquet table, (our culture!) taking the places and
resources reserved for our children? A culture is the banquet table of human
life. It is in our culture, where we as human beings are able to bring about
economic prosperity and social tranquility, loyalty to our ancestral trust, and
devotion to our children and to our God. Culture is the fulcrum of human
existence.

From the biological realm of the *Caucasus Mountains* (the wilderness)
where the seeds of the *Caucasian Fematrix* would emerge and flower
into being, a race of people was born, a proud race, and from them, from
this small realm of biology, would flow the many tribes of the *Caucasian
Fematrix*.

These tribes, driven by the three laws of life, then engaged life and
all its opposition,...to the North, the South, the East, and to the West, they
migrated, moving to the constant rhythm of their racial spirit, acquiring the
knowledge and skills they needed to survive. This migration was anything
but a joyous dance; rather, it was a -*Trail of Sorrow*- that followed their
journey.

Their journey into the vast wilderness was nature's (the sisterhood's)
rite of passage. Under the indifferent eyes of nature, they ran a gauntlet of
predators, predators that awaited them at every turn, around every corner,

and behind every rock,...predators relentless in their savagery and predation.

Such was the price of admission to nature's great bounty, a bounty never given away!...a bounty that must be taken!

The places are few, and the mouths are many. The fate of those who do not gain admission to the banquet is to fall back onto the menu of life, for nature to devour. There are only three positions in life: (1) those being served to? (2) those doing the serving? and (3) those being served up?

All of life revolves around these " Three" primitive positions, they are not fixed positions, but constantly in motion, constantly dynamic and shifting.

They are the life cycle itself, and the position that one holds at any given moment is determined by one's skills in understanding the *Fematrix* life cycle and its truths.

Each species, each race (subspecies) and life form, must develop, sustain, and safeguard it own banquet table (culture).

Failure in this regard would bring about the complete destruction of the socio-economic bond, along with the vision of the whole, and as a result, the complete collapse of the social contract, and the dispersion of its many members would soon follow.(the downfall of all empires!...and bio-dynasties)

The mind set of all order, whether it be the microscopic atomic structures or the universal biological tropism, consists of basic fundamental absolutes, or laws that have themselves been predetermined and fixed by the *Fematrix*.

The careful observation of emerging societies, as well as those long existing, will reveal the very close observation of those laws. However, even close observance to these laws cannot guarantee survival?

Life, as is clear to all with eyes to see, is a constant, unrelenting battle to push back the darkness.(the unknown!)

These laws are guiding lights toward that end, which is why they are referred to in "Caucasianism" as the laws of light, for by them a greater darkness can be dispelled, the darkness of the mind.

The Alpha's view: No people, no community, no pattern of life, may build and maintain a civilization unless they are supported by a system of-

Rational Ideas! A positive attitude to life that is rooted in a living identity. Precisely herein lies the danger of a destabilized people, a destabilized community, a destabilized cultural tradition. A people that have been- Deracialized!..and removed from their biological and cultural mandate, the core belief of their civilization!...well become bearers of a failed value system" that well ultimately overwhelm and destroy them. This is truth, this is reality!

State Of The World

~~~

(the Caucasian world initiative)

The concern for the environment and the global situation is honorable. We are all for a better environment and high bio-diversity, and against poverty,...not to mention the growing awareness of a perceived global climate change?

The Alpha does not argue against these legitimate concerns. He argues against those who feel strongly about the ills of poverty and the environment and who always emphasize how deep and wide-spread it is, because of exploitation by advanced *Caucasian States* throughout the world.

But they seldom if at all mention, that if not for the Caucasian states throughout the world, there would be- *No*- technological advancement and no environmental or poverty concern!

A similar observation applies to those who care very deeply about human rights. Once again, if not for the Caucasians world community there would be -*No*- concern for human rights! And as for the *African, Asian,* and *South American* (Amerindian) communities, and their participation and concern for these matters?

Virtually- None!

But yet! The Caucasian world community is in a constant state of defending itself from these *African, Asian,* and *South American*- no-shows, and let us not forget the righteous tirades from their Caucasian neo-socialist handlers, (liberal zealots) who along with the crisis-focused media have created images of a rapidly deteriorating world?

Nothing could be further from the truth! On the development side, our traditional problems like- *Food*, *Energy*, *Water*, and *Pollution* are being tackled, and in many cases (world wide) have been managed already. Again, thanks to the Caucasian world community, and no other!

It is crucial to the discussion about the state of the world that we consider the fundamentals. This requires us to refer to long-term regional and global trends, considering their importance especially with regard to human welfare.

People debate and participate in decision making processes, but it is also crucial that we cite figures and trends which are true, and not any- *Organizations Propaganda* of a doomsday belief (environmental mythmaking!) and their unfor-tunate frequency of blatant errors.

This demand may seem glaringly obvious, but the public environment debate has unfortunately been characterized by an unpleasant tendency towards a rather rash treatment of the truth. This is an expression of the fact that the *Liberal Litany* has pervaded the debate so deeply and for so long that like their *Racial Tirades,*(racial equality) their blatantly false claims can be made again and again, without any reference, and yet still be believed? (truly absurd!)

Although economists have long acknowledged that the fear of running out of resources is erroneous, it has had an almost magical grip on *liberal Intellectuals* as liken to their *Racial Phobia,* and its backdrop of arguments pointing back to the incessant and erroneous claims of *Slavery* as if that world enterprise only shackled the welfare of *Sub-Saharan Africans* and no-other?

In the longer run, it is likely that we (Caucasians) will change our energy needs from fossil fuels towards other and cheaper energy sources- maybe renewable, maybe fusion, maybe some as of now-unimagined technology. Thus, just as the *Stone-Age* did not end for lack of stone, the *Oil-Age* will eventually end, but not for lack of oil.

Rather, it will end because of the eventual availability of "Superior Alternatives", again!..Caucasian technology.

The *Alpha's* basic argument, both from *Biology* and *Economics,* is that the focus should be on making the best possible regulatory system. But we also need to realize that no system can provide absolute certainty. Science cannot always prove that something is not dangerous.

Technology cannot always provid absolutely "Safe" products. Hence, environmental as well as our technological sciences are not risk-free.

Thus, choosing sensibly in this debate requires us to see the risks but also compare them thoughtfully with all other risks. We as Caucasians need to know how we have handled past problems.

We must be able to dispose of the many myths but also face the true challenges in order to make the most informed decisions. Consequently, we Caucasians must stop giving our environmental thinking a *Doomsday* perspective.

It is imperative for us to see the environment as an important, but only one important part of the many challenges we as Caucasians must handle to create an even better world.

The Alpha's view: If we of the Caucasian American com- munity are to continue on with our bid for a secure future, by upholding our "Biological Mandate" it stands to reason that we must put the welfare of our community First and Foremost!...and not let any kind of subversive alien trademark of- Victimhood?..a delusive moral ruse!..to lure us to submit to their "Parasitic" agenda. We the Caucasian American community must always remember that we are the- Caucasians!..a Biological Racial Dynasty! (subspecies) A unique and one of a kind occurrence, and as such!...if we fail to understand this life's competitive (predatory) nature!...of malevolent biological dynasties (species and subspecies!) we Caucasians, like all who came before us, will be consumed by the hunger of its truth! And like all of life's misguided, we also will descend into the shale of the earth, never to be seen again!

"In The Arena Of Life, There is Only One Reality"

- Survivability-
(Encounter - Analysis - Strategy)

Biological Competition

(Racial Rivalry)

Racial possession: is the right of racial competition, and the defeat of racial opposition; hence, the establishment of the rights of the- *Victorious* social will, over the desires of the- *Defeated* social will. This is the social arena of all biological life, which has no preference for any life other than the *Victorious*!

Which in human terms is ultimately determined by the *Racial Combatants Themselves* through their social discipline and by the legacy of their forbears, thereby establishes the stability of their society and its social direction?

The society that does not establish *Biological Discipline* in its social order has failed to understand the basic fundamentals of life itself. And a society that establishes biological disciplines on the grounds of "Superiority" has not failed to understand the basic fundamentals of life.

Life, you see, has no equals!

What life deals in is quite simply the dynamics of- *Biological Difference*, and the survival of superior biological difference. (Eugenics- well born!) The vitality of one's "Racialness" constitutes an important part of one's *Social* and *Spiritual* reality. A society that threatens the survival of dynamic racial difference in its social philosophy and makes the preference for one's own kind - a crime?...is operating from the political halls of *Intellectual Capitulation*, by virtue of the fact that *Eugenics* and *Dysgenics* are the true fulcrum of all biological life. (no exceptions!) Superiority: is the ultimate arbiter of all biology. (the supreme goal!) this is truth, this is reality!

Caucasian Supremacy?...Absolutely!

Alien Invasion

(Predatory Colonization)

The Alpha tells us; In Caucasianism you cannot deny the truth of kind!(bio-differentia)...and you cannot deny kind's right to exist. To do so would be to invoke the annihilation of all that is. For all there is, is kind! There are three things a living kind must accomplish in its first life. The first thing it must accomplish is to learn the ways of its kind. (bio-cultural fusion) Until it does this, it merely flounders through some passage of time, always vulnerable to its own destruction, and often responsible for the unwanted and unnecessary destruction of others.

The second thing it must accomplish is to bring others of its kind into the world; only in this way does a *kind* or *Race*, continue! The third thing it must do for its kind is to grow and expand its predatory opportunity-*Hunting* and *Gathering* range; for the benefit of its kind. (food and territory)

Competition
(the right of suppression)

The Alpha tells us: In life there are basic rules, *Run* if you can!... *Fight* if you must!...Survive at all cost! And these rules apply to that most unavoidable and everyday encounter "Competition" and its desired outcome "Suppression" in other words, in a competitive world for *Limited Resources* the principle of *Competitor Suppression* for both *Domestic* and *Alien* alike, is the standard for all living things!

Therefore, you will either defend your way of life, (ancestral life strategy) your Culture, that which is yours, or you will lose it all to "Alien Conquerors" and their right of *Suppression*!

Case in point: Alien- *Immigration* or *Invasion*?

When a person or group of people come to the borders of a country who's society and people are of a deferent *Race* and *Culture*, only two scenarios will present themselves.

Number One: they have come as alien *Immigrants*!...in which they have entered the host country legally and intend to except the *Suppression* of their culture (language included) in favor of the host Country?

Number Two: they have come as alien *Invaders*!...in which they have entered the host country illegally and intend to resist the *Suppression* of their culture and language, thereby undermining the host Country, and in fact declaring a state of hostility or war, (predatory colonization) you will either vanquish them, or they will subjugate you through *Political Hostility* (majority rule?...the *Achilles Heel* of democracy!)

This is truth, this is reality!

The Alpha's view: the wide range of variation between racial populations (human kind!) in their physical characteristics and diversity of the gene frequencies is identifiable, measurable and assignable. Thus, for the liberal zealots erroneous claim that human race's do not exist? Therefore no subspecies competition?...is an anthropological impossibility. There is but one identifiable bio-group which fits that ubiquitous designation of occupying the four quarters or hemispheres of the Earth, they are the three remaining subspecies of homosapiens, (human species!) Negroids – Mongoloids – Caucasoids, and they like all of life!..are in direct competition for the "Supremacy" of their own Biological Dynasties and Fematrix Mandates.

The
Pseudo Guilds

(political house's of human deception!)

The Alpha tells us: Yes!...we humans have our very own groups of *Political* and *Intellectual* "Chameleons" who have continued "Ritualistically" through false appearance and statements; to *Mislead and Disguise* the political, social and international reality of *Sedition* and *Treason* now facing "Caucasian America" and her sister states throughout the world.

And the mere knowledge of these facts within itself, is no more powerful than one being lost in the wilderness. For neither can find a solution until the release of courage though intelligently directed action. The purpose of political house's (the Senate and Congress.) is to represent and carry out the will of those people who created the Nation and the seats of power in it?...not, a Senate or Congress that has taken on the status of *Street Venders* (donations!) and state government contract deals (gratitude-envelopes!) Yes, this is all very alive and well, completely out of control and totally Criminal!

The
Political Purge

"We can do it if we believe in our future!"

The purpose of intelligent action and the value of the law lies in the using of it. For you see, a society that gets out of the habit of expressing it self in "Action" finally atrophies and becomes closed to many of the vital facts of life. (what's going on around them!) And, Americas political house's of the *21st* century have registered no signs of action?..against an "Alien Invasion" yes, that's right!..an "Invasion" and their psychology of inaction is nothing short of-*Treason!*..yes, the time has come to clean up the- *Garbage!*...in both Political Houses, and drive out the Vermin!...the obnoxious *Socialists* and *Progressive zealots* collectively.

Thereby, restoring our Caucasian American *"Constitutional Dynasty."*

- Territory -

(the bio-haven)

Life is not static, and so a living force cannot be static, but must grow and adapt for its own benefit and the benefit of its kind. In this regard, there are three things that are understood by all of nature (the sisterhood,) from the pinnacle of creation that is man, to the lowliest creature crawling across the face of the earth.

These three things are the *Taking*, the *Holding*, and the *Losing* of territory.

All living things must build a safe place to live, a nest or den! This nest or den is like no other place on earth; it is most revered, in that it is the sacred domain of the female, of birth, of regeneration. It is the center of life, the *Bio-Haven*. The area around the bio-haven is its perimeter. Without question, the greater the perimeter, the more secure the bio-haven. No living creature, allows perimeter trespass, for the perimeter has the same sacred quality as the bio-haven itself, and as such must always be defended to the death. Therefore, a perimeter breach cannot be allowed or be occupied by competitive beings. (alien emigration)

To allow such trespass would place the very future of its kind (race) in mortal jeopardy. This then is given, *Racial Havens* (homes, towns, and nations) are sacred and must be defended against alien aggressive immigration.

Furthermore, what is true of one living entity is also true of others. Case in point, let us consider the *Destruction* of our Caucasian neighborhoods in America! People cringe in horror when confronted with the possible destruction of the *Spotted Owl's* habitat, they mock the very assertion that the *Lion* should be relocated to *Tiger* territory, or that the *Baboon* should be forced to live with the *Chimpanzee*.

Why then, do they suffer the awful hypocrisy that all humankind should live together?

Even then, there are reserved hypocrisies. Aren't these same liberal thinkers trying to preserve the cultures of the *Aborigine*, of the *Amazon*

Primitives, of the *North American Indian?* Do they consider these "Tribal Ethnics" to be mere curiosities? Do they believe that they can be categorized along with all the other life forms in this earthly zoo, but that we "Caucasians" are somehow exempt?

That is preposterous! Why isn't the same concern for *Caucasian Survival* by our social scientists extended to the Caucasian race and its cities, towns and neighborhoods?

Is this not the race that gave them life, that taught them love, and that educated them in the ways of their science and art, and, that sponsored their passage in the world?

Why do they disregard the well-being of the Caucasians, their own-*Posterity?* Why the insidious desire to *Destroy* the Caucasian culture and way of life, by forcing unwanted alien racial "Trespass" into Caucasian territory?

If this same *Social Terrorism* were perpetrated on any other species of life, there would be an outcry.

Why not for Caucasians?

I call on these intellectual utopian architects, these keepers of the ultimate fallacy "Equality" to answer these questions. I call on these liberal grim reapers, these Caucasian men and women without *Racial Loyalty*, to justify their *Cowardice* and *Capitulation*.

Where will they be!..when our Caucasian neighborhoods (bio-havens) have been brought to ruin by alien others?

Will they endeavor to rebuild that which alien others cannot rebuilt?...or will they step back and applaud their obscene and cruel course of Caucasian-*Cultural* and *Social-* destruction? We cannot, and must not allow decisions that affect our very existence as a people to be in the hands of liberal zealots subversives! If we as a people do not put a stop to the loss of "Caucasian Neighborhoods" to an "Uncontrolled Alien Invasion", then our "Culture" along with our "Children's Future" will be lost.

Friends, there are evil forces at work, evil forces determined to bring down Caucasian cultural life in America.

These forces must be exposed for what they are,(liberal zealot progressives!) and then they must be stopped! Only when we Caucasians are convinced of the necessity to recover and preserve that which is now being *Politically Hijacked* right out from under us,...will we be assured of a strong and positive future.

We must inaugurate Caucasian political and social necessities! We must have the will and the courage to carry them out to the very end. For some five thousand years, the race known as the Caucasians has written a legacy for the entire world to see, most of all, for its children and their future generations to see.

The purpose of this legacy is a lesson, a lesson not to make the same mistakes that have already been made in past- *Caucasian Civilizations!*

The legacy cries out; do not repeat the mistakes of - *Alien Racial Emigration*!

Do not force yourselves to suffer the pains of an altruistic social delusion by- *Liberal Zealots*!

Alien Racial Emigration: to Caucasian American lands, is nothing short of *Culturally*, *Politically* and *Economically* deadly!...for the Caucasian American community.

Hence, leading to *Alien Predatory Colonization* and the belligerent and violent displacement of all Caucasian people and their culture!...example: *South Africa!*...total- Caucasian Capitulation!..and lose of their future. (this is their reality!)

The great Caucasian minds of the past, know perfectly well of our impetuous nature to push aside the warnings of "Reality" for the desires of the present and the visions of the future. They were themselves part of their own "Alien Emigration Folly" as they did not heed the warnings themselves, and became victims of their own voracious liberal social egos.

A racial society is governed by the field of biological human play, with a variety of ethnic social zones. Each one of these zones can be further divided by alien racial emigration, which was not a big factor in past history,(racial sensibility) but is now a major factor in all Caucasian societies throughout the world, by liberal zealots placating- *Invading Aliens!*

Because of the lethal social virus "Equality" a political and socially engineered morality by liberal zealots, alien racial emigration has been able to storm the gates of Caucasian societies throughout the world with devastating political and social results, leaving the modern Caucasian world to face the newest social and liberal political compromise, the most recent capitulation to history.

Again, a biological (racial) kind's society is woven in its likeness. It is its major poem, a social biography, and mental definitive. The cup of history is overflowing with the sweet and bitter wines of long-gone societies. Some were just societies; some were evil; some were known for their military conquests, while others were known for their intellectual conquests. Human society, unlike any other social order, is hampered and enriched at the same time with unspecialized individuality capable of anything, the total social nightmare, and as history has revealed, the perils of the *Caucasian Human Journey*, our social nightmares, is no less a burden!

Hence, *Political-Correctness, Affirmative-Action, Multi-culturalism-* all alien pandering!...all having become the new liberal *Political Sermon* in their never ending quest for that which they could never achieve "*Racial Equality*" being, that it has no foundation or truth! But, remains a fortress for their political and cultural subversion.

Furthermore, If the American *Liberal Zealots* are about to embark on a real "Equality" voyage for a *Multiracial State*? They are heading into some very *Subversive* and *Dangerous* uncharted social waters!...*Racial Storms* of unprecedented fury, and *Political Upheaval* of great magnitude await these social mariners. (biological reality contempt!)

It will truly be a voyage, by a ship of fools! A race of people as a general rule, owes very little to what their born with- A race of people is what they makes of itself.

- Truth -

(The addiction of the mind, compass of the will!)

The Alpha tells us: In life there is the phenomena of *Truth*, both for the animal kingdom, as well as for the human kingdoms. And of this *Truth*, there are "2" one being *Fundamental Truth*, and the other being *Ideological Truth*, and of all known life!...only one living group possesses both, and that is the *Human Species*,...animal species/subspecies, only possess and operate through *Fundamental Truth*!

In Caucasianism, the study of *Truth* and its evolution from *Fundamental Truth*, being *Hardwired-Imprinting*- 99 and 9/10% of all living things?...to *Ideological Truth* being *Human Intellectual Theater*, and the only group being 99 and 9/10% free of *Imprinting*?

All this taking place in a world where a 100% of all living things (in the billions!) who's communication with each other, is nonexistent?

Hence, these intelligible anomaly; humankind's lack of imprinting? (being the only one!) And a world with life forms in the billions, and no *Cross-Species* communication,...none!

These truth's needs to be understood!

They will bring *Acumen* to the survival of the *Caucasian* world community.

And, as Caucasians, our future will never be found in those who have not acquired the habit of taking the initiative.

"Truth"
Though Often Difficult, It Must be Upheld!

- Hatred -

(Emotional Antipathy)

It was an enlightened war correspondent who gave us this sincere testimony: The potency of *Hatred* is that it allows us to make sense of *Mayhem* and *Violence*. It gives a justification to what is often nothing more than gross human *Cruelty* and *Stupidity*.

The Alpha's point: When we allow hatred to rule, as it almost always does in a society that has "Competing Racial Groups" then there is only one solution for all!- Separation.

It continues: But the goal we seek when we embrace hatred is impossible to achieve. Hatred never creates the security or the harmony we desire; it disguises our powerlessness and hides from view our own impotence. By finding our identity and meaning in the hatred of others, it makes communication impossible, it exposes the capacity for- *Evil,* which lurks not far below the surface within all of us, and this is why for many people hatred is so hard to discuss once it is discovered. In the rise to hatred we become smaller, hatred absorbs us, and once hatred is attained we are often its pawn. Our *Understanding* and *Compassion* may not always triumph, but it keeps us human. Along with- *Reasoning*- it offers the only chance to escape from the contagion of hatred. It is perhaps, the true and only antidote.

There are times when faced with hatred, when remaining in one's spiritual faith, is the only victory possible. We are tempted to reduce life to a simple search for *Happiness.*

Happiness however, can wither if there is no meaning, the other temptation is to disavow the search for happiness in order to be faithful to that which provides *Meaning*! But to live only for meaning, indifferent to all happiness makes us fanatic, self-righteous, and cold. It leaves us cut off from our own humanity and the humanity of others. We must hope and keep faith with our *Spiritual Reason*, for our lives to be sustained by moments of *Meaning* and *Happiness.*

The Alpha's view: Lacking a historical insight, which is fostering their ignorance!..our "Enemies" of the 21st century have taken our Caucasian kindness for Weakness!..and if this is true?..then it is in our best interest to convince them of their error! And in response to those who believe that liberal zealotry is not a hatred?...and a conspiracy against the Caucasian world community, are ignorant and racially inattentive. Hence, Caucasian America is also being easily misled by the liberal zealot conspirators (progressives) who have dedicated themselves to the willful destruction of the Caucasian American community! Furthermore, the history of the world for the past several centuries and current events at home and abroad have confirmed this treasonous cabal! And why is it?... that our Caucasian American politicians appears to be more ignorant or more indifferent about this Hatred and Treachery than the average Caucasian citizen? And would you be shocked to learn that there are Caucasian American subversives among us?...who have been aiding abetting and conspiring with the dedicated enemies of the Caucasian American community! Therefore, for the sake of our future and that of our children's, we must not!...and can no longer Placate the liberal zealot subversives and their alien cultural marauders!...the time has come to make clear our future!...or the liberal zealots will make it for us, and its called- Extinction!

"Caucasian Patriots"

We must safeguard our children's future, or by the will and action of alien others, we will lose it! Therefore, we must invoke our resilience, to harness our inner strength for the battles that are on the horizon.

"Blessed are the Caucasians"

The Caucasian Empire

(Democratic Racial Monarchy)

The
-Caucasian Imperium-

"Declaration Of Empire"
Empire State - Democratic State - Religious State

-The Quest-

{-Caucasian Racialocracy-}

Racial Sovereignty- itself is, of course, not subject to law, for it is the *Author* and *Source* of all law.(the lawgiver!)

We, the people of the "Caucasian Race" in order to form a more perfect world, establish justice, ensure domestic tranquility, provide for the common defense, promote the general welfare, and secure the blessings of our *Caucasian Fematrix*, "Caucasia" and of liberty to ourselves and our posterity, do *Ordain* and *Establish* this Democratic Racial *Monarchy* "Caucasianism" our Sovereign Racialocracy!

- Preamble -

The Alpha speaks: Behold the "Caucasian Idea" and never let its position be compromised. All that is lives, and all that lives are ideas, and they abound in the endless struggle for the position of their choice.(free will!)

In the beginning was the great void, and in this great void is the spirit of the creator, the *Fematrix*, her will has brought about the beginning of all that is and all that will ever be, and by her will, the fabric of the living being was woven, and into its biological mechanics was placed the gift of the creator,(choice) its own free will, and so it came to pass that all of life would race forth into the bio-cosmic universe, weaving its own will and destiny in the spirit of the creator, the *Fematrix*. Life is the arena of biological opposition, the caldron of physical aggression, where *Inequality* is paramount to survival, and where *Independence* and *Difference* is its most precious fruit. From a wake in this arena of life came forth the Caucasians, a race of people endowed with the spirit and form of its creator, its *Fematrix*. (Caucasia!)

Believing in the Sovereignty of our difference from all others, we the Caucasians have established the Empire of Caucasian tribes and set our course to explore the wonders of life, so that we can be one with *Our Creator*. Therefore, we the Caucasian race seek the survival of our kind. We will meet *Peace* with *Peace, Aggression* with *Aggression,* and will not be diverted from our course. We will abide by our- *Sovereign Biological Mandate.* (so say we all!)

The Quality Of Life

Free will is the foundation for the degree of quality in any and all life forms; therefore the guidelines that are developed in free will are referred to as *Laws* and *Rules* that are the restrictions of the physical expression of free will! And thereby, will ultimately determine a life's failures, its accomplishments, and it overall destiny.

Restriction Of Free Will
(Birth of Direction)

Free will has no center and is without a compass, but restricted will has a point of origin, a center, the sense of limitation, the realization of opposition, and a willingness to comply with or resist that opposition. This is what constitutes a society in its reality, whether primitive or modern.

Whether for man or beast, the restriction of the physical expression of the will is paramount to the survival of the Caucasian race, its society, and the future of its world.

The Alpha
(Lord of the Caucasians and Guardian of the Race)

One man is more capable than a number of men. One man can see the unified view without the clamor of many voices. One man can see in a single glance what a hundred eyes might overlook. You see, authority comes from common interest, from the unified vision. If we wish for The Valorous to be administered well, then the authority must be in the hands of a single individual whose primary thought is our religious race, who cares only for the race's glory and greatness, which is of course, also his own. The *Alpha* is the head of the *Sovereign Racialocracy*, but he is also an elected body; he is elected by the *Monarchy*, the council of *Regents*, and presented to the *Empress* for conformation for the head of the *Sovereign Racialocracy*.

The *Empress* is the divine symbol of the-*Caucasian Religious Racialocracy* and its *Democratic State*.

The *Alpha* is free of the ties that bind each citizen to a particular part of the *Caucasian Empire State*. The *Alpha* cannot have more than a general view, cannot have other interests than general sovereign racial interests, to guide his actions regarding the *Caucasian Empire State*. Only The *Alpha* has, in legislation, the right to mediate and veto. In him alone reside executive powers.

The difference between the powers that make the law and the powers that execute the law is that the former should be divided, so that every question of royal and public interest is completely discussed and analyzed, while the latter should concentrate on a single point, so that the executive action will be unified.

The Hall Of Caucasians
(The Arena of Social Debate)

In the same way that a question to be grasped as a whole should be examined with singularity of view by an individual, so, too, the attention that allows no detail to escape and weighs all with equal precision can belong only to an assembly. The Hall of Caucasians is composed of delegates from all the Caucasian nations (nationalities), members of all the corporations who together represent every kind of local or particular Caucasian interest.

This Hall has, like The *Alpha,* mediation and veto rights in legislation. It possesses the authority for democratic particular interests, because each of the members is obliged to consider, first and foremost, the interest of the persons who elected him or her as a member.

This process, which allows for all three, The *Alpha, Chancellor*, and the *Caucasian People*, to participate in the making of laws, guarantees that no measure of public interest (political) is carried out if it harms the majority of the Caucasian peoples particular interests (people's domestic interest), and no measure of public or domestic particular interest is put into force if it is contrary to the interests of the Caucasian race as a whole, the *Monarchy*, the *Sovereign Racialocracy*, the *Caucasian Empire*.

The Chancellor
(Defender of the Democratic State)

The *Chancellor* is the chosen representative, elected by the hall of Caucasians and appointed by the *Empress* as head of the *Democratic Party* and chief administrator of the *Democratic State*. This position, like that of The *Alpha*, can be held only by a male Caucasian. As stated in the office of the *Chancellor*, if we wish the *Democratic State* to be administered well, then the authority must be in the hands of a single individual whose primary thought is the Democratic Social State of the Caucasian people.

The *Chancellor*, like The *Alpha*, is free of the ties that bind each citizen to a particular part of the *Democratic State*.

Again, the *Chancellor* cannot have more than a general view, cannot have other interests than the Caucasian peoples general democratic interests, to guide his action regarding the people and the *Democratic State*.

The *Chancellor* has, in legislation, only the right to mediate and veto. In him alone resides executive democratic power. The authority of the *Chancellor's* office comes from the common interest of the Caucasian people and their unified *Democratic Vision*.

The Lords
(The Guardians of Balance)

There remains, of course, the danger that The *Alpha* and the *Chancellor* might influence the decisions of the people or conversely, the people might influence the decisions of The *Alpha* and the *Chancellor*. There is the danger that The *Alpha*, the *Chancellor*, and the *People* might deceive themselves regarding the true interests of the *Empire* of *Royal* and *Democratic Individuals*; therefore it is necessary to ensure against such errors, either deliberate or unconscious. A body of man highly esteemed by reason of their public service, academic, or economic achievements shall be placed between The *Alpha*, the *Chancellor*, and the *People*, to examine decisions taken, to balance them, to correct them, or to propose fresh legislation.

This body will exercise this power from another point of view, from the *Hall* of *Lords*. Checks are made on the *Alpha*, the *Chancellor*, and the *People*. They will balance and check the natural tendency on the part of individuals and corporations to grope toward absolute power.

The *Hall* of *Lords* creates real limits because the interest of the *Lords* is in preserving the privilege that makes them an independent corporate body.

Should this balance be destroyed, say by the *Alpha* or *Chancellor* dominating the *People* or by the *People* dominating the *Alpha* or *Chancellor*, the *Empire* would become either *Despotic* or *Democratic*. In either case, each peer would cease to be a member of the government and would be forced to descend to the level of *Courtier* or *Subject*.

It is not enough to establish this constitution on its foundation. It is necessary also to ensure that the foundation itself cannot be shaken!

The *Alpha*, (elective) represents the interests of her Majesty- the *Empress* and the *Racialocracy* as a whole, the Religious Racial Monarchy. (The Caucasian Empire!)

The *Chancellor*, (elective) represents the interests of the *Democratic State*,

The Hall of Caucasians, (elective) represents the interests of each part of the *Democratic State*. (the Caucasian people's special interest)

The Hall of Lords, (elective) is the- "Racial Fulcrum" upon which the three are balanced.

The Empress
(Descendent of the Sovereign, the Caucasian Fematrix)

The root of moral racial purpose (hereditary racial survival) is the domain of the hand that rocks the cradle. It is her, and the preservation of her kind, (her bio- mandate!) that the true light of morality shines upon. *Hereditary Racial Survival (bio-kind!)* is the ultimate truth of all that is, and all that would ever be.

Hence, the will of all life!

The descendent of the hereditary racial right weaves the fabric of society. All must go through her to alter or change the purpose, direction or pattern of her social fabric. The laws and rules that govern this *Religious Racialocracy* are fixed and cannot be altered. They are *Hereditary* and *biologically* fundamental.

They are *Eternal!*

The *Caucasian Empire* (*Caucasianism*) consists of two *Social States*: The *Sovereign State*: (religious racialocracy) the *Empress,* (hereditary-female) sovereign of the state, the office of the *Alpha*, head of state, and the *Council* of *Regents*, governors of the- *Twelve Provinces*. Their duties consist of all- *Foreign Policy* and *Social Domestic Law*.

The *Democratic State*: the people (Caucasian Political Party) The office of the *Chancellor*, governor of the democratic state.

The *Congress*: the elected representatives to the *Hall* of *Caucasians*. Its duties consist of all- *Democratic Policy* for economic and civil domestic growth.

The *Hall Of Lords*: They are appointed by the *Empress* (nominated by the people) The *Lords* see to it that the economic and civil domestic growth is not infringed upon by the foreign policy and social domestic laws of the- *Alpha* (sovereign state) and the *Foreign Policy* and *Domestic Social Laws* are not infringed upon by the *Economic* and *Civil Domestic Growth* of the- *Chancellor* (democratic state)

If the *Empress* lacks the necessary talent for her position, if she is unjust, then the sovereign power she wields will be used for personal vengeance and arbitrary acts.

To avoid this situation, the *Monarchy* is divided into two part. One comprises the *Royal Pomp* and *Circumstance* of the *Religious Racial Fematrix*, the "Empress" and her court.

The other is the business of the *Racialcratic Government*, the 𝔄*lpha*, and his cabinet. (sovereign racialcratic state),

The *Chancellor* and his cabinet, head of the *Caucasian Party* (democratic state).

The *Lords* protect the people against the abuse of power.

The advantages of *Female Hereditary* succession remain in place, (the Empress) while the advantages of election and the choice of the people remains firmly entrenched as well.

The Caucasian people will be governed democratically by a *Parliament* of their choosing with supreme democratic legislative powers- *Culturally, Economically,* and *Civically*.

The 𝔄*lpha* (sovereign state)

The 𝔠*hancellor* (democratic state)

The 𝔏*ords* (the fulcrum, balance of power)

The 𝔠*ouncil* of 𝔯*egents*: the *Regents* are comprised of twelve elected *Caucasian Females* from the- *DEN,* the sacred chambers of the sisterhood of the *Caucasian Fematrix*.

Each *Regent* is assigned to one of the twelve districts in the *Empire*. She is the *S.G,* or *Social Governess,* of that district. The *Regents* have absolute investigative power in both states (sovereign and democratic). They carry the shield of the *Empress*.

The 𝔠*aucasian* 𝔓*arty*: the Caucasian political party is dedicated to the *Caucasian Democratic Commonwealth* and the survival of Caucasian cultures and their institution throughout the world. The *Caucasian Party* is the only political party in the *Empire*. It is comprised of many special interest groups that elect representatives to the Hall of Caucasians (the People's Congress). The Hall of Caucasians is where the People's Congress legislates the *Economic* and *Domestic Rules* and *Laws* that guide the everyday life of the Caucasian citizen. It is in the Hall of Caucasians where the *Will* and *Democratic Social Debate* of the people is heard.

"Blessed"
-Is Our Caucasians Racial Sovereignty-

"So Say We All"

The
Caucasian Dominion

-Hall Of Religions-

The *Hall of Religions*: the Empires religious leaders (of all Caucasian religions) have a seat on the *Council of Religions*- known as the- *Caucasian Dominion*!

This council, along with the *Sovereign State* (the Alpha), makes all the Empire's social laws. Along with the *Sovereign Laws* of the *Caucasian Fematrix*, they are the *Supreme Laws* of the *Empire*; hence the *Democratic State* can make no *Civil*, *Domestic,* or *Business Law,* that will be in conflict with the Laws of the- *Sovereign State*.

-The Human Endeavor-
-Those who Create – Those who Serve – Those who Mendicant-

The Alpha tells us: In the human endeavor there are three class's or groups that make up its social construct, and it has always been the evolution and social position of these three that ultimately determine the final destiny of all human societies.(their success or failure?)

-Those Who Create-
(The Visionary!)

Of all humankinds intellectual achievers, none has had a greater affect on the human journey then the will and drive of the *"Visionary"*, a single human will that transcends the physical world and portrays a wider vision of awareness and acute foresight, with clear ideas of the future and how to bring it about!

Hence, they have been called- *Kings, Queens, Conquers, Presidents, Explorers, Scientists,* and *Industrialist,* and let us not forget our *Spiritual* and *Religious Icons*- those who brought us out of darkness and into the light of *Reciprocity* and *Charity,* yes!...all have contributed substantially to the foun-dation of the human enterprise.

Therefore, it would not be a stretch of the truth to declare that without this small community of revered and exalted intellects running our human enterprise, (very few being their equal!) the human position would be greatly wanting!

-Those Who Serve-
(The Believers!)

Just as the human enterprise could not exist without its small community of *Intellectual Icons*, you must not think for one minute that these *Visionary's* don't have their needs?

These revered elites need a group to assist them in bringing their vision to reality? A group who understands and believes in the meaning and direction of the "Vision," hence willing to work for and serve the purpose of the Vision, with their loyalty and dedication.

(the Unified Vision: the Society!)

But, the human unified society is not simply a process of visionary elites?...but rather an extensible framework which is customized by and for those who are unified in *Body* and *Mind,* a human racial framework that we are all born with, a *"Biological Vision"* of a predetermined kind!

Yes!...Our *Human Racialness* and its social order is *Decided, Determined,* and *Established* in advance of our arrival. Yes!...all living things bear the mark (likeness!) of their Fematrix will!...the "Visionary Core" of all life!

-Those Who Scavenge-
(The Alien Malcontent!)

The *"Alien Racial Opportunist"* (the parasitic equation?)

The Alpha tells us: the *Alien malcontents* having no interest or regard for the Caucasian society's *Cultural, Moral* or *Political Ideology,* other then to plunder its *Charitable Coffers*, and if possible to establish through the country's *Liberal Zealot Fraternity* the moral ruse of *"Equality"* (equal human outcomes?) all this intended to subjugate the Caucasian public will through a very clever psychological-assault!...by declaring the *Wealth* and *Prosperity* of the Caucasian world community- as Criminal?...is this not -*Sedition?*...a deliberate "Racial Assault" against the lawful authority of the- Caucasian American Community? (the founders and builders of America!) by groups of culturally and economically non productive- *Alien Malcontents!*

Fostering a very deep sense of "Guilt" in the weak mind of the liberal zealot elite, thereby gaining free access to the- *Governments Coffers*?..the "Holy Grail" for all- *Alien Opportunists*? (a sense of weakness!...creates great peril!)

The Fatal Process

-Failing To Act!-

The Alpha tells us: our passed human history not only tells us the story's of its *Great Empires,* but more important at this time in our history, are the facts of their tragic failings! Like, *Biological Heredity*, a society must pass on its core construct, its learned and imbedded strategy for the survival of its *Posterity-* (its kind!) its future leadership.

And this can only be accomplished by having a *Posterity* that is acclimated, understands, and is loyal to that strategy! It is the *421*st century of the *Caucasian Conquest of Earth!*...and thou, those who founded the great societies of the Caucasian world (having the vision!) have long passed on leaving their legacy and making places of leadership available to those loyal supporters of the vision and its strategy.

But, these new leaders of the *21st* century would develop a fatal intellectual flaw!...*Liberal Zealotry?*

You see, it is one thing to believe in *Human Rights*, and an other to believe in- *Racial Equality?* (equal racial outcomes?)

By advancing and promoting this *Liberal Fallacy* and its dogma to the level of an *Ideology*, it wasn't long before- *Alien Parasitic Preachers-* would seize this opportunity, using it as their *Moral High ground* to obligate and exploit the *Caucasian Liberal Zealots* into *Demonizing* their own society and to *Betray* their own- *Racial Sovereignty!*

(Hence, *South Africa-revisited*!)

Enter- *The Alien Racial-Opportunist:* (the plunderer!)

It is the *21st* century, and the modern Caucasian world has allowed its *Liberal Zealot Elites* to legislate and enact its ultimate- *Destruction?* (*Alien Racial Equality!*)

Having now betrayed its biological mandate (*Caucasian Racial Sovereignty*) by permitting *Alien Subversives* to enter and participate in Caucasian *Cultural* and *Political Chambers* of power, the Caucasian American community, along with its *European* sister states, will now pay the ultimate price to learn history's unsympathetic truth: When Alien races infiltrate the territory of another race, their intention is always *Predatory, Plunder* and *Subjugation!*..and no amount of liberal*"Utopian-Amends"* will alter the outcome of this truth!

The Alpha's view: You cannot turn "Aliens Races" into Caucasians! And this is why: Alien races don't think like Caucasians, act like Caucasians, build like Caucasians, explore like Caucasians, and they lack

our great inquisitive nature both in the Sciences, as well as the Humanities just to mention a few! In other words, they are unequivocally not of our Caucasian kind!...in either body or mind. And if the Caucasians of the 21st century continue to disregard natures wisdom of "Natural Distance" (territory!) between apposing life strategies (bio-kinds) we will fare no better then all those who in denial of their sacred kind!...would lead their children to their demise in the name of "Racial Equality" the ultimate intellectual ruse!

The Military

"Defenders Of Our Racial Dynasty"

The Alpha tells us: All societies are the products of their own biological mandate, (historical journey) and part of this mandate is its core initiative- defending its *Biological, Social,* and *Cultural Subscription* through its life strategy. Hence, the union of related defenders, known as- *The Military!* That which is authorized by its greater society to use *Lethal Force!* including *Weapons* of *Death* in defending its- *Sovereignty*!

The Military Mandate

"Victory"

The Alpha tells us: It is a grave error for any society to not keep its people disciplined for war! For in what person should a society look for greater faith than in those who have promised to die for it! Hence, *the Solder*!... defender and keeper of the- *Sovereign Frontier,* the boundary between the *Caucasian State*, and all other adjacent *Alien States*!

The Purveyors of "Victory": The *Caucasian Solder*, whether against an *Enemy* in battle or the endless encounter's in life's elimination tournament, (the world conquest!) he or she has always through their *Ability*, *Integrity* and their *Unassailable Courage!*...given to all- *Enemy Combatants*?. their superior principles of- *Discipline*, *Command*, *Respect*, *Assistance*, and *Mercy!*...Hence, their mandate for- "Victory"

Our Caucasian Eternal Debt
(To Our Noble Military Heroes!)

To all our *Mothers* and *Father*, *Sister* and *Brothers* who gave it all!... their *Wellbeing*, their *Futures* and their *Lives*, so that you and I, their posterity, would in their name! ...measure all our actions by the unalterable rule of our Caucasian right to survival!...and that we will take care of the *Families* of those who give their lives, and oversee the *Rehabilitation* and *Recovery* of all those who suffer from the *Pains* and *Injuries* of war, bringing them back to the *Loving* and *Grateful Arms* of their people, and reassure them of their future, by supporting and making their path to a productive and meaningful life.

-This we do Swear before our Nation and our Faith-

"So Say We All"

League Of Caucasian States

(The Union of Empire)

The *Caucasian Empire* is a body comprised of Caucasian *Tribal* and *Ethnic* States throughout the world. These States are the source of Caucasian America's eclectic culture and religious reason.

The *United States of America* is a Caucasian state, and considered by the *Caucasian Empire* to be the *Consummate* Caucasian State. Founded by

Caucasian European Explorers and settled by Caucasian religious pilgrims on their journey to freedom. America has become the spirit of Caucasian social, intellectual, and political reality. But America is only one of many Caucasian states throughout the world.

Hence the *League of Caucasian States*. A Caucasian world political body that leads the world in economic and financial development, not to mention the pursuit of excellence in the arts and sciences, from 40.000 BC to the present day.

As all Caucasians of historical intellect know, the Caucasian States throughout the world have been head and shoulders above all rivals when it comes to significant technical and social achievements.

It is Caucasianism (our faith!) that recognized the validity of the racial will to a degree as to concede to that will the right of *Racial Sovereignty*, and *Racial Sovereignty* cannot suppress itself. If we look at the matter from a purely Caucasian point of view, *Racial Sovereignty* is inalienable. For decades, and even for centuries the Caucasian people continue to endure passively outworn *Political* conditions which greatly impede social and moral progress.

Therefore, one would be unwise (Alien or Caucasian!) to believe that we Caucasians will not take up the battle for our own Existence!

Thus, the Caucasian world must come together as one United Racial Empire! A *League of Caucasian States,* that will take its place as the "Guardian" of the Caucasian Empire.

The Alpha's view: the premise of any life, is survival of its biological blood line.(unique kind!) For that reason, a life forms physical presents is a manifestation of what it believes!..and therefore, a notable strategy for the survival of that which it believes. The value of this truth is to be estimated according to its tendency to promote improvement, either in Racial Virtue, or in those qualities which render Intellectuals extensively useful in Caucasian society.

-Truth-
"Is History Teaching By Example"

Lex Sacrata

(Sacred Law)

ARTICLE - I -It shall exist

THE GREAT SEAL OF THE CAUCASIAN EMPIRE

The great seal of the Empire will be referred to as the star of the Caucasians, it will consist of a- *Sixteen-Pointed Gold Star.*

This *Gold Star:* will symbolize the ever enduring spirit of the Caucasian people and their *Fematrix.* (Caucasia!)

This *Gold Star:* will sit on a *White Background,* which symbolizes the light that all life moves toward, it will have *Two Red Lines,* one above and one below. These lines are the symbol for all those Caucasians who lost their lives and shed their blood in the defense of the Caucasian way of life.

This great seal shall also be on the *Flag* of the *Caucasian Empire.*

ARTICLE - 2 -It shall exist
Seal Of Religious Sovereignty

The great seal of Religious Sovereignty: shall be referred to as the *Will,* and it represents the community of *Caucasian Religions* that forms the moral backbone of Caucasian society. The *Will* shall consist of the symbols of the *Great Caucasian Religions,* each joined to the other in their rightful progression.

This sculpture of *Gold* and *Silver* shall sit in the center of the *Caucasian Star* upon a *White Background,* for it is the true light against the darkness.

It shall also have *Two Red Lines,* one above and one below. This is the symbol for all those who stood by humankind in its darkest hour and gave their lives to bring them into the light. This great seal shall also sit upon a *Flag* that will honor the *Great Hall of Religions.*

ARTICLE - 3 -It shall exist

Caucasianism: is the religion and social philosophy of the Caucasian people who believe in, and have formed a sovereign political racial state, a democratic racial monarchy. (a racialocracy!)

A *Caucasianest*: is a person who believes in and practices Caucasianism as the only legitimate Caucasian social order in the world.

The *Caucasian Empire!* Is the *Sovereign Racial State* of the *Caucasian Democratic Commonwealth*.

It will be referred to as the "Caucasian Empire" comprising the social, economic, and political institutions that have been established by the various Caucasian people and their cultures.

The *Caucasian Party*: is the only democratic legislative body of the *Caucasian Empire*. It will be referred to as the *Democratic State*. It is an elective political body and serves the economic and domestic special interests of the Caucasian people.

The *Laws of the Caucasian Fematrix:* the life force must be known to all. These laws are grouped into three, and they are called the *Sovereign States of Life*.

ARTICLE - 4 -It shall exist

The *First Sovereign State*: "Physical Racial Inviolability" is the sacred heritage of *kind*, of *Identity*.

It is the established mark of the *Caucasian Fematrix* "Caucasia" her biological mandate.

SECTION 1: Race is not deducible from anything else, it is the self-establishing life of the female will. In this regard, let it be known! To compromise or undermine the sovereignty of the Caucasian Race for personal or material gain is forbidden and falls under the rubric of treason, morally, spiritually, and biologically. It is punishable by excommunication from the race and from its society.

SECTION 2: Any individual who embraces the philosophy of racial denial and racial compromise must be considered to be mentally disturbed and must be treated accordingly.

$SECTION 3: Any individual who is not of Caucasian biology (kind) will be considered an alien (non-Caucasian) and will be accorded all the rights of alien social status.

$SECTION 4: Those individuals having one Caucasian parent (mixed racial origin) are considered *Recessive's or non-Caucasian*, and will have no social distinction as a Caucasian, or Caucasian citizen.

$SECTION 5: It must be stated explicitly!...that any kind of willful *Procreation* between *Caucasian People* and *Alien Races* (miscegenation) is *Caucasian Racial Treason!* Furthermore, all those Caucasians outside of the *Empire*, who entertain the idea of *Miscegenation*!...the death of their own race! Must be, and will be *Shunned*!...by the Caucasian world community as-*Subversive Racial Nihilists*.

ARTICLE - 5 - It shall exist

The Second Sovereign State: **Culture.** All cultures of Caucasian origin are welcome into the Empire as long as they do not violate any of the three sovereign states or laws of the empire.

$SECTION 1: Under no circumstances will a cultural act of *Female* abuse or bondage be tolerated, nor will it be tolerated against *Children, Men,* or *Aliens.*

$SECTION 2: All children and adults, regardless of their cultural origin, will be indoctrinated into Caucasian society. Any cultural laws that they follow that may be in conflict with the laws of the Empire will be subject to termination or cultural readjustment.

$SECTION 3: Any and all *Females* in the Empire are recognized as the life force of the Empire and therefore their status overcomes all cultural differences without exception.

The *Female* and her children are the supreme catalyst of the Empire. Their position therefore, can never be compromised!

$SECTION 4: All cultural *Holidays* and *Festivals* will be legislated by the said cultures that share a seat on the *Cultural Council*, in the Hall of Caucasians.

$SECTION 5: No culture will obstruct or prevent the full and desired education of any and all persons in the Empire. No culture will prevent any person from performing any *Public Service* for the betterment of the Empire.

$ECTION 6: All *Aliens* are considered *Guests* of the Empire, and they will be treated with *Respect* and *Dignity*. Any and all Aliens that will not comply with the laws of the Empire will be deported.

$ECTION 7: All Caucasians whose *Culture* or *Political* philosophy prevents them from abiding by the laws of the Empire will remove themselves from the Empire or they will be removed.

$ECTION 8: It is the will of the Empire that all the people, *Caucasians* and *Alien* alike, are able to speak their own *Ethnic Language*, but, to communicate in a *Common Language*! Therefore, *English* is the official language of the Empire. It is and will be the *Umbrella Language* spoken in the Empire.

$ECTION 9: *Cultural Tolerance* is the law of the Empire, and all cultures must conform to the laws of the Empire; none will be in conflict.

ARTICLE - 6 -It shall exist

The Third Sovereign State: **Religion.** The Caucasian race holds the freedom of religion to be paramount to the existence of the Empire. All religions are welcome as long as they do not in any way *Debase*, *Degrade*, or *Destroy* the human spirit.

$ECTION 1: *Religious Persecution* will not be tolerated; nor the debase-ment or destruction of religious property.

$ECTION 2: Because the human spirit is *Sacred*, any religious cult established for the purpose of personal gain or human bondage will not be tolerated.

$ECTION 3: In order to demonstrate respect for diverse religious expression, no public display of religious symbols or articles will be allowed. Such displays will be restricted to those places designated by the *Council* of *Religions*, at the Hall of Religions.

$ECTION 4: All *Donations* and *Finances* given or acquired for religious purposes must, as a matter of law, be channeled back to the community from which it came. This is the *Sovereign Will* of the race, and all religions must comply.

SECTION 5: All religious *Holidays* and *Festivals* will be legislated by the said religions with a seat on the *Religious Council*, in the Hall of Religions.

SECTION 6: All religions will conform to the laws of the Empire. When religious law is in conflict with the law of the Empire, that religion will be subject to *Religious Readjustment* or *Termination*.

SECTION 7: All *Females* in the Empire are understood to be the life force of the Empire, and as such, enjoy a status that overcomes any and all *Religious Differences*, without exception!

SECTION 8: No religion may *Prevent* the full and desired education of any person in the Empire. No religion will *Prevent* any person from performing *Public Service* for the betterment of the Empire.

SECTION 9: All visiting aliens who are members of a *Different Religion* must comply with the laws of the Empire. Those who cannot or will not will be denied entry into the Empire.

SECTION 10: *Tolerance* and *Respect* for the diverse religions of the Empire is the law of the Empire, and no *Person* or *Group* of persons will be in conflict with that law. These *Three Sovereign States* and their laws of light are the foundation of all laws of the Empire. They represent the Caucasian way of life.

These laws derive from the will of the *Caucasian Fematrix*, and therefore serve neither man nor nation, but only the existence of the *Female* will and its creative force. It would be well to recall that the first sound a living thing hears upon entry into this world is the sound of a *Fematrix* crying, and upon leaving this world, the last sound one is likely to hear is the sound of a *Fematrix* crying.

Only the life force is present at both gates.

The Alpha's View: It is necessary that if one is to study the "Fematrix" it should be according to a Religious-Scientific plan; for this science, more perhaps than any other, is liable to perversion from its proper understanding. With some, it is no better than an idle amusement; with others it fosters the prejudice of gender, and leads to female bigotry. The sources of prejudice are infinite; and the mind of one's faith should not be left undirected!..It is dangerous for those who, even with the best intentions, seek for "Fematrix knowledge" to pursue the study without a guide; for no science has been so little methodized. Besides the importance of being able to discriminate truth from falsehood, the attention ought to be directed only to useful truths. There are many difficulties which attend the attempt of forming a proper understanding of the Fematrix; for we are all of her, and by her!

Caucasian Civil Rights

(The Social Fulcrum)

The code of *Caucasian Civil Rights* is fundamental for the social stability of the Empire. The Caucasian people must have an understanding of their Rights under the law.

Caucasian civil Rights are divided into categories that comprise the whole of the *Caucasian Empire* and its people.

This is a general review of those *Rights*.

The First: And most elemental *Right* of all Caucasian people is the *Right* of "Freedom of Speech" (and the right to hold it accountable!) *Heredity Transmission*, the transmission from parent to offspring or from the race to its descendants of all *Rights, Territories, Possessions,* and *Privileges* of the Caucasian race.

To this end, women have some special- *Rights*.

They also enjoy the *Right* of *Self*, of *Truth*, of *Entity*, of *Grievance*, of *Satisfaction*, of *Destination*, of *Association,* of *Privacy*, of *Property*, of *Social Assistance*, of *Social Custom*, and of *Homage*.

Woman will be *Respected* and *Honored*! They are the life force, the *Caucasian Fematrix*; they weave the fabric of life. Through them the race is educated and regenerated.

Children, likewise, enjoy some special *Rights*. They enjoy the *Right* of- *Divinity*, for they are the gift of the *Caucasian Fematrix*. They enjoy the *Right* of- *Social Custom*, of *Truth*, and of *Education*, education by which they can rightfully claim all other *Rights* and *Privileges* while coming to understand their responsibilities.

Just as women and children have clearly their absolut *Rights,* so too, do the men of the Caucasian race.

Men have the *Right* of- *Hereditary Transmission*, of *Self*, of *Truth*, of *Entity*, of *Grievance*, of *Satisfaction*, of *Destination*, of *Association*, of *Privacy*, of *Property*, and of - *Chivalry*, which is simply the *Right* to be men.

In addition to these *Rights*, the *Caucasian Race* as an entity has some *Additional Rights*, those of *Divinity*, of *Covenant*, of *Coventry*, of *Empire*, of *Court*, of *Course*, of *Heroism*, of *Heraldry*, of *Law*, of *Consecration*, of *Arms*, of *Sentinel*, of *Auction*, and of *Property*.

The *Right* of heroism deserves special elucidation, for it reserves for the parents the *Right* to defend the *Rights* and privileges of the children and the race, while it reserves for the children and the race, the *Right* to offer the selfsame protection and defense to the parents. In these matters there is no room for compromise.

Defense and protection of all that is dear to the Caucasian race is- *Inalienable*! All individuals of the race have the *Right* to seek to improve themselves, both mentally and physically. Every individual has the *Right* to the knowledge of the *Truth*, regardless of how offensive or painful that truth maybe!

The *Right* to believe in any and all entities is fundamental, contingent upon the caveat that none of those entities *Debase* or *Degrade* the race or the individuals of the race. Each individual or group has the *Right* to have its grievances heard by an *Impartial Court*, whether those grievances are *Domestic* or *Political* in nature.

This holds true to crimes committed against an *Individual* or *Group*.

The *Right* of *Satisfaction* decrees; the individual or group offended will determine the fate of the offender upon conviction, the parameters of that fate defined by law.

There exists the *Right* of "Ritual Empire" which guarantees the *Protection*, *Enhancement*, and *Glorification* of the mark of the will. We are a people of movement, and therefore the *Right* of *Destination* guarantees us the right to come and go as we see fit, without being detained or obstructed by anyone without clear legal cause. Likewise, we have the *Right* of *Association*, a right not to be infringed upon by any person unless that association or those associations are detrimental to the individual or to the group as a whole.

These *Rights* are in part protected by the larger *Right* to *Privacy*. Unless authorized by a *State* of *Emergency* or by a *Court Order*, the right to privacy is *Unassailable*!

Every individual and corporation has the *Right* to acquire *Property* according to need; however, under no circumstances may an *Individual Person* or *Persons* be considered property to be owned! In addition, no one may possess property that is appropriately considered to be a *Weapon*, unless he or she is a licensed-hunter, officer or a soldier in the service of the Empire.

Land: when acquired by persons for private dwellings, shall not be *Taxed*. In the event of death or abandonment, when there are no legal claimants, the property will become the property of the Empire.

No person residing in the Empire shall suffer the indignity of lacking *Food, Shelter* or *Medical* services. Every individual, whether *Caucasian Citizen* or *Alien Resident*, has the *Right* to *Social Assistance*. In the same way, each individual has the *Right* to- Die? (Euthanasia)

The determination of the appropriate quality of life is the *Right* of the afflicted individual, and upon review by an "Impartial Medical Council" his or her wishes may be carried out by a *Physician* or *Proxy* according to those wishes.

The *Caucasian Race* has the *Right* of -*Divinity*. This right belongs to the *Race* and the *Children* and their *Children*, the supreme virtue of the race. These represent the future of the *Caucasian Fematrix* as well as her greatest works and should therefore be worshiped.

The *Right* of -*Caucasian Consecration* belongs solely to the Alpha. This *Right* is a sacred ceremony of honor for the leaders of the race. So too, the *Right* of *Covenant* belongs to the Alpha.

This Right binds the accountable three, the Alpha, the *Hall* of *Caucasians*, and the *Hall* of *Lords*, to the doctrines of the Caucasian Empire.

The *Right* of -*Chivalry* also belongs to the Alpha. This is the sacred ceremony of men being given the rank of *Centurion* the guardians of the race and enforcers of the law.

The *Right* of -*Heraldry* also belongs to the Alpha, ensuring the authenticity of the science that is devoted to the coats of arms, *Genealogies*, as well as the ritual pomp and circumstance that accompany it.

The *Right* of -*Reverence* is the sacred Right of the *Caucasian female*. She is the weaver of the Caucasian social fabric. As such, she is the center of all things and must be served by both Man and Empire.

So, too, does she hold the *Right* of -*Homage*. This is the sacred ceremony of public avowal of allegiance to the *Caucasian female* and *Her Children*!

The *Right* of *Arms*- belongs to the *Centurion*, the guardian of the race and the law. A codicil of this *Right* is that individuals of the Caucasians race may *Bear Arms* for sporting occasions and in the event of war.

The *Right* of -*Court* belongs to all Caucasian people.

In the Empire, there are three courts- the *Civil*, the *Criminal*, and the court of the *Empire* (𝔄lpha). It should be noted that *Alien Residents* are also subject to the jurisdiction of these three courts.

The *Right* of -*Law.* All people, *Caucasian* and *Alien* alike, must abide by the laws.

Each individual has the *Right* of -*Course*, the guidelines in the manifesto that are fixed for the Caucasian Empire.

If individuals, for whatever reason, choose not to abide by these laws, then they must remove themselves from the Empire.

The *Right* of -*Education* ensures that all Caucasian children will receive the *Finest Education*!

No Caucasian *Child* or *Adult* will be without *Formal* or *Vocational* schooling in accordance with the person's individual skill and ability.

The *Right* of -*Auction* belongs to the Empire, allowing the Empire to dispose of all property that it deems unnecessary for its appropriate function.

The *Right* of -*Sentinel Authority* defines the *Rights* of the *Centurion*, who is given the sacred task of keeping the Caucasian people safe and out of harm's way.

They are the keepers of the law and the holders of the *Sacred Shield* of the *Centurion*.

Because all knowledge is not instinct, it is vital to the Caucasian race that ceremonies exist to mark the attainment of certain degrees of knowledge. The ceremony that marks the entry of *Men* and *Boys* into the *Brotherhood* of the race so they may step forward and stand beside their *Brothers* and *Fathers* in welcoming their responsibilities to their *Caucasian Racialness*, its *Integrity* and its *Central Throne,* is a rite of passage.

There are, in the Caucasian race, three *Rites* of passage.

The *First* and *Second* ceremonies are officiated by the initiates *Brother* and *Father*. In these passages there are three classes of which two must be successfully completed in order for the initiate to receive his *Armor* and his *Weapon*.

The *Third* ceremony is officiated by the- *Throne*. In this ceremony, the initiate will undergo trials of *Mental* and *Physical Oneness*. The initiate must pass this metamorphosis, this *Spiritual Trial* of oneness, with the whole, in order to receive the *Helmet* and the rite of *Passage*!

If the initiate *Fails* any of the three trials, then he has failed them all. So it is written.

Any man over the age of *Eighteen Years* may apply for the rite of passage, which is given yearly during the *Summer Solstice*. Those who pass receive the junior title of *Centurion Cadet*, and they are then required to attend the *Gathering* that takes place once a year after the *Rites* of passage.

For those who attempted the *Rites* of passage but failed, another opportunity is available to them the following year.

No *Man* or *Boy* can be refused the trial unless he has been deemed unfit by the *Centurion Tribunal*, whose judgment is absolute and final.

The Three Levels Of Life
(The Journey)

Life level One: *Barbarism*, the Hunter.

With one single desire, to consume, this level serves only itself. It is at this level that the greatest amount of opposition is endured. At this level, the will is tested to the limit of its capacity. This level requires the greatest amount of biological information for human evolution, this level is the root of human evolution.

Life level Two: *Laborer*, the Builder.

This level is called the labor level. Once biological consumption has been satisfied and secured, a break can be taken in the struggle. What this break allows is time, time to think, time to understand, time to build. This is the level where the first glimpses of *God* are seen. This is the level of art, the level of compassion, the level where all the nation of humankind are born.

Life level Three: *Science,* the Vision.

At this level, the concept of life is put into focus, and a direction is taken on behalf of the race. It is on this level that the physical and intellectual change places. Consumption and production being satisfied, this level is free to embark on almost any path; it depends only on the quality of leadership, this level is capable of real greatness, of absolute greatness. It is also capable of absolute tragedy.

The Three Laws Of Life
(The Quest)

These three laws govern all forms of life, all levels of life, and all dimensions of life. They are the very blueprints of all that is. Depending on the quality of these three laws in any given life form, its span is determined.

LAW ONE: *Consumption.* The Conflict! The taking of life to sustain life, this is the strongest of all laws. This law allows for no compassion or guilt. It exists to allow the taking of prey.

LAW TWO: *Production.* The Advantage! The making of recognizable racial kind, (the distinction) the state of getting special recognition, the art of offense and defense, the making of the weapon, fangs, claws, knives, spears, and guns.

LAW THREE: *Direction.* The Colonization! The Social growth, it is this law that tests the will of man. This law is the Creator and will of conflict in all living things. Man is the Least specialized, thereby increasing his ability to survive.

The Three Times Of Life
(The Gathering)

THE PAST: The well of *Knowledge.*

From the knowledge that time past has given us, we, the Caucasian people, are capable of drawing from this vast well the answers that are needed for the many obstacles that life will put in our way. The study of one's own people and their history are a people's greatest gift to their children. It is their only true light in the darkness.

THE PRESENT: The *Cauldron*.

The living force of competition, all that is, stands opposed to all that would be. The present is the living arena where all the forces of man and all the forces of nature take part in the great exchange, the wars of will and nerve, the clash of law and desire, the assault of weather and storm.

From these inherent violent roots, all life takes it future direction.

THE FUTURE: The *Vision*.

The individual races of humanity, plus all the other forms and species of life, possess the vision, the desire to live in freedom and safety, to pursue that direction which they have chosen for themselves, their children, and their prosperity. To create the institutions of learning where by their children can come to an understanding about the sacrifices that were made for them, and the sacrifices that are expected of them. Life is an individual experience in a group setting. The race sacrifices for the individual, and the individual sacrifices for the race. Henceforth, the eternal joining of generations, the *Past* and the *Present,* join to become the parents of the- *Future.*

Foreign Affairs
(Alien Social and Political Diplomacy)

Foreign affairs are the sole concern of the *Sovereign State* (the Alpha), and no other government body can supersede the sovereign state's authority in foreign affairs.

Alien social and political diplomacy, after all, is what foreign affairs is all about, and it is the Alpha's duty to see to it, that the *Caucasian Empire*, its people, and their best interest are looked after in any and all negotiations with aliens. (non Caucasians!)

ARTICLE I
(Alien Encounter)

When in the course of Caucasian events they should encounter an *Alien Race*, they shall raise their *Defensive Shields*, and these shields shall remain in effect until the alien's *Intentions* and *Direction* have been determined? And at no time in the encounter, shall the *Sovereign Directive* be waived!

SECTION 1: If Aliens have taken a hostile stance, all shields must remain in a defensive position.

Any and all hostile advances are to be repelled with *Extreme Force*, unless otherwise instructed.

SECTION 2: Aliens having expressed a *Willingness* to exchange goods and services for a *Peaceful Coexistence* will be welcomed to the Empire and can apply for alien residency.

SECTION 3: Aliens seeking entrance into Caucasian lands for the purpose of *Colonizing* will be informed of the law *Forbidding* the acquisition of Caucasian lands by aliens.

SECTION 4: Aliens seeking entrance into Caucasian lands for the purpose of *Citizenship* will be informed of the law that *Strictly Forbids* alien application for citizenship in the Caucasian Empire.

SECTION 5: Alien nations having a *Peaceful Coexistence* with the Caucasian Empire (a social treaty) shall establish their *Embassy* in Caucasian lands.

- Taxation -

(The Social Commonwealth)

The Taxes, or the *Commonwealth* of the people, after all, that is what "Taxes" are! They are administered by the elective government, which is a tool of the people, and it is the job of the elective government to collect the taxes and invest the taxes to the benefit of the society and the will of the people as a whole, not according to the will or the benefit of the people's representatives?

It is because of the neglect of the people that their representatives abuse their office, this is truth, this is reality.

The people must not only be *Governed*, they must also do the *Governing*, for it has been this failure of the people to oversee their *Chosen Representatives* that has caused many great Caucasian Empires to fail!

It is true, that *Representative Democracy* is not a true democracy? But, due to the great numbers of people, it is a *Necessary* and *Logical* compromise, this of course providing that the Caucasian people hold tightly to the reins of those who represent them. (by being attentive and knowledgeable.)

Terror By Taxation
(Individual Government Intimidation)

Taxes are collected for the direct benefit of the people and society as a whole and taxes must not and cannot be allowed to terrorize the very people they were designed to help. Terror by taxation is government out of control. Let's look at this social demon, and let's also get right to the three parties that are participants in this social joust.

They are, for all practical purposes, the poor class, the middle class, and the rich class. Let it be said right from the beginning that all three of these parties are innocent and naive victims of a government out of control. There are no villains, only a frightened and inattentive public.

The Deficient Class
(limited social opportunity)

Poverty: It is a word that is understood by all humanity and invokes the same image, regardless of race, culture, or religion. All societies have felt and are still feeling its deadly grip.

Its appetite is unequaled by any predator, whether real or imagined. But what actually is poverty?

Some say that it is ignorance! Some say that it is laziness! Others say that it is genetics. The real fact of the matter is, it is none of these things, the Alpha tell us: that its true cause can be put into a single category - Unavailable Social Opportunity.

It was Martin L. Gross: a great American who gave us the truth of the- *American Impoverished.*

We can't demand charity from the Salvation Army, although it seldom refuses. But state charity what we call *Welfare* is a different proposition. In modern society, we consider that a right of the poor. So really big charities become an *Involuntary* activity, one whose goals are decided by our politicians, our duly elected representatives.

Most citizens go along, to a limit. They gladly pay taxes for some social programs, including sustenance for the blind and disabled, unemployment insurance for the out of work, and various other fringe programs, such as student loans. But, state welfare is still not fully trusted! The country didn't become great because the government gave anybody welfare.

And surely no one ever became rich on the dole. If the millions who struggled their way through *Ellis-Island*...Irish, Germans, Jewish, Italians, Polish, Greek, Hungarians (Caucasians all!) had been given welfare, they'd probably now be victims of capitalism instead of its masters.

Taxpayers are convinced that all is not quite right with the Governments attempts to stem poverty by handing out checks!

They grumble: What is going on?

Is it true?

Is the government mishandling the system meant for the poor? And if so, how?

To answer that, we should first explain that since there's no bottom line, government lives more off perceptions than reality. And behind that is the federal government's attitude about virtually everything.

It is based on two premises: (1) good intentions; (2) bad theory.

The great question of the 1960s- What about a plan to *totally eliminate* poverty in America?...asked our politicians.

Yes, most enlightened Americans answered, that's a good idea!...but, how would it be done?

The *Search* for the *Poorest:* who are the poorest and the most disadvantaged of all?

Generally those young people who are fatherless and whose mothers are unemployed.

How can we lift them out of despair?

Education surely!...but, the schools are failing?

Then try this idea!...the social theorist said, as if shouting *Eureka.* Let's find the young men and women of these disadvantaged families and encourage them (by not enforcing moral behavior and responsibility) to engage in premarital sex at an early age! We know the inevitable result: teenage pregnancy, high school dropout, and child birth out of wedlock.

Now the government has isolated its clients both *Caucasian* and *Alien,* for its system of state "*Government Paternalism*" unwed mothers and fathers, teenage and older, with small children, with no socio-cultural commitment!…in other words: not only physically destitute, but now thanks to the Government, "Mentally Destitute" as will!

And yes!...*Pay Them!*...first with cash, then food and housing, then with a marginal life-style. How do you do that?...Just add money and rewards for each additional child born out of wedlock, making sure the system helps the young women avoid marriage, and than make it jump from generation to generation, and of course, now there is more poverty instead of less?

Hence, the liberal theory didn't work!

Yes!...it all want wrong, and in its fulfillment, it has become perhaps the most destructive social concept in the history of American society.

If truth be known, it has been the greatest creator of "Poverty" ever conceived, and the destroyer of *Families*, *Social Civility* and *Dignity*. And what happened to the original intent of- Curing Poverty?

It got lost in the *Social Work Theory* that the poor are "Clients" that need to be rehabilitated? The evidence seems quite clear, "Welfare" (public assistance without accountability) as we all now know it, is the true- Villain!

The Alpha's view: If the present Caucasian altruistic trend of -Alien Welfare- (unaccountable alien paternalism) continues into the future in the same direction and at the same rate?...the Caucasian world Community as well as the Caucasian American Community being what they are to-day,(a bastion of liberal zealotry!) will have disappeared from the face of the earth. Simply speaking, it is not possible or in the power of anyone or any Nation to create a - Sanctuary - for the multitudes of human misery without becoming its victim! In the arena of life, all must play their part, all must exhaust their will, and all shell create their teleology, on the path to their fate?

The Productive Class
(The Socio-Economic Well!)

This social class may also be called the "Tax Well" or for a more explicit term, the "Tax Trough" and the bearer of all social pressures.

It is this social class called the "Middle Class" that holds and maintains the very organs of Caucasian society, and if it were ever to rise to its full "Intellectual Potential" the world would take on a social renaissance unequaled in human history.

But it lost its concept of the social whole and chose to plunge itself into the shallow halls of liberal individualism, thereby leading to the authorship of its own social nightmare.

Because of this liberal social concept of the individual taking precedent over the whole, terror by taxation is only one of the many social demons born of this utopian fallacy.

By allowing the taxing of an individual's personal income, you have allowed yourselves to be singled out for any reason under the heading of "Tax Discrepancies", just the sheer accusation! And what that actually means is a full-blown investigation into the corridors of one's life?

And make no mistake! Under this *Terror Tax Act*, all your rights are usurped, and no one can stop it! Case in point, by putting the burden of an

"Income-Tax" on every individual, the government can and does use this *Tax* as a *Passkey* into the lives of everyone!...and it doesn't need anyone's permission to use the "Tax-Passkey" to enter your life; hence, *Tax Terrorism*!

You can be targeted and separated for harassment and reduced to a submissive bewilderment, with the terror tactic of holding all your "Lifetime Achievements" hostage!

There is no mistake about it; they like doing it!...so if you are part of the middle class,…there is no escape!

You just wait for your turn to be called to the Dungeon of Taxation and hope you can survive the Inquisition of Terror.

The systematic subjugation of the middle class is due, in fact, to this system of terror by taxation. Day by day, more and more people are being stripped of their dignity and their worldly possessions by a government out of control. The middle class has become completely overwhelmed by the terror of government taxation. People are *Threatened* and *Bullied* by Time, Dates, and Deadlines, not to mention the *Penalties* that await all those who-file late!

The Wealthy Class
(Financially Affluent!)

Of all the position in the human social order, it is the position of financial independence that is most desired; in other words, to be "Rich." Although some question the wisdom of great wealth, because of its relation to power in general, but the truth is, they are not twins.

The use of wealth or power is neither good nor bad, in and of itself. It is what the individual brings to these states that make them what they are. Hence, I've chosen here to address the abundance of good will that the rich and their social institutions have given to humankind as a whole.

Let me lay out their credentials, for they are impressive indeed! The average person of wealth who runs or owns a business, whether large or small, is a person of special qualities, though these qualities by no means imply superiority, but they are unique. And it is this uniqueness in their character that sets them apart from the rest of us.

They are the top players in the greatest game that has ever been played in the history of humankind.

Mercantilism- the prime mover of all social order without exception.

Mercantilism, which we will now refer to as the merchants, competes on a scale that encompasses all *Social* levels, all *Political* levels, and all *Economic* levels, not to mention the infamous terror tax that even they have no immunity from.

The Merchant: he or she creates the products, the indus tries that make the products, and the jobs that support the dreams and hopes of millions of people.

They are also the targets and scapegoats for the failures of those dreams and hopes, not to mention the endless laws, regulations, legal assaults, and the latest social bias legislation (affirmative action, or alien job quota bill!) that is thrown into this great arena. There are no ballads sung to the credits of the merchant.

That is the saddest part!

There is no cause in the social agenda that does not receive the financial goodwill or personal time of these special individuals. From a political dinner, to a cake sale, or to benefit a sick child, the local merchant is always there, willing to lend a strong, sturdy hand. In all social human affairs, we, like water, seek our own level, for contrary to popular belief, there are no equalities. We all live by our mental and physical abilities, and that is the only true great equality, our common inequality.

This has been an introduction to the three major players in the world of taxation. These three social groups comprise the wealth the government manipulates in its tax strategy. The time has come for some serious scrutiny about our taxes. This is what I propose: First, *Eliminate Tax Terrorism*.

This can be done only by eliminating *Personal Income Tax* and *Personal Property Tax*. In other words, when you purchase a home, you pay a one-time purchasing tax, and the seller pays a one time sales tax, and this is the only tax you ever pay on this property.

To be more precise- *You Own It*, with no other tax obligation, so when you get into your golden years, no one can take your home away, for nonpayment of back taxes. This of cause, applies only to private property, not commercial.

The elimination of personal income tax works in the same manner; the tax base from personal income taxes can be shifted to a *Purchasing Tax*. This way you do not have to pay personal income tax or fill out tax forms every year; hence the elimination of terror by taxation, and no more tax burden on the individual.

You would pay taxes on only *Purchasing, Sales*, and the *State* or *Federal* "Municipalities" (police, fire etc.) and "Capital Projects" (roads, bridges, water etc.) This would also increase the incentive to save and stimulate consumer buying power, thereby stimulating the economy. In the case of a "Farm," the residential part of the farm cannot be taxed, only the land that is in "*Seed*" for the market-place can be taxed, not the land untilled.

Just as it is necessary to lift the burden and responsibility of taxes off the shoulders of the individual citizen, it is also necessary to do the same for *Industry,* which is constantly being called upon to make sacrifices, adjustments and demands for *Better* and *Cheaper* products.

The *"Caucasian Industrial Complex"* with it added assault of alien competition, not to mention its immense tax burden, is beginning to sound the alarm to- *Abandon Ship!*

The economic seas in America are just too rough, and they are being swamped. Of course their government is without any contingency plan to rescue them.

Even though their SOS has been picked up, and the loss of - *American Economic Life* - in great numbers is most assured, their government will not act, to relive the burden of its oppressive corporate taxation.(out of control!)

There isn't a person who does not relate to terror by "Taxation" whether its the *Poor Class* that never gets elevated!...the-*Middle Class* that has been enduring taxes in the form of a plague with casualties to match, and lest we forget the *Rich Class*, that endures endless false accusations of tax breaks and loopholes, as if it had some secret formula to avoid the- *Tax-Terrorism-* of the government.

It is absurd. All one has to do, is calculate the cost of doing corporate taxes.

It is an industry in and of itself.

The people in all walks of life must come together to break the *Stranglehold* of *Taxation*, and this must be done in three areas, *Personal Income Tax*, *Property Tax*, and *Corporate Tax*.

This *Legislative Piracy* must be- *Eliminated!*

"The Government- *Is Not A Growth Industry"*

- Radicalism -

(extremism - zealotry - militancy)

The Alpha tells us: That *Radicalism* weather it is *Political, Economical* or *Social,* is part and partial to the advocacy and attitude of *Sweeping Change!* ...which is not traditionally supported by the main-stream cultural populous.

In other words an *"Aggrieved Group?"* Case in point: the *Caucasian American Community,* and its *Undeclared War* of more then 50 years against its greatest *Radical Enemy*, an enemy so *Degenerate* and *Ruthless* that it uses *Alien Racial Militancy* as its "Vanguard" in its *Socialist Assault* against its very own Caucasian American community!...Yes, *Cauca- sian Liberal Zealots*? (liberal progressive socialist's) making claims for minority races of being wronged, and thwarted, suffering and deprived of their ambitions, has decided to challenge the ruling cultural direction of "Caucasian America" (the founders of America!) with bogus public accusations of *Caucasian Racism, Caucasian Privilege, Caucasian Supremacy,* and the *Seditious* legal action by liberal *Appointees* who head the *Justice Dept*, and the *Internal Revenue Service*, threatening "Prosecution" against all Caucasians in both *Academia* and *Corporate America* with charges of *Racism!*...if they check, or act on the bad behavior of both domestic or foreign- Aliens Races?...is this not an oppressive power?...a Tyranny? (we must be vigilant!)

Hence, it is no surprise to any *Caucasian American* or for any observer to see that the domestic alien violence, and the on going *Alien Invasion* in Caucasian America is completely out of control, and even their "Sponsors" the *Democratic Party* are themselves at a loss, on how to stop their violence, and the invasion?

But, it is not the only field of *Alien Intrusion* in which we Caucasians must be on guard against!...Alien political intrusion: "Alien Political Radicals" who are being hustled in by *Liberal Subversives* for no other reason but their Vote? (Caucasian Americas destruction by any means!)

We in the Caucasian American Community must begin to prepare ourselves to understand that it requires the staunchest and most unshakable character to become a defender of the truth!...because it can be *"Fatal"* to those who challenge the *Liberal Zealot Radicalism* of the *21st* century.

The Alpha tells us: It is one thing to wage war against an oppressor, a tyrant, (cruel and unjust!) but, it is a whole other thing to conspire with *"Alien Races"* to overthrow you own race!...and destroy its *Culture*, its *History* and its government for the purpose of their total elimination!... and this, has but one name: "Genocide" the deliberate and systematic extermination of the *Caucasian American Community*- by a very extreme cabal of Caucasian *Liberal Zealot?*-both in *Academia* and the halls of *Political Power?*...this is truth, this is our reality!

Forgoing a call to arms?...for that storm is already gathering, and like all natural occurrences it will have it way through the corridors of *Retribution* and *Revenge*, driving before it all those *Caucasian Traitors* and *Alien Subversives* who misjudged the *Fighting Will* and *Fortitude* of the greatest biological will in all of creation!...the *Caucasians*.

Therefore, in the coming purge to *Restore* and *Realign* Caucasian America, and her sister states throughout the world!

It will be of the utmost importance that in search of the *Facts*, *Nature* and *Course* of this-*Liberal Radicalism,* it will be necessary (for justice!) to gather them through the sole source of *Knowledge* and *Experience* of others.

It will then become necessary to examine carefully both the *Evidence* submitted and the *Person* from whom the evidence comes, for it is a *Common Human Tendency* for men and women to find nothing but evil in those whom they do not like or trust! So, the object of the search in the name of *Justice*, for the *Caucasian American People* is just that! "Justice" the impartial adjustment of conflicting claims, through the conformity to *Truth*, *Fact* and *Sound Reason*.

Finally, don't overlook this very important point!...The *Caucasian Race* and their ongoing conquest, their *Biological Mandate!*...has been *Pushed,*

Lifted, Dragged and *Defended* for more then 40 thousand years, we know who we are!, and we know where we're going!

"Blessed are the Caucasians"

The Alpha's View: For more then 10,000 years; The race of people known as the "Caucasians" and their historical world conquest, have been the primary driving force for the survival of humankind. Hence, the object and general purpose of this stated truth!..is the following; The superior efficacy of example to precept is universally acknowledged. All the Caucasian laws of morality and rules of conduct are verified by experience, and are constantly submitted to its test and examination. Caucasian history, besides its general advantages, has a distinct species of utility to different races, according to their places in Nature and cultural direction. In Caucasian society; it is an indispensable duty, for every one of Caucasian birth to be acquainted with the love for liberty and the blessings of our- Caucasian Racial Dynasty.

Racial Apostasy

(He or She who forsakes their biological racial dynasty!)

- Apostate -

A person or persons of a bio-historical ancestry and heritage, with *Opinions*, *Beliefs* and *Acts,* contrary to the biological, cultural, economic or political "Survival" of their *Bio-Racial Dynasty!*...having no, or caring not!... in the realization of what their *Biological Dynasty* hopes and works for.

Caucasian Apostasy

For a Caucasian To: Deliberately compromise the very safety and social stability of the Caucasian race.

For a Caucasian To: Deliberately advocate the dismantling of the greater Caucasian society.

For a Caucasian To: Become a subversive agent against Caucasian society, for the benefit of alien others.

For a Caucasian To: Advocate Miscegenation or interracial union. (marriage)

For a Caucasian woman To: Give her *Eggs* to an alien.

For a Caucasian man To: Give his *Semen* to an alien.

For a Caucasian To: Advocate and promote the denial of Caucasian racial and social sovereignty.

For a Caucasian To: Champion the cause of alien races against the interests of the Caucasian race.

For a Caucasian To: Encourage abdication of Caucasian authority and socio-political power over its Empire.

For a Caucasian To: Advocate the social fallacies of the liberal utopian zealots and alien racial subversives.

For a Caucasian To: Incite Caucasian ethnic social bigotry in the Caucasian race.

For a Caucasian To: Deny one's loyalty to their Caucasian race.

For a Caucasian To: Deny one's social obligation to their Caucasian community.

For a Caucasian To: Deny one's moral obligation to their Caucasian ancestral trust.

Of all the threats to the Caucasian race and its great society, it is the "Caucasian Apostate" that poses the greatest danger, for *He* or *She* has been mentally castrated by the "Liberal Zealots," becoming the "Vanguard" and "Gate- Keepers" of their *Social Fallacies* and *Cultural Subversion.*

"Beware of "Evil Patterns" in the liberal social fabric"

- Feticide -

Feticide: the deliberate and systematic destruction of human genesis

Feticidelist: A person or persons who believe in or advocate feticide.

Feticidelism: the political and social agenda of female liberal zealots and their co-conspirators for the destruction of human genesis. Of all the evils committed against human kind and of all the plagues that laid siege to human existence, none, if even combined, could have the destructive force of feticide.

The very act of feticide goes beyond rational moral understanding, proclaiming its legitimacy from the temple of individualism, as if it were the fruit of human intercourse and not childbirth itself. It became the right of choice; this was the cry of the female liberal zealot, but that cry (the right of choice) is a cloaking device skillfully applied to the public ear, in order to deny their responsibility for their sexual behavior and to hide the most evil and most despicable act of any human being, the selfish and immoral destruction of human genesis because of its social inconvenience and burden.

The Right Of Choice

(The Burden of Result)

In the human heart, the right of choice has always had a special place and has always been one of the foundation blocks of a democratic society

The right of choice also comes with the burden of result and the right to disregard future circumstances for short-term pleasures. But where human life is concerned, future circumstances cannot be disregarded for short-term pleasures.

When a *Male* and *Female* are engaged in *Sexual Activities* and

135

contraceptive precautions have been taken, then it can be said, no, they are not reaching for life, and that is their choice.

But, when a *Male* and *Female* are engaged in *Sexual Activities* and no contraceptive precaution have been taken, then it can be said, yes, they are reaching for life, and that is their choice.

Let it also be noted that even with the best contraceptives, *Fertilization* can still take place, and that is the chance you take, for all *Sexual Intercourse* has but one course, and one course only, and that is to reach for- "Life" there is no other reason for *Sexual Intercourse*, regardless of any proclaimed cultural *Fallacy* or *Fantasy*.

The Alpha's View: Among the many sins of the 21ˢᵗ century, the distorted reality of "Woman's Rights" has become the greatest Transgression to the meaning of that which brings us life!...if birth is not the purpose?...and the magnificent being that brings it, has lost the spiritual understanding of her task and its fulfillment!..diverting her purpose?...do to the weakness of political and cultural debauchery!...beliefs and desires in extreme forms of personal vanity, sensuality and seduction. Hence, the crime of mass human genocide, absolut and unrestrained "Abortion-Mania" the systematic elimination of future Caucasian generation- in the millions! A crime!..of unprecedented magnitude, and beyond atonement.

The Right To Life
(The Ancestral Trust)

In the dominion of human biology waits the spirit of human determination, and from its very beginnings, it is a contest of an unprecedented magnitude.

So precious is a single human life and the journey to that life, that to destroy it in the name of *Individual Choice?*..constitutes a direct moral violation of our *Human Sovereignty* and the code of *Human Evolution*.

And this is not to say that the destruction of human genesis for the preservation of humankind is not warranted; unfortunately, in certain *Medical Circumstances* it is!

𝔗hose 𝔚ho 𝔚ait
(The Cherished)

𝔄nd so it is to those who wait on a distant biological shore for their turn, their right, that we will fulfill our evolutionary obligation and prepare a place for them, just as once a place was prepared for us.

And when their journey begins, we will honor that journey and see to their safe arrival.

This is the sacred right of those who wait. Human genesis is the greatest single event of the human heart, and the greatest single achievement of the human will. The journey of human genesis brings with it that which links all social order and fires the machinery of all human discourse, the arrival of the newborn child. Therefore, any man, woman, or politician who chooses to debate the journey of human genesis and its right to take place undertakes a debate of profound intellectual weakness, itself, born in the cesspool of elitism.

𝔊ender 𝔐orphosis

(Sexual Confusion)

𝔊endermorph: A person or persons that are afflicted with the prejudicial illness of gendermorphosis! (homosexuality and/or lesbianism)

𝔊endermorphosis: The biological and/or psychological illness of gender confusion, in both male and female humans.

The Gendermorph has existed in human societies for as long as human societies have existed, and it has always been an illness of debilitating social circumstance, not only for the person who is afflicted with the illness, but also for the families and loved ones of the afflicted.

And if those who are afflicted are, or become- *Political Leaders*?...they will seek to infect the *National Culture*!... and this pathological (intellectual) change is called by the 𝔄*lpha* "Caligulaism" a code of subversive and pervasive laws establishing "Sexual Degeneracy" (unnatural and abnormal behavior!) and all that it implies as a social rightfulness? A legitimacy? This of course is absolutely absurd!...and is due in part to the nature of the morbidity, which is concentrated in the area of mental sexual perception!... an illness, a mental disorder!

There are many theories on the existence of *Gendermorphosis*, and twice as many books and opinions, from childhood mistreatment to the hallowed halls of *Freudian Enlightenment*, not to mention the politically correct and their assertion that it is merely a *Different Lifestyle*?

So let us descend to a simpler mental plane, and that is this: *Males* do not mate with males! And *Females* do not mate with females! And this is the very uncomplicated truth of it all! For you must see!...I can love someone and never consider having sex with them!...and I can have sex with someone and never consider loving them!..there for, love and sex are mutually exclusive!

The Gendermorph, whether the illness is brought about *Biologically*, *Culturally*, *Mentally*, or a combination of the three, is best left to those in these sciences, but what is not in doubt is the existence of the illness itself, and the social persecution that is bestowed upon those who suffer from it, and not to mention the public's fears and confusion about *Unnatural Sexual Acts,* and their exposure to their children.

Let it be said right up front, this is a legitimate fear by the public, for there is a large movement, in fact a campaign, by gendermorphs to deny the existence of their illness and a political attempt on their part to legitimize their- *Unnatural Behavior*. This can only come about by the cowardly nature of the modern-day politician, and it does not take much observation to see the extent of their cowardice.

Our Caucasian ancestral trust tells us: If you distroy the "Moral Fabric" that binds a people and their culture to a Nation, those people and that Nation will fail!

This Is Truth, This Is Reality!

The Alpha's view:When the basic understanding of one's "Morality" the differentiation of intentions between those that are good.(intention, decision, and action!) having the manner, character, and proper behavior of what is right, according to one's natural biological imperative (deductive commands!) and honoring that reasoning to a state of Religious Validity when the truth of its premise accurately corresponds to the truth of its conclusion in the real world, then it can be said: that a Nation and its people will know the true measure of its future! But, if it fails to honor its basic morale foundation-the family!...the union between man and woman,..and so chooses a degeneracy with an appetite for the Unnatural? It will have surely found its road to "Hades," and thereby, its unavoidable extinction.

The Public Media

(The Guardians of Social Focus)

There are three mental nourishments: *Identity*, *Sexuality*, and *Crisis*. Each one of these mental nourishments can also be divided by three, thereby enlarging the media's field of play.

Identity: Your identity, identity of your love ones, identity of your enemies.

Sexuality: Your sex, the opposite sex, sexual behavior. (moral, cultural, religious)

Crisis: Individual crisis, local crisis, foreign crisis.

This is and always will be the blueprint for social, political, and economic media control over any and all societies. Add to this blueprint the four delivery vehicles, television, radio, newspaper, and the Internet, and you have a power that exceeds even the gods of legend. The one who controls and manipulates these four social appetites the best can accomplish anything, for it's all in how you present it! When a group of people can control how much of this mental nourishment you get and in what configuration you get it in?...there should be no doubt in your mind as to the power that is wielded by the- *Public Media!*

The Medias Target
(The Public Joust)

The control of the public's focus is the fulcrum of all media, and when you add the right of accusation and declare yourself and your source immune to accountability, it then becomes apparent that the club of terrorism can be grasped by many other hands other than your standard social fringe.

Freedom of the press? What does that actually mean?

And in whose hands is it to be perceived as being free? Is there a living being without racial, cultural or political bias? Is there a human will void of emotional offense? Can media freedom possibly become an institution of information pandering?...and should we not question this?

Trial by public opinion is one of the many aspects that take place in the arena of media freedom, and guilt or innocence does not matter. It is the accusatory torment of the media's target that stimulates the public's demeanor.

The American citizens who were unfortunately dragged into the media's arena to be tormented and branded by the media's weapon, freedom of unconfirmed accusation, will never fully recover their dignity or their good name, but go through the rest of their lives with scars that were inflicted by a social evil cloaking itself in that greatest of mystical hungers, freedom?

Let it be said right up front, freedom has no loyalty; it is without a center. It is neither good nor bad, but is desired greatly by both; in other words it is what the individual or the group brings to it? (American media seditionism!)

Only restriction can give freedom a direction. And it must be the good will of the people that guides that direction. So once again, the *Caucasian People* must do what is necessary to balance the liberal fallacy of freedom and give restriction to public media's biased public manipulation, its *Information Pandering* and *Public Accusation* with no accountability-*Source Anonymity.*(the modern inquisition!)

The public media of today is no longer the champion of the human cause.

It no longer possesses the integrity and balance of men and women whose integrity and balance were the pillars of their professional character.

Today's media is a totally different type of animal, *Rarely* if ever do the heads of major media have any *Printers Ink* in their veins. They are more likely to be a type of Multi-Conglomerate Engineer that acquires and exchanges monetary risk at the multibillion dollar level.

So you see, if you change the nature of the enterprise, that nature being media, for the sake of an informed public (just the facts!) and not the *Political, Social,* or *Economic* manipulation of the public ear for *Personal* or *Political* gain, (media default!) you no longer have, and the American people no longer have, a once world-envied and longstanding ally, the American public media?

"A public "Reevaluation" Seems Appropriate"

- Caucasian Education -

(the sacred well of the race)

"Knowledge Is Our Treasure"

Among all the great gatherers of the fruits of life, it is perhaps those who gather the waters of racial and cultural history, so it can be stored in their social well of education, that are most sacred to the lives and futures of all people.

What is drawn from this well nourishes the most important force of them all, the mind! It has been said that in the root of the tree, in this lies the strength of the tree! So it can also be said that for the well of education, in this lies the strength of the human mind.

The Caucasian well of education is perhaps the oldest and sturdiest institution in all the world, bar none. It is because of its well of education that the race of people known today as "Caucasians" has advanced and prospered so far.

The Caucasian well of education has also been directly responsible for the gathering and documenting of the *Histories* and *Cultures* of all alien races throughout the world.

These alien races, having no written language or well of education other than language folklore, have had their histories preserved, and they owe that preservation to the Caucasian educational well.

History and culture are the parents of education!

Together they sing the *Songs* and write the *Poems* of life's journey, both good and bad, both creative and destructive. From this well, many come to draw their understanding and their spiritual nourishment, to sustain themselves on their journey through life. But for some, the waters of the Caucasian educational well are not always sweet and satisfying, sometimes its truths are bitter to the taste of *Alien Races* and their Caucasian *Liberal Eunuchs* who serve them.

The Guardian Of The Well
(the Caucasian teacher, the educational steward)

For some 40,000 years, the race of people known today as the Caucasians, have contributed to their sacred historical and cultural well of education. And they have bestowed upon certain individuals in their race, the stewardship of the educational well, this most vital of institutions.

Therefore, these most trusted individuals must never, under any circumstances, violate their sacred trust. They must never subvert (poison) the sacred well of Caucasian education for the social, political, or economic ambitions of alien races. (alien radical revisionism)

Academic Betrayal

The sabotage of Caucasian Education, as stated in the poisoned well.

I am sorry to say, it has already begun and will lead to the total dismantling of Caucasian cultural society.

Alien Multiculturalism and its academic anarchy have now taken hold!

The social and political wars of *Cultural Dominance* have begun! And the most respected political and or academic individuals will be powerless to stop it.

Let it be said to the *Caucasian People*: Your own "Academic Leaders" yes, the ones you trusted and voted for, pulled the *Liberal Zealot Horse* - "Multiculturalism" through the gates of Caucasian education, knowing perfectly well that in its belly lies the seeds of your *National Destruction!*

The
Utopian Liberal Zealot

(the absurdity of racial equality)

It has been said: there are none so blind as those who will not see, and there are none so deaf as those who will not hear! This is the affliction of the utopian liberal zealot, the most absurd of social individuals.

They set themselves apart from the active realities of social life and create a mental social fallacy devoid of biological rhythms, prints, and wakes; in other words, the belief that a square peg can fit into a round hole. And these liberal zealots will not be dissuaded from this belief, for they are always trying to convince the races of humanity that it can be done,(racial equality?) in spite of its obvious absurdity.

There is also the other side of the liberal zealots, and that is their *Racial Abolitionist* view, their ultimate social fallacy; hence the belief that they owe nothing to that specific biology that gave them life and continues to sustain them as one of the whole. This unconscionable liberal arrogance cannot and must not go unchallenged by the Caucasian people.

To continue to tolerate the further existence of their malignant political cult in Caucasian society, which has already destroyed the social structures in many Caucasian neighborhoods, is to abdicate the future of our children to the authority and cultural direction of- alien racial pretense.

The deceit of the racially uncommitted, the Caucasian liberal zealot, weighs heavy on the Caucasian heart, for they enjoy the safety of the racial society of their birth, but like a parasite, they gorge themselves on the cultural wealth of the Caucasian community, and then leave their host badly wounded (culturally and racially betrayed!) in return.

And if everything that sustains them (their Caucasian culture) should become threatened and needs to call on them for its defense, these liberal zealots, these
*Caucasian Apostates!...*will deny their allegiance and their association with the very force that gave them life.

Their cowardly demeanor is only equaled by their deceit, and always, in conflicts of *Race* and *Culture*, do these Caucasian liberal zealots both *Violate* and *Deny* their "Racial Ancestral Trust" as if it were a badge of courage, but in fact, they are arrogant cowards, and at the first sign of conflict, they start to preach utopian liberal zealotry, (equality?) the shelter of cowards.

And, it will greatly benefit the *Caucasians American Community* to deny association and renounce any and all Caucasians who are *Racially Uncommitted*, for they are of the philosophy that it is *Permissible* to bite the hand that feeds you?..and that it is "Okay" to deceive the committed people of the race, and derive benefit from their sacrifices!

The racially uncommitted Caucasians are strictly social opportunists, and their deceit and contempt for Caucasian society is well documented. These *Caucasian Apostates*, (liberal subversives!) with their emaciated mental illness of *"Racial Guilt"* are just what the local *Alien Anarchists* and *Alien Invaders* have been cultivating! Therefore, it is with great importance and expectation that the Caucasian people in "America" and throughout the world will come to see the light of *Truth!...*and that truth being?...is that some *"Prominent Caucasians"* have been *"Racially Castrated"* and have become *Racial Eunuchs* for *Alien Invaders* and their *Political Machine*, and like all *Aliens!...*these "Caucasian Apostates" have no sense of *Loyalty* or *Dignity*, other than their own- *Selfish Needs* and *Opportunities.*

The Alpha's view: The "Betrayal" of Caucasian America and its related states throughout the world by a cabal of Caucasian liberal zealots, is the breaking of a presumptive sacred moral trust, their Bio-dynastic Loyalty! Thereby, they are Deliberately and Criminally engaged in the willful destruction of our- Caucasian Dynasty!..of it's Allegiance, Devotion, Duty, Cause, Support, Pride, Belonging and Love of Kind!...They would distroy it all!...some 40 thousand years. Alas, for this crime above all!... there must be and will be a just "Retribution" for all- Caucasian Apostates.

- The Fringe -
(the fourth social zone)

The social order understood by most societies consists of three social zones, the rich class, the middle class, and the poor class. But the Alpha submits to you that there is a fourth social zone! He calls it, the *Fringe*, and it has a very distinct nature. It has no economic status, no political status, and no social status.

It does not vote, it does not hold office, and it lives on the outside looking in!

Maybe you know a fringe?...a person from the outer edge- the *Fourth Zone*.

The Alpha thinks most people know one or two, and those of us who don't know a fringe personally have surely passed a few in our travels- *Train Stations, Street Corners*.

They are the most diverse people in the world, these people from the fringe! Without exception, they always have the appearance of- *Nonconformity*. They are always assaulting the senses; it is their trade-mark. The fringe, unlike the other three social zones, has no social philosophy and is basically a social paradox! The fringe is a place where some are driven, and where some flee, a place of physical and mental distance, a rough and rugged land of no expectations. It is a place of great genius and madness, a frightening wilderness to the socially committed.

It has no *Heroes* and no *Villains*; it neither praises *Success*, nor condemns *Failure*.

It has no altar to worth! The fringe is not without its explorers from the ranks of the socially committed. They have erected many outposts and have sponsored many expeditions into the fringe. These outposts and expeditions have met with only moderate success in solving their preconceived social theories of the fringe.

The *Religious* expeditions into the fringe are by far the more successful out of the two, the other being the *Government*, and that is due in part to the nature of their religious expeditions approach, which is purely spiritual, as opposed to that of the government, which is a maze of mindless bureaucratic abuse and intimidation.

145

The fringe and its inhabitants have existed as long as humankind has existed.

It is a natural biological occurrence in all social orders. It is the rejection of difference and the withdrawal from competition by those who can no longer agree with or sustain the social drive. They retreat to that land where the human excess is left to graze on the barren slopes and valleys of large metropolitan cities, and where a cardboard box becomes a welcome sight on a cold winter's night!

The fringe, even in the heart of the poet, is the mystical pebble of defiance thrown into the human pond, sending its ripples through the lives of others.

The Alpha tells us; that it is a paradox of human discourse to the social architects and their high priests, the *Sociologists*, and *Psychologists* who are forever stumbling over their own guidelines of social truth.

Therefore, The Alpha, must now put his own beliefs before you, and it is his belief that the fringe is a vast mental ghetto that humans either fled to for sanctuary or were driven to by poverty.

He further believe that the fringe is a reservoir of great human resource some forty million strong that has been waiting in silence for a distant purpose, which the social architects of today have failed to understand or express in their modern social mythology.

A nation, or a government, is a body in motion without a soul; it has no compassion. It is a mindless bureaucratic machine that is often operated by *Special Interest Groups*- that do not comprehend the common good.

Not knowing weather by design or by circumstance, but history tells us that its warnings have often been ignored by the politicians- *Violent Social Revolution*, the dark side of the fringe! The fringe and its historical explosive nature have been well documented throughout the lives and times of human existence.

The symptoms of its social upheaval have always been the same and easily read by all political and social architects.

This also brings to mind their historical incompetence and cowardice when confronted with the final countdown to social destruction.

But, it also is the Alpha's belief that these great social upheavals throughout human history are a natural part of human cultural evolution, brought about by unstable forces, in large numbers at the fringe. So he gives this aggressive warning to the social architects of America and all other betrayed Caucasian states!

Do not disregard or fail to diagnose the "Symptoms" coming from the-Caucasian worlds social fringe!...alas, your demise.

The Caucasian Pathfinder
(the hunger of curiosity)

The pathfinder is a person or persons of great daring and courage. It is from the mental and physical hunger of such persons that a race of people, or a social order, derives its evolutionary progress.

The wilderness is not only a term for the vast stretches of untamed *Physical Landscape*, but its greater meaning is of a *Mental Wilderness* that comprises an endless array of interdimensional horizons.

This then draws its perceptions from that most human of mental activities, and the main driving force of the pathfinder, *Exploration*. If not the enduring will of the pathfinder, then who does academia owe its existence to? In this question, there can be no intellectual joust! For every science that ever was and for every science that will ever be, it will be that enduring will and that staunch courage, the mark of the *Caucasian Pathfinder*, that will light the way. If ever the truth be expressed to the greatest of pathfinder's, that honor would unequivocally rest with the Caucasian race.

For unlike any other race, the Caucasian race and its pathfinder's have from the very beginning understood the union of intellectual hunger and social direction.

This lead to the birth of *Western Civilization*, whose social, cultural, and scientific leap created a vacuum that diverted the entire social direction of humankind.

Hence, the list of achievements by the Caucasian pathfinder's has filled the shelves and corridors of all the libraries throughout the world, from the Quark to the greatest island galaxies and all that they encompass, it has been the Caucasian pathfinder who has explored their veiled mysteries and revealed their true spirit to humankind.

The Police Officer

(the holder of the sacred shield)

The *Sacred Shield* is the symbol worn by the defender of the social will. The sacred shield is bestowed upon that men or women who, by having those most desired of human qualities, *Courage*, *Compassion*, and *Loyalty* to the common social good, will serve with dignity.

Under the gaze of their sturdy presence, a society draws its social confidence, for they are the true champions of the people, these officers, the men and women of the *Sacred Shield*.

If not the police officers, then who will defend the common good? Who stands between the social predator and its victim? Who will confront criminal death when it calls, and who will defy the odds to save a single life?

There is no doubt; it is those very special people who wear the *Sacred Shield*, the police officer.

Of all the human souls that have ever endured the slings and arrows of social persecution, when a society needs a scapegoat to unload its social ills, the lamb of political choice on many occasion are the holders of the *Shield*, for they must stand in silence, when their political accusers wash their dirty hands in the waters of public denial.

It is a dark day! And we hear the sound of the *Celtic Pipes* and the thunder of the March! A *Shield* has fallen, and a watch stands empty! Once again, a very special person has given it all to the *Shield*!

And if we could, we would say to the family of this *Fallen-Knight*, that the world is a poorer place upon the passing of so noble a spirit, and that the light of this fallen spirit will shine forever in the hearts and minds of a most unworthy society. For if it were not for the noble spirit of the Shield!...this unworthy society would have long perished.

Although, I the 𝕬lpha speak as one, I speak also for many, and when my children ask of me- what shall I be in life?

I will tell them of the *Sacred Shield*, and I will remember those noble spirits who served.

The Alpha's view: Throughout Caucasian history there has always been those- Special People: Policemen, Firemen, our Solders, and let us not forget Doctors, Teachers, Nurses, Paramedics just to mention a few, and Yes!...when we were most in need?...they were always there!... always engaged in their noble craft of generous Unselfishness, (Magnanimity) and their loftiness of spirit, enabling them to bear the misfortune of others calmly!...bringing to them the gifts of- Help, Order, and Peace of Mind! And thou not often stated, they are truly loved!...and will always be throughout the Caucasian World Community, the measure of a true and heartfelt gratitude.

- Leadership -

(the social reliance)

It has been The Alpha's observation that a people or race measures its gains and its losses (the social confidence) against the gains and losses of its leaders. A strong leader makes a strong race. A weak leader, a weak race! Therefore, the leader must recognize his or her profound *Responsibility* to the race.

The race can only succeed if its leaders are strong and if they carry out their responsibilities of office, seeking first and foremost the good of the race.

However, the greatness of a leader is in part his or her ability to achieve these noble aims while functioning within clearly defined parameters.

A race is not a cult, and it cannot rely on charismatic leadership alone. Ultimately, a leader is answerable to the people he or she leads. To this end, leaders must be bound by traditions of office to establish and follow the order under which the Caucasian people are judged, rewarded, punished, and constrained. The Caucasian people are a people of laws and morals, laws and morals that restrict and define appropriate actions. Even more so than the people they lead, leaders must understand that it is their action, not their words, that establishes the moral integrity and sense of justice by which those subordinate to them live.

Leaders cannot say one thing and then do another. Such behavior contradicts the mandate of leadership. Leaders must value the highest standards of behavior and performance and show no tolerance for those uncommitted to the cause.

By their action, consistent with their words, leaders must provide direction.

Leaders must value and respect the high moral ground of their office and never form selfish relationships or take advantage of any other person.

To do so would undermine the moral authority necessary to lead. Likewise, leaders must hold their commitment to duty above all other ambition.

Leaders must never be satisfied with being followed blindly. They must encourage creativity, freedom of action, and innovation in those they lead.

However, they must provide guidance to ensure that these activities remain consistent with the noble goals of the race. The sense of trust comes from the top!

Leaders must establish and foster a sense of trust. For these efforts and others, leaders have the right to expect their subordinates to demonstrate continual improvement in all facets of their lives. As they improve, subordinates should be allowed a greater of decision making authority.

Only those leaders who are truly weak reserve all decision making for themselves. Control is kept by moral strength and example, not heavy-handed suppression. By the same token, leaders must never delegate decisions for which they are directly responsible. If a subordinate has attempted in good faith and to the best of his or her ability to carry out a delegated responsibility but has failed, the leader should not punish, but use this as an opportunity to teach and guide.

Leaders must avoid decisions that favor them over the Caucasian people as a whole.

Every decision that confronts the leader is an opportunity to improve the conditions of Caucasian society and the race.

Leaders must understand that, ultimately, the spirit of the law far exceeds the letter of the law, and they must therefore bow before the spirit of the law as they honor the letter of it. Too often, history has marked the decline of a glorious civilization by the empty lives of decadence its leaders have engaged in.

These leaders have lost their moral compass and their moral integrity. As a result, they hold onto power for power's sake, disregarding the needs of the people. Success is never built upon the shifting foundation of political maneuvering. It is built only upon responsibilities properly carried out.

Civilizations do not collapse from the bottom up, but from the top down!

Despotic Leadership

The
"Death Of All Empires"

All "Biological Empires" (life!) are the unions of many "Distinct" living forms, which are induced with *Purpose, Design* and *Obligation* to their own inherited strategic life essence, this being the driving "Sacrosanct" force in all.

Therefore, having expressed this truth, this reality for the *21ˢᵗ* century, the Alpha is giving a *Clarion Call!*...so as to give a "Dire Warning" to the average Caucasian, both in "America" and throughout the Caucasian world community.

Do to Caucasian- "Moronic Leadership" (*Liberal Zealots!* and *Conservative Apathy!*) and their years of *Corruption* and *Scandal* which can hardly be *Argued* or *Defended*, has lead to the complet breakdown of *Intellectual, Moral,* and *Civil Discourse*- in most, if not all!...Caucasian state communities.

Alas, this trait of - *Betrayal* and *Subversion,* along with *Alien- Sedition,* against the Caucasian world community, must by all Caucasians, be *Resisted* and *Defeated!* (no compromise!)

"Leadership Through Racial Faith"

Caucasian Leadership Through Racial Faith: involves a principle that is so far reaching in its effect that no man or woman can say what its limitations are or whether it has limitations.

Caucasian Racial Faith: is the lodestone though which all who have it may turn the base metals of their life into pure gold. Without your Caucasian racial faith, you have nothing, you are nothing, and you can be nothing.

Your Caucasian racial faith is that which you cannot buy, you can only get it by building it, through your own thoughts and by your own deeds, and in no other way.

Social Extortion

(the art of the moral magician)

The Caucasian American people and their society are waging a major war against one of its greatest enemies, the social extortionist. To fully understand this war, it is necessary to first explore the art and craft of the *Social Extortionist*.

The rules of extortion, or for any type of extortion to take place, you must have four essential ingredients. (A) a crime, (B) a victim, (C) a criminal, (D) a court of judgment.

And in the case of courts of judgment, there are two, the court of established judicial law and the court of public opinion. In the arena of legal debate, the moral magicians (liberal zealots) have cast their spells of moral social fallacy over the mind and will of American judicial sanity, thereby coercing both courts to participate in the social extortion against the Caucasian American people and their society.

This came about in part by the poetic moral social fallacy that - *All Men Are Created Equal?*...and it is this type of *Political Fallacy* that is tailor-made for the Social Extortionist!...and the alien opportunist!

When a society decides that social truth is to be made criminal and social fallacy is to be exalted as truth, then that society has created the ultimate social nightmare.

Instead of the old accusation of *Witchcraft* and being a *Witch*, its modern version is *Racism* and being a *Racist*.

Instead of being *Tortured* and *Stoned* in public, the "Modern Version" is you are stripped of your *Job* and *Livelihood* and made to *Apologize* to the offended public *Moral Fallacy*. The art of the *Moral Social Extortionist* is simple: first you establish the society's *Cultural Standards*, then you mount a counter cultural campaign, both *Legal* and *Moral* to have the *Dominant Culture* declared as morally and socially oppressive?...thereby establishing through a clever subversive accusation, and a "Stacked Judicial Deck" the *Caucasian American Community*,(our founding culture!) as being criminally oppressive?

The results of this legal and political charade is the modern American social dilemma, which is now so submerged in its *Legal Social Anarchy* that even rational solutions are beyond its reach.

Therefore, the Caucasian American society, not being able to disregard its culture, has become a victim of its own paranoid moral cultural denial. In other words, it has become a social and cultural nervous wreck, always defending itself from the moral and criminal accusations of the *Social Extortionists* and their bag men the *Caucasian liberal zealots*. The success of the social extortionist is made possible only by an extreme weakness in the intellectual fabric of the social order that is under attack. And it derives this weakness from a social misconception of life in general and social structure in particular.

If there was one thing- the *Alpha* would say to Caucasian America, it is this: the *Fematrix* will tolerate many things in the lives of her creations, but *Equality* is not one of them!

Equality is a term that has no life beyond the mystical mind of the poet.

Equality is a fallacy unsurpassed by even the greatest of impossibilities, and it is this very *Fallacy* of "Equality" (equal human outcomes?) that is destroying our social will to reason reality, and thereby, allowing this ruse of -*Equality* to become the "National Anthem" of the- *Social Extortionist!* (expose the *Extortionists*!..seek out life's *Truths!*

The
Human Fematrix

(the bio-cosmic life force of humankind)

Any race has to define certain realities and certain mysteries to the extent that they can be elucidated.

To this end, we begin with a discussion of the human entity herself.

Life!...What does it mean? Why are we all here? And what force is behind it?

The answer to these complex questions lies not in the word *life*, but in the eternal being that encompasses it, the "She" (Fematrix) creator of the- *Seed*, guardian of the bio-cosmic well, the source, the origin, the harbinger of the ancestral trust, the keeper of the nest, (the need), the creator of time and space, the architect of man, and of all other worlds.

She: is without doubt a force with no equal.

Her tears are your first greeting when you come into the world, and her tears are your last farewell when you leave the world.

All serve her will. All seek safety and comfort in her presence. In between, she sets directions and alters destinies. Those who bow to her and recognize her centrality in their lives will evolve, for only through serving her, her needs, and the life she brings into the world can we find the true meaning of life.

Those who deny her and do not recognize her throne will not evolve, but will become stagnant and socially sterile.

The She Spiritual Force: is the- *Fematrix*! And, that is how we will refer to the "Female Spirit" from now on!

Without a doubt, she is the most loved, the most emotional, and the most scrutinized subject that has ever preoccupied life, and that is as it should be.

The *Fematrix* is the author of all that is and all that will ever be, yet the *Fematrix* has remained mysterious and elusive and has kept out of human reach and is subject to *False*, *Deceptive*, and *Misleading* interpretation by the weakness of male zealotry.

The essence of life declares that the *Fematrix* is everywhere, and most if not all must agree with this spiritual observation, for all of us have felt her oneness, her beauty, the feeling of her presence, her greatness, in all living things.

And like so many others, The Alpha was also over whelmed by this timeless and dimensionless sensation radiating from her life force. And yet he could not touch her, nor could he see her, and oh, how he longed to do both of these things. But this of course was the rhythmic essence of the *Fematrix*, and at that time he like so many others did not know of her existence.

The Dilemma Of The Fematrix

Imagine a world where there was only the *Fematrix;* in other words, imagine a world where I kept emerging, but never becoming? (no form, life without body?) A conciseness without ability, an observer who's moment was shorter then its emergence. (the cosmic Fematrix).

The Fematrix Transition

There is the realm or dimension (void matrix) where the creation of the *Fematrix* takes place, the birth and death of Stars! (heavy elements - inorganic matter) The *Cosmic Fematrix,..First Transition*, then there is the realm where the *Fematrix* reigns supreme, Earth, (biological elements, organic matter) the Bio-cosmic

Fematrix- Second Transition.

The *Fematrix* is not the creator of her world; she also must evolve (from cosmic to biologic!).

The *Fematrix* is only supreme in the world she has created; in other words, the *Fematrix* draws her power from the world that created her- Void Matrix, …Origin: the *Elementals!* and brings it to the worlds she has created (authored bio-cosmic matrix...Earth!).

In the *Fematrix* world, there can be only the *Fematrix* in her original state (cosmic energy...heavy elements), no dimension, no form. Therefore, the *Fematrix* must leave her world, if she is to create something other than her original self.

The Second *Transition* of the *Fematrix* was the transformation from inorganic matter (cosmic) to organic matter (biological) form, or interdependent, dimensional existence, which allowed the *Fematrix* to go from restricted directional dimensional movement, to the complete freedom of directional, dimensional movement, bio-cosmic form, or biological life. (the becoming!)

The Third and final *Transition* of the *Fematrix*, was the creation of the servant male being "Man" (her fifth force in the bio-cosmic universe). This male being only exists in the organic dimension; he is a specific and unique creation of the organic *Fematrix* and exists in no other dimensional life, and he is the final inter-dimensional phase and evolutionary stage of the bio-cosmic *Fematrix*.

The *Fematrix* is life, and life is a single consciousness with a multitude of forms and shapes that span the realms of inter-dependent dimensional being (bio-cosmic), henceforth the races of humans and animals in an organic dimensional life.

The divisions of the bio-cosmic *Fematrix*, and especially the last organic *Transition*, were totally and completely misunderstood by humans, and especially by those who attempted to interpret the meaning and laws of life.

Life is a single pulse, a bio-cosmic hunger.

You would have to think of an existence that has no form in and of itself, but has endless inter-dimensional substance, that of itself, has that single pulse.

That pulse is the hunger to create and to bring about an acquired inter-dimensional self. (form!) And so it is to this spirit that brings forth the self, from the self (rebirth) that we celebrate as the living female will, the "She" (*the Fematrix!*)

The Alpha's view: This truth of the Fematrix will not be completely understood until you shall have made your choice and purpose in life, so as to be in harmony with her training and education, (her enlightenment!) to attain the object of her purpose! As has already been explained else-where in the "Holy Valorous", the term- Caucasianism- and its organized effort means that you must develop the strategic ability to direct your efforts in such a manner as to take advantage of her awareness and the wonder of her increasing return. This calls for the highest order of your cooperative ability, hence being furthered by the entire trust between Caucasian and Caucasian, and the social disorganization that follows universal untruthfulness, thereby emancipating oneself, not only from primitive superstitions but from more developed superstitions, so as to be no longer influenced by them. And this implies the trait to which I am drawing attention. The conception of the "She"- Fematrix Causation, is so imperfectly developed, that there is only an indistinct consciousness that throughout the whole of human conduct necessary relations of her intentions of causes and effects prevail, and that from them are ultimately derived all moral rules. Of course, there are some Caucasians who will get the wrong conception of the principle I am here trying to make clear, I hope that you are one of those who understand the reality of her existence, and to which all bio-life is based upon. Yes! we look at her success in the creation and spirit of "Man" and "Civilization", wondering how she did it, and overlooking the importance of her methods, and the price she payed to give us the fruits of her effort.

Man Kind

~

- The New Being -
(the sacrificial flesh)

The Fematrix herself is now a- *Biological Imprinted kind.* Brought about by her inter-dimensional cohesion, she would find herself overwhelmed by her newfound physical and mental task. The first *Fematrix's* were limited in their ability to fend off their hungry sisters who, like themselves, needed to consume great amounts of biological energy to sustain their physical forms in their new dimensional life.

This biological dimensional life of the *Fematrix* would in fact come to dominate an entire planet, with endless physical configurations of the sisterhood, not to mention the first wars of configuration domination (survival of kind).

In the very beginning, the life span of many in the *Sisterhood* was short lived; they would no sooner birth their young (themselves), then the young would be consumed by their much larger sisters. So it came to pass that because of this high rate of offspring predation, a unique occurrence would take place, the creation of the *Sacrificial* being!

The first sacrificial beings looked just like their sisters, but they were in fact empty shells. They could not reproduce, and they were not mentally imprinted.

They were in fact-*Food Decoys*, birthed first, to divert the *Predatory Sisterhood*, so that the real *Fematrix's*, who were birthed after them, could escape.

This diversion system of sacrificial beings became very successful and was quickly adopted by all the rest of the *Sisterhood*, and would have a profound effect on the entire dimension of biological life, leading to the establishment of sexuality, and the male-created being.

- Man -
(the ultimate bio-cosmic machine)

The *Female* being (Fematrix) is the original being and the only natural being.

The *Male* being (mankind) is a creation of the *Female* (Fematrix). He is not an *Original Being* of himself, but is a *Modified Female* brought into being by the *Fematrix* (the Sisterhood) to perform the duties of *Servitude*, *Sacrifice*, and the gathering of *Genetic Information* for distribution to, and processing by the *Fematrix*.

The *Human Male* in fact is born into the world an empty vessel, and it is to this lack of mental imprinting in her male creation, her instrument, and her means to an end, that would prove to be her greatest bio-cosmic achievement.

Though both male and female receive long-term parenting, it is the male that requires more extensive female attention, not only because of his slower maturity, but more to the fact, of his intended sacrificial purpose. She, his mother, knows instinctively that one day he will be called upon to sacrifice himself on behalf of the sisterhood of his race.

This is the true legacy of the male being!

In the case of the young female, her fate is that of her mother; she is the *Fematrix*, the highest form of life, and she will perpetuate the legacy of her throne. She, unlike her brother, is mentally imprinted and knows exactly who and what she is. With minimal guidance from her mother, she will grow to maturity and select a male suitor (serf) to serve her will. It is this process of male servitude to the *Female Will*, and how the *Fematrix* developed the male character, especially in the human male, that is pure genius.

To fully understand the great achievement of the *Human Fematrix*, I think we should examine the creation of her *Sacrificial Flesh*, man, and the very special gift that she gave him. This will give us a deeper insight into her world.

The creation of the male being, by the *Fematrix*, as I stated previously, was the answer to the female state of physical and mental limitations. For you see, life has two frontiers or wildernesses, the physical and the mental. Both complement each other to create dimensions, and it is these dimensions that require an author (creator) who is both physical and mental.

Therefore, if there is no original form of life, no blue-print, so to speak, then any life form is possible. Hence, the great diversity of the *Fematrix* in form, but not in being the only being! In other words, she is still the only *Living Being*, and is still only creating herself, but now, in many different biological forms.

The equation of the *Human Fematrix* is the birth of human biological preferred form (racial kind: subspecies!) through and by a *Life Strategy,* and the mental and physical ability to overcome *Predation,* for the survival of their kind. (races, families, clans, tribes and nations)

The Alpha's view: To understand the beginning?...one must first under-stand that,...there was no beginning? Yes, that's right, there was always the Void!...the existence of the state of nonexistence! Called in Caucasianism, the Age of the Non! And there are 3 Ages in all. First: is the Age of the Non? ...the existence of an endless nonexistence!...the Void. (unsolvable Emptiness!) In other words, how does one find when and

where nothing began? Second: is the Age of the becoming?...the- Author Particles!(elementals) The parents of subatomic particle evolution, the existence of form by chance. Third: is the Age of the Observer? The emergence of biological Life! The "She"- Fematrix!...the only "living thing" the existence of form through need, by cognitive choice, the process of elimination by competing forms!...is the fematrix life-strategy for her- Immortality!...for all living things are of her, and by her!

The Mental Wilderness

(the final frontier)

In the great living realm of the sisterhood, only one being, is born into the mental wilderness, and that being is *Man*. Even *Man's* creator, the *Fematrix*, will stop, gaze, and resist venturing into the mental wilderness, for it is void of direction, and only those born without direction (no mental imprinting) can enter. In the realm of beings, there are three mental states.

The First: Total bio-mental directional imprint
The Second: Partial bio-mental directional imprint
The Third: No bio-mental directional imprint

Though the three mental states comprise the totality of authored life as we now know it, it is the third mental state that is only comprised of a single being, and that being is *Man*!

Uncharted mental direction, no bio-imprint, no maps, no sensory compass, the total wilderness and the final frontier of all life, and it was the *Human Fematrix,* and the *Human Fematrix* only who dares to explore this boundless wilderness. She herself hesitates to enter, for like the rest of life, she possesses direction, and therefore could not survive the mental wilderness. But unlike her sisters, the *Human Fematrix* would send her *Sacrificial Flesh*, *Man*, to explore this wilderness and return with its bounty.

In her great wisdom, the *Human Fematrix* knew that if *Man* was to survive, he must not be bio-imprinted mentally, like her and the rest of life. This was the key to his survival and to her evolution.

Therefore, for the first time in bio-mental evolution, a *Fematrix* would create a being of *Non Specialized* free mental will, the ultimate consumer and retriever of knowledge and the only living being to enter and retrieve the fruits of the final uncharted wilderness, the Mind!

Only *Man*, and *Man* alone, seeks to know what you know and why you know it! "Man" her *Sacrificial Flesh*, her alter ego, the ultimate biological machine, the guardian of the nest, the servant of her will, the receiver of her favor.

Because of *Man*, her *Ultimate Creation*, the *Human Fematrix* has been able to gather immense wealth and increase her territorial range far beyond that of her sisters.

But this greatness does not lie in him alone, for he is the receiver of a force that even he cannot comprehend, but must obey! And that force is in and of itself inimitable in its being, for all must yield to the will of the female! (the Fematrix!)

The Caucasian Faith

(religion of the Caucasian fematrix)

THE CAUCASIAN: A person bearing the mark of the *Caucasian Fematrix*, her racial kind and culture, this mark is a biological distinction and recognizable by all Caucasians.

CAUCASIANISM: Religion of the *Caucasian Fematrix- Caucasia,* (female will) and its democratic racial monarchy (the Caucasian Empire)

THE CAUCASIANEST: One whose faith is *Caucasianism* and who works for the good of the *Democratic Racial Monarchy*. One who wears the Caucasian *Star* and keeps a Caucasian home, having a reliquary to the Caucasian Fematrix, *Caucasia,* and who honors the Caucasian calendar and its social and cultural rituals.

MONASTIC CAUCASIANISM: The monastic order of the *Caucasian Fematrix*, *Caucasia,* the Caucasian *Female will.* The teachings of the Holy Valorous; the writings and labored understandings, social philosophies of the Alpha!

The
- Summons -

(The Alpha's Revelation)

Emerging from the fires of the core into the sea, the "Transcendence" creating the beginning of her becoming!

-The Fematrix Vocation-
"Life"

Having been sentenced to silence by the powers that be, in the year 41968, and lost in the wilderness of reason, he, *Rolland*, son of the Caucasians would cry out into the vastness of his solitude: I know you are there! And I know, you are not man! I see you, but there is no image? I hear you, but there is no voice? I feel you, but there is no touch? Your sent crowds my mind with unfulfilled hunger.

Please, I beg of you, your image! And after a long agonizing wait, with his spirit departing,...her voice reached into his mind, and she said,...you ask for what all others fear!

You ask for me,..oh son of the Caucasians! Fearing his own madness,

Rolland cast the voice out of his mind, only to have it return,...fear you should not, for I am your mother, as I am the mother of all things. And because you are of me, I will calm your soul, and for three nights at this time, I will give you answer. Realizing his issues, in his desperation his mind gathered the questions.

Issue (1) of Life: And *Rolland* asked of her, who are you? And she said to him, I am born of my mother, the *One,* I am her, I am her need, I am her desire, I am the beginning and the end, I am life, I am a daughter of the *Fematrix Vocation (life!)* I shall be called by the name of my creation, my kind, I shall be called Caucasia, and all shall come to know me.

And *Rolland* asked of her: what of your image? And she said to him, do you not know the face of your mother?
For she is of me, and I am of her, to see her, is to see me, to touch her, is to touch me, to love her, is to love me, for we are of the one,...the Fematrix.

And *Rolland* asked of her: who am I? And she said to him, you are man, born of my need, born of my desire, and all shall come to know you.

And *Rolland* asked of her: who are we? And she said to him, I am of my mother, as you are of me, your mother, and we are of the *One,* the Fematrix,...and all shall come to know us.
Issue (2) of Purpose: And *Rolland* asked of her: what is my purpose? And she said to him, you are man, born into the service of my need, born into the service of my desire, only through you, "Man" is our immortality possible.
And *Rolland* asked of her: how shall I serve? And she said to him, you shall seek out those who oppose us, and render them null. You shall seek out those who befriend us, and render them fit. You shall create the covenant in our name, the "Caucasians." And with the *Gift* I have given you, you will come to follow the-*Word?*...it shall be of your hand and of your heart, making secure our journey to immortality.
And *Rolland* asked of her: what is the gift? And she said to him, what is the question that none can ask but you?

"Why" is my gift to you, it shall be by this freedom, this boundless gift,...that all things are possible.

Being anxious to ask her another, *Rolland* sensed she was leaving, calling to him from what seemed to be a great distance, she said,...gather what you seek,...return again I shall! As her light faded from his mind, her *Gift* began to whisper,... Why here?...Why now?...Why me?

The Second Night

Having been unable to sleep from the night before, and spending all day fighting his reasoning, thinking himself mad, he would never the less return to the place, the place of her light, the place that touched his soul. Sitting in the darkness and clinching the questions in trembling hands her voice eased into his mind. So madness is what you think, *Rolland*, son of the Caucasians. I assure you, it's not madness that make you tremble, it is truth, a truth so deep and so profound, that to actually know it,...is to bring all that you think you are, and all that you believe about the world to a state of silence, a truth so submerged in the essence of being,...that to deny it, would mine the undoing of the universe and all that it implies. But that is for another day, let us give you answer ho *Rolland,* son of the Caucasians.

Issue (3) of Destiny: And with a trembling voice *Rolland asked of her:* what of my fate? And she said to him, you are man my greatest creation, my supreme instrument and means to our end. For you see, your destiny, like no other, will be free of all that binds us. Only you, *Man* can explore and retrieve the wonders of the *Void,* and only you, will make the way for us to follow!

And *Rolland* asked of her: what of the end? And she said to him, you will know of the end, when the need has been met, the desire has been pleased, and immortality is our state.

And *Rolland* asked of her: what of today? And she said to him, today is the beginning of your service to me- your Caucasian Fematrix, Caucasia and that of your family, your race, and your nation. Repeat after me,...Blessed are the Caucasians,...for by these words, all shall came to know you.

Issue (4) of Race: And *Rolland* asked of her: what of our race? And she said to him, I am the well of my own existence, my race is created through me, of me, by me. It is life of the self, given form by my need and desire, I am *Caucasia* all that I bring into this world are called by my name *Caucasians* and have my mark, and are of my will. Our destiny is our own!

And *Rolland* asked of her: what of your well of *Existence*? And she said to him, I am of my mother the *Fematrix,* life can only exist in my presence, life can only come into being through me, in me, lies the womb of my matrix.

And *Rolland* asked of her: what of your *Matrix*? And she said to him, my matrix is of myself, and that of my chosen male, by him, through me, I create us both, and all our kind.

Again, the sense of her presence began to fade, he called to her,... *Caucasia,* she whispered ,...tomorrow!

Writing as fast as he could...her answers to his questions, *Rolland* began to realizes the true magnitude of this, his enlightenment, but, was he dreaming? ...was he awake?

Then, his reason began to guide him through the dark corridors of human mental frailty, its faults, failings and inabilities arising from such weakness, and bringing him to the core of *Being* the eternal light of *Female Absolutism,*...the *Female Being,* the *Fematrix.* (the only living thing!) He had come full circle, from birth to reason, and his spirit was humbled by the majesty of her truth, her creations, and her origin.

The Third Night

Again, having been unable to sleep, he worked through the night finishing her answers, by day break he had become mentally fatigued and fail off to sleep. But, this third night would come quickly, and *Rolland* would be awakened by the calling of his name,...*Rolland*, awake, it is our time.

He awoke suddenly, with the new questions held tight in his hand, and she said to him, ask of me what you seek?... oh son of the Caucasians. Clearing his mind, and with a new understanding he began!

Issue (5) of Death: *And Rolland asked of her,* what of death? And she said to him, of this death you know not, I cannot die, and you are of me, so nor can death be of you. We do not come from this world; we have come into this world. It is through me, through the birth that I bring all to this journey, and until immortality is mine, all of man must return to me the knowledge of survival for my next generations to come. It is this cycle of entering and leaving this world and man's sacrifice that can only be stopped by that which I seek,...*Immortality*.

And *Rolland* asked of her: what of the journey? And she said to him, I carry the seeds of our first beginnings, my mother has created the physical world from need, and I have created you, *Man* from need, and it is you man who will give us immortality in this *Dimensional* world, this is what we seek, this is our journey, this is our destiny.

And *Rolland* asked of her: what of our very first beginnings? And she said to him, in the beginning was my *Mother* (the one!) she emerged from the fires of the core, into the cold darkness, and all about her was darkness, she knew not of sound, sight, or touch; she was alone in the void with no physical form, or sense of time. She was, and is the *One,* she is the light; all are of her, and by her.

As *Rolland* was about to ask again, she called for his silence, and she said, you, *Rolland,*...son of the Caucasians, have asked me much! And I your *Fematrix* have given you much! And so I say to you, enough of what you seek,...and more to what you must do! *Rolland,*...son of the Caucasians.

Hear me now! For what I speak will determine our fate, and that of all human destiny! You must seek out all my posterity, and ready them for a *Great Racial Storm* that comes their way. It is a storm like no other, for what drives it is the alien demon "Invidia" (envy-jealousy-hatred!) and with her overt "Caucasian Apostates" (Caucasian liberal zealots!) this cabal of "Invading Aliens" will bring *"Death"* and *"Destruction"* to our great-Caucasian Journey!

And make you no mistake, these - *Alien Forces*- are led by this demon, and driven by her will, these opposing forces will settle for nothing less than the complete destruction of the- *Caucasian Quest*, and its people.

And be you very afraid!,...son of the Caucasians, for time is not on your side,...*Dark Alien Forces* are gathering!

And in less then- *Forty Seasons*, this racial storm of "Alien Invaders" (in the millions!) will lay siege to our Caucasian world community. (our bio-dynasty!) They bring a collective *Impoverished* and *Hyenic* mindset of *"Cultural Sedition"* and *"Political Mayhem"*. And in less then-*Sixty*

Seasons, if you have failed me in this greatest of quests, to rally my children to their own survival, all will be lost, and *Immortality* will not be ours, humankind will descend into oblivion, and none, not even the beasts of the earth shall remember us!

As silence lingered, *Rolland* realized she was fading, he cried out, wait, don't leave yet! I don't know where to start?...and I don't know the Word! - *What is the word?*

As he knew he would never hear from her again, panic filled his mind,...but, return again she did, calming his panic she whispered the word "Valorous" by this word, our "Empire" shall be, and all shall come to know us!

The Quest For Her Immortality

(from 40,000 to the present)

It is the year of our *Fematrix*: 42009, and it has been 40 years since *Rolland* was Summoned by Caucasia to create the *Holy Covenant* (the religious order) and to create the *Written Word* (the religious book) for the Caucasian people, so that they may come to know and embrace their destiny, and prepare for the trials and social storms that she, Caucasia has foreseen in their future. For 40 years, *Rolland* has gathered the *Knowledge*, *Truth*, and *Understanding* of his world, that she, Caucasia has demanded of him, and now upon its completion, their names have been declared, The Religious order shall be known as Caucasianism- and its written word, shall be called the-"Valorous". And by these names, the Caucasian world community and their posterity shall come to embrace them, and stand together as one people, united by their "Ancestral Trust"...and forever being *Unfaltering* and *Faithful,* to the survival of their *Caucasian Racial Dynasty* and its *Historical Journey* of more then- *40 Thousand Year!*

Caucasianism: (the religion of Caucasian Fematrix Theology (*CAUCASIA*)

Founded By: John P Rolland, United States Of America (The year of our Fematrix 42007)

World Population: Abundant

Sacred Text: The Valorous. A collection of the Alpha's social commentary, his philosophy, teachings, and a vast body of political and social truths- maxims.(reasoning's)

Organization: The basic institution is the *Caucasian Holy Sanctum* This is the predominant house of Caucasianism through which the Caucasian social and religious traditions are passed to each generation by the female monastic order, which in Caucasianism is both democratic and authoritarian, and have authority only over those who accept it.

Practices: Among traditional practitioners, all areas of life are governed by a strict religious racial discipline. (the12 Caucasian defenders or virtues)

The chief annual observations are the *Winter* and *Summer Solstice*, plus a variety of rituals, primarily passage rites. (initiations, birth, marriage, death, est.)

And daily devotion, plus ceremonial dinners for the various holidays on the Caucasian social calendar.

And the faithful must make at least two visits a year, to the *Holy Sanctum* if possible.

Divisions: Caucasianism is an unbroken spectrum from Conservative to Liberal, largely reflecting different points view regarding the binding character of the *Caucasian Race*, and the greater world around them.

Location: United States of America.

Beliefs: Strictly Monotheism; there is only one divine principle: The *Fematrix Vocation,* and life in all its forms, *Races* and *Species* (different female life strategies) are aspects of the *Female Divinity*. She is the creator and the absolute ruler of the known universe. Man, (her sacrificial flesh) is her greatest creation.

The emphasis in Caucasianism is on *Ethical* racial behavior, and among the Caucasian racially fundamental, careful monastic racial obedience (anti-miscegenation) as the true worship of the Caucasian Fematrix- *CAUCASIA.*

The Holy Sanctum

(the house of Caucasia!)

-The Domicile Of Caucasian Worship-

The Caucasian Holy Sanctum: the sacred religious domicile of worship for the Caucasian people who practice and obey the religious order of Caucasianism, and its *Fematrix Theology.*

Article I

The Caucasian Holy Sanctum:(domicile of religious- worship) shall consist of two rooms, the first room (outer room) Auditorium is for gathering, and the second room (inner room) *Holy Sanctum* is for worshiping.

The Outer Room: this room (the Auditorium) is for the casual gathering of the Caucasian faithful, their friends and families, Furthermore, this room will exhibit Caucasian eclectic art and culture

The Inner Room: this room (the Holy Sanctum) is for the solemn worshiping of Caucasianism (our Fematrix Caucasia) and all the self-sacrifice made by our ancestors (our ancestral trust). Furthermore, this room will consist of twelve megaliths in a circle (a Stonehenge) each stone will represent one of the 12 moral defenders- *Megaliths of* Caucasian *Religious*

Racial Faith, and upon which a sacred maxim is written on each!

Caucasian Racial Communion-   Caucasian Racial Virtue-
Caucasian Racial Love-   Caucasian Racial Faith-
Caucasian Racial Education-   Caucasian Racial Fidelity-
Caucasian Racial Duty-   Caucasian Racial Honor-
Caucasian Racial Survival-   Caucasian Racial Charity-
Caucasian Racial Law-   Caucasian Racial Justice -

Article II

The Holy Sanctum: At the East End of the Sanctum, an oriel shall be in place to receive the light of days.

Furthermore, below the oriel and in its path of light, will stand the *Alter* to the Caucasian Valorous, and to which the Valorous (Caucasian Manifesto) shall sit upon. About the *Alter*, shall be a sitting amphitheater (half circle) for the contemplation of the Caucasian way.

Article III

The Holy Sanctum: At the center of the Sanctum, and on the floor, shall be inscribed the Star of the Caucasian Empire and at the center of the Star shall sit the eternal well of fire, honoring our Caucasian ancestors. Furthermore, there shall be only one entrance and one exit, and they shall not be reversed.

Article IV

The Holy Sanctum: At the West End of the Sanctum, the shrine to *CAUCASIA* our sacred *Fematrix* shall be in place, before it,...shall sit the reliquary of sacred lights and burnt offerings (prayer candles and incense devotions) at the center of the reliquary will sit three candle, these candles are referred to as the Lights of the Covenant (light of the Caucasian sisterhood, light of the Empress, and light of the Caucasian brotherhood)

Article V

The Holy Sanctum: At the entrance to the Sanctum shall stand the

Paladins (guardians) only through them, may the faithful pass.(enter the Sanctum)

Holy Sanctum Services

(observances - ceremonials - rituals)

"The Observances"

The Caucasian Sabbath: In Caucasianism observant Caucasians come to the high Mass on the last Saturday night of each month for prayer, and the Alpha's social sermon, plus his ritual reading from the judicious Valorous (adults only)

Proper Dress: No one may inter the Holy Sanctum, unless they are properly dressed in the Holy Sanctums religious robs, there are two types of robs, *Laity* and *Guest.* All people interring the Holy Sanctum must be robed. (the Holy Sanctum will provide robs upon request)

Electronics: No electronics of any kind are permitted in the Holy Sanctum, phones, cameras, radios, visual or audio equipment.(unless officially permitted by the Religious Regent)

The Ritual of Silence: talking of a soft nature while in the Holy Sanctum is requested.

Children: the sound of children shall reign free in the Holy Sanctum, and none shall oppose them.

Proper Behavior: All boundaries (both physical and ceremonial) in the Holy Sanctum must be honored.

The Burnt Offerings: Any *Laity* or *Guest* may light a candle or incense to honor the spirit of CAUCASIA, their ancestors or love ones.

Furtherance: At no time shall food, beverages or smoking be permitted in the Holy Sanctum, unless officially authorized by the- *Religious Regent.*

Accessibility: The Holy Sanctum will be accessible to all *Laity* 7 days a week 24 hrs. a day.

Personal Services: The office of the *Religious Regent,*(Sister of the Den) administrator and caretaker of the Holy Sanctum, tends to the scheduling of religious services and rituals,...Birth, Death, Marriage, Religious Schooling, Caucasian Imperial Initiations.

Sponsored Guests: No *Inquirer* may enter the Holy Sanctum unless sponsored by a Laity. All sponsored guests (inquirers) must sign the- *Book of Inquirers*

The Laity: (la-i-te) All registered Caucasians practicing the religion of Caucasianism.

The Prelacy: (prel-a-se) All religious rituals in *Cauca- sianism* are performed by the "Caucasian Female Prelacy" the female monastic order in Caucasianism. All sisters of the monastic order are ordained with the title *Prelic* (prel-ik) Caucasian Priestess, keeper of Caucasianism and its laws of Caucasian racial fidelity.

Duties of the Prelacy: Besides their performance in religious ritual, the Prelacy is also the holy conservator of the miracle spheres, the Caucasian females *Eggs* and their sacred laws of moral interdiction.

Racial Fidelity: It is the obligation of all Caucasian males and females to practice and preach the holy union of Caucasianism both in their public and privet lives. And if at all possible, to bring about no less than 3 children in to the world, thereby insuring the numerical stability so integral to

Caucasian racial survival.

Racial Infidelity: The Caucasian female's *Eggs* and the Caucasian male's *Semen* are the sole property of the Caucasian race. Hence, any and all Caucasians who offer their eggs or essence to alien races (Miscegenation) implies an overt act of *Racial Infidelity* in violation of the sacred allegiance and religious vows to our Caucasian *Fematrix*. (evoking excommunication from the race)

The Prime Directive of the Prelacy: To uphold the honor and dignity of the *Holy Empress* through the worship of the *Caucasian Fematrix CAUCASIA* to participate and guide in all the religious and sovereign services. Furthermore, to declare the light of Caucasianism as the true profession of faith for all Caucasian people. In addition, every morning with the rising of the sun, the Prelacy shall avow the wards *Blessed are the Caucasians* and perform the holy ceremony of *Birth,* proclaiming the sacred right to *Life.*

"The Ceremonials"

Ceremonials: an assembly of many participants. In the everyday life of the Caucasian people there must be a since of *Purpose* a desire to *Contribute*, to *Participate* in the social union of the *Caucasian Family* and its greater community.

And therefore, in the spirit of Caucasianism we honor through the unity of *Ceremonials* Birth, Death, Marriage, Holidays, and the *Seasonal Thanksgivings* etc. Furthermore, due to a great many ethnic and cultural contributions over the past millenniums, a rich and wonderful social and cultural *Calendar* has been created by the *Caucasian Religious Faith* "Caucasianism" to bring *Racial, Cultural,* and *Spiritual Union* to our Caucasian world community.

"The Ritual"

Ritual: an individual observance. In Caucasianism, and in accordance with the *Faith*, an individual observance can be performed in the home; this comes about by the existence of the *Reliquary* a shrine placed in the home for religious observance. Furthermore, and in accordance with the *Faith*, all homes of the faithful must have the *Star* of the Empire at the entrance to their home, so when entering the home, all Caucasians may acknowledge the *Faith* by bringing ones hand to their hart, then touching the star, and speaking the words, *"Blessed are the Caucasians"*. This is the ritual of *Caucasian Faith* and *Respect*, when entering the home of the *Caucasian Faithful*.

"Profession of Faith"

The avowal of belief in Caucasianism and its *Fematrix Theology*.

The prelic asks the Question: Are you ready to make the profession of Caucasian faith?

The Inquirer Answers: Yes, I am ready.

The Prelic Declares: repeat after me (The Profession**)** I have no greater devotion, than *CAUCASIA* and her poster- ity....Blessed are the Caucasians!

"The Caucasian Vows"

The verbal oath and promise of allegiance to all of the Caucasian community.

"The Oath"

The prelic asks the Question: Are you ready to take the Oath?
The Inquirer Answers: Yes, I am ready.
The Prelic Declares: repeat after me: (the Oath) I (your name) a son/ daughter of *CAUCASIA* declare my allegiance, and pledge my honor to the *Caucasian Empire* and its world community. So I pledge unto *Caucasia*.

"The Promise"

The Prelic Asks The Question: Are you ready to make the Promise?
The Inquirer Answers: Yes, I am ready.
The Prelic Declares: repeat after me: (the Promise)

I, (your name) do solemnly promise to honor and obey the laws, rules, and protocols of Caucasian society,...until death do us part. So I pledge unto *Caucasia.*

"The Anointing"

The Prelic Asks The Inquirer: Are you ready to be anointed by the spirit of *CAUCASIA* and take your place with your brothers and sisters in the greater Caucasians society?

The Inquirer Answers: Yes I am ready.

The Prelic Asks The Inquirer: to extend his or her hands with palms facing up, and with the waters of life, the prelic cleanses the hands of the *Inquirer,* calling to all Caucasians of dissent, to speak now or forever hold their peace.

Then, under the guise of silence the prelic will ask the *Inquirer* to stand, and declaring to all "Caucasians" their new title of *Laity* a *Parishioner,* a *Brother* or *Sister* of Caucasianism.

"Ethical Caucasianism"

(the social demeanor)

How we should live as Caucasians: The Alpha till us that all living societies are structured products, brought about by the laws, courtesy, and religious teaching or spiritual journey of its people. And this intern is greatly influenced by its overall understanding and perception of the world around it. As a whole, Caucasianism is unlike most religions, this comes about through its religious doctrine of *Fematrix Theology* (bio-female absolutism!) the *Spiritual, Intellectual,* and *Ethical* belief in that all life comes from a single bio-female entity- The Fematrix.

Furthermore, in Caucasianism, life, as well as the human purpose has no mystical debate, life is seen through clear eyes, it is a single arena of predatory competition and consumption between the daughters of the Fematrix (plants, humans, birds, insects, reptiles etc. All sisters, all having their own life strategy, all competing for the top spot of *Immortality.* Moreover, truth is not lost to the Caucasians in this great struggle, Caucasianism demands the truth,...for truth, in the struggle for immortality is its only salvation.

"Monotheistic Faith"

Caucasianism: is a monotheistic faith, but, its supreme being the *Fematrix* plays no direct role in the social formulas (life strategies) of her daughters.

Though she has created their task in life, that of *Immortality,* she takes no part in their destiny,...life, death, what they accomplish and become are in their own hands, it is after all, a *Competition* for immortality!

Furthermore, the issues of *Sin* and *Evil* have no spiritual mining in Caucasianism, right and wrong are a matter of human law, and are not elevated to the *Spiritual* realm.

In Caucasianism, the spiritual realm is of the *Positive* and *Negative* in nature, and are both celebrated in the truth of their existence, not as mystical, but as practical forces in the realm of all existence. Hence, the "Mystical Force" in Caucasianism is the *Fematrix* herself, through the Alpha's declaration of her (the female) being the only living thing in the universe. One of the basic tenets of Caucasianism, is that *Female Absolutism* (Fematrix Theology!) supports and is the foundation of all known life,...this is the greater ethical teaching in Caucasianism.

"Caucasian Ethical Canons"

In Caucasianism there is a tradition of sacred obligation, of the path to racial salvation and enlightenment that all Caucasians of faith most walk. Thus, the *Ethical Canons* remind the Caucasian people that it is much better for Caucasian society at large, if they accept and obey through their faith in Caucasianism, the social obligations of racial harmony and respect, both in their communities as well as for the many different communities of the world.

Canon 1. *Being a Caucasian means:* Having compassion and charity for all living things.

Canon 2. *Being a Caucasian means*: The Conducting of one's self with dignity and discretion.

Canon 3. *Being a Caucasian means:* Self-improvement through education and discipline.

Canon 4. *Being a Caucasian means:* Having respect for, and adhering to all society's laws.

Canon 5. *Being a Caucasian means:* Honoring and fulfilling your Caucasian ancestral trust.

Canon 6. *Being a Caucasian means:* Treating all human diversity with dignity and respect.

Canon 7. *Being a Caucasian means:* Serving all of the Caucasian family with devotion and love.

Canon 8. *Being a Caucasian means:* Coming to the defense of Caucasian society when in need.

Canon 9. *Being a Caucasian means:* Honoring Caucasianism, its laws, and spiritual creed.

Canon 10. *Being a Caucasian means:* Honoring the obligation to truth, and Caucasian survival.

"Prayer"
(spiritual faith within)

Prayer: the living faith within one's self, the personal manifestation of the divine acceptance of Caucasianism. The belonging to the *Caucasian Spiritual Community* that contemplates their religious text, reading passages from the Holy Valorous and asking the question:

What is the Alpha saying? And what is the Alpha saying to me?

Furthermore, *Prayer* is the most intimate connection with the divine "CAUCASIA" by opening your heart, your mind, and your soul to the truth of her enduring spiritual light,...you will come to feel an intensely personal experience.

When the Caucasian person of faith needs to pray surrounded by the spirits of their love one's, it is always to the *"SANCTUM"* the Caucasian house of worship that they must come, for this is the *Spiritual Fulcrum* of the Caucasian community. The most intimate connection to "CAUCASIA" and her spiritual wisdom is found in one's *Personal Prayer* through the serenity of the- Holy Sanctum and its stations of Spiritual, Cultural, and Historical Truths.

Hence, *Spiritual Faith Within*, by truth, through prayer.

"Caucasian Acquiescence"

- Death of the Caucasian will -

The Alpha tells us: It is the *21st* century, and it has come to pass that the Caucasian states throughout the world are now under *Siege* by alien race's through *Cultural Attrition* and *Domestic Social Assault!*

The aliens strategy is simple: *Isolate*, and *Infiltrate* all Caucasian communities, by disrupting our *"Cultural Bonds,"* demonizing our *"Racial Union,"* deconstructing and subjugating our *"Educational System,"* intimidating all our *"Intellectuals,"* and infiltrating and subverting our house's of *"Political Power!* And most of all!...cutting off all our will to resist!...by spinning our *Moral Sense* of *Right* and *Wrong*, and thereby creating little concern for the- *Truth!*

Hence, our *"Acquiescence"* as a race of people in the face of- *Alien Subversive Thuggery.*

So, to all Caucasians, let it be said, that wrong does not cease to be wrong because the majority share in it!...and the fact that we Caucasians as that majority are participants in our own- *Social Demise!* ...through our own *Acquiescence* because over the years we have been *Morally Intimidated* by an alien campaign of - *Equality Subterfuge!*...there being no doubt as to its *Social Treachery*, and to which no Caucasian can deny!

Hence, bringing us now to the obvious question of how do we ride ourselves of this- *Parasitic Alien Dilemma?*

There is no other way but through- *Honorable Racial Separation!* (separate sovereign states) Because the alternative

"Alien Political Rule" which fundamentally would not be able to *Produce* or *Govern* an *Economic, Cultural* or *Politically* sustainable future, for the- Caucasian American Community?

It is one thing for an *Advanced Cultural People* to rule over an *Inattentive Cultural People!*...but the reverse?

That would be absolutely "Cataclysmic" for the future of the *Caucasian American People* and their Community.

And that is a future?...that we "Caucasians" can not, and absolutely will not- *Entertain!*

"The Caucasian Pilgrimage"

(the cleansing of the mind)

The *Pilgrimage* in Caucasianism is a journey into truth, into the historical properties of a given biology, (the Caucasian race) it is a journey that bears witness to one's ancestral struggle, their reason, their faith, their courage.

The *Caucasian Pilgrimage* begins with the 3 questions of life, *Who am I?* (the beginning) *Why am I?* (the reason) *Where am I?* (the journey)

And, if *Reason, Faith,* and *Courage* is of you, and in you, the answer will bath you in the light of eternal truth, and you will inter the Holy Sanctum to behold the sacred fire of *Caucasian Rebirth*, and bear witness to the- *Pillars* of *Sacrifice,* hearing further the- *Sacred Hymns*, sung to the departed Caucasian souls, that have brought us closer to that which she seeks- *Immortality,* and the end, to the shackles of time!

"The Beginning"

Who am I? Of all living things, only humankind comes into this world accompanied by this question.

It is for all humans, a profound individual mental task, it is a question of their-*Existence?*...which has been given to them by their *Fematrix* (female will) in the form of a permanent flashing mental beacon- *Why?* And this mental novelty exists in the minds of no other living things.

But, there is an understanding, and this understanding of the *Why?*...can be found in the religious enlightenment of Caucasianism. And it is only in and by the teachings of Caucasianism, were the mental beacon- *Why?*...is explored.

Furthermore, though my first question on my Pilgrimage may be-*Who am I?* I must look to the next question of -*Why am I?*...if I am to get the answer.

"The Reason"

Why am I? Unlike other religions, who answer this question through faith, and faith alone, Caucasianism answers this question by and trough-*Physical Existence,* and the *Spiritual Faith,* in that physical existence. It is studied in Caucasianism as *Female Absolutism*, the belief in a single physical living thing, that all other thing are derived of, called and studied in the religion of Caucasianism, as *Fematrix Theology* (the divine female will!) she is both- *Physical* and *Spiritual*, both *Individual* and *Multiple*, both *Male* and *Female,* both *Life* and *Death.* She is the will and the reason of all things; all are of her and by her!

So, the questions of- *Who am I?* And -*Why am I?* Can be found and studied in the *Spiritual* and *Physical* beliefs of Caucasianism*?*

But, if I am to have an answer to this *Why?* a complete understanding of me! I must therefore have the answer to the third and final question of- *Where am I?* The place of my environment, my surrounding circumstance, my friends, my family, my enemies, that which influences and affects me, for without this understanding, my Pilgrimage as a "Caucasian" into a Rational, Spiritual, and Moral being!...would be unfulfilled.

"The Journey"

Where am I? The most intimate connection is found in the birth! And from the moment we are born, we are cast into a series of truths and fantasies, a cloistered world submerged in culture, religion and politics. All in all, the *Human Journey* unlike the rest of life is in a constant state of inquiry, humankind not only labors physically, we also labor mentally. So, the *Where am I?* and all that it entails, is paramount to the religious teachings of Caucasianism.

The world we live in: the *Journey!*..imagine a world, were the beings that live in it, are 99.9/10% mentally feral, and neither recollect their past, or contemplate their future, and with absolutely no dialogue between species?...it is an arena *of Savagery!* This is the world of the Caucasians,... our truth, our reality.

Having said all this! It is only therefore right that we confirm it, so as not to bring confusion to this truth, and all that it implies for the human species, as well as the Caucasian world community.

We as Caucasians most now put aside the mental trappings of the liberal utopian vial,(the political and social masquerade of brotherhood?) to revile the genuine beneath, and that truth is this- *Life* has a foundation, and that foundation is - *Competitive Predatory Consumption,* the taking of life to sustain life!

In other words, were all on the "Menu" and if for any reason you are in doubt?...of this-*Ultimate Truth!*...a trip to your local "Supermarket" to observe its offerings, should correct any misconception.

Therefore, the answer to *Where am I?*...brings us full circle back to-*Why am I?*...and *Who am I?*- completing the *Pilgrimage,* and cleansing the mind of *Religious*, *Cultural,* and *Political Fallacies.* Yes, understanding the truths of life, and one's *True Place* in that life!...are the teachings of Caucasianism.

The
Transcendence

(Journey of the Becoming)

The Alpha tells us: That in "Caucasianism" there is the- *Journey of the Becoming*, albeit in Caucasian religious terms the- Transcendence, (going beyond!) is used by Caucasians with reference to the "Fematrix" and her relation to the world is particularly important in-*Caucasian Theology.* Her *Transcendence* means that the "Fematrix" and her origin are completely outside of and beyond our world. But, she is manifested and fully present in our world. In the Alpha's words: if our "Fematrix" (Caucasia!) is situated in our world, she is *Immanent;* if her origins reside outside of our world, she then is both *Immanent* and *Transcendent.*

Therefore, the Alpha compels us, the Caucasian people to understand and contemplate the *Truths* and *Realities* of "Transcendent Knowledge," that which, going beyond all possibility of experience, strives to determine the nature of things as they really are in themselves. Along with our need for "Immanent Knowledge" which keeps within the bounds of the possibility of experience, but thus, can speak only of phenomena. Hence, the hypothesis of the - *God gene?*

Which some geneticists propose, that a specific gene, called- *"Vesicular Monoamine Transporter(2)"* predisposes humans towards *Spiritual* or

Mystic experience.

In other words, a *Mental* and *Physical* connection with the- Creator! This is not an incorrect definition of the connection, her genes are in us all, for we are all of her and by her, she is not a-*God!*..for they come and go! She is the- *Life Spark*, the "Fematrix" and her *Spirit* is hardwired into our genes. She is the harbinger of all transmitted "Consciousness" and her claim on all of life and its destination, is absolute.

Articles Of Caucasian Faith

Article (1) Faith in Race: Through its many social and historical accomplishments.

Article (2) Faith in Religion: Through its spiritual enlightenment, by the truth of its path.

Article (3) Faith in Family: Through its union of love, understanding, and devotion.

Article (4) Faith in Tradition: Through the acceptance of honoring historical achievement.

Article (5) Faith in Truth: Through the enlightenment of understanding by reasoning.

Article (6) Faith in Charity: Though the enlightenment of what is right and good action.

Article (7) Faith in Community: Through the participation of work and social union.

Article (8) Faith in Education: Through and by the teachings of social and historical truth.

Article (9) Faith in Sacrifice: Through the understanding of Caucasian social survival.

Article (10) Faith in Authority: Through the leadership of Caucasian social enlightenment.

Article (11) Faith in Duty: Through the understanding of social need and dependents.

Article (12) Faith in Morality: Through the enlightenment of ethical intellect and righteous behavior.

The Alpha's view: In the faith of "Caucasianism" there is the act of – Toleration - for those Caucasians and Aliens of other faiths or of no faith? This act is a safeguard to their liberty, and it must be, and will be uphold by all! (Monarch or Democrat) Therefore,"Caucasianism" thou the founding principle and intellectual faith of the Caucasian Empire, understands and willingly acknowledges the Civil, Moral and Spiritual lessons of other religious faiths, or those of no faith,...finding them unassailable!..if righteous in purpose.

The Nexus

(Age of the Caucasians)

The Alpha tells us; We are the "Caucasians" and the- *Nexus;* (the bridge!) between what was!.. what is!.. and what will be! In other words; the "Architects" those *Instrumental* in serving as a crucial means, and the *True Agents* of the *Active Principles* of the human journey. Furthermore, manners, genius, laws, and government of the Caucasian Nations, form an important object of inquiry, from their influences on the *Manners* and *Policy* of the modern Caucasian states.

In the delineation of Caucasian history, the leading Caucasian Nations of attention are more various; the historical scene is often changed; by Nations, which for a while occupy the chief attention, become for a time subordinate, and afterward reassume their rank as principle; yet the same plan is pursued as in the department of *Ancient History*; the picture is occupied only by one great Nation at a time, to which all the rest hold an inferior rank, and are taken notice of only when connected with the principle. The rise and progress of the *Caucasian Monarchies*, (the Caucasian Conquest!) and the splendor of their dominions, was the origin of *Chivalry*, *Art, Science*, *Literature* and *Modern Democracy*.

Therefore, it is necessary that the study of Caucasian History should be prosecuted according to the truth; for the science of history more perhaps than any other, is liable to perversion from its proper use. The Caucasians owe their civilizations to the life strategy of their "Fematrix,"(Caucasia!) and the rise of her independent states in the *Caucasus* and *Europe who's Spirit* and *Truth!*...will lay sedge to the rest of the- *Universe.*

The
Human Apocalypse

The Alpha tells us: Throughout human history, and in most, if not all of their cultures, there is the legend or prediction of the coming "Apocalypse" and in all, human fate will be brought to its "Demise" by the wrath of the Gods? (storms, plagues, earthquakes, fire!) a biblical reference to the end of- Humankind. And yes, the Alpha agrees, but, his understanding is not *Supernatural* in origin, he does not assign the end of *Humankind* to the Gods, No!...that honor will strictly belong to- *Humankind Alone!*...and it won't be by any disasters of legend?...it will come about by three intellectual emerging's- *Reality, Fantasy,* and *Artificial Intelligence,* and it will be a combination of these three mental configurations that will command and repurpose the wilderness of- *Pleasure and Reason!* ...which at this time has already infected most if not all of the-*Civilized World?* (in the billions!) Its "Intoxication" has even made inroads into the halls and chambers of our "Government" fostering a utopian social edict of "Racial Equality" (a fantasy!) while disregarding the truth of "Racial Competition" (a reality!) and ignoring these simple facts of absolut truth: if it looks different!..act different!..and produces different!...then it is different!...yes? And if you believe in the reality of difference?..and all that it implies, then you cannot in good conscience deny "Competing Races" with different life strategies, (incompatibles!) and their truth of "Racial Sovereignty" (their own racial state!) and their right of- *Destiny!*

"*Sovereign bio-identity!*..is the principle of all living things"

- Robotics -
(A.I. artificial intelligence)

The Alpha tells us: That "Life" has properties unique unto itself!...and some of these are "Inter-dimensionally" inherited!...and what that means is they cannot be recreated?

In other words- Human Emotions: *Sorrow, Passion, Love, Hatred, Envy, Desire, Purpose,* and let us not forget-*Need!*...just to mention a few, are all roots of the human intellectual endeavor, for these and others like them, form the intellectual chamber of the *Self* - in *Mind!*...which *Drives* and *Navigates* all human reason. Therefore, it now becomes fitting to address one of the most important questions of the *21st* century, that is now and will be in the future paramount: "Robotics" (automation!) and its A.I. or "Artificial Intelligence" and that of its *Purpose?*...and its *Future?* First- "Robotics" and its A.I. are revolutionizing the human world both in their *Industrial* and *Domestic* endeavors! Think about this!...by the mid *21st* century, the world will have *Built* and put into *Human Service* more then-100 million *Domestic, Industrial*, and *Military* robotic units!

The Alphas Warning! Do not fail to understand that *Robotics* with

"Artificial Intelligence" are not living things and have neither *Human Reason,* nor *Compassion,* and can be commanded and put to purpose, by both *Good* and *Evil!*

Therefore, their-*Creators, Programmers* and *Directors* must be held accountable, "Humankinds Necessity" must not fade in the shadow of the-*Machine!*

The
Caucasian Acclimation

(Caucasian racial alignment)

The Alpha's lore: Blessed are the Caucasians, for none shall know a more *Nobler Spirit* then theirs!

As the Alpha, I will put before you what is already known, it is the year 2016, and all the Caucasian communities throughout the world are under sedge by three deadly- *Intellectual Ventures.* (liberal-zealotry!) (moral-enervation!) (alien-appeasement!) Because of the wild and extravagant liberal Caucasian worlds democratic social notions, a runaway social fallacy!(the equality mantra!) Caucasian America and her sister states throughout the world are now being directed by their elected political leaders to accommodate hostile alien concessions, *Political, Cultural* and *Territorial.*

In other words- *Complete Caucasian Submission?*...and thereby putting the entire Caucasian world community on a-*Suicidal Path!*..to their own destruction.(South Africa?)

Furthermore, by losing (abdicating!) its *Social Compass,* (it's bio-identity) the Caucasian world community is completely out of- *Survival Alignment,*...And, it is the job of all Caucasians throughout the world to unite and rectify this deadly situation. Alas, all will be lost!

"Racial Lore"

(biological enlightenment)

To fix that which is broken: We must first understand what it is, what it does, and the very environ-ment it functions in! And in the case of the Caucasian race and their many Societies, this also applies.

So, let us begin by descending to a simpler mental plane or understanding, so as to not cloud our analysis with the trappings of scientific and moral leaps of faith. For all practical purposes there are only two types of existence in our known world, and they are organic structure (biological cellular) and, Inorganic structure (elemental particles) Though it is true, that organic matter is comprised of inorganic matter, but it is only organic matter that has a-*Collective Intellect*, the *Fematrix*, and is capable of deliberate conscious self-regeneration. In other words, she can think and act on her own behalf,...she makes choices, she selects, she favors, she discriminates, she rejects, she decides, and all of this is unique to herself. (her own free-will) Having said all this, let us now get to our subject, the *Human Species* (homo sapiens) and its three races (subspecies) *Negroid, Mongoloid,* and *Caucasoid.* There should be no doubt in anyone's mind, as to the differences between biological beings! Or the truth, that their everyday life and its subsistence is based on decisions made for them and by them, their life strategy (cognitive ability) Evolution, or the path to survival, ultimately depends on a *Life Strategy,* different environments invoke different life strategies, hence, whether human or animal, these strategies both form and alter all mental and physical being, they are embedded (DNA) and uniquely individual to each life form, and are directly responsible for all biological *Success* or *Failure,* this is truth, this is reality. These truths are self-evident, and all those who champion truth, will align themselves with it. Furthermore, it has been said, that the stability of a society is ultimately determined by that which supports it,...its *Life Strategy.* And, it is this truth that applies to all three human races as well. In defense of our racial kind: *Negroid, Mongoloid, Caucasoid,...*simple terms, at least most people would think so, but are they? In a world plagued by endless difference, does not the term *Racial Kind* pause the mental traffic, and bring focus to the meaning of ones being?

Is it not true, that I am human, and therefore of a racial kind!...a *Biological Determinant,* and does not the word "kind" imply the existence of others, others of racial difference and determination? All that is,...lives, and all that lives,...are different *Fematrix Life Strategies*, and they are bound in the endless struggle for the positions of their choice. Each human race has but a single premise, and that premise is its very own "Survival" through and by its own "Fematrix" life strategy. (this is truth, this is Reality!)

Racial Indifference

(Caucasian society's greatest enemy)

Survival, this was, and is the first law of the living *Fematrix* in her pursuit of corporal being, and all other laws are subject to it. Furthermore, Caucasian racial kind is a product of its *Fematrix* (Caucasian female will- Caucasia) and her *Life Strategy,* as the female will is the common denominator of all living things. This is truth, this is reality.

The Alpha tells us: there is a condition brought about by ones belief in their supreme cognizance, leading to a deep mental arrogance, (intellectual inebriation) that fosters a false since of social liberality, thereby enabling the destructive advance of *liberal zealotry* and its cult of *Equalitarianism* (human equal outcomes?) and their drive to shackle and silence–*Veracity!* Intellectual Racial Disdain: the Alpha asks us this troubling question, what in all creation, would make a Caucasian person deny the essence of their own being?

In other words, what would cause an otherwise rational individual to repudiate their own *Biological Inheritance* (racial kind) and cultural essence (ethnic heritage) for a broader and neutral identity, of human equality?

The Alpha tell us, that for any Caucasian to take the position of- *Racial Nonpartisanship* or if you like,...racially neutral?, hence, having been born of *Caucasian Parents*, fed, housed, nurtured, and educated by *Caucasian Society*, being in fact, their ultimate social investment, would constitute an act of cowardice and betrayal beyond measure.

Furthermore, any male or female Caucasian that denies his or her duty to uphold the self-determined right of Caucasian racial existence, whether for political, economic or intellectual reasons must be hold morally and historically accountable. The *Alpha* further declares, that it is the supreme calling in all Caucasians, that they stand ready to challenge any and all Caucasian "Enemies," whether foreign or domestic, whether political or ideological, whether they be Caucasian or alien,..none shall pass, all shall be arraigned.

Biological Fematrix Dynasties

(the driving force of all life)

The Alpha tells us: that all life, and its fate will be determined by the *Success* or *Failure* of its *Biological Fematrix Dynasties*: For more than a billion years, war has been waged between- *BioSpecific Life Strategies*, or as called in Caucasianism "Biological Dynasties" forged and ruled by the "Fematrix" (female entities!) with their own unique life strategies for "Supremacy" and their goal of- *Immortality*! In the last billion years!...the list of known biological dynasties (Microbe, Bacteria, Plants, Insects, Reptiles, Birds, Fish, Mammals and Humans) has been more than impressive, (in the tens of billions!) and it would be safe to say, thou impressive!...never the less, all have failed! ...and are the symbol of the fate that awaits 99 % of all the living biological dynasties of our *21st* century. But, having said all this!..there are three "Human Dynasties" that have great promise, *Negroids-Mongoloids-Caucasoids*. And all three are *Races* (subspecies) of the same species (homo-sapient) and if history has taught us anything, it is that of the three, only one will prevail?...laying claim to the *Universe,* and the *Teleology* of the *Fematrix* (immortality!)

The Alpha's view: Can the three come to terms?- creating a future for us all?..he believes that we of the 21ˢᵗ century are at the crossroads, that will unequivocally decide the fate of all- Humankind

- Miscegenation -

(destruction of hereditary ancestral descent)

Hereditary ancestral descent (Fematrix biological kind) or *Racial Inherency* is the harvesting of knowledge that fills the genetic depository (innate DNA) of all living thing. Hence, providing a living thing with all of its unique in- grained qualities, character and physical form.

In other words, DNA is a created biological blueprint, made up of two submitted specifications or needs, both *Male* and *Female* for biological structure or restructure, thereby increasing the *Survival* of their kind

The *Alpha* tells us in the interest of historical accuracy, *Interbreeding* between *Species*, *Races,* or direct family members -*Incest* has always been as a rule *Objectionable* and *Harmful,* a very destructive act, with a serious and costly out- come,...it is *Biologically Stunting* for all who partake of it!

And for any *Race* or *Species* the act of *Miscegenation* is an immediate death sentence, for in this dance of *Sinful Trespass* will culminate in the death of two, for the birth of one! A male or female of a *Species* or *Subspecies,* will never surrenders their *Eggs* or male *Essence* (the very future of their kind!) to alien others!...this is an unassailable truth!

In the religious faith of -Caucasianism- the willful act of *Miscegenation* is regarded as *Subversive Treason* against the *Caucasian Community* and its *Posterity*!...punishable by the public declaration of one's -*Excommunication* form the greater Caucasian society. (persona nongrata!)

A living being; made up of elements originally from different *Races* or *Species* is referred to as a *Hybrid* and their mixture brings nothing positive to the biological equation of whence they came, they are in fact the harbinger of death for the biological lines of their parents. Biological Substance: a million years or more of physical and intellectual evolution (knowledge and judgment) is primarily the definable essence or form of a living thing, and the preservation of their biological journey. The *Alpha* tells us, that all life is in a constant state of predation, (to eat, and not be eaten) and in a world where everybody is on the menu; a *Life Strategy* is paramount for *Survival*. Having said all this, let us now bring into the light the subject of "Miscegenation" (interbreeding of racial differentia!) and its relation to survival. When one speaks of human racial kind, one has entered a social, political, and scientific mind field, were the *Intellectual* has become subservient, the *Sociologist* has been repressed, the *Politician* has become obedient, and the *Scientist* has bowed to self-censorship.

In no other field of the *Intellectual Kingdom* does this malignancy exist. (unrestrained liberal zealot tyranny!) But, it is not within the enduring Caucasian spirit to yield to threats and intimidation, while in the pursuit of truth, because that truth does not align itself with the uneducated notion of a *Mystical Racial Equality*! Having expressed this in the full spirit of a *Caucasian Inquiry*, let us now look into this forbidden dark realm, and unveil the truths and fears by bringing them to the unforgiving- *Reality!* Forgoing a biological debate as to the complex mechanics of life, and the now excepted fact by most if not all, that *Intellect* and *Genes* are the harbingers of biological evolution, let us descend to a simpler and novice understanding of human kind, we now know that all life on this planet has a common denominator. (a single source!) We know this because in our endless search for life, we have never encountered any life contrary to the life we already know? (biological-life?) So, if this is true? We are now faced with the reality that all life on this planet is related to each other? And if we are all related to each other!...than why is there difference *?*

Biological Differentia

(a fematrix life strategy; offensive-defensive)

Having now established the fact that all life on our planet is related; the obvious question is why then are we all different? The Alpha tells us: from the moment a life comes into the world, it is immediately under assault by other competing life forms, and from the moment its born, its bio-imprinted code, its inherited *Fematrix Life Strategy* come to its defense. And if this is true,...which it is! What is this life strategy, is it universal to all life?...and if it is, how did we acquire it, and by what means?

The Fematrix life strategy: Bio-Metamorphosis through needful cognizant deliberation, (biological evolution) all life on our planet is in a constant state of mental and physical adjustment to defeat and control *Biological Predation,* and to find or produce shelter from the elements.

Failure in ether one of these life challenges,...is fatal!

Mental and physical adjustment through *Need,* in other words, what one must have both mentally and physically if one is to survive against the forces that oppose it?

Furthermore, of the two forces only the biological is of *Mental Intention*, and therefore like one's self, having a life strategy. While the elements though having no intention, are never the less a great physical and deadly force to be reckoned with. Thereby, making it apparent that biological difference or the differences that appear in groups of living things are a manifestation of physical and mental changes brought about by a need for *Predation*, *Competition* and *Cooperation*. In other words, physical and mental differences in living things implies deferent survival decisions, and the differences between them are the outcome of those decisions.

Futhermore,their appearance and mental prowess are for all practical purposes the symbol of their success, and their needful cognizant deliberation. (their life strategy!)

Alas, we now return to the detriment of *Miscegenation,* for millions of years, the primate species has been roaming the continents of our world, in a constant state of multiplying, subdividing, winning and losing.

Then, somewhere along this great primate journey, in very distant and remote lands from each other, would emerge three *Human Races*, (subspecies) *Negroid, Mongoloid* and *Caucasoid*, three different races, (physically distinct!) three different cognizant deliberations, (environmental opposition!) three different life strategies (survival solutions!).

The biological core: the center of inherited biological navigation, the central core of acquired biological knowledge (100 thousand years +) and its transformation into a life strategy, a species or races cognizant direction. It is this biological core in each living thing that makes them what they are. Furthermore, in this core, is the essence of their ancestral racial being, the total of their own biological historical journey. When you bring different dominant racial groups together,(with millenniums of isolation) and miscegenation takes place, the outcome is always gene frequency digression, and recessive racial character.

Hence, the creation of one, by the sacrifice of two!

All hybrids are a forfeiture of *Racial Character*!

In other words, the biological racial core (ambition, cognizance, aggression, etc.) of both parents is lost in the process, and their offspring emerges with no trace of "Racial Character" they have been biologically *Alloyed,* and that implies that the ancestral core of each race is not passed on to the miscegenated off-spring, leaving them in a state of biological exile, socially repelled and racially wanting. Hence, this truth!...no liberal utopian socialism of a "Racial Equality" (equal racial outcomes?) being an absurd intellectual artifice, is at any time and in any way, ever going to be able to resist successfully, the onslaught of "Life's" (the- *Fematrix!*) unforgiving competitive reality of *Winners* and *Losers.* (the rule of life's- *Arena!*)

Social Imperative

(The Need To Survive!)

It is considered by most, to be true, that life has a single premise, and that premise is its *Survival,* the universal term or as referred to in **Caucasianism**, the *Need toSurvive!*

All humans, as well as all living things are dependent upon a foundation of mental or intellectual ability, and unlike other societies that are fixed and their social paths are stayed,(imprinted!) the human society is constantly shifting and its properties are both *Radical, Fractional*, and in an endless state of repair. But, it is the humans union of social focus on behalf of its intellectual ability (education!) that ultimately determines our human adherence to the universal term. This is truth, this is reality!

Furthermore, though all societies whether human or animal, have as their primary drive the survival of their *Fematrix,* and are as a whole, fierce competitor in the game of predation,...it was out of this competition that one of them would far exceed the ability of all the others?

Hence, the emergence of the *Caucasians* (the valorous race!) and in the spirit of truth further determined, there has never been a race of people who have conquered as much, created as much, or given its good will as much too human kind, as have the Caucasian race of people. They have far exceeded their biological precept, and all this has been to the credit of their supreme being, their *Fematrix,* the *Caucasian Sisterhood.*

The Alpha tells us, that *Caucasian Racial Faith* should be based on the truth of knowledge which is further determined. He also tells us that *Caucasian Racial Faith* is power, and that the power of *Caucasian Racial Faith* for its own sake can be destructive if the knowledge that guides it is misleading, false, or the deceitful preaching of its interpretation by- *Sinister Racial Zealots.* (hate-mongers!)

Therefore, *Caucasian Racial Faith*, though often corralled by visions of mystical beginnings and endings, our "Ancestral Mythology" is by far the true medium by which all Caucasian enterprise is possible. (our love and racial self-esteem!)

Caucasianism, is the faith of the Caucasian whole, the final understanding of racial union, the spiritual empire of the Caucasian line of *Fematrix* biology, only through the enlightenment of Caucasianism, and one's adherence to its religious faith, its righteous path, can one fully bathe in the light of its eternal truth.

We are the Caucasians, and all shall come to know us!

Caucasian Judicious Tolerance
(prudent racial diplomacy)

It is in Caucasianism where the religious enlightenment of *Biological Difference* and its social theology (fematrix differentia) both on the part of the life sciences and human races is explored.

Biological Antagonism: Competitive production and consumption between different living beings, and their physical difference being a manifestation of their mental difference, and that intern brought about by millenniums of *Positive* and *Negative* encounters. (creation by priority)

So, how a living thing approaches its life is ultimately determined by its ancestral trust. (its bio-acquisition)

Hence, biological difference through survival resolution, this is truth, this is reality. Having now established to the satisfaction of any rational being, the truth of difference, the *Alpha tells us*: In life, there is this universal premise, and he states- Were there is difference?...there must be the "Identity" of that difference!

Therefore, "Classifying Opposition" is paramount and any life form that fails to do so, has disregarded its own "Survival" and all that it implies.

Hominid Differentia
(the two-legged primates)

The Hominid line of living things include a vast number of primates and subprimates such as Homo Sapiens (humankind) Great Apes, (gorillas, chimpanzee, orangutan) Monkeys,(baboons, capuchin, colobus, marmosets) plus additional groups of early humans, Peking, Erectus, Ne- anderthal, Cro-Magnon just to name a few.

Though their bioline is great, and they are all directly related to each other, they are also *Completely Different* from each other, both in physical anatomy and mental capability.

Which intern brings us back to the reality of *Biological Difference* and its relationship to survival, its meaning, and its classifications.(Fematrix life strategy)

Human Races
(Negroid, Mongoloid, Caucasoid)

Homo Sapiens: *Humankind.* After more than a million years of *Fematrix Evolution* (biological competition!) the human species has been reduced to three competing races- *Negroids, Mongoloids* and *Caucasoids.* In other words, if you are a Human, you are either one of the three?...or a combination of the three? (there are no others!)

This is truth, this is reality.

It is clearly understood in "Caucasianism" through the enlightenment of *Fematrix Theology* that the three remaining races are the last vestige of hope for the human journey.

And as is intended by the *Fematrix,* in this great arena of human racial competition,...that only one of them will emerge as the victor, and it will be a victory of *Destruction,* and human failure, or, it will be a victory of *Preservation,* and human *Immortality* and creative guardianship, the fate of all humankind will be determined by this conflict, and it's out come? For in *Fematrix Theology*- the victor will take custody of the *Universe*!

The Ancestors
(the sacred well of sacrifice)

The Ancestral Trust: The Holy Obligation of all Caucasians to be in the service of their- *Biological Mandate*- their Fematrix- *Caucasia!*.. and her quest for our immortality.

Our Race, Family, Religion and Bio-Dynasty, these are the sacred pillars of our Caucasian social structure, and not the least of which, should we ever forget our- *Ancestral Sacrifice,* the very bad rock upon which we all as Caucasians stand!

Furthermore, let no Caucasian man, woman or child, in the comfort of their modern-day life, relinquish their sacred obligation to their *Ancestors.* An obligation of *Spiritual Caucasian Loyalty,* and the continuation of their further *Sacrifice* for the future of Caucasian posterity.

- Racialship -

(loyalty and service to our Caucasian life strategy)

The Alpha's concept of Racialship is a wide one, and can be seen from the divisions that he makes between different types of- Racialship!

Racialships of- *Utility:* in which people do not love their race for what it is in itself, but only for the advantage which they receive from it. Such Racialships are necessary to people, since people are not economically self-sufficient.

A Racialship through business would be of this type.

Racialship of- *Pleasure:* These are founded on the natural delight that people take in the society of their race, and are characteristic of the young, for young people live by feeling, and have a main eye to their own pleasures and to the present moment. But both these types of Racialship are unstable, for when the motive of the Racialship - Utility or Pleasure- is gone, the Racialship also is destroyed.

Racialship of- Spirituality: This type of Racialship is perfect Racialship and endures as long as both retain their *Character* and *Virtue,* it is everlasting.

As we would expect, the *Alpha* makes a few observations on the subject of Racialship, which, if not profound, are shrewd and to the point, and which are applicable not only to a natural Racialship, but also to a supernatural Racialship with Caucasia, our *Fematrix.*

If Racialship is activity in accordance with virtue, it is reasonable that it should be in accordance with the highest virtue, and this will be that of the best thing in us.

Racialship, is, according to the *Alpha,* the contemplative faculty, by which he means the faculty of intellectual Caucasian racial activity, thus showing the intellectualist Caucasian racial standpoint which he shares with the Caucasian people and their world community.

Reason is the highest faculty of humankind, and Racialship contemplation is the highest activity of reason.

Racialship is one of the elements of happiness, and is admittedly the most pleasant of the activities in which human excellence manifests itself. The pleasures of *Racialship* at least appear to be wonderfully pure and reliable, nor in deed is it surprising if the life of him or her who knows of their *Racialship* is pleasanter than that of the *Racial Gainsay*. It is in the exercise of *Racialship,* then, and in the exercise of that *Racialship* concerning the noblest objects,(the Caucasian family) that a Caucasians complete happiness is found. Such a life expresses the divine racial element in us, being Caucasians, and to mind things that are Caucasian.

Racialship: is a great part of us; in *Power* and *Value,* it far surpasses all others. Moreover, it would seem to be the real self in each of us, since it is sovereign overall and better than all. And accordingly, it would be very strange if we as Caucasians were not to choose the life of our own true selves, but of something other than ourselves. The highest object in our society is our *Caucasian Racialship* and our religious adoration to "Caucasia" our Deity. (*Fematrix!*)

The essence of the *"Beatific Racial Vision"* consists in the act of our intellect on the truth of *Fematrix Theology* (female absolutism!)

" What becoming is to being, truth is to belief "

The Alpha's view: the initial issue that first brought attention to the Alpha was the liberal debate over - Civil Rights- that over a short period developed into -Racial Equal Rights and has now become – Racial Equal Outcomes? ...and along with this fallacious intellectual indulgence, there would also emerge the liberal papacy, elite Caucasian liberal zealots with their racial minority cabal of victim hustlers on a Crusade of Exorcism, to ride the Caucasian American community of its demonic possession- Racial Privilege? The Caucasian American community should be Horrified by the behavior of these 21st century liberal elites, with their preaching being not only a fallacy!...but a direct subversive assault against the Caucasian American people and their community, of which the Nation owes its creation and to which all aliens others draw their security and livelihood, need reminding: the United States of America is the sole creation of a "European Caucasian Diaspora" having its own biological mandate for survival.

-First And Foremost-

-We Are The "Caucasians," We Will Defend Ourselves!-

"So Say We All"

The
-Caucasian Fematrix Monarch-

"Caucasia"
(our Caucasian Sovereign life force!)

In the realm of the *Fematrix* (the sisterhood) by far the greatest and most powerful of them all is the *Caucasian Female* (fematrix) Caucasia!

Her daughters, with no doubt, are a force with no equal!

They have mothered the greatest *Nations* and *Empires* of our world. Their needs have given rise to all the great industries, and their appetites for the trinkets of the craftsmen have led to world commerce.

The evolution of the *Caucasian Fematrix* is perhaps the most incredible biological event in the history of life.

The *Caucasian Fematrix*, unlike her sisters, has employed a greater amount of color in her off-spring.

In fact, of the three *Human Fematrix's*, she is the only one to have, multicolored eyes, multicolored hair, and multicolored skin.

These bio-characteristics (native traits) are uniquely inherent only to the *Caucasian Fematrix*, and do not appear in the natural offspring of her sister races. The *Caucasian Fematrix* has also excelled in the development of her *Male Vessel* in ways that are uniquely hers.

Though all of the Sisterhood of the *Fematrix* has created a male being of their own, none had been as responsive to the will of its *Fematrix* like that

200

of the *Caucasian Male,* this is do in part to the great ability of the Caucasian *Fematrix* to fully understand the importance of the males indoctrination to the- *Females Will!*...and the control of his direction in reference to her needs and that of their offspring.

To gain an even greater insight into this miraculous *Caucasian Female,* we must go back to the beginning of a specific biological pulse that took place in the great mountains and forests of the- *Caucasus, Asia* and *Europe.*

It is said that man became great because of his ability to use and make tools; therefore, if tools are the criteria for greatness, then the *Human Female* must be the greatest of them all. For man is her created tool, the most versatile in the living universe. And the most gifted user of this tool called "Man" is, without a doubt, the *Caucasian Female*-(Fematrix!)

She, above all other females, has created and set the standards of *Social, Political,* and *Economic* life in the human species. There is no realm of human life that does not have her influence or does not benefit from her will. Europe is the *Intellectual* and *Cultural* cradle of the Caucasian race, the biological site of the *Caucasian Female* (Fematrix), though the exact place of the first tribe of the *Caucasian Fematrix* is not known. There are significant signs of her presence in the habitats of the *Caucasus, Western and Eastern Europe,* and other *Asian* locations at or around 400,000 years.

And if a people's history begins with writing or art, then the date is 40,000 years in parts of *Europe,* for it is in these areas that the most accomplished *Paintings, Stone* and *Ivory Sculptures* have been found.

These are the site of the most ancient habitats of the *Caucasian Fematrix.* It has always been the 𝔄*lpha's* belief that it is from these *European* region that the *Caucasian Fematrix* set out to dominate her world. With her culture firmly rooted in her male creation, and the *Caucasian male* balanced in his devotion and direction to his *Fematrix,* her realm, her symmetry to his being, the *Caucasian male* and his kind would set out to gather the fruits of her will, to lay siege to a world of resistance, with multitudes of different life forms and cultures.

The human world is for sure, "Understood" by its *Geological, Biological,* and *Archaeological* information. It is through these *Sciences* and other phenomena that the path of the *Caucasian Fematrix* has been charted in great detail.

But like the opposing forces that fuel life (diversity), the minds of the learned sciences are also at odds with one an other over the beginning and source of life?

There are those who would go as far as to give the *Female Spirit* (Fematrix) a second-rate position in the realm of life? And, as absurd as that may seem, there are learned minds that follow this philosophy.

Therefore, how one sees and interprets their information, will determine his or her truth. The nations and kingdoms founded by the *Caucasian Fematrix* and her sacrificial flesh, the *Caucasian Man*, have been the catalyst in the history of all humankind. From the ancient caves of *Western Europe* to the *United States* of *America,* the *Caucasian Fematrix* has sat on every throne, she has ruled over every nation. Her cultural creations are an exercise in social evolution.

Therefore, even those who have suppressed her rule, and have enslaved her power to deny their people the gift of her social evolution will admit to her power, which beckons them to serve her, even in her bondage.

When you think of the *Fematrix* (the female spirit) you will have to perceive beyond the infinite universe, to encompass its whole. In her lies the beginning and the end to all things. There are only two gates in a dimensional life, one for entering, and the other for leaving, and it is her spirit and her will that operates both.

In the sisterhood of the *Fematrix*, it is the human sisterhood that has taken its place at the head of the biological table. And of this great human sisterhood, it is the *Caucasian Fematrix* (Caucasia!) that rules, and has set an historical social standard, and modern direction for all of humankind.

This has been made possible through her sacrificial flesh, the *Caucasian male*, which has dominated the entire world for more than five thousand years.

The *Caucasian female* is the most powerful *Fematrix* on *Earth!*...and it was due to the great ability of the *Caucasian Fematrix* to maintain her elevation in the different tribal cultures, which led to a common social order, that is often referred to as "Western Civilization" but, is in fact the biological civilization of the- *Caucasian Fematrix*.

Man does not serve man,...no!

Man only serves his *Fematrix*, this is truth; this is reality, and only through her can reality be fully realized.

For life can only exist in her presence, the ultimate cultural and social being, the eternal life force!

To gaze upon the modern *Caucasian female* (Fematrix) surrounded by the symbols of her wealth and status is to be bound by true power, the likes of which has never been seen on this planet since the beginning of time.

The modern *Caucasian Female* (Fematrix) reigns over her world like no other, a complete social agenda backed by the cultural diversity and economic wealth of her race, her creation, her soul,...the *Caucasians!*

The Alpha's view: I see her every day!.."Caucasia" *and I marvel at her stamina, and in awe of her stealth, her appearance of commonality, her ability to take second place in a world she and her sisters have created. Yes!..life has but one living thing, the "Fematrix" (the imperial being!) and it is only through her extended self (her daughters!) that life and its diversity is possible, for all are of her!- through them, and by them. And so it is my hope that one day in the life of man, that he shall come to see what I have seen, and what I now know! For in her, and from her, comes the true meaning of all things, the eternal idea,"Life" the light in the darkness! Furthermore, make sure that your "Caucasian Racialness" is constructive, that its attainment will bring hardship and misery to no one, that it will bring you peace and prosperity: then apply, to the limit of your willful understanding, the principle of "Caucasianism" for the speedy attainment of its purpose.*

"Overcoming Our Inner Disturbance"

Caucasian Ascension

~

"Monarchy"
(Our monastic discipline of imperial racial faith)

The word *Caucasian* is the name given and accepted by a multiethnic race of people who bear the biological mark of their *Fematrix*. Furthermore, the monastic sacred devotion to the study of the *Caucasian Fematrix* and her race is paramount to the socio-cultural "Dynasty" of the Caucasian people.

The Caucasian individual sees his or her race and takes it for granted; the Caucasian public desires racial enlightenment but is afraid to embrace it. Both equally need guidance, the Caucasian individual must be obliged to his or her racial ancestral trust; the Caucasian public must step beyond its "Fears" and embrace the racial enlightenment it desires.

There is thus a profession of racial faith that is purely civil and of which it is the 𝔄*lpha's* function to determine the articles, not strictly as religious, but as expressions of racial conscience, (Caucasian Nationalism!) without which it is impossible to be either a- *Good Citizen* or *Loyal Caucasian.*

The general Caucasian public's will, is always rightful, but the judgment that guides it is not always enlightened, there must be racial covenant and positive law to unite race with duties and to direct justice to its object.

To discover the rules of a society that are best suited to a race of people, there would need to exist a compassionate intelligence, one who could understand the passions of the people without feeling "Overwhelmed" by them, who had an affinity with our racial nature and know it to its fullest, who would make our happiness his concern, who would be content to wait in the fullness of time for a distant glory, and to labor in one age to enjoy the fruits in another. This is the true creed of the 𝔄*lpha*, the one who would shape a natural racial society, its government, and its future.

The Caucasian race must be shown the good path it is seeking and secure itself against seduction by the desires of individuals; it must be given a sense of its racial situation and season, as to weigh immediate and tangible advantages against distant and hidden evils. Such Caucasian enlightenment would produce a union of understanding and a will in the social body, bring the parts into perfect harmony, and lift the whole to its fullest strength.

Hence the necessity of "ℭaucasianism" the precept of *Caucasian Racial Faith*! What then is correctly to be called an act of Caucasian racial faith? It is not a covenant between a superior and an inferior, but a covenant of the Caucasian racial whole, with each of its members. It is a legitimate covenant, because its basis is the racial social contract; an equitable one, because it is common to all Caucasians; a useful one, because it can have no end but the Caucasian common good; and it is a durable covenant, because it is guaranteed by the love for the Caucasian race.

Each to all, and All to each; from this it is clear that the "Racial Faith" of the Caucasian people, wholly absolute, wholly sacred, wholly inviolable as is, must come to understand the oldest of all societies, and the only natural one, "Family" (bio-haven!). The *Race* and the *Family* are one and the same!, in and of its- *Natural Existence*.

"This is our truth, this is our reality"

-Henceforth-
-Declaring The Words Of Our Union-

"Blessed are the Caucasians"

The Racial Principle

(biological covenant)

The *Racial Principle*, or the *Biological Covenant* of the race, is to watch over its own preservation; its first care it owes to itself; and as soon as it reaches the age of reason, it becomes the only judge of the best means to preserve itself.

Life is constantly changing it social mode of existence, and since we are all part of this life force and are bound by the biological laws of the *Fematrix,* how to find a form of association that will defend the person and goods of each member with the collective force of the whole.

This is the fundamental problem to which the biological racial contract holds the solution. The articles of the biological racial contract are so precisely determined by the nature of the act that the slightest alien modification, *Miscegenation*, must render it null and void. It is such that, though perhaps never formally stated, the biological order in races (subspecies) and species of all life are everywhere the same (survival of the seed, their kind!) everywhere tacitly admitted and recognized. In fact it can be stated that life has a *Universal Covenant*, and it is the same for all!

When a life form *Specific* and *Unique* from all others encounters obstacles to its *Preservation,* its *Universal Covenant* will invoke its *Racial Social Covenant* to act, and that act becomes the accumulated focus of pure survival.

Each one of us, puts into our - *Racial Faith*- all our power under the supreme direction of survival of our *Seed,* our *Caucasian Biology*, and as a *Social Racial Body*, we incorporate every member as part of the whole. Therefore, it is imperative for any racial group (human-subspecies) to keep its *Core Identity!*...its unifying biological mandate (love of kind!) as the idol of its *Survival Initiative*, without its promotion and dedication there can be- *No Union, No Community and No Future.* This is the fulcrum of Caucasian *Racial Faith,-* Caucasianism!

Our Caucasian Fematrix Liturgy
(symbol of the Caucasian female spirit)

THE CAUCASIAN STAR: The Caucasian star (called the origin!) is the name of the *Sixteen-Pointed Gold Star,* symbol of the *Caucasian Fematrix* and the state crest of the *Caucasian Empire.*

THE CAUCASIAN FEMATRIX LITURGY: The *Caucasian Fematrix Liturgy* (the social formula!) having three levels of knowledge: *Devotion, Understanding, Obligation*, and sixteen points of *Enlightenment.*

It has always been the Alpha's belief that each day the human mind sets out on a journey, and that a mental posture is taken for each journey, and that all journeys are imprinted with this mental posturing and then stored away.

He also tells us that each journey develops its own separate type of personality (by way of information gathered on the journey), and each journey begins to develop a degree of importance, a kind of pecking order. So when one enters another person's journey, the personality of that specific journey will come into play.

First level: The four enlightenments of devotion include *Racial Kind*, *Racial Sovereignty*, *Racial Education*, and *Racial Defense*.

Second level: The four enlightenments of understanding include *Religion*, *Culture*, the *Law*, and the *State*!

Third level: The eight enlightenments of obligation include *Man To Woman*, *Woman To Man*, the *Family*, *Parent To Children*, *Children To Parent*, *Oneself*, the *Law*, and the *Commonwealth*!

"Devotion"
(first level, four enlightenments)

Racial Kind: All things are born into the world of their kind, their *Fematrix* (female will) and all have her mark and are recognized by her kind, the social order of racial kind, recognized kind, mental kind, one in accordance with kind, in accordance with order, in accordance with direction, in accordance with the whole. In its reality, biological society both human and animal, their cultures, and their directions are a oneness with the whole of their likeness.

Race: Is the *Sacred Heritage* of kind, of *Identity*. It is the established mark of the *Fematrix* and not deducible from anything else. It is the self-establishing life of the *Female Will*. To this will, power has been allotted and assumed.

Racial Sovereignty: The *Fematrix* (female will) is the creator of life! All things she creates are of her image, unique and separate from all other living things, the only one of its kind. Therefore, the highest priority must be given to its survival. A race is its own source; it alone carries the blueprints of its likeness.

The belief in the sovereignty of kind (race) is paramount to the survival of any and all living things. This is truth; this is reality, and no amount of political fallacy can alter this ultimate truth!

Racial Education: The education of racial identity and the part it plays in the understanding of racial diversity and social community is paramount for social stability. This racial education can be achieved only through the teachings of the *Fematrix*. Only by understanding the *Fematrix* (female will) can biological difference be understood!

The fear of difference is manifested through ignorance, and those who drink from the well of ignorance will find it often bitter and desperately unsatisfying.

Difference, and the recognition of that difference to have its own destiny and right to survive, is racial education well served.

Racial Defense: All that is stands opposed to all that would be! Kind feeds upon kind. Race wars against race.

Difference seeks opportunity over difference. A race having the mark of its kind (it's Fematrix), which symbolizes a communion of bio-cultural direction, is also seen as standing competition and opposition in the eyes of other races.

Therefore, if a race of people fails to understand or realize this truth and act accordingly, this would ultimately mean the destruction of its social order and the consumption of its future by the predatory ambitions of other races.

The sacking and plundering of societies throughout human history has always been a requisite of kind, racial kind, tribal kind, ethnic kind, cultural kind, political kind.

On that premise if your kind (race) is to survive, it must be defended! This is truth; this is reality.

"Understanding"
(second level, four points of enlightenment)

RELIGION: In the dark uncertain storms of life, there is a great desire to anchor the human spirit in a safe harbor, and that harbor is religion. The story of human religion is a social journey with no equal, and its spiritual, cultural, and intellectual expressions are the very fulcrum of human social evolution.

Though religion is the harbor of the human spirit, that harbor has not always provided shelter for those seeking spiritual refuge, for on many occasions the dark storms of life have breached its hollowed walls, and yet, even these violations could not stem the human desire to be one with the creator.

CAUCASIANISM: The religious institution that holds the belief that the *Caucasian Female* (Fematrix) and all other females are manifestations of the *Supreme Being.*

The *Fematrix* adjusts and structures her own form; she alone decides what it will be and what path she will take to achieve her destiny; Hence the great diversity in the biological sisterhood. There is only one absolute driving pulse in the all embracing sisterhood of the *Fematrix,* and it spans the wilderness of good and evil, man and beast, space and time. That absolute driving pulse is the survival of her kind, which is the creation of her will and carries the distinguished symbols of her chosen biology.(form!)

CULTURE: Culture is the ritual communication of human society, the very heart of social unity. There are three types of culture, civic culture, nomadic culture, and barbaric culture. The differences between the three cultures has nothing to do with superior or inferior social airs, but rather, the degree to which each of their Fematrix's is out of line with their social center.

Civic culture: confronts opposition (on center) **Nomadic culture:** avoids opposition (off center) **Barbaric culture:** parasitic hyenic (no center)

Human evolution is a product of confrontation, of meeting opposition head on, and this is what "Civic Culture" is all about. It is the establishment of a fixed place and social direction upheld by ritual communication and a willingness of the whole (the people) to stand and overcome all opposition to their social direction.

THE LAW: The law is the socio-cultural boundaries by which human societies are governed and determined.

-There Are Three Types Of Laws-

Natural Law- or laws of life: (Kind, Consumption, Production, Direction)

Sovereign Law- or laws of social survival: (Alien Treaties, Treason, Murder, Rape, Kidnaping, Capital Punishment)

Civil Law- or laws of social direction (Cultural, Commerce, Contracts, Building)

Although the two human laws, *Sovereign* and *Civil* are in fact manifestations of the *Natural* laws, they are uniquely human in their makeup and adherence. The human social order, unlike any other, is always reinventing itself, and therefore human laws are always in a state of evolution. It is to this fact of social reinventing by human societies that make their laws either a social *Triumph* or a social *Tragedy*, and this ultimately depends upon their understanding of the natural laws!

THE STATE: The state, second to the family, is the highest form of social order. It is the focal point and instrument of the collective social will. The state can only be what the collective brings to it! It is in fact an empty vessel, with no life of its own. It can perform no task other than the task that has been willed for it. The state is the vehicle and guardian of a social direction legitimized by a diversity of social wills.

This is truth! This is reality!

Therefore, if the state is the manifestation of collective social will, then what is the collective social will? The social will of the human state can never be of a single pulse, but will always be of conflicting wills. In other words, the common thread of the social will is to create the desire in others, for the preservation of others. Hence, the preservation of oneself!

It is the understanding of self-preservation, which in turn manifests social preservation in the group and gives rise to the social will.

The social will is, in fact, a group of differences that have come together for the sole purpose of a common preservation, and because of their individual compromise, this bond has led to the establishment of a socio-cultural direction under the guardian ship of the vessel known as the state.

The sole purpose of the state is the preservation of the social direction, and it is the will of the whole that is the spirit of the state and its direction. Therefore, if the will of the whole fails, the state fails and ceases to exist, leaving the socio-cultural direction unprotected and vulnerable to anarchy. The state reflects the best and worst of the human spirit; it is our mirror image.

This is truth! This is reality!

"Obligation"
(third level, eight points of enlightenment)

MAN TO WOMAN: For one to fully understand man's obligation to woman, it is first necessary to understand the true nature of man and maleness. The debate over man and his origin has long been the exclusive debate of man, by man!

And that is most unfortunate, for you see; man is not the product of man!

Man is the product of woman! In fact, and in reality, man is a *Modified Female*. Man is not a natural being in and of himself! Man is a created being, a modification of the natural being, the *Female*. Man was created for the express purpose of servitude and sacrifice. He is a biological serf, and this is the male's natural state throughout his existence. This fact, on the contrary, does not diminish man's stature or his greatness in any way whatsoever. In fact, if fully understood, man is the greatest creation in the universe, even surpassing his creator in ability and intelligence.

Man is the ultimate of creations, and this ultimate creation is wielded by the greatest force in the universe, the *Fematrix* (female will)! Man's obligation to woman: This most misunderstood of human encounters and actually begins at birth. From man's very first days of life, he will encounter the love, the discipline, and the unyielding demands of his mother the *Fematrix*.

She will become the center of his existence. The first years of his life will be spent completely submerged in the spirit of his mother. This envelope of protection and communication will establish the foundation upon which his perception of his socio-cultural world will be erected.

His long years of adolescence will be spent in the introduction to his mother's culture and the adherence to its rituals and social conduct. It is in fact the skill with which his mother teaches him her culture that will ultimately determine his level of obligation to a woman in a family setting.

So it can safely be said that the obligation of a man to a woman is determined to a great degree by the teaching skills of his mother and his acquired cultural imprinting.

Therefore, this brings us full circle. Man's relation to a woman in a social setting is a learned thing, not an instinctive thing, and cultural compatibility, or the lack of it, plays an immense part in the relationship between man and woman.

It is now possible to turn to the heart of this subject, the Caucasian man's obligation to the Caucasian woman. The Caucasian male is a product of a racial *Fematrix* and her culture!

First Obligation: to educate himself in the ways of his Caucasian culture.

Second Obligation: to educate himself in the ways of the *Caucasian Empire* and its moral codes of chivalry.

Third Obligation: to educate himself in the ways of his duties of servitude to the *Caucasian Female* (Fematrix), her family, and her society; to protect it, provide for it, and if need be, to die for it!

WOMAN TO MAN: To fully understand the woman's obligation to man, it is first necessary to understand the true nature of women. Woman (Fematrix), and the debate over her origin, is so obscure and intellectually barren that even women in general don't know who they are!

This phenomenon is very unfortunate for all of humanity, for woman (the Fematrix) is beyond any doubt the greatest living force in the universe. All that is, comes through them! Life can only exist in their presence.

Woman is the doorway into dimensional life; their spirit is the living covenant of all life.

In the *Fematrix* is the *Sisterhood*, the direct descendants of the entity herself, the author of all that is.

This is truth! This is reality!

THE GIFT: In the realm of the *Human Fematrix,* there are three great-*Sisterhoods*, the *Negroid*, the *Mongoloid*, and the *Caucasoid*. These three sisterhoods comprise the total of the human species, and all three have created a male serf, but unlike the male serfs in the animal sisterhood who have partial or total mental imprinting, the human male has virtually none. At first glance, this lack of mental imprinting in the human male serf would appear to be a defect, but in fact, in a forever changing world, this absence of mental imprint is a gift beyond measure.

Unspecialized, totally free mental will, a gift, even denied the human *Fematrix* herself! And let there be no mistake and no doubt, this is a gift from the *Human Female* (Fematrix) to her male serf. No other living thing possesses this gift! Man is born into the world an empty vessel, by design of his *Fematrix,* and in this lies his greatness.

But besides her gift, he, like all serfs, is male, and this is biologically reinforced sexual bondage with a single drive, and that drive is to copulate with the *Female*. Man's interest in the *Female* does not go beyond the sexual act itself; his interest in family is coerced by the *Female*, and he must be guided through its rules.

Man has no instinct for children, unlike the *Female* who has child imprinting, the male's loyalty to his children is learned; he must be introduced to his children and guided in his behavior and duty by the *Female*. The longer he is with his children, the more loyalty he will develop for them man's contact with children is never independent; it is always through the *Female* and subject to her observation and discretion. Children do not exist in man's inner world; they are completely outside of it. He has a natural resistance to cater to the weak and helpless; therefore, he is coached by the *Female*, into accepting and serving it, rather than adhering to his natural contempt for it.

Man's world is filled with sexual compulsion and the arena of male-to-male physical conflict. He has no true connection with life and death, hence his quickness to take life and his compulsion to risk his own!

So what is the *Female's* obligation to her created vessel, man, this greatest of all living serfs?

First Obligation: She must educate herself in the ways of her- *Caucasian Fematrix Culture*.

Second Obligation: She must choose a male who responds to her Caucasian culture and educate him to family life.

Third Obligation: She must perform the duties of her *Racial Fematrix*, uphold the socio-cultural direction, create the family unity, and hold her male serf to the will of the *Caucasian Fematrix*.

THE FAMILY: The *Family* is the undisputed core of all creation, the junction that all life must pass through. The *Family* is the consummated realm and holy ground of the *Female!* It is from this, her nucleus, that the living social order is received, formed, and directed. Therefore, it is the will of the *Female* and the power of her eternal spirit that fires the engines of all social discourse.

Whether man or animal, commoner or king, all are schooled and graduate from the socio-cultural academia of the *Family* (the bio-haven).

If the truth be known, it is the governing faith of the sovereign *Family* that binds all humankind to the social order, for if the *Family* fails, the human social order fails.

This is why the status of the *Family* must be the highest and most honored position a man or woman can attain in Caucasian society.

The social status of the *Family* must take precedent over individual status, and the individual must be made to understand that the higher rewards of Caucasian society are reserved for those who have made a commitment to the *Family*. This is not to say that the individual in Caucasian society will not receive his or her earned or achieved social rewards; on the contrary! The achievements of the individual are the very rewards of the *Family*. It is for the purpose of enhancing the desire in men and women to create the *Caucasian Family Structure* that certain social rewards have been set aside.

This in turn brings an added strength to the biological racial base, making a more secure Caucasian social structure.

A nation or a race of people that does not hold the *Family* to be its highest moral and social institution is a nation or race in moral and social decline.

A *Family,* like a garden of rare flowers, must be cultivated and socially tended to, if it's going to produce the highest quality of humanity that has been entrusted to its care.

The *Caucasian Family* is the nursery from which all good Caucasian social order evolves. It is the academy of cultural and moral discourse.

Those who tend to the maintenance of the *Caucasian Family*, tend to maintain the *Caucasian Future*!

Obligation to the Caucasian Family: The preservation of the *Caucasian Family* is a moral obligation beyond measure, and it is the duty of all Caucasians to align themselves with and to this obligation.

PARENTS TO CHILDREN: The union of the parents creates the social well from which the child draws, in his or her pursuit to gain social status.

Therefore it is the quality of this *Parental Union* that ultimately determines the child's adjustment to his or her society. In the final analysis, the *Parental Union* must be able to inject five basic social reasoning's into its child: obedience, compassion, persistence, mutual aid, and sacrifice.

Obedience: the ability of the child to understand the value of social rank and the servitude to its authority, regardless of personal ambitions or opposition.

Compassion: the ability of a child to feel a genuine loss for the destruction of life and a great sorrow for the injury to life, whether physical, mental, or social.

Persistence: the ability of the child to stay the course and strive to overcome obstacles, no matter how difficult, no matter who the opposing force.

Mutual Aid: the ability of the child to understand the value of the whole (Caucasian society) over the individual and the value of the individual in the service of the whole.

Sacrifice: the ability of the child to understand the forgoing of his or her own needs for the benefit of others, and that the quality of their own life will be enhanced by his or her sacrifices. The children's social direction will be socially enhanced or degraded by the cultural understanding and development they receive through the teachings of their parents.

This is the chief foundation for the social quality of society. The greatest threat to any society is the emergence of social fractures in the philosophy of the *Parental Union*, for where this occurs, the children lose all direction and become lost in the wilderness of social fallacy, a world where the lives of children are sacrificed wholesale on the altar of moral anarchy.

Therefore, the *Parent Union* is paramount to the very survival of *Caucasian Society*, and this union is, in fact, a *Sacred Obligation*- to the service of *Childhood* and all that it implies. In the case of physical divorce between parents, their sacred obligation to their children must be and will be honored in the atmosphere of *Parental Union*. In this, there will be no compromise!

CHILDREN TO PARENTS: the social obligation of a obligations. Children, just as previously stated, are a product of their parent teachings and their understanding of the socio-cultural order, of which they are a part.

Therefore, the child, like its parents, will become the keeper and messenger of the *Socio-Cultural Faith* and this is where the obligation of the child to its parents comes into play.

The child is, in fact, for all practical purposes, the vessel of the continuum of the biological and cultural self, and although children, *Male* and *Female* have different obligations to their *Parents,* these separate obligations are in fact a single pulse of racial survival.

The common obligation of the child to its parents, therefore, resides and is received in the family. It is in the sacred family where the socio-cultural *Scepter* (cultural responsibility) is passed to the child, freely given and freely accepted.

This passing of the socio-cultural *Scepter* is in fact the agreement to accept those socio-cultural obligations of their parents and to take their place in upholding its social and cultural laws, which have sustained and provided for them.

Therefore it is the obligation of the children to sustain the sacred heritage of their kind, and passing that socio-cultural heritage on to their children is fulfilling their obligation to their parents and to that sacred state, the family, which brings the union of the sacred three; past, present, and future, to a single social direction, the- *Caucasian Way!*

The success of any and all societies is ultimately deter mined by its socio-cultural transference; in other words, the transfer of cultural way and means from one generation to another. But the success of this transference is determined by the child's understanding through the teachings of the parents.

The dual nature of human obligation, parent to child, child to parent, is a prerequisite of human evolution and socio-cultural evolution. And its certainty is without question, not chiseled in stone, but Caucasian society rests on Caucasian culture, and you cannot alter one, without altering the other! Caucasian cultural transference, and its acceptance by Caucasian future generations, is paramount to the survival of the- *Caucasian Racial Continuum!*

⊕BLIGATION TO ONE'S SELF: Before you can have good foreign relations with others, you must have good domestic relations with yourself. The obligation to oneself is a manifestation of self-preservation and personal identity; these two needs motivate personal worth, and also help to develop one's individual social image.

The social order in a society is a direct reflection of the individual quality of the citizens that make it up. The true quality of the individual, and the ability of the individual to express that quality, is a direct result of the socio-cultural education available to the individual. The search for the ideal social order has always been, throughout human history, a permanent expedition into the social wilderness of educating the individual. For you see, the problem has always been how to balance education with social restriction.

These have always been the horns of the social dilemma! But, the social dilemma of educating the individual in today's modern society is even more confounding, brought into being by an academic weakness- *Utopian Liberal Zealotry*!...which is a liberal educational philosophy that aspires to the fallacious belief that all people are *Created Equals*?..and if the madness of this educational philosophy happens to escape you?...all one has to do is observe "America," and the madness becomes Apparent!

Be all you can be! This, without a doubt must be the educational philosophy for the Caucasian individual in the modern Caucasian society!

But education of the individual is a byproduct of an even more cherished mental acquisition, the cultural racial whole of the- *Caucasian Fematrix!*

Therefore, to be all you can be, or the obligation to oneself, in reality, is of a dual purpose. Education is a generational gift, knowledge of the past, given by the present to the future, and the obligation to oneself is the acceptance of this generational gift.

The obligation to oneself is to identify the self and establish the self within the boundaries of that cultural biological order that sponsored your life, to which you, the hope of its future, must now fulfill that legacy passed on to you with- *Dignity, Loyalty,* and *Courage.*

OBLIGATION TO THE LAW: Of all human endeavors pursued, it is by far the laws of society, and their constant evolution that try and exhaust the human social will. Laws are the guidelines of human social discourse. If they are just laws, they will channel the social direction of the whole to a point of union with it members. This in turn motivates in the common citizen an obligation to obey the law.

But if they are unjust laws, they will channel the social direction of the whole to the point of a social rebellion, and the common citizen will forgo his or her obligation to obey the law. The obligation of the citizen to obey the law is derived from a point of social fair play on behalf of its elected government and or political party.

Therefore, it is not difficult for one to recognize bad social laws. All one has to do is just take a survey of the work load on the court calendar and review the budget to see how many new *"Prisons"* are on the social drawing board.

This has always been a reliable yardstick by which to measure the social pulse toward good or bad laws. A nation's life force is its laws, and these laws are brought about by the desires, ingenuity, and goodwill of its citizens. Justice under the law is the mortar of all social structure and the high altar of the common will.

*Bad Laws***:** These are laws that serve the interests of a specific group of the society, at great expense to the whole of society (affirmative action laws) (racial job quota laws) (racial equality laws). These are laws that unjustly qualify the unqualified! These are laws that serve more to split the society than bring union to it.

Good Laws: These are laws that serve the interest of society as a whole and serve the individual as well as the group through the interests of the whole and not outside of it (religious freedom) (cultural freedom) (educational freedom).

These are deliberate laws that serve the whole and foster union in the society, rather than division.

The compromising of the law: This is the greatest of social evils, when laws can be trifled with, manipulated, and undermined for purposes of wealth, convenience, politics, or personal revenge. It is these types of legal subterfuge that can undermine or even destroy the common obligation to respect and obey the law and leave anarchy and lawlessness in their wake.

THE COMMONWEALTH: The obligation of the individual to his or her society is an obligation to its whole, its commonwealth. This commonwealth is comprised of four social elements, race, culture, religion, and politics, and it is around these four social elements that all human societies revolve.

Therefore, it is up to the individual to establish his or her obligation to these four social elements. The first three are relatively easy, for they are elements of birth, and one can no more deny their obligation to them than they can to themselves.

But the fourth, *Politics*, is a vast wilderness, and it dominates the social commonwealth of all societies and their directions. Politics!...is in fact, the very machinery of the commonwealth, so if one has an obligation to the commonwealth, it can safely be said one has an obligation to politics.

But when the politics of the commonwealth begins to lose its center, its common bond, and drifts into the wilderness of social fallacy, because of individuals who have been seduced into social heresy by the lore of personal gain, the commonwealth will begin to lose its union of social direction, and the society as a whole will begin to fracture. This in turn will lead to the collapse of its defensive instincts, which are needed by a society if it is to survive. Therefore these persons must be identified and held up to *Public Ridicule* and prosecuted to the full extent of the law.

In the final analysis, the social commonwealth must always maintain in the four social elements the sense of *we, the whole*, and that no amount of individual wealth is worth the destruction of so noble a social bond. The maintenance of the commonwealth is the job of all its people and the quality of that job can best be measured by its less fortunate individuals and how their day-to-day needs are met by the more fortunate segment of that commonwealth.

The commonwealth draws its quality from its people, and that quality is expressed through the four social elements that its people live by. The Caucasian commonwealth, whether in *Europe*, *America*, or anywhere else, will depend ultimately on the loyalty of its people to maintain its ancestral trust, its social direction, and to provide a future for its children. This is our truth; this is our reality!

The Alpha's view: Our Caucasian character is but the crystallized reflection of the thoughts that dominate our minds and the deeds we perform. We Caucasians have within us the power to select the material that constitutes the dominating thoughts of our minds, and those thoughts that dominate our minds will bring us Success or Failure according to their nature. (thought control!- self control!)

The Sacred Warnings

I, the Alpha, protector of the racial spirit and keeper of the social path do now call upon the Caucasian people to uphold the sacred warnings and heed their knowledge.

"The First Understanding"

LIFE: Life is the need, and the need is the Fematrix (the female will!).

She is the creator of kind, and kind is the existence of her will. All that is comes from her, and all that is must serve her. This is truth in reality!

SACRED WARNING: Be free of those who do not recognize and will not serve their racial Fematrix and her social code (the cultural family), for they are sterile beings and have no purpose.

"The Second Understanding"

THE RACE: The race is the multiplication of the self by the living will of a Fematrix. What she brings into life bears her distinctive marks, which identify her specific biological kind and cultural direction, unique and separate from all others.

SACRED WARNING: Be free of those who do not honor their race and have no allegiance to their- *Fematrix.*
These are sinister beings that lack a social orbit and are lost in the dark, mental wilderness of self-delusion.

"The Third Understanding"

THE CAUCASIAN EMPIRE: The Caucasian Empire is the biological and socio-cultural state of a racial kind and its Fematrix (female will). The cultural teachings of the "Caucasian Fematrix" is the foundation upon which the state and it social direction must rest! Therefore the Caucasian Empire's survival is ultimately determined by the loyalty of its citizenry and by the teachings of its racial and cultural Fematrix.

SACRED WARNING: Be free of those who preach the gospel of the Multi-racial state and its lies of racial equality. These are the evil seeds of the liberal zealots, who roam the intellectual wasteland of social fallacy.

The Sacred Seed

(Biological Dominion)

In all of existence, there is only one truly sacred threshold, and that is the dominion of the sacred seed (biological idea), the seed of biological history; the sacred seed of kind, racial kind, mental kind, physical kind, spiritual kind, identifiable kind.

The seed of Caucasian ambition, is of its will, of its self- determination, and once fertilized, it brings forth a million years of biological enterprise, a million years of trial and error, a million years of opposition, and conquest.

All of biology is ruled by the same living spirit, the Fematrix, or Female Will.

She is the crucible of gametogenesis (the process of life to birth); only she holds the miracle sphere (the egg) only she controls its essence (by choice of males) and the miracle sphere can be activated by only germ cell information (DNA) brought to her by her gatherer, her chosen male.

She decides what she will be, and only she decides what we will be.

This is the realm of the *Caucasian Seed*. It is the realm of all living seeds, from microbes to plants, to humankind; all are born of their own unique seed, a one of a kind Seed forged in the biological crucible of its Fematrix, its female will.

So if truly understood, there should be no doubt as the special nature of a race of people or a species of any kind.

We are all fragile, and we all share a common deno- minator, we are forever on the hunt and forever being hunted!

Caucasian Sacrilege

(Liberal Desecration of the Caucasian Race)

It is the *21*st Century, and the Caucasian American dream is beginning to unravel. The social will of Caucasian America has been smothered by a sinister political ideology, liberal totalitarianism (liberal zealotry).

Under this political banner of extreme paternalism, the American liberal class has begun to put into force a decree that all Caucasian Americans must abandon their identity and surrender their culture, the reason? Because, Caucasian American identity and their culture is offensive to racial minorities, and therefore politically incorrect?

Do they really think that we Caucasian American are going to surrender our very existence?

Abandon our biological seed?

Desert our ancestral trust?

What arrogance!...What political hubris!

To believe that we the "Caucasians" will not defend our *Seed?*...is to be in total denial of- *Caucasian history?*

The American liberal zealots are about to make the greatest mistake of their entire political existence, and like others before them, who have betrayed our trust, and subverted our good will, they more than anyone else, because of their *Racial Treason* and *Political Sabotage*, will bear the full and justified weight of Caucasian Americas political and social wrath!

To think that there are "Caucasians Americans" who would seek the destruction of their own *Biological Origins*, *Social Structure*, and *Cultural Heritage* is beyond rational reason. But yes, they do exist, and they are in high political office throughout the *City*, *State*, and *Federal Government*, working deviously behind the-*Political* and *Cultural* scenes with *Alien Radicals* to overthrow the Caucasian American social order, and their first (main!) objective is to *Demonize* and *Demoralize* our- *Caucasian Racial Identity!*

Why?...simple!...destroy the very root of their social foundation "Their Racial Identity" then you can dismantle their- *Social, Cultural and political Loyalty*,...thereby leaving the Caucasian people and their community with no social cohesion! And it becomes even more sinister when our Caucasian political representatives (the one's we put in office!) put aside their loyalty to the people who were loyal to them, and become self-seeking "Political Freebooters" which, as we all can see, they are quickly becoming!

This in turn provides a large window of opportunity for absurd and destructive legislation intended exclusively for the dismantling of Caucasian America by racial minorities, with help from Caucasian cultural renegades, liberal zealots, and intellectual deviants. The question?...now is this: what can the average Caucasian citizen do to help restore the Caucasian American Com-munity's *Social* and *Cultural* fabric? Although at first, it may sound awkwardly bold, given the political and social circumstance, but we, the *Caucasian American People* and our society are now under "Alien Siege! We have no other choice but the following.

First: we must ask and insist upon from all those who now represent us, and from all those who wish in the future to represent us, to *Declare Themselves*?

What does this actually mean? When a politician asks for your support, always remember, you are a "Caucasian American" and part of a community with *Social* and *Political* interests that are submerged in Caucasian American culture and history. It is what we are!, and who we are!, and it's referred to in Caucasianism as our- *Ancestral Trust*!

Second: Just as *Nations* are separate social entities and negotiate with each other on behalf of their own self interest, the very same thing applies to *Different Races* as well. We, the Caucasian Americans as a race of people must negotiate with other races on behalf of our own- *Vital Racial Interest.* (on this, there can be no compromise!)

So, when a politician asks for your support, you must ask them to *Declare Themselves?*...and this is what they must declare: "I am a *Caucasian American* and loyal to my *Ancestral Trust*." I will continue to advance and support all Caucasian American interest, locally, nationally, and internationally.

And if that personal declaration is not openly stated, you must, as a conscientious "Caucasian American" withdraw your support.

Third: Be not afraid!...Declare yourself!– Declare your-self!...a "Caucasian Racial Fundamentalist" who's *Religious* and *Political* base is an interpretation strictly in compliance with Caucasian racial doctrine, and our historical- *Dynasty's Life Principles.*

We Can Get To Were We Want!
By
Being Who We Are!

"The Caucasians"
-This Is Our Political Mission-

The Journey Into Self

(the Alpha's intrinsic accord)

The truths and realities of biological origins, let alone our own human origin, have always seemed obscured by some lack of focus or scientific procedure or professional confusion. Not wanting to cast a dark shadow on the veiled evidence that our distinguished and most illustrious scientific community has laid before us on the matter of human origin? But, to think that because you have unearthed some old primate bones doesn't give you the bragging right, nor does it indicate discovering the holy grail of our existence.

This is an arrogant scientific leap of faith, if you find evidence of humans in North Africa, Southern Europe, or Central America, regardless of their age! It says but one thing and one thing only, and that is that humans or the likeness of humans were there. It speaks to existence; it says nothing of origin!

Truth and reality are things that the perceiver brings with him or her to an event; in other words, it is an individual experience. The human brain is constantly adding more pieces to the puzzle of one's existence. And why not? No one has ever come close to completing this puzzle, and it seems to me that no one ever will. However, there are absolute truths, and what I mean is that some truths don't yield, no matter how you fit them into your puzzle of experience; they will always remain the same.

First let me say this: There are absolute truths, and second, these truths can be understood by human thought. For example, I base much of my own personal truth on the philosophy of absolute difference. I grapple with difference.

Why does it exist? What brought it about? What is its root? In this grappling, I have gained a deeper self-existence, which is always the case when one grapples with absolute truth. By examining difference, I have been lead to the boundaries (and beyond) of my own reality and forced to behold the true maze of life,...Culture!

Like a vast directory, it put me on the path to where *Moses* got the Ten Commandments, *Einstein* learned the theory of relativity, *Aristotle* conjured up his thoughts, *Shakespeare* drafted his plays. *Mozart* composed here, *Dante* wrote, and *Galileo* searched for the stars!

This Sanctuary "Culture" encompasses the outermost reaches of the mental capacity of humankind. And like the others before me, I recognize that I have come to a mighty place, a place of awe, a place on the precipice of eternity, here, one must find one's own map, to mark one's own way.

- Culture -

(survival of the unified)

In the realm of all living beings lies the dominion of culture. It carries within it the very essence of biological direction, the very blueprint of all human social structure.

Culture, though a simple term, is by far one of the most misunderstood and misrepresented of all human creations.

To truly understand culture you must first and foremost understand that culture is a mental submergence in its purist form, and that submergence is survival of kind.

This is its root, as is the root of all living things!

Culture, simply stated, is organized mental direction (choice), or for a better term, discrimination.

This being true, therefore it must serve two forms of existence, the first being biological organized direction (race) and the second being social organized direction (political); hence, if race and politics are the parents of culture, then it stands that culture is the vehicle by which we enter and determine our future.

It is the business of *Racial* and *Political Survival*, the true social compass.

Culture, does it have an overall plane or destination?

It is my belief that all cultures have but one plane, one destination, the unification of *Race* and *Politics* into a single force,..*Empire!* (the union of conquest)

Cultural Literacy
(the civil religion)

In the Caucasian Empire, the *Alpha* has determined that a nonsectarian "Civil Religion" must be put in place to secure a good and harmonious-*Democratic State.* Since the Caucasian people are to govern themselves in the democratic state, they must govern on high, broadly moral principle for the larger public good as well as for their own private good.

This civil religion will honor the values of *Tolerance, Freedom, Patriotism, Duty,* and *Cooperation*: it has symbols and rites like the *Flag, Public Oaths*, and the *Holidays.*

Its book of *Genesis,* a knowledge of which is at the heart of their cultural literacy would of course be the Valorous, which is also the simplest, clearest, most comprehensive yet briefest telling of the *Caucasian Idea*, and along with their *Democratic Declaration* (the democratic state) that is understood to be amendable because it serves a principle more ultimate than itself - that of the sovereignty of the Caucasian people. And in turn, is based on fundamental principles of *Justice* and *Freedom*, thereby, permitting progress and change, lending coherence to the larger Caucasian public culture and is the basic source of Caucasian American values.

- Language -

The *Alpha* is not, of course, directly concerned with the question of *Bilingualism*. But he knows that well-meaning bilingualism could unwittingly erect some serious barrier to Caucasian cultural literacy among our young people and therefore create serious barriers to Caucasian universal literacy at a mature level.

In Caucasian America the reality is that we have not yet properly achieved *Monoliteracy*, much less *Multiliteracy*.

Because of the modern demands created by technology we need effective *Monoliteracy* more than ever. Linguistic pluralism would make sense for us only on the questionable assumption that our civil peace and national effectiveness could survive *Multilingualism*. But in fact, *Multilingualism* enormously increases cultural fragmentation, civil antagonism, illiteracy, and economic technological ineffectualness.

Because of modern economic needs, the goals of language standardization and universal literacy become even more urgent. Hence, cultural literacy is the central requirement of all industrial societies.

The employability, dignity, security, and self-respect of individuals, typically, and for the majority of man and woman now hinges on their education.

A man or woman's education is by far their most precious investment, and in effect confers their identity on them.

Literacy: Its chief reason is broader; the complex understanding of modern life depends on the cooperation of many people with different specialties in different places.

Where communications fail, so do the undertakings.

Our chief instrument of communication over time and space is our standard national language- *English*, which is sustained by national literacy. All human communication is dependent upon the essence of Cultural literacy and lan- guage. This is truth, this is reality!

The Alpha's view: Place in your mind, through the principle of Biological Suggestion, the positive, constructive thoughts that harmonize with your definite purpose in life, and that mind will transform those thoughts into

physical reality and hand them back to you as finished Cultural products.
(how different is the culture of self-control!)

Unified Cultural Empire

"Opposition and Conquest"

The truths and realities of life are often bitter fruit, especially to the Caucasian utopian liberal zealots who spend most of their time in a state of perpetual guilt, apologizing to any and all minority races for the success and accomplishments of their own!

They are an intellectually arrogant lot, who, if left to their own social delusions, would surrender the very spirit of the Caucasian people to the sacrificial altar of liberal social fallacy, to calm and appease the hyenic behavior of the savage minority.

As the *Alpha* has stated before; *All That Is, Stands Opposed to- All That Would Be!*

Life demands adherence to its truths, and that *Predatory Cultural Assault*, the "Conquest" is one of them, and it is this form of predatory social compulsion (to Conquer!) that runs very deep in the character of all human societies.

The *Alpha's* sympathies go out to any society that in its ignorance (Caucasian South Africa!) fails to understand the *Terrible Truth* and *Reality* of *Predatory Cultural Assault* by an invasive species or subspecies.

Think of this: there are two types of *Cultural Assault*, the first one: is when an opposing culture comes at you by means of straight out warfare!

But the Second one: is much more sinister: *Parasitic*!

First, it gets inside your culture, (mistakenly brought in!...judicially put in!...or invited in!) and forgoing a debate on the ignorance that let it in?

Once inside, it begins to grow, invading the major organs of the culture, like the *School System* and the *Municipalities*, breaking them down, changing their vital structure, altering their direction, sapping their very life, leaving a wasteland of shattered dreams, broken wills, and wasted efforts. (Detroit?) And in the end, it will keep getting bigger, and so will its appetite!

Two choices: You will either get the courage to cut it out?..or you will become just another *People* and *Culture,* plundered and laid to waste by- *Alien Parasitic Conquest.*

Culture is the unity of physical and mental struggle for social direction; it's a society's directional idea; it is the very vehicle by which the future of their kind is possible.

This is put in place by a unified body of contributors who are themselves tributaries of their *Ancestral Racial Trust*, and like those before them, they are also willing to sacrifice themselves on its behalf.

It is the 𝔄*lpha's* belief; that it is not possible for an individual, let alone a society, to go down two politically different roads at the same time! And so it is with culture!

Culture is the fulcrum of all societies, from the most *Primitive* to the most *Advanced*, it encompasses all that we have been, all that we are, and all that we hope to be!

The *Caucasian Cultures* were built by the hands and hearts of a thousand generations and a million social debates. Like no other racial cultures, the Caucasian cultures have evolved into a beacon of light, and it was this light, and this light alone, that pushed back the moral and intellectual darkness for all humankind.(Liberty - Democracy!)

Now, for some personal insight, after years of personal struggle with the ups and downs of his own identity, the- 𝔄*lpha* had reached a measure of his own mental pursuits, "ℭulture" and it was a very humbling experience. The more he studied his culture, the more he realized that a life force millions of years old was confronting him, assaulting his senses, demanding his attention.

How could I have been so blind?...he asked himself over and over, how could I have placed so much faith in misguided social appetites?

However, the task of understanding his culture was before him, and it was there, he had to turn his attention. He learned of a race of people, (his own!) their culture and their passionate desire for life to succeed.

Yes, he had found himself,…he wept tears of joy, of relief, of humility! And he said: This is for sure, I will never complete my own puzzle! I have added a few more pieces, and I see the world a little more clearly, and the difference between my school of thought and that of others, is that mine is based on the truth of - *Race*, (human subspecies) and all that it encompasses. To know my truth, you will have to travel down the historic corridors of the *Caucasian Race*, (my people!) but to understand their journey, is not for the faint of heart!

However, culture is the key to the maze of life, and the journey through this culture is one filled with endless *Detours, Dead Ends*, and *Social Scarecrows*.

For one to go down this road, is to know the fallacies and truths of life, the whole of life. These fallacies and truths will exact a powerful toll on your mental well-being, for throughout the long history of *Religion, Intellectualism,* and the *Arts,* lies a vast wilderness littered with the broken spirits of all those who chose these paths.

There is an inscription, I would like to put over the doorway to culture.

It is a message that everyone would do well to consider; ***"The secret of life's complexities lies in its simplicities."*** Although this message strikes one at first glance as being a trivial riddle, it is so much deeper!

We all complicate the simple things and forget to simplify the complicated ones, but that is, after all, part of culture's mystique. We Caucasians must realize that still waters run deep, and that the truly complex can be addressed in the most simple and straightforward terms.

When it has all been said and done, when the last vestiges of a liberal social fallacy (racial equality?) has crumbled of its own structural and intellectual absurdity, then and then only will the "Caucasian American Dream" come into its own. Furthermore, let me say to all Caucasians, a "Culture" is what defines and gives a race of people merit.

-𝕴𝖙 𝕴𝖘 𝕺𝖚𝖗 𝕾𝖔𝖈𝖎𝖆𝖑 𝕭𝖆𝖓𝖓𝖊𝖗, 𝕺𝖚𝖗 𝕸𝖔𝖘𝖙 𝕻𝖗𝖊𝖈𝖎𝖔𝖚𝖘 𝕴𝖉𝖊𝖆!-

The Sins Of The Father

(quondam intellectual default)

History! It is a two-sided coin. On the one side, because of our actions, it brings us *Pride* and *Joy,* and on the other, because of our actions, it brings us *Tears* and *Remorse.*

There is no *Nation*, no *Society*, or *Race* of people that can exclude itself from this human phenomenon.

As the Alpha, I must tell you that the good and bad we humans have done to each other, and are now still doing to each other, like it or not are the *Biological Dictates* of the *Evolutionary Process*, and it is not limited by any means to just humans. This *Aggression* and *Carnage* in its various forms, such as *War, Hunger, Slaughter,* and *Slavery,* just to mention a few, seems to be a prerequisite for all *Sociological* and *Biological* change, and if that is so, are we of the future libel for the sins of our *Forefather's* history?

Reparations to others for bygone deeds?

Are there a *People* or a *Nation* whose historical hands are so clean that they can make such a claim against another *People* or *Nation?* This could never be from an intellectual or historical point of view, a valid claim!

Like it or not, predatory deeds, such as *Slavery* and *Slaughter* was and still is the nature of life throughout our world, and yes!...their primitive afflictions can be found in the "History" of every living person today! (no exceptions!)

Therefore, there is no group of people who have the exclusive on "Victimization," whether its *Slavery, Slaughter*, or *Starvation.* All predatory instincts and their extreme deeds, have been a part of the human, as well as all of biological life's experience for millions of years. But alas, all those who would make clams from the future!..for the deeds of the past?..are attempting to mislead by false impression and are the true purveyors of a-*Ruse!*

"This Is Truth, This Is Reality"

Sovereign Directive

(alien encounter!)

When in the course of Caucasian exploration an alien people and their culture are encountered, the following procedure (sovereign directive) must be observed:

Protocol - 1 - All defensive shields must be raised.

Protocol - 2 - Make contact with alien culture.

Protocol - 3 - Determine alien cultural demeanor (friendly or hostile).

Protocol - 4 - Analyze diplomatic contact.

Protocol - 5 - Do not interfere with alien social or political order.

Protocol - 6 - When alien analysis has been completed, the principal will submit all information to the empire for further determination.

Protocol - 7 - Do not lower shields until further determination has been received from the empire.

The
Caucasian Mandate

(a biological mandate)

The Alpha tells us: It is the twenty first century and the Caucasian world community is beginning to lose its biological mandate? Alas, for more than forty thousand years, the Caucasian people and their future has always been contrived by the capability that the Caucasians might not live there after as a people being ransomed for a price, and the matter is noteworthy, not only with reference to today's modern occasion, the Caucasian worlds "Liberal Zealot Dementia" but also as it bears on the methods generally followed by these modern day Caucasian states, (Caucasian suppression!) for we almost never find Caucasians seeking freedom or purchasing peace with money to alien races, but always confiding in their own warlike valor: which could be said of other racial states, as their competitive ambitions unfold.

The
Caucasian Male Canon
(reason- action- conquest)

The Caucasian male principle: *Caucasian Survival* is the inalienable right and eternal will of their Fematrix Caucasia.

Hence, ordinary morality agrees that the world owes no one a living, and there is no reason to assume alien criteria for personal goodness to coincide with our Caucasian *Kantian Values*. Furthermore, our "Homo Sapiens" diversity, (racially different life strategies!) their dimensions of value and operational sense are factual issues, empirically decidable. In other words, we Caucasians have one advantage no one else has: and that is do to our "World Conquest Experience" which is "Unequaled" and unique to us alone. (our racial character!)

Caucasian Reason

(40.000 years thereof)

The ultimate truth: *Life* (competitive predation) is the empirical reality for all living things biological.(there being no other) By the light of Caucasianism, and its moral racial principle, let it be understood that, Caucasian mothers believe their first obligation is to marry their own kind, (Caucasian male) and second, to care for their children through their own effort and those of their husband.

Furthermore, Caucasian fathers believe their first obligation is to marry their own kind, (Caucasian female) and second, the survival of their family (wife and children) through the cultural values, religious morality and the defense (preservation) of the Caucasian community.

Caucasian male racial patriotism: loyalty to his Caucasian biological origins, (racial identity) and his fematrix- *Life Strategy* of more than 40.000 years is the racial, cultural and moral political mandate of the Caucasian male-for his existence, continuation, and salvation,...this is his divine reason, and if so, can we as Caucasians say that the divine reason of *Racial Kind* is not the ultimate exemplary cause, but also the ultimate productive cause of the Caucasian male and his success?

The Fematrix and the racial-soul (biological life strategy) represents together the divine reason immanent in the world, and mankind her supreme instrument is expressed by his need (through her) to exhibit intelligence and design (principle of order) in his achievements. This truth is expressed in the Valorous by saying that the sensible Character of man's place in his race (subspecies!) is dependent on his *Fematrix* (bio-sentient female will!) and her life strategy, which is inherited (bio-imbedded) in him to serve her Survival, and therefore the survival of her race (her chosen form) and its direction. Hence, the Caucasian man is the great *Paladin* of his race, and therefore, by his *Loyalty* to his racial *Fematrix* (Caucasia) and her sovereignty, will ultimately determine the future of our children, and thereby the survival of the Caucasian race,...this is our truth, this is our reality.

Caucasian Action

(strategy-behavior-engagement)

The ultimate action: *Survival* of one's *Self*, one's *Family*, one's *Kind*, all determined by the principle of *Intelligent Action,* it success or failure.

Hence, living beings embody the principle of order, they are for example, instances of the logical *Biological Universal* and tend towards the realization of their form: they are the embroidery of intelligent need, and exhibit their own strategic design. (physical being!)

This truth is expressed in the HolyValorous by saying that the sensible characteristics of all biological life are dependent on their *Fematrix* and her strategic counter (opposition) to the forces of *Bio-Predation* and the *Elements*, both of which compel a living thing to *Action* if it is to survive

The Alpha has been disappointed by the political conduct of the Caucasian world community in general, and epically by his disappointment in Caucasian America, but he is not actively hostile to this failing Caucasian world; on the contrary, he desires to train statesmen of the true type, who would as it were, carry on the work (action) of Caucasianism in bringing *Racial Order* into *Racial Disorder*.

He is hostile to the Caucasian political actions only in so far as they are *Racially Disordered* and *Fragmented*, out of harmony with or not expressing what he believes to be stable

Racial Realities and *Stable Norms* of Caucasian racial values and its universal significance. If a Caucasian man or woman is going to talk at all, he or she is certain to make value judgments, judgments which presuppose objective norms and standards, values which can be apprehended with varying degrees of insight, values which do not actualize themselves but depend for their actualization on human life.

The Alpha's point is not so much what actions contributed to the political formation of- *Racial Nihilism* through out the Caucasian world, whether as *Causes*, *Conditions* or *Occasions*, as to the question: does the *Alpha* prove his position or does he not?

And with this question all of humanity must come to terms. Furthermore, the Caucasian world community cannot afford to dismiss the notion that what there is of racial order and its intelligibility in this world has an objective foundation in *Action*. All human happiness or misery takes the form of action; the end for which we live is a certain kind of activity, not a theory.

The Alpha not only attained a considerable measure of truth in his *Racial Metaphysics*, but also goes a long way towards showing that it is the truth!

Caucasian Conquest

(a bio-principle objective)

The Conquest: Is the biological act of sustaining the *Becoming*. (Evolution) all participate, but not all succeed!

The entelechy in life, the *Fematrix* (intelligible principle) expresses herself in organic function, unfolds herself in matter, organizes, molds and shapes matter, tends toward an end, which is the adequate manifestation of her essence, of her *Idea* in all life forms. (Immortality) All life is conceived as a hierarchy of species, each of which the essence tends toward its full actualization in a series of bio-forms, (life Strategies) by the pursuit of *Conquest* and its sensible objective *Survival* through selective *Predatory Acquisition*.

This formal principle realizes itself in the activity of all living organisms.

Hence, the *Conquest* is thus a dynamical process of species *Self-Perfection* and *Development*, and this supreme actuality has meaning and value, for none can escape their participation, it is immanent, and operating in our world.

Survival Reasoning

(a biological vested interest)

Biological life: Is that which promotes personal and group advantage, and is an established and forever binding right that cannot be eliminated, (a world submerged in a survival free for all) due to its intrinsic *"Predatory"* character.

This is an elemental truth, in the Caucasian world's inescapable reality. And if life's character is *"Predatory"* than that would explain the circling of the bio-wagons into defensive distinctive groups (biological strongholds) *Species* and *Subspecies* with different life encounters, hence, different life strategies, with both physical difference and difference in cognitive imprint. (mental demeanor!)

Altruism
(liberality)

Concern for others: (generosity, kindness, tolerance) the social doctrine that the general welfare of society is the proper goal of an individual's actions. But, let us not forget its extreme, by adding to this a little *Passivity, Submissiveness,* and *Acquiescence,* and you have consent without protest. (liberal zealotry) Or, as nature likes to call it: a *Predatory Opportunity-* easy pickings, a society lost in the wilderness of its own intellectual fallacy.

The renunciation of one's own social interest for the benefit of *Alien Others-* is a social philosophy that biological life will not entertain, for in biology, *Unselfishness* (unguarded self-interest) brings misery and death to all!

Racial Society
(a kindred life strategy)

The Biological Essence: The indispensable conceptual characteristics of cognizance into *Form* (totemic-unite) by its survival strategy. Hence, the

Racial Society descended from a common *Female* emergence. (fematrix absolutism)

The Alpha's contribution and emphasis on the development of the *Caucasian Race* as a uniquely individual subspecies under his understanding that *Homo Sapient* subspecies referred to as *Races -Negroid, Mongoloid, Caucasoid* have an inborn instinctive tendency to follow their own proper development.

Furthermore, from this perspective of biological history, his conception of natural racial growth (bio-vested interest!) a society of related individuals or kindred communities that are imprinted with a *life Strategy,* and have the mark (physical appearance) of their *Fematrix* (living female will) has been for him, the most decisive influence on human social theory.

The Alpha's view: the word "Racialness" has reference to all people who try to enlighten others by logical argument or appeal to self-interest. We are all "Preconceived" through a biological life strategy of our own making. And yet!..have you observed how few there are who understand this? The ability to enlighten others without friction and argument is the art of Tactful-Patience, when presenting its Truths and Evidence .(all predicated on the reality of racial identity!)

"God"
(The Unbeknownst!)

The Alpha tells us: One cannot produce a "Physical Harvest" without first producing an "Intellectual Harvest."

And in the realm of humankinds nature, has resin an intellectual spirituality called "Religion" and its harvester, go's by the name of - God! (the Unbeknownst!)

Do Gods Exist?

"Absolutely"
-Gods Are Operas Of The Mind, And Not Of The Flesh-

Intellectual Spirituality: It is said by the Alpha, (without malice or aversion) in his reference to humankinds quest for their *Gods,* and that which their *Gods* demand of them?

That!...he does put all "Human Gods" to the discretion of the one "Unforgiving God" (Reality!) who cares not for humankinds trappings of their Gods mystical beliefs, nor the coming of their *Wrath* or *Judgement,* that is, if they ever find the time to bless us with their presence? (how long on our knees, must we wait?) After all, it has been for all of them, some two thousand years or more!...but, like it or not!...the Alpha thinks that their *Credibility,* along with their *Believability,* is to say the least, running out!...this being the historical handed down fate of all mystical (Omnipotent, not understood!) gods of legion! Alas, it is time to-*Upgrade* their ancient hold on use!...to "Caucasianism" (Reality!) if we are to survive the coming inevitable plague of "Liberal Zealot Progressivism" you know! "Socialism" the subspecies of "Communism" and its septic degenerate lamprey-Caligulaism. (unfettered sexual degeneracy!)

The Alpha tells us: It is the *21st* century, and for all those Caucasians who are in great denial and refuse to believe that the "Caucasians World Community" is now on the road to its "Annihilation" must now, if there is just an ounce of "Love and Compassion" for the future of our children, by forgoing the mystical path and thereby engaging the *God* that gives us reason!- For it is only this *God,* "Reality" that can save us all from the *Antiquated* and *Caligulaized* "Governments" of the *21st* century and their lying and fraudulent *Political* and *Media Cabals.* And alas, let us not forget the rising tide of alien collective ambition!...and violent aggression! (war like?) We must be more vigilant! By the very nature of the subject of "Race" it can never be finished, for it leads into the heart of all human activities. Its purpose is to cause you to take the fundamentals on which it is based and use them as a stimulus that will cause your mind to unfold, thereby releasing the latent forces of "Identity" that are yours. This inquiry by the Alpha was not written for the purpose of teaching you, but it is intended as a means of causing you to teach yourself one of the great truths of your being!...You are a "Caucasian" and in all of known life, there is no *Equal!*

And when you deliver the best "Loyalty" of which you are capable, to your "Caucasian Racial Dynasty" you are making use of the highest form of your "Definite Purpose" (your biological mandate!)

It is only through the delivery of such service that your -Truth Of Identity- can be attained. The weakness of our "Racial Attitude" becomes the weakness of our "Racial Character." We Caucasians are the product of our thoughts. *What we think, we become!*...nothing was ever created by our "Caucasian Racial Dynasty" that was not first created in our imagination through our desire and then transformed into reality.

Do not underestimate the "Power" of the *Caucasian Racial Will,* because it did not come to you clothed in mysticism or because it is described in language that all who will may understand. The truth of "Caucasian Greatness" is simple in final analysis and easily understood.

Use your "Caucasian Racial Understanding" with intelligence, and only for the attainment of worthy ends, and it will bring you enduring happiness and success. Make your "Caucasian Racial Excellence" not an act, but a habit!...thereby freeing yourself from- *Self Identity Trepidation.*

Alien Rivals

(persona non-grata)

It is the 21st century, and all of Caucasian America as well as her sister states throughout the world are living in the midst of an *"Alien Invasion"* of both the physical and mental.

Furthermore, Caucasian religious houses, politicians, journalists and educators (academia) are all promoting a view of the world that is as damaging to us, as would be an ideology imposed by a conquering power.

Of course, only a minority of Caucasians recognize we are under *Alien Siege* and many Caucasians are unwitting collaborators in a liberal system that will prove *Fatal* to our Caucasian civilization. But what of those Caucasians who recognize the dimensions of the crisis and have the choice of acquiescence or resistance?

When the opposition (liberal zealotry) is in control, the rewards of collaboration attract the *Cowards*, *Conformists*, and the *Racially Unprincipled*.

And those Caucasians who are loyal to the memory of older and better Caucasian ways must be ready to sacrifice!

But, which sacrifices are meaningful, and what should be the price for *Alien Collaboration*? (Caucasian treason!) It is these questions that the Caucasian American people and the greater Caucasian world community must reckon with?

In the case of "Caucasian America," we are struggling with an outright "Alien Invasion" being sponsored by a cabal of - *Liberal Zealotry,* a form of *Regurgitated Communism* with a progressive agenda of *"Racial Nihilism"* against the Caucasian American community. And by getting all their support through the leisure class, who have accommodated themselves psychologically to a alien occupation. (sanctuary cities!) Further more: "Our Caucasian American National Character*"* is being challenged in a lightening campaign in which our society's *Dedicated Statues* and *Places of Honor* are being destroyed, creating an- *Alien Hyenic Province?*

But how are the average Caucasian Americans feeling today about their *Occupation* and coming *Social Demise*?

They take it badly, said the 𝔸lpha, *Badly* in more ways than one. They feel helpless and they are *bitter-bitter* in a useless kind of way that produces no great resolutions?

How did it all happen? Caucasian America is being beaten down because *Wealth* and *Luxury* has made them *Soft*, *Indifferent* and *Dismissive,* all this leading to the lose of their racial-bred suspicion: for the old insular belief, equally grounded on insular lack of knowledge, that most *Racial Aliens* were *Amiable*, good people?...who only needed to be talked to and patted on the back to become your *Friends* and *Benefactors*. (this of course is absurd!)

Hence, the 𝔸*lpha tells us:* we, the Caucasian people of the world are not prepared to accept *Alien Aggression* on our knees: we know our racial neighbors and are under no illusions about them. (Negroids and Mongoloids) We know what to think of them, we as Caucasians know what we want in this world, and we know what they (aliens) want: that knowledge does not sand us flying at each other's throats, but it does, and should keep us from growing soft!

The *Alienquest* (alien frontline strategy!) can be sumed up as thus: *Promote* and *Advance* the liberal ruse of *Racial Equality* (equal racial outcomes!) through the liberal corridors in *State* and *Federal* agencies, and by *Accusing* and *Branding* all Caucasian American opposition as *Racism* and *Hatred*.

Furthermore, the alien and liberal zealots recognize that the older Caucasian generations will never be won over, (to forsake their race!) and therefore, if they are to subjugate Caucasian America, it will be necessary to cultivate (indoctrinate) their young!...today's Caucasian youth, the generation that is at the threshold now!...it is this Caucasian youth that the *Alien Races* and their *Liberal Racial Nihilists* must capture and turn! (through shame and guilt!)

They will teach them to believe in *Social Fallacy,* by using the ruse of *Racial Equality*? And coerce them into betraying their *Caucasian Ancestral Trust,* by demonizing their own history, and thereby creating a pathway by which *Alien Parasitic Races* can infiltrate and subvert the good will and charity of the *Caucasian American community*, and the truth of this *Liberal Pathology* and the fate of Caucasian societies that are infected can be observed in the modern Caucasian state of- *South Africa.* (parasitic alien invasion,...*Death!*)

Indeed, as we Caucasians Americans know, if a generation is gotten hold of early enough, by any *Social Radicals* with a will to teach them to question their racial history and coax them into accepting an *Alien Other*, a great people can be made *Submissive* in just a few decades.

Hence, the Alpha tells us: clearly, there are no answers here to the question of whether so many Caucasian Americans have come under the spell of an alien *Moral Deception,* (the ruse of racial equality!) that liberation is impossible?

However, once enough Caucasian people are prepared to collaborate with the unthinkable, (their social capitulation) then the act (surrender) becomes routine!

There will be no *Assimilation* by *Alien Races* into the Caucasian American Culture, for like all predatory groups, they don't want to conform, or be absorbed,...they are not Caucasians!...they just want to *Feed* and *Take*!

They are here because of our *Weakness*, our *Stupidity*, they see the gains of alien others through- *Hostel Occupation*, *Legal Manipulation*, *Hatred*, and *Racial Malice*. In other words, a continuation of the present social process of- *Alien Racial Militancy* with the usual renegade Caucasians and alien suspects: *Equality Hustlers - Racial Nihilists - Liberal zealots - Elite Academics,* and let us not forget the politi-cal highwaymen- *Federal & State Legislatures-* all of which have played their sinister part in the assault against the "Caucasian American Community." Yes! all turning their backs to the - *Alien Invasion!* Alas, disregarding Caucasian Americas future demise, its lose of "Sovereignty" in its own state! Yes, "Alien Tribalism" will impose its desire...and the Caucasians will once again "Rise" to defend their- *Dynasty!*

Alien Discourse

- Alien-
(any and all who are not Caucasian!)

The Alpha tells us: the word "Alien" mines not of us! (Caucasians) It is not a derogatory term, though negative in origin, and that is do to the fact of it being a *Species* or *Subspecies* (races) with different cultures, religions, languages and their potential nature, which history has put before us, in the form of *Competitive Predation*? Hence, the following three alien subjects, for the benefit of the Caucasian world community!

- Alien Migration -

The Alien Migrant Worker: It has always been the way of human nature, as well as all of nature to sustain it self by migrating to places that afford it the ability to feed and protect their families.

But, in today's world there is no more unclaimed wilderness, all *Lands* and *Sea's* have been claimed and chartered by the Nations of the world.

Thereby, making those people who live in these lands locked in as either natives or citizens. So, all migration is now from one country to another, and for one to do this, they must apply for documents from both countries.

A set of documents for leaving a country, and a set of documents for entering a country. (a passport or if looking to work, a work visa!) It is now a world of Nations!...with no freedom to be had.

- Alien Refuge -

The Alien Refuge: *War, Poverty, Persecution*! Hence, this dilemma: Not all nations and governments are capable of *Feeding* or *Protecting* their citizens, (poverty and dictatorships) and in some, nor do they care! And this social dilemma has infected more then 50% of the Nations around the world, leaving millions of people in a state of *Despair* and *Flight*. And this flight with its third world cultural pathology is lining up at the gates of *Caucasian America*, and her sister states throughout the world.

- Alien Invaders -

The Alien Invader: Any and all who enter a Nation through *Subversive* or *Culvert* action, (unlawful-undetected entry!) Is a *Criminal Invader*, and an enemy of the state, (they are not refuge's or immigrants!) and must be immediately apprehended. Furthermore, any and all those who assist or harbor an *Alien Invader* will be considered a *Co-Conspirator*, and subject to lose of *Citizenship* and /or *State Excommuni- cation*

𝔗he
ℭaucasian 𝔏egion

(brotherhood- honor- sacrifice- conquest)

𝔗he Caucasian Brotherhood: Of all the contributors to the human struggle and of all the sacrifices made on its behalf - None, not even the gods of legend, could have attained the glorious heights of the- *Caucasian Brotherhood.*

They above all, have fare exceeded their biological mandate. They above all, by the will of their *Fematrix* and for more than 40 thousand years, have brought - Honor, Sacrifice, and Conquest to the human species. This is our truth, this is our reality.

𝔅rotherhood
(the Caucasian male covenant)

𝔗he ℭreed: We are the sons of the Caucasians, and none shall break faith!

Let all who take part of this document: Come to understand that we the *Caucasian Brotherhood* sound of body, mind and faith, do solemnly pledge our *Will* and *Obedience* to our *Caucasian Fematrix,* her *Heritage*, and her *Posterity*, making our union with our brothers, a great wall of Caucasian *Faith* and *Strength* that our enemies will break themselves upon, bringing their *Conspiracies* and *Ambitions* to an end.

This we do pledge, before our posterity and our god!

𝔥onor
(loyalty and integrity)

𝔏et all who take part of this document: Come to understand that we the *Caucasian Brotherhood* sound of body, mind and faith, do solemnly pledge our Honor, Loyalty and Integrity to our *Caucasian Fematrix,* her *Heritage,* and her *Posterity*, never faltering in our obligation or sense of propriety. And, always promoting Caucasian *Self-respect*, *Morality*, and *Duty*. Hence, upholding the code of Caucasian social homage.

This we do pledge before our posterity and our god!

Sacrifice
(contribution and forbearance)

Let all who take part of this document: Come to under Stand that we the *Caucasian Brotherhood* sound of body, mind and faith, do solemnly pledge our *Sacrifice, Contribution* and *Forbearance* to our Caucasian *Fematrix,* her *Heritage*, and her *Posterity*, never faltering in our obligation to stand fast, and defend Caucasian freedom and its *Fematrix* given right of survival. And may all Caucasian males both young and old take part in the *Caucasian Legion* protecting the social will of a free sovereign Caucasian state.

"This we do pledge, before our posterity and our god"

Conquest
(victory- achievement-colonization)

Let all who take part of this document: Come to understand that we the *Caucasian Brotherhood* sound of body, mind and faith, do solemnly pledge to be *Victorious* against all the *Enemies* of the *Caucasian Empire,* and through our *Victories* and *Achievements* we as a race of people will be better suited and positioned when we seek the *Colonization* of the Earth's Oceans and the not too distant planets of our Solar System.

Hence, in the spirit of truth, it was our *Victories* against our *Enemies,* and our *Achievements* in the *Sciences,* and let us not forget the *Social Humanities*?...and the world health programs: **Starvation, Disease, Natural Disasters**. Yes, all being of the Caucasian worlds social initiative, and all deriving from the spirit of the- *Caucasian World Conquest!*

This Is Our Truth, This Is Our Reality.

Victory or Death
(the contest!)

The Creed of life: you are either the Victim or the Victor!

The Alpha tells us: life is the supreme engagement, and in Caucasianism the *Conquest* has great meaning, both in *Life,* and in Caucasian *Spirituality,* because it is the prime enterprise of both *Success* and *Failure* in all living things.

That having been said, let us now pursue what we as Caucasians know to be true: In life, living things (different species or subspecies) are endowed with special qualities- they can fly, run, swim, climb and build, all of which is con- sidered in Caucasianism to be a segment of their given (Fematrix) life strategy.

Furthermore, let it be said, that of all the human subspecies and their quest for life, *None* have embraced the *Conquest* on a nobler course then that of the Caucasians, their itinerary (course of pursuit) has no equal in the modern era, whether in the sciences or social humanities, the Caucasian race and its *Fematrix Mandate* of *Conquest* (its biological commission) has given all humankind its *Social Contract* with a view of *Security, Peace, Value* and *Truth.*

The Caucasian state: the maintenance of the *Caucasian Racial State* is a direct underlying principle in the continuation of the *Caucasian Conquest.*

Therefore, a failure on the part of any Caucasian society to uphold the sovereignty of their *Racial State* is the equivalent of generational betrayal and biological treason. Thus, we Caucasians have to be careful not to allow insistence on the rights of *Alien Races* and the importance of their *Equality Plea* to lead us to minimize or mutilate the racial character of the Caucasian state, which has been rationally formed and organized according to the ideal *Caucasian Pattern* and not left to the fallacious play of irrational alien causes, hence, the *Conquest* having the Caucasian peoples historical welfare as its end, and exhibiting the divine will and spirit of the Caucasians unyielding racial soul.

-This Is Our Truth, This Is Our Reality-
"So Say We All"

The
{- All -}

～～

(realm of the Light and the Dark!)

"There Is No Other"

The Alpha tells us: That in the realm of the- "All" there is the *God* of-*Reality!*...and it is this *God,* that hold sway over the "All." It's character is without judgement, for it is the guardian of "Chance," and the caretaker of "Outcome," it knows neither "Malice" nor "Compassion," it reveals what- "Is" and cares not, for what- "Isn't." Yes!, there are other *Gods?*...but they are gods of "Purpose," of "Wrath," of "Compassion," gods of one's Soul, gods of one's- Hope.

They are the Gods of "Fear," Gods of the "Observers."

The Gods of- *Judaism, Islam, Christianity, Buddhism, Hinduism,* and, less we forget, the thousands of legend?...who have battled, and still to this day!...among themselves for the right of "Supremacy" through the *Physical* and *Mental* hosts of- *Humanity!* Gods, who like their predecessors- being of a "Metaphysical Speculation" will fade into the shall of the earth when their hosts become "Enlightened" (reality!) by not surrendering themselves to the childhood fears of an imaginary- *Absolute God!* (the divine being!...is not a God!)

Meanwhile, the Alpha makes it known that he does not need the "Pardon" of any- *Omnipotent Being!*...for declaring the absolute *Sovereignty* and *Supremacy* of the "Caucasian-Dynasty" and its *Biological Mandate.* (its life strategy!)

Yes, that which is held by the "All" to be the fundamental premise of a life-forms pursuit, the reality of its-*Teleology!* The appalling circumstances of the Caucasian world community in the *21ˢᵗ* century, being both *Political* and *Cultural*, is not going to correct itself by waiting for-*Divine Intervention!* (God is not coming!) And therefore we have but only one solution!...and that is, as it has always been, to- *Fight Back!*...stop retreating, turn and face our- *Enemies!*... invoke the spirit of the "All," create the out-come?...bring the fight to them!

-Blessed Are The Caucasians-
"So Say We All"

Caucasian Racial Autonomy

~

(racial self-determination)

-Racial Liberty-

One must have a need to be strong, otherwise one never will be! We are the Caucasians; we know well enough how remote our place is, hence, our conscience of truth that has remained unheard. We have discovered our happiness; we know the way; we got our knowledge of it from thousands of years in the wilderness. We have our inclinations, born of strength, for questions that no other has the courage for; the courage for the forbidden; predestination for the wilderness.

Our truth belongs to the rarest of Caucasians, perhaps not one of them is yet born. It is possible that they may be among those who understand our *Quest,* our grand manner to hold together our strength, our enthusiasm,...our reverence for race; love of race; absolute freedom of race. Let us look each other in the face, we are the Caucasians, we know what it means to maintain ourselves against all opposition, we understand the will to *Power,* even if in an altogether different manner than our enemies assume.

Caucasianism: (racial enlightenment) sees humankind in the light of their natural and historical ties. It is this racial enlightenment which strengthens the inclination toward concern of a racial self, towards one's psychological racial analysis and biographical examination. Caucasianism is by no means of a religious sentimental character.

It believes in reason, it is *Rational*, and it is *Political* only in that it denies *Liberal Zealotry* (equality fascism) as it opens our eyes to the reality of us, our past, our ancestors, the mythologies and the hero's. It is a new spiritual movement that is still fully alive seeking not Caucasian redemption, but rather that we Caucasians have entered into a new relationship with our past, that our view has been cleared for what was truly forceful in the past but which had been clouded by a liberal zealot ideology.

In a word from the *Alpha*, we Caucasian have discovered new possibilities for understanding the essence of our existence.

The *Alpha* makes this clear: First and above all is the *Caucasian Race*! And that means *Racial Love*, *Racial Security*, and *Racial Prosperity*! The accompanying faith will come by itself- of that you can be certain.

The *Alpha* opposes the liberal zealot proscription of the political sphere, of the sphere of *Racial Equality* altogether, with the thesis that also overcomes the contrast between *Liberal Zealotry* and *Democracy*. (Socialism and Liberty)

One has to train oneself not in the strengthening of the state of *Equality* (a fallacy) but in the state of *Racial Liberty* (a realty) one must come to understand.

In this way we reestablish the purity of the sphere of action, in the political and social realm.

We must call an individual or a group corrupt, when it loses its vital instincts, when it chooses, when it prefers what is injurious to it?

In **Caucasianism** life itself is an instinct for growth, for survival, for accumulation of force, for power: whenever the will to power fails there is disaster.

It is the *Alpha*'s contention that the highest values of the

Caucasian world community has been emptied of this will, that the values of *Social Decadence,* and of *Racial Nihilism* now prevail under their sacred name. If one measures the effects of *"Liberal Zealot Equality"* by the gravity of the reaction it set up, its character as a menace to all human social standing appears in a much clearer light.

Many misguided Caucasians Americans and their sister states through out the world have ventured to call the seduction of *"Racial Equality"* a virtue?...in reality a great Perjury! But, let us always bear in mind that this is from the standpoint of a *liberal zealot philosophy* that champions both *Diversity* and *Equality,* and upon whose shield the denial of their intellectual hypocrisy, (apposing realities- polar opposites!) is inscribed.

Hence, that by means of equality, "Racial Liberty" is denied, and made worthy of denial through the intellectual deception of a "Moral Fallacy" a declaration of Caucasian American subjugation. Equality is the very "Technic" for *Caucasian Racial Abolition*!...this is truth, this is reality.

The thing that sets liberals zealotry apart from social reality is not that they are unable to find *Race,* ether in history, or in nature, or behind nature, but they regard what has been honored as *Race,* to be not a reality, but as socially injurious?

Such liberal reasoning, which does not touch reality at a single point and which goes to pieces the moment racial reality asserts its rights at any point, must be inevitable the deadly enemy of the wisdom of this world.

And they (liberal zealots!) will give the name of *"Good"* to whoever serves to *Debase* and *Cry-down* all matters of Caucasian racial conscience, and noble freedom of mind. Hence, liberal zealotry as an imperative vetoes science in praxis, lying at any price!

The experience of all disciplined and profound minds teaches that humankind has had to fight for every atom of truth, and has had to pay for it with almost everything that their hearts, their love, and their trust clings to.

Greatness of soul!...is needed for this venture: the service of "Racial Truth" is the hardest of all services.

What then, is the meaning of integrity in things- racial?

It means that a racial being must be severe in his or her racial understanding, that they must scorn *Racial Nihilism* and that they make every *Yea* and *Nay* a matter of racial conscience! It is necessary to say just who we Caucasians regard as our antagonists: all *Racial Nihilists* and all who have any *Racial Nihilistic* blood in their veins.

One must have faced this menace at close hand, better still; one must have had experience of it directly and almost succumbed to it, to realize that it is not to be taken lightly.

Upon this- *Liberal Racial Nihilism!*...we Caucasians must make war: for we find the tracts of it everywhere!...and they are *Shifty* and *Dishonorable* in all things.

The pathetic thing that grows out of this condition is called *Liberal Zealotry,* in other words, closing one's eyes upon one's self- once and for all, to avoid suffering the sight of their-*Surrounding Reality.*

They have erected a concept of social morality, *Racial Equality,* upon this false view of all things; they ground good conscience upon faulty vision; they argue that no other sort of *Social Vision* has value anymore, once they have made theirs *Sacrosanct* with the name of- *Equality.*

We unearth this liberal zealot ruse in all directions: it is the most widespread and the most *Subterranean* form of *Falsehood* to be found on earth.

Wherever the influence of liberal zealotry is felt there is a- *Trans valuation-* of values, and the concepts of *True* and *False* are forced to change places: whatever is most *Damaging* to life is there called- *Truth?...* and whatever *Exalts* it, *Intensifies* it, *Approves* it, *Justifies* it and makes it *Triumphant* is there called- *False?*

When *Liberal Zealots* working through the consciences of people, stretch out their hands for power, there is never any doubt as to the fundamental issue: their will to make an end to all *"Caucasian American Identity"* and their communities, and it is this Liberal Zealot will, that exerts that power.

Caucasian Racial Autonomy: When a race of people are on their downward path, when it feels its belief in its own future, its hope of freedom slipping from it, when it begins to see a submission to *Alien Races* as being a first necessity and the virtues of submission to *Alien Races* as a measure of *Self- Preservation,* then it must overhaul its sovereign racial entrust, its state of- *Caucasian Survival!*

A race of people that still believes in themselves hold fast to their own- *Sovereignty!* In them, it does honor to the conditions which enable them to survive, to their virtue they project their joy into their racial self, their feelings of power, into a "Racial Being" to whom its children may offer thanks. Hence, this unassailable truth: Remove from this world all things- Caucasian!..and then give me a measure of what remains?..are we "Caucasians" not the wellspring?

The Enlightenment

(reason and experience)

Racial Perseverance: Or for a relative term, our *Biological Resilience.*
This is the supreme challenge for all Caucasians of the *21st* century.
It now seems that the power of natural law that cannot be other than it is;
Natural Racial Causation, the physical compulsion placed on humankind
by nature (the Fematrix!) giving division (racial-subspecies) to humans and
their separate destinies (over 200 thousand years!) has now been declared
a moral sacrilege by the liberal zealot fraternity. Hence, determined to
remake humankind into their utopian image (equal racial outcomes?) by
the reliance on liberal dogma (their mystical equality) and a tradition of
demonizing the progress of the Caucasian world and its communities,
these harbingers of benevolent liberal despotism (alien paternalism) are the
advanced representatives and an indication of what will follow in the future
if we Caucasian Americans continue to tolerate the existence of this liberal
Canker, this intellectual corruption that is gradually destroying Caucasian
Americas academic intellectual courage. If we should lose "Caucasian
Academia" to liberal villainy?...Caucasian America, will descend into
infamy, a social wickedness so perilous and infamous, that a *Civil War* will
be the least of its engagements.

Many Caucasian people are badgered by *Alien Races* to think of
"Caucasian-Racialism*"* as malice?...and Caucasian social standing as-
White-Entitlement? In fact, what their reacting to is reality's intrusion on
their contrived social fallacy- "Racial Equality? Causing their cloistered
intellect to lose its way in life's preservation ordered reality of an absolute
- *No Equality!*

This universal liberal zealot ruse of - *Human Equality?...* is also very
dangerous for our children, it will stunt their ability to comprehend that
alien others do not feel, think, or live the same way we Caucasians do. It is
dangerous because of its deceptive intent, acting "Destructively" upon our
Caucasian - *Racial Identity?* (our Origin, that life to which we are obliged!)
To help elucidate this reality, let me say this- the liberal zealots of the *21st*

century are about to throw our children morally naked and intellectually defenseless, into a world of "Aliens" who are going to vengefully humiliate them.

Fortunately, our "Caucasian Traditions" survives in our subconscious perennial tradition, our inherited biological mandate, our unique way of being Caucasian *Men* and *Women* in the face of a world influenced greatly by the chaos of alien others. Therefore, as the Alpha, perceiving these historic disruption has been at the very heart of my work "Caucasianism" and its light of "Caucasian Sovereign Identity" it continuity and the resurgence of our civilization having its roots in time immemorial. It is important that all Caucasians see themselves as the *Sons* and *Daughters* of "Caucasia" (our Fematrix!)

The Sacred Race

(the biological endowment)

We are all living being, born into this world of a kind, a breathing, thinking, biological kind which has been ordained with a path, a direction, a life strategy unique unto itself, a bio-singularity comprised of body, mind, and spirit, a preconceived production who's function is to carry the living spirit of its kind into the future, and by the sacred link of its ancestors the divine right of "Caucasian Survival" which transcends all and every contrary.

All civilizations are the direct result of a definitive biological group, with a clearly defined physical identity. (common corporeality)

Hence, the emergence of the physical symbol of a life strategy in kind, (color, form, course) called in Caucasianism the *Becoming*- the drive for biological survival through the union of identifiable kind. (species or subspecies)

Thus, for millenniums, we have been born, structured, and corrected by our own hand, our own will, desiring no other outcome other than that which we have made. And seeing ourselves in the new *Birth* our newly born,..is that which fills and strengthens our racial resolve, our spirit, our soul. Yes, we are the *Proud Caucasians*, and all shall come to know us!

The
Human Requisite

(the essential-essential need)

Humankind, like all life, is driven by a *Mental Draft,* and that draft consists of three elements- *Consumption*, *Production*, and *Direction*, and it is these three essentials that form the universal will to survive in all living things called in Caucasianism the-*Need*!

In other words, life and only life has need! And therefore it is the degree of recognition, understanding, and the fulfillment of that need, which ultimately determines a life's *Success* or *Failure*.

This is our truth, this is our reality.

The
Caucasian Principle

(a living struggle)

The Caucasian Principle: Gives us the stimulus to reflect on ourselves, as a one of a kind racial group of people, (the human subspecies Caucasoid!) and our more than 40 thousand years of struggle that has been formed by the laws of nature and her cosmos, by the hand of our Fematrix *Caucasia* and according to her will. (her life strategy)

The Alpha tells us: the Valorous leads us to the beginning of our universe, for a universe can only exist in the eyes of an observer. To her (the one!) who came into existence through that star (our sun) which the atoms essential to her being were cooked (for billions of years) and brought to fruition, the living molecules by which she would create the becoming of her *Formulated Self*- the Fematrix.(the One!)

From the beginning, her formula was a direction for her survival, through *Form* and *Duration* would come her evolution. In other words, when *Form* and *Duration* reached their limits, she would evolve,(rebirth through self!) shading her past, for her future, and always working towards her new arrival, and her final destination.(her evolution - immortality)

For some, this means succumbing to a not yet understood- ultimate truth,...the *Fematrix!*

The Fematrix: the measure of all things determined. On earth, it is the Caucasians who have made the world self- aware, or self-cognizant.

This Caucasian cognizant's (self-awareness) has become known as Caucasianism. Hence, the existence of the Caucasian race limits the cosmos and nature in their ability to be different from what we actually observe.

So, is the Caucasian race the measure of all things?

Are we Caucasians as a unique race of people the yard-stick by which we should assess all natural phenomena, particularly one in which *Deadly Competition* is possible?

The result is the racial doctrine presented in this book: *Competitive Racialism* (human subspecies) as we know them is only possible in the world we know!

Thus, an answer to the question why the human racial groups we observe today are as old and different as they are, could be?

Because if they were not, humankind would not be here. (Fematrix diversity through Need!)

It is not an exaggeration that human life only exists because the universe and the physical world have certain special characteristics and arrive at the following claim: the universe and the physical world must, taken as a whole, be constructed in a certain special way to be able to produce at least one type of intelligent life form!(biological)

The new approach Caucasianism (fematrix theology) seek to draw scientific benefit from the fact and the characteristics of human existence. The reversal of the usual way of looking at things that involves at least as far as the origin of *life* and *Racialism* is concerned is not without a certain boldness: indeed, if taken to its logical extreme it would bring about a historic turning point in the evaluation of humankinds place in the cosmos.(Caucasian conquest of space) Undeniably, we as Caucasian racial beings are here, observing the universe. Taking this as our starting point, the *Caucasian principle* does place our race in the central position with respect to physics and cosmology, giving us a special role, and since our existence, at least on this planet, we are without question something special. The Caucasian race of people have existed for some 40 thousand years, and for the last five thousand years their *Civilizations* have become the most scientific, and socially advanced of all humankind as well as all living things. Though a humble achievement in bio-cosmic terms, compared with the age of the earth, some five billion years, the Caucasian race never the less, in a world with more than a billion competitive life forms, developed the first *Technological* "Civilization" of the *20th Century* more then one hundred years ago, and as a "Civilization" created on this level (human liberty!) we Caucasians and our world communities, not-withstanding all other life forms, are a very rare and unique phenomenon.

The
Caucasian Survival Initiative

(a sovereign Caucasian dominion)

- Empire -

The majority of the Caucasian people of the world want *Peace,* wherein lies the possibility of its attainment! But, the Caucasian Nations of the world stand today as so many disconnected units of power, and it is not overstating the possibilities to say that, if these units were connected, through allied effort, the combined power of the Caucasian racial alliance could influence the world, and there would be no opposing power on earth that could defeat it!

At first thought, it seems too much to expect that the Caucasian Nations of the world can be induced to pool their power and subordinate their individual interests to those of a Caucasian Civilization (Empire!) as a whole. But this seemingly insurmountable obstacle is, in reality, no obstacle at all because whatever support this plan borrows from the Caucasian Nations it gives back to them a thousand fold, through the increased power the Nations attain. Let us see, just what advantages the Nations will realize by participating in this plan to establish- The *Caucasian Empire* as a world ideal. First of all, it will be clearly seen that no individual *Nation* will lose any of its advantages by allying itself with other Caucasian ethnic and religious denominations in establishing this Caucasian world ideal. This alliance in no way changes or interferes with the *Creed* of any Nation.

Every Nation entering the alliance will come out of it with the power and advantages that it possessed before it went in, along with the additional advantage of greater influence, which the Nations as a whole, will enjoy by reason of having served the leading factor in bestowing on Civilization the greatest single benefit it has enjoyed in the history of the world. (A Caucasian Unified Empire)

By, and through this alliance, the Caucasian world community will have grasped the far reaching significance of the principle of a Caucasian organized world effort, which is by far the greatest potential power in the world today, but its power is merely potential and will remain so until it makes use of the principle of Caucasian organized effort, that is to say, until all Caucasian ethnic and religious denominations formulate a working agreement under which the combined strength of Caucasian nations will be used as a means of bestowing a higher ideal (Caucasianism) upon the minds of the Caucasian young.(inheritors of the future!)

The Caucasian quest for *Empire* is the greatest potential power in the world, and this power grows out of their Caucasian biological mandate(fematrix life strategy) which manifests their peerless sense of-

Reason! Reason rules the world, and the Caucasians race of people rest their civilization solely on their power of - *Reason*! The Caucasian race has the power to harness and direct the reasonable forces of civilization because reasonableness is controlled by analytical logic and racial faith. (biological esteem) And by this, the Caucasian world community has become a great organized body, in which the reasonableness of the world is now centered. It is in no way a discouraging spirit, that this statement is followed by another which may seem more radical.

The task of bringing about this alliance of the Caucasian Nations in support of the Caucasian world ideal- a *Caucasian United Empire* must rest upon the *Female* members of the Caucasian race because the abolition of separate Caucasian nations promises advantages that may be prolonged into the future and that may accrue only to the unborn Caucasian generations.

The 𝔄lpha tells us: In terms that are uncompromising, a truth upon which the hope of our *Caucasian Civilization* rests when he declares that the race is always to her more than the individual, and being the natural enemy of man's ambitions because of this inborn trait of placing the interests of the race above those of the individual, it seems a reasonable prophesy to suggest that Caucasian civilization must pass into a new era, beginning with the future *Survival* of the Caucasian race, in which the Caucasian woman is destined to take into her own hands the raising of *Ethical Racial Standards* in the Caucasian world community.

This will be a hopeful sign because it is the Caucasian woman's nature to implant in the minds of her young, *Racial Ideals* that will accrue to the benefit of Caucasian generations yet unborn. Caucasian Social Heredity (Race-Family-Culture- Empire)

The 𝔄lpha tells us: If the *Caucasian World Community* is to ultimately survive, then its *Social Heredity* (Race- Family- Culture- Empire) must be preserved at all cost as a Caucasian national ideal. But, this of cause must come under the rubric of freedom of choice- for any and all Caucasians, for this is the Caucasian way! As to those Caucasians who do not want to take part in the new -*Caucasian Empire*? We wish them well, and will pray for their return.

Social Heredity: is the sacred guiding principle of the *Caucasian Fold,* as well as all living things, and none can survive or prosper without its

Indoctrination- biologically (physical) and cognitively, (mental) this is our truth, this is our reality!...social heredity is survival indoctrination!

It is in fact, a bio-cultural mandate (social rules) by which all societies and nations participate, and to which is developed institutions and professions for its *Teaching* and *Enforcement* (Religions- Governments- Schools- Universities and the Press) so as to bring the idealism of the whole people to a conception of and to a support of the national policy of their *Racial Social Heredity*.(their biological lagacy!)

If one would study the effects of Caucasian social heredity today, as it is being *Overturned* and *Corrupted* by the liberal zealot ideal of *Human Equality* through equal racial out-comes? The nature of which it requires no master analyst to interpret this *Degenerate* and *Subversive* ideal, that has been fully developed and implanted in our present, with the hope of creating a path of *Infection* into our future generations? All of this!... represent exactly what a *Liberal Zealot Government* want it to represent- the complete and willful destruction of the *Caucasian American Racial Spirit*, and its *Community*, from the inside!...and by its own hand!

The "Alpha's Question"

~

Do we the "Caucasians" (the Conquerors!) being historically and rightfully the greatest and most "Magnanimous" of all - *Biological-Dynasties,* and creators of the *Modern World, are* now going to Abdicate our authority over the Nations we have justly inherited from our ancestral trust?...I think Not!...but, life is about Evolution!..and historically, evolution is a parting of the ways, a reformation, a committed process of departure one from the other, or others. (free from hostile alien input!) Yes, it is time for the "Caucasian Race" to pursue and control its destiny, as they see it, and on their own terms. (Caucasian Empire!)

Caucasians!...What Say You?

Caucasian Exceptionalism
(The Criterion)

The Caucasian archetype (biological pattern) is the same for them, as it is for all living things- the preservation of their *Racial Paragon* (visual racial character) their chosen biological model or pattern of needful perfection, through and by their historical existence.

Caucasian Prime: *Comprehension*- their great capacity to *Understand,* to *Conceptualize, Formulate,* and *Invent,* is an exceptional and unique nature (bio-characteristic) inherited by the Caucasian people, giving them a special historical role in world affairs.

Furthermore, in the light of truth further determined, the world of humankind has received no greater gifts, then those given by the *Caucasian Conquest* (Charity-Freedom- Science- Culture-Education-Religion) all part of our human prosperity, and all brought to a higher social state by a greater Caucasian intellectual and spiritual mindedness.

Superiority
(the biological mandate)

In its truth further determined - *Preponderance*, in the biological arena (competitive predation) is the absolute goal (intention) of all living things, whether human or other, life's aim is to overcome opposition and to entertain and satisfy ambition. Hence, *Superiority* is the elixir that free all from doubt and anxiety, giving the mind comfort and support, helping to quiet its fears, lighten its burden and strengthen its survival resolve. This is truth, this is reality, and there are no living biological exceptions to this truth, all are bound, and must comply. Furthermore, for one to not understand this rudimentary bio-premise (fundamental survival) is a fault, a delinquency unto their death!

Caucasian Racial Delinquency
(ancestral desecration)

As in Caucasianism, *Racialness* is also sacred in biology, for the *Fematrix,* (the One!) the diversity of her daughters and sons, and their loyalty to a biological journey of their choice, in the name of their *Caucasian Fematrix* (Caucasia) is essential to her and our immortality.

So if a Caucasian *Male* or *Female* decides to abandon their-"Biological Heritage" (their racialness!) for whatever reason they have "Betrayed" their *Ancestral Racial Inheritance*, and thereby forfeiting their place in any and all Caucasian societies.

The "Betrayal" of one's race! (biological-treachery) is the *Evilest* of disloyalties and the most *Unforgivable* act of all!

The Alpha view: We as Caucasians!...of the 21ˢᵗ century- most not under any circumstances entertain or pander to the social elusions or intellectual incompetence of either Caucasian "Liberal Zealots" and their bio-fallacy? (racial equality?) or "Alien Races" with bogus accusations of Social Oppression? (white privilege?) For both of these subversive social enigmas are just that!..a direct criminal conspiracy by both to foster the "Derailment" of our Caucasian American society and its destiny!..and therefore, if we Caucasians as a sovereign race of people, fail to recognize these Truths! ...and act accordingly as with all such declared enemies, our future and that of our children will be in great peril!...all brought about by the iniquitous intellectual disease of– Liberal zealot Socialism, and its Lamprey - Caligulaism.

Caucasian Salvation
(racial redemption)

It is the millennium of our fematrix - 42 AC (After Caucasia) and the demon *Invidia* having detected a weakness in the Caucasian world, (egalitarianism) has begun her assault,...leading her menacing hordes (emulous alien races) into Caucasian lands, with no intention to assimilate, but only to accumulate and establish their own alien culture and territory through socially hostel and legal militancy. Hence, this alien invasion and its future demise is the direct result of an intellectual hubris by Caucasian liberal zealots, the disdain of Caucasian elites and their self-importance, and the political state and federal circus that now masquerades as our government.

We the Caucasian Americans, and our sister states throughout the world are *Failing*. Yes, we are failing our - Children, we are failing our- Ancestors, and most of all we are failing our race. (ourselves!) We are the Caucasian!

And for Caucasian sake!...what are we doing by putting our very existence in the hands of militant - *Alien Races*? Is the fate (survival) of the Caucasian people: when put in the hands of alien races not obvious?..asks the Alpha, which is clearly apparent and observable in his eye's, and to which he gives this grave warning and truth. In biological life (and we know no other) the nature of competing groups is -*Predatory*. (think of it!) Therefore, *Tragedy, Sorrow,* and *Death* will be visited upon all those who are unprepared and weak!

"This Is Our Truth, This Is Our Reality"

Racial Endearment

(the cradle of racial dynamics)

Blessed are the Caucasians: These are the words of the Alpha, declaring his honor, love, and devotion to his *Fematrix* (Caucasia) and his oneness (union) with her life force.

Racial Nihilism: What living thing denies its own existence?...asks the Alpha, and can that denial be conducive to its survival?

The Alpha tells us: if it were not for the fact, that a certain Caucasian elitist group *Liberal Zealot Academia,* who have set out on a course of -*Caucasian Racial Nihilism*- (Caucasian racial destruction!) we as Caucasians would not have cause for alarm, nor for the call to action by the

Caucasian community (a clarion response) on behalf of our own survival.

Furthermore, we as Caucasians both in America and throughout the world must promote our own Caucasian *Racial Endearment* if we are to counter this liberal zealot cabal and its evil plot,...its scheme of Caucasian *Social Prostration* through deceit and betrayal.

Our Caucasian *Racial Endearment*: Born of our kind, (bio-providence) and with love of family and community, we the Caucasian people celebrate our singularity (bio-distinction) in the universe of beings.

By invoking the words of the Alpha -*Blessed are the Caucasians* we remind ourselves of the spiritual nature of our being (biological spirituality) and its source of historical racial ancestry.

Furthermore, in the- Holy Valorous (our path!) one can find a maxim that says- A single living thing is the total of its biological idea. It is a symbol of a way of life,(its life strategy) identifiable from all others. Hence, race is at the center of our spiritual life, to believe in ones racialness and to be of the Caucasian faith (Caucasianism) are synonymous.

The virtue of *Racial Being* is not only rooted in the nature of our *Fematrix* (Caucasia) but also in the experience of the Caucasian people as a social embodiment in the spirituality of being.

We Caucasians are *Unique* in this world of living beings; we are distinguishable and peerless in our understanding of life and its vast complexity, and this all having been brought about by our *Biological Mandate* and *Racial Spirituality,* it being the foundation of all the rest.

Hence, every racial group of people and their traditions are interested in the welfare of their people.

In the Valorous the command to pursue the survival of our race is absolute and is the just thing to do, for it is what our *Fematrix* requires and demands of us!

By pursuing our racial survival, we as Caucasians attempt to imitate, honor, and reflect our *Fematrix* who made us.

In essence, Caucasian acts of racial survival merely mirror that of their *Fematrix* through the dictates of their conscience and their Caucasian racial faith.

Caucasianism doesn't require blind obedience to secular laws. When the law of the land is *Ruinous* obedience to that law (alien equality) is also immoral. In that situation, the Caucasian people should obey the dictates of their Caucasian racial faith. In this way Caucasianism can be a force for positive change.

The virtue of Caucasianism doesn't require just racial survival, the will of combat: is the action for the defense of the common security of the Caucasian race. But, it also requires "Benevolence" doing good and respecting the sanctity of all living things by treating them well, in a proper and fitting manner. (but not equal!)

In Caucasianism, understanding and implementing the virtue of *Racial Sovereignty* has been a struggle and the topic of intellectual, theological, and political debate. These social icons have traditions that support armed resistance as well as laws that demand respect for life.

The question then, is when (if ever) is the armed defense of *Racial Sovereignty,* survival of one's kind morally acceptable?

The Alpha's defensive accord: If you as a Caucasian take up arms to defend your life and the freedom of your race, (against alien invaders) you're protecting yourself and those you love from an unjust assault.

The combat therefore, is in self-defense. Hence, the self-defense argument defends your rights not just to respect the lives of others, but also to respect your own life and the lives of your family, friends and fellow Caucasians who have been unjustly attacked by alien marauders.

In Caucasianism, respect and tolerance for all is paramount. But, it doesn't teach pacifism or absolute nonviolence. Turning the other cheek so that an oppressor has free rein over you is not considered a virtue!

In Caucasianism, the point is to do what is right; some times, doing what is right!...requires the use of force within the law of moral standing.

Caucasian Racial Ethics

(acceptable behavior)

In Caucasianism; racial ethics are the moral principles that guide the Caucasian community and that set the standard for what is and isn't acceptable behavior. These fundamental principles flow from the core beliefs and ancient wisdom of more than 40 thousand years of teaching and tradition. The Golden Rule: *"Love Your Race, As You Love Yourself"* this is the first ethical principle and the foundation of all the rest.

Hence, *Race, Family, Respect, Compassion, Humility, Honesty* and *Gratitude* command us as Caucasian racial beings, that which hurts us, hurts others, and that which heals us, heals others.

Reality is the foundation, the premise in Caucasianism, and so its ethics, virtues and social principles take shelter under reality's prime consideration *"Survival"* to which all living things must submit. Furthermore, the principle of *Survival* (life!) and its common understanding leaves no room for *Intellectual Fallacy* nor any mystical wanderings, survival demands *Vigilance* and *Self-Defense,* and of those who fail to comprehend,...will descend into the depths of woe. Therefore, the ethics and virtues in Caucasianism are not based on a *Mystical Becoming*, or a *Pacifist Enlightenment*, but a cold and unforgiving reality (competitive predation) that has been put upon all, and to which the Caucasian world community has been (up to this point) able to defend against.

So, what of our salvation?

In Caucasianism racial honesty goes beyond telling the racial truth, racial honesty is living that truth: it's not just our right racial speech, it's also our right racial action!

If Caucasianism is about seeking racial truth, seeking racial salvation?... then the tools of that quest are spiritual racial questions! The virtue of racial curiosity isn't the same thing as doubt or lack of racial faith. Questions!...help a racial seeker understand more deeply or enable a teacher to explain more fully an aspect of *Racial Faith*. For this reason Caucasianism encourages active questioning and curiosity about the world, about the *Fematrix* and about the sacred teachings of our- *Caucasian Racial Faith*.(Caucasianism!)

Caucasian Ancestral Gratitude
(ancestral obligation)

The appreciation and acknowledgment of our *Caucasian Ancestors* spills over into *Rituals, Blessings*, and *Ceremonies*, bringing us to the union of - *Caucasian Racial Spirituality*. The field or circle of Caucasian gratitude for their ancestors, yields endless illumination, and this dialectic of gratitude is a gift; in this sense they have given us the intimation of order within disorder, stability within instability and a great rendezvous with intelligibility.

This gratitude should be present in all dimensions of Caucasian life, Intellectual, Interpretive, as well as *Emotional* and *Religious.* And if we Caucasians for whatever reason, now or in the future, fail to honor our *Ancestors* it will be a sin that will precipitate our demise!

- Purpose -
(life's teleology)

The Alpha asks this question: Dose life, have a destination? And if so, what is it?

The Alpha tells us: there are three great questions in life.

(1) In our biological life there are 2 existing realms, one of *Intellect* and the other of *Form,* and if that is so (which it is!) was there a time when there was just *One,* and if so, what was it? (2) In our biological life (and we know no other!) *Male* and *Female* are the norm, but, was there a time when there was just *One*, and if so, who was it, and why is there now two? (3) If biological life is all we know, (and it is!) and this biological life is fueled by *Competing Intellects* (which it is!) and its history having declared there can only be one winner, what is the competition for?

In other words, what prize or prizes awaits the victor? The Alpha's thoughts: In biological life, there are (3) great competitions, (1) is for the survival of *Kind* (species or subspecies- created by different life strategies) (2) is for the possessor of the *Egg* (the female) and (3) is for the *Egg* itself, and all three are male competitive pursuits. In competition for the survival of his *Kind*, (human species) and his *Racial Subspecies* (Negroid, Mongoloid or Caucasoid) he directly takes part, as well as his competitive pursuit of his racial females. (females of his kind!) But, as for the *Egg* he knows not, having deposited his biological line (his essence with multiple heredities) and each one having to compete on its own to join with the *Egg* ,(first one to gain entry) and when a winner emerges the *Egg* will immediately lockout all other competitors.

And if this is so, and the *Egg* is the ultimate prize, (and in that, there is no doubt!) then what does it offer? And who created this *Egg* and the cultural and biological *Tournaments* that compete for it? (Who is the creator and controller of life's Colosseum?) This great understanding can only be found in the forbidden truths of the *One!* (the Fematrix) and only those Caucasians who take up her quest (racial spirituality) and make the journey to her enlightenment will know the wonder of life's teleology.

The
Caucasian World Dilemma

(liberal zealotry, and its war against reality)

At the time of this writing, some well meaning but ignorant Caucasian liberal zealot is in the aimless service of a mystical fallacy- *Racial Equality*- and do to their propaganda of demonizing the wealth and prosperity of their own people (Caucasians) these liberal zealots in the tens of thousands have declared war against the forces of reality.

Like all mystical social cults, this liberal colony of *Equality Worshipers* and their many charismatic leaders who have indoctrinated them with their extremist equality views, are themselves the very purveyors of alien racial elitism. (their racial future in their hands) That's right, it is a scam by racial minorities to attack gullible Caucasian liberals to serve their hidden true agenda, and if you are a student of social reality, (and we hope you are!) Then you know exactly what that agenda is! (racial, political and social domination by an alien race!) Within a single Caucasian generation, alien races have advanced from passive minorities to the ranks of an aggressive racial force that cannot and will not be subordinated to the norms of Caucasian society. (no assimilation!)

Far from being shocked by this significant press for unaccountable social and political power by minority races, even the majority of the media (news broadcasts, and news papers) have succumb to their mystical spell of

Equality, hence, leaving Caucasian social heredity to fend for itself!

The very possibility of racial war exists as a stern reality today solely because the principle of social heredity (racial homogeneity) has been violated.

So deeply seated has the violation become that we as a race of people (Caucasians) are perfectly willing to cut our selves to pieces in political and social warfare so long as we do not interfere with our scramble for *Racial Equality*. It is not necessary to dwell at length on this description of our social demise or to offer evidence in support of its existence because its existence is obvious, and as well understood by the ignorant as it is by those who make a pretense of thinking accurately.

Nor is this the saddest part of the indictment that we might render against ourselves, for we are not only willing to engage in our own social demise, but the future of our children and grandchildren will fall into the hands of *"Alien Races"* that will have diverted back to *Hyenic Tribalism* once the Caucasians are no longer in control!

This is truth, this is reality.

One may deny this indictment if one chooses, but the facts do not support the denial! However, the problem is to extend the principle of Caucasianism (Caucasian Racial Sovereignty) so that the Caucasian people will subordinate their individual interests to those of the *Caucasian Race* as a whole. The question then arises,...How can this be done?

Before we answer this question, let us again define the term *Caucasian Social Heredity* and find out what its possibilities are?

Caucasian Social Heredity: is the principle through which the young of the race absorb from their environment and particularly from their earlier training by their *Parents, Teachers*, and *Religious Leaders*, the *Beliefs, Tendencies* and *Rules* of the adults and their society who dominate them.

In other words, we as Caucasian parents and community leaders must cooperate in this vital task of creating a *United Caucasian Empire* (our sacred mandate, our biological dynasty!) by *Defending* and *Preserving* what we as a race of people have created!...if our children and their children are to have a future!...in their own hands?

It is the Alpha's hope that you as a Caucasian, recognize the fact that you are a Caucasian!...and conduct yourself accordingly, and within the spirit of your *Ancestral Trust*!

Therefore, nothing more of value can be said on the subject of the *Caucasian World Community* and its overall survival!...except what you say for yourself?

The privilege of thought and discussion of this vital subject is now surren-dered to you!...and may its truths bring to you a spiritual racial clarity, so as to inspire an unwavering devotion to your "Caucasian Dynasty" and its "Bio-Mandate"

"Blessed are the Caucasians"

The Alpha's view: Knowledge of an Aliens Nature? Ability to accurately analyze "Alien Others" and the courage to see in them what is there instead of that which one would wish to see. Many a Caucasian has gone down to defeat through misplaced confidence in "Alien Others" for no other reason than that of seeing in them those qualities that were never there. And if you aspire to "Caucasian leadership" I would urge you to study alien others, by determining the workings of their Minds and the outcomes of their Ambitions.

The Mind
(in search of its reason)

All of earths biological beings, (and we know of no others!) have no recollection, and can find no physical record of their beginning? In other words, all have no idea why their here?...or how they got here?

Hence, the Alpha's question: Is all of life's *Collective Amnesia* an accident!...or is it by design?

Therefore: It is imperative that we Caucasians start from what we understand, and that understanding in our cultural society is called "Science" the pursuit of why! (causality, purpose, motive) a great task to be sure,... so, let us begin!

First Question: Was the *Entrance* of matter into the Void an *Explosion* or a *Breach*? In other words, if it was an explosion of a "*Subatomic-Cyst*" in the void (a mass of subatomic particles?) then its expanding perimeter should be *spherical* or round in shape, and what some considered to be the time of that event some 13 billion years ago, it stands to reason that a field of complete emptiness of billion of light years across exist at its center. (an expanding hollow ball) But, if it was a breach?... a *Tear* or a *Rupture* in the membrane (barrier) of the *Subatomic Cyst?*...then its flow into the void would be slower and there would be no center, and its outer perimeter would be very inconsistent in form and have a "stream" from the breach to the field body, it would be in fact a "Pond" in the Void.

Second Question: Is it possible for a Vortex to materialize in a Void?...a phenomena known to science as a Black Hole? (a state of reconfigured emptiness?) But, taking the phenomena a bit further, maybe what were looking at is something even more amazing, but much more understandable!...is it possible that it could be an immense- Black Sun?... that takes place without any prevention by which light cannot escape (a barer) a kind of *"Electromagnetic Gas or* dense *Particle Field"* between the core and the surface, either *Deflecting* or *Disseminating* all light back into the suns interior?

Third Question: If sub atomics exist?...and we now know that to be an absolut! Then it stands to reason that the vastness of open space is not a void?...but a great expanse (pool) of dimensional subatomic extremophiles- were *Size* and *Stability* have no meaning- the dominion of celestial chance!

So, then it can be side, that we of the *Biological* are no exception!...and we must also take our place in the struggle, for you see, for us, its about choice of form and its freedom of movement. The union of *Thought, Form* and *Motion!* (the biological idea!) for are we not also the children of the- *Extremophiles?*

The
Biological Domain
(the most extreme of the extremes)

-Life-
(the Fematrix: Creation by choice)

Let it be understood by all!...that of all the known Extremophiles: only one is capable of self creation though the extreme capability of "Mind" (Consciousness) a process of sensory awareness, brought about by a central core called the "Self " which is a manifestation in housed in an organ known as the "Brian," being the newest of the *Extremophiles (the biological Fematrix!)* and a child of them all.

Having side all this, let us examine this- *Fematrix* "Self" and her properties, for we "Humans" are our selves, of her, and by her!

The 𝔄lpha tells us: that we of the- *Biological Domain,* are not only the *Newest* but also the most extreme of all that has ever existed in the great Void!...for we are the *Caucasians!*...the *Observers!*...the

Witnesses for all that have no "Voice," and for all those that have *Come,* "Participated" and have *Gone!*...we, will tell their story's, and build monument to their passing, for we Caucasians have been found-*Worthy!*... and have inherited from our *Fematrix* (ℭaucasia!) the stewardship of the- *Universe!*

Therefore, let us now explore some of the properties, no, the *Wonders!*... of the one who brought us all here- *Our Fematrix!*...and the magnificence of her being!...and all that she has achieved.

𝔅ehold 𝔥er 𝔚onders 𝔒f 𝔗he 𝔐ind
(All are of her, and by her!)

-𝔗he ℭorridors-

Self * Thought * Love * Faith * Hope * Kindness * Fear * Sight * Hearing * Touch * Laughter * Sex * Sadness * Aggression * Language * Hatred * Forgiveness * Goodness * Creativity * Art * Tools * Music * Literature * Exploration * Building * Learning * Purpose * Win * Questions * Curiosity * Need * Science * Sharing * Schools * Friendship * Motherhood * Fatherhood *

Progress * Children * Reproduction * Life-Strategy * Family * Enemy * Teaching Satisfaction * Desire * Relationships * Morality * Work * Appetite * Intention * Right * Imagination * Care * Human * Demand * Law * Standards * Answers * Society * Racialness * Us * Concepts * Behavior * Conscience * Giving * Remembering * Conversation * Willpower * Lose * Effort * Culture * Kindness * Learning * Manners * Words * Strength * Weakness * Discipline * Past *Worthless * Courageous * Spiritual * Precious * Quality * Life * Objective * Overcome * Elusion * Information * Origin * Preservation * Deception * Reality * Belief * Absence * Acceptance * Truth * Falsehood * Rejection * Alien * Tragedy Food * Obligation * Leadership * Conquest * Difference * History * Defense * Health * Death * Present * Future * Migration * Survival * defeat * Them * Recognition * Accuracy * Play * Value * Wrong * Decisions * Taking * Life * Obedience * Respect * Pride * Achievement * Loyalty * Success * Failure * Responsible * Meaning * Understanding * Beauty *

The Alpha's view: There should, and can be no doubt!...by any one!...as to the extreme intellectualism and capability of the "Caucasian Race" (our human subspecies!) which far exceeds all other biological endeavors, whether other humans or animals. This of course has the sting of one's racial pride!...but, it is free of arrogant malice and corruption, do to the fact that it is true!...having created the greatest and only intellectual phenomena of its kind, Caucasian Science! (the world knows of no other!) Therefore, it is imperative for the Caucasian race, as well as the rest of the world to not "Hobble" this greatest of biological journeys - the Caucasian Conquest!...for it needs to succeed if the "Biological World" (the Fematrix!) is to survive! All living things have an inherited intellectual path, an acumen of embedded distinctive perception, (life strategy!) a keenness and depth of discrimination, of discernment, especially in matters of one's future and the survival of one's unique and incomparable bio-racial kind!

The
Caucasian Acquisitions

~~

Health - Wisdom - Wealth

The Alpha tells us: that in Caucasianism there are three social edicts called the *Acquisitions*!...they are *Health, Wisdom,* and *Wealth.* And it is the duty of all Caucasians of the faith to aspire to, and comply with these three acquisitions if they are to achieve happiness and tranquility in their Caucasian life.

Health

The Acquisition of Health: In Caucasianism; there is no greater attention, then there is to one's over all well being! Hence, this understanding: One cannot serve his or her *Family, Culture,* or *Nation,* (racial society) unless they see first to their own *Physical* and *Mental* health? Therefore, the first attention of any living thing, is to it self! (self- preservation!) And only through this understanding is all other Caucasian endeavors possible. (the maintaining of one's physical and mental health is imperative!)

Wisdom

The Acquisition of Wisdom: In Caucasianism; there is a true understanding of the obstacles that all of life must face in its becoming! Hence, this understanding: All of life is dependent upon a single factor, and that factor is *Decision*?

Therefore, if *Decision* is the ultimate factor in all of life and its destiny, what constitutes or fuels it? Decision is the *Harvesting Engine* of need, and what feeds this engine is knowledge, and knowledge refined is *Wisdom,* the ultimate fuel of the mind. Right thought, right understanding, right decision, right outcome! ...*Wisdom,* the true oracle of the human journey.

Wealth

The Acquisition of Wealth: In Caucasianism; there is the understanding of life and its becoming, its accent in to the vast wilderness of *Needs*? Hence, the term *Wealth*,...being in the possession of that which is needed to sustain one's *Life* and *Future*,...as to *Poverty,* a life or lives on the precipice of death, those who fail to understand, having no expectations, neglecting their charge, and unable to meet their needs, thereby succumbing to natures unforgiving end. In human life, as well as in all life, there are no equals, all are on their own! Furthermore, there are two types of *Wealth - Personal and Community,* and they come in many different forms, such as *Food, Shelter, Land, Children, Knowledge*, *Religion* and *Culture*- these being even more paramount then precious metals. The Alpha tells us: All life, weather *Species* or *Subspecies* must harvest the *Wealth* and *Means* for their future,... failure, is not an option!

The Alpha's view: Our Caucasian Organized Effort means that one must develop the strategic ability to direct one's efforts in such a manner as to take advantage of the Law of increasing returns, and this calls for cooperative ability of the highest order, this being in harmony with one's racial faith, and the object of that purpose.

"This Is Our Truth, This Is Our Reality"

E. R. S. Proposition
(Equitable Racial Separation)

This great and multifarious battle for the right of our *Racial Sovereignty*!...in which such various points are at issue, *Alien Cultural* and *Educational Debauchery!*...and the counterfeit social direction of *Liberal Zealot America*, has plunged *Caucasian America* into a very dark murky pool of *Political Cowardice!*...and intellectual degeneracy.

Thereby creating an alien racial- *Hyenic Distain!*

Hence, this *Manifesto* and the Alpha's eagerness to let the Caucasian

Americans know the intellectual and social perils that lie ahead for them if they fail to address these vital issues. Only through the recognition and acceptance of the true racial circumstance plaguing Caucasian America can one hope to pierce the cloak of human racial discord.

As was related to in C847, it is the *Alpha's* belief that *Equitable Racial Separation* (into their own states) by and through political means is the true and only honorable answer for the Caucasian American racial dilemma as well as its sister Caucasian states throughout the world.

By good will, treaty, and contract, let the American people create two new *Sovereign Nations*, a *New Asia* and a *New Africa*, thereby giving both the *Asian* and *African* people a sound and rooted foundation for political and socio-cultural development. (their future, in their hands!)

The deepest issues will lie between those who conceive a society as having a biological foundation to which its socio-cultural direction is given form and image, its racial identity, and those *Aliens* and *Caucasians* (liberal zealots) who think of freedom as having a purely banquet existence, a society to be plundered, to be restructured, rerouted, for their form, their image, their identity?

Lurking beneath the surface of every racial society, including ours, is the passionate yearning for a cause that exalts us, the kind that our *Race Alone* is able to deliver. It reduces and at times erases the anxiety of our individual consciousness.

We abandon individual responsibility for a shared, unquestioned communal enterprise, our- *Racial Survival*!

Hence, the cosmology of *Titus Lucretius,* makes life's conflict of opposites the principle of growth and decay in our ever present universe... *Creativity* struggles against *Destruction, Kind* wars against *Difference,...* *Life* against *death.*

Death dealing motions the poet writes, cannot keep the mastery always nor entomb existence for evermore, nor on the other hand can the *Birth* and increase giving motions of things preserve them always after they are born.

Thus the war's of *-Biological Kind-* and its first beginnings (competitive predation!) waged from eternity is carried on with dubious issue: now here, now there, the life- bringing elements of a kind get the mastery and are over- mastered in turn.

Furthermore, by recognizing and understanding the truth of life, and by countering its absolute *Negative* of *Someone Must Lose*?...in its arena of *Competitive Predation*- we must learn to apply to human races (our-subspecies!) that which we now recognizes and create for- *Animals,* their own biological sanctuaries.(survival preserves!)

And for humans- their own *"Sovereign Racial States"* for those that desire it, and seek to preserve their unique (one of a kind!) biological heritage and its chosen course.

Therefore, we as Caucasians, and our crusade for the preservation of *Caucasian Societies* throughout the world, our unassailable right!..will either happen at the table by *Ink* and *Treaty?*...or in the streets by *Arms* and *Blood?*

But, it will happen!..that's for sure, the countdown has already begun,... this is our truth, this is our reality!

Hence, the wisdom of –*Equitable Racial Separation!*

The Caucasian World Conquest
(A Means to Subsistence)

The status of racial biology is differentia, and its act of existing is its essence.

The Caucasian racial differentia, and its beginnings, as previously stated, has been lost in the mists of time! But its legacy of subsistence, its eclectic cultural history, is in fact a biological singularity of unprecedented human magnitude.

Historical Focus
(Caucasian cultural genesis)

Is Europe the cradle of Caucasian civilization? Hence, the great debate!

Alas, once again, we must descend from the sacred halls of scientific speculation to a simpler realm of what is known.

And what is known is this: At or around 40,000 years ago in an area known today as the European continent, there emerged a bio-cosmic genesis, a *Fematrix Caucasian Homo Sapient*, and there were three known types, *Mediterranean, Nordic,* and *Alpine* Caucasians.

This is not to disregard their predecessors, *Erectus, Habilis, Cro-Magnon* etc.

But it was these three *Fematrix Sapient* lines of biology from which the learned sciences say, that modern *Caucasian Humans* emerged, the Caucasians homo sapient *Race.*

Having been forged in nature's caldron of predation, this Caucasian race would emerge, and that emergence would sweep all before it! Having said this, let us begin. As most already know, life's very foundation is predation. In other words, the bio-task of eating. Hence, the eternal struggle of who eats whom and as stated before, life is sustained by the consumption of life. Furthermore, life does not surrender it-self to the hungry without a fight! This is truth; this is reality!

The
Quadrisect Of Life And Death
(the bio-gauntlet)

Of all life's encounters, it is the bio-gauntlet and its four deadly forces, *Hunger, Competition, Exposure, Disease,* that preoccupy its mental and physical pursuits; for all four forces of the gauntlet must be defeated if a life force is to prevail. They were and still are the true adversaries of the Caucasian Conquest.

Hunger
(the first adversary)

Eating? The taking of life to sustain life! And as stated before, contrary to popular belief, eating is a violent act!

A very violent act! So, as to the pursuit of life-giving sustenance, it seems that everyone is on the menu, and that no one is exempt. In other words, everyone is eating everyone, and even cannibalism, although not practiced today, was, at one time in human history, an unholy deed!

In the human equation, it is believed that originally scavengers, humans developed into hunter gatherers, and so it is from this evolution of *Scavenger* to *Hunter Gatherer* that the Caucasian journey begins. Having no great physical powers or bio-weapons such as fangs, claws, or great size, the Caucasians had to rely on the one thing that the rest of biology didn't have, and that was the great gift from their Fematrix, the gift of a *-Free Mind-* the ability to out think your opponents! (un-imprinted mentality - no boundaries!)

So the Caucasians and their boundless mental ability set out to conquer hunger. And this is what they did! Hunting 40,000 years ago was, at the time, haphazard, to say the least, although man had made weapons spears, knives, and clubs, most game animals had the advantage of speed and could easily out run man's attempts at deadly pursuit.

The Dog
(rival domestication)

In all of its history, one of humankind's greatest adversaries was the wolf, for unlike bears, lions, and a host of other predators, wolves, like humans, were social animals, and both hunted in groups or packs.

The wolf was a very successful predator, and on many occasions driven by hunger, man and wolf would find themselves fighting over the same kill. Sometimes the wolves won, and sometimes man won!

And it was this fierce competition that would lead to one of the most formidable unions in all of biology, the union of wolf and man, the domestication of the wolf into what is known today, as the dog.

This union of man and dog would dislocate the predatory balance and make mankind the top predator, for no animal can outrun a dog, and no animal can withstand the onslaught of man's weapons. But even with the dog as his partner, man found that hunting was still no easy task; if game was to be gotten, man and dog had to travel long distances, which sometimes meant being away for days at a time, leaving family members alone and unprotected.

Farming
(domestic human culture)

The hunter gatherer and his dog, though a formidable team, still had to cope with the seasons and the migration of game animals, not to mention human territorial squabbles that were, for the most part, also deadly.

Within a short period of time as a hunter, man began to realize that there were other animals (like the wolf) that could also be trapped and tamed for his use, either as food or labor; hence the beginnings of -*Animal Domestication.*

In the first periods of *Homo Sapient* Caucasian social development, there would emerge three types, the *Cave Dweller*, the *Forest Dweller*, and the *Nomad*, and although each one had its advantages, it would be the *Forest Dwellers* that would prevail in the end, and it was these forest dwellers that would come to be known as the *Caucasian Farmer*, the forebears of all modern Caucasian societies! The farming history of the *Homo Sapient Caucasian Race* and its beginning is still to this day unfolding.

Recent archaeological studies and excavations around the world are starting to make a different picture.

It now seems to point to animal domestication preceded by a few thousand years plant domestication (farming), but all the facts are not yet in, and until then, we will have to wait! Be that as it may, the farming ability of the Homo sapient white race known today as the Caucasians is an achievement without equal! As all human history has shown, no other Homo sapient species (Negroid or Mongoloid) has ever created a farming culture as proactive in fighting hunger and as productive in the raising of either plants or domestic animals as the Caucasian World Community.

Competition
(the second adversary)

Competition is the catalyst of all living things, the natural by-product of a world composed of different and unequal forces (elemental and biological).

There are no equalities on the playing fields of life; all is unequal. Hence, the competition of it (opposing force) to be better than it, to overcome it, to defeat it, to consume it, and in the case of "Homo Sapiens", there are three *Competitive Races*: *Sapient Negroid*, *Sapient Mongoloid*, and *Sapient Caucasoid*. It is these three competing *Homo Sapient* races that comprise the modern day human story.

Equality
(Intellectual default)

Of all humankind's political, cultural, and moral pursuits, none are as fallacious as the pursuit *Human Equality*?

Hence, the very term *Equality* (equal with) if applied to biology, eliminates the very nature of biological existence, which most of us know as- *Difference*, and if things are different, they cannot be *Equal*.

Hence, equality cannot be applied to difference! And to do so is to submerge one's mind into the dark pool of intellectual wanting. We as Caucasian want to succeed, and we want others, as well, to succeed!

But the lack of such in others does not call for the disregard of reality, because one does not respond well to the truth. And by the way, the term is - *Human Respect*,...not equality?

The philosophy of the lie is that the road of the lie, only leads to the next lie, and once a society starts down that road, it will lose its social bearing, becoming morally disoriented and lost in the wilderness of its own intellectual cowardice.

The only logical explanation for technological racial gaps is that certain types of cultures, or civilizations, are the products of certain types of racial people representative of the innate potential of any given group of racial people. While this is currently deemed a political incorrect point of view, the facts of historical development support no other conclusion.

What use are educated beliefs, if they are excluded from the public square by the suffocating conformity to a *Phantom Racial Equality*, imposed by an ever vigilant *Thought Police* (political correctness!) backed by armies of predatory lawyers?

Caucasian America is no longer a society in which its people feel free to hold whatever private views they have on human groups and their behavior.

Caucasian Americans are being persecuted for their personal beliefs, and fearful to disclose them, are we as Caucasians supposed to respect groups with high crime statistics, groups that spread disease, or groups that hate Caucasians? The answer, as we all know, according to the liberal orthodoxy of tolerance is- *Yes*.

The American liberal orthodoxy not only wants to stamp out private opinion on the subject of *Racial Competition* but the actual facts as well.

The liberal taboos against the strong biological basis of human nature and of racial difference in behavior and cognitive processes, which are the very basis for racial competitiveness has, in the Alpha's mind, eliminated American academia as a significant source of rational intellectual influence and has, in fact, defaulted on its social contract with the Caucasian American people. Alas, let it be said that the conspiracy of social and cultural sabotage against Caucasian America by the liberal orthodoxy and the neo-socialists will not go unchallenged!

Exposure
(the third adversary)

Rain, wind, cold, and heat, these are the powers of nature's fury. It was and is, by their very combination, what the world and all that it implies must struggle to overcome.

Furthermore, in the realm of physical supremacy, it has no rival. To escape the harsh elements, the Caucasians at first retreated into natural caves, and for centuries these caves were their dwellings, and many prominent caves dating back to some 30,000 to 40,000 years can still be visited today at various locations throughout Europe.

But cave dwelling was not to last!

Not too distant from the last Ice Age, the Caucasians began to leave the caves and build dwellings out of stone and wood throughout Europe, the Near and Middle East.

The Village
(the birth of Caucasian culture)

The union of related members was the union of relatives that would became known as the village, and from this social union the cultural story and appositional conquest of the Caucasian race of people begins.

As the Ice Age began to recede, milder weather beckoned the Caucasians to leave their caves. Hence the Caucasian forest dweller, late "Paleolithic Era," began to emerge.

These first settlements lead to a shift from food gathering to a food-culti-vating society, and the appearance of crops and the domestication of animals other than the wolf (dog) became features of their way of life. This change in the Caucasian culture is called the Neolithic Age. The first Caucasian Neolithic continental settlements can be said to have been established around 10,000 BC in Europe (Ireland) and 5,000 BC in the Near and Middle East (Mesopotamia, Egypt), all of Caucasian origin.

A regular and continuous food supply created by the establishment of farming meant that bigger Caucasian populations could live in settled, more secure areas, and this marked the first time that the luxury of non-food producing professions within Caucasian society became possible, the mining of Gold, Copper, and Iron, and the manufacturing of Jewelry, Pottery, Weapons, and Tools.

From about 20.000 to 4.500 BC the- "Lascaux Cave Paintings",the "Azilian Script", and "Tartaria Tablet" were painted and written, and they are some of the oldest Caucasian paintings and writings on earth.

Disease
(the fourth adversary)

The unseen adversary: Of all of humankind's adversaries, it is the unrelen-ting peril of disease (microscopic organisms) and their adaptive predatory strategy that makes them so formidable and feared. For millions of years, human biology has been the victim of a microscopic predatory assault, and for millions of years, humankind has defended itself by various means and with various methods.

From witch doctors of old to modern day institutions of scientific study, the battle to stem the tide of disease in the human species has led to some of the greatest achievements in Caucasian history.

Of all the races, it's been the Caucasians who have opened up a vast battlefront in the war against the world's most formidable diseases, such as *Smallpox, Typhoid Fever, Asian flu, Syphilis, Aids, Tuberculosis, Cholera, Malaria, Hepatitis, Meningitis, Alzheimer's,* and *Cancer*, just to mention a few.

Leading the war on disease, the Caucasian world community has made a few significant breakthroughs, but like all diseases, social or biological, it is an uphill fight and not for the weak of heart or the timid.

As of the Caucasian year 42005, new and more sinister diseases are starting to raise their ugly heads, *Ebola, Anthrax,* and *Hemorrhagic fever*, not to mention the new strains of *Tuberculosis* and *Hepatitis* that are resistant to all antibiotics! (we as must stay the course!)

The Law of Competition

(the Fematrix strategy of Winners and Losers!)

The Alpha tells us: That, in the realm of biological life, and we know no other!...there is the act of "Competitive Consumption" or the process of consuming other life forms to sustain one's own life!...plus, the engagement of physical and mental strategies to defend one's group,(biological line!) their way of life, their cultural beliefs and spiritual truths, and to defeat any and all *Competitive Opposition* to their *Existence*!...and life strategy. This is truth, this is reality!

Furthermore, the fate of the loser, is always in the hands of the winner!... this is an unsalable truth, and by no means does it exclude humankind and its *Racial Subspecies*!

For humankind by far, and more then any other, have shown their

Merciless Competitive Nature, not only to the *Animal World,* but to *Themselves* as well.

Thereby, leaving no doubt in todays *21st* century as to giving "Mercy" for that *Racial, Ethnic* or *Religious* group that fails to recognizes or defend themselves against *Alien Subversives* and their front groups, that penetrate and manipulate *Ideological Weakness* (liberal zealot equality) in existing political parties. Translation!..for control of their *Social* and *Political Action,* (their Cover and Voting Power!) to incite and bring about an outright-*Territorial Invasion*! (immigration ruse!)

It worked well in the Caucasian state of *South Africa,* annihilating its *Cultural Civility,* and destroyed the *Future* of the *Caucasian Afrikaner Society*!...and like some kind of *"Poetic Justice"* this very same deadly *Suicidal Pathogen* (racial equality!) has now infected the Nations of *Europe* and *America,*..yes, those very same nations that sponsored South Africa's *Death* and *Destruction*?..yes, they are now themselves "Infected," and in a fight for their very lives!

And if for any reason, should *Caucasian America* or *Europe* fail to defend themselves? (by not expelling the alien invasion?)...like the- *South African Caucasians!* they will also find their place and future in *Hades!*

"The Fematrix Never Weeps For The Loser"

The Alpha's view: Our Caucasian history spans some 40 thousand years!.and if we as a people (one of a kind!) for what ever reason?...do not recognize or understand the value of our struggle? Than it stand to reason that we have through our intellectual hubris (our fallacy of equality!) failed our "Fematrix"! (through cultural and political "capitulation" that favor hostile alien others?) And if that is the case?...then I the Alpha, must in the name of my people (the Caucasians!) and our posterity resist our demise, and -Confront and Defeat- all those "Caucasian Seditionists" and their "Alien Subversives" who conspired in creating the "Trojan Horse" (racial equality?) telling us it was a wondrous gift?...but knowing very well that its true nature was a hostile ruse!...a precursor to an "Alien Invasion" that numbers in the Millions! But,..to all the wayward Politicians, Liberal Zealots, and Progressive subversives who have taken part in this- Treason! Understand this: A great storm of "Caucasian Patriotic Defense" is gathering!...there will be no escape!..our stated "Enemies" both citizen and alien alike, must and will be held accountable by law, for their deeds!...this being the will of- Caucasian America!

"So Say We All"

The Caucasian Racial Expression

⌒

(Our Manifest Destiny)

The Alpha tells us: the human expression is, "the motion of emotion," the presentation of a vast complexity of physical actions which are directly caused by psychic activities. The objective phenomena are manifest of subjective racial experience, and the conception of our racial expression does not need to be established by argument; it only needs careful observation.

As we study further, we can see that *Racial Expression* is not peculiar to human kind. Thus the facts can be seen on every side in the most familiar actions of both *Humans* and *Animals*. Racialness!...is revealed *per se* to our sense, its phenomena being *Seen, Felt* and *Heard.* (an outward sign of an inward substance) In biology there is nothing manifest without "kind in form".(our Caucasian racial identity!)

The Alpha, would like to hand on, to a world where Caucasian rationalism is today finding itself in dire straits, do to the *Ruse* of "Racial Equality" the fallacy of *Liberal Zealots* and *Alien Radicals,* having now taken up a deliberate position of *Subversive Malice* against the rationale right of *Caucasian Racial Identity* and its *Culture.*

Thereby, compelling the "Alpha" to give them the "Valorous" and its journey, evoking a figure little known to the present generation; and to reconsider and recapitulate our *Caucasian Universal Conquest!* Its object is to reassert the idea of the connection between our "Fematrix" (Caucasia!) and our manifest *Racial Destiny.*

Our Caucasian Contribution

~~

"Conquest"
(Empire- Truth- Law- Education- Liberty)

The Alpha tells us: The following contains an outline of Caucasian General History. He has composed these elements principally with the view of furnishing an aid to the Caucasian World Community, and hoping to be useful even to those who have acquired a competent knowledge from the perusal of the works of detached Historians.

As the progress of the human mind forms a capital object in the study of the *Caucasians* and their contributions to the Arts, and Sciences, their Religions, Laws, Governments, and as already stated; The superior efficacy of example to precept is universally acknowledged!...and in most Caucasian societies all the laws of morality and rules of conduct are verified by experience, and are constantly submitted to its test and examination.

The Caucasian contribution to the *Human Struggle*, which adds to our *Modern Experience* an immense treasure of the experience of others, furnishes innumerable proofs, by which we Caucasians may verify all the precepts of our own every day-*Morality* and *Prudence!* Therefore, in *Caucasian America,* it is an indispensable duty of every *Man* and *Woman* of *Caucasian Birth* to be acquainted, in a certain degree, with the science of *Politics*; for history is the absolute school of politics. It opens to us the springs of human affairs; the cause of the rise, grandeur, revolutions, and fall of empires. It points out the reciprocal influence of government and of national manners: it dissipates the prejudices, nourishes the love of our *Racial Union* and directs to the best means of its improvement: it illustrates equally the blessing of our *"Caucasian Culture"* and the miseries of *Political Factions;* the danger of *Uncontrolled liberal Zealotry*, and the cold debasing influence of *Despotic Power.* Caucasian history, besides its general advantages, has a distinct species of utility to different "Alien" racial groups according to their several ranks in history, and occupations in their struggle for life.

What is our "Racialness?"...the subject matter of our racialness, and indeed the judgments we build up on it, are as we now see in the modern world, are inadequate as a means of grasping the attributes of our *Caucasian Creation?*..in and of itself, this being the true essence of the modern world. (twenty first century!)

Even the most convinced and convincing, the most deeply experienced definition of that which underlies the manifestation of creation, does not avail to get at the root of our *Racialness,* and draw it into the light?

They are of no avail as objects of actual knowledge, for they are the servants of a distant past, advocates, keepers of *Ancient Dogmas,* professing the esoteric, mystic fallacies of *Man* and *Gods, Redemption* and *Salvation?*...never to realize the reality of their *Bondage,* and a *Deliverance* that will never come. Obviously, it is our Caucasian spirit and ancestral inheritance (training) which teach us to subordinate to our *Racial Identity*; which attribute *Truth* and genuine *Significance* to it alone and adhere to the contemplative abstraction and spirituality of a biological racial reality.

But, it is precisely in the *Pessimistic* hue of our own *Caucasian Journey* that our humanity and spirituality lie; in the fact that our great Nation (Caucasian America!) practiced in suffering and wielding the prose of an enduring cultural epoch in human history, lifting the human soul out of the biological sphere of nature, and seeing in our *Caucasian Race* the savior of the *Fematrix* endeavor.

Yes, our *Racial Character* (our Fematrix spirit!) is not a mere objectivation of "Biology" but the fruitful union and interpenetration of both spheres, immensely heightening to life and more fascinating than either can be by itself!

The Alpha, as the purveyor of "Caucasianism" and the voice of the "Caucasian Race" tells us; there is no disputing the fact that the advancement of human life has nothing to fear from the "Caucasians" yet the anti-Caucasianism of our day is a "Liberal Subversive Experiment" a one sided answer to the eternal question as to the nature and destiny of- Humanity, and we palpably need a corrective to restore the balance, in other words, his existence as the "Alpha" may help to bring to birth a new humanity of which we stand in need, and to which they are akin: a humanity above dry reason on the one hand and at idolatry of instinct on the other, for "Race" accompanying humankind on their painful journey to self-realization, has always been before them at the goal.

The
Indo-European Migration

(born of the Caucasus)

Although parts of Europe had been settled by Caucasians of Mediterranean and Nordic stock and later to become Alpine (old world late Paleolithic, 35,000 BC to Neolithic 10,000 BC), it wasn't until around 5,600 BC that a great wave of Caucasian tribes swept into Europe from their place of origin, the Caucasus Mountains, hence their (our) racial name, Caucasians It is believed that this great migration of Caucasian tribes had come about by the flooding of the Black Sea Basin from the Mediterranean Sea, a factual occurrence around 5,600 BC. The rising waters of the Mediterranean Sea burst through the narrow neck of the Bosporus, destroying the Caucasian civilizations ringing the fertile Black Sea Basin. It was this catastrophe that triggered the great Caucasian migration into Europe. With the aid of the horse, this great Caucasian migration moved in all Directions, disrupting the slow but steady pace of development everywhere they went. Large numbers settled in Northern Europe, staying there until they later began to move south.

Other tribes moved off to the Middle and Near East, while others ventured west, crossing into Britain and Spain. Europe was completely settled by four main Caucasian hordes- the Celts, the Germans, the Balts, and the Slavs.

In the south they settled predynastic Egypt and the Middle East, penetrating, India (indo-Aryans) Afghanistan (Aryans), and parts of

China (Tocharian Celts), xian in Qui Chan province and the Wapu region. Furthermore, we must not forget to mention some of the most recent Caucasian discoveries in the Canary Islands and in North America, also thousands of years old.

Knowledge of these Caucasian migrations has been lost for centuries, and some for thousands of years, but due to relatively recent archeological finds, they have now been rediscovered. The discovery of these *Mummies* and *Settlements* show without question that early Caucasian migrations took place 10,000 years ago, across seas and continents.

Caucasian Revelation

(religion, art, science, government and law)

It can be stated, that the first signs of Caucasian cognizance (knowledge) appeared in Willendorf Austria; Sungir Russia; Lascaux France; plus various other sights in the Czech and Slovak republics, in the late Paleolithic era, 30 to 15,000 BC, but it wasn't until the Neolithic era, 10,000 BC, that the "Caucasian Race" began to emerge from its long dark journey of subsistence living, and into the light of their *Intellectual Capacity,* a gift of their "Fematrix" (Caucasia!) and her miraculous life strategy. The particulars just considered is what formed the ground work of what the Alpha has termed "Natural Religion" the conveyance of the "Fematrix Will" by means of "Facts," is the foundation of what he terms "Revealed Religion" hence, a Natural and Revealed Religion such as "Caucasianism" can never be contrasted; but there is a real, although it is but a relative contrast between the channels through which they are conveyed, between *Nature* and *Revelation*. How then, are they related; and where in *Nature* can we recognizes a "Supreme Activity" other then that exhibited in the order of the universe.

The Alpha's view: Nature and Revelation alike proceed from the "Fematrix," and, consequently, if their relation to each other be correctly expressed, all semblance of absolute opposition must, of itself, disappear. We have, therefore, to seek for some point in which they both unite; in which Nature assumes a Religious Aspect, as plainly as Revelation presents itself as a matter of Fact! Hence, that which reveals the "Supreme Being" and thus mediates between both the Fematrix and Humankind, is the Logos, or Created Word, which proceeds from the essence of Deity! And for the Caucasians Race; it's the "Holy Valorous," its Social, Cultural and Religious Instructions. Instructions: effected by "Direct Revelation" through the Alpha's: Spiritual Encounter. Hence, it is that the active revealing power in Nature, and the historically revealing elements in Religion, having one and the same principle. Revelation: properly so called, is distinguished in Scripture into Revelation by Word, and Revelation by Act– the Act, or Spiritual Insight, representing and expressing, in the world of sense, what the Word, or knowledge communicates, expresses in the world of thought: the former being to the ordinary law of Nature, what the latter is to the light of Reason. Therefore, in one point of time, and in one form of life, both these elements have found their perfect union. Yes, both have been united in The Holy "Valorous" the "Eternal Word" by the spirituality of our Fematrix- "Caucasia," who is the subject Miracle and Holy Inspiration of the Creative and Animating Voice of the "Alpha," bringing the Light of Truthful Revelation, dispelling the darkness of the world.

The Caucasian City State

(civilizations)

The growth of the Neolithic settlements in Europe were matched by the growth of similar settlements in the Middle and Near East, and by 7,000 BC, in addition to such towns as Jericho in Palestine and Anatolia in Turkey, a major city, Catal Huyuk, was built. By 5,000 BC, all over Europe, the Near East and Middle East, farming villages were established upon which the non-food producing professions could be built. The growth of the Neolithic age laid the foundation for the next great leap in Caucasian history, the creation of Caucasian civilization. The creation of a system of literacy and civil law established a formal social contract between the individuals making up the communities, the city state.

Civilization
(the Caucasian golden age of city states:5,000 BC to AD 100)

Celtianians, Germanians, Baltannians, Slavannians, Aryans, Sumerians, Tocharians, Ubaidians, Indo-Aryans, Cretans, Trojans, Egyptians, Mycenaeans, Akkadians, Dorians, Corinthians, Spartans, Etruscans, Romans, Carthaginians, Babylonians, Phoenicians, Athenians, Guanchians, Assyrians, Mesopotamians, Judaians, Persians, Macedonians, Scandinavians, Brittianians, Arabians, Chaldeans, Hittites, Philistines, Kassites, Medeans, Scythians, and Chaldeans: Are just some of the many *Caucasian Tribes* that established some of the first and greatest city states throughout the world.

Although many have been defeated by time and war, their legacy is still to be found in the *Laws, Cultures*, and *Histories* of all modern day Caucasian states.

They are our- Ancestral Trust!

What is meant by *Civilization?* One of the better definitions comes from a great Caucasian patriot, Arthur Kemp, whose great truth is here quoted: Many definitions of civilization are subjective in nature, classifying nations by technological advances or other narrow factors. Civilization should be taken to mean the entire gambit of social and cultural manifestations that are characteristic to any particular nation or racial group. It is therefore possible to talk of a Japanese civilization, an American Indian civilization, a Polynesian civilization, an Australian Aboriginal civilization, a Negroid civilization, a Caucasoid civilization, and a Mongoloid civilization, without being subjective about any of them as to their existence.

Alpha And Omega
(the rise and fall of civilizations)

When reviewing the historical development of all nations, quite often mention is made of a rise and fall of particular civilizations. This, then, poses a major question: Why do Japan, Sweden, England, and Germany (as examples), all nations with limited natural resources, still have progressive, active cultures after more than 2,000 years, and then why did such mighty nations as Rome, Greece, Persia, and India, among others, produce active vibrant civilizations for a few centuries, and then fall, never to rise again? Politically correct historians blame the rise and fall of great nations of the past on politics, economics, morals, lawlessness, debt, environment, and a host of other superficial reasons; however, Japan, England, Sweden, and Germany have gone through crises of these nature scores of times, without those countries falling into decay.

It is obvious that there must be some other factor at work, something much more fundamental than just a dip in politics, morals, lawlessness, or any of the other hundreds of reasons that historians have attempted to dream up.

An Intellectual Reasoning

(each society, unique to each people)

Herein lies the key to understanding the rise and fall of all civilizations, no matter where they are or who they are. In any given territory, the people making up the society in that territory create a culture that is unique to themselves.

A society or civilization is only a reflection of the population of that particular territory. For example, the Caucasian civilization is a product of the Caucasian people and is a reflection of the makeup of the population living in Europe.

The Caucasian civilization is unique to the Caucasian people. They made it, and it reflects their values and norms.

As the Caucasian people made the Caucasian civilization, it logically follows that the Caucasian culture would disappear if the Caucasian people were to disappear.

Currently the overwhelming majority of Caucasian people live in Europe, creating the Caucasian civilization in that land. If, however, Australian Aborigines had to immigrate into Europe in the millions, and the Caucasian population had to dramatically reduce in numbers, and then in a few years the character of Caucasian civilization would change to reflect the new inhabitants of the territory.

In other words, the society or civilization of the territory would then reflect the fact that the majority of inhabitants were now Aborigines rather than Caucasian people.

If Europe had to fill up with Aborigines, this would mean the end of Caucasian civilization. Aborigines would create a new civilization that would reflect themselves and not that of the Caucasian people.

That this should happen is actually perfectly logical.

It has nothing to do with which "Culture" is more advanced or any notions of superiority or inferiority; it is merely a reflection of the fact that a "Civilization" is a product of the nature of the "People" who make up the population in that territory.

To go back to the Caucasian example, if all Caucasian people on earth had to disappear tomorrow, then fairly obviously, Caucasian civilization and culture would disappear with them. It is exactly this startlingly obvious principle that determines the creation and dissolution of civilizations.

Once the people who create a certain society or civilization disappear, then that society or civilization will disappear with them.

If the vanished population is replaced by different people, then a new society or culture is created, a society that reflects the culture and civilization of the new inhabitants of that region, whether good or bad, progressive or regressive.

There are numerous examples of this process at work throughout the Caucasian world. There are those that are familiar to all of us, such as the collapse of the alien emigration system, both in Europe and the United States.

The great shift in the North American and European alien emigration policy will reflect the fact that by the *Year-2075*, the majority of Caucasians, both in *Europe* and *North America*, for all practical purposes will have disappeared?

This effect, the displacement of Caucasian Americans and Europeans and the subsequent disappearance of their civilization, will have a direct implications in racial terms. So the rise and fall of any particular civilization can therefore be traced not by the economics, morals, etc, of a particular civilization, but rather by the actual *Racial Presence* of the people themselves. If the society that has produced a particular civilization stays intact as a racially homogeneous unit, then that civilization will remain active and prosperous. If, however, the society within any particular given area changes its *Racial Makeup*, through invasion, immigration, or any decline in numbers, then that civilization they produced will disappear with them, to be replaced by a civilization that reflects the norms of the *New Racial Inhabitants* of that territory.

The Alpha view: Of all the sins that can be put upon a race of people, none are more detrimental in its quest for survival then an ideology of- Passive Assent!…a docility, a readiness or willingness to yield to the hostel wishes of -Alien Others without protest? As there is in law, so to is there also a Promissory Estoppel in biology, a living organism is brought into the world with an implying promise stating the terms by which its Inherited Contract (its D-N-A life strategy!) will be fulfilled. And if for any reason an organism fails to understand its- Life Contract?...it is an indication that something is likely going to happen to it!...and that something is always-Extinction!...and for the record: more then- 99% of all the Species and Subspecies that have ever existed on our celestial body are now extinct!- in other words, in our world of "Competitive Predation"(we know no other!) It can now be said, without any sense of ambiguity, that the "Extinction" of "unvigilant" life forms, is quite common! Therefore, the principle of our "Caucasian Racial Effort" is lost sight of, and instead of laying hold of life's Truths that are in evidence all around us and permitting those Truths to carry us to the heights of a greater understanding of our Caucasian Racial Dynasty and its Destany, we

*have defied them?...and they have now become forces of our destruction!
Hence, the development of our Caucasian self-confidence starts with the
elimination of this demon called "Racial Equality" and this demon is
getting into close quarters!...Political, Cultural, and Economical...yes!
we must put this demon to flight!...for if we do not? It will be to our own
detriment and that of our children's future.*

-Into The Darkness-
(the plight of the Caucasians)

The Alpha tells us: it is the *21st* century, and *Liberal Zealotry* (equality
virus!) as previously stated has become the Caucasian worlds *Deadliest
Pathogen,* an intellectual virus so infectious that the producing agent-
Liberal Academia has itself become infected losing all its ability to prevent
the virus from distorting not only its *Racial Understanding*, but now, their
own cognitive ability to reason?

The *Equality Virus* and its *Effects*: it has now become apparent that the
Caucasian World Community is now under direct attack by *Alien Races*
(non Caucasians!) who have discovered a "Psychological Weapon" that can
alter the ego-mindset of *Caucasian Intellectualism* (the mental pathogen-
Equality?) who's mystical basis (utopia- we are all the same?) can be used
to inflect very high degrees of "Moral Guilt" (*racism-hatred-slavery?*)
weakening and defeating liberality's good common sence, and once a *Person*
or *Group* becomes infected a pattern of *Self Oppression* (pathological guilt!)
develops that is excessive and systemic, a form of *Delusional* alien racial
appeasement. (the collapse of reality!)

Where the liberal sence of *Truth* is turned inside-out?...were the obvious
is shunned, truth no longer speaks, and reason has lost its way.

Therefore, we Caucasians who remain in the light of our historical reason,
and its hold on a superior conviction, a belief in our distinct *Caucasian
Racialness* and its evidence of natures intention: "Survival of the Fittest" (a
life strategy!) must wage "War" against this alien racial absurdity if we are
to be successful in freeing our *Liberal Brothers* and *Sisters* from this deadly
"Equality" pathogen.

The
Sovereign Supremacy

"Caucasian Racial Survival"

It is the *21st* century, and for same 40 thousand years the race of people known as the Caucasian have endured the *Trials*, *Hardships* and *Assaults* of life's coliseum, always *Engaging*, always *Risking*, always *Exploring.* But never, ever yielding, surrendering, or relinquishing their destiny!

The Alpha tells us: that *Life's Colosseum* is not by chance!...but by "Fematrix" design?...yes, it is a multidimentional arena?...that creates both *Winners* and *Losers*, and only the *"Winners"* advance to the next dimension.

For you see, her daughters and their males compete on all levels, displaying before her the fullest extent of their *Ability*, *Value* and *Worth*?... hundreds of millions and their life strategies have competed and perished in their bid to create her future! (all dead ends?)

All having failed the Competitive right of passage through which all of us, and all that we would be, must travel. Our world (*21st* century!) is plagued by greater and greater divisions within not only all the *Nations* of the world, but far more by the three remaining *Races* of humanity, they are all in a hostile state of total- *Political*, *Economical*, and *Cultural Competition!*.. and the level of *Conflict* between them is higher than ever, and they have now: (all three race's) *Internalized* their hostility for each other in their every day lives. This is Nature's way of telling us (the three races!) that it is time for our *Separation*!..time to *Evolve*!..time to go our own separate way's, we are not, and have never been- *Socially Compatible!*

Our separate destiny's await us?...and if we fail to understand this by not dividing "Civilly" into separate racial states!..none will escape the outcome?..for as we should all be aware!- in life's coliseum there can only be one winner!

The Alpha's view: As Separate and Distinct groups of life mature, so does their Talents and Ambitions, not to mention their lack of tolerance

and distain for their relative Competitors? And this also applies to the three Human Subspecies (races!) Negroids, Mongoloids and Caucasoid being no exception in this biological equation. In fact, these three now find themselves at each others hostile and vengeful antagonism, do to their failed experiment in "Racial Equality? (the fallacy of equal racial outcomes?) This of course is a vital lesson for those who think they can rewrite the rules of life?...and, like all those before them, and all those yet to come, the rules will forever prevail!...identify and contain your enemies, and if need be, defeat them!..or be destroyed by their hand.

- Science -

(systemizing principle knowledge)

Science is of culture, and culture is a product of racial cognizance, which determines the nature or principle of that which is being observed or studied. Of all the great sciences, *Mathematics* has been found to be the fulcrum upon which all the others must rely. It is the validating utensil of all truth!

The beginning of Caucasian science was the first step into the light of discovery for the Caucasian people in particular and for the rest of humankind in general. It was and still is the Caucasian people's inquisitive intellect, their biological cognizance, which gave rise to the understanding of the *Living Universe* and all that it encompasses.

The achievements of the *Caucasian Intellect* need not be discovered, for they are for all practical purposes the very bedrock of all known *World History* and *Science*! The *Caucasian Pathfinder*, (Caucasian scientist) from the archeological finding of the first humans, to the education of the masses, and on to the secrets of - *Interstellar Space*, the Caucasian scientist has created a vast reservoir of knowledge and has pioneered the creation of technological institutes to develop and apply that knowledge for the benefit of all humankind.

We Caucasians have unprecedented access to the best that survives of everything Caucasian, and in every cultural achievement over the past ten thousand years, and we as a people retain the conditions for continued great accomplishments and vast new- *Terra Incognita* to explore.

The structure of the Caucasian scientific method is self-renewing, certainly in its constant creation of important new tools and crafts, but also in its refinement of relentless reexamination of its principles.

The Arts
(human metaphysical excellence)

Access to transcendental goods has most of its effect on the enduring quality of- Art. Where artists do not have coherent ideals of beauty, the work tends to be *Sterile*. Where they do not have coherent ideals of good, the work tends to be *Vulgar*. Lacking direct access to beauty or good, the work tends to be *Shallow*, the accomplishments in the arts that are *Sterile*, *Vulgar* and *Shallow*...will not endure! *Charles Murray*.

Age Of The Caucasians

(a biological-Dynasty having no equal in this world!)

"Intellectual Conquest"
(the elixir of all life!)

The Alpha tells us: It is the- *Caucasian Century 421Ac,* and in the attestation of the truth and origin of the facts on which the Caucasian world community relies, no more convincing proof can be alleged than the endurance of such *Trials* and *Triumphs* thus achieved in 40 thousand years of their existing- *Dynasty!*

The proof, too, is one of which *Caucasian Apologists* (liberal zealots!) in every age have not been slow to avail themselves. But, the *Alpha's* argument should not pause here. It exhibits his belief in the sacred character and inspiration of the Holy Valorous, (Caucasian scripture!) no less than in the truth and historical origin of its contents.

The course of our inquire respecting the *Inspiration* of the Holy Valorous has brought us to the examination of the- *Caucasian World Dynasty* - itself. We have now to seek for the intimations given by the *Alpha,* as to the nature of the influence by which it was actuated. On such evidence we are entitled to assume the- *Genuineness*, the- *Authenticity*, and the- *Perfect Truthfulness* of the book to which the name of Holy Valorous has been assigned. Therefore, we regard the sacred book, in the first instance, as historical documents drawn up by the *Alpha* whose honesty and truthfulness rest upon the ordinary grounds of human belief, and whose qualifications are further attested by that *Society*, to whose charge the writings which he composed have confessedly been committed. Still less, can any objection be made to his drawing inferences as to the nature of the influence under which the Holy Valorous was composed, from the phenomena which its pages present to view, or its contents record.

Such a process of reasoning is as sound as it is philosophical.

Therefore, being convinced of the authority of the Holy Valorous, that its doctrines are revealed, and that its facts are true, we can feel no scruple in admitting as accurate the character which its own author the *Alpha,* ascribes to it.

A Billion Years Of Life
(a billion life forms that failed!)

The Alpha tells us: Yes!...its true, life has existed on our planet for more than a "Billion Years" and whether we like it or not- 99% no longer exist, and it is a fact the we- (humankind!) should not ignore. Therefore, the obvious question for all of us is- *What Happened To Them?*...and the answer is straight forward, plain and simple- they were *Defeated!*...Yes, defeated by their own bio-mandate (life-strategy!) with an evolutionary acquired- *Dead End?*

It is needless to inquire to what extent we are to look upon such conclusions as the result of a false conception of life, or how far it may be traced to certain dogmatic points of view on religion, it is more to our purpose to examine whether such sentiments have any foundation, and, if not, to expose their falsehood. Let us then examine, in the first place, under what aspect the Human Race is presented to us in their true life giving position?...and inquire, secondly, whether a comparison of the three remaining *Subracial Divisions*: –*Negroid*, *Mongoloid* and *Caucasoid,* last of the *Homo-Sapient* species offers such analogies, as may justify maintaining our *Partnership* for a foreseeable future?- or is it better for us!...that we depart to our own *Separate Destinies*?

It is not forgotten that the Caucasian people themselves, their history, their rituals, their world conquest, all present one grand understanding of their- *Biological Dynasty!* From what has just been said, it will appear that the character of the 𝔄*lpha's* influence, under which the "𝕳oly 𝖁alorous" has been composed, is absolutely unique, and a great deal different from all those assisting the progressive "Cabal" of -*Alien* and *Caucasian Subversives*.

The *Inspiration* of the 𝕳oly 𝖁alorous is altogether both *Objective* and *Subjective,* and directed to the *Moral* and *Ethical* improvement of the Caucasian individual, (Subjective!) and the survival of their- *Biological Racial Dynasty.* (Objective!) Therefore, the Caucasian sacred narrative - the *Survival* of our *Biological Dynasty* decides the question: "When will we as "Caucasians" come to our own defense?...and counter all those who seek our demise!

Such failings are generally noticed, as we should say, in the most cursory manner. The sinful act is dwelt upon, and the violation of our "Caucasian wellbeing" and the degeneracy of its defense is the deepest root of evil cultivated by our representative leadership.

Have these leaders no obligation? Has their mode of life bereaved them of the common *Sympathies* and *Sensibilities* of their Caucasian loyalty? Nay, when we bear in mind that so many astonishing "Alien Assaults" are now being committed against the "Caucasian American People," as well to mention the Caucasian world Community, which is highly credible and fully conforms to any inquirer. When we read these accounts, so *Troubling* and *Distressing*, of the various disclosures which the 𝔄*lpha* has brought into the light!...we naturally expect, to find information on the matter in the pages of the daily press? But, the "Very Reverse" is more the case, and, were the Holy Valorous altogether silent upon this disturbing and depraved subject of: Alien Cultural *Sedition!*...and Caucasian Liberal Zealot- *Subterfuge!* We can easily picture to ourselves the use which would be made of such "Facts" if they were committed against the wellbeing of the very same people who are now *Deeply Involved* and *Committed* to the destruction of "Caucasian America" and its racial identity!..is this not so? This truth, indeed does no more than apply the general principle laid down by the *Alpha* that we as Caucasians should not pause to consider the *Objections* which have been urged against the rendering of our right of "Racial Sovereignty" and our *Separation* and *Departure* from: *Alien Cultural Marauders* and *Caucasian Racial Nihilists.*

Furthermore, it must also be understood that the "Caucasian World Dynasty" liken to all other bio-dynasties has among its many conquests a much deeper "Intellectual Reason" and "Inquisitive Spirit" which in truth has benefited humankind far-beyond the beneficial offerings of "Alien Others" both *Passed* and *Present,* being expressed without malice to those of its wanting.

Caucasian Scripture

"Voices Of The Caucasian Age"

The *Alpha* tells us: the designation of "Sacred Writings" refers to the human recognition of those sacred compositions; which are, accordingly, elsewhere described by some as containing the ancient covenant between humans and their gods.

We are also to note how the *Alpha* unites his instructions to his beloved people and successors; and how he combines an assertion of the practical value of "Sacred Writings" with the statement of the source whence their vitality is derived: *Language, Religion, History, Science.*

Sacred Writing, he argues have power to make the wise seek salvation, and open the eyes of the skeptic, because "Scripture" in all its parts, is given by inspiration of the divine! The transformation of the whole nature of the Caucasian race has followed their higher- *Religious Ascension!* We find these Caucasian communities whose whole tone of thought and line of conduct before their racial enlightenment had remained so true to the character of "Unlearned and Ignorant Souls," changed suddenly into the courageous rivals of their *Enemies* and *Cultural Subversives* of their age.

We see them, at first restless from doubts and fettered by prejudice, now immovable in their *Racial Convictions* and alive to each new aspect of their- *Racial Truth!* Formerly timid and wavering, they now are *Fearless* and *Resolved.* Their understanding of their *Racial Deliverance* becomes a real assurance of the *Salvation* of their future.

One of the services which the 𝔄*lpha* has unconsciously rendered to the Caucasian cause is the clear light in which he has exhibited the alternatives between which we have to choose.

ℭaucasianism: to borrow the 𝔄*lphas* own description – firmly maintains the historical truth of the "Fematrix" narrative, weaving it into one consecutive, chronological arranged detail of facts; but he does not deny divine agency! ...only- Cryptic supernatural intervention.

Supernaturalism: Cryptic Gods, not of this world!...a narrative irreconcilable with the known and universal laws which govern the course of all- Existence!

ℭhe 𝔄lpha's view: the passages of "Human Scripture" which bear upon this spiritual subject may be reduced to two classes. The first class illustrates the harmony which is assumed to subsist between the "Devine" and that of "Human Intelligence;" and affords a striking confirmation of the view respecting inspiration which have been advocated in these- Discourses. The second class of passages exhibits the manner in which inspired humans claim infallible authority for their own words and writings. In the first place, the texts already quoted, and especially those from the 𝔄lpha, imply that the presence of the, Fematrix Spirit (ℭaucasia!) would abide with her chosen witnesses, bringing about a dynamic instance of Inter-dimensional Interpenetration of the Human Spirit by the Divine. It is to be inferred, therefore, that the effect produced in every such case by the Divine Spirits influence was a completely harmonious blending of human and divine intelligence, and that the result of this combination – whether we speak of the old or the new, is that distinct energy which has received the name of- Divine Inspiration! The Holy Valorous writings therefore, with reference to its inward principle, is described as given by inspiration of the "Jematrix" and thus the Caucasian people can say, this was done, that it might be fulfilled which was spoken of "Caucasia" by the Alpha. From all such passages its clear, that no line is to be drawn between the "Caucasian World Community" and the elements of - Caucasian Scripture; while the Holy Valorous itself presents the-Alpha's Revelation- to our view as it is incorporated with the reality of human life by means of "Righteous Instruction" and "Righteous Acts." The language and the conduct of the "Caucasians people" therefore, become the channels whereby "Caucasia" communicates her will; presenting, in some cases, a certain enlightenment to that will: while in others we find perfect submission to the training and the guidance of "Caucasianism." This spirited relation of the Caucasian people to the "Alpha's Revelation" that the Holy Valorous exhibits, not only under the form of external events, but also by means of dramatic "Pictures" of the inward life of the Caucasian soul; as in the "Imperial Holy Valorous" the Second Book (a family book of Caucasian-Visual History!) presenting to each of us a mirror wherein we can see reflected the emotions of the Caucasian soul, a family's "Reliquary" to their Caucasian religious faith, presenting to the gaze of all, the great journey of our Caucasian race, guided by the Omnipotent Spirit of "Caucasia" and the express statements of the- Holy Valorous itself.

The World Reckoning

"The Facing Of Unpleasant Truths"

The Alpha tells us; the *21st century,* is going to become the "Final Battle" for *Racial, Cultural*, and *Religious*- Supremacy!

Yes, more and more conflicting power is emerging form these-*Tree Combatants,* and this will come to represents an "Equality and Homogenization" enigma!...one, that the 𝔄*lpha* believes will change the course of human history forever, despite what the worlds corrupt elites would like us to believe.

It is, and should be to anyone with a modest intelligent empathy!... that the bringing together and mixing of fundamentally deferent- "Racial Groups" with deferent bio-imprinted historical norms, (values, customs, traditions and religion,) in other words an arena of Incom-patibles?...defying the common logic, that if they were meant to be together, they would have never become separate?

Therefore, "Forced Racial Mixing" (humankind!) as well as the mixing of other different life forms, is truly a vile, cruel and treacherous- *Social Experiment!*...who's only outcome is that of all-Combative Arenas: *Mayhem, Fear, Hatred, Injury, Revenge!*...all being favorable to no one.

However, make no mistake: those elites in authority who are allowing this to happen!...in the 𝔄*lpha's* eyes, are themselves responsible and must, and will be held accountable. Therefore, having expressed this understanding and the need for "Evils" demise is one thing!...but, actually bringing it to *Fruition-* is another? ...and that's when the *Caucasian Racial Spirit* is called upon!... Yes, summoned by the needs of its people, for the world and its multitudes has once again begun to move, entering a new and unpredictable future?

It is not impossible to sum up political and ideological currents in the world, and it is important to remember that *Alien Racial Groups* have been shaped by very different historical and political circumstances. And furthermore, let it be said that "Economic Systems" do not determine "Representation" and nor dose it determine "Ideologies." Rather, it is those of the latter that determines- *Economic systems*, giving rise to "Ideas" like the reorganization of world geopolitics around the engine of economic globalization "Anglo- American Finance" becoming decisive historical forces. But, make no mistake!...Alien forces, even as we criticize them, do not lack the ambition to imagine a truly dominant future?...putting aside the Caucasian model in their quest for modernity, and fresh from the escape of "Maoism" and the delirium of "Communism" the Alien will of the *21st* century has decided to creat their own path, maintaining an authoritarian political system, making it, in essence, their return to- Conquest!...with great hardship to follow.

In spite of all the differences, let's us go back to what the 𝔄*lpha* calls the-*Siege of Caucasian America?*...shaken by the retreat of its political will to repel an Alien Invasion?...and its legal system not being able to oppose it? Caucasian America is unwittingly undergoing a social trauma so immense it has lost faith in its own values, which it no longer even knows, even lacking the freedom to imagine a truly Caucasian American future.

Therefore, there must be a new Caucasian Order!- under the influence of the "𝔥oly 𝔙alorous" without being able to appose it. We must not become "𝔙ictims" of our own lack of *Identitarian Memory?* When we analyze our downfall we can only do so in terms of *Political* and *Moral* failure.

This must and will end!, however, faced with Alien cultural subversion and Caucasian liberal zealotry, we will have no choice but to call upon our spiritual racial strength, that strength from which the primordial impulsion of our "Caucasian Civilization" once surged several millennia ago, and which has continued to "Animate" the world in the Caucasian way, by the spirit of its *Homeric* thinking!..for we are in possession of a *Racial* and *Spiritual Heritage* that has nothing to envy in those of other racial civilizations. To this massive crisis of - *Caucasian Racial Nihilism,* in America and throughout the world, we as Caucasians must provide our own answers. Caucasians exist only by what distinguishes them; *Race, Clan, Lineage, History, Culture,* and *Tradition.* There are no universal answers to the question of existence and behavior. Every civilization has its *Truths* and its *Religions,* all respectable so long as they do not threaten our existence, every racial civilization creates its own answers, without which the individual, man or woman, lacking identity, is thrown into a world of chaos!...for like plants, humankind cannot exist without roots!...and every individual must discover their own.

One's racial "Identity" after all, is the very *Irreducible,* begetter present and active in every single one of us, the impelling force producing the whole visible world of us and them?...for, it is "Identity" that guides the will to live.

This is our truth, this is our reality!

"Caucasians"

〜

-Our Time has Come-
-We Must Evolve-

"Renounce The Ruse Of Equality"

"Caucasian Imperialism"

〜

(Our Rightful Future)

The Alpha tells us: we the Caucasians are the products of a will!... and her name is "Caucasia" (our Fematrix!) and she always wills only one thing: "Life."

And why?..you may ask: because it afforded those of her (the Elementals!) a form through which "Dimensions" could be breached? (life in form!) This understanding of which, has already been discussed, needs no further light, thereby giving us a clear path to the list of *Demands* and *Questions* of our future?

The First-Demand: is that all those of the- *Caucasian Racial Dynasty!* (regardless of their religious faith!) declare their political allegiance and fidelity to their "Caucasian Racial Identity"and its historical journey.

The First-Question: how do we, the Caucasians, free our-selves from the "Racial Quagmire" our bad judgment has put us in?...and with a desire to be reasonable and a willingness for an honorable outcome. We as Caucasians must accept no apologies on the ground that neglect of it was unavoidable, or that the reason for neglect was noble. The direct and indirect sufferings caused by non-conformity to the laws of life are the same, whatever induces the non-conformity cannot be omitted in any rational estimate of conduct. If the purpose of ethical inquiry is to establish rules of right living; and if the rules of right living are those of which the total results individual and general, direct and indirect, are most conducive to our Caucasian wellbeing; then it is absurd to ignore the immediate results and recognize only the intended results.

The Second-Demand: That all Caucasians regardless of their historical- "Culture" or "Faith!...must take part in the support and service of the Caucasian- "Democratic Racial Monarchy" (a Constitutional-Racialocracy) thereby, returning the Caucasian people and their great and noble journey of same *40* thousand years!...back on course to "Their" destiny!

Thereby: sheading all "Alien" *Cultural, Political* and *Economical* inclusion and pandering

The Second-Question: Creating the "Caucasian Empire" (our manifest destiny!) Government?...If the Caucasian world community is to have a "Representative Government" other then what has served it for the last- "Two Hundred Years" it must come to terms with the reality of *Checks* and *Balances* that cannot be *Broken*, and needs *Little* or *No Interpretation.*

The Third Demand: that every and all Caucasians having neither "Loyalty" nor "Gratitude" for their "Racial Heritage" or their "Ancestral Trust" must be completely- *Shunned!*..on the premise of their biological, intellectual and moral betrayal, by aiding and abetting "Alien Enemies" in the commission of "Subversive Criminal Acts" (Caucasian Racial Nihilism!) against the Caucasian world community.

The Third Question: Can the "Caucasian Dynasty"(a biological- rex!) continue its cultural, scientific, and moral evolution in the grip of a- *Compatriot Biological Treason?* By one's subversive promoting of- *Racial Identity Nihilism?*

The Alpha View: this social madness of "Race Mixing" by force!..was and is a "Mission Impossible," neither being sanctioned by Nature! or favored by its Reality! And we of the 21ˢᵗ century, have been stricken by Civil Racial Violence and Moral Cultural Rebellion. Therefore, with a very deeply felt conviction and a knowledge of our human history, Warfare!...on a terrible level would seem now to be the only outcome? Yes, you may ask, is there or can there be a more civilized outcome?...and as the Alpha, I must tell you, that would be a maybe!…if the combative racial groups were not so Fallacy

Entrenched, but, whether the alternative is War or Peaceful Compromise?... one thing is for sure: Total Separation of the "Racial Groups" into "Separate States" will be the ultimate outcome! Hopefully bringing an end to this unproductive social-jam, this liberal zealot racial discord, and once and for all, letting go of that Fallacious Intellectually barren idea "Equality" thereby freeing the last three human racial spirits - Negroids, Mongoloids, Caucasoids- of the biological "Homo-Sapient Dynasty," so as to fulfill their destiny, and that which is willed by their "Fematrix," to continue their separate journeys, to find their-Place!, their-Utopia!, their-Teleology! In the vast wilderness of being. (the rooted code of all life!) Yes, I know, that its easer said then don!..but, not if one understands the true nature, of that which needs to be governed! Whether human or animal the rules need to be Simple and Clear, and above all understood; to the legal mind, this would appears to be vague and ill-informed, and that is because as of now, the "Law" and its vast realm of- Legal Technicalities and Reevaluations is far beyond the average citizens ability to comprehend, and that is exactly the problem! But for now, we are going to address the structure of Government for like the law, it also has a tendency to grow out of control, and what needs to be understood, is that neither one of them is a growth industry! Therefore, having said all this, The "Caucasian Empire" is not going to be your average political "Government" and that is because it consists of both a- Sovereign State! and a- Democratic State! The truth that the ideal Government is one in which the political equilibrium is perfect, or approaches nearest to perfection, becomes, when translated into physiological language, the truth that it is one in which the appreciation of all it citizens are duly fulfilled. But it is none the less true that always some disorder results from Excess or Defect, that it influences every function, Politically and Socially, and that it constitutes a lowering of the political will for a time. Hence, the politician is one whose function many and varied in their kind, as we have seen, are all discharged in degrees duly adjusted to the political conditions that exist. And this conception of political conduct in its ultimate form implies the conception of a nature having such conduct for its spontaneous self serving outcome, the product of its normal activities. Strange as the conclusion looks, it is never the less a conclusion to be drawn, that the performance of every politician is, in a sense, a moral obligation. It is usually thought that *morality requires us only to restrain such vital activities as, in our present state, are often pushed to excess, or such as conflict with average welfare, special or general; but it also requires us to carry on these vital activities up to their normal limits. All the Moral Functions, in common with all the Righteous Functions, have, as thus understood, their imperativeness. While recognizing the fact that in our state of political transition, characterized by very imperfect adaptation of constitution of conditions, moral obligations of supreme kinds often necessitate conduct which is physically injurious; we must also recognize the fact that, considered apart from other effects, it is immoral so to treat the "Caucasian World Community" as in any way to diminish the fullness of their vitality for the benefit of "Alien" others! All this being a concept that penetrates deeply into the modern social will, bringing to mind the Political Fraud and Betrayal, by all those who declared their-Allegiance?..and their Service Solutions?.to help meet growing social needs of the people. Yes, you know them, those in the "Congress! and the "Senate!.. those persons who make their "Deals" in the shadows, filling their coffers with the funds of the public fraud, or the quick "Pro-Quo" at the expense of their constituents. Yes, a "Government" out of control, this complete "in its selfness" of things, existing outside of sight, greedily, ruthlessly, disregarding its pledge of service, as though there was no force to make it accountable? A government should not be born of Greed and Compulsion for in the end it forgets its original unity and becomes divided against itself, its houses fall upon each other. And lastly, the politician sees the whole created for his or her use but in their turn makes frightfully explicit the horror of the struggle of all against all, the division of the political will against itself, constantly, setting its teeth into its own flesh. Hence, this is the Political Creed of the modern governments of the 21st century. All of "mixed race" all in denial of life's truths, and believing that the platitudes of utopian reason (liberal zealotry!) will suffice for the yoke of equality they must bear to satisfy the ungrateful "Alien Hordes" that will in the end, devour them and their children, at their own table. Here might be urged the necessity for preluding the study of Racial Science by the study of Biological Science. Here might be dwelt on the error that "Liberal Zealots" make in thinking they can understand those special phenomena of human life with which "Racialness" deals, while paying little or no attention to the general phenomena of human life, and while utterly* *ignoring the phenomena of life at large. And, doubtless, there would be truth in the inference that such acquaintance with Kind and Identity have played in organic evolution, would help to rectify these one-sided liberal conceptions of- Racial Nihilism? (and in the Caucasian sense, racial treason!) It cannot be held, however, that the lack of racial knowledge is the sole cause, or the main cause, of their - Treason. For facts of the kind above instanced, which, duly attended to, would prevent such distortions of racial theory, are facts which it needs no intellectual inquiry to learn, but which are daily thrust before the eyes of all. The truth is, rather, that the general "Liberal Zealot" consciousness is so possessed by sentiments and ideas at variance with the conclusions necessitated by familiar evidence, that all the evidence gets no attention. Therefore, we must infer that like a purer social creed and a better "Government" a truer "Racial Ethic" belong to a more advanced social state. The science of "Racial Sovereignty" has to take account of all consequences in so far as they affect racial wellbeing, personally or socially, directly or indirectly; and by as much as it ignores any class of consequence, by so much does it fail to be a science, and to be so adjusted is to have reached the goal toward which the evolution of racial sovereignty tends.*

The
Survival And Sovereignty
Of
Our Caucasian Racial Kind

"Is Our Most Sacred Duty"

The Alpha tells us: Of all bequests of parents to children, the most valuable is a sound- *Racial Constitution*. Though a persons soul is not a property that can be inherited, yet their *Racial Constitution* may fitly be compared to an entailed *Biological Estate*; and if they rightly understand their duty to posterity, they will see that they are bound to pass on that estate uninjured if not improved. To say this is to say that he or she must be racially egoistic to the extent of satisfying all their desires associated with the due performance of their culture. Nay, it is to say more. It is to say that they must seek in due amounts the various pleasures which a true racial unified life offers. For beyond the effects these have in raising the tide of life and maintaining a *Racial Constitutional Vigor,* there is the effect they have in preserving and increasing a capacity for receiving *Racial Enlightenment* and its *Truths.*

The
Caucasian Assembly
(a summit to discuss matters of great importance!)

The Alpha tells us: The "Caucasian Assembly" when called to attend!... is the most important of all Caucasian gatherings, it is in fact, a signal of common purpose, prior to an- *Event?* or *Threat?*...to which the entire "Caucasian World Community" will be affected!

Preamble: to the "Caucasian Assembly" in the year- *2020,* a succinct by the Alpha; to bring *Clarity* and *Direction* to what he understands to be our greatest "Peril," and one in which if not acted upon with an unfaltering determination! ...will bring the Caucasians and their journey of some- *40* thousand years, to a complete End!

Our Peril!

"Caucasian Liberal Zealotry"
(an illness that induces intellectual fallacy)

Symptoms: Equality Euphoria, Caligula Moralism, Economic Socialism, Intellectual Marxism, Alien Political Inclusionism, Racial Nihilism, and

Alien Cultural Concessionism.

The 𝔄lpha tells us: it is the *21ˢᵗ* century, and the great Caucasian liberal experiment of "Race Mixing" has proven to be an absolute failure!...and this is no surprise to anyone who has the slightest understanding of "Life" and its rules of engagement when it comes to millions of years of "Biological Diplomacy," and for the record, just what was their desired end? Did they really think for one moment they could change life's demeanor for- *Predatory Engagement?*..the rule that has sustained life for millions of years?...or, the fact that "No" you cannot strip a life of its "Identity" its union of kind, for the erroneous purpose of a utopian society?...an Equality?...a social fraud, understood by all who are forced to participate.

Life's journey for "Billions" has been a journey of separate and unique unto-themselves life forms, never to be repeated, and once gone, never to be seen again!

For life determines what it is, and that of its fate, by what it does!

- 𝔗his is our truth, as it is the truth of all life! -

𝔗he
𝔠oming 𝔖truggle
(racial separation and departure!)

𝔗he 𝔄lpha tells us: there is no going back!...we as a race of people are about to evolve?...and we must see it though to the end! Yes, the time has come to shed the burden of the social fallacy "Obligation" to any other life form, other then the life form we are of!...and to whom we owe our existence, and to whom by their gifts of *Love, Sacrifice* and *Guidance* we have made our way in this world.

This our final "Evolution" will require everyone to make sacrifices.

No sacrifice is too great when it comes to the future of all our children.

There are obvious social effects of a kindred nature. Most Caucasian people now recognize the demoralization caused by indiscriminate- *Alien Charity*.

They see how in the *Alien Mendicant* there is, besides destruction of the normal relation between labor expended and benefit obtained, a genesis in the expectation of the alien mind that others shall minister to their needs; showing itself in the venting of physical assaults on those Caucasians who refuse.

Therefore, *Racial Egoism* precedes *Liberal Altruism* in order of imperativeness, is thus clearly shown. The acts which make continued life possible, must, on the average, be more peremptory than all those other acts which life makes possible, including those liberal acts which benefit alien others.

Turning from life as existing to life as evolving, we are equally shown this. Sentient beings have progressed from low to high types, under the law that superior shell profit by their "Superiority" and the inferior shell suffer from their "Inferiority." Conformity to this law has been, and is still, needful, not only for the continuance of life but for the increase of wellbeing: since the superior are those having faculties better adjusted to the requirements,.. faculties therefore, which bring in their exercise of *Greater Progress* and *Less Failure*.

More special considerations join these more general ones in showing us this truth. Such *"Racial Egoism"* as preserves a vivacious mind in a vigorous body furthers the wellbeing of descendants, whose inherited constitutions make the labors of life easier and strengthened their resolution; while, conversely, *Misery* and *Failure* is entailed on posterity by those who bequeath them constitutions injured by self-neglect. Lastly, we come upon the truth that undue *Liberal Altruism* increases *Racial Egoism* both directly in contemporaries and indirectly in posterity.

And now observe that though the general conclusion enforced by these special conclusions is at variance with nominally accepted beliefs, it is not at variance with actually accepted beliefs. While opposed to the doctrine which we are taught should be acted upon, it is in harmony with the doctrine which we do act upon and dimly see must be acted upon. For, omitting such abnormalities of conduct as are instanced above, every one, alike by deed and word, implies that in the business of life, one's being of kind!...and its welfare is the primary consideration. In other words, one's biological kind and its sovereign existence does not answer to a democracy!..one does not get to vote on it! And, above all!...one does not put themselves in the position where "Alien Races" get to vote on it? (hence, Caucasian America's liberal zealot nightmare!)

Now that moral racial injunctions are losing the authority given by their sacred origin. The *Nihilism* of racialness is becoming the new creed. Few things can happen more disastrous than the intellectual decay and moral death of a society no longer fit, before another and fitter enlightenment has grown up to replace it. Thus, between these opponents, there is an Honorable Solution: " Separate Sovereign Racial States." Both sides contemplate a coming change, which the one wishes and the other fears. As the change which promises or threatens to bring about this state, desired or dreaded, is rapidly progressing, those who believe that the changes can come about, and that it must come about, are called on to do something in pursuance of their belief.

To this more special reason I may add a more general reason. Great mischief has been done by the repellent aspect habitually given to "Racialness" by its liberal zealot expositors, and immense benefits are to be anticipated from presenting "Racialness" that attractive aspect which it has when undistorted by liberal malice and fallacy.

If a government, sternly enforcing numerous laws, some needful and some needless, adds to its severe control a behavior wholly unsympathetic; if its people have to take their pleasures by stealth, or when in need of assistance, ever meet a dismissive glance or more frequently- disrespect! This government will inevitably be disliked, if not hated, and the aim of its people will be to evade it as much as possible.

Contrariwise, a government who, equally firm in maintaining restraints needful for the well being of its people or the well being of visiting others, not only avoids needless restraints, but, giving its sanction to all legitimate grati-fications and in some cases providing the means for them, looks on at their gambols with an approving nod, can scarcely fail to gain an influence which, no less efficient for the time being, will also be permanently efficient.

The control of such two governments symbolize the control of Morality as it is, and Morality as it should be. But just as the rampant perversion of liberal *Race-Mixing* is not to be remedied by a higher moral reasoning that liberal zealots repudiate, so to, we as Caucasians need to adhere to our "Moral Racial Precepts" a society that corresponds with the "Holy Valorous" and its social doctrine of "Caucasianism" (racial sovereignty!) that gives us our *Social* and *Moral* rules of- *Direction, Action* and *Conduct.* The relation between the individual and the state, considered as representing all individuals, have to be deduced an important and relatively difficult matter.

What is the ethical warrant for government authority?

To what ends may it be legitimately exercised?

How far may it rightly be carried?

Up to what point is the citizen bound to recognize the collective decisions of other citizens, and beyond what point may he or she properly refuse to obey them?

The Alpha tells us: "Justice"..which formulates the range of conduct and limitations to conduct hence arising, is at once the most important division of *Ethics* and the division which admits of the greatest definiteness.

That principle of equivalence which meets us when we seek its roots in the laws of individual life, involves the idea of *Measure;* and on passing to social life, the same principle introduces us to the conception of equity or *Equalness,* in the relations of citizens to one another; the elements of the questions arising are *Quantitative,* and hence the solutions assume a more scientific form.

Though, having to recognize differences among individuals due to race, age, sex, or other cause, we cannot regard the members of a society as absolutely equal, and therefore cannot deal with problems growing out of their relations with that precision which absolute equality might make possible; yet, considering them as approximately equal in virtue of their common human nature, and dealing with questions of equity on this supposition, we may reach a conclusion of a sufficiently definite kind.

The division of *Races* considered under their absolute forms, has to define the equitable relations among their perfect individuals who limit one another's spheres of action by coexisting, and who achieve their ends by cooperation.

They have to do much more than this. Beyond justice between *Race* and

Race, justice between each *Race* and the aggregate of *Race* has to be dealt with by it.

You are a "Caucasian" is the right way of looking at yourself and others. Human Racialness: is a "Reality" it is our ultimate message!

- The End Game -

"Racial Separation"

The Alpha tells us: By association with *Rules* and *Laws* that cannot be obeyed, rules and laws that can be obeyed lose their authority.

Having said all this, let us now make clear our coming journey, and put to "Truth" its final outcome!...if certain things are not corrected in the Caucasian world Community?

(1) Caucasian Racial loyalty!
(2) Caucasian Cultural loyalty!
(3) Caucasian Political loyalty!
(4) Caucasian Economic loyalty!

If we Caucasians in America and throughout the world, do not stand united (one people!) against our enemies and defeat their marauding invasions, our posterity will lose their future, do to the *Cowardice* and *Incompetence* of our response, and we will deserve not pity, but contempt!

Caucasian America!...is at this very moment in the middle of an undeclared- War?...Yes, with many casualties, and No, its not in a far-off land, it is the war no one wants to see?...No one wants to know? A war created by the wishful thinking of a class of "Caucasian Americans," a cabal of intellectual elites, that has lost complete control of "Alien Cultural Subversives." The Caucasian liberal zealots: will not defend Caucasian America!...no, not now, and not in the future, they will never admit to being wrong about- Race-Mixing?...they will continue *Paying* the aliens off,...

with more *Social Programs* and greater- *Political Inclusion?*

In other words, they have betrayed us?..we are being served up to our enemies! Yes, the greater "Caucasian American Community" has been infiltrated by "Caucasian Renegades" (liberal septic-infiltrators, educational and cultural saboteurs!) who are working with a cabal of *Liberal Zealot Elites*, and *Alien- Subversives!...*they all being Committed to the *Destruction* of - Caucasian America!

There is no hope for them, "Liberal Elites," they have sold their soul to the "Aliens Subversives" for a few more years of peace?..but we, the common-*Caucasian People!..* will not be afforded that luxury, as the years go on; alien aggression will become more *Numerous* and more *Violent,* and much more resistant to *Legal Compliance* and *Civility!..*that's for shore!..it has already been incubated in- *Alien Strongholds!* throughout "Caucasian America" (sanctuary cities?) This is our truth, this is our reality!

None of us will be spared, but, we are the "Caucasians" and we will not go down without a fight, and that is also for shore! Yes, this is only one future scenario!..but, it is the one that is now in play!...and if the alien invaders from south America and around the world (in the millions!) join with the native alien subversives?..and it looks like, that could become a reality! We Caucasians may be in an all out-*Racial Civil War* in less then 20 years?... and if for any reason you think this a-fallacy? Just think for a minute on this truth: Right now, and at this time in *America* there are many "Alien Lawless Strongholds" in most, if not all of our major cities; yes, Alien Communities that are *Socially*, *Cultural* and *Morally* unaccountable?...and off limits to all Caucasians?...not because your not allowed to go there, but, because if you do, you will be come a victim of assault or much worse!

For these are by no means- *Caucasian American Neighborhoods?* they are large "Unassimilated" pockets of aliens! ..with a common bond of colonizing, not assimilating.

These are breeding grounds for- "Alien Sociopaths" and if you need a second opinion?...just ask any school teacher who was given the *Distressing* and *Impossible* task of teaching there! So, where does this live us?...one might ask, unfortunately, as of this moment: not in a good position! But, all is not lost, at least not yet?...it all depends on what we as a people do now, before the window of opportunity closes for ever!...and understand this: that window is already in its closing mode!

Therefore, this is what is proposed: first, we most creat a coalition of dedicated Caucasian *Men* and *Women* under the leadership of the "Caucasian Empire" and its-*Democratic State*, for the purpose of soliciting aid from the "Caucasian World Community" for an earnest and formal declaration: for the separation of combative "Human Races" (Subspecies!) known as- *Negroid, Mongoloid, Caucasoid-* into their own "Sovereign Racial States" giving each one their right of "Sovereignty" that is understood in juris-prudence as the full right and power of a governing body, to govern themselves without any interference from outside sources or bodies.

We need to *Separate!!*..this is absolutely and unequivocally essential! We "Caucasians" have acquired capacities for other appropriate activities and accompanying pleasures, to which "Alien Races" have shown no capacities for, and whereby "Alien Social Strategies" are not *Suited* or *Conducive* for the ways of our Caucasian Society.

Clearly major, along with many minor differences in our social, cultural and intellectual life strategies conform to the activities appropriate to our different needs as- *Sovereign Biological Entities,* which confirms our separate evolutionary modes, thereby, putting any encounter between us in a confrontational and uncooperative turbulence.(competitive opposition!) Of self-evident truths so dealt with, the one which here concerns us is an agreement of "Honorable Racial Separation" must be reached, before it can be acted upon, from this it is a corollary that the acts by which each race maintains its own "Life" must, speaking generally, precede in imperativeness all other acts of which it is capable. This is to say, the Ethics of all the races participating must recognizes the truth, recognizing that "Racialism" comes before "Altruism." The acts required for continued self-preservation, including the enjoyment of benefits achieved by such acts, are the first requisites for a *Sovereign Racial Kinds*-welfare. Therefore, under its biological survival aspect, which the 𝔄lpha has presented his proposition for "Racial Separation" cannot be, and should not be contested by those who agree in the doctrine of evolution, and as already said, the law that each "Race" of people shall take the benefits and the losses of its nature, be they those derived from ancestry or those due to self-produced modifications, has been the law under which life has evolved thus far; and it must continue to be the law, however much further life may evolve. Whatever the outcome of the- Alpha's honorable call for "Racial Separation" and its natural course of action may now or hereafter undergo, is a biological inevitable, for race mixing is an-*Unnatural State!*...and the longer it remains undone?...*Misery, Hatred* and *Violent Resistance* will prevail.

Hence, "Racial Separation" will be don through the goodwill and pleasure of all in agreement, or by "War" and the blood of patriots?...and yes, one or the other will absolutely take place! For, just as one has the right to believe in a religion, or choose not to vote for an apposing social or political idea, all under the heading of *Accepted* or *Rejected* "Association" a freedom of choice!.. which no one should be in doubt!...or hesitate to believe that this same life giving right also applies to one's biological choices in association!..for after all, it can be safely stated that one's choices (to accept or reject!) are the fundamental acts of their well being, and that of their posterity.

The Alpha's View: let us make "Reason" for life!...and not welcome death. But, if reason should fail!...then the evil twins of Violence and Death will demand an audience. And as history has often assured us: they will not be denied! Now, not only is it rational to infer that changes like those just mentioned which are fundamentally needed if our Caucasian Civilization is going to continue to be socially viable, and those who "Doubt" that Caucasian adaptation will go on is absurd. Those who lack our faith in the future evolution of "Caucasian Civilization" as shall harmonize its nature with its conditions, adds but another to the countless liberal zealot illustration of inadequate consciousness of causation. (we the "Caucasians" will prevail!)

The relations of this work prior to the works preceding it in the book are such as to involve frequent reference Containing as it does, the outcome of racial principles set forth in each of them, I have found it impracticable to dispense with restatements of those racial principles.

Further, the presentation of them in their relations to different ethical racial theories, has made it needful, in every case, briefly to remind one and all Caucasian readers of the "Truth" of what they are, and how they are derived. Those who have followed with assent the 𝕬lpha's recent course of thought, do not need telling that throughout past eras, "life," vast in amount and varied in kind, which has over-spread the earth, has progressed in subordination to the law that every individual shall gain by whatever aptitude it has for fulfilling the conditions to its existence. As exhibited in past chapters, the compromise between the claims of the Caucasian social world and the claims of Alien others seems to imply a permanent antagonism between the two. The pursuit by each of their own wellbeing while paying due regard to the wellbeing of their fellow humanity, apparently necessitates the ever-recurring question- How far must the one end be sought, and how far the other: suggesting, if not discord in the life of each, still, an absence of complete understanding.

This is not the inevitable inference, however. When in the principle of "Racialness," the phenomena of "Race-Maintenance" among living things at large are discussed, the development of its domestic relations might be the better understood, it has been shown that during evolution there has been going on a "Conciliation" between the interests of the *Races,* the interests of the *Parents,* and the interests of the *Offspring.*

Proof is given that as we Caucasians ascend from the lower form of social life (rule by brutality!) to the highest (rule by empathy!) our race-maintenance is achieved with a decreasing sacrifice of life.

We saw this, with the very progress of our "Caucasian Civilization," and the alike changes among alien others; that the highest domestic relations are those in which the conciliation of welfare within the family become greatest, while the welfare of the society is best subserved. Here it has been shown that a kindred conciliation has been, and is, taking place between the interests of each Caucasian citizen and the interests of Caucasian citizens at large; tending ever toward a state in which the two become merged in to one, and in which the feelings answering to them respectively, fall into complete racial concord.

We the Caucasian race of people (a biological dynasty with a living mandate!) must take everything history has to offer in order to see the present clearly and properly anticipate the future. We cannot ignore the history of events.

It shows us that in life, the unexpected is king and that the future is often unpredictable. Therefore, concerning our "Caucasian Civilization" it seems as though we will be forced to rise up and face immense challenges and fearsome catastrophes even beyond those posed by our resent *Alien Invasion!*...but these hardships will present the opportunity for both a *Rebirth* and *Rediscovery* of our *Racial-Selves*.

And, these motions can be made to work in favor of a Caucasian world awakening as our *Spiritual*, *Cultural* and *Racial Leviathan* begins to come to our defense.

Hence, the Caucasian American order is truly in crisis, the concept of "America" rests upon the civilizational values shared by its ruling elites.

Yet since the beginning of the *21ˢᵗ* Century, this notion of shared values was brought into question by "Liberal Zealots" who were, and are!... the main "Architects" of this- "Pox," this utopian fallacy this -*Racial Equality?*...a socialism, being not a fruit of our *Caucasian Civilization*, but of its Corruption, a downward spiral leading to a widespread national catastrophe.

This of course is the actual goal of every liberal zealot both in the halls of *"Academia"* and *"Government,"* and let us not forget *"Religion"* with mystic beliefs, but historically short sighted in their own *Moral* and *Charitable* compliance concerning the cause, nature, and purpose of the universe.

On the topic of "Caucasian Racial Loyalty" what role does it play in Caucasian America?

Without falling into naïve idealism, we can note that *Racial Loyalty* was not simply a matter of birth, but also of merit. This implies not only a constant renewal, but also the transmission of a code of ethics and behavioral rigor.

The function of *Racial Loyalty,* when it is indeed worthy of the title, is to command and protect. It also serves to offer a living example of a higher ideal.

In Caucasianism, it repeatedly affirms the fact that *Racial Loyalty* can only be conceived in relation to duty, and that the service of racial loyalty and human dignity are not opposed to each other.

The Alpha's View: It is the 21ˢᵗ century: And we as the Caucasians (a Sovereign Race of People,) are now with our backs to the - Precipice of a

social, cultural and economic disaster?...and yes!...it is of our own making! We trusted and put our fate in the hands of "Liberal Zealots" not realizing that their social-stratagem of "Equality" was a Fallacy!...an evil deception, a means to gain an end!...and that end is the rebirth of "Socialism" under the new name- "Progressivism" an artifice!...an intellectual ruse, but still the purveyors of- Communism!...that age old social ideology of "Human Equality" through the elimination of free human potential, and its individual reward. In other words classless ownerless and raceless! Having said all this!..let us now face the foreseeable future? Survival!... is the final criteria for all life, there is no reasoning contrary to this truth, whether "Human" or "Animal," whether in the Past or the Future! Therefore, as the Alpha, I am dedicated to the truths of my age, and all it represents to my- Race!, and my reason for living, this is what I see:...a great unavoidable- "Racial War" is beginning to gather, and its encounter will call for our- Caucasian Dynamic Behavior!...(racial loyalty!) This coming war!...will never be forgotten, and neither will the Caucasian heroes who will fought it, and therefore, one must understand this: there will be no neutral ground.

"So Say We All"

Calibrating Who We Are
(the Caucasian religious and cultural calendar)

-January-

January 2 - 4 is the Perihelion (we are nearest the sun), the day we celebrate the origin (the collision), the beginning of the universe, the birth of the Cosmic Fematrix, the first solar sun, the life force.

-February-

February, the second Sunday is the celebration of the sacred and fruitful union, marriage between Caucasian men and women.

-March-
March 20 is the beginning of the Spring Equinox and the celebration of the reincarnation of the self through the birth (children), the sacred journey.

-April-
April is Caucasian History Month, celebrating Caucasian racial and ethnic pride and giving tribute to our educational and cultural achievements.

-May-
May, the second Sunday, is the celebration of the Creation by the Cosmic Fematrix of our Holy Terrestrial Globe, the Earth

- June -
June, 20 - 21, the beginning of the Summer Solstice, is the celebration of the bio-life force, the *Biological Fematrix.* (femaleness).

- July -
July 3-7 is the Aphelion (we are farthest from the sun) the day we celebrate the Full Radiance of the Caucasian female, our life force (Caucasian Fematrix), creator of the Caucasian race.

-August-
August, the second Sunday is the celebration of the Caucasian Male and his great contribution and sacrifice to race, nation, and family (the Sacrificial Flesh).

-September-
September 22 - 23 is the beginning of the *Fall Equinox* and the Caucasian dedication to racial and cultural survival (repledging our Caucasian racial vows).

- October-

October, the second Sunday is the recognition of Caucasian Heritage, our Ancestral Trust, and the honoring of loved ones who have passed.

-November-

November 24 is the celebration of Thanksgiving for Caucasian America, its health and survival.

- December-

December 21-22 is the beginning of the Winter Solstice, honoring the contributions of all Caucasian religions and the Caucasian international family.

-The Exchange-
(life's eternal act!)

The Alpha tells us: That all of life, has but one *Mandate?*..and that is *Survival!* And this survival has a fundamental "Strategy" with four under-standings-*Need, Encounter, Exchange,* and *Form.*

And of "Exchange" there are two, *Predatory* exchange, (no-compromise!) and *Reciprocal* exchange. (a desire permitting both to exist!) Therefore, whether one is *Human* or *Animal?*...where there is *Need*, there is *Encounter*, and where there is encounter, there is *Exchange*, and on the "Outcome" of exchange, "Life" will take its- *Form!*

We Caucasians directly and within reasoning, that the in-itself of our own manifestation is also that of others, therefore, the will to live, which constitutes the inner nature of the *Exchange-* lives in all, and we find the *Exchange* (in the widest sense of the word) occupied with the explanation of the living phenomena in the world. For it explains itself by something still more unknown than it is, itself; by laws of nature, resting upon forces of nature, to which the power of life also belongs.(the fematrix!) Hence, It is rather the case that the greatest advances of the *Exchange* will make the need of the *Exchange* even more felt. The task of the *Exchange* is certainly the outcome of its particular experience, and the correct explanation of its experience as a whole. Therefore, humankind, like that of all, carries within them the "Exchange" and this is accessible to them in the most immediate manner; so it is only here that they can hope to find the key to the mystery's of the world and gain a clue to the nature of all things. Thus, the special province of the "Exchange" certainly lies in what has been called its analytical principle- *Mental Reasoning* on the subject of life's eternal "Conflict" comprised of different life forms and their- *Opposing Life Strategies!*...all in accordance with the survival of one's own kind! (one's biological mandate.)

The
"Nemesis Gauntlet"

Life's Affliction

{-Need-}

Needs Affliction

{-Encounter-}

Encounters Affliction

{-Decision-}

Decisions Affliction

{-Outcome-}

Outcomes Affliction

{-Reality-}

The Alpha tells us: If one is to ever understand their place in "Life" (the Biological Cosmos) one must first in the broadest sense cover a variety of very difficult approaches: *Religious, Philosophy, Science.* All having a common attempt to understand the implicit order within the whole of our- *Being?*

Therefore, It would behoove us to descend to a simpler plan, other than the "Cosmic Universe," one that after all is of us and by us, our own- *Bio-Universe,* that which holds the comprehension- of who, what, and why we are?

- Immortality -
-Exemption From life's Cessation-

The Alpha tells us: "*Truth Suggestion*" is one of the most subtle and powerful principles of psychology. We are making use of it in all that we do and say and think, but unless you understand the difference between our *Negative Truth Suggestion,* and our *Positive Truth Suggestion,* you may be using it in such a way that it is bringing you defeat instead of success. Science has established the fact that, through the *Negative* use of *Truth Suggestion*, life may be extinguished!

This principle applies to and controls every sense impression that is lodged in the human mind, this is a point that I would stress with all the power at my commend.

It is a point that I repeat over and over again in teaching the Holy Valorous, for it is not so much the *Truth* you say, as it is the *Tone* and *Manner* in which you say it!

It naturally follows, therefore, that sincerity of purpose, honesty, and earnestness must be placed back of all *Truth* that one says, if one would make a lasting and favorable understanding.

One cannot successfully teach others, without first successfully teaching one's self! And what!..dos all of this have to do with "Immortality" one may ask? Alas, If you would plant a deep suggestion of "Immortality" and mix it generously with enthusiastic "Truth" the understanding of its fruition will be made clear, for "Immortality" is the "Elixir" of all life, it's why were here in this Dimension!...its in the "Biological" arena, the proving grounds so to speak, for the human mind is a marvelous piece of machinery!..and that's where the true answer for "Immortality" lies, not in the product per se, but that which desires or needs the product?

Hence. It stand to reason if two living bio-constructs exist, and they are related, but one lives and function a great deal longer then the other, and it is consistent?...then the deficiency lies not with the product, but that which created it!...its cognizant life strategy.(the mind!) For all of life's choices are calculated solutions to its encounters!..and likewise determining its functional and physical form. In other words, the fruition of our "Caucasian Immortality," unequivocally lies with in our own "Intellectual" capacity and competency.

- 𝔉ailure -

⌁

(Teaching the needed lesson!)

𝔗he 𝔄lpha tells us: Neither temporary defeat (unforeseen occurrence!) nor an intellectual misconception, amounts to failure in the mind of *He* or *She* who looks upon it as an important moment in one's determination, an "Enlightenment" so to speak, that has taught us a needed lesson.

Every "Defeat" every "Reverse" usually teaches us a valuable lesson that could be learned in no other way. And just remember that many of the greatest Caucasians in all of history were the products of their own *Determination!*..and Determination you know, is born in the grip of- *Adversity!*

"𝔚e 𝔄re 𝔗he 𝔠aucasians"
"𝔑one 𝔖hell 𝔅reak 𝔉aith, 𝔖o 𝔖ay 𝔚e 𝔄ll"

𝔗he
𝔠aucasian 𝔠ontinuum

⌁

-𝔗he 𝔉uture-

𝔗he world we know is fueled by the competition of unequal forces; it is the lifeblood of evolution. One does not seek to become equal with another, one seeks to become better than the other, and this is the true pulse of life. There are those who would try to make a case for the pursuit of equality, and because of their political cowardice and intellectual poverty, these political sultans and their utopian scientists have set out to dislocate the universe. But it will be a futile effort, for the road they take leads to the wasteland of political and social fallacy, the final resting place of fools.

The world is now under great strains to support its billions of people, out of this immense number, more than two thirds are on or below the poverty level.

Add to this more than 500 different languages, over 1,000 different cultural societies, not to mention five major and a dozen minor religions.

And if this is not enough to overwhelm an intelligent mind, you should think of this: All the world's wealth, and all the world's hopes and dreams are in the hands of less than-1,000 people? Therefore, we are left with this simple observation: The only conceivable equality in all of life, is the sheer fact that we are all- *Equally, ..Unequal!* Hence, the time has come for Caucasian men and women of substance, Caucasian men and women of courage, to speak the truth, and to "Hades" with the liberal *Moral Fallacies* that have entombed our social and political thoughts.

The three races of humankind are on a collision course of great proportion and magnitude, and I am sorry to say, of all the places that will engage in *Racial War*, it will have its greatest physical climax in Caucasian America.

The Social breakdown and racial nightmare that is new engulfing America cannot be denied, and it has become now, even to the most casual observer, socially and politically irreversible. Religion cannot stop it!

The government cannot control it! The liberal zealots have failed and are now themselves casualties of their own utopian meltdown. There are two words chiseled on the altar of biological survival: *Advantage* (domination) and *Disadvantage* (subjugation), and it is without a doubt the understanding of these two life forces, the *Positive* position, and the *Negative* position, that determine the destiny of all life.

This is an eternal truth.

The Caucasian race is about to pass through one of the darkest periods in its history, and may even prove to be the most tragic period of all. The raped development of the material side of the Caucasian world left little time for the true and real problems of- *Racial Conflict*, two different paths may eventually lead to the true comprehension of our *Racialness.* The first is- *Racial Revelation*, a direct spiritual road, but, its closed to a great many people and is independent of our every day thought, though those who are in touch and can make use of it are fortunate. The second, on the contrary, is strictly agreeable and scientific. It considers race as one of the *Elements* of the whole, the universe of kind, and it studies this racial element as a function of the external world. This is why I say that in order to really understand the "Racial Phenomenon" we should know not only its *Objective* (external) cause, but also the relation that binds it to the *Subjective* (biological, psychological) phenomena that accompany it. This is a course that should be pursued by all Caucasian men and women of intellect.

There is no other way toward *Racial-Solidarity* but the search and respect for individual dignity. (self-identity!

If you as a Caucasian were bold enough to extrapolate at long range on the basis of the ideas expounded in this book, you might say that in prudent words, everything takes place as if the descent of the material universe toward an inert chaos and annihilation are in fact compensated by the simultaneous ascent of an imponderable life force, that of the- *Caucasian Racial Spirit*, whose harmony and perfection would endure and rise from the competitive organic world. The destiny of the Caucasian race is not limited to its existence on earth, and we as Caucasians!...must never forget that fact, for "Outer Space" is the final physical frontier, and it is there "Outer Space" where the Caucasians are looking! Once again, we are gathering our ships and crews to set sail into the unknown.

Once again, the great wilderness beckons us to come and seek its treasures and its mysteries. Let every Caucasian man, woman, and child remember that the destiny of our race is incomparable, and that it depends greatly on our will to collaborate in the transcendent task.

Let us remember that the law is and has always been to *Struggle*, and the *Fight* has lost nothing of its *Violence*.

Let our own dignity, our nobility as Caucasian racial beings emerge from our efforts to liberate ourselves from our *Enemies* and to obey our deepest aspirations. And above all, never forget that the divine spirit of our *Fematrix* (𝕮aucasia!) is in us, and guiding our race.

If this is not in reality a prayer; it is a creed, a creed that, by expressing faith in the dignity of our race, addresses itself beyond itself to the great entity from which we have received it, our *Fematrix!* (the Caucasian female will!)

The time has come for the races, as well as individuals, to know what they want. If the races of humanity want peace, they must understand that the problem must be and can be approached basically. To attain this, there is only one method, which is to reestablish the path of historic truth and the path of individual racial dignity. We as Caucasians are now close to the end of our great journey in the *Caucasian Continuum*.

As the *Alpha*, I never thought, that the guiding thread, I have suggested would explain everything or that it would be our final definitive.

It only represents, in my mind, a step in the direction of truth, which may never be attained by some. But I firmly believe that no progress will be made unless the ultimate solution is sought in the extrusion and understanding of the concept of "Fematrix Racial Theology" to the whole of life, including *"Humankind"* and their intellectual and moral development. Some readers may have been surprised and even shocked by the fact that this *Fematrix Racial Theology* has been extended to the *Moral* and *Spiritual* realm, but this was entirely logical.

Indeed, as we are led to accept the facts of- *Racialism*, in which to be in a bio-racial group is to be in unison with the creation and its life force, the *Fematrix*. (female will!)

Evidently this *Fematrix Racial Theology*, some will say, is based on a declared postulate; (racial fundamentalism) however, this postulate seems to me to be the only one that gives humankind a reason for existence and attributes a definite significance to our lives.

Therefore it is scientifically useful, and it throws light on many previously obscure social problems. Finally it has the further advantage of linking the Caucasian biological mandate and it inner activities to evolution as a whole, and thus rationalizing *"Caucasianism"* and its spiritual support.

-Racialism -V- Altruism-

The Alpha tells us: If insistence on them tends to unsettle established systems of belief, self-evident truths are by most people silently passed over; or else there is a tacit refusal to draw from them the most obvious of inferences.

Therefore of self-evident truths so dealt with, the one which here concerns us is that- *a being must live before it can act!* From this it is a corollary that the acts by which each maintains his or her own life must, speaking generally, precedes in imperativeness the acts which maintain life; and if this, accepted as a general law of conduct, is conformed to by all, then by postponing the acts which maintain life to the other acts which make life possible, all must loss their lives!

That is to say, "Our Ethics" has to recognize the truth, recognize in- *Unethical Thought?*...that "Racialism" comes before "Altruism." The acts required for continued self- preservation, including the enjoyment of benefits achieved by such acts, are the first requisites to universal welfare.

Unless each duly cares for their own bio- *Racial kind,* their care for all other kinds of life is ended by death!

This permanent supremacy of one's- "Racialism" over "Altruism," made manifest by contemplating existing life, is further made manifest by contemplating life in its course of evolution. And, those who have followed with assent the "Alpha's" recent course of thought, do not need telling that throughout past eras, that life, vast in amount and varied in kind, which has overspread the earth, has progressed in subordination to the law that every individual living thing shall gain by whatever aptitude it has for fulfilling the conditions to its existence. In the foregoing, the case on behalf of our "Racialism" and that of "Altruism" have been stated. The two conflict; and only your Caucasian ethical understanding!..have now to consider its- *Verdict!...what say you?*

Racial Collective Vision
(union of racial determination)

Strength of will, perseverance, conviction, and let us not forget, courage, these are the mental attributes that are required by a race of people if they are to survive in a world of competition against alien rival antagonists who strive for the same *Prize, Position,* or *Objective,* and usually not in accordance with any rules or goodwill?

The *Caucasian Collective Vision* (western civilization) having reached a high stage of social and cultural devel opment in language (a literate society) and by advances in the *Arts* and *Sciences,Government* etc, the modern world has come into being.

Hence, add to this- *Caucasian Racial Prime!* (bio-work ethic) that gave the human mind it greatest Possessions

Culture, *Religion*, and *Science*, the three spiritual tools of the human quest. And was it not *Caucasian Racial Prime* that gave the world, its greater humanity? And is it not our *Caucasian Racial Prime!,* that gives the world a promise for a greater future?

Furthermore, permit me as the *Alpha* to recommend that you plant in your mind the seed of a desire that is constructive by making the following your creed and the foundation of your code of ethics!

- The Caucasian Creed -

I wish to be of service and uphold my *Caucasian Racial Legacy* as I journey through life.

To do this, "I have adopted and pledged myself to this "Creed" as a guide to be followed in dealing with my fellow beings, to train myself so I never disrespect my fellow beings because of their *Race, Religion* or *Culture,* as I expect them to be respectful of mine. And, to be a loyal citizen of my *Caucasian Community,* to speak of it with praise and act always as a worthy custodian of its good name. To avoid *Hatred* in all its forms, to be honest and fair in my profession, and above all to be faithful to my sworn allegiance to my *Caucasian Ancestral Trust.*

Yes!...these truths are mine! And I align myself with them! Therefore, the time has come again, to refresh the memory of the *Nonbeliever!*...both *Alien* and *Caucasian* alike, giving to them the "Truth" of our unassailable "Caucasian Racial Dynasty," being "Unprecedented" in its continuous *Spiritual* and *Innovative Supremacy!*...thereby, the premier force of human existence, never failing to rise as "One" to the challenge of its rivals!

"So Say We All"

The
- Caucasian Trinity -

"Racial"
Loyalty - Compassion - Sacrifice

-UPHOLD THE CAUCASIAN IDEA!-

-KEEP OUR FUTURE IN OUR HANDS!-

-NEVER IMPERIL OUR POSITION!-

"Who Will Stand With Me"
John Rolland- THE ALPHA (LOC)

{- Caucasians -}

-Social and Political Guidance-

The following social *Maxims* and *Aphorisms* are the Alpha's thoughts and knowledge: All living things must create their own journey!

Therefore, it stands to reason that all journeys will sooner or later encounter many life altering Intersections!...places of *Confusion, Evaluation,* and *Decision.* The Alpha, wants all Caucasians to think of these *Maxims* and *Aphorisms* (guiding principles!) as *Road Signs* when encountering "Life's Intersections" and thereby to be considered and studied by both *Young* and *Old* throughout the Caucasian World.

There is not a truth existing which I fear or would wish unknown to the whole world- Thomas Jefferson.

This book of - Maxims and Aphorisms will be known and referred to all as- **"CAUCASIANS"**- C1, C2, C3, etc.

C1. First and foremost is the *Maintenance* of racial health.

C2. All that is, stands *Opposed* to all that would be.

C3. A race superior in patriotism, fidelity, obedience, courage, sympathy, mutual aid, and a readiness to sacrifice for the common good will *Survive Longer* than a race poorer in these qualities.

C4. It is a law of nature that territorial animals, whether individual or social, live in *Eternal Hostility* with their territorial neighbors. Seek peace!..through understanding, if possible?

C5. We must become the first down payment for the future.

C6. Life comes into the world *Predetermined*; therefore, life must have an author.

C7. If there exists in the world of social animals a biological right of privacy as expressed through either the private territory or through individual distance, it is of infinite concern to contemporary societies. Natural arrangements confirm that such a right exists, and so it must have *Biological Value*, although to my knowledge that value has never been explored.

C8. What the holding of territory ultimately promises is the high probability that if *Alien Intrusion* takes place, war will follow.

C9. The racial confusion in the Caucasian intellectual is more *Ominous* than all alien physical destruction, for where it persists, we can have no *Valid Hopes* of recovery.

C10. The real test of a system of the Caucasian sort is in its response to crisis, when its *Necessity* must govern it.

C11. The human world, like their lesser works of art, expresses and reveals all its values, principles, ambitions, virtues, and vices. They make it in their *Racial Image*; it is their major poem.

C12. Like animal life, human life is affected by evolutionary forces that blindly fit the organism to its environment. Human history, however, involves also the unfolding of a visionary imagining. To create a desirable *Caucasian Future* demands more than foursight; it requires a vision.

C13. When the spirit of greed and violence abounds, it is because it has been well housed and fed, and it is triply *Dangerous* when it is well *Armed* and *Drilled*.

C14. Identification! is a most important thing, in the fight for survival.

C15. You must always fight your enemies on your terms.

C16. There is no sure success, except in the more patient passage of time, or perhaps in a *Racial Conviction*, for those who are so fortunate as to have it.

C17. A single living thing is the total of its biological idea. It is the symbol of a way of life, *Identifiable* from all others.

C18. The racial issue is a trial and burden, and humans will take it up only if they are convinced that its demands are rational. But Caucasian morals must rest on Caucasian beliefs, and Caucasian beliefs must be sustained by Caucasian doctrines. If Caucasian doctrines were shed, Caucasian morals would remain only as convention, surviving at convenience.

C19. If our Caucasian American culture begins to disintegrate, (by alien intrusion!) the Caucasian community's social and political position will become desperately difficult. Thereby, creating a Caucasian defensive will!

C20. When a society does not know what it wishes it's young to know?...it is inflicted and suffering from *Moral* and *Spiritual* disorder. Giving rise to social incoherence.

C21. We Caucasians must screen those more closely who represent us in *Politics* and make them more accountable to us and to the *Sovereignty* of our race.

C22. Racial development (spiritual racialism!) has fallen grotesquely short of social, economic, and cultural development. Where the interests and influences of races overlap, we have here problems of *Racial Education* and *Enlightenment*, that the leaders of the various races have not even begun to address? These are problems arising from the fundamental conflicts of - *Racial Competition* and the truth of its- *Subspecies Principle.*

C23. We Caucasians must never cease to respect ourselves as a *Race of People,* and never cease to *Cherish* our history.

C24. If an individual is to survive, he or she must see to it that his or her *Race Survives*. Individuals must also suppress many desires of individual expression in favor of the good of the race, when its survival depends on its unity.

C25. Who can say how many good ideas are lost because of the inability of men and women of *Intellect* to agree as to ends and means?

C26. A race of people are fortunate, when they are able to channel their *Prime Energies* (united will!) into collective achievement and common goals.

C27. The person who knows least about a subject may in his or her *Ignorance* feel fully qualified to make a judgment on the matter; after all, these people don't even know enough about it, to realize how little they know.

C28. If the races of humankind are to survive?..they must not compromise their *Unique Separateness,* by denying the intrinsic value of –Racialness- and the right races have to their own territory, and to prevail as a living force.

C29. To suppress our right of *Racialness,* is to suppress our life's greatest expression.

C30. Consumption and Production: In these lie humankind's greatest fears and its greatest hopes. Hear a balance must be understood, and struck.

C31. All biological ideas, and we know of no other kind of ideas!(fematrix life strategies!) Are all, advanced planned journeys through *Time* and *Space* by mind.

C32. For us Caucasians, *Knowledge,* is a thirst that can never be quenched.

C33. Life is the struggle for the survival of different biological ideas. (a fematrix life strategy!)

C34. There will always be some in our race who believe that the momentum of past achievements can best be continued by not *Touching Anything* and letting well enough alone. Our job is to show and explain that this possibility does not exist.

C35. Racialness; is the very *Nucleus* of human experience, the irreducible root.

C36. The final authority on one's own likes and dislikes, pleasures and pains, is one's self.

C37. The total or *Root Instinct* may be called the will to live. It may better be called the will to do one's living well and to realize the idea of one's *Racial Survival* in one's career. To this instinct there corresponds a feeling of the total compulsories of life; it may be called the sense of reality!

C38. A Men or women may be too wise to be angry? They may also be too stupid!

C39. All good things should be able to endure the test of *Ridicule* and come through it unhurt.

C40. If intellect is cold, it is not merely because it lacks emotional color; it is because it lacks truth.

C41. The whole significance of the efforts to know the laws and things of nature lies in its indifference to our wishes.

C42. Truth must be *Cumulative* in the race, but to accumulate there must be an element of *Permanence* in what is gained. If what we learn by experiment is to be at once unlearned, the motive to learn it is destroyed at its root.

C43. There is always a standing opposition, without resolution, and it is a condition that human thought unwillingly will entertain forever.

C44. Truth is the service of our *Survival,* thereby occupying the first place, and, then of all other well beings.

C45. As sunlight dispels shadows, truth dispels falsehoods.

C46. Racial fallacies have explored and enslaved the intellectual nature of all liberal zealots.

C47. Where *Reason* fails, opinion has the upper hand; where *Will* fails, there is domination; where *Reality* fails, there is extinction.

C48. Racial deception and distortion are always on the liberal menu.

C49. Intelligence identifies itself with *Origin* and restores the center of *Gravity, Principle,* and *Mind Vision.* Unless we Caucasians extend our *Racial Roots* and reestablish ourselves with its moral potencies, (fematrix reality!) we will become *Enslaved* unto our death, by liberal moral fallacies.

C50. Humankind is blessed, by its capacity to know fear.

C51. Unenlightened people are notoriously confident that they have the monopoly on truth. If you need proof, feel the weight of their knuckles.

C52. The truth of our *Racialness* (bio-subspecies) is much broader than any average individual's conception of it.

C53. Before we can honestly breathe the words *Caucasian Racialness,* we must acquire a deeper understanding of the immortal spirit (our Caucasian Fematrix!) that originally inspired it, and the mortal obligation that keeps it alive.(the Caucasian family!)

C54. Our *Personalities*, far from being self-created substances, are *Fabrics* woven on the looms of other personalities, from the *Cradle* to the *Grave*.

C55. Life becomes distorted, not merely for *Adults*, but for *Children* as well, when situations of *Racial Reality* and its *Truths* emerge, and are unwisely handled.

C56. The modern Caucasian man must never make a God out of comfort, and grow afraid of facing reality in all of its depths.

C57. Race cannot be made the *Scapegoat* for the evils that individuals commit.

C58. We must have good domestic relations with ourselves, before we can have good foreign relations with others.

C59. If you want to capture a liberal mind, bait the trap with guilt!

C60. It is *Analysis* that leads us most assuredly to reality.

C61. Commonsense, can be no final criterion of truth.

C62. Humankind is only *Sincere* when they are able to distinguish genuine *Cognition* from mere possibility.

C63. All Caucasian men, women and children, have an obligation to their *Historical Ancestral Trust*, for this is the sacred well that *Nurtures* and *Sustains* their being.

C64. Religion is a *Flower* that *Blooms*, brings *Life* and *Beauty* to where nothing else will grow.

C65. Our Creator- the *Fematrix*!..the great living entity is called by many *Names*, and seen in many *Different Ways*. And it is only her spirit, that can touch the human soul.

C66. Only *Religion,* can quench humankinds greatest thirst.

C67. In Caucasian society *Quantity* must never overshadow the great importance of- *Quality*.

C68. The best will in the world does not accomplish anything if it remains blind to the *Fundamental Vices* that paralyze its action, before it can even be felt.

C69. Only through the schools, can we undo the *Liberal Zealot Harm* that the schools have done.

C70. When a Caucasian child begins to speak and to think, we must not be afraid to make his or her brain and memory work. The quality of a child's memory can be surprisingly and rapidly lost.

C71. Only a highly evolved *Caucasian Man* or *Woman* is willing to *Defend* the *Liberty* of others.

C72. The *Highest Duty* of every *Caucasian Person* is to contribute to the best of his or her ability to the *Survival* and *Spiritual Evolution* of their race.

C73. The Caucasian race as a *Living Reality* is the limit at which something that is more than life itself determines life through the will of the *Caucasian Whole*! The Caucasian race is, in virtue of its power, the supreme authority for decisions in one's- *Caucasian life*.

C74. Those wishing to find their way to the origin of the *Racial Crisis,* must pass through the *Lost Domain* of *Truth* and must strip off the trappings of the *Liberal Masquerade* in order to disclose the *Genuineness* that lies beneath.

C75. Criticism is certainly the precondition of a change for the better, but it is not itself- *Creative*.

C76. The *Caucasian Home*: herein we discern the most essential elements of our- *Caucasian Racial Humanity* - being the foundation of all the rest.

C77. When the average *Functional Capacity* has become the *Standard* of *Achievement*, the individual is regarded with indifference.

C78. The realities of the world cannot be evaded. Experience of the *Harshness* of the *Real* is the only way by which a Caucasian *Man* or *Woman* can come to *His* or *Her* own self.

C79. True *Heroism*, so far as it is *Possible* to modern man, is displayed in

Inconspicuous Activities, in the work that does not bring fame.

C80. There is no *Worse Injustice* than to treat unequal causes-*Equally*.

C81. In *Humankind*, the many *Groups* and *Races* are all *Discernible*, and each has an equal chance to qualify as an element of- *Moral Evolution*. But, for those who do not seize this chance?...and fail to understand *Instinctively* or *Rationally* the significance of their-*Barbarism*, it denotes they are not fit to play their part, in the human journey.

C82. The sanest judgment is- *Always Questionable*, because it is impossible to always assemble all the elements required to give it an *Absolute* value.

C83. All societies have the same problems, selfishness of the individual, and all have to induce in him or her the same idea of justice, that of applying to themselves the rules they recommend to others.

C84. Our interest motivates the questions, but it does not determine the answers.

C85. The principle of truth is that no human interest, however great, can outweigh any item of evidence, however small.

C86. To know that one does not know is a highly important kind of knowledge. It starts one on the right road to gain genuine knowledge.

C87. There is- *Illusion* for the will as for the intellect in the whole scheme of nature, and the wise person will all ways keep his or her *Desires* and *Hopes* in check.

C88. Humankind may escape *Emotion* with their lips, but they cannot do it with their deeds. For it is the *Dynamic Energy* that vitalizes every aspect of their many cultures, and every creation of their civilizations.

C89. Poor indeed, are those *Caucasians* who live only in their own time.

C90. It is very important that all *Caucasians* become wise enough to recognize where they can go *Astray* in their attitudes between themselves and alien others, and how they can become *Enslaved* to- *False Liberal Notions* of what they are, and what they ought to be.

C91. We should not demand of ourselves more than our *Racial Fematrix* (Caucasia!) herself will permit.

C92. The history of science is the history of human opinion on the question of - *Certainty*.

C93. The Alpha tells us: A better understanding between the *Human Races*, does not necessarily result in, much less determine changes in the- *Policies* of their respective elites.

C94. The *Caucasian Race,* and its *Families* are the chief surviving resorts of its *Creative Social* action.

C95. All those Caucasians in denial of- *Racial Values*, are *Selfish, Shortsighted*, and given over to social disorder and conditions with *Ruin* and *Wretchedness* in their wake.

C96. In the *Complexities* and *Perplexities* of modern life has grown a non-suspicious awe of the- *Expert!* Government has largely fallen into its hands, and the expert is of all, the last to take the *Broad View*, or permit the rugged intrusion of - *Common Sense,* on their- *Veiled Mysteries*.

C97. The Alpha tells us: There is only one way for our *Racial Progress*. It comes in our *Caucasian Moral Efforts* that have sustained us in the long stubborn struggle of our *Fematrix* (Caucasia) and her ends perceived,(life strategy!) but by some, never wholly realized.

C98. We Caucasians must strengthen our *Racial Resolve*, by the true measure of - *Racial Logic*! We must learn to act, not from the *"Racial Abolitionism"* the *liberal zealots* created, (a social fraud!) but, by the light of - *Living Reality*.

C99. The Alpha tells us: To love one's *Cultural, Idealistic* and *Racial Heritage*, to swear to pass that heritage unimpaired to one's children, to *Fight*, and if need be to *Die* in its *Defense*, all this is *Eternally Right* and *Proper*, and no amount of *Casualty* or *Sentimentality* can alter this- *Truth*.

C100. To those who swear to the new religion; *Racial Equality*, it will have the *Briefest Life*, of all the- *Liberal Heresies*.

C101. Human affairs are best conducted where there is a proper balance between- *Imagination, Experience,* and *Enterprise.* Having all governed, by a *Sound* and *Orderly Judgment.*

C102. Deferent *Racial Encounters* are not the cause of war per se. But, they can become the cause of war, in the sense of *Racial Territory.* What *Racialness* promises is the high probability that if an *Alien Racial Intrusion* takes place, (predatory invasion!) a war for survival will follow.

C103. Equality: If one becomes infected by its pathogen, (epistemic-nihilism) *Intellectual Delusion* will be their fate.

C104. The Courts must *Apply* and *Inforce* the law! But, never become the *Social* and *Cultural Sculptors* of the Law!

C105. Those who are not true to their- *Racial Soul* will inevitably lose it, and they will fall! For that which gave them balance is no more.

C106. Peace, a cool drink of water on a break in the battle for life. It is but for a moment, and then the battle rages on.

C107. The 𝔄lpha tells us: In our eternal search for Truth's "Presence" (all intellectual encounter!) We should at least introduce or suggest those things that seem wise, and of a value to our need! When we do this, we do all that we can.

C108. We *Caucasians* have don much to determine our future, but we have been lacking a *Spiritual Consistency* about our-*Racialness?* We must *Shun* the voices of *Racial Nihilism,* and embrace a moral standard of- *Racial Values!*

C109. Our *Caucasian Fematrix* greatest achievement was the creation of the *Caucasian Man*, her means to the end.

C110. Reasoning is hard work, which explains why *Weak Minds* prefer the *Status Quo*, as soon as they successfully adjust to it.

C111. The shock of *Social* and *Culture Dislocation*- by a Nation that has been invaded by - *Racial Aliens* - will produce- *Hatred, Suspicion*, and *Paranoia,* leading to extreme damage to its *Social Civility* and *Cultural Unity,* and thereby making the emerging culture-*Warlike!* (cultural supremacy!)

C112. We are all guilty of coasting, after we have attained a certain intellectual speed.

C113. Truth: is a perceived finality of cause and effect.

C114. We must reach back into the midst of the creation, to understand the beginning.

C115. Enlightened and persistent criticism is of fundamental importance in the- *Caucasian Empire.*

C116. Matters that are beyond our senses of- *Experience* and *Reasoning;* things based on this, cannot be final.

C117. The ultimate state of *Bondage* is - *Ignorance.*

C118. Short lived are both the *Praised*, and the *Praisea.*

C119. When a *Race* of *People* are without an *Intellectual Central Core,* (a throne!) they will not develop a *Mature Culture.* The-*Throne;* is the reference point that a society builds from.

C120. If the *Premise* of one's reasoning is false! Then the conclusion will definitely, and logically be false.

C121. The Alpha tells us: It is the scale of our observation that creates the phenomena. Every time we change the scale of our observation, we encounter new phenomena.

C122. The splendor of our world is born from the impact between it and our- Coercion.

C123. Memory is an *Essential Condition* for the persistence of living things.

C124. The moment humans ask themselves the question whether an act was *Good* or whether another was *Better*, they acquire a *Liberty* denied to other living beings.

C125. As in the past, human social progress can take place only by *Struggle, Competition*, and *Selection*.

C126. Action follows- *Conviction*, not knowledge.

C127. A certain amount of *Obstinacy* is necessary, as is salt in our food, but its absence is more fruitful than its excess.

C128. If a people disbelieve in *God?* Let them proclaim it and give their reasons. If they do not have *Faith*, let them ask themselves *Honestly!*...what can- *Replace Religion?*

C129. Intelligence alone is- *Dangerous!*...especially if it is not subjected to the- *Intuitive* or *Rational Perception* of *Moral Values*.

C130. None of us are individually *Indispensable*, yet none of us are *Useless*. Therefore, the degree of our usefulness depends on our will.

C131. We Caucasians must not allow our young to become infected with- *Alien Multiculturalism* and its many useless details while Caucasian- *Educational Essentials* are passed over in silence.

C132. Social Extinction: When *Environmental* or *Physical* impression becomes suddenly altered, a society of largely *Specialized Persons,* whose avenues of possible change are limited can be wiped out. *Over-Specialization* can trigger social extinction.

C133. Great *Epochs* have faded into the past, but each has left its *Legacy* to the- *Caucasian Experience*.

C134. The creation of race is a *Biological Imperative*, and its character is shaped by the *Needs* and *Limitation* of its existence.

C135. Childhood: Is the *Prolonged Immaturity* we must have in order to embrace our- *Racial Heritage* and learn what went before us, before we can become a part of it, in one or another of its many aspects.

C136. The Alpha Tells us: That the very *Laws* upon which *Social Explanation* must rest, (the natural order!) are themselves the subject of *Frightful Liberal* discussions.

C137. Refuting an opponent's- *Case?*..is not and should not be looked upon, as *Establishing* your own.

C138. Curiosity: Is to the *Mind,* what appetite is to the *Body.*

C139. The Mind: The *Archive* and *Purveyor* of one's own bio-historical consensus,(intellectual character) a subspecies unanimity on the order of its- *Survival.*

C140. The Alpha tells us: Too often the shelter of childhood becomes the prison of maturity.

C141. All those who strive for total- *Repression* and or total- *Expression* of their *Impulses* in the realm of their *Imagination* will- *Wreak Havoc* on both their *Bodies* and their *Minds.*

C142. The Caucasian self is not a *Gift,* it is an *Achievement.*

C143. The Alpha tells us: A society loses its sense of direction when the *Compass* of its being is not magnetized by some great *Human Star* within the orbit of its- *Experience.*

C144. The Alpha tells us: It is *Imitation* that is responsible for both the *Tragedy* and *Glory* of our existence.

C145. It is not merely what we- *Do!*..but also what we- *Are!* that *Influences* our- *Whole Environment.*

C146. Treachery: Is the *Teacher,* making us aware of the *Fragility* and the *Nobility* of the- *Caucasian Dream.*

C147. The Alpha tells us: Ours is a *Universe* where everything has a *Price!*.. and we cannot expect to purchase the *Fragile Beauty* of our- *Caucasian Racial Consciousness* without the suffering of *Racial Transgression* and *Betrayal.*

C148. The Caucasian- *Racial Spirit!*...is not a municipality that can be *Bribed* to overlook- *Violations* of *Principles* upon which the Caucasian- *Race* and its *Culture* must rest.

C149. We Caucasians shall become *Free* of inner *Conflict* and *Burden* only when we have *Enunciated* our very own *Racial Faith,* and persuaded ourselves that it is *Essential* for the fulfillment of - *Our True* and *Permanent Happiness*.

C150. Anyone can- *Complain*?..but to see precisely what is *Wrong!*..is a gift.

C151. If a *Belief* has been accepted on *Deficient Evidence*, its pleasure is a theft of ego.

C152. Every Caucasian *Man* and *Woman* has the task of arranging their lives into a pattern of- *Racial Unity*, but that *Racial Unity,* will always be a unity of- *Diverse Parts*, a *Harmony* of many varied- *Social* and *Cultural Elements*.

C153. The 𝕬lpha tells us: Caucasian *Racial Teachings,* should always emphasize that-*Inner Justice,* is always the creation of *Proportion* and *Harmony* between our *Fear*, *Aggression*, and *Love*. And that an individual Caucasian's successful living is dependent upon the expression of the proper- *Quantity* and *Balance* of these qualities.

C154. One's *Excessive Preoccupation* with *His* or *Her Drives* and *Impulses* is the- *Enemy* of their inner peace.

C155. A true- *Racial Philosophy* encourage its people to Realize that they must anticipate many *Deserts,* as well as some *Oases,* in the *Social* and *Cultural* terrain of their lives.

C156. The "True" social idea- Aids Survival, the "False" social idea- Aids Wasted Effort, and Death.

C157. The 𝕬lpha tells us: Caucasian thinking must first achieve not only *Courage* and *Independence*, but also a sufficient body of coherent historical *Racial Knowledge* to propose a contracting world view.

C158. All conversation tends to transmit- *Philosophy*, and this process, when it becomes the conversation between one generation and another, is what we call *Tradition*, from which everyone selects what appears as *Valid* or *Fit*. It is the chief original source of *Belief* in the form of *Prejudice*.

C159. There are ways of living that are in *Harmony* with the *Divine Fematrix*, and there are other ways that are out of harmony. The ways of *Harmony* can be known.

C160. We Caucasians are not justified in deferring to our children the *Justice* that is our duty to create in this life.

C161. The reality of our *Racialness* consists in its being willed by the creative mind of our *Fematrix*.(Caucasia!)

C162. The Caucasian *Man* and *Woman* are not the creators of the world, but are *Apprentices* in creativity. Learning how to produce "Their World" from their own mental store.

C163. The use of force is but- *Temporary*. It may subdue an alien opponent for a short time, but it does not remove the necessity of subduing again? An alien group cannot be governed that is *Subversive!*..and must be *Continuously* subdued. Therefore, *Territorial Separation* has always been the norm in life, for competitive being.

C164. Respect for "All" must stand at the beginning of any *Honest* fraternity.

C165. Social planning is indispensable in our crowded *Caucasian World,* but if our society is to remain viable, our planning must recognize our non-material needs more than it has. And it must offer us worthwhile goals without exhausting one at the expense of the others.

C166. When the load becomes too heavy for the *State,* "War" we should remember, is a common- *Escape!*

C167. The *Caucasian Race* must be willing to meet all the *Challenges* to it way of life. It must be willing to *Sacrifice* on behalf of its-*Children*, and above all!...it must never "Compromise" the *Wellbeing* and *Future* of its children.

C168. A living thing owes its *Allegiance* to the *Survival* of that "Biological Idea" that gave it life.

C169. A "Race" of people that has no more respect for its *Ancestors?*...and no more pride in its *Racialness,* deserves the "Extinction" that surely awaits it.

C170. The *Mind* that experiments must *Remain* the same and *Mean* the same by its inquiry when it *Ends* as when it *Began;* otherwise the experiment is a- *Fraud.*

C171. The unfavorable answer is taken as well as the favorable one. It is the duty of science to tell us the *Worst* as well as the *Best* about "Ourselves" and the world.

C172. All- *Laws, Conventions,* and *Institutions* can be like "Language", either *Bonds* or *Wings,* according to one's degree of mastery.

C173. The 𝔄lpha tells us: In life, there are no *Trackless* happenings, there is a- *Caucasian Racial Whole!* Freedom and "Racial Wholeness" are both to be had.

C174. The 𝔄lpha tells us: If we Caucasians should *Cheat* our children of the *Splendid Promise* of a *Caucasian life,* we shall be to blame, and deserve not *Pity,* but- *Contempt.*

C175. Race and Mind: are the *Odyssey* of the spirit.

C176. All the issues between *Wisdom* and *Folly* or between *Right* and *Wrong* can be put in these terms: What *Goods* do you seek, and what *Means* do you use in obtaining them?

C177. Race is *Necessary,* in order that *Mind* may qualify as will.

C178. Honor is simply the *Flower* of self-respect; it may lead a character into regions where neither the *Social Standard* nor the *Aesthetic Standard* alone would suffice.

C179. Space and time present *Mysteries* for any view of the worlds order. They have no-Evolution; they are Changeless! For all "Beginnings" are in Space and Time, and space and time, therefore, is *Before* and *After* every- Beginning. Time measures all change, but for that reason, the time order itself cannot change.

C180. One's *Philosophy* is something more personal than the truth of a science; it must be made not of things learned, but of your own seeing.

C181. Intuition is not wisdom, and intellect is not wisdom. Wisdom: is the *Union!..*of intuition and intellect.

C182. The *Fematrix* implies- *Continuation!..*among all of her phenomena.

C183. To make a *Principle* of the relative truth of all principle?..is to- *Surrender Principle.*

C184. Character: Whether of *Men* or *Philosophy*, is shown as much in what one *Denies* as in what one *Affirms.*

C185. We Caucasians are today the *Inheritors* of all types of *General* and *Extensive Knowledge*, of both *History* and *Thought,* and also, the accumulative *Debates* that support their- *Continued Existence.*

C186. The details of *Law* may blind the *Skilled Jurist* to the intention of *Human Justice*, and this may be so prevalent an-*Occupational Defect!...*that the common citizen may come to dread the courts of law as places in which justice only- *Occasionally Emerges*, as it were by accident from beneath the mass of - *Technicalities.*

C187. The 𝔄lpha tells us: The *Value* and *Meaning* of things proves to be not in-*Themselves Alone!..*but, more to the fact of something that the *Perceiver* brings to them.

C188. Idealism: Can never be a "Substitute" for- Religion! For only in *Religion* is -*Metaphysical Truth*- truly known.

C189. The 𝔄lpha tells us: The difference between *Religion* and *Science,* is the degree of one's mental poverty.

C190. The 𝔄lpha tells us: One of the *Realities* of one's "Racialness" is the sum of all the *Meaning* that can be found in it, and taking *Race* in this way, it and its *Laws* become an expression of one's *Ultimate Purpose* and *Significance.*

C191. In Caucasianism: the word "Racialness" indicates chiefly that the mental life within the world has unity, and that all meaning of things cohere in a *Single* biological will.

C192. The "Human Paradox" is: that no one *Sees You,* as you see yourself.

C193. Racialness exists, because it is a *Necessary Condition* for "Identification," a visual and psychological orientation of the self, and their union of "Sameness" in their journey.

C194. Race is necessary, in order for one's mind to attain self-consciousness, and self-possession,(identity!) thereby bringing union to one's historical-*Biological Journey*.

C195. Human feelings appear to contain some rudimentary essential elements of *Truth!*...that are needful to our adjustment to reality.

C196. Tolerance is the meeting in perfect harmony of earnest conviction and personal indulgence.

C197. Humanity is the carrier of health and disease, either the divine health of *Courage* and *Nobility* or the demonic disease of *Hatred* and *Anxiety*.

C198. If you pray at the altar of *Survival*, you will learn of its two greatest wisdoms, *Opposition*, and *Advantage*.

C199. Those who come in contact with us are either the *Beneficiaries* or the *Victims* of our presence on earth.

C200. We must always realize that we need not measure our *Values* by the yardstick of our- *Fallible Neighbors*.

C201. Unexpressed *Emotion* ultimately takes its *Vengeance* in the form of *Mental* and *Physical Illness*.

C202. You must remember that what you do is like the pebble thrown into the pool, making *Larger* and *Larger Ripples* in the waters of other lives.

C203. We must always remember this about the world we live in. That values keep *Emerging* as we enlarge our capacity, and learn to adjust our own instrument of vision.

C204. The great thing about *Life* is that as long as we live, we have the *Privilege* of *Learning*.

C205. We as parents must never let our children become the *Tragically* lengthened shadows of- *Our Failures*.

C206. The answer to the *Mysterious Complexity* of the *Fematrix* !...lies in her *Simplicity*.

C207. It is in our *Children* who are touched by the *Flame* of our *Caucasian Spirit* that we live on and find our *Eternal* and *True Significance*.

C208. Caucasian *Men* and *Women* willultimately benefit from the interlocking of their *Destinies*.

C209. Our *Children* must never lose their "Place" at the banquet table of life. and we as *Caucasian* must never "Surrender" their *Future* or betray its- *Moral Purpose*.

C210. Our *Children* are the symbol of our *Worthy Totality,* which in turn confers *Worth* and *Love* upon- *Our Race*

C211. Death, there is as much *Oblivion* about the last hours. As about the first, and therefore, humans fill their minds with *Mystical Specters* that have no reality.

C212. In life, every one of us leaves a trail, either *Modest* or *Brilliant,* and this conviction should make itself felt in all the *Acts* of our lives.

C213. Seek *Peace,* and *Understanding* with *Alien* others, but never *Pretend Peace*, when there is- *No Peace*.

C214. Every human being does in time come to recognize that their *Race* has a claim on them, and that they ought to be a *Serviceable Member* of it; this is a natural *Social Ethic*.

C215. Freedom applies immediately to the *Sphere* of one's own *Choices*. It gives an absolute mastery of nature outside of self; we can directly control nothing but the meaning we make our deeds carry. There remain countless things not within our power; there are tides of *Physical* and *Social* circumstance, such as *Age*, *Disease*, which no human has yet been able to row against. Death conquers *Idealists* and *Realists* alike.

C216. Racial Fundamentalism; (bio-spirituality!) must not be viewed as a competitor of *Religion*, any more than the science of *Optics* should be regarded as a competitor of- *Normal Vision*.

C217. The human flock obeys an obscure order; it must *Rise!*...and it cannot do so without a- *Leader*.

C218. When a society is like a vessel that has no pilot or lacks a skilled pilot, it will eventually crash.

C219. The fittest of a race line can eventually give birth to children destined to- *Disappear* or *Vegetate*. This will take place if the external cultural conditions are modified or if other races more apt from the final *Teleology* point of view displace them.

C220. The strength of nations of *Prey* and of fundamentally *Bad-Men* is drawn in part from the relative *Immunity* derived from the *Humanitarian Sentiment* of their- *Victims*.

C221. The world is moved by *Religion* and *Love,* the great fortifiers for the crisis of- *Human Existence*, and all kneel before them in awe.

C222. Individual immortality escapes rational conception, but it is hardly questionable if we admit the *Reality* of the *Wake*.

C223. We must never forget the *Gratitude* we owe the *Caucasian Trailblazers*. They are with us all the time. The modern Caucasian men and women are tributaries of the most distant past and linked to their most remote ancestors by an immaterial but unbroken thread more durable and more impressive than the great pyramids.

C224. No Caucasian *Man* or *Woman* can never disappear completely if he or she has strived to do well and has expected no reward outside of the joy of having contributed to the progress of their race.

C225. As long as the *Caucasian American Community* remains without a *Collective Racial Conscience* rendering their race, the social engagements taken by their representative treaties with *Alien Races* will without a doubt, constitute- a *Tragic Comedy*.

C226. Superstition of all kinds will spread much more easily than *Truth* or *Rational Doctrine,* because undeveloped minds still constitute a majority.

C227. Intellectual and Spiritual weapons (Truth! and Compassion!) are without strength against- *Fanaticism*.

C228. We cannot conceive any limit to the development of ideas, because the limit we might conceive would obviously be conditioned by the actual state of our mentality.

C229. Conscience, like intelligence, is very unevenly developed among humans; however the sincere and sustained effort of a moderately intelligent being can have a more efficacious radiation than that of a great brain.

C230. To love to eat, drink, and amuse oneself are not acts that are reprehensible in themselves, as long as they are practiced with moderation, and the word *Moderation* implies a moderator, which is the conscience, the sense of dignity.

C231. The progress and happiness of the Caucasian people can be obtained only by an improvement in the individual, and this improvement can be based only on a high and noble racial discipline, not only freely accepted, but understood.

C232. We must educate ourselves and our children to live amid *Uncertainty* and *Temporary Truth*.

C233. Without the *Joining* of *Man* and *Woman* in moral ceremony, (the union of marriage) life would be one of immediate appetites, immediate sensations limited to a past shorter than their own life-times, and at the mercy of a future they could never anticipate, never prepare for.

C234. There is no such thing as a permanent *Superiority* or *Inferiority* among the *Races* of the human Fematrix, nor in other living thing. Fore it implies a finality, and that does not exist, unless you know the summit of your being?

C235. Never are the facts so certain that the probability of their being false, is zero.

C236. Evaluation without facts is blind prejudice.

C237. People will continue to commit *Atrocities*, as long as they believe in *Absurdities*.

C238. Human understanding is by its own nature prone to abstraction, and supposes which is fluctuating to be fixed.

C239. The social habitat of the *Liberal Utopian Zealot* has determined a whole system of opinions and theories that appear to them as unquestionably true or self-evident, and therefore no intellectual bridge may exist, and no rational plea possible...the total intellectual meltdown.

C240. The Alpha tells us: that *Time* shouts the truth much louder, than words often do.

C241. You cannot preserve the *Core* of a culture when all of the important technical props have been removed.

C242. Race hides much more than it reveals, and strangely enough what it hides, it hides most effectively from its own progeny

C243. In the balance of life, the use of space is one of the most delicate in all of nature.

C244. The history of man's past is largely an account of his efforts to wrest space from others and to defend space from outsiders.

C245. Humans operate on three different levels; the *Formal*, *Informal*, and the *Technical*. Each is present in any situation, but one will dominate at any given instant in time. The shift from level to level is rapid, and the study of these shifts is the study of the process of change.

C246. Biological Racialness is communication at its best, and communication at its best, is *Biological Racialness*.

C247. The laws of order in a society are those regularities governing changes in the meaning when order is altered.

C248. There is in our world, no experience independent of racial biology, (kind identity) against which racial biological can be measured.

C249. There is a *Relative* principle in *Racial Biology*, just as there is in physics and mathematics.

C250. Experience is something humans project on the outside world as they gain it in its racially determined form.

C251. We must never assume that we are fully aware of what we communicate to someone else. There exists in the world today tremendous distortions in meaning as humans try to communicate with one another.

C252. Race is not an exotic notion studied by a select group of people, it is a mold in which we are all cast, and it controls our daily lives in many unsuspected ways.

C253. Morals and values will persist in a society only in the measure to which socialization of offspring succeed.

C254. We seem to be on firm ground when we assert that ideas and systems of belief determine human action, not to the exclusion of other factors such as heredity and role experience, but above their influence, of far greater consequences for action than other factors are the beliefs that direct effort and give them a sense of rightness.

C255. Human groups cannot effectively carry out acts for which they do not have a system of beliefs.

C256. Humans have no rights other than the rights they take by *Force* and maintain by *Force*.

C257. The greater or lesser degree of vigor in a race depends ultimately on the power of its vital instincts, of its greater or lesser faculty for adopting itself to and dominating the conditions of the moment.

C258. It is not because a race ceases to believe, that it falls into decay; it is because its social politics are in decay that it abandons the fertile dreams of its ancestors without replacing them with a new dream, equally fortifying and creative of energy.

C259. It is the nature of states founded on *Socialism* to content themselves with a hand-to-mouth social policy without general views based on reality, always satisfied with immediate gains and unable to prepare against a distant future.

C260. Let it be understood that aliens are perfectly justified in trying to win broader opportunities in Caucasian lands. But we Caucasians are equally justified in keeping these opportunities for ourselves and our children. The hard facts are that what Caucasians bring about is Caucasian, and when the enormous pressure and outward thrust of an *Alien Population* bursts into a Caucasian land, it cannot let live, but automatically pushes Caucasian people out from the land forever, first the Caucasian laborer, then the Caucasian merchant, and lastly the Caucasian aristocrat.

C261. Racial biology: is in fact the *Principal Project* of the mind, and the ulti-mate expression of the mind.

C262. The racial peril has three facets: the peril of migration, the peril of mar-kets, and the peril of arms.

C263. The Fematrix is inexorable; no living being stands above her law, neither protozoan nor demagogue. If they transgress, alike will perish.

C264. We must come to know that the whole of the earth is made of ashes, and that ashes have a meaning.

C265. Cohesive instinct is as vital to the Caucasian race as gravitation is to matter. Without it, *Disintegration* would likewise result.

C266. The longing to hack a path to greatness will always lurk in the minds of humanity.

C267. Let it be said, that to transplant the beliefs and institutions of a race of people to another race of people in the hope of transplanting its virtues and civilization is the vainest of follies.(different bio-core life strategies!)

C268. One must not violate the greatness of racial teachings by prostituting them for personal gain.(by hatred!)

C269. Those who deny consciousness of race and its value must deny genetic instruction, the caretaker of all that is.

C270. To the archenemies of the Caucasian race, the renegades, the traitors within our gates, those who would betray the race and degrade the very fiber of our being, you will be known, found, and banished forever.

C271. We Caucasians must never cease to proofread that which goes into our society.

C272. You have to understand the past, to know the present.

C273. Caucasian racial solidarity must never be compromised.

C274. The Caucasian race must never cease to colonize, for it is this movement that expands our survival.

C275. Even the sound of a bell leaves its likeness behind it.

C276. The psychology of predetermination in life is based on the uncertainty of the outcome of conflict and the preservation of the mark of the Fematrix.

C277. Biological racial kind is the work of the free mind; it is the physical artistic expression of necessity, desire, and choice.

C278. You must never deny the intentions of your enemy for the sake of peace.

C279. Time: is the great destroyer of nations.

C280. Technology flourishes when society nurtures it.

C281. The key to survival is to know when you have the advantage and when you don't.

C282. The Caucasians; will always be a race in battle.(the spirit of- Encounter!)

C283. Human knowledge is transferred to the field of free opposites by the field of joined opposites.

C284. Success in *Being;* is the Union of Opposites.

C285. Race; is commanded by an *Involuntary Defense*, when it is in the presence of another- *Alien Race*.

C286. You must never deny the nature of the- *Beast*.

C287. Make no mistake, if weakness is seen, it will be acted upon by all opposing forces.

C288. The price our enemies pay for their aggression must always be severe and unprofitable.

C289. The Caucasian Empire is the body, and the race is the soul.

C290. A race of people elated by pride or soured by discontent is seldom quali-fied to form a just estimate of its actual situation.

C291. Never seek to justify the *Caucasian Empire,* or that of our *Race,* to the non-believer. (a racial- Apostate!)

C292. Let the punishment bring justice to the crime, for it is by this wisdom that mankind will check its ways.

C293. The Alpha is the lord of the Caucasians and the keeper of the eternal light and spirit of the race.

C294. It is to the great religions that humankind owes its allegiance, for it was religion that stood by their side in their darkest hour.

C295. In the end, its reality, not abstract theories, that decides.

C296. Migration, like other natural movements, is of itself a blind force.

C297. It is the Caucasians divine privilege as well as duty to direct their socialization with aliens?...by rejecting the bad and excepting the good, for the evolution of their higher and nobler destiny.

C298. Caucasian cultural existence is the wellspring of our being, the sacred heritage of our children.

C299. The Caucasian Empire, in it, all things are possible.

C300. The Dark Ages will come again to humankind, and like the first, it will completely overwhelm their world.

C301. Competing races view the symbols of other races with contempt!... looking to put up their own.

C302. Words can be like drugs; they have the power to make pain as well as to reduce pain.

C303. Beware of moral accusations; their impressions can mislead your reality.

C304. The Caucasian race must not let alien races use the accusations of victimhood? (ethical deceit!) to breakdown their principle defenses. For their intention are to slay the Caucasian *Racial Spirit*!...and put their own in its place.

C305. The Caucasian people must become aware of those Caucasian subversives?...who are serving the ambitions of "Alien Races" in their society.

C306. There are "Caucasian Apostates" in our communities?...who have been *Betraying* the Caucasian American people, by placating *Alien Victimhood*, and especially by offering them their *Service* and *Political Allegiance*. (reality!)

C307. To all Caucasians who think they are safe from outside danger, you possess a false sense of security. (an alien invasion has begun!- year 2019)

C308. To all Caucasians who are lost. Come back to the enlightenment of your *Racialness!*, your *Caucasian Fematrix!*, and discover the source of all things.

C309. The Caucasian people must never let an alien race become parasitic in their society. For when one race becomes parasitic on another, the host race becomes increasingly debilitated, and the cultural castration of that society is the ultimate result. (self-Destruction, by Compassion!)

C310. Beware of those Caucasians who hold the fate of their own people in contempt and would sell them out to a moral fallacy for a few pieces of political silver

C311. The Caucasian society belongs to a scheme of things that embodies the wisdom of generations.(our greatest- Treasure!)

C312. Reasonable Force; is the midwife of society; and never has change been accomplished without it.

C313. The Caucasian society and its people must become aware of misguided and mentally disturbed Caucasians who have become *Treasonous Subversives* by the political propaganda of alien races.

C314. There is, according to the Alpha's view, one simple chord and one only, which the great organ of society is adapted to play, and it is the business of our elected legislator to see to it that it is played right, the chord of Caucasian racial survival.

C315. It is the Alpha's wish! Take the place you can, enjoy the authority you can win, and let our laws express and protect the balance of forces in our society.

C316. Let the avenues to political influence be open to all Caucasian men and women of goodwill.

C317. The *Evils* of the day call for the *Remedies* of the day.

C318. The Caucasian policeman is the holder of the sacred shield and therefore his position of honor must always be upheld. Through him, the weak rule strong, the few rule the many, and the intelligent rule the fools. It is through him survive those whom the struggle for existence would have eliminated. Police officers are our society's true champions.

C319. We must always realize that the whole structure of society rests upon rational habits. Hence a new society must here fore grow the new *Rationality*

it will need to support those habits.

C320. A man or woman knows nothing but what he or she has been socially practicing; and in every branch of work, only those are fitted to direct who are themselves the workers.

C321. Caucasians must be free of those who are inflicted with the disease of *Racial Hatred*, for it destroys the desire to *Reason* and cripples the spirit of *Compassion*.

C322. Anarchy is not the absence of order, it is absence of force; it is the free out flowing of the human spirit into the forms in which it delights, unaware of its evil.

C323. In the biological world of souls and in the hierarchy of the human spirit there is a need of man no less than his Fematrix. Her station and social gravity will determine his acceptance, and the antagonism that keeps them apart also knits them together.

C324. Unfortunately for many of us, the most important things are often the last to be known about, and it is exactly when it is most important to act, that our ignorance is most complete.

C325. Our eyes must also be on the coming generations; in them centers our hopes and our future.

C326. We know what we do or fail to do, matters.

C327. Our aim must be fruitful, and to be fruitful through criticism

C328. Collectivism, Order, Anarchy, and Liberty, each is held as a *Faith* and propagated as a *Religion*.

C329. The greatest social duel, which runs through history, has always been *Intellect* and *Passion*.

C330. We as Caucasians must always feed, clothe, and educate our children, to make them better than ourselves, and in doing it, to find our own life and our own satisfaction. This is our task and our privilege.

C331. It is for wise direction that the coming Caucasian generations cry, and it is the business of Caucasian society to see that they get it.

C332. It is a Caucasian's duty to be socially cautious, for great ideas naturally suggest practical application, and it is here that the 𝔄lpha foresees difficulties.

C333. One must not waste his or her time by decorating the image of a sinking ship.

C334. It is the things that the liberal mind calls *Good*, even more than those they admit to being *Bad*, that make the 𝔄lpha despair.

C335. The end of America will come when *Racial Treason* is eternalized and Caucasian political power is lowered to annihilation.

C336. We project into the future the perfection we miss in the present, and did not have in the past.

C337. The *Literature* and *Art* of our Caucasian past, are the gifts of *Love* to a *Caucasian Eternity*, one has only to gaze upon them, and their journey is yours.

C338. Life is raw material for the artist, whether he or she is the private person carrying out his or her own destiny, or the states person shaping that of a nation. The ends perceived by the artist in either case are the good life, and on his or her own conception of that will depend the value of their work.

C339. Those who commit great crimes against *Caucasian Society* must come to know and feel the full fury of the Caucasian people; in this there can be no compromise.

C340. If you substitute the mass for the patron, you will eliminate taste, the artist perishes, and the charlatan survives and flourishes.

C341. We must work not with, but against tendencies, if we would realize anything great.

C342. Power is the center of crystallization for all good, given that you have morals, art, and religion. Without it, you have nothing but *Appetites* and

Passions. Power then, is the condition of life.

C343. The artist is the rarest, the most choice of men and women. Their senses, their perceptions, and their intelligence have a natural and inborn fineness and distinction. They need a class to appreciate and support them.

C344. When you do away with aristocracy, you do away with responsibility, which is the salt of privilege. When there is no core, your standards, dignity, manners, nobility, and common honesty itself will rapidly disappear from among you.

C345. To those how would build an equitable society in which everyone will do productive work and nobody will live at the cost of others?...let me warn you of this: beware of the liberal doctrines of utopian zealotry.

C346. The Caucasian race must sooner or later wake to it *Imperial Mission*!

C347. Caucasian American dependencies must never fall to alien races.

C348. The dust of oblivion will bury our debates.

C349. None can anticipate with advantage, the necessities of the future.

C350. A race of people like an individual has a personality to maintain. It must be its objective not to accumulate wealth at all cost, but to maintain the capacity to be powerful, energetic, and above all, *Racially Conscious*.

C351. We Caucasians have faith; our faith is built upon our *Race*, and it's a faith which will endure forever.

C352. It is because of our Caucasian diaspora, having divided ourselves into Nation?...that we must endure the *Oppression* of *War* and *Armaments*.

C353. Intellectually as well as morally, liberal zealotry (Egalitarianism!) is eter-nally bankrupt.

C354. The work of destruction is a necessary preliminary to the work of creation.

C355. Passion without intellect is mischievous.

C356. Dismiss truth if you like; where then will you turn?

C357. All the races of humanity must be responsible for their own destiny?... and Caucasian territory must not become the *Promise Land!*...for everyone who may imagine they can better themselves by migrating to it.

C358. The idea of progress comes of taking the values out of the *Past* and *Present* in order to put them into the future, hence the foundation of a new beginning.

C359. Those who have eyes to see have always admitted and always will, that life's driving force is- *Survival!*...the conflict between competitive kinds.

C360. Discrimination, take away that!..and you take away life itself.

C361. The degree of enthusiasm that accompanies a belief is in direct proportion to the intellect that holds it.

C362. A society without religion is a society without a soul.

C363. The real *Good!*...is open to all, and the more a man or woman has of it, the more he or she gives to others. This good is the love of their race, and through the love of race, the love of all living things, this is eternal.

C364. Will, is more than knowledge, because will creates what knowledge records.

C365. Faith, Hope, and Charity, of them justice is born, the plea of the many against the few, of the future against the present, but being seeds of themselves until they reach the fertile ground of wisdom, beauty, and love.

C366. Doubt is a horizon, and on it hangs the star of hope.

C367. The Caucasian Empire is the well of the race. Hence, the Alpha calls on all Caucasians to draw from this well.

C368. If our Caucasian *Racial Creativity!* disappears, there will soon be nothing left that seeks the stars.

C369. I say unto the Caucasian people, do not allow alien races, to *Disadvantage* your children?...and dislocate them from their future.

C370. Each *Biological Idea!*...has its own quest for immortality, and none are the same, they are as different and numerous as the sands of a desert.

C371. When you look into the eyes of a child, you are looking into the center of life itself, where all concepts of life merge; where the hopes of the past, the desires of the present, and the visions of the future become one. You are in the presence of the supreme idea, the *Future!*

C372. Those who would take from you by *Force!*...what you have are obeying the weakness that you project.

C373. To successfully defend your socio-cultural way of life against *Opposing Forces*, you must apply a force greater than the force oppressing you. Evolution has decided that "Prey" will be determined by the stronger bite.

C374. There are three levels of human life: *Barbarism, Labor,* and *Science.*

C375. The three laws of life: *Consumption, Production* and *Direction.*

C376. There are three times of life: our *Past, Present*, and *Future.*

C377. There are four educational pillars of life: *Levels, Laws, Times,* and *Kinds.*

C378. Whenever we feel initial certainty, we require an argument to make us *Doubt!*, not an argument to make us *Believe.*

C379. The Caucasian people must not put their *Future!*..in the hands of- *Alien Races.*

C380. Communism; is a *Crippling Political Disease* that affects human mental evolution, and in its most severe form, it reduces its host to a- *Stagnant, Useless Mass.*

C381. Democracy; a *Slow Illusionary Political Disease* of the intellect, who's most severe form is political impotence leading to *Liberal Anarchy* and the death of the society.

C382. To all the young and restless Caucasian children, you enjoy a freedom you did not earn. Your freedom has been bought and paid for with the blood and sacrifice of your Caucasian forebears.

C383. Hatred, for whatever reason, is a disease of the mind that will not allow the healing of wounds, thereby diverting the human spirit from its good path and into the dark wilderness of self-pity and revenge, a detriment unto all.

C384. Should one worship the symbols of others, or should one put up his or her own?

C385. Life has to be what it is, swirls, branching, and cell groupings, it has been predetermined, it has an author.

C386. We must never lose the wisdom to match the technology that we create.

C387. Racial identity!...means a psychological accuracy.

C388. The clarity of race removes all blindfolds and dogmatic obstructions, weeds out mental distress, unlocks all doors, and resolves all problems, for all things revolve around its origin.

C389. Hunger and love move the world.

C390. Race is the influence that civilization owes its origin to.

C391. Our "Instinctual Passions" are much stronger than our reasonable interests.

C392. If you transgress racially, many penalties await you.

C393. Race transcends all man's fallacies of - Utopia.

C394. Race is the symphony, the harmonious composition of human biology.

C395. Compromising the moral righteousness of race will bring about social caducity.

C396. Only those suffering from moral fallacy would dare challenge the Caesarism of race.

C397. Race, or kind, is the sanctified sphere of biology.

C398. To depart from one's race, is likened to losing one's compass in a great forest.

C399. Racial dereliction; is the most unforgivable of all.

C400. Those who would divide our race with the fallacies of *Equality* are filed with jealousy, and mental distortion.

C401. All races had their biological designation made many millions of years ago by the wisdom of their Fematrix.

C402. Race having a fixed value must therefore also have a determination.

C403. The Caucasian Fematrix; (Caucasia) she is the soul of our creation.

C404. It is most essential that the Caucasian people do not become the scapegoats for the social and cultural failures of alien races.

C405. Biological exclusion, (alien others!) is a natural right of all living things.

C406. Self development of civil behavior, and its intellectual disposition is an essential human process

C407. Freedom is the most misunderstood of all social states.

C408. Liberty is the root social desire of human evolution.

C409. Family is the core of education, the temple of culture, and the well of the Caucasian race.

C410. We are relative and not absolute creatures; everything we do is tinged with imperfection.

C411. The Alpha tells us: Slavery is Humankind's vilest work.

C412. Justice is the keeper of social equilibrium.

C413. You must draw from the small realm to produce in the vast realm.

C414. You are assaulted by things smaller than you and things larger than you, and both these forces seek no greater purpose than to consume you.

C415. Once a thing has shared its direction, then all other things can be shared.

C416. One of life's greatest merits is its many differences.

C417. We know that we have will, and that will may be directed by reason, and that the end to which reason points is the progress of the race.

C418. Simplicity and immediacy are the characteristics of all passionate convictions.

C419. The intensity of life is not to be measured by the degree of oscillation, for it is at the stillest point that the most tremendous energies meet; and such a point is Caucasian intelligence open to immortality.

C420. I would point out that neither liberty nor order is sufficient ends in and of themselves, although each, I think, is part of the end. The liberty that is desired is that of good people pursuing good in order; and the order that is desirable is that of good people pursuing good in liberty.

C421. A man or woman who is not constantly reiterating the process of criticism is a man or woman who has no right to enthusiasm, for he or she has attained it at the cost of drugging their minds with passion.

C422. If liberty be taken on its own merits, how is it to be distinguished from anarchy? How, but by the due admixture of coercion, and that admitted, must we not descend from the mountaintop of prophecy to the dreary plains of political compromise?

C423. Beware of alien races that would destroy the Caucasian image in the eyes of the world. The downfall of the Caucasian social order is their reword.

C424. Swift public punishment to those who abuse our children, morally and physically; in this there can be no compromise.

C425. We must never cease to colonize, for in colonizing we are assured a better chance of survival

C426. There is no sense in deluding ourselves; alien races have a political and social agenda, and it is based on Caucasian social and political demise.

C427. It is not, perhaps, unreasonable to conclude that a pure and perfect democracy is a thing not attainable by humankind, constituted as they are of contending elements of vice and virtue, and ever mainly influenced by the predominant principle of self-interest. It may, indeed, be confidently asserted that there never was that government called a republic that was not ultimately ruled by a single will, and therefore (however bold may seem the paradox,) virtually and substantially a monarchy.

C428. It is by conflict that the higher emerges from the lower, and the Great Spirit herself (Fematrix), it would seem, does not direct but looks on, as her world emerges in painful toil from chaos.

C429. Search all the human records of history, and you will seek in vain for *Prosperity* so immense, so continuous, as that which has blessed the Caucasian race.

C430. The Caucasian possibilities that lie in the womb of the race (its culture) are greater than we can gauge; we can but facilitate their birth. We may not prescribe their future.

C431. To precipitate organic change is to court reaction; that is the lesson of all revolutions.

C432. I sympathize with the somewhat extreme view of the ancient world that those who are engaged in trade ought to be excluded from public office.

C433. The Caucasian people should always look to the end, and this also applies to race relations, striving both to limit and express by our institutions the forces with which we have to deal.

C434. Let our racial constitution express the balance of forces in our society.

C435. We must never substitute the unfit for the fit; this would dislocate the human social universe.

C436. When we are convinced of our necessities, we must inaugurate them wholeheartedly and carry them through to the end.

C437. We have come to believe that alien races will adapt Caucasian social policy, but why should they, unless it is to their advantage? We Caucasians adapt to it because we think it is to our advantage, and we will abandon it, if we ever change our minds.

C438. The forces that move the politician's world have passed out of their control, and it is only where the forces are at work that the living ideas move upon the waters. Politicians don't study science; that is the extraordinary fact, and yet every day it becomes clearer that politics is either an applied science or charlatanism.

C439. That which shelters our weakness must be torn down, if we would face the truth and pursue our destiny. There we shall see amid the blinding storms of hatred and fear, of dark suspicion and indifference, the direction our road lies across. Then, and then only will we come to understand the true spirit of our race.

C440. Appetite, this is the strongest predetermined need.

C441. All life is lived in degrees, densities, and dimensions of matter.

C442. The needs of life are determined by the environment the determiner finds itself in.

C443. The Caucasian people and their society must never let an alien race become autoecious on them, for like all parasites, they will destroy the life of their host.

C444. The Caucasian race carries with it, its own certainty, and on that rests the certainty of Caucasian society.

C445. To change institutions without changing hearts is idle arrogance.

C446. It is her will to create one who has the power to create himself. If he falls, she fails; back goes the metal to the pot, and the great process begins anew, but if he succeeds, she succeeds, and her fate is in his hands.

C447. Yet still, after centuries of social stumbling, reason is no more than the furtive accomplice of habit and force. Force creates; habit perpetuates; reason the sycophant sanctions; and so we drift!

C448. Nature watches humanity in anguish, self-forbidden to intervene, unless it is to annihilate.

C449. The man that is to be, comes at the call of the man that is.

C450. We must not give the social reins to liberal zealots; they will drive us back to the abyss.

C451. Race: the aim is perfection; the method, selection. Science is its minister; ethics its lord. It spares no prejudice, respects no habit, and honors no tradition. Institutions are stubble in the fire it kindles. It throws the present and the past into the jaws of the future without remorse. It is the angel with the flaming sword, swift to dispose of the nonbeliever.

C452. Let us be patient and follow each his or her path, waiting on the word of the Alpha, until he is pleased to reveal it, for his way is not hard; it is joy and peace unalterable. Those in faith, will be blessed with the knowledge of - *Race*.

C453. We must be critics with a full consciousness that we are part of the absolute principle of - *Racialness*.

C454. To deny kind is to deny the essence of life itself.

C455. Beware of moral illusions; these are the most dangerous of all self-inflicted mind drugs.

C456. The unity of race is the unity of history.

C457. Biological (racial) survival is the principal project of the mind.

C458. The large gap between mind and matter has been filled in part by new views on mind, but much more by the realization that physics tells us nothing as to the intrinsic character of matter.(is consciousness a natural attribute of matter!..or is it a parasite?..and matter, just its host?)

C459. All Caucasians must become aware of the tools of the moral magician

C460. America, the Caucasians newest social child, conceived and raised by Caucasian culture, it was this social child that gave the greater promise of a Caucasian future, but fate would strike a terrible blow upon this newborn. It has developed moral and social insanity, the prognosis, suicidal.

C461. All Caucasians must prepare for the coming of the New Caucasian Empire.

C462. When the children's worth is compromised, the end is near; there is no turning back.

C463. In the end, Caucasianism will rise from the bottom and seek the top, and all will fall before it.

C464. Those who do not possess the star of the Caucasian Empire will not receive the benefits of the empire.

C465. Only a spiritual Caucasian racial union will prevail in the end.

C466. The true poverty of mind is the absence of origin.

C467. Those Caucasians who believe in the empire will believe in themselves.

C468. The greeting to all Caucasians of the empire will be done with the right hand clinched in a fist, brought to the heart, and then brought back up with an open palm, to hail the empire. This is the ancient salute of our forefathers.

C469. The new Dark Age will last until the Caucasian nations are united under a single- *Empire.*

C470. All Caucasians in the empire shall humble themselves before the golden star, the symbol of the Caucasian Fematrix, and our racial spirit.

C471. In the end, the empire will prevail. Truth will prevail, and the Caucasian race will prevail.

C472. The right of laying down the rules of a society belongs only to those who created the society.

C473. The general will of the people is always rightful, but the judgment that guides it is not always enlightened.

C474. The Alpha tells us: The *Entity Particle*?...the becoming (by chance!) of the creator; A one time singularity in the depths of the infinite molecular cosmos, having never been before, nor will ever be again! the becoming of the bio-cosmic being...the Fematrix, (the female will!) and the birth of her intention?

C475. There must be racial covenant and positive laws to unite rights with duties and to direct justices to its object.

C476. We must join divine worship to a love of our race, and in making the race the object of the Caucasian people's adoration, it teaches that service to the race is the service of the spiritual whole.

C477. Everything is hopeless. Nothing legitimized has any force, once the laws have force no longer.

C478. Reform the opinions of a person, and the person's morals will be purified of themselves.

C479. To judge morals are to judge what is honored; to judge what is honored is to look to opinion as law.

C480. It is useless to separate the morals of a race from the object of its esteem, both spring from the same principle.

C481. The moment the government usurps the sovereignty of the race, the social pack is broken, and all the ordinary citizens will recover by right their natural freedom.

C482. The body politic, no less than any other body, begins to die as soon as its born and bears within itself the causes of its own destruction.

C483. As soon as someone says of the business of the state, what does it matter to me? Then the state must be reckoned lost.

C484. Every action has two causes that concur to produce it. One is moral, the will that determines the act; the other is physical, the strength that executes it.

C485. What makes the task of the lawgiver so difficult is less what has to be established than what has to be destroyed, and what makes success so rare, is the impossibility of binding the simplicity of nature together with the needs that society creates.

C486. Whoever wills the end wills also the means and certain risks; even certain casualties are inseparable from these means.

C487. Just as an architect who put up a large building first surveys and tests the ground to see if it can bear the weight, so the wise lawgiver begins not by laying down laws good in themselves, but by finding out first whether the people for whom the laws are intended are able to support them.

C488. Whoever wishes to preserve his or her own life at the expense of others, must give his or her life for them when it is necessary.

C489. The nearer human natural powers are to extinction or annihilation, and the stronger and more lasting their acquired powers, the stronger and more perfect will be their social institutions.

C490. What does the Caucasian race gain, if it's very condition of civil tranquility is one of saver hardship? There is a peace in dungeons, but is that enough to make dungeons desirable?

C491. When the Caucasian race reaches a point where the obstacles to its preservation in a social state proves greater than its strength to preserve itself in that state, beyond that point, the Caucasian social order cannot endure, for the race will perish if it does not change its mode of existence.

C492. Every human has the right to risk his own life, in order to preserve it.

C493. Victory is the object of war, not lengthy operations, no matter how brilliantly conducted.

C494. Weapons are ominous tools to be used only when there is no other alternative.

C495. In the administration of rewards and punishment, there must be reliability.

C496. Racial kind is the work of the free mind, the physical artistic expression of necessity, desire, and choice.

C497. Do not charge people to do what they cannot do; select them and give them responsibility commensurate with their ability.

C498. What is essential in the temperament of a leader is steadiness.

C499. The race that is united in its *Social Purpose* will be victorious in its com-petitive ascent.

C500. Humankind in its awkward thrust toward the stars may repeat itself in vastly separate times and places, driven by the same longing to create a beauty that will survive its passing. *Character* and *Wisdom* produce an individualized truth and each person his or her own measure.

C501. When principles are *Established* or *Recognized*, we the Caucasian people must sacrifice accordingly.

C502. All Caucasians have an obligation to their ancestral trust; it is the root of our social and cultural being and the religious covenant of the Caucasian female, our sacred Fematrix.

C503. The right rewards for the right behavior get the right results.

C504. We Caucasians need cohesive competition, not divisive confrontation.

C505. The Caucasian people will exchange their hard-earned money for only two things, good feelings and solutions to problems.

C506. Every Caucasian man born of his Fematrix is entitled to success. It is your birthright; not to pursue it is folly.

C507. Caucasians must not engage in self-delusion when it comes to alien interest.

C508. In political parties, the Caucasian people must be watchful where integrity ends and fraud begins.

C509. All Caucasians must remember that making poor but popular decisions leads to unpopularity when the poor results of those decisions finally catch up with you.

C510. A trusted and respected leader is more effective than one from whom followers withhold information in order to protect it.

C511. Caucasians prone to political maneuvering may gain power and influence by appearing to have abilities that they in fact lack.

C512. A well-trained child won't always make the best choice, but an untrained child is not likely to know a good choice from a bad one.

C513. The Caucasian man must understand that the Caucasian woman will listen to what you say, but they will believe only what you do.

C514. The courage that takes one into the unknown usually supplies the skills and ability to sail successfully through strange seas.

C515. Learn how to say no. Anyone can say yes; it's easy, but too many of us have never learned the art of saying no, the world has instant respect for the person who can say no.

C516. Initiative; turns you into a free person, a person of pride and honor.

C517. The first key to real Caucasian kinship is the magic word *same*. Same is the connecting principal and psychological climate of all living things.

C518. The Caucasian family meal is at its best when the food is mixed with great conversation. Draw your children into a conversation with yourself. Children are funny, clever, and witty. Your family dinner will change into a magic, thrilling place; a miracle will happen, the union of family.

C519. Life, it is a compounded inner-dimensional existence.

C520. We, the Caucasian males, must always be in the service of the need, and that need is the Caucasian female, our Fematrix.

C521. Most, if not all people will behave the way the reward system teaches them to behave.

C522. The Caucasian woman must understand that the Caucasian man is her greatest asset. In him lies her future and that of her children, and without proper management, man tends to wander.

C523. True friendship is a sheer miracle, and no one can tell another how to make a friend or where to find one.

C524. When you acknowledge that the very attempt to give compassion calls from you an important expenditure of your best faculties of understanding, boldness, and intelligence, you will put the value in, and the value will come out.

C525. No matter how commonplace, no matter how stale, empty, or totally irrelevant, become irresistible. Honor the opinions of others.

C526. If you are as missing in kin as you are in friends, prepare now to do something about it. As a member of the Caucasian race, you already have within you all the elements of Caucasian kinship. All that is needed is the desire of union, for the miracle to be yours.

C527. In trying too hard to prove your ability so as to make everyone like you, and you'll find that nobody likes you.

C528. No matter how colorless or unremarkable your past history is, it is loaded with gems of experience that can be turned into practical benefit. This is the genius within. It was not born into you; you made it yourself. Remember this: genius for the most part is the brave use of past experience.

C529. A Caucasian lady is a woman who gives a man chance to be a gentleman.

C530. The more you give constructive feedback to your children on how they are doing, the harder they will try to do better.

C531. Children must be trained to serve the family's interest, so that when they are tempted to make a quick personal gain at the expense of the family, they will instead do as they have been taught.

C532. Caucasians who are vulgar and unpleasant gain neither trust nor respect.

C533. Caucasians who criticize successful people give to unaccomplished and lazy people a rare opportunity to feel important, thereby undermining the morale of the competent majority.

C534. High-handed parents thrive on confrontation. They have closed minds and make terrible models. We need high-minded parents, not high-handed ones.

C535. Your dreams should always exceed your grasp, and your perfection in leadership is an ideal to move toward, not a goal you should expect to reach.

C536. The fortunate Caucasians will reject fantasies that they are invincible.

C537. An alien race's responsibility to and for itself should never become the burden of the Caucasian people.

C538. The Caucasian people should not be made to suffer, while their leaders increase their own wealth and privilege.

C539. When the Caucasian people reap the rewards of their race's successes. They should also be accountable for their race's problems and failures.

C540. A Caucasian child should learn early in life that not everyone will be his or her friend, and a child who is not a friend need not be an enemy.

C541. When a female tells a male where his performances is substandard and what he must do to meet expectations, it is a great day, but when a female fails to tell a poorly performing male how to meet expectations, it is a bad day. In the first instance, the male learns that the female is not happy and what steps to take to make the female happy. In the second instance, the male learns only that the female is not happy.

C542. Listening is never a waste of time, if you engage in it actively.

C543. All Caucasians have been helped by teachers, mentors, and more capable leaders willing to take a chance on our unproven skills. We are all successful by the hands and hearts of others.

C544. Learn and get better from complaints.

C545. We Caucasians must toil in the present to teach our children to solve their own problems in the future.

C546. In order to fulfill the expectations of parenthood, a parent is sometimes a very different person in public from the person he or she is in private, but no worthy parent disgraces the title, even in private.

C547. You can deal with bad advice, but you cannot act wisely without good advice.

C548. It is a prudent Caucasian parent who promises a child only that which can be delivered and then delivers all that has been promised.

C549. The fewer facts available, the more people will assume, and the more they will be wrong.

C550. If you must be your own person, that's fine, but keep in mind, standing out does not mean you will be respected or admired; it has its own demons.

C551. Children rarely understand the subtleties of complex problems. Women too often allow subtleties to obscure the solution. Males who understand the subtleties of a problem will expedite a solution.

C552. Your children are going to have a much better chance at success if you are successful. Your example in making something out of your own life will always be the best and greatest teacher they will ever know.

C553. As long as we keep rewarding pathological behavior, we will keep getting more of it.

C554. Most successful people have a competitive spirit. They like a test of skill, a showdown of some kind. But the more seasoned the success, the more reason comes into play to subdue this competitive instinct.

C555. The term Caucasian kinship means the union of all Caucasians for the preservation and maintenance of the eclectic cultural climate within the Caucasian race.

C556. Compassion is a great and noble thing. It is human-kind at their best. It is self-rewarding because it so clearly justifies your status as a human being.

C557. All they want to do is talk about the past, thus they are confessing to me they have nothing to offer.

C558. Act to prevent the weak defender of a good point from being defeated, and you will be loved by all and long remembered.

C559. Never ask yourself can I, because you may not be able to show all the experience to prove that you can. Make the question will I.. Say yes to it, and things you never knew you could do become easy, with the application of a little study and intelligence.

C560. What's the cost of audacity? Nothing. They will cheer you almost as loudly if you fail as if you succeed.

C561. As you force yourself to hear the frayed old opinion, you believe you are in for a bad time, but honor it; you are giving care and thereby winning care. Nothing is wasted; much is gained.

C562. To improve oneself is a commendable thought, but it's too vague to be a good goal.

C563. The Caucasian woman must never let her man lose face, as with most men it is vital to be courteous of their feelings and to listen. All they really want is someone to hear them out and respect their point of view, and as a Caucasian woman, you can give them that.

C564. The mark of true Caucasian parents is that by their conduct, they give their children excellent values for their everyday lives, as their children perceive that life.

C565. When you are afraid of failure, you can sacrifice the possibility of success.

C566. Because all Caucasians like honor, they will acknowledge that other races like it too. Hence, Caucasians must honor all humankind without regard to their economic importance, racial difference or social significance, unless their aggression dictates otherwise.

C567. If a Caucasian is free enough to make a promise, he or she should be dependable enough to keep it.

C568. Pompous, sanctimonious individuals are clearly out to sell themselves, and they think their pomposity impresses people. Actually it only estranges them.

C569. The basic principle for developing racial kinship is to forsake shame. Drop your guard that futilely tries to protect you from the misguided feelings of racial guilt and false shame. This tactic of fostering racial guilt has been put upon all Caucasians by parasitic alien races and their liberal political eunuchs. (these are sinister being!)

C570. Once you have thoroughly convinced yourself that you are a legitimate member of the Caucasian racial family, the scales will fall from your eyes, and you will come to recognize that the greatest enlightenment of all lies in just being yourself.

C571. In a Caucasian life, you must regard each crisis as part of your education. Fear it, if you must, but insist that you can learn something from it. You will recover, you will live, and this crisis will help you immensely in avoiding the next.

C572. Any and all Caucasians are instantly on their way to being successful the moment they decide to use the gifts their Caucasian Fematrix gave them, the way they were intended to be used.

C573. If you have a definite handicap or deficiency, study it for its possible advantages. In every deficiency there is a compensating asset. Before surrendering to disaster, be sure to examine the deficiency thoroughly for its potential success content, and remember this: A man who couldn't walk turned his handicap into an asset and was elected president of the greatest nation in the world four times.

C574. The most important place to cultivate good relationships in any field is at the point of personal contact.

C575. As every superior skill a child develops can be turned into an asset, sensible Caucasian parents insist that their children be taught by the very best teachers.

C576. All Caucasians must keep the Caucasian Empire's major goals in mind. Get hold of them and study them, as with your personal vision, your short and longterm decisions and plans should support them.

C577. Caucasian parents should meet with each one of their children to speak about goals and standards, get their opinions, and get agreements as to what is expected of them. Caucasian parents should not try to spell out their children's future in minute detail, so that their children don't have any room to use their own talent and creativity.

C578. Obsolescence is not a quality we should reward in our leadership.

C579. All the money, all the resources, and all the good will can serve as no substitute for personal responsibility.

C580. The Caucasian attitude is to build your confidence and your image by going for the most positive attitude you can. To do that, try your best to have a Caucasian social vision; think Caucasian race and its future.

C581. Anything a Caucasian parent can do to infect their children with a love for words, is a direct contribution toward their children's future success.

C582. If you dwell on failure rather than success and your mental choice is that it's all *over,* I'm *a* loser, I'll never be much good, and begin to act accordingly, you are sacrificing your self-image on the altar of self-pity, and you deserve nothing but contempt.

C583. Showing your children that you are approachable with their problems is much more effective than saying it.

C584. The Caucasian man must be patient with his wife. Most wives are ready and willing to be managed, providing that the man does it with common sense and keeps the wife's ego in mind.

C585. The less time you spend discussing with your children what you expect them to accomplish, the more chance there is that they will accomplish something else.

C586. On the backs of the brave, the ordinary person comes to experience the pleasures of freedom.

C587. The Caucasian people must never allow themselves or their social ascension to ever become subordinate to subversive alien races, by their preaching of white guilt.

C588. Caucasian men should realize that Caucasian women respond also to positive feedback, and they will try hard to believe it, if it sounds halfway sincere.

C589. Make them feel good about being your children. Always thank them for the opportunity to help them, always reassure them that they make a wise choice when they come to you with their problems, and then back up those words with actions.

C590. Your life is in the control of any fool who makes you lose your temper.

C591. Caucasian men and women must cultivate the habit of intelligent persistence when dealing with the opposite sex, but, there are times when giving up on a particular prospect makes good sense. There's a fine line between persistence and foolishness.

C592. Intelligent Caucasian people will become winners when they realize that the way to become a winner is to make it okay to lose. Learn from the experience and move on.

C593. Learn to live with yourself; learn to converse with yourself. If your own thoughts and deliberations, your inward personal conversation can satisfy you, you will not be too expectant when you meet strangers.

C594. Everything that is a plus inside you can be exploited and should be exploited. To transfer the good inside you is to sell yourself and to win, thereby creating the success that is your proper due.

C595. All Caucasian business people, whether in top jobs or minor ones, realize that talent is by far the best connection of all.

C596. The fastest way to get ability is through study and practice. Everyone will place a bet on the person who studies and practices.

C597. You are not required to account to your friends for any self-improvement you engage in; it is all your own business and none of theirs.

C598. Your clumsy accent, your big nose, your moles and freckles can be turned into capital, if you will use them instead of merely hating them.

C599. One of the great travesties of life is that we all think we think alike, and therefore speak accordingly. The same misconception pertains to race, when we think that the races are the same and don't have *Separate Destinies*. But actually we all feel the same about race, a deep personal private feeling of one's own, of one's belonging to a separate biological social direction, one that is different from all others. Yes, our race is our passport to enduring kinship.

C600. Without boldness in the heart of the possessor, money itself loses a great deal of its power.

C601. The will to win is meaningless without the will to prepare.

C602. To motivate children you must let them know what's expected, keeping them informed, giving them some control, giving start-to-finish everyday responsibility, helping them learn and grow. And by always being approachable, you will create an environment that is stimulating to your children.

C603. Obligation through identity of kind is intrinsic to all life.

C604. While the skills of reading, writing, and speaking are taught in school, listening rarely is. Poor listening equals poor performance.

C605. Truly successful Caucasians learn from failure and use what they have learned to do better in the future.

C606. The Caucasian man must show that what he is suggesting will benefit the Caucasian woman and her family. Make it clear you are trying to do better and better work to make the family successful, and that the woman's help is necessary and valuable. Do this with sincerity and confidence, and you will be surprised how well your wife will respond to your leadership.

C607. For one to understand life, one must first learn how to disassemble that which is not physical.

C608. People in general don't buy goods; they buy solutions to problems.

C609. When Caucasian men offer Caucasian woman solutions to their dilemmas, he should state them positively and tell her what you can do, rather than what you cannot do.

C610. It will give you and your family a source of pride and confidence when you as a parent make the effort to learn and reach each of your children's needs. Time and again it's been shown that children will not resist someone who sincerely wants to help.

C611. We as Caucasians have an obligation to safeguard our racial and cultural heritage.

C612. Because people accept competition as an inevitable part of life, they look for ways to excel at it.

C613. Rewarding a Caucasian woman at the initial moment of truth begins long before she ever appears or agrees to see a man. For him, it takes a sound well thoughtout strategy and a good deal of groundwork to make the first contact successful.

C614. A Caucasian woman not only wants quality in a man, she also wants a meaningful dialogue with a man.

C615. Caucasian parenting; by reacting helpfully rather than defensively, keeping your cool, and listening for the facts with true empathy, will always help resolve family complaints or problems.

C616. Creativity is the ability to free yourself, from any imaginary boundaries, to see new relationships and patterns, and in that way, accomplish the new things of immediate and future value.

C617. Children need feedback like they need food; they want to know how they're doing. It helps them correct their performance problems and motivates them to build on their strengths. Feedback is not hard to give out; make sure you as a parent are giving it on a regular basis.

C618. Keep it small, keep it simple. These are two valuable skills for you to master and use.

C619. For better or worse, your children have an opinion about the world around them, and collecting, gathering, and measuring those opinions on a regular basis provide the crucial information that Caucasian parents need to adjust their parenting compass.

C620. Never underestimate the value of listening to children.

C621. Managing and guiding the Caucasian man; this is the Caucasian woman's greatest challenge.

C622. What does success mean to you? Think in terms of work, family, hobbies, sports, community activities, and your religion, and then think of the three pillars they rest upon, *Responsibility, Discipline,* and *Faith.*

C623. The Caucasian man must remember that how a Caucasian woman reacts to bad news depends largely on how you tell her. You can't always tell women what they want to hear, but you can tell them in such a way that they will want to listen. Nothing turns a Caucasian woman off faster than giving her a flat No or bad news at the outset. Set a positive tone at the outset.

C624. The single greatest obstacle to effective performance in most social states is the great mismatch between the behavior needed, and the behavior rewarded.

C625. Children respond in astounding ways, the moment they are given control, even a little, over the work they do. Having some say over how they do the work is a great motivator.

C626. Putting off today's decisions can ruin tomorrow.

C627. Victory is often won late in battle.

C628. You can't change your basic personality, but you can bend or modify it. Think about your irrelevance.

C629. Some men and women just cannot be managed in a family setting. They are too stubborn, insecure, emotionally disturbed, frightened, or worried about their spouse emerging as a competitor and will not respond to any reasoning. This kind of intimate relationship should be terminated.

C630. What is the value of an art that converts a person of sense into a fool?

C631. We as Caucasians must share only with those whose contribution to the welfare of all Caucasians in both mind, body, and spirit is equal to ours. (racial benevolence!)

C632. Caucasian women should realize that strong men are good for them, though, a hard but manageable man will be a challenge, keeping you stretching, and trying harder than you would otherwise. You can learn and grow a lot with a spirited man of mettle and vigor.

C633. The racial commonwealth is the educational belief that the ideas and skills basic to our- Caucasian race, should be taught to all in the race by time tested methods.

C634. Racial fundamentalism; (Caucasianism) is a religious movement of the belief that the female of a race or species is the highest form of life and is directly linked to the universal life force The Fematrix (female will) and that each different race or species led by its female has its own destiny and must be worshiped accordingly.

C635. Identity of kind is intrinsic to all life.

C636. When a woman is critical, she is giving information. A man must con-centrate on listening for information that will help solve the problem, rather than taking the criticism personally.

C637. If change bothers you, don't worry; it bothers every one, but it is foolish to battle change, because change is inevitable. Make change work for you. (reason its benefits!)

C638. Many of the things we consider a disgrace for others has actually hap-pened to us! Every living person, rich or poor, is subject to temporary defeat and to the imaginary disgrace that goes with the defeat, if it reaches the public ear. This then, is the time to give your friend the gift of your personal presence, not your sympathy, but rather your encouragement or practical help.

C639. Never ask from another; information that you yourself would refuse to give, if you were asked the same question!

C640. We as Caucasians cannot understand either the broad political, religious or social issues of today, without some understanding of the earlier stages of human association, and that involves the understanding of- *Racial Origins*.

C641. The 𝕬lpha: is just a guide who brings his race at last to the present edge, the advancing edge of socio-cultural things, and stops and whispers to those beside him, behold our racial inheritance!...and all that it implies.

C642. One's first obligation is to their "Racial Mandate" (biological dynasty!) and its historical life strategy.

C643. We Caucasians have found from the records in the rocks that there have been long periods of expansion and multiplication. When life flowed, abounded and varied, and harsh ages when there was a great weeding out and disappearance of species, genera and classes, plus the learning of stern lessons by all that survived.

C644. What are a man's political activities, but the expression in action, of his inheritance of ideas?

C645. It must be borne in mind that great changes of our climate have always been in progress, sometimes stimulating and sometimes checking life. Every species of living thing is always adapting itself more closely to its conditions. There is no finality in adaptation. There is a continuing urgency toward change.

C646. We as "Caucasians" must maintain the integrity of our racial difference!...and its laws of forbiddance.

C647. In a vast variety of forms, the appearance of kings and priests and magic men was happening all over the world, everywhere humankind was seeking where knowledge, mastery and magic power might reside; everywhere individual people were willing, *Honestly* or *Dishonestly*, to rule, to direct, or be the magic being who would reconcile the confusion in their world.

C648. Unfortunately the Caucasian race's most devastating enemies! ...may also be those sworn to serve them?

C649. Caucasian liberals zealots have destroyed the heart and soul of their (liberal) general population, being content with the "Cultural Sedition" they had made, until the end, liberal zealots thought they could go on buying minorities (alien races!) to defend them against their enemies without, and "Caucasian Patriots" within,...they were wrong!

C650. A society that does not feel secure is difficult to lead.

C651. The Caucasian people must learn to build a problem solving approach into their lives. They owe it to themselves, their families, and their society.

C652. When the people lose faith, the leaders lose power!

C653. It is almost impossible to deal with either the *Literature* or *Art* of America as a thing in itself; both are a continuation and part of a much greater and more enduring- *Caucasian Eclectic World Culture.*

C654. Truths Protection!...under no circumstances, should now or ever be entrusted to- *Cowards.*

C655. Hatred is one of the passions that can master a life, and there is a type of temperament prone to it, ready to see life in terms of vindictive melodrama, ready to find stimulus and satisfaction in frightful demonstrations of justice or revenge, "Reason" is the true inoculation against hatred!

C656. The essence of our social failure will be that we did not sustain a Caucasian unity of "Opposition" in the face of an "Alien Invasion" into-*Caucasian Lands!*

C657. There is bitterness in acknowledging and correcting our mistakes, but to do so, is our only salvation.

C658. Beware of those who collect symptoms and effects, just to suit their own arguments.

C659. A "Serious Defect" has a very direct way of helping you take notice of your limits.

C660. The Caucasian people must never make laws that will endanger the sovereignty of the Caucasian race.

C661. There are two types of alteration in life, alteration by "Chance" and alteration by "Choice."

C662. If we the Caucasian people are ever to become whole in our social journey, we must erect a temple to the spirit of the Caucasian female, our "Fematrix," the life force of our ever-enduring biology.

C663. Education is a possession that no one can take away.

C664. You are not the only person in the world who is internally conscious of his or her own fears, inabilities, humble surroundings, holes in the socks, worn-out lining in the coat, mistakes in grammar, poverty-stricken vocabulary, and a feeble ignorance on most subjects. These, contrary to what most may think, are universal human conditions. In the act of being a Caucasian man or woman, you can break these shackles. Success is the property of any Caucasian being with enough love and compassion to embrace the spirit of the Fematrix.

C665. Life is often thought of in terms of position and loss of possession.

C666. The Caucasian citizen must beware of undemocratic acts and scenarios emerging from the shadow government of political bosses.

C667. A nation without borders is not a nation.

C668. Historians are, for the most part, very scholarly men nowadays; they go in fear rather of small errors than of disconnectedness; they dread the certain ridicule of a wrong date more than the disputable attribution of a wrong value.

C669. It would seem that in the modern marketplace of ideas, there no longer remains a place for *Integrity* and if this loss of the social compass integrity is true, then the next obvious question is what now will guide us through the wilderness of human social intervention?

C670. Sometimes we have to reach into the past, to recover the future.

C671. The best way to incorporate dependability in your own person is to make good on all your own private resolutions, and remember this: you are always in danger of unselling yourself and forfeiting many hard-won gains through a sudden exposure of undependability.

C672. Beware of changes made with reckless impunity; look to the facts.

C673. Social attitudes on the part of the public become the basis for political attitudes, and personal attitudes arise from personal experience, not from what some may believe, such as abstract thinking or facts.

C674. There is only one great miracle, and that is the miracle of birth (the journey). It is life's starting point and its final destination. All roads lead to the birth, and in the service of its living author, the Fematrix (female will), the meaningful joy of life, is revealed.

C675. Life struggles to contain itself in that which does not contain.

C676. A certain level of conflict is often present between a leader and those ambitious to lead.

C677. There is no such thing as a little self-improvement. The tiniest, most insignificant act that improves you is a huge gain. It immediately puts you into the plus column. It also puts you on intimate terms with self-progress and self-respect, and it gives you a new taste of success, and every taste of success is a firm step toward your goal.

C678. Defining makes you think. Because you cannot think without words, defining makes you handle your words with extreme care.

C679. All Caucasian men will sooner or later come to realize that the Caucasian woman (our fematrix!) doesn't want reasons; what she wants is results.

C680. The future of Caucasian society must never be put into the hands of socio-political cowards.

C681. If it is not a Caucasian?...then it is an- Alien!

C682. You have a mind, you have a heart, you have an emotional system and a wealth of many other highly personal tools for making yourself respected and honored. The fact that others have these same tools but rarely use them with real efficacy should make no difference to you. The defection of others is no excuse for your own conduct in the Caucasian world.

C683. Self-exposure of the heart and the emotions is a magnet that draws all people to you. (caution is advised!)

C684. Focusing on long-term family goals will keep you from becoming side-tracked by short-term frustration.

C685. Stop despising yourself. Self-denunciation is a very perverted form of pride. Every time you say things like, I am a loser, I haven't the guts, I can't cope with life, and you are indulging in a foolish form of obnoxious pride. You can never justify yourself with puny little words of self-effacement. Your ultimate duty in life is to be *Available* and *Productive* to your race.

C686. Never advise others in conversation tell they demand advice; advice is ordinarily resented, though its temptation hovers over every conversation.

C687. Caucasians must risk ridicule by proposing a move that is a radical move, but that they believe is right.

C688. Natural selection (will of the Fematrix) is a slower process with humans than with any other creatures. It takes sixteen years or more for an ordinary human to grow up and reproduce. In the case of most animals, the new generation is on trial within two years or less.

C689. The record of the rocks is like a great book that has been carelessly misused. All its pages are torn, worn, and defaced, and many are alto-gether missing. The outline of human history is being pieced together slowly and painfully in an investigation that is still incomplete and still in progress.

C690. The fear of the old man, your father, was the beginning of wisdom, and long after the old mans passing, Mother would continue to convey to the children how awful and wonderful he was.

C691. The love for Mother (your Fematrix) is to be in the presence of great power and mystery. She is the teacher of fear and obedience, love and compassion, and even the old man is in awe and bends to her will, for she is the Fematrix (female will), the demander of beings and spirits, creator of the musts and the must-not's. Her wonderful secrets have been and are still being discovered by her sacrificial flesh, man.

C692. Religious Intolerance and Moral Accusation, are the natural weapons of the envious against great leadership.

C693. Man's ambitions are likely to reflect the standards of their intimates.

C694. When people are held in a network of illegal restraints that make them unhappy and spiritless, this universal question will come up: What must we do for salvation? The common answer, a frequent and natural consequence, is to throw the imagination forward to an after-life that is to redeem all the miseries and injustices of this one. This belief in such compensation has always been a great opiate for current miseries.

C695. If our Caucasian society fails?...and falls into the hands of alien races, henceforth it can be said that the essence of its failure was the inability of Caucasian citizens to maintain their loyalty to their "Ancestral Trust" and therefore, could not sustain a political and cultural Caucasian unity!... deserving not pity, but contempt!

C696. In one field of knowledge particularly, we might have expected "Caucasian Intellectuals" to have been more alert!..to the serious reality of-*Racial Competition* in an-*Unnatural Multiracial State?* Does not our political and cultural interest demand it?...and is it not after all a point of *Racial Confrontation!*...and all that it implies?...and yet, to this very day, an inquiry or analysis has never been made?

C697. People are sometimes ruled by their emotions, for emotions are contagious.

C698. The future belongs to those people who see possibilities before they become obvious.

C699. Since humans have lived on earth, they have seen and wondered about rainbows. Who could have told them that those bands of color held in them a promise that one day they would be able to analyze the stars?

C700. The essence of leadership is the ability to articulate a vision and then get people to follow it.

C701. If you have a skill or an ability that appeals to the public, by all means display it anytime you are invited to do so. The public loves skill and instantly bows to its possessor. But be careful never to make a public demonstration of your lack of skill!

C702. One fails toward success.

C703. Any craftsperson, once he or she sees you as a sincere inquirer, will begin to tell you about their work. They want to pass on to other worthy souls some of the fine things that they know; this is true conversation.

C704. Children who feel confident act with confidence; it's a principle of self-perception.

C705. The law cannot think. Only people can think.

C706. Wrongful laws of discrimination will destroy candor in the social structure.

C707. Certain racial conditions we are now beginning to perceive in a Multiracial state (America) have absolutely and unequivocally confirmed the biological imperative of species domination, and it is this dose of biological reality that the political leaders have failed to bring to light. The pursuit of this social truth will be laborious, difficult, and uncertain, but we Caucasians understand that the attempt must be made, because no other prospect before us gives even a promise of happiness or self-respect or preservation of our kind.

C708. Never allow, Alien Revisionists a foothold into the affairs of our Caucasian culture.

C709. When we realize the uninspiring quality of the Multiracial State with its parasitic-hyenic subculture and its political cowardice that gave birth to its criminal indifference, we will be able to account for the failure of Caucasian America.

C710. Victory is won not in miles, but in inches.

C711. The greatest economic security in the world is to find something to do that people are willing to pay for, and then do it extremely well.

C712. A first-class image, it's not a frivolous expense, it's an investment.

C713. Caucasianism is the doctrine of racial immortality and salvation. All man serve their *Fematrix* with all that they have and with all that they are. This is the only righteous life for all mankind.

C714. Joining the Alpha on his great campaign of racial salvation can mean the successful remaking of your whole life.

C715. Caucasians should avoid doing battle, when both winning and losing will cost too much.

C716. Truth, can you afford not to learn it?

C717. If you can't take the best advice and forgive your enemies, then take the second best and forget them. The only way you can achieve true revenge is not to let your enemies cause you to self-destruct.

C718. There is no more certain recipe for disaster than a decision based on emotion.

C719. Creativity achieved at the expense of "Efficiency" is counter-productive.

C720. What makes loneliness so unbearable is the loss of one's self, which can be realized in solitude, but confirmed in its identity only by the trusting and trustworthy company of friends. In this situation, we lose trust in ourselves as the partner of our thought and the elementary confidence in the world that is necessary to make experience at all. Self and world, the capacity for thought and experience, are lost at the same time.

C721. Sometimes our sense of worth of an object is not derived from its intrinsic value, but from the demand that has been created for that object.

C722. Of all useless, time-consuming behavior, the most dangerous, expensive, and self-destructive habit of all is wasting time.

C723. Idealism, foolish or heroic, always springs from some individual decision and conviction and is subject to experience and argument.

C724. The attraction of evil and crime for the mob mentality is nothing new. It has always been true that the mob will greet deeds of violence with the admiring remark. It may be mean, but it is very clever and profitable.

C725. People participate emotionally and justify with logic.

C726. Authority, no matter in what form, always is meant to restrict or limit freedom, but never to abolish it. Totalitarian domination, however, aims at abolishing freedom, even at eliminating human spontaneity in general, and by no means at the restriction of freedom, no matter how tyrannical.

C727. Everyone who claims social benefits must also accept its risks and responsibilities.

C728. Loneliness is not solitude; solitude requires being alone, whereas loneli-ness shows itself most sharply in the company of others.

C729. Democratic freedoms may be based on equality of all citizens before the law, yet they acquire their very meaning and function organically, only where all the citizens belong to and are represented by groups or form a socio-political hierarchy.

C730. Evil can become possible in total loyalty only when fidelity is emptied of all concrete content from which changes of mind might naturally arise.

C731. The aim of an arbitrary political system (totalitarian), without doubt, is to destroy the civil rights of the whole population.

C732. Perception is the mental consumption of existence.

C733. Insist on sampling every fear you have. Test it; probe it for its pragmatic possibilities.

C734. Politicians have always been somewhat deceptive, and if we fail to monitor, hidden agendas proliferate. More and more, the lying will become pathological.

C735. We must never allow our representatives to exclude themselves from the laws and rules they would bestow upon us.

C736. When thinking of our government, we must always remember that a representative democracy (democratic state) is the making of sound legislation, not the development of reckless spending.

C737. When thinking of our empire, we must always remember this: The female hereditary monarchy (sovereign state) is the spiritual and physical core of our socio-biologic wholeness, not a despotic exercise of power.

C738. The need to feel good about ourselves should never replace inner convictions so as to satisfy our charitable instincts without ever considering the value of what they're doing or its harmful results.

C739. The eternal life force (Fematrix) is a transforming illumination that brings harmony, peace, and attunement to the world and the individual's place in it.

C740. Biological laws (racial) do not depend upon our intellectual acceptance of them in order to operate in our lives.

C741. Caucasian illumination brings about calmness and the spirit of serenity, and the actions that are based on Caucasian illumination and racial attunement stem from the great divinity of the Caucasian Fematrix. (Caucasia!)

C742. The eternal life force (the Fematrix) is the spiritual energy behind all things, in all things, controlling all. She is the fundamental power of the universe. Through Caucasian attunement we are able to be conductors of her power, so that it flows through us and remains with us. She is by far the very center of our being; she is our very soul.

C743. When you understand the dynamic laws of the racial self, you can then direct your life toward your most cherished fulfillment, and by tapping the hidden power of your own racial spirit, you will come to know where you stand in the total scheme of all things.

C744. A life transformed by Caucasian attunement begins with a search, a search for the truth of your being.

C745. Always remember this: people become committed to answers, answers that benefit them the most.

C746. There is as we are seeing, no social order, no security, no peace or happiness, no righteous leadership or scholarship, unless humankind loses itself in something greater than itself. To submerge oneself in greater or righteous interests is to know true freedom.

C747. There seems to be no limit to the lies that stupid disciples will tell for the glorious image of their masters, and for what they regard as the success of their propaganda.

C748. In the twentieth century a dark theology grew up about race. The theories grew and flourished; each new step, each new hypothesis, demanded another; until the whole sky was filled with forgeries of the brain, and the nobler and simpler lessons of race were smothered beneath the glittering mass of intellectual fallacies.

C749. What were slight and shallow impressions on their predecessor's cultures are now deep and intricate grooves, worn throughout the intervening centuries, generation by generation.

C750.Making a decision is one of the duties of strength.

C751. As the idea of *Caucasian Identity* begins to fail and fade before the onslaught of *Political-Correctness*, there remained still an inner, that is to say a real racial unity in the Caucasian American community. A spiritual racial unity, reaching out to Caucasian man and woman who tend more and more to retreat into *Racial Guilt* fostered upon them by the *Sinister Liberal Zealots* among them.

C752. If Caucasian America is to survive, there must be a common socio-political idea in the minds of all Caucasian Americans, an idea of their race, thought of as the personal possession of each individual and as the backbone fact of their scheme of duties.

C753. Much mischief results from our taking a moral position on matters that are not basically moral matters at all.

C754. If every time children come up with an opinion they are squelched and put in their place, they will learn that it is right for them to be a nobody, and wrong to want to be a somebody. Such a distorted and unrealistic conscience does indeed make cowards of us all.

C755. Having a goal and understanding the situation are not enough. You must have the courage to act, for only by acting can goals, desires, and beliefs be transformed into realities.

C756. Faith, does not believe something in spite of the evidence; it is the courage to do something regardless of the consequences.

C757. Nothing in this world is ever absolutely certain or guaranteed. Often the difference between a successful person and a failure is not one's better abilities or ideas, but the courage that one has to bet on his or her ideas, to take a calculated risk and to act.

C758. We can destroy our self-confidence by remembering past failures and forgetting all past successes. We not only remember failures, we impress them on our minds with emotion. We condemn ourselves. We flay ourselves with shame and remorse (both are highly egotistical, self-centered emotions), and then our self-confidence disappears.

C759. The cause of Caucasian difficulties in dealing with all alien races is not a deficiency of power but an excess of the wrong kind of power, which results in a feeling of impotence when it fails to achieve its desired ends. Inadvertently; we Caucasians have reduced some of the intended beneficiaries of our great generosity to a condition of dependency and self-denigration.

C760. In a democracy, dissent is an act of faith.

C761. The great value of history is not what it seems to prohibit or prescribe, but its general indication as to the kinds of social policies that are likely to succeed and the kinds that are likely to fail, or its hints as to what is likely not to happen.

C762. The historical question of this Caucasian age is whether a change radical enough to close the gap between traditional political behavior and the requirements of racial survival is possible within the limits imposed by a judicial fallacy.

C763. It seems that in the twenty-first century, neither the government nor the universities are making the best possible use of their intellectual resources to deal with the problems of the Multi-racial state. Both seem by and large to have accepted the idea that the avoidance of racial war is a matter of skillful crisis management, as though the law of averages hasn't already been more than kind to us.

C764. A problem is the difference between what you have and what you need.

C765. Despite its very dangerous and unproductive consequences, the idea of being responsible for the whole world seems to be flattering to Caucasians. Sincere though it is, the Caucasian effort to remake other races in its own image is nothing short of a fatal impact resulting in accusations of cultural genocide and submergence into pathological racial hatred on the part of alien races toward Caucasians.

C766. Facts, exist independent of motives.

C767. The most valuable public servant, like the true patriot, is one who gives a higher loyalty to his or her country's ideals than to its current policy, and who therefore is willing to criticize as well as comply.

C768. A political or social consensus must be understood to mean a general agreement on goals and values, but not necessarily on the best means of realizing them. Then and only then does it become a lasting basis of national strength.

C769. Freedom of thought and discussion in a society always diminishes the danger of an irretrievable mistake, and it introduces ideas and opportunities that otherwise would not have come to light. We Caucasians are much in need of this benefit, because we are severely, if not uniquely, afflicted with the habit of policymaking by historic guilt, through liberal zealot accusation.

C770. The responsibilities of high office are burdensome indeed, but they are borne, let it be remembered, by men and women who actively sought or freely accepted them, men and women who accepted not only the obligation to use power, but also the obligation to account for its use.

C771. A revolution, after all, is not in itself a blessing; it is the product of social and political failure, and its sole merit is that it provides the means to dispose of atrophied institutions and introduce the hope of social justice. It is important, therefore, that we Caucasians set aside false analogies put upon us by the architects of the Multiracial state and recognize the eternal importance of our ancestral and biological trust.

C772. The university cannot separate itself from the society of which it is a part, and neither can the community of scholars accept existing public policies as if they set limits on responsible inquiry. The proper function of the scholar is not to exclude certain questions in the name of practicality or in the name of a spurious patriotism, but to ask all possible questions, to ask what has been done wisely and what has been done foolishly, and to determine what the answers to these questions imply for the future.

C773. The Caucasian people must never fail to support the act of dissent in the democratic state; a true consensus is shaped by airing differences rather than suppressing them.

C774. Politicians have no right to ask that they be absolved from public judgment; they may hope, however, that they will be fairly judged principally on the basis of their performance in the areas of their principal effort.

C775. The Alienquest [ale-in-kwest] alien races and their attempt at world conquest is a great hunger and a very particularly enticing vision of their social direction. The evil in the Alienquest is not doctrinal content, which at worst is a social fallacy, but more to its fanatical certainty, of its parasitic hyenic cultural zeal.

C776. It is not the child who is taught about love, but the child who has experienced love who grows into a healthy, happy, well adjusted adult.

C777. The self-image is the key to human personality and human behavior. Change the self-image, and you change the personality and the behavior. Self-image sets the boundaries of individual accomplishment. It defines what you can and cannot do. Expand the self-image, and you expand the area of the possible. The development of an adequate, realistic self-image will seem to imbue the individual with new capabilities and new talents and literally turn failure into success.

C778. Despite our genuine sympathy for those who cry out against poverty and social injustice, and despite the material support that we Caucasians give to many of the world's poor (90% being of alien racial status), we Caucasians are finding ourselves and our societies in a constant state of alien parasitic siege, and its greatest impact overall is being felt in Caucasian America, where the affliction of Multiculturalism, a form of liberal utopian dementia, has severely infected the body politic, causing severe *Logic* and *Economic* hemorrhage.

C779. The first step toward acquiring knowledge is the recognition of those areas where you are ignorant. The first step toward becoming stronger is the recognition that you are weak.

C780. Historians today still discuss the problems raised by Burckhardt, but they are also learning to view those problems from a new perspective. They are exploring aspects of Caucasian society and social experience inaccessible to Burckhardt and many other earlier social historians.

C781. Humanism means classical scholarship, the ability to read, understand, and appreciate the writings of our Caucasian ancestors. In classical antiquity, and again in the Caucasian European renaissance, educators called this Caucasian curriculum most suitable for the training of free and responsible persons (the studies of the humanities). This curriculum was designed to develop in the student primarily those qualities of intellect and will that truly distinguished men and women from animals, and to its greatest champion, Petrarch, we Caucasians give our love to he who so clearly understood love.

C782. Unsettled religious spirit, a religion that fails to console is a religion in crisis.

C783. Without a disciplined and unified view of the world, attitudes toward war, love, and religion lose balance, and disordered behavior follows.

C784. Racial criticism, in short, is more than a right; it is an act of patriotism.

C785. Relations among races, between enmity and amity there must be a period of disengagement, a period in which passions cool, perceptions change, and new perspectives are formed. I do not think Caucasians should be in a precipitate hurry to convert their current animosity to hostile alien races into warm friendship.

C786. Of all the traps and pitfalls in life, the lack of selfesteem is the deadliest and the hardest to overcome, for it is a pit designed and dug by our own hands, summed up in the phrase, it's no use, and I can't do it.

C787. Sometimes how you do something is more important than what you actually accomplish.

C788. What is revered and rewarded in our culture can be an open invitation to disaster in another.

C789. We Caucasians are shaped by our values, interests, and customs, and like our churches, universities, and political parties, we have been formed by past experience. Both individually and collectively we use the past to explain and justify our hopes and ambitions, our fears and conflicts. We use it to define who we are, to connect our personal experience to the history of our race.

C790. The Caucasian family creed: What does the family need that's not being provided? How can I serve them better?

C791. If you are continually being mistreated, chances are you're cooperating with the treatment.

C792. A college course is not the only way to build a personal culture; neither is history the only path to integrated knowledge. Racial illumination and its social grace is to experience the study of Caucasianism as one of the vital intellectual activities by which we Caucasians come to know who and what we are.

C793. Complacency breeds failure, and self-dissatisfaction is the key to improvement.

C794. The Caucasian experience, far from being unified has always been deeply divided in its social quest. The point that I wish to make is not that Caucasianism is a vital social revolution, (which it is!) but that the future of a strong Caucasian state is more desirable, from the viewpoint of Caucasian interests, than a weak non-Caucasian state (Multiracial State) whose very weakness and disunity forms a vacuum, inviting cultural conquest and moral subversion.

C795. The person in whom the capacity to enjoy is dead can find enjoyment in nothing; no goal is worth working for; life is a terrible bore; nothing is worth while. But the truth is that joy is an accompaniment of creative function, of creative goal-striving. It is possible to win a fake success, but when you do, you are penalized with an empty joy.

C796. The individual who is actively engaged in a struggle or in striving toward an important goal does not come up with pessimistic philosophies concerning the meaninglessness or the futility of life.

C797. One of the biggest mistakes we as Caucasians can make is to confuse our behavior with our self, to conclude that because we did a certain act, it characterizes us as a certain sort of person. Being realistic, to say I failed, is but to recognize an error and can help lead to future success. But to say that I am a failure does not describe what you did, but what you think the mistake did to you. We also seem to recognize that all children, in learning to walk, will occasionally fall. We say he fell or he stumbled; we do not say he is a faller or he is a stumbler.

C798. Conscience doth make cowards of us all. So said the great Caucasian dramatist Shakespeare. Conscience steers us, or guides us, down the straight and narrow to the goal of correct, appropriate, and realistic behavior insofar as ethics and morals are concerned. But if we are to let our conscience be our guide, our conscience must be based upon truth.

C799. Properly directed and controlled, anger is an important element of courage.

C800. The yardstick for judging emotions is not goodness or badness, as such, but appropriateness and inappropriateness.

C801. Resentment: is an attempt to make our own failure palatable by explaining it in terms of unfair treatment or injustice. But as a salve for failure, resentment is a cure that is worse than the disease. A vicious cycle is often set up. It can become a way of making one feel important, a perverse satisfaction from being wronged. The victim of injustice, the one who has been unfairly treated, believes he or she is morally superior to those who caused the injustice. Habitual resentment invariably leads to self-pity, and emotional habits of resentment and self-pity also go with an ineffective, inferior self-image. You begin to picture yourself as a pitiful person, a victim who was meant to be unhappy.

C802. The purpose of emotions is reinforcement, or additional strength, rather than to serve as a sign of weakness. The real problem is not to control emotion, but to control the choice of which tendency shall receive emotional reinforcement.

C803. When you experience Caucasian illumination, your internal machinery is set for success, and you will also experience winning feelings, self-confidence, courage, and a faith that your future will be desirable.

C804. The building of an adequate Caucasian image is something that should continue throughout your lifetime. Understanding the psychology of the Caucasian self can mean the difference between success and failure, love and hate, bitterness and happiness. On another plane, discovering your real Caucasian-self, means the difference between freedom and the compulsions of *Political Correctness* and its conformity to a liberal fallacy, the Multi-racial state.

C805. This self-image (your Caucasian illumination) becomes a golden key to living a better life because of two important facts, as follows: (1) All your actions, feelings, behavior, even your abilities, are always consistent with this self-image. It is a premise, a base, or a foundation upon which your entire personality, your behavior, and even your circumstances are built. (2) The self-image can be changed (your ego ideal), but to change it you must find and identify its root, its point of origin. Personality, after all, is an assay system of ideas, and these ideas are formed on the understanding and identity of origin. If the understanding and identity of origin is wrong, the ego-ideal or self-image will also be wrong. The answer is kind; we are all of a biological kind, a racial kind, upon which all else is built.

C806. Those who made the revolution thought they saw clearly the reason for it. They were rising against tyrannical government in which the people had no voice and against injustice, in which taxes were imposed or benefits distributed unfairly. Caucasian American leaders in the twenty-first century have become confused and indecisive men and woman, much preferring to enjoy their corporate junkets and political perks, than to supervise closely the routines and social direction of government.

C807. Prisons, or houses of long-term criminal confinement in a society, are signs of social failure. The idea of human justice is the assignment of *Merited Rewards* or *Punishment* under the law, and I must emphasize punishment for it is this task that seems to have escaped modern intellectualism.

C808. Prisons, case in point America, have now taken on the status of a dual society, with a population of more than a million, and an inner structure of schools, daycare centers, and industry. This, the prison society, will prove to be a social formula of cataclysmic disaster for America.

C809. If it has committed a crime, punish it. Do not warehouse it?

C810. The rise of crime in a society is likened to a fever in a child; it is a symptom or by product of a greater illness.

C811. When a society (Caucasian America) begins to breed into its academic circles; groups of *Intellectual Cowards* with no stomach for their cultural defense, that society has betrayed its *Ancestral Racial Trust*, thereby warranting a *vote of confidence!*...the right of the common Caucasian citizen.

C812. The amazing results that follow from developing an adequate and realistic Caucasian image come about not as a result of self-transformation, but from self-realization and Caucasian racial revelation.

C813. Your racial-self right now is what it has always been, and all that it can ever be. You did not create it. You cannot change it. You can however realize it and make the most of what already is, by gaining a true mental picture of your Caucasian racial self.

C814. The Caucasian racial self is not a static but a dynamic thing. It is never completed and final, but always in a state of growth.

C815. You cannot correct your course if you are standing still.

C816. Societies, like individuals, can endure a limited dose of virtue and high ideals, only so much of the effort to bring heaven to earth. When societies have had their feel, the revolution abates, and the terror gives way to the thermidorian reaction.

C817. The study of any past epoch requires an effort to balance the work of death and renewal. In very few periods of Caucasian history does death and renewal confront each other so dramatically as in the years between AD 1300 and 1600. Through hunger, malnutrition, war and plague, the merciless hand of death was correcting the ledgers of life, balancing the numbers of people and the resources that supported them. It is wise to reflect on this period.

C818. Sooner or later the law of averages will turn against the Caucasian Americans, and the law of averages will be greatly influenced by alien racial numbers.

C819. The first step toward control of alien races and their competitive instinct is to acknowledge it? No Caucasians however, whether politicians, or social architects, have yet undertaken a serious and concerted effort to put the survival of our Caucasian American culture on a more solid foundation! This is for sure: we Caucasians have somehow got to try to grasp the idea of Caucasian cultural destruction by some means other than actually experiencing it.

C820. In racial politics, as in domestic economic's, competitive instincts are natural and within limits creative, but so prone are they to break out of those limits and to wreak havoc that Caucasians must maintain means to confine them to their proper sphere, or alas, our society will be destroyed.

C821. There is, in the matter of race relations, a strain toward consistency that leads a race, once it has decided that another race is good or bad, peaceful or aggressive, to interpret every bit of information to fit that preconception, so much so that even a genuine concession offered by one is likely to be viewed by the other as a trick to gain some illicit advantage. Obviously this human tendency helps to explain the savagery of war and the psychological phenomenon of antagonists to dehumanize each other.

C822. Ideology influences perception; perception shapes expectation; and expectation shapes behavior, making for what is called the self-fulfilling prophecy. Thus, for example, aliens fearing Caucasians, but lacking power, threaten and bluster, confirming the Caucasian fear of aliens and causing them to arm against them, which in turn heightens alien's fear of Caucasians. Each has filtered information from the real world through its ideological racial view, selecting the parts that fit, rejecting the parts that do not, and coming out with two radically different interpretations of the same events; hence, racial (or kind) ideology.

C823. We Caucasian Americans must dissolve the Multiracial State and come to realize that *Racial Paternalism* is no longer a workable basis for our relations with alien races. The combatant races in America desire true political and economic independence; they want their own socio-racial system in their hands!

C824. The emerging alien insurrection (political correctness) in the Multiracial state of America is developing and will continue to develop into a parasitic-hyenic entrenched culture. The hard fact of the matter is that conditions are deteriorating in the Multiracial America at a pace and on a scale that outweighs all current efforts to reverse the tide. Hence, this truth: you cannot govern a people who do not recognize your authority.

C825. Hostages of the Multiracial State, brotherhood and freedom, which are the creed of the Multiracial State, are a cruel social fallacy that can never be realized, due to the absolute principle of species domination. The truth is that only one racial culture can lead or rule a nation, and if for some reason there happens to be other races in that nation, those races will be culturally dominated or held hostage. This is an absolute necessity for the survival of the dominant racial culture. It is hoped that Caucasian America will come to understand the truth of this scenario and work toward the equitable dissolving of the Multiracial State before it is engulfed in racial fire and death.

C826. It is an established psychological principle, or for that matter, just common sense, that the strongest and most viable human bonds are those that are voluntary, a voluntary bond being, by definition, an arrangement that one is free to enter or not to enter.

C827. The cultural war in Caucasian America (and it is a war) as now being fought is open-ended. With little prospect of either negotiation or effective legislation, the conflict is gradually expanding in scale and intensity, raising two distinct and exceedingly distasteful possibilities: either it will remain a protracted endurance contest in which Caucasian lives and culture are sacrificed in small but unlimited installments while the politicians and liberal zealots stand aside, or that it will explode into an all-out war with aliens and their liberal Caucasian allies as well. But what is apparent is the level of alien violence and Caucasian cultural capitulation has become so high that either Caucasians will rise to the occasion or they will lose their nation!

C828. The crusading Caucasian American spirit has had a great deal to do with some of the regrettable and tragic events in Caucasian America, no doubt! By a sincere desire to bring *Freedom* and *Justice* to all, we Caucasians lost sight of the *True Nature* of man, and that nature being that it will simply not allow itself to be instantaneously remade, and has a list of failures, Desegregation, Great Society, Affirmative Action, Multicul-turalism, and Political Correctness, are all bewildered testimonies to that nature.

C829. Caucasian racial solidarity has been outlawed in the Caucasian America home, their children are now forbidden to think in terms of their-*racial identity?* Hence, "Caucasian Racial Persecution" is now a fact in America. Alas!...our Caucasian survival?..is it not time to- *Rethink it!*

C830. The conspiracy of guilt that has been fostered upon Caucasian Americans by its own government for being white is a modern lesson in racial treachery. Hence, Negroes and Asians may make race the centerpiece of their identity and their racial solidarity as a healthy expression of pride, but Caucasians racial pride is punished by being labeled as racism, hatred, and bigotry?...our *Enemies* are at our gates!

C831. Unconditional economic support (welfare) for aliens as well as Caucasians is to this very day an unwise social doctrine. Aside from its negativism as a social aim and the fact that it has submerged certain alien and Caucasian intellects into a parasitic-hyenic culture, those that are receiving it become addicted and lose their vital creative instinct of social ascension, and hence, deteriorate to the level of all other dysfunctional dependent souls.

C832. Caucasian America, in the words of John Quincy Adams, should be the well-wisher to the freedom and independence of all, but the champion and vindicator only of her own! Not the Multi-racial state.

C833. Our Caucasian economy is geared to human acquisitiveness, and our politics to human ambition. Accepting these qualities as part of human character, we have been able in substantial measure both to satisfy them and to civilize them.

C834. The realism about *Alienquest* will prove in the long run to be our greatest asset over liberal fallacy, which can deny and denounce, but even with all the liberal zealots subterfuge!...they cannot remake human racial nature.

C835. The true difficulty about liberal noble deeds has not been in its motives, but in the very perverseness of human nature, in the regrettable fact that most liberal legislators are loutish and ungrateful when it comes to improving their own souls and more often than not have to be forced into their own salvation.

C836. Who are the self-appointed liberal crusaders in Caucasian America? They are men and women with liberal doctrines; men and women of faith and idealism; men and women who confuse power with virtue, who believe in social fallacy without doubt, and practice that belief without scruples; men and women who cease to be Caucasian racial beings with normal preferences for their culture and racial identity, but have become instead a living, breathing embodiment of some- *Paternalistic Ideological Fallacy*.

C837. From the destruction of the Caucasian American culture onto the parasitic-hyenic, Multiracial State, liberal paternalism is the extreme practitioner of the arrogance of Multiculturalism that is spearheading the capitulation of Caucasian American identity and its culture. This is being done in a way that has never been known to a rational Caucasian world. The elements of this liberal fanaticism must be brought into the light, challenged, and removed, if "Caucasianism" (our destiny as a people!) is to survive.

C838. The cause of the cultural change in Caucasian America society is an ideological crisis. The result has been an unhinging of *Traditional Relationships* such as family, husband and wife, children and parents, citizen and government, and the forum of diverse opinions in the academics between the races has degenerated to the point where truth is now being sacrificed on the altar of- *Intellectual Cowardice*.

C839. We Caucasian Americans would do well, however, to stop deluding ourselves about the likelihood of racial brotherhood. We would do well, for example, to stop proclaiming the mystical triumph of social equality, when the more pertinent fact is that neither brotherhood nor equality exist; they are strictly tools used in the crafting of social guilt, and Caucasian identity capitulation.

C840. It would require a great deal of optimism to expect alien races in Caucasian America, beset as they are with problems of poverty, over population, and declining education, to achieve by peaceful means what other people with greater advantages were able to achieve only by violent revolution. This is the true curse of the Multiracial State. Truth, in the end, will begin to undo a nation, when its foundation rests upon the sands of social fallacy.

C841. The *Criminal Act* versus the *Wrongful Act* means in the committing of a crime, besides the basic question of who did it, there is a second question of was it deliberate. Though the act itself is always punishable, it is the so-called status of the act that determines the severity of punishment. Hence the criminal act is an act of intention, while the wrongful act had no such intention.

C842. Trial by jurist (law judge) versus trial by jury (average citizen) this has always been an intellectual joust in the arena where commoner versus baronage. It has always been a question of the honorable pursuit of truth and who is best suited to that task. It is my belief that it is the jurist, and not the jury system, that is best suited for the pursuit of truth, because of the legal educational pursuit and the large appointments of commoners to the jurists position. Though the baronage still possesses its great wealth, and that is good, the law has now become the sovereign of us all, and it is the commoner in our modern world who now interprets and enforces that sovereign will.

C843. Criminal punishment, In Caucasian society there are six types of punishments for crimes against the people, death, banishment, castration, flogging, public service, and monetary restitution. *Imprisonment;* should not exist in Caucasian society.

C844. The great challenge in Caucasian law is to make certain that the major strand in our law, the strand of judicial steadiness, does not falter under the weight of individual interest or personal vendetta, and by keeping the law an icon we can hold to and believe in, we, as Caucasians, and our society will prosper.

C845. It is the Alpha's belief that the man who makes the best contribution to his race, is the one who begins by meeting his responsibilities to himself and to his own family. By analogy, it seems to him that it is unnatural and unhealthy for a race to be engaged in global crusades for some principle or ideal while neglecting the needs of its own people. Indeed, it seems far more likely that the race that does most to benefit itself in the long run is the race that begins by meeting the needs of that portion of humanity that resides within its own biology.

C846. In the struggle against the *Alienquest* of 1940 to 1945, the Caucasian Americans and their Caucasian brethren throughout the world rose to meet this deadly alien challenge. It was a long, bloody struggle, but in the end we Caucasians were victorious; our enemy was defeated. The moral of such a conflict is to recognize the truth of the *Alienquest*. It is true that one cannot undo the past, but the assessment of past errors is absolutely indispensable to efforts to correct them and to avoid their repetition.

C847. In both psychological and traditional political terms and which could serve as a workable alternative to the Multiracial State of America and a possible plane for peace between the warring races, the key to peace is a mutual disengagement (divide the country) or E. R. S. (equitable racial separation) through political arrangement. This idea is not as radical as it may seem. India (a democratic nation) did it because of its uncom-promising religious conflict, and though very socially traumatic at first, it proved to be very successful. If religion can do it, then why not race?

C848. Pavlov, on his deathbed, was asked to give one last bit of advice to his students on how to succeed. His answer was passion and gradualness.

C849. Creativity is certainly one of the characteristics of the life force. As a group, Caucasians, research scientists, inventors, painters, writers, and philosophers not only live longer, but also remain productive longer when being creative and goal oriented. (Michelangelo at eighty did some of his best work; Edison was still inventing at ninety; Picasso, past seventy-five, dominates the art world today; Wright, at ninety, was still a creative architect; Shaw was still writing plays at ninety. The Caucasian people must develop nostalgia for the future, if they want to remain productive and vital. Develop an enthusiasm for life, create a need for more life, and you will receive more life.

C850. Uncertainty is a way of avoiding mistakes and responsibility. It is based upon the fallacious premise that if no decision is made, nothing can go wrong.

C851. There is within each Caucasian person a life instinct that is forever working toward health, happiness, and all that makes for more life for the individual. This life instinct is the life spark of your Fematrix that gives racial illumination through the teachings of racial revelation.

C852. Simply stated, a delusional thought is a fixed, false belief. The person cannot be talked out of it; this is why it is called fixed. Also, it does not conform to reality and therefore considered false. Do not try to reason with delusion. It has no grain of merit or reality to it. Sincere as such efforts may be, they are a waste of time and devotion. Never let the delusional person act out his or her delusional thoughts. This is where you must be alert, anticipate the acting out, and seek professional help.

C853. Build your listening skills: Make sure you can hear what's being said. Actively focus on what's being said. Becoming a better listener will help you all day, every day.

C854. Once you have asked a person for his or her opinion on a problem, you take on a sacred obligation to listen.

C855. Don't waste your time and effort working on things that don't matter or struggling to handle events you can't control.

C856. Opinions will differ from person to person; facts stay the same. Get the facts.

C857. Remember, doing nothing is almost always an alternative, especially if solving the problem would be too difficult, too costly, and more than it's worth.

C858. When defining a problem, be careful not to settle for symptoms. Symptoms help you see that a problem exists, but they aren't the real problem. They are not definitions.

C859. Don't let assumptions stifle your creativity. Wrong assumptions set up imaginary boundaries and restrictions that suppress innovative thinking.

C860. The powerful bonds that integrated Caucasian America, bonds of law, common values, centralized and standardized education, and cultural production, are breaking down. All this explains why cities suddenly seem to be unmanageable and our universities unaccountable. The methods based on uniformity, simplicity, and permanence is no longer effective against the *Parasitic-hyenic* liberal plague that is now ravishing Caucasian America. The Multiracial theorists, the very architects who unleashed this alien hyenic cultural plague, will have much to answer for.

C861. The split-up of the races in Caucasian America is precisely analogous to the process of growth in biology. The entire march of evolution, from virus to man, displays a relentless advance toward higher and higher degrees of differentiation. Thus it is not accidental that we witness hostile trends toward *Equality* in the relationships between the races, and this is why it often seems to us that our society is cracking at the seams. It is!

C862. For Caucasian America, this leap to a new level of racial differentiation (parasitic-hyenic behavior) holds awesome implications. The Multiracial theorists (liberal zealots) in their attempt to stem the social meltdown have erected two more social barriers, Multiculturalism, and political correctness. But these two additional attempts at containment will only increase the pressure; socio-structural failure in America is imminent.

C863. No previous Caucasian generation has ever faced the social task of the twenty-first century in Caucasian America. It is only now, therefore, in our lifetime and not only in the Caucasian American society, has this potential for mass racial destruction crystallized. Thus, we Caucasians need neither blind acceptance nor blind resistance, but an array of creative strategies for shaping, deflecting, and defeating the- *Alienquest*!

C864. Toffler said in one of his great works, change is the process by which the future invades our lives, and it is important to look at it closely, not merely from the grand perspective of history, but also from the vantage point of We!...the living, breathing individuals who experience it.

C865. It is important to be very clear about what is meant by Caucasianism (religious racial nationalism). It has been best described by, as a state of mind that regards the race as the true source of all creative cultural energy, and of economic and spiritual well-being. Understood in this way, Caucasianism is true racial patriotism. You identify your- self with the race and its mystique, with its eclectic cultural state of mind, which more than any other in our time, has inspired the Caucasian people to acts of loyalty, bravery, creativity and a union of self-sacrifice- *Caucasian America.*

C866. It was *Fulbright* who said; it seems obvious that almost all of us acquire our ideological beliefs not principally as the result of an independent intellectual process, but largely as the result of an accident of birth. And psychologists say that the appeal of an ideology is that it shields the individual from the painful fact that his or her life is a minor event in the ongoing universe. The Alpha also upholds these truths but must interject the wisdom of root; the root of an ideology determines its social and spiritual truth.

C867. It is of the greatest importance that Caucasian societies throughout the world begin to shade the liberal social fallacy of the Multiracial State and embrace the true spiritual light of their Fematrix (female will); the real destination of racial union, a *Biological Nation*, the only- *True Nation.*

C868. It is only by generating the truth of race, defining it, embracing its true light, that we Caucasians will become synchronized with our Fematrix, as some already are. In such a world as we are now in, the most valued of our moral and intellectual pillars are beginning to fail, and this is due to a lack of social maintenance, not design. The social problems of tomorrow, especially those of Caucasian America, will require not a romantic fallacy of brotherhood, but a critical judgment of what the Alpha calls root identity (racial core belief) for on that and that alone rests the future of a people and their nation.

C869. Caucasian America is not alone in its struggle against the Alienquest. This liberal nightmare has infected all the great Caucasian nations in the world. Like Caucasian America, her sister states are also suffering from Multiracial delirium and are becoming societies that can no longer agree on standards of conduct, language, and manners, or on what can be seen and heard. It is these symptoms, the loss of social consensus, and moral values, that speak to the greater danger of the *Alienquest* in a Multiracial state.

C870. In psychology, they have coined the term *cognitive dissonance* to mean the tendency of a person to reject or deny information that challenges his or her preconceptions. We don't want to hear things that may upset our carefully worked out structure of belief. Hence, "Caucasianism," it threatens to undermine the liberals zealots carefully worked out fallacious concept of- *Race!*

C871. Knowing what to do isn't enough, if you haven't developed the self-discipline to do it.

C872. It was Jefferson's warning, reminding us that a wise and good government shall not take from the mouth of labor the bread it has earned. He was advising our founding fathers to be watchful of taxes. The government could not afford to impoverish its own citizens. What happened to his counsel? In 1913, a great fiscal spell was cast over America. The Sixteenth Amendment and its evil appetite can be matched only by its lack of compassion in its destruction of human lives. And hence, its new title by the beleaguered middle class, tax purgatory.

C873. When a rational racial conviction has been arrived at, it is necessary to dwell upon it, to follow out its consequences, to search out in oneself whatever beliefs are inconsistent with the new conviction that might otherwise survive. Never allow contrary irrational racial beliefs to pass unchallenged or obtain a hold over you.

C874. The sale of public office has always been a diabolical disease of all governments, but in America, the political arena has become the premier employment agency to the tune of one billion dollars. Think of this: The average person elected to Congress spent half a million dollars to get his or her job; typical senators can spend upwards of five million dollars or more for their jobs. Disgraceful, you say, well, between the PACs and the soft money schemes of both the Democratic and Republican parties, it has become campaign budgets, not the government budget; the American politician is ultimately concerned with.

C875. The root of functional existence is mind.

C876. The ₴ANCTUM, this is the temple to Caucasian birth, and its Fematrix, the holy center of ₵aucasianism, the fulcrum of Caucasian religious belief.

C877. Dimensional ascension, this subject is perhaps one of the most vital, if one is to understand life. Hence this truth! If you do not have the hunger to go there, you will not seek the means by which to go there. So in fact, dimensional ascension is a process fueled by desire, by way of mind, and thereby subject to the three levels of thought, which are in turn determined by the mental alchemy of a Fematrix, who measures the degree of belief in her sacrificial flesh man, thereby determining his ability to conquer the mental and physical wilderness.

C878. Culture; the machinery of dimensional ascension, the barometer by which dimensional ascension can be measured. Culture is the final product of the mental alchemy of a Fematrix, and it is to culture and its single driving force of identity aggression and its three elements that comprise the total social direction of the human Fematrix and all others of the sisterhood.

C879. The mental crucible, and the art of mental alchemy are the very source of social direction, and it is the skill and artistry of the Fematrix (female will) that provide the vital mental formula for the journey into the mental and physical wilderness. It is at her knee that the *Conquest* of *Dimension* forged the following: (1)three biological mental imprints, total directional imprint (reptilian), partial directional imprint (mammalian), and No directional imprint (man) (2) three socio-cultural beliefs, ego belief (self), union belief (bonding), and authority belief (trust) (3)three aggressive natures, consumption aggression (lethal), competitive aggression (dominance), and conformative aggression (obedience) (4) These are the three elements, and nine ingredients that comprise the mental alchemy of the Fematrix.

C880. Examine and reevaluate your beliefs. One of the reasons that the power of rational thinking goes unrecognized is that it is so seldom used. Trace down the belief about your- self or the belief about your world or other people. Perhaps you secretly feel unworthy of success or you have become anxious and fearful for no good reason. Don't pass these feelings by casually. Wrestle with them, think hard on them, and do not cheat yourself. But always remember this: both behavior and feeling spring from your beliefs. To root out the belief that is responsible for your feeling and behavior, ask yourself,…Why?

C881. Truth in reality does not exist, because one chooses not to acknowledge it!

C882. Do not let emotional scars alienate you from life. Many people have inner emotional scars who have never suffered physical injuries. Hence a woman who has been hurt by a man takes a vow never to trust any man again. A child who has had his ego sliced up by a cruel parent or teacher may never trust authority in the future; therefore, to guard against future injury from that source, an emotional wall is built through which neither friend nor foe can pass, cutting them off from their real selves and keeping them out of touch with life. Thus they drive away the very people who would love them and could help them, if given half a chance.

C883. The political class in America will all sign on to a bipartisan fiasco of anti-government rhetoric when the Caucasian middle class (tax base) begins to speak out loud about the government's inefficiency. This knee-jerk reaction by the politicians is without merit; they will never downsize their operation to one that the Caucasian American people can afford. Fiscal stonewalling has always been a good defense against an inattentive public.

C884. The will of the people, or the people's initiative, this is the vital tool that is missing from the people's state legislative toolbox; no fiscal repair is possible without it.

C885. The will of the people, or the people's referendum, this is the vital tool that is missing from the people's national legislative toolbox. No congressional repair is possible without it.

C886. It is the young Caucasian of little racial faith who says, I am nothing. But it is the young Caucasian of true racial conception who says, I am everything, and then goes on to prove it. That does not spell conceit or egotism, for we as illuminated Caucasians know that it means faith, trust, confidence, the Caucasian expression of our Fematrix within us. She says, Do my work, Caucasian eclectic cultural work. Do it with a zest; keenness, a gusto that surmounts obstacles and brushes aside discouragement. Be true to your racial self.

C887. Happiness is not something that happens to you. It is something you yourself do and determine upon. If you are waiting for happiness to catch up with you or just happen or be brought to you by others, you are likely to have a long wait. Every day is a mixture of good and bad; no day or circumstance is completely good! Good is as real as bad. It is merely a matter of what we choose to give primary attention and what thoughts we hold in our minds.

C888. Poverty, the true remedy is to abolish it and put in its place a national infrastructure work program like the WPA, rebuilding facilities, highways, as assistants for various public institutions throughout the states, and offer decent paying jobs. The details of AFDC and day-care for single parents and the disabled can be worked out. This back to work plan will also supply health insurance and a return on its investments in the form of less crime and more human productivity, taxes, and economic infusion on the retail level. And on the contrary, this can all be accomplished for one-half to two-thirds (it's all in the numbers) of the cost of what Americans are now spending for nothing in return.

C889. An impoverished people are a sign of a nation's failure, and are its ultimate disgrace. Poverty is curable only if it is attended to by honest and dedicated social practitioners.

C890. Accountability must be the ultimate rule of all forms of government, for people on the road to government can find it a very tortuous path without it.

C891. Influence peddling by elected officials can become a severe political illness in the body politic; therefore, it becomes necessary to be on the lookout for symptoms of this illness, before it can take hold.

C892. Immigration to Caucasian America has become the focal point of the *Alienquest* (lethal alien migration). Shackled with the standard liberal unwritten rule- Do not offend the alien minorities, Caucasian America has been refused the legislative material it needs to repair the illegal fractures in its migration dam. This act of political cowardice and the Caucasian politicians who initiated it must be brought into the full light.

C893. Immigration has fatal impact, in numbers, finances, and culture. Both illegal and legal alien immigration will overwhelm Caucasian America by the next quarter century. Hence, by the year 2025, the Caucasians in America will have dropped to less than sixty percent of the American population. And not long after that, Caucasian Americans will become a minority in their own country. A democracy is ruled by numbers?

C894. Our errors, mistakes, failures, and sometimes even our humiliation were necessary steps in the learning process. However, they were meant to be means to an end, and not an end in themselves.

C895. It is not knowledge of actual inferiority in skill or knowledge that gives us an inferiority complex and interferes with our living. It is the feeling of inferiority that does this. And this feeling of inferiority comes about for just one reason: We judge ourselves and measure ourselves not against our own norm or par, but against some other individual's norm. When we do this, we always, without exception, come out second best. All this comes about because we have allowed ourselves to be hypnotized by the entirely erroneous idea that I should be like so-and-so or I should be like everybody else. It is a fallacy. If analyzed for its truth, you will find that it is individuality in a group setting that governs and moves the world.

C896. If you are going to spend time in worry, why not worry constructively? Begin to imagine what the desirable outcome would be like. Go over these mental pictures and delineate details and refinements. As they are repeated over and over again, you will find that once more, appropriate feelings are beginning to manifest themselves, just as if the favorable outcome had already happened. This time the appropriate feelings will be those of faith, self-confidence, and courage, all wrapped up in one package, that winning feeling.

C897. The great philosopher Plato put it best. Neither must we cast a slight upon education, which is the first and fairest thing the best of man can ever have, and which, though liable to take a wrong direction, is capable of reformation. And this work of reformation is the great business of every man while he lives.

C898. Each one of us has in our character two counselors, both foolish and antagonistic. We call one-*Pleasure*, and the other-*Pain*.

C899. There are two kinds of fear. There is the fear of expected evil, and the fear of an evil reputation, or shame. Both are greatly honored, for they preserve us in so many ways. What is there that so surely gives victory? Is it not confidence before our enemies and fear of our disgrace before friends?

C900. There are two great cultivation's in the human soul by our Fematrix; first, the Greatest Courage, secondly, the Greatest Fear.

C901. The great Fematrix oracle Diotima of Mantinea, who instructed Socrates on the subject of love, said the object in love is birth in beauty. And all men are bringing to the birth in their bodies and in their souls love of kind, Generation, and Immortality.

C902. In the quest for the soul, it eluded all the learned minds as they journeyed into the wilderness of being, not ever realizing the beauty of its simplicity and the ease of its accessibility, for you see, the 𝔄lpha also speaks of this great quest, and he tells us, Soul, is to embrace the need (the 𝔖he!)and to be in her *Service* and *Devotion*. In other words, soul is the great desire to labor for the need. Hence, if it labors, it must therefore have a soul.

C903. Argument is unprofitable; worse than that, unintelligible, when opponents do not share some common ground. Between the complete skeptic who denies reason's competence and the philosopher or scientist who appeals to it, no common ground exists. Between the man or woman who obeys the rule not to contradict themselves and the man or woman who finds nothing repugnant in answering yes and no to the same question, there can be no argument. There is an issue between them, but the position each person takes reduces the other to silence.

C904. There are three great mental trials in human existence: *Religion, Philosophy*, and *Science*. Each appeals for allegiance not merely on the grounds that they can answer fundamental questions, but also because of their contributions to human life and culture. But the 𝔄lpha tells us, in their competition for supremacy was lost intellectual steadiness on the compatibility of *Reason, Faith,* and its concluded certainty.

C905. Is there any one of us intended by nature to be a criminal, and for whom such a condition is expedient and right, or is all criminality a violation of nature? Criminality is a term most misunderstood. Criminality is an alternative to social union, or treaty, as it applies to its true state. When a citizen recognizes authority but rejects it, he or she becomes a criminal. But in the case of an alien, the dominant race and its cultural authority is almost never recognized! Therefore, they cannot be criminals. The rotation of alien being in and out of prison for the rejection of the dominant race and its cultural authority is an intellectual form of alien subjugation; hence the social dilemma of the multi-racial state.

C906. No man can be useful or faithful to his race without a balance of *Temperance* and *Courage*.

C907. Theology, it is the sweetest of intellectual fruits, and to those who question its place in science, the Alpha tell us it is the root of all science. It is the ultimate intellectual joust for reason, the true fleece of knowledge. Hence, did not Plato say; Who can be calm, when one is called upon to prove the existence of the gods?

C908. Beauty, because of its relation to the cognitive powers, Aquinas defines the beautiful as that which pleases upon being seen, and the same as the good. The notion of good is that which calms the desire, while the notion of the beautiful is that which calms the desire by being seen or known. There is a mode of truth peculiar to the beautiful as well as a special kind of goodness. Therefore, it may be asked, what in the object is the cause of the peculiar satisfaction that constitutes the experience of beauty? The Alpha also speaks of beauty. He believes beauty to be rooted in sight and sight to be the ultimate junction of the senses, and these senses have become a union of labor to form the soul. It is through this junction of sight that the soul beholds accomplishment (others, as well as its own) and then bestows the crown of beauty upon its perfection.

C909. Mental Imaging is a tool of the mind that offers us an opportunity to practice new traits and attitudes. It opens new mental windows to success and happiness. Successful men and women have, since the beginning of time, used mental pictures and rehearsal practice to achieve success. Napoleon for example, practiced soldiering in his imagination, for many years before he ever went on an actual battlefield. And many great musicians, composers, actors, and entre-preneurs have practiced mental picturing for success.

C910. Daily living also requires courage, and by practicing courage in little things, we develop the power and talent to act courageously in more important matters.

C911. We cannot feel anything about other people unless we stop and think about them. In your treatment of other people, have regard for their feelings. We tend to feel about objects in accordance with the way we treat them.

C912. The real racial self is not derived from the great things you've done, the things you own, or the mark you've made, but from an appreciation of yourself for what you are, a child of your Fematrix. When you come to this realization, however, you must necessarily conclude that all other people are to be appreciated for that same reason.

C913. The right of greater importance, when in the cause of a dispute between parties and no direction is clear, and all is in disarray, a person (single) may call for the right of the greater importance be established. This is done by a majority vote of the combatants.

C914. Montesquieu put it best: When virtue vanishes from the republic, ambition enters hearts which are capable of it, and greed masters everyone... so that the state becomes everyone's booty, and its strength now consists only in the power of a few citizens, and the license of all alike.

C915. It was Clemenceau who said. War is too serious a matter to be left to generals. Experience also showed that it was too serious a matter to be left to statesmen.

C916. The great failure of the peacemakers is that peace conferences rarely concentrate on the great questions that seem to deserve their attention. They are usually distracted by same topic that has little significance for later generations. But it is also a warning that unified idealistic principles are still far from being accepted by the peoples of the world.

C917. Men are reluctant to believe that great events have small causes; therefore, when the Great Racial War begins, they will convince themselves that it must be the outcome of profound forces. The liberal statesmen will have miscalculated their instruments of liberal social bluff and threat that proved effective on previous occasions. This time, things will go wrong. The liberal social fallacy of equal rights and brotherhood that they relied upon will fail to deter alien ambition and racial unrest, and hence, the liberal social zealots will receive their just due and become the pariahs of modern social intellectualism.

C918. The liberal zealots of America will have to recognize full liability for the Caucasian casualties brought about by their programs of social debauchery and moral capitulation.

C919. Peace between the races in America has altogether vanished beneath the horizon of an alien parasitic-hyenic culture, and a deeply entrenched racial hatred is now the menacing sound that mans the racial blockade. And for all those Caucasians who think that they can seek the shelter of neutrality in this cultural war, understand this: the very fabric of Caucasian America is the sacred fabric of our Caucasian ancestral trust woven by our Fematrix (female will), and any attempt at neutrality by a Caucasian will be seen as cowardice and Caucasian heresy.

C920. Only on the sands of fallacy would an immature liberal mind attempt to build a castle of racial brotherhood and equality, just to watch it fall to pieces of its own absurdity by the unforgiving tide of reality.

C921. Journalism; is the art and craft of mental nutrition. Every day, we, the populous, sit down to two meals, one of the body, and the other of the mind. But unlike the meals for the body, which are of free choice, the meals for the mind are prepared for our consumption. Therefore it is the recipe (social agenda) of those in this craft that must be bought into the light.

C922. Since man wishes to be judged in accordance with his own self-determined choices, man's worth is estimated by reference to his inward action and hence the standpoint of morality is that of freedom aware of itself.

C923. Attention must be directed to the importance of the infinite difference between a principle in the abstract and its realization in concrete. In the process before us, the essential nature of freedom, which involves in it absolute necessity, is to be displayed as coming to a consciousness of itself, for it is in its very nature self-conscious and thereby realizing its existence. It self, is its own object of attainment and the sole aim of spirit. This result is the process at which the world's history has been continually aiming and to which the sacrifices humankind has laid on the vast altar of the earth.

C924. The good is the truth of the particular will, but the will is only that into which it puts itself; it is not good by nature, but can become what it is only by its own labor and by inwardly specifying what good is, is conscience.

C925. The intrinsic worth of courage as a disposition of mind is to be found in a genuine absolute final end, the sovereignty of the racial state. The work of courage is to actualize this final end, and the means to this end is the sacrifice of personal actuality; a sacrifice that is the real existence of one's freedom.

C926. The racial state is mind in its substantive rationality and immediate actuality and is therefore the absolute power on earth. Race is autonomous.

C927. The history of a race is its own act. A race is only what it does, and its act is to make itself the object of its own consciousness. In life, the racial act is to gain consciousness of itself as a kind, to apprehend itself in its interpretation of itself, to itself.

C928. Since races are related to one another as autonomous biological entities, and as particular wills on which the very validity of treaties depends, and since the particular will of the whole is in content a will for its own welfare pure and simple, it follows that racial welfare is the highest law governing the relation of one race to another.

C929. Sacrifice on behalf of the individuality of the race is the substantial tie between the race and all its members, and so is a universal duty. Since its tie is a major aspect of the mind as part of reality and so are subsistent particulars, who are in form a class of their own with the characteristic of courage.

C930. The matters of issue and disputes between races may be only one particular aspect of their relationship to each other, and it is for such disputes that the particular class devoted to the race's defense is principally appointed. But if the race's autonomy is in jeopardy, all its citizens are duty bound to answer the summons to its defense, and then it becomes a war of conquest.

C931. Does race manifest itself? One element in race is that it produces itself, makes itself what it is, and the other is that it is original, and that this originality is its nature and its idea. There is no essential existence (that which preserves existence) that does not manifest itself.

C932. Since racial subjectivity is not comprehended in all its depth by the human spirit, the true reconciliation was not attained in it, and the Fematrix (female spirit) has not yet asserted her true position. This defect shows itself in fact of fate, as a perceived male superiority to the female; it also shows itself in the fact that men derive their resolve not yet from their Fematrix (female will) but from their male oracles.

C933. Truth is the idea further determined, the unity of the concept of the will with a particular will. It is not something abstractly right, but something concrete, whose contents are made up of both right and welfare alike.

C934. It is the absolute right of the race to step into existence in clear-cut laws and objective institutions, beginning with marriage and migration, whether this right be actualized in the from of divine legislature and favor or in the form of force and wrong. This right is the right of races to found states.

C935. The concept of race and its objective existence are two sides of the same thing, distinct and united, like soul and body. A soul without a body would not be a living thing, nor would a body without a soul. Hence, the objective existence of the concept is its body, while the body obeys the determinate soul that brought it into being. The unity of determinate and objective existence, the concept, is the racial idea. The idea of race is kind (identity), and if it is to be truly understood, it must be known both in its concept and in the determinate existence of that concept.

C936. Just as civil society is the battlefield where everyone's individual private interest meets everyone else's, so here we have the struggle of private interest against particular matters of common concern, and both of these together against the organization of the race (sovereign biological state) and its higher outlook. The organic unity of the powers of the race itself implies that it is one single mind, which both firmly establishes the universal and also brings it into its determinate actuality and carries it out. It lays claim only to a single form of riches, namely, its biological mandate of racial kind.

C937. Liberal subjectivity is manifested in its most external form by the public undermining of the established life of their race, by defeatist opinion and utopian ratiocination when they endeavor to assert the authority of their own vacillating character and so bring about their own destruction.

C938. Racial sovereignty at home is a reality in the sense that the moments of mind and its actuality, the race, have become developed in their necessity and subsist as the organs of the society. Mind in its freedom is an infinitely negative relation to itself, and hence its essential character from its own point of view is its identity, an identity that has incorporated these subsistent differences into itself, and so is a race, exclusive of other races. So characterized, the race has individuality, and individuality is in essence individual.

C939. Individuality is awareness of one's existence as a unit in sharp distinction from others. It manifests itself here in the race as a relation to other races, each of which is autonomous visa vie the other. This autonomy embodies mind's actual awareness of itself as a unit, and hence, it is the most fundamental freedom that a people can possess, as well as also its highest dignity.

C940. The destiny of a race is linked to its individuality; they are one and the same. This relation and the recognition of it is therefore the racial individual's substantive duty, the duty to maintain this substantive individuality, the independence and sovereignty of the race, at the risk and sacrifice of property and life, as well as opinion and everything else naturally comprised in the compass of life.

C941. Racial self-determination, the future could be made secure only by an assertion of this moral principle.

C942. Statesmen are expected to build the peace of the world on idealistic foundations, yet at the same time to satisfy the bitter resentments of warring parties and to promote the interest of their respective countries. It is truly the business of magicians, a Merlin. No wonder the public's conviction that all statesmen are wicked.

C943. No treaty after all can provide that it will be enforced when those who benefit from it are too supine to enforce it.

C944. Reparation for slavery has now become the political cry of the *Alienquest* in Caucasian America. It is, of course, absurd, but this absurdity comes as no surprise to Caucasian Americans. It is, in fact, just another fallacy in a long line of fallacies by a race of people lost in the wilderness of liberal dementia.

C945. The envious person bends the facts out of shape in order to justify his or her position. Hence, the Alpha tell us this same enviousness can take hold of a much larger groups of people (races) as well as the individual, and he refers to it as racial envy, dementia. This envy is a byproduct of group competition, and its most modern classic case can be found in *Minority Races* struggling to compete with Caucasians, in Caucasian America.

C946. In the multiracial state of America, the competition between the races has been divided into a feel-good *Truth Distortion* by one racial group,... and we have done wrong, *Delusional Guilt* by another racial group. The Alpha tells us, that the real culprit in this *Social Illness* is the liberal zealot's social swindle of *Equality*, and speaking of social reality?...in the attempt to attain the unattainable equality, minority races now mistrust everyone who is not of their kind. Purging their leadership, exiling their intellectuals, they have now put their social and political fate, into the hands of street hustlers, who are themselves the profiteers of human misery.

C947. In the Multiracial state of America, the Caucasian population is now being assaulted by an evil liberal conspiracy. Case in point, the Caucasian community is being given large injections of historical guilt of wrongdoing (slavery) to create an alien moral high ground. These injections are designed to create failure in the Caucasian social and cultural will, and fracture the Caucasians ability to defend themselves against alien cultural subversion and liberal zealotry. This assault by Caucasian liberal zealots on the Caucasian people to undermine their society is the equivalent of treason!

C948. In the Multiracial state of America, the alien social intent and agenda is *Cultural Sabotage*, pure and simple. They see the world through a clear eye and a fixed direction, *Cultural Conquest*. A steady diet of Caucasian cultural weakness feeds their hunger, knowing that those who control the culture control the future!

C949. Depression closes the gap against self-doubts. The essence of help for depressed persons is to shore up their strengths and praise their efforts and block out their doubts. And remember this, when you educate the depressed person to a healthier mode of adaptation, you are rewarding yourself too, because you are doing one thing more, helping to prevent future depression in that person.

C950. Hatred, and even love endure, but there is in the human make-up that which is unwilling to bear the burden of being grateful to anyone for very long.

C951. The *Alienquest* agenda in Caucasian America loses its importance and scrutiny by most, if not all Caucasians. The efficiency of the *Liberal*

Zealots and the absolute loyalty to their social fallacies are what drive the *Alienquest*. Make no mistake; whoever misunderstands the *Alienquest* hunger for cultural dominance and its ability to position itself in strategic places for that purpose will come to learn firsthand what the term *affirmative action* really means? And along with the liberal zealots, their sinister strategy is long-term and targeted at Caucasian universities and Caucasian identity capitulation, thereby doing with liberal legislative street vendors what they failed to do by rioting and civil disobedience, American cultural domination by strategic subversive legislation. Those who control the culture, dictate the terms of the future.

C952. There are three perils in the *Alienquest,* the peril of migration, the peril of markets, and the peril of arms. All three are the horns of the Caucasian social and political dilemma.

C953. To uphold and defend one's racial dignity and the convictions of its destiny is to be in unison with all of creation.

C954. Learning: it was Aristotle who once remarked; Learning is accompanied by pain. Hence, through education, the Alpha speaks of liberalism and its great contribution to the stability of humankind. True liberalism is by no stretch of the imagination the modern zealotry of political correctness, and if it could be recaptured, we would all be blessed by the excellence in ideas. The true liberal educated man or woman seeks not to make real the dreams of the mystical social poet, but to regard humankind as an end, not as a means, and to regard the ends of life and not the means to it. Its true object is the excellence of humankind as human and humans as citizens. We all practice the liberal arts, well or badly, all the time, every day.

C955. To proclaim the necessity of observing the facts and all the facts is not to say, however, that merely collecting facts will solve a problem of any kind. The facts are indispensable, but they are not sufficient. To solve a problem, it is also necessary to think, and it is this thinking, and its present-day direction, which the Alpha tells us is now in great peril due to a severe intellectual neurosis (equality) in the liberal arts.

C956. No age speaks with a single voice, and no society so determines intellectual activity that there can be no major intellectual disagreements in it. We should not reject the help of sages of former times; we need all the help we can get.

C957. Montesquieu once said that as the principle of an aristocracy is honor, and the principle of a tyranny is fear, so the principle of a democracy is education. Learning (liberal arts) is in principle and should be in fact the highest common good, to be defended as a right and worked for as an end.

C958. A frantic concern by Caucasians to understand aliens will lead us nowhere, unless Caucasians bring to these problems skills in analysis, order in valuing, knowledge of racial history, and such alien social experience, whereby we can form a basis for judging what we as Caucasians find out about aliens.

C959. There is no apparent reason why Caucasians Americans, should feel they must apologize for a determination to retain a sense of their own character and their own social range. The Caucasian civilizations are the greatest civilizations to date, and this statement is not said in the spirit of arrogance, but in the spirit of a concern that nothing good be lost for the future. We Caucasians should take to all our meetings with aliens a full and vivid sense of our own achievements.

C960. The very deep problem of racial relations in America must await the racial spiritual recovery of the Caucasian Americans. And he or she does not know the truth, who believes that the Caucasian Americans do not have in their own tradition the means and power whereby they can once again be true to themselves.

C961. A civilization in which all people are compelled to agree, is not one in which we would care to live. The only civilization in which a free person would be willing to live is one that conceives of history as being one long conversation leading to clarification and understanding. Such a civilization presupposes communication; it does not require agreement (democratic state).

C962. The Caucasians are the most powerful race in the world. We have been a world power for a very long time. We have centuries of education, experience, and responsibility that have given us the kind of maturity that the current racial crisis demands of the most powerful race in the world. We Caucasians bear no ill will toward any other people. Since we Caucasians are devoted to our own kind of society and government, we do not want any other race to threaten the continued survival of our society. Hence, any military moves made by the Caucasians against alien races will only be made by the conviction that they are necessary for the defense and or survival of the race.

C963. The religion Caucasianism symbolizes the civilization of the Caucasian race. It promotes the realization of the racial civilization here and now. *The Valorous* is organized on the principle of attaining clarification and under-standing of the most important issues pertaining to our Caucasian society as stated by the Alpha through continuous discussion. Its objective is to project Caucasianism into the future and to have all Caucasian people participate in its social quest.

C964. The essential ingredients in Caucasian social strength are trained intelligence, love of race, the understanding of its ideals, and such devotion to those ideals that they become a part of the thoughts and life of every single Caucasian man, woman, and child.

C965. A civilization in which there is no moral union or core belief is not a civilization in which we as Caucasians would choose to live. Morals or core beliefs in a civilization and the agreement of a population to abide by such, is the very root of all human social order, and without it, no social order is possible. Hence, a civilization is the embodiment of a core agreement, a union of the minds of the whole (society) to uphold the sovereignty of the whole over individual interests. Therefore, it is that which symbolizes the true union of the whole, the core of all life, the *Female* (Fematrix) and her *Racial Kind*, that is sovereign. Caucasianism, (the Caucasian racial female will) is the royal crown and hence, the sovereign state.

C966. The truth of any statement is its conformity to reality or fact, and in that sense, experience is required to discover the particular matters of fact that test the truth of general statements about the nature of things.

Hence, lack of experience diminishes our power of taking a comprehensive view of the admitted facts. And it was Aristotle who insisted that theories should be credited only if what they affirm agrees with the observed facts, and the Alpha also declares that to test whether anything has been well or ill advanced, to ascertain whether some falsehood does not lurk under a proposition, it is imperative on us to bring it beyond just the facts, but to the proof of sense (thinking) and to admit or reject it on the decision of sense.

C967. The Alpha speaks to the Multiracial State and its social dissectors and politically correct drill masters. The liberal zealots have overpowered the good will of the Caucasian Americans with their social subversion of mystical equality and legal debauchery, hence bastardizing moral code and casting liberal arts into the hyenic pit, alas, getting rid of Caucasian cultural and racial pride. But all is not lost, the Alpha's tell us. This evil plane by the liberal zealots has failed; a Caucasian revolt is imminent and justified. The restoration of Caucasian America will take place, and the liberal zealots will have a lot to answer for!

C968. The Alpha states that the racial ideal toward which the Caucasian Americans, as well as all Caucasian people, should strive is the ideal of racial fundamentalism, a distinct, biological determination through form, or its common name, race, and the illumination of one's race through love, devotion, and sacrifice. This is the sacred ideal to which he speaks; therefore he asks, if not in its racial difference, then where lies Caucasian truth and beauty?

C969. The intrinsic nature of a society is its unified identity, and without it, societal survival is not possible.

C970. The great Caucasian books of ethics, philosophy, history, and literature do not yield up their secrets to the immature. In Caucasian America, if these works are read at all, they are read in the schools and colleges with a very restricted curriculum, (Multiculturalism) where they can be only dimly understood, and hence, deprived of the light they can shed upon our current problems. The great proliferation of the curriculum of Caucasian American schools, colleges, and universities is the result of intellectual cowardice and the evil purse of *Affirmative action*, which was proclaimed the great cure for *Alien-Autolysis*, but it became in fact, the lysis, which is now eating the very heart out of Caucasian education in America. The 𝔄lpha tells us that if you distort your education, you distort your culture (racial ascension), and if you distort your culture, you lose your future.

C971. When asked of the youth of his day what could make them better, Frost once said, give them the hardships which made us rich. The 𝔄lpha speaks to this great wisdom and tells us the great struggles of the Caucasian social legacy has almost disappeared from American education and is now being replaced by inferior substitutes bent more toward making people feel good rather than developing the mental instrument needed to understand the here and now. The 𝔄lpha regards this modern element of education as an aberration and not as an indication of progress, but as an error, unjustly conceived, and therefore it must be corrected.

C972. Whitehead called it the habitual vision of greatness. He of course was referring to the great books, or as often referred to as the great conversation. As put by their authors, these books are the means of understanding our society and ourselves. They contain the ideas that dominate us with out our knowing of it. And the 𝔄lpha tells us that Caucasian American society is the prodigal child of all these eclectic Caucasian works. And like all prodigals, modern Caucasian America needs to be reminded of the winter of its racial and cultural discontent, and to the necessity of its education. Copernicus, Vesalius, Kepler, Galileo, Newton, Darwin, Pascal, Freud, Euclid, Dante, Plato, Aristotle, and a host of others, hence, the great enduring legacy of Caucasian education, and its social ascent, and make no mistake, this legacy will be defended.

C973. Sexual hunger and the need to control it are paramount to the survival of all life. In most living creatures, sexual behavior is strictly regulated, and few if any can violate it. But in humankind that strictness does not exist. Human sexual control is cultural and not biological. Therefore, human sexuality poses a much greater inquiry as to its impact on social, cultural, and political outcome in human societies. Unlike the Fematrix (female will), in the majority of living things that control male sexual aggression by chemical stimulation (total control), the human Fematrix has no such control, and hence is in a constant state of self-defense and must rely on her society's cultural laws to control male sexual aggression.

C974. Unlike her sisters in the animal world, the human Fematrix relies on the union of monogamy as the root of her society. And it is this monogamy that is largely responsible for human success.

C975. Whether its controlled by chemicals or by laws, ultimately the Fematrix (female will) controls birth and the male's relationship to that birth, and so in the final analysis, social stability, cultural creativity, and the overall determination of a society hinge on the ability and social craftsmanship of its Fematrix. The positioning of the male by the female in society is the key to its success or failure.

C976. Irresponsible alien birth in the Multi-racial state, you would be hard pressed in any rational social state to make the case that one race of people should be held entirely responsible for the welfare of another race of people and their children. But think of this: in the Multiracial State of America, this socioenigma has become the norm. Reckless and promiscuous sexual behavior (sexual misconduct) by large numbers of alien females, plus, desertion by their males after impregnating women, has now reached epidemic proportions in America. The entire burden and cost of this social folly has been placed on the backs and shoulders of a compassionate Caucasian America. The 𝔄lpha tells us this is an evil burden, and Caucasian society must never become the safety net for any alien race's irresponsible and arrogant disregard for human dignity. Therefore we as Caucasians must resist alien social debauchery.

C977. The great issues of the *21st* century issues of life and death for the Caucasian American people and their civilization call for mature minds. The 𝔄lpha tells us nobody can make so clear and comprehensive and accurate a statement of the basic issues of human life as to close the discussion. Every civilization calls for explanation, correction, modification, expansion, or contradiction. So in an attempt to be rational, the 𝔄lpha speaks to an alien socio-hyenic culture of moral dilution, social decay, and sexual misconduct that is expanding and which politicians and intellectuals have failed to socially counter on behalf of Caucasian Americans.

C978. Caucasianism is the ultimate unifying social system for all people of Caucasian descent, for its social and spiritual context is rooted in the very beginnings of life. Hence, Caucasianism operates on three basic principles: survival of kind (biological idea), survival of the whole (socio-cultural direction), and survival of the individual (freedom of ambition). These guiding principles are the foundation of Caucasianism and its two political states, the sovereign state (rights of the whole, the race) and the democratic state (rights of the individuals, their ambitions). The traditions of a religious eclectic morality are embodied in the social spirit of Caucasianism.

C979. In the political states of Caucasianism, each state has a social mandate, and each mandate has a single common principle, public accountability.

C980. Caucasianism is the socio-political and moral light for the Caucasian people and their social direction. Therefore, to all those who embrace the Caucasian light and its moral path, your future will be spirited and fulfilled by a sense of *Caucasian fundamentalism* and racial illumination.

C981. In the quest for moral government, intellectual evolution has always played its part, but at the same time, intellectual evolution, if anything, has proved that moral government is one of the most shy and elusive of creatures in all of human nature.

C982. The greatest illness in any society comes about when it develops an inattentive public, which in turn leads to the loss of social vision, hence, the veering off course of social direction. As history has shown us, most if not all of these past societies would come to create new spectacles of social vision, *Democracy, Feudalism serfdom, Constituted Monarchy, Fascism, Communism, Socialism*. All of these social visions have been woven into the fabric of the human soul; therefore it can be safely stated that all of them, even modern democracy (American mystical equality) has failed to maintain the course to human salvation. But all is not lost, for there comes a great truth, a great moral enlightenment, Caucasianism. It will prove and come to be the final and greatest *Enlightenment* and the steadiest *Social Navigator* of all!

C983. Let the light of Caucasianism go out to our Caucasian cousins in

Europe, Asia, the Middle East, North and South Africa, North and South America, and wherever the Caucasian spirit is engaged. Let the proclamation go out to them all, Cleanse yourselves, your societies, of liberal zealotry and the evils of its multiracial doctrine, for it is your very future and that of your children's that hangs in the balance. Hence, step out of the social darkness and into the true enlightened spirit of Caucasianism, the final destination, in your pursuit of racial illumination, dignity, and the sanctity of individual liberty.

C984. We as Caucasians people must never mislead ourselves by the conspiracies of races, one against the other, to outwit the other, outmaneuver the other, defeat the other, and in some cases, destroy the other. The Alpha tells us this is the mind set of bio-engagement, and that in this game of real life, there are no *Level Playing Fields*, nor will there ever be.

C985. The triumphs of Caucasian civilization that made the American dream and its expansion possible resulted from triumphs of culture and law that rested on the triumphs of morality and which were promoted by Caucasian religions. This is truth in reality.

C986. The Alpha asks why racial education disappeared. He attributes this phenomenon to two factors: (1) internal decay, liberal zealotry (mystic equality) and (2) external alien debauchery (parasitic-hyenic subculture). No one can deny the evil social curriculum of these two, not to mention the many blind alleys, absurd social legislation, and intellectual cowardice they have woven into the Caucasian American social fabric. A spirited scent of revolution is in the air. It is the revolution of Caucasianism and its affirmation of race.

C987. The aim of Caucasianism is human excellence, both private and public (for Caucasians are a racial kind). It strives for a grasp of the methods by which racial solutions can be reached and the formulation of standards for testing racial solution proposed.

C988.The Alpha believes that *The Valorous* should be read and studied by all Caucasian adults and their children all their lives. He concedes that this idea has novel aspects. The racial education of adults and children is paramount to the future of all Caucasian societies. What is here proposed is an international racial education. The trials of the Caucasian citizen of today surpass anything that previous generations ever knew. Private and public liberal propaganda beats upon them every day, and so it is hoped that a strong dose of racial education through the *Holy Valorous,* can inoculate them to withstand the great illness of "Liberal Zealotry" and its paternalistic cult of " Equality" a *Social Fallacy.*

C989. Every Caucasian ought to push toward the horizons of their intellectual powers all the time. The most that we can hope for from these chaotic periods of life is that during them we will be set on the right path, the path of realizing our human possibilities through intellectual effort and an appreciation of racial aesthetics. The Alpha tells us that racial education ought to end only with life itself.

C990. It is now necessary for all Caucasians to try to live at the height of their times. The Caucasian social enterprise in America is imperiled if anyone of us says, I do not have to try to think for myself, and the death of Caucasian America will be a slow extinction from apathy, racial indifference, and intellectual default.

C991. The decay of racial education in Caucasian societ- ies is felt most profoundly in America, undoubtedly making the task of understanding Caucasianism and The Valorous more difficult. In one way The Valorous is the most difficult and in another way the easiest book for any of us to read. It is the most difficult because it deals with the most difficult problems that Caucasians can face, and it deals with them in terms of the most complex ideas. But treating the most difficult subjects of racial thought, The Valorous is the clearest and simplest expression of the best thinking that can be done on complex racial matters.

C992. The criteria of The Valorous is immediate intelligibility on the aesthetic racial level, increasing intelligibility with deeper reading and analysis, leading to maximum depth and maximum range of significance, with more than one level of meaning and truth.

C993. The fabric of our lives is full of the images and the myths of ambition.

The minds of so many are full of shadows and reflections of things they cannot grasp. It was Scott Buchanan who once said, popular science has made every man his own quack. Hence the cult of learning around liberal zealotry and the cult of ignorance around race are phenomena of the vicious specialization of scholarship. But the Alpha tells us that the educational apparatus of liberal zealotry is a product of its own social quackery, and it is sinking into the intellectual darkness of its own social fallacy.

C994. The spirit of Caucasianism and The Valorous is the spirit of racial inquiry. No racial proposition is to be left unexamined. The exchange of racial ideas is held to be the path to the realization of the potentiality of humankind and its social dialogue.

C995. The conservative and the radical, the practical person and theoretician, the idealist and the realist will be found in every society, many of them conducting the same kinds of social, political, and religious arguments that have been carried on for decades. Although humankind has progressed in many spectacular ways up to the *21st* century, (medicine, transportation, science, sanitation) it cannot be denied that they are today worse off in many other ways, some of them more important than the ways in which they have improved. Taxes, criminal justice, poverty, education, race relations, and political conduct all are in direct and dire need of reform.

C996. The Alpha tells us that in a final simplistic social analysis, if a society is to survive and continue its ascent, it must step from the shadows of denial and cowardice into the light of truth and courage. In our rush to the promised future, we must stop and take a reading of our Caucasian social compass, so as not to get lost in the wilderness of political haste and its folly.

C997. Caucasianism and the light of its Fematrix bring our future into focus, a future of economic progress, racial dignity, and academic enlightenment.

C998. In the future, the twenty-first century and beyond, all of the Caucasian states throughout the world will come to find the social concept of the Multiracial State in default. Racial hostilities against Caucasians will render an alien forfeiture of their rights in Caucasian societies; hence, the Caucasian social awakening to the- *Alienquest.*

C999. The Alpha tells us, democracy is a social term with no face or form. It is the social fleece of legend, and the tales of its social healing ability have filled the hopes and dreams of all humankind; hence the great quest to possess it. Throughout human history, many nations have bragged of its capture, just to have it slip away once again on its journey to worthiness. It is elusive, but once captured, you must understand its needs, or it cannot be held!

C1000. The Alpha tells us: that in the realm of life, there are no equals, and that today is the furthest point of the human journey. In the confusion and madness of opinion, nothing is rooted; all seems lost to *Ego* and *Envy* in the modern intellectual joust. But all is not lost. We as Caucasian must lift our heads and stand in defense of our *Racial Ancestral Trust* and shed the cloak of *Guilt* that has been put upon Caucasian success, by the failure of alien others. Your future, my future, and that of our children depend ultimately on our courage to seek out, and defend the truth.

C1001. Wars are won in the will; find the will, strike the root.

C1002. Only by removing ambition can you establish equality, but, biology without ambition cannot exist.

C1003. When one seeks to recreate a balance in life by the forging of equality (fantasy) and difference (reality) together, the outcome is mental debauchery, a form of intellectual castration. If they are equal, then they cannot be different, and if they are different, then they cannot be equal.

C1004. Who among the races of humankind, let alone the individual, will forgo ambition, to establish equality? The answer is so obvious: No one.

C1005. In the twenty-first century, the joust for political power has no true substance. It is a sleight of hand and a verbal shell game. Before the election, now you see it. After the election, now you don't. It is referred to by same as a political loop, an endless repeating cycle of social, economic, and legislative lies and a public so deeply and completely inattentive that it lacks a genuine social focus to counter this political ruse.

C1006. No leader can escape dependence on those he or she leads.

C1007. There are forces that are compelling the Caucasian people to re-examine and ultimately to reinvent themselves. The nineteenth-century structures and methods that still define the way most Caucasians work simply are not adequate for the radically intensified competition of the twenty-first century.

C1008. Life pushes us all around so much that passivity can easily masquerade itself as wisdom.

C1009. The process of transformation requires a personal commitment and the willingness to persevere. It begins with the recognition that change is necessary. For any Caucasian with a sense of racial pride and who wants to keep that pride, this is a challenge that must be faced.

C1010. If you weren't already a Caucasian, would you want to be one today? This question should be pondered deeply, and then you must act on the answer, for racial awakening requires a frontal assault on the status quo. My goal as the Alpha is not to frighten, but to arouse the emotional energy of the entire Caucasian race. That energy, which manifests itself first as fear and later as a personal commitment to a plan of action, is the only fuel that can sustain a foreseeable future.

C1011. Replacing the old way with the new does not happen at the touch of a button. It requires deep convictions, enormous upheavals, a vision of what lies ahead, and perseverance, even when the pain seems unbearable.

C1012. A vision can't be acted upon until it is shared.

C1013. You can't deny reality and control your destiny at the same time.

C1014. Facing reality in good times and bad is an ethical obligation for elected officials, indeed, for anyone whose actions affect other people, and if that sometimes requires indicting oneself, tough; it comes with the territory.

C1015. We must demonstrate by talking to the people and by asking them what to do about some things and then do what they suggest. If we do, our society will normally run better. It's a simple idea that some politicians with IQs of 110 can't bring themselves to understand.

C1016. The worst sins are committed in boom times, when the society at large feels satisfied. That's when our politicians get fat and arrogant.

C1017. Events justify their foreboding. Displays of racial hatred are counter productive and serve no purpose other than to torment one group, so as to relieve the frustration and mental agony in the other. It is this type of racial joust that fosters mistrust, closing the door to common ground, leaving no intellectual bridge.

C1018. New technology and increased world trade are causing social structural change. Computers, fax machines, and improved telecommunication services are reducing the difficulties in doing business. Hence, we are now forging the links to an integrated world economy. Good, you say. Good, I say. But make no mistake; this is a new class of social animal. We have yet to learn of its appetite, not to mention the fact that instant communication between large corporate groups is a very sharp double-edged sword, International economic power cartels the ultimate predators.

C1019. The competitive environment doesn't allow for complacency, and globalization still presents a challenge, a challenge substantial enough to preoccupy those nations who see the future as being anything but compassionate.

C1020. In America, there's a place called the halls of Congress, but it's true demeanor is more like someone taking a lunch order in a factory. He or she starts out with the original order, (a bill) and goes from person to person (committee to committee) altering this order, so at the end of this political harvest, we no longer have lunch, we have a banquet.

C1021. Elections in the United States are not won, they are bought. Although ideology counts, success measured in money is infinitely more important.

C1022. Welfare, public assistance is a noble goal, as long as it serves and does not capture those it was designed to benefit. We must not let welfare go from a service to a master.

C1023. When a people become productive, they gain control of their destiny.

C1024. Anger and resistance, a massive change in the culture of hundreds of thousands of people does not take place without it.

C1025. When money becomes the lifeblood of American politics, America, the nation that gave birth to liberal democracy, will be, in the end, managed by the mentality of panhandlers.

C1026. False ideologies have replaced inner convictions in the American politician, both Left and Right, hence leading to the birth and acceptance of social distortion, where marriage and not illegitimacy has become a dirty word.

C1027. When there are no statesmen to counter false ideologies in the drive for power, participating governments rob the people of their power by making them pay for their own oppression: *Income Tax.*

C1028. Unfounded mandates are the true weapon of choice for the destruction of state sovereignty by an unstable and politically bankrupt American government by making a mockery of their constitution and reducing states to colonies, the citizenry to subjects, and never have so many people paid so much and received so little in return, from those in control of their nation.

C1029. Change can be terrifying, and anyone who hopes to revolutionize an entire nation had better know how to cope with change on a personal level, and just as important is the belief in an unambiguous distinction between right and wrong.

C1030. We Caucasians and our allies believe in the paradox that change and that which is sacred function collectively as one direction and individually as many directions at the same time. For us, culture means leading while being lead.

C1031. We Caucasians believe in the sharing of our values, because we believe they are fair, effective, and socially stabilizing. But we also realize they are not for everyone. Therefore, individuals whose values do not coincide with ours will more likely fare better outside the Caucasian society.

C1032. The Caucasian community must come to understand that there are no textbook answers to the problems we will face in the twenty-first century. We will have to write our own textbooks every day.

C1033. When left to themselves, some people will ignore warnings of danger, scorning vital opportunities to change early.

C1034. The real Caucasian American issue is facing reality about a troubled political situation. Stand back, look at where you are as a Caucasian now, and probably more important, where you and yours will be in the very near future. Can you play in that future arena? Are your enemies going to push you out? The implications should be perfectly clear, unless the political street vendors that now run America get a religious experience and reverse their plunge into the social void, Caucasian America will continue to be feasted upon by hyenic malicious minorities, and let there be no mistake. It is the politicians that you elected that are selling the tickets to this feast.

C1035. There are now cultural attitudes in Caucasian America that are guiding Caucasian society to critical mass. Hence, a culture begins to shift its moral phase to appease the belligerence of a minority group that is attempting to dislocate the society's moral bridge by mounting a public campaign for legitimacy through that most mystical of social conduits, *Equality*, which has the highest degree of suppressing any challenge to it by the very fools who created it. The Alpha offers this caution, already successful in driving a number of wedges into Caucasian America's moral foundation without any real difficulty or opposition coming from the *Political Cesspool* that now passes for our leadership. The battle to hold America's moral gates has failed, and the *Liberal Fifth Column* (liberal courts, liberal dissidence, and minority activists) have joined the moral marauders in their brutal assault on human dignity and moral integrity. Furthermore, with a bewildered sadness, I must tell you this: Even the great religious houses, have *Fallen Silent*, so the Alpha concludes that when the controlling mechanisms in a society can no longer sustain a rational intellect, and the stink of *Social Caligulaism* begins to fill the American Forum, then the law of opposites, *Critical Mass*, will prevail, and social revolution will engulf us all.

C1036. Recognizing the growing importance of the American cultural and moral inner conflict, we Caucasians must recognize the need for action.

We must respond with an aggressive campaign of communicating what's at stake for Caucasians in this critical phase of American history.

C1037. The Alpha wishes to point out that the American cultural and moral conflict can be broken down into three interesting questions: (1) what do we Caucasians want to happen? (2) What can we Caucasians do to make it happen? (3) What will we Caucasians do when it happens? The first question should be answered by a set of carefully thought out and clearly stated cultural and moral objectives. The second question really concerns the role of a cultural and moral strategy, decisions about how to use specific advertising techniques to accomplish stated objectives. The third question: means that we Caucasians must consider the effects of our cultural and moral campaign in the long term and make sure those different elements of Caucasian society will support one another along the way.

C1038. Decline of the work ethic and rise of the leisure ethic in today's modern working class is creating great stress in the well-oiled American system, which once thrived on the work ethic as its principle social icon.

C1039. The appearance of integrity has become the key to success in America's entrepreneurial politics, so long as it has no real moral bite in the influence-peddling world.

C1040. When a government operates on the principle of no accountability, with entrenched political big bosses in the leadership (in absolute charge) holding the elected Congress by the political throat, this is what's called a self-destructive operation with no unifying intellect other than greed.

C1041. It was James Madison who warned us about a tyrannical and overly expensive government, and it requires no great intellect to see the proof of his prophecy.

C1042. The Alpha asks, do the Caucasian Americans deserve the government they created? No, but they are responsible nevertheless for the shrewd political party's fiscal and political unaccountability. The federal elected government, the state houses, and the town halls, at all levels, like it or not have become commodities for sale on the American market.

C1043. When you find yourself in a *Threatening Environment*, do you come up with a new approach? That's the test!

C1044. Trust is enormously powerful in a social group, let alone a nation of diverse people. A willingness to listen, debate, and then accept the best ideas is achieving the union of intellect, which in turn lays a foundation for common ground upon which trust and stability can be realized.

C1045. The Alpha tells us: that the Caucasian people have the responsibility to respond to any challenge, whether that challenge be to their culture, their economy, or by a group of parasitic, hyenic, social marauders. If the challenge is the size of a storm, then the response should be the size of a hurricane.

C1046. The Alpha tells us: that the darkest days will begin to materialize in Caucasian America when in the cause of criminal legislation, laws will be enacted to suppress and ultimately to abolish "Caucasian identity". This will of course, plunge America into a social dilemma of unprecedented magnitude (civil war!) or as the Alpha calls it, the war for- Caucasian Preservation.

C1047. Educating the young for their role in society is by far the most important cultural task a race of people can institute. And so important is this *Education* that a group of very special people are chosen because of their cultural and historical knowledge, and their ability to communicate that knowledge, they are given the title of *Teacher*. The *Teacher* is the fulcrum by which the future is determined; they are the builders of the mind.

C1048. Education through discipline; all children and for that matter, most of us adults, have had attention deficit in one form or another throughout our lives. This in turn leads me to the subject of the modern classroom and its discipline deficit and the flaunting of student individuality. Taking on the atmosphere of a theatrical audition, the students in to day's modern classrooms (in America) have been allowed to violate the very principles of their own social integrity by their language, their behavior, and their overall disregard for traditional values. This in turn has led to the derailment of liberal authority and resulted in the competition between students and teachers for control of the American classroom. Hence the calamity of uncontrolled youthful liberty!

C1049. There is an unforgiving tide rising against the educational system in Caucasian America, and in this tide, there are two very sinister culprits, mental poverty, made up of alien racial hatred and envy, and intellectual cowardice on the part of liberal educators. When will the scales fall from our eyes?

C1050. The twenty-first century is already showing signs of moral and cultural capitulation by elected officials as well as those seeking to become elected officials. This disregard of the moral and civil majority by the two political parties in power points to, and makes very clear, the low caliber of persons seeking to be elected and being elected to leadership positions in large metropolitan cities.

C1051. The Alpha tells us: there's a political trend toward election for election's sake; in other words, no higher calling other than a paycheck (political street vendor), and it has led to the emergence on center stage of sinister subgroups (moral despiser's) with what the Alpha cal their Caligula platform, a political attempt to make moral and civil law expendable by demanding public acceptance and wanting to be included in all cultural and social activities under their own contemptuous immoral banner of Caligulaism. This, of cause, is without a doubt not acceptable to Caucasian Americans as well as all people with a sense of social dignity and integrity.

C1052. Ethical nihilism, or *"Caligulaism"*, as the Alpha calls it, is alive and well in America. This is due in part to the mind-boggling system that now passes for the law, and a judiciary that has become lost in a dark labyrinth of mandatories, statutories, admissibles, and let us not forget everybody's favorite, constitutionals. And all are receiving their legitimacy from that most trusted of legal icons, the Supreme Court interpretation, or to be more precise, the generational Supreme Court interpretation.

C1053. The American- *Civil Liberties Union* (ACLU) is a private group of legal and constitutional missionaries, who the Alpha believes are true American heroes, even though he finds himself in disagreement with some aspects, never the less, it's their noble, unbiased mission, that of bringing all the American people *Judicial Salvation* and leading them out of the maze of *Legal Mischief* as well as *Legal Procedure Abandonment,* gives them unprecedented merit.

C1054. The Alpha states categorically that the health system, or for a better word, industry in America has become an uncharted landscape with no one willing to venture into this wilderness of divided professional kingdoms, not to mention the army of subgroups that service them. The American health system, in spite of the lack of professional union by its health providers, is second to none. In fact, it is without equal. But it is of no worth to those who cannot afford it! We need a national health plan (not a shell game from the federal government), and I say it can work with minimal impact. First and foremost, bring together all of the health industry doctors, nurses, hospitals managers, clerical workers, aids, rehab workers, x-ray technicians, etc. Second, bring in the HMO insurance companies and the outside drug and medical supply companies. The ultimatum; tell them this; you have three years to put together a national health plan that is fair to all parties involved. But at the end of that time period, if you do not have a plan to submit, the federal government will institute its own. And we all know what that will mean! (make it happen for all of us)

C1055. Euthanasia, the Alpha tells us that of all the many inevitabilities in life, it is the end of life that poses the most spiritual and intellectual difficulty for us all. This confusion is due in part by the sheer fact that coming into life and leaving life is not at all a democratic process. When it comes to life and death, we must all stand on the side lines with virtually no vote. But there is the question of the quality of life?... and do the people with terminal (no cure!) agonizingly painful illnesses have the right to take their own life or to die if they so choose? Although there are many intellectual arguments for No, and they are not without their merits, I must tell you that we all make life-threatening decisions every day, both conscious and unconscious. Furthermore, is it not also true that we ask others to put their lives on the line for us?...to walk through death's door, to defend our nation, or at the risk of their own lives, save ours, from fire or criminal behavior? Life is about decisions, and you cannot ask people to make decisions to sacrifice their lives on your behalf, and then deny them the right to make a decision on their own behalf. The answer is yes!...It's their right.

C1056. Social misanthropy is a form of mental illness that can not only take hold of a single individual, but in its worst form, an entire society, divide and conquer, an old, and very reliable means by which a government can bring a society to heel. A house divided cannot stand? Not so if that division is a cleverly worked out plan of controlled confusion and misinformation, to create a cultural rift of mistrust, so as to prevent political union. So I ask, in this arena of sponsored American misanthropy, who are the spectators?

C1057. Racial nihilism, the culture of social dereliction, it has been said that the road to hell is paved with good intentions, and in the case of our "Caucasian America" and its road to hell!...it's being paved with *Intellectual Failure*, *Political Default*, and *Social Debauchery*. All self inflicted!..all part of a lost identity?..a great lose of love of self, in union with our -*Caucasian kind!*

C1058. The American democratic illusion is the loaded political deck, keeping the independent and third parties at bay by a gauntlet of carefully tailored state and federal laws (the numbers game), requiring hundreds of thousands of signatures to get on the ballot. Democracy, you say. But was it not John Taylor who spoke of political parties and their tendencies to degenerate into aristocracies of self interest and questionable integrity? When will the scales fall from our eyes?

C1059. The root problem in the modern American social system stems from the failure to *Recognize* and *Uphold* its *True-Purpose!*...which is the newest- "Empire Nation" (a bio-cultural tributary!) and part of the 40 thousand year "Caucasian Dynasty". (it is not an alien joint venture!)

C1060. Due to the unlikelihood of a moral epiphany by American political leaders, it then becomes imperative for the Caucasian American people to close ranks and make a stand for the moral right. Without moral productive growth, it is possible to lose in a few years the very cultural and social stability that took endless centuries to build. Productive moral growth is not only essential to a society's survival, it is paramount.

C1061. Power without morals, though it may have a short-run success, fails to secure and combine the strength that resides in free men pursuing a course to protect, defend, and advance their common good. This is not only a compelling moral ideal; it is also a natural characteristic of man as a human being, a force for undoing oppression.

C1062. The correction of errors in a nation's racial policy is greatly assisted by the timely raising of rational voices of criticism within the race.

C1063. It is only when the Caucasian people fail to challenge Congress and its executive branch; when the opposition fails to oppose; when politicians join in a spurious consensus behind policies of economic and cultural assault against Caucasian America; when institutions of learning sacrifice traditional functions to the short-term advantages of association with the policies of political cowardice and intellectual failure, that the campuses, streets, and public squares of Caucasian America are likely to become the forum of a direct and disorderly democracy.

C1064. There is an essential truth, which is appropriate in referring to a democracy as an experiment; it is the obvious fact that an experiment can fail! A society organized by democratic political institutions can move in a democratic direction or in a more or less frightening way in a direction away from democracy. It is true and wholly consistent with a democratic experiment that there will be degrees of democratic realization and degrees of democratic failure. Difficult as it may be to demarcate without a margin of theoretical dispute what separates a democratic from a non- democratic society, it is a problem that cannot be sidestepped and it clearly relates to the defense of freedom as the end and standard political action.

C1065. All men are fallible and likely to blunder because of their failure of knowledge or their lack of objectivity, face to face with issues that affect them closely. Let us limit the extent of their blunders, and above all, let us keep open the channels by which they can be pointed out.

C1066. The scholar can ask what is wrong with the other side, but he must not fail to ask as well, what is wrong with our side. Remember always that the highest devotion we can give is not to our race as it is, but to a concept of what we as Caucasians would like it to be.

C1067. It was Fulbright who once said that free and open criticism was a therapy and catharsis for those who are troubled by something their country is doing; it helps to reassert traditional values, to clear the air when it is full of tension and mistrust.

C1068. It was Jared Taylor (American Renaissance) a great Caucasian American Patriot, who once said it is in race relations that America has gone most obviously wrong, yet it is about race that we dare not think anything new or different. If there is a body of thought that shows all the signs of doctrinaire rigidity, willful ignorance, and even duplicity, it is what is thought and said about race. It is where we are failing the worst, that honesty and clear thinking are least welcome.

C1069. It was-*A Koch* who spoke of the great American experiment and its timeless philosophers, from Jefferson to Dewey, and their distinctive works. America's version of philosophy has variously been called pragmatism, instrumentalist, naturalism, and experimentalism, but it may be usefully summed up under the last of these labels. The term *Experiment* implies systematic investigation guided by an idea or hypothesis, rather than random activity. It suggests organized social inquiry in a setting that recognizes that everyone shares in some degree, the supreme political power. It envisages the resolution of political problems in a social environment of intellectual freedom, criticism, trial and error, and a continuing process of self-correction.

C1070. The rewriting of history, the Jefferson Memorial in Washington, for example, falsifies the third president's views of sub-Saharan Africans. Inscribed on one of the interior walls are these words: Nothing is more certainly written in the book of fate than that these people (sub-Saharan African!) shall be free. When Jefferson wrote those words, he did not end them with a period but with a semicolon, after which he wrote: nor is it less certain that the two races, equally free, cannot live under the same government.

C1071. President Lincoln is likewise falsely portrayed. He was certainly opposed to slavery, but he did not want free sub-Saharan African living in the same society as Caucasians. As president he asked Congress several times to appropriate money to send them back to Africa, and even argued for a constitutional amendment for that purpose.

C1072. Was it not the Kerner Report, many years ago, (1968) that said America was becoming two societies? I say it was wrong, America has become three separate societies, Mongoloid, Negroid, and Caucasoid, and all three have a rigid self-righteousness, a racial orthodoxy that is monolithic and unforgiving. They will not, and cannot, become anything other than what they are, opposing forces, hence forced to take part in the liberal social masquerade and dance the dance of brotherhood, while waiting eagerly for the dance to end, so as to get back to what they know is real, the business of racial competition.

C1073. It is interesting to note that in America it was the liberals who championed the color-blind constitution and the Fourteenth Amendment that compels the states to be color-blind as well. But when minority races started to benefit from reverse discrimination, those same liberals for-got all about the color-blind constitution, and without the slightest hint of guilt, they joined forces with the minority revisionists and the federal government in their quest to embrace Black color consciousness and wealth redistribution. All of this was, and still is, promoted under the most enlightened of democratic epiphanies, affirmative action (reverse discrimination).

C1074. People that do not believe themselves to be free, can ever be free!

C1075. Racial quotas, sensitivity training, and lowering the standards are the tools of a failed liberal intellect and the siege engines of minority cultural raiders. They are the saboteurs of education, family, and moral decency.

C1076. Reckless procreation and abortion lie at the very heart of America's degenerating moral climate.

C1077. To admit to fault is to accept the need for work, effort, and responsibility. It's far easier to blame someone else for one's failings, and much more satisfying.

C1078. Victimization, (the shell game of racial guilt) has now become an exclusive minority illness. So deeply is its penetration into the minority culture that all of the culture's hard-won social benefits have failed to stem the tide of unwed mothers, fatherless children, and the flight of intellectual responsibility.

C1079. The shackles of a delusional ideology, when some one begins to believe that a *Street Education* is more appealing than the enlightenment of credited teachings, it can then be said that this person or person has failed in social reasoning. The ways of the street, are the ways of the hustler, the thief, the mugger, and the drug dealer. Hence, all of which will graduate to a life in prison or, for a more ceremonious ending, an early funeral.

C1080. The stigma against bad language has collapsed. If there is a single statistic that underlies a failing culture, it is the bastardization of its language.

C1081. Perhaps worse than even race relations is the illegal drug epidemic in America. It is believed by some that America consumes more than 50% of all illegal drugs in the world, heroin, cocaine, pot, crack, amphetamines, crank, LSD, hashish, opium, and we must not forget the newest of the feel-good demons, ecstasy. In confronting the drug problem, we Americans are emotionally and intellectually handicapped, because we lack the stomach for what has to be done. Just say no! That's not going to do it. Long-term mandatory sentencing! That's not going to do it. There is only one way, banishment for life. Cast out those who bring death. Cast out the destroyers and enslaver's of the human spirit. Cast out those who would profit from the deliberate poisoning of society.

C1082. Once again (drug problem) there appears to be a discrepancy between liberalism and reality, between the liberal perception and a situation as it actually exists. Once again, it seems that the source of the distortion is the ideological prism through which liberals look at the world.

C1083. One cannot defend human values by calculated and unprovoked violence without doing mortal damage to the values one is trying to defend.

C1084. It was Edmund Burke who once said, Magnanimity in politics is not seldom the truest wisdom; and a great empire and little minds go ill together.

C1085. In race relations, as in our individual lives, we must strike a balance between our aspirations and our limitations. Our aspiration is toward a peaceful world community of races, but we must seek it within the limitations of a world divided by ideology and racial nationalism.

C1086. Cooperation, like conflict, tends to feed on itself.

C1087. It was *Aldous Huxley* who once said, organized slaughter or war, is the result of arguments about such questions as the following: Which is the best nation, the best religion, the best political theory, and the best form of government? Why are other people so stupid and wicked? Why can't they see how good and intelligent we are? Why do they resist our beneficent efforts to bring them under our control and make them like ourselves!... Sound familiar?

C1088. The human and cultural resources that make for a great society are produced by a racial union. Therefore, an ambitious racial policy built on a deteriorating domestic base is possible only for a limited time; it is predestined to come to an end. Hence it is at this very end that the Caucasian American people must be united.

C1089. All rational people know there is no alternative to work and family.

C1090. As the violations of the Constitution continue daily, the theory that made America great is rapidly being lost.

C1091. It was Pierre Carron who once said; the dignity of humankind, the excellence and perfection of humankind as humankind, are based on an ethic that issues in the ancient virtues of prudence, justice, fortitude, and temperance. If knowledge does not function to make our lives happier, it is a small and sterile good, and may on occasion be even worse than that. Wisdom must be active, ready to control and govern things.

C1092. When knowledge guides our will and choices are made after we have examined the good or bad of what we desire, we are at once free and on the road to true happiness.

C1093. Contemporary theories of personality have made us all familiar with the idea of humankind as interpersonal beings characterized by the capacity and need for both intelligence and love. Even psychoanalytic theory envisions the mature, aware, and self-realized person as the one for whom the pursuit of happiness is an open avenue, not a fatal cul-de-sac, as it is for the neurotic, the mentally sick.

C1094. Happiness eludes those who expect to seize it directly.

C1095. Racial enlightenment is something that must be established by men and women who cherish it, and it must be maintained by a society that concedes it value.

C1096. The captive intellect that submits to *Fallacy* cannot follow nature in the wise man's way.

C1097. It was Jefferson who wrote; Agreeable society is the first essential in constituting the happiness and the value of our existence.

C1098. Those Caucasians, who defend affirmative action, have to pretend that there is no injustice in it.

C1099. To *Jared Taylor*, a true Caucasian American hero, there are no words that can truly express the gratitude owed you by so many people, for your courage, your intellect, and steadfast approach on the subject of socio-racial politics in America. You have truly been a light in the darkness, a beacon in an otherwise cloudy and often stormy social direction, and as for your books, they should be required reading, with a mandatory essay by all high school students.

C1100. When a society or a group of people fail to address deliberate transgressions put upon them by a declared hostile adversary, it is courting a disaster. If there was ever a sign that all the world knew, recognized, and searched for, that sign would be weakness; weakness of body, weakness of mind, weakness of will, weakness of courage. It is universal to all living things. Find the weakness. This is the one unchanging supreme rule in all of nature: find it, strike it, and victory, or the advantage will be yours. This truth is the bedrock of life and has not changed in a million years, and I am sorry to say there will be no change in the next million years. Therefore, my fellow Caucasians, the point is this: in the last fifty years or so, the Caucasian culture, which is the primary force in America, has been projecting signs of political and cultural weakness to some very *Dangerous Groups* of people. They are an underclass without *Rules* and no *Family Values*. They have presented the Caucasian Americans with social and moral problems we cannot fix! They want society to change; they want uncontrolled self-expression; they are now refusing to be *Family Accountable* and *Morally Responsible*.

C1101. A lie requires many words in its own defense. Truth is like a silent light; it needs no clumsy structures about, it simply is.

C1102. Three things in the world evoke silence: *Fear, Beauty*, and *New Born*. Fear paralyzes into silence all that does not immediately contribute to self-preservation. Beauty makes words superfluous, even inopportune. The New Born creates in the depths of the soul the silence of adoration.

C1103. A life without recollection runs the risk of real failure.

C1104. Caucasians must respect the silence in which prayer can thrive, which alone gives value to activity.

C1105. The ignorant person is so full of themselves that no space is left for intelligent intervention.

C1106. Caucasianism is the courage of truth.

C1107. The greatest disaster brought about by our lack of racial pride is that it gives alien social and political dialogue an undeserved advantage and makes the Caucasian social and political position impossible.

C1108. Where race is denied, there also the genuine concept of family is altered, whereas where race is honored, there also the family is sought out and rightly celebrated. Who could ignore this link that binds race to the family in the races throughout the world?

C1109. Caucasianism in its multiple aspects has given us a beautiful image of union, the *Holy Union of Race*! Let us Caucasians keep it close to our hearts; let us hold on to it, so that with its protection we can be preserved in the light of its truth.

C1110. The Greeks of old employed the word for being reasonable and meant speaking out the truth. If today we speak of *Racial Confrontation*, then let us call to mind that it means giving *Vital Racial Witness*, in contrast to other ways of thinking or acting, that in no way indicates a preformed inimical judgment to be cast at the opposition.

C1111. The ignoring of a vital element (our race) is always death-bringing. Only biology is fertile, life- bringing.

C1112. Sorrow and love are correlative terms. Without love there can be no true life, and without suffering there can be no true love. If we as Caucasians want to live for our race and love it, the way is the same for all: sacrifice.

C1113. Racial faith is the empowerment of Caucasian intellect. It is the lamp of our life that makes clear the meaning of our existence. It is the light of truth.

C1114. Caucasianism unifies, it integrates. It is the sanctuary of Caucasian racial fruitfulness, the mark of social maturity.

C1115. Efficient activity needs three things: meditation, decision, and action. And meditation is the key to the other two.

C1116. Silence helps us enter into the realm of ourselves. I must stand still, if I wish to examine my own image; I must reach inner silence, if I want to examine my soul.

C1117. The liberal zealot, despising counsel from others and disdaining the practical and logical view, become isolated, frustrated, and impoverished in social enterprises.

C1118. The best way to predict the future is to invent it!

C1119. The Caucasian race awaits our collaboration in the building up of the Caucasian World Empire. And as sons and daughters of the Caucasian race, we ought to regard this as our duty and honor.

C1120. Let all Caucasians be apostles of racial goodness, mediators of racial virtue, and ministers of Caucasian racial faith.

C1121. The world is saved by those who pray and sacrifice.

C1122. The word *Race,* in the hearts of those who are receptive, is peaceful and fruitful.

C1123. The pure enlightenment of race produces only good effects.

C1124. It is by example that racial notions turn into racial convictions, that racial knowledge turns into racial wisdom and racial wisdom turns into a social and cultural way of living.

C1125. All Caucasian will live a full life when they use their wealth, their thoughts, and their words in the service of their *Racial Convictions.*

C1126. Our racial nobility is in direct proportion to our capacity to love our race. Life is an exchange. When we as Caucasians shut ourselves off from our race, we bring death, but when we open ourselves to our race, we bring vitality and fulfillment.

C1127. The law of race is as fundamental to the world of humankind as the law of gravity is to the world of physical bodies.

C1128. Racial faith makes us collaborators in the work of Caucasian racial salvation.

C1129. Racial Faith; is neither the mortification of thought nor the pruning of scientific research nor a useless dead weight attached to the gossamer of modern spirituality. It is a light; it is a voice that enhances our racial souls and makes life and the world comprehensible.

C1130. What does it imply, living in racial faith? To live racial faith means ultimately to entrust and devote oneself wholly to our racial Fematrix.

C1131. Racial faith is adoration! Accepting the truth that racial faith tells me, that I know the end result of interracial conflict, because racial faith makes it known to me.

C1132. Authority without liberty is despotism, but liberty without authority is only anarchy. Together, authority and liberty work to become totally creative. Past and future enrich the present, though each keeps its own character and function.

C1133. Action without meditation, or meditation without its projection into behavior; each remains sterile without the other.

C1134. Form in art is significant only when it gives shape to thought and inspiration that are the content of art.

C1135. Racial joy brings us together; racial suffering unites us.

C1136. Those who have no racial spirit will not understand the racial spirit of others.

C1137. One who has a racial spirit is able to participate in the racial spirituality of others.

C1138. The participants in racial love communicate with the deepest, most indestructible part of humankind, their soul.

C1139. If intellect is the bread of humankind, race is the grain from which it is made.

C1140. In our teaching on racial truth, we must always present our mission as a spiritual quest. Our teachings must guide the racially faithful to the understanding and devotion of their Caucasian Fematrix and her mysteries.

C1141. Caucasianism is more a way of life than a system of doctrines. Our racial life is modified not so much by books and sermons as by the devotion of racially dedicated personalities.

C1142. The word of the Alpha, sown in the hearts of those who are racially receptive, is peaceful in its growth and fruitful in its intellectual harvest.

C1143. We as Caucasians can teach or counsel others racially by words, but we help those most of all by our good racial example.

C1144. Our Caucasian racial vocabulary, impoverished as it is by the narrow range of our actual racial interest, needs to be enriched by the vocabulary of Caucasianism. Then, perhaps, we as Caucasians might find the words of racial truth that the Caucasian world about us actually needs.

C1145. Our Caucasian racial example will prompt our children to cultivate a fruitful, active race in which we can with clear vision and honesty measure our racial progress or regression in our Caucasian moral and spiritual life.

C1146. All our life, with its mistakes and vanities, is an unceasing lesson in humility.

C1147. All those who condemn our Caucasian ancestors and the past have this in common: they wish to see Caucasian racial devotion disappear.

C1148. If you find that all is not well in your life, look to it and see how you stand with regard to racial devotion and Caucasianism.

C1149. The lives of our children show us that to be devoted to our race, to be united with it, is the most reliable guarantee of an authentic Caucasian life.

C1150. Our race exists so that we as Caucasians can know more intimately the spirit of our Fematrix.

C1151. It may appear that other races hostile to us have the upper hand, but our Caucasian spirit has so often overcome heresy in the past ages that even today we will not leave the field open to our enemies. If we are faithful to our racial, social, and political cause, we as Caucasians will bring about victories greater than anything we have yet known.

C1152. There is no surer, quicker way to unite ourselves to a great and ever-lasting Caucasian future and to find all the good that's in it than through the teachings of Caucasianism.

C1153. Let all Caucasians endeavor to live in complete and joyous racial harmony, the bond and foundation of all other virtues, the touchstone of authentic social sanctity.

C1154. To think of others is very good; to pray for them is better; to love them in a practical way is best of all.

C1155. All gifts are dead, if love is not animating them.

C1156. All Caucasians in their earthly life have the power to think, compare, and decide how to behave. All Caucasians in their spiritual life should occupy themselves with one activity: loving in racial faith and hope.

C1157. Let all Caucasians remember this: In life we as Caucasians begin to act foolishly when we stop praying.

C1158. If today Caucasian people are suffering a social and racial crisis that threatens them to their very roots, this has been caused chiefly by a lack of racial spirituality. We as Caucasians must therefore strive to ensure that in our modern generations the light of love and devotion to our race does not grow dim, but is ever more strongly rekindled.

C1159. All Caucasians reflect what they choose; they are what their desires make them. Of course, the real dynamic quality of freedom does not consist solely in shunning evil. It rather involves a sustained choice of things conducive to the goal we set for our life.

C1160. Every Caucasian child has his or her own message to give to the world. History necessarily unfolds from the present to the future. Each child who comes into the world is a link joined to another link, or like a hand that clasps another hand to form a biological pilgrimage marching on the way to immortality.

C1161. The highest prerogative of the Caucasians is undoubtedly that of being a Caucasian, and it is the history of the world that reminds us of that privilege.

C1162. The human soul fears a void (loss of identity). When the Caucasians have lost the taste for the presence of race in their life, everything will becomes very difficult, and their world will suffer a crisis of social and political folly, and darkness will descend across their society, because without the root of race humankind cannot understand itself.

C1163. So often we Caucasians approach our racialism with the mentality of the tourist, out of sheer curiosity, interested but detached. How often have we examined our race and gone away confident and proud, but afraid that someone will notice?

C1164. The Alpha's reflection and note of caution: In any human society, we can never separate our interior racial qualities from the exterior society and its activities.

C1165. A practical means of being an authentic Caucasian is to accept and preserve the biological ideals embodied in the very architecture of our race. In its biological form, what is a race? It is first and foremost a desire and a decision on the part of the builder (Fematrix). Race is also a challenge; it stands out from all other races as the custodian of a different biological kind.

C1166. Faithful Caucasians who are truly devoted to their race believe always, hope always, and love always in the spirit of their Caucasian racial faith.

C1167. Being a Caucasian reminds us that we must be sons and daughters in the spirit of the race, before we proceed to any worldly activity.

C1168. We as Caucasians believe that our race is the embodiment of hope counteracting the pessimism inherent in the world. A true democracy cannot exist as a permanent form of government. It can only exist until the voters discover that they can vote themselves largesse from the public treasury. From that moment on, the majority always votes for the candidate promising the most benefits from the public treasury, with the result that a democracy always collapses over loose fiscal policy followed by a dictatorship. The life cycle of civilization is from bondage to spiritual faith to great courage to liberty to abundance to selfishness to complacency to apathy to dependency and back into bondage.

C1169. If we as Caucasians enclose our society into a social fallacy of mystical equality and lose sight of our racial centeredness, we make a grave dogmatic error.

C1170. Every race is a unique creation; nature never repeats itself. But all races share in common a longing for happiness. Each race picks out its own path, yet all wish to arrive at the same destination, the threshold of prosperity.

C1171. The modern Caucasian may ask: Why is there so much sadness and pessimism in the Caucasian world? No doubt if we were to draw up a list of the causes of our grief, we would discover that we ourselves are at the root of much of it. Our wrong choices often bring us distress. At the root of racial unrest, of individual discontent, we should place a gross mismanagement of our society. The affliction of many of us is an ethical illiteracy, racial atrophy, if not downright opposition to Caucasian racial spirituality (identity).

C1172. A race whose soul is not in order, not open to true racial value, will never know or be able to radiate true social harmony.

C1173. No doubt in human society many a disaster is inevitable, even fatal, but the affliction of political cowardice on the subject of Caucasian racial identity and its right thereof is a mindset of treasonous racial treachery.

C1174. It was Mark Twain who once said; In the beginning of a change, the patriot is a scarce man, brave, hated, and scorned. When his cause succeeds, however, the timid join him, for then it cost nothing to be a patriot.

C1175. In the mists of history, one once wrote: Remember, O Lord, what has happened to us; look and see our disgrace. Our inheritance and our land have been turned over to aliens. Our fathers have sinned and are no more, and we bear their punishment. Aliens rule over us, and there is no one to free us from their hands.

C1176. In the words of the Alpha: Among other evils that being *Racially Unarmed* will brings you, it causes you to be despised.

C1177. We as intelligent Caucasians know that to stabilize the "Alien Population" among us, is a condition of- *Our Caucasian Survival.*

C1178. The load of *Mystical Equality* for aliens in Caucasian lands would impinge in unpredictable and destructive ways upon the Caucasian race, undermining their life support systems. There is a threshold beyond which liberal social desires and curiosity cannot be pushed.

C1179. All in all, when alien migration to Caucasian lands is not put into check, we as Caucasians must conclude that it will be impossible to meet such a rate of alien expansion. And there are two things not in doubt, a vast increase in capital cost and a massive impact upon the cultural domain. There is a very great impetus given to equality, but are we running out of common sense? And what will aliens make available to take its place?

C1180. Those who understand the past will dominate the future.

C1181. It is perhaps at this point in Caucasian history (*21st* century) that a general difficulty in *Racial Calculus* should be examined. By our relative neglect of our racial identity, by treating our race and its liberal future as proverbial, we as Caucasians have accustomed our-selves to a method of measuring our society that gives us all the good (liberal utopianism) in our Multiracial state and tends to leave out all the bad (alien cultural differences). Indeed, it includes such irrationalities as making no subtraction for racial competition, ambition, social objectives, and the alien's appetite for power as a racial whole?

C1182. The *Alien Social Toxicity;* (cultural militancy!) in Caucasian America and its byproducts is not in doubt. But, what is the scale of all these risks to Caucasian use of their liberal social fallacy- *Racial Equality*? One way to measure *Alien Toxicity* is by the amount of *Political Animosity* (malice toward Caucasians!) that alien leadership promote in their name.

C1183. We find once again the phenomenon of the biological social threshold. Few if any Caucasians suspected in the 1960s that in a dangerous sense, the attempt to standardize all the cultures of the different races in America (melting pot) would lead to cultural blight, and the delicate balance between the races would be decimated, leaving a bewildering degree of racial nationalism to fire the American social psyche.

C1184. The Alpha, would like The Valorous to issue a more forceful warning, a clarion call that present racial and cultural trends cannot continue much longer, because liberal Caucasian America is on a course of self-destruction. The Alpha did not want The Valorous reduced to a mere recital of facts, because America's social salvation will ultimately depend on an emotional awakening of the Caucasian racial spirit.

C1185. An extreme form of social shock (political desertion) occurs when there is a breakdown of the natural mechanisms (racial loyalty) built into a race of people for self-protection and self-renewal. This type of upheaval follows the sudden introduction of some new social factor, political alien pandering, Caucasian identity capitulation, which has no established link with existing social or cultural patterns of survival.

C1186. The extraordinary development of the Caucasian mind has lessened its dependence on animal instinct, but it is also the root of the Caucasian's creativity and destructiveness. Caucasians can modify more drastically than any other animal the conditions they find unsuitable. And having found their first experiment unsuccessful, they have far more immediate freedom to cast about and try something new. But they can also carry their experiments to disastrous point of no return when instinctive reactions might have held them back.

C1187. Human freedom and social experiment has its counterpart. Some form of order must be imposed on such a range of possibility and risk. No social unit, not even one as small as the family, can live on permanent change of social innovation and liberal experiment. The instinctive response had to be supplemented by elements of social and physical design, first for kind preservation (racial survival) and then for all other extra dimensions of meaning (culture) that Caucasians could conceive and therefore, in varying degrees, realize.

C1188. From the very start of their existence, the Caucasian race has innovated in social forms, and in technical improvements. But today, as we Caucasians enter the new decade of the twenty-first century, there is a growing sense that something fundamental and possibly irrevocable is happening to the Caucasian people and their relation to their world? In the last forty years the extent and depth of their intervention in the natural social and biological order seems to presage a treacherous and fraudulent new epoch in human history, perhaps the most infamous the liberal mind can conceive. The liberal mind seems on a planetary scale to be replacing biological truth (racial competition) with a social fallacy (racial equality), and it is promoting this *Social Malignance* with a speed and depth of intervention unknown in any previous age of human history.(it must be stopped!)

470

C1189. All living things have to be adapted to their surroundings in order to survive and produce their kind. Natural selection is the *Fundamental Mechanism* of this adaptation. But this phrase gives little idea of the infinite variety of stratagems by which living things come to occupy different niches and to produce the incredible variety of shapes, colors, movements, patterns of courtship, of escape, and challenge that make up the richness of the *Fematrix Mystique*.

C1190. Natural selection involves, of course, different racial groups in conflict for limited amounts of food and space. Competition in this sense exists between all human races, and it does not lack in ferocity, as some may think. Prudence, cooperation, indifference, parasitism all play a part in the human world drama.

C1191. A different race introduced, a social balance upset, a political eruption, the slow onset of fear and hatred, all such disturbances can elicit so violent a response that the social system may not be capable of returning, by itself, to a desirable and stable society. There are many potential paths toward points of irreversible no return, and this social and cultural weakening unleashes the capacity of races to destroy each other and themselves at will. And therefore, the self-repairing cycle underlying the race, the unities of the dynamic racial balance we call Caucasian Culture, cannot survive indefinite, unaddressed alien racial hostilities.

C1192. The Caucasian race has survived the glaciations, the volcanic convulsions, the earthquakes, typhoons, and tidal waves that have torn through its social history, and this, for all practical purposes, brings us to a final intellectual balance. If these are the lessons learned, they teach surely one thing above all, a need for extreme caution, a sense of the appalling vastness and complexity of racial forces when brought together, and the violence they can unleash when forced to compete in a society for the right of one racial culture to rule over another.

C1193. There exists a single unified *Biological Force* from one end of our biological cosmos to the other; and in the final analysis everything human or not, comes under the regenerating power of the *Female Will*. (Fematrix) And this brings us to the final balance; the intimate, inescapable in- terdependence of all living things implies a certain stability, a certain dynamic reciprocity for the survival of one's biological (racial) Fematrix. All knowledge, Science, and Technology derive from her and through her unparalleled intensity of material wants and needs.

C1194. In an age dominated as never before by separate racial aspirations and pretensions and by the liberal promise of a mystical equality between all races, how can cogent arguments be marshaled for social balance, for cooperation, for that awareness of racial reality that all the great sages of humankind, without exception, have held to be the root of human wisdom and hence of human survival? And if their witness has been largely in vain, how can we Caucasians hope now for better racial insights and a better or stronger unified Caucasian racial will?

C1195. In all this racial debate, one thing is certain. The ordinary Caucasian citizen cannot judge the political racial facts (double talk). What they can and must do is bring their reason and common sense to bear on their country's whole approach to the racial problem. The first act of racial sanity is to insist, with all possible urgency and influence, on the need for caution. We as Caucasians are not making a simple calculation of gains or conveniences. We are confronting our own survival and that of our children and grandchildren and the whole Caucasian race.

C1196. This perhaps is the ultimate meaning of Caucasianism and its preservation: to remind an increasingly urbanized Caucasian community of the delicacy and vulnerability of its social humanity and political reliance. The lessons in Caucasianism are obvious. How many essential Caucasian cities, neighborhoods, schools, and jobs have vanished before we discovered that our social humanity had brought about unmanageable threats to our future? And as we observe the political arena, we must remember that we, too, are part of this social betrayal. We as Caucasians let it happen! We allowed racial betrayal! We allowed political treachery! We allowed cultural subversion. Yes, it is uncomfortable, the truth always is! We must not break down too thoroughly the biological, social, and cultural rhythms and needs of the Caucasian world. For if we do, we may find we have destroyed the ultimate source of our own being.

C1197. Preservation is the first need. It is race that must be protected against the liberal social architects, these master less men and women, these dark lords and ladies of social alchemy. The unraveling of liberal American society and the unfolding of Caucasian racial nationalism thus offer a remarkable paradox. On the one hand, liberal social and political power is giving America the means of self-annihilation. On the other, Caucasian racial nationalism, brought about by the liberal pandering of alien races, is offering the Caucasians a racial perspective they need, to avoid social suicide.

C1198. The Alpha's method employed now (The Valorous) to decipher not the separation but the interconnection of Caucasian society can provide Caucasians with better, more reliable, and wiser means of working within their society against unstable, unpredictable, and violent alien political and social facets. The Alpha's warning remains. Political liberal powers on such a scale require the furthest reach of wisdom, social political union, and racial respect in their exercise to combat this liberal power. If Caucasian Americans continue to let their behavior be dominated by false accusations of racism, guilt by racial prosperity, and fail to counter this moral social mugging by alien races, Caucasian society will become encircled! Once encircled, aliens will bring Caucasian America to a brutal violent end.

C1199. At the core of the new Caucasian American situation (liberal equality epoch) is the interaction of increasing alien people in great numbers, all tending to draw together in urban regions, all concentrating to a wholly new degree the racist by products of their political activities, their demands for unjustified social concessions, their political and cultural demeanor cloaked in their own racial rapture, their intellectual default and moral delinquency on behalf of their children. And the most challenging of all, these alien insufficiencies and social desires will never be addressed by the *Political Derelicts* that now run the Caucasian American dream!

C1200. In The Valorous, the role of the Alpha is more accurately described as a creative manager of a cooperative racial process, one that engages many of the Caucasian world's leading authorities. His aim as the Alpha of the Caucasians is to reach out for the best advice available from the Caucasian world's intellectual leaders in providing a racially conceptual framework for participants in a united Caucasian world conference, or C W C (the Caucasian World Conference, held once every four years) and the Caucasian general public as well. Members of the conference will be asked to review the state of the Caucasian race and offer criticisms and contributions. The greatest value of this conference would be that it will represent the knowledge and opinions of the Caucasian world's leading experts and thinkers about the relationship between the Caucasian race and the rest of the world. Unless the feeling of solidarity with our Caucasian kinsmen is awakened, we as Caucasians Americans will perish! Facts and forums are equally important, but we must awaken the blood as well!

C1201. The man or nation who is possessed by the unbridled lust for self-assertion is driven headlong into reckless self-confidence, and so to destruction. Blind passion breeds self-confidence, and overweening self-confidence ends in ruin.

C1202. Every race of people is in a natural state of war with every other, not indeed proclaimed by heralds, but everlasting.

C1203. The biological race that combines both aspects of human life must also recognize the position and right of the supernatural society, the church. Yet we have to be careful not to allow insistence on the rights of the church and the importance of humankind's supernatural end to lead us to minimize or mutilate the character of the biological race, which is also a perfect society, having humankind's temporal welfare as its end.

C1204. To challenge Caucasian racial identity as incompatible with America's democratic nature would be to eviscerate America's Caucasian nature.

C1205. In modern-day America, the fear Caucasian society feels is exactly what's intended by our enemies. They know that fear of being called a racist is so powerful that even smart and principled Caucasians can be scared into staying home and remaining silent.

C1206. Remember, there is no loyalty to nations or people. As corporations have gone global, they have simply ceased to be part of any nation or to identify with any people, race, or civilization! A world economic labyrinth is the new world order.

C1207. It was Garrett Hardin who once said: Noble intentions are a poor excuse for stupid actions. Man is the only species that calls some suicidal actions noble. The rest of creation knows better. To Hardin's words we would add: The penalty for those who fail to grasp nature's realities is the same as it is in the animal kingdom, disappearance.

C1208. To judge the morality of a policy, it may be remembered that in all ethics a balance must be struck between different values, different rights. Absolute right for one may mean tremendous injustice to the other.

C1209. Realistically, Caucasian American dominance, achieved more through excellence than conquest, although embodying elements of both and characterized by paternalism has for almost two hundred years left alien races in a dependent and subject role. Obviously, this is a condition that could be changed, if that is what the Caucasian American people desire. There is a possible rational approach to such a guest. America could be partitioned into several sovereign racial states, with each racial state enjoying full sovereignty over a part of what is now the United States of America. This plan would certainly not rule out the retention of a common market, coexisting with the current whole.

C1210. Who are the alien Invaders? They are not Caucasians, and they are not successful. Successful people do not leave their country, they like their country! These aliens who are sneaking into Caucasian America are uncultivated, and uneducated in our Caucasian cultural ways. They will not assimilate, and they show signs of becoming another *Unsalvageable* underclass.

C1211. A word on alien assimilation: Assimilation is proportional to contact. When a minority race is sufficiently large and sufficiently concentrated, the consequence is not assimilation, but the establishment of a sort of country within a country. Do not expect assimilation.

C1212. When alien assimilation fails (as it always does), the laws of the primary society (Caucasian) are no longer respected, and the incarceration of aliens becomes an industry, with alien prisoners in the millions, and the cost to the Caucasian society is more than that of educating its own children.

C1213. The Alpha; standing sadly before the world's greatest symbol of *Freedom* and *Humanitarianism*, (Caucasian America) found that questions assailed him that must have occurred to many others as well. Of what utility is all this Multiculturalism, other than Caucasian racial suicide? Of what profit is it in the overall social Caucasian cosmos? Is there any constitution or concept of government whose defense can justify the Caucasian people's destruction of their own country? Whether morally or intellectually, singly or collectively? (it is an illness unto death!)

C1214. Is there any Caucasian who can justify before his or her God and all futurity the *Immolation* of his or her entire race, so that alien races can be established in Caucasian lands?

C1215. No one can doubt today that Caucasian liberal zealots (American leftists) have taken the path of *Cultural* and *Moral Genocide* against their own people and are willing to sacrifice them to the extent of putting the soul of Caucasian America (their identity!) upon the sacrificial altar of an erroneously conceived fanatical idealism- *Racial Equality*?

C1216. Caucasian America is now being herded into a multicultural future that it never wanted and was never asked to choose. As the American civic moral order is in danger of collapsing, the politicians have not grasped that the center of political gravity has also shifted. This in turn means that the traditional moral values that have long underpinned the Caucasian American nation, including the maintenance of high education, the civilized standards upon which the racial minorities rely for the maintenance of neighborliness and tolerance, are also undermined. In other words, left liberalism has already shattered our bedrock norms of respectability and responsibility.

C1217. The political cowards of both parties (Democrats, Republicans) have actively promoted this moral slide and with drastic effects on the Caucasian American social order and national character.

C1218. Racial minorities will never ask themselves whether they have contributed to this new seedy moral order. Alien communities, after all, depend upon a degree of social cohesion, and that in turn rests on a critical mass of familiarity, shared language, and traditions (non-assimilation).

C1219. A degree of diversity, as between tribal variations of the same racial stock, is very good for a country, but not extreme alien racial diversity pushed through at an alarming rate. As of the *21st* century Caucasian America is becoming *Dysfunctional*, and that hints to Caucasian American society becoming a failed state. Life in the big cities will become increasingly unpleasant for all Caucasian citizens!

C1220. Is it moral to survive? To even ask the question is to reveal the extent to which our instincts, as well as our powers of rational thought have been corrupted. Leaving aside debilitating liberal zealot platitudes, one thing is certain; those who do not seek to *Survive* will not do so!

C1221. Those who demonize racial identity are being disingenuous. That which is built inextricably into the laws of the universe cannot be immoral. The- *Our Race*! And the- *Other Race* distinction will always be. And any idealistic racial group that unilaterally dismantles its own racial identity will be the loser in this new form of racial competition.

C1222. The competitive exclusion principle, in the competition for living space and resources between two species (or two races that occupy the same ecological niche), one will inevitably eliminate the other. In a finite universe, and the organisms of our world know no other, where the total number of organisms of both kinds cannot exceed a certain number, one race will necessarily replace the other race completely if the two races are complete competitors living the same kind of life. Hence, for both to survive they must separate!

C1223. One need not yield to the liberal zealot's condemned stereotypes of superiority and inferiority to justify the distinctiveness of the world's peoples. Distinctiveness is an inseparable part of human nature, a heritage we have an unalienable right to preserve. The unpleasant truth is that all people are not equal, either by standards of objective reality or by their own perceptions, and the very fact that other races are attracted to us is proof that our racial character, and the way of life it has created, is different, and therefore worthy of preservation. But one of liberalism's most poisonous evils is that it condemns such racial loyalties as morally wrong?

C1224. To attempt to destroy a race's identity, whether out of social ideology or out of something altogether much more malevolent, is an act of aggression. Whether distinct groups be called Tribes, Nations, Religions, Ethnic groups, or Races, they are still worthy of respect!

C1225. Because the Caucasians are productive, they have something other races want. Because they are kind-hearted, they are vulnerable to appeals of conscience.

C1226. In Caucasian America there is a vast reservoir of disaffected alien minorities whose role is to function as a social and political battering ram in the service of whoever is able to secure their allegiance?

C1227. As of today, by de facto controlling America's educational system, the liberal zealots have managed to muzzle the minds of millions of young Americans who have been conditioned to not question certain revealed truths, particularly those related to Race, Intelligence, Immigration, and social reality.

C1228. When the whole state is on the right course, it is a better thing for each separate individual than when private interests are satisfied but the state as a whole is going down- hill. However well off men or women may be in private life, they will still be involved in the general ruin if their country is destroyed.

C1229. A man or woman of politics who has the knowledge but lacks the power to express it clearly is no better off than if he or she never had any idea at all. Men or women who have both these qualities but lack patriotism could scarcely speak for their own people as they should. And even if they are patriotic as well but not able to resist a bribe, then this one fault will expose everything to the risk of being bought and sold.

C1230. In order for the Caucasian race and its culture to survive, its social and political elite must focus not only on its own needs, but on the needs of the less affluent and more numerous citizens. And if our elites had not been so self-absorbed and had worked to prevent the worst excesses of th purveyors of cultural and moral decline, perhaps the harsh edge of The Valorous *(Caucasian Manifesto)* would not be necessary

C1231. In today's Caucasian America, there is not a single statement about public morality, not a glimmer of recognition that welfare mechanisms of liberal democracy are fast destroying Caucasian America at will. Ironically the only thing that Caucasian wealthy and successful politicians are capable of articulating is the politics of their own personal frustration. What they want from politics is validation of their own personal choices and loud public approval of their self- centered existence.

C1232. Social policies that cripple and destroy others are the natural byproduct of aggressive feelings of racial or ethnic minorities. (self-interest) A more serious problem, because of a lack of any obvious motive, is the anger of Caucasian American elites toward their own culture and own kind?

C1233. What you and I, the average Caucasian American, must understand is that *Minority Elites* will always speak to each other of truly important and subversive things in code. After all, when they debate among themselves just exactly how they must deal with us (Caucasians), it may be very risky if we hear and understand.

C1234. Speaking in code is the sign of a subversive culture, a culture with an egregious intent. To remain ignorant of the truly *Important Discussions* going on around us dealing with our socio-political fate is a sign of a weak culture, one that is easily destroyed?

C1235. The last defenders of racial integration and pluralism are the liberal zealots and their neo-conservative allies. Caucasian America is entering a time of flux and danger. Racial minority elites and their allies are becoming more desperate and more dangerous. We as Caucasians Americans can weaken our enemies by unmasking their agendas in public.

C1236. We as Caucasian Americans must change. We must learn how to think like alien minorities. We must develop powerful code-speak antenna. We must understand the real agendas behind the words and images racial minorities place before us, so that we can defend our own social culture.

C1237. Diversity worship is the new liberal zealot's social newborn right out of the Supreme Court. Born of judicial cowardice, it will now take the place of equal treatment under the law. Hence, equal protection under the law no longer pertains to Caucasian Americans.

C1238. Did you know? As you walk up the steps to the building that houses the U. S. Supreme Court you can see near the top of the building a row of the world's lawmakers and each one is facing one in the middle who is facing forward with a full frontal view, it is Moses and he is holding the Ten Commandments! And the wall right above where the Supreme Court judges sit is a display of the Ten Commandments!

C1239. Did you know? Every session of the United States Congress begins with a prayer by a paid preacher whose salary has been paid by the taxpayers since 1777. Thomas Jefferson worried that the courts would overstep their authority and instead of interpreting the law would begin making law, an oligarchy, the rule of the few over the many. How, then, have we Caucasian Americans gotten to the point that everything we have done for 220 years in this country is now suddenly wrong and unconstitutional? If I remember correctly, this great Caucasian nation was built on In God We Trust!

C1240. The Orthodoxy of Tolerance, liberal zealots are so arrogant they seek to stamp out not only private opinions, but also actual facts. Under their relentless pressure private beliefs fade from all but the bravest hearts, to be replaced with the state approved formulas: diversity, inclusiveness, equality, Multiculturalism and affirmative action. This being the arsenal of Caucasian America's greatest enemy!

C1241. Liberal taboos and their enforced political correctness have turned against the strong biological basis of human nature and of differences in behavior and cognitive processes between races. This is having the effect of eliminating American academics as a significant source of intelligent science.

C1242. The strongest argument in favor of racism is that it is adaptive; it is natural, healthy, and necessary for survival. Those who oppose it must argue that people should act in a maladaptive way, against their own interests of surviving and reproducing. Thus to argue against racism is to argue for extinction.

C1243. Miscegenation is an increase in human entropy, a death of information; information contained in the separate races is lost. It equals the end of both races that engage in it. To do it deliberately and to advocate it without knowing its implications is completely unscrupulous.

C1244. In the realm of natural eugenics, homo-box genes play a greater role than was once thought; they are a class of highly conserved regulatory genes. Conserved; means that they have not changed much over millions of years. They are important because even a small difference in only one could make a huge difference in the way a biological organism develops, or what it becomes.

C1245. One common concept of *Racial Psychological* warfare is the great war of *Words* in which peoples racial loyalties and conviction are manipulated on a mass scale, and to which it makes falsehood as effective as truth in influencing a people's racial reality. If your faith dos not hold the survival of your race to be its *Highest Virtue*, then your faith is suicidal.

C1246. Part of becoming a race of people with a will to survive is learning to understand alien races and their hidden agendas, and having the will to unmask them in public.

C1247. In Caucasian America, schools, governments, and public institutions have come to view tolerance and diversity as weapons with which to control the Caucasian American majority, narrow Caucasian options, and extract additional tax dollars for the support of their hyenic integration liberality.

C1248. Because of the inherent economic bias against the effects of traditional Caucasian culture, the print and broadcast media will always become a haven for minority races and their elites who are comfortable carrying out their veiled attacks, not only for economic reasons, but for reasons of cultural and racial aggression as well.

C1249. Ironically, the defenders of racial integration are morally out there alone twisting in the wind, with the shrill and obviously self-interested racial minority elites desperately trying to keep the old integration flame alive. In other words, the liberal myth of racial integration is now dead.

C1250. In their heart of hearts, Caucasian American elites have become aware that exclusion and discrimination at the hands of emerging alien elites of international commerce is a virtual certainty. Hence the alarm at the large *Fifth Columns* of these new alien elites already within our borders. The silence of Caucasian elites now speaks volumes.

C1251. Because of encroaching alien elites, the new world Caucasians might someday be confined to working among and organizing the economic activities of their own kind. A global racial empire would be the best defense, and the continued goodwill of the average middle-class Caucasian American would become critical in an unknown future. It would seem an asset these Caucasian elites would not wish to destroy.

C1252. As Reivilo P. Oliver said: You may search the vast and respectable literature of China in vain for any trace of compassion for suffering per se!

C1253. An Islamic Europe? Remember, Islam, to this very day, has no history of *Democratic Credentials*, and if a large population of Islamic people legally invade Europe, the next logical question is whether Islam gets Europeanized, or Europe gets Islamized. And there are those who believe that once Islam takes hold, Europe will not have the ability to reject it or socially steer it. And then, which Islam, sharia- Islam or Euro-Islam, is to dominate Europe?

C1254. Muslims are very passionate about their faith and highly fertile. Has Europe lost its *élan vital*, its Christian life force? Is it as the poet Yeats wrote, that the best lack all conviction, while the worst are full of passionate intensity? Is it possible that Europe has lost the will to ensure its own survival as a Christian civilization?

C1255. Is Caucasian America at any less risk than Caucasian Europe? What Caucasians brought to America was not only their genes and a shared vision of their future but a shared heritage from the past (Europe). That heritage included a work ethic as well as an ethic of creativity and cultural dynamism that is unique to Caucasian civilization. Today in Caucasian America, not only has mass immigration and differential fertility started displacing the Caucasian people who carried that vision, but the vision itself is being discarded as well. Hence, either you have Caucasians and the America they created, or you have the Third World from which a non-Caucasian America will emerge.

C1256. So, as to the European Caucasians and the American Caucasians, are their best days behind them? Has the world Caucasian Community finally started to figure out that as a result of their liberal delirium, and social fallacies of alien mass immigration and the implosion of the Caucasian birth rate, that the future doesn't belong to their decedent?

C1257. Race, it has now pretty much been proved, is not just a social construct, but a fact of nature having both a socio-cultural and biological meaning, and yes, while Caucasian Europe and America have historically been the lands of futurists and dreamers, that place where dreams come true and the future really happens, these Caucasian lands are now increasingly home to political and cultural pessimists, with the Caucasian classes whispering about Paradise Lost and the coming racial Apocalypse.

C1258. Empathy is a rare quality indeed in most of the biological world, so it stands to reason that Caucasian empathy for other races, and the world biological community in general must be a type of gene with a selective advantage in the Caucasian population. Empathy is surely a good thing, but it loses its advantage when it is bestowed on all those who break through the back door.

C1259. It was Clemens who once said that some ideas are so stupid that only highly educated people can believe them (bio-egalitarianism).

C1260. Liberal zealotry is a self-destructive ideology, a form of mental illness. Abortion, for example, they push it because they believe it shows compassion toward women who may be in some kind of short-term distress (children...inconvenience or burden). But ultimately, in a declining population, if you keep supporting abortion you will simply abort yourself out of existence and remove your racial bio-ideology from the gene pool.

C1261. Being overly generous toward alien races is another example of liberal zealotry and its mental illness. A sound individual or group would favor their own. But the liberal zealots (leftists) have it completely backwards. They abort their own children and favor (support) the uncontrolled birth rate of alien races that are most unlike themselves. In the mind of all zealots, there is always a defect.

C1262. In today's Caucasian America, we cannot reasonably discuss things like race because the liberal social agenda has so corrupted the pertinent vocabulary that young Caucasians who have spent many years in liberal draconian universities will be bringing this *Pavlovian conditioning* into our public schools, foundations, media, courts, and government. At encountering the word *discrimination* they will follow the example of university administrators that newly classified phylum of invertebrates, and assume a fetal position.

C1263. In Caucasian America today, we are forever being told not to do this, not to do that. Foremost among the no-no's is to legislate morality. That sounds so tolerant, so if not morality, then just what are we to legislate-Interests, Prejudices, the public interest however determined? (this can be little more than the toting up of special interests.) In practice, the stricture against legislating morality is now restricted to sexual morals because sex is the last respectable appetite in our national pantheon. Most of those who insist we tolerate same-sex marriage also regard Affirmative Action as moral imperatives. So when a liberal zealot says you cannot legislate morality, his or her unspoken code is, but I as a liberal can?

C1264. In America today, some have taken to referring to public schools as government schools. This name is appropriate, to be sure, but given the power of their employees, more accurate still is union schools. But none approach the size or clout of the National Education Association. So dominant is the- NEA that at the national level, it owns and operates the PTA. So the most accurate term is NEA schools?

C1265. Civil Rights, the liberal packaging of something as a Civil Right by co-opting the jargon, personalities, organizations, presumptions, and odor of sanctity left over from the liberal movement's glory years. Unlike the bill of rights, these newer rights are not aimed at protecting citizens from their government, but rather at using the power of government to obligate other citizens and their property. In other words, these new rights, their jargon, and so on are enlisted in purely liberal seditious interests against the majority of Caucasian Americans. The subversive redistribution of monetary, political, and cultural wealth to alien others?

C1266. The enemy of subversive thought is not suppression, but publication: truth has no need to fear the light of day; fallacy withers under it.

C1267. It was Sir Stanley Unwin, who once said that the unpopular views of today are the commonplaces of tomorrow, and in any case the wise man or woman wants to hear both sides of every question.

C1268. For Caucasian America to resist the liberal zealots and their social fallacy, they must see that stealing is just as wrong and destructive to their society when it is done by their government as when it is done personally. If you have needs, you cannot seize your neighbor's money, but you can vote to have the government seize it and give some of it to you. Then you don't have to realize that you are just hiring a thief. But most people don't want to understand something that will reduce their take.

C1269. If Caucasian American intellect shifts more and more toward those who cannot comprehend the destructiveness of liberal zealot ideology the politics of America will become a game of you trying to form political alliances to steal more from others than they can steal from you. And when the government is hired to do the stealing, most of the stolen funds go to the government.

C1270. There are limits to taxation. People in business add taxes in as a cost of doing business, and if those costs mean that the profits will be puny, they find something else to do. Alas, the productive people who are keeping the economy working will shrug and no longer do so. Hence, the Government borrows. But eventually, interest payments on the money borrowed become so large that they can no longer be paid out of taxes. Then the Government's only alternative is to print the money, which is called inflation, and that action results in higher prices. Of course the lenders aren't stupid, and they raise interest rates to include the inflation rate!

C1271. When liberal zealotry has failed and there are no alternatives left and their access to real wealth diminishes, these liberal rulers will have to choose between guns and butter. That is, when they can no longer meet the demands of the alien needy and maintain a social fallacy to keep themselves in power, there will be alien riots, and the liberal government will collapse.

C1272. The slogans of the American liberal zealot are Equality, Diversity, Multi-culturalism, Inclusion, and we must not forget, Affirmative Action. Translated, that means that all those Caucasian Americans who are capable of creating wealth will have most of that wealth taken away from them by force, and it will be given to all those alien races that cannot or will not create it. Free health care, education, housing, food, and on and on, because alien racial needs are endless. Isn't that exactly the social program of both the Democratic and Republican administrations? They differ only in small points, such as whether the taxes will be paid by Caucasian Americans now living (Democrats) or more by Caucasian Americans not yet born (Republicans).

C1273. Kin-based altruism has profound implications for explaining social cooperation and group cohesion among cultures, races, and tribes. It has exposed equalitarian dogma as the scientific hoax of the twentieth century. The liberal zealot doctrine of human equality, that races, cultures, and individuals have equal genetic potential for intelligence and other traits valued in human society, has not only unraveled but has been thoroughly demolished as a viable theory of human nature.

C1274. No two human beings are created equal. Individual, and thus racial, inequality is simply an iron law of nature. The persistence of group difference has undermined the liberal fable that all races and ethnic groups are created equal. Despite overlaps in the trait distribution for IQ and other valued traits, there are large and persistent differences between races and ethnic groups in the ability to create and adapt to the advanced civilizations of the modern world. Ethnic and racial group competition merely confirms the maxim that humans are inherently unequal.

C1275. Human inequality in general, and racial inequality in particular, will end the liberal zealots ironclad dominance of what might well be the most destructive social dogma among the utopian ideologies.(equality!)

C1276. Caucasian altruism or The Guilt of Superiority, no healthy race of people doubts its own legitimacy or even its superiority. Every race or ethnic group of people thinks itself better than its neighbor, and every race or ethnic group is right. Not even the most primitive tribe of New Guinea is likely ever to take an inventory of its characteristics to determine whether or not it should step aside so other people can take its place. All living thing act this way. Neither man nor beast tolerates alien incursion, displacement, or Multiculturalism. They fight them instinctively, without having to explain to each other why they must fight them and why they should survive as a people. Only the liberal zealots pretend that pluralism and displacement are good things and that the measures necessary to ensure group survival are immoral.

C1277. The matter of Caucasian American capitulation is the most troubling of all, but its explanation may lie in a better understanding of the distinctive traits of Caucasians. In describing the ways of our people we may find that the very things that set us apart from other races are the very things that paralyze us. What we ordinarily think of as our virtues have become, through degeneration, our greatest weakness. This may help us to understand why Caucasians all around the world seem to have lost their racial consciousness and will to survive as a group. We Caucasians have brought dispossession upon ourselves, so we as a race of people must look to our own natures if we are to understand why we have done so.

C1278. Racial Nepotism; or old fashioned racism as the liberals like to call it, and to which they are not excluded, is the human tendency to favor our own people. This discrimination is deeply rooted in our animal past and thus rests on a direct genetic foundation. *Racial Nepotism* isn't a metaphor. It's a reality. And we'd better accept it whether the politicians think it would be good for their careers or not.

C1279. Humankind is more social even than social insects, because our social life is based on knowledge of right and wrong (bio-cultural nepotism). Those who promoted the social development of the bio-cultural state are humankind's greatest benefactors, because of the encouragement given to virtuous living. Justice is one of the ends for which the bio-cultural state exists, but humankind detached from the bio-cultural state and its control means household, village, and government become more depraved, more wanton, covetous, and violent.

C1280. The bio-cultural state is thus natural, the logical sense of being the end on which all human development is converging. And what Caucasian Americans refuse to imagine is the rootless liberal individualists who today parade their antisocial nature and call it libertarianism truly deserve the withering description of a derelict intellect.

C1281. Caucasian America is beginning to suffer an epidemic of mental illness, through racial dispossession. Mental health requires grounding, for the individual as well as the racial community.

C1282. Caucasian American, as well as European education, is having its freedom of expression suppressed. Liberal zealot indoctrination has now been substituted for reasoned analysis by extreme liberal ideologues who pose as scholars and even scientists. Freedom of expression and scholarly impartiality are out. Instead, dogmatic, unsubstantiated beliefs are imposed on students. There was a time when universities were the strongholds of truly liberal ideas. Then, liberal meant what it says. It meant free inquiry into every opinion and a willingness to give all views an opportunity to be heard. That no longer exists.

C1283. The uncontrolled alien racial migration into Caucasian lands does indeed carry with it the potential for catastrophic social and cultural disaster. The solution is for the world Caucasian community, and that means us, to acquire governments possessing the will to defend Caucasian frontiers and place firm barriers against further alien racial migration, while taking all necessary steps to remove all those who have illegally entered Caucasian territory in the past.

C1284. The duty all Caucasians have, in a world in which human fertility outstrips economic resources and therefore ensures that some will not survive, is to ensure that we as Caucasian will be among the survivors.

C1285. The liberal socio-cultural illness, the multi-racial state, and the low fertility rates among Caucasian people throughout the world pose a great threat to us, our lands, and our resources. This in turn with each generation makes our nations progressively older and thus weaker in vitality, energy, productiveness, and the capacity for self-defense. If we Caucasians have lost the instinct to produce children and welcome them as additions to the family and national racial strength, as did our ancestors without even needing to think about the matter, we will surely die out eventually, even if the final self-extinction is not witnessed by those currently living. So I say again, putting it in another way: the socio-cultural pressure and its eventual catastrophes are of our own making. They are socio-cultural pressures and catastrophes created in the liberal zealot's mind and made real only by the Caucasian community's paralysis.

C1286. There is one further thing Caucasians must do. We Caucasians, both here in America and throughout the world, cannot and should not take on responsibility for alien races and their problem of overpopulation, and we most certainly can and should reverse what threatens to become our own problem of under population.

C1287. Once it is accepted that true Islam does not recognize a prior, the right of any other religion or world outlook to exist, least of all the atheistic secular humanism, a serious anti-terrorist strategy will finally become possible. This message is a huge problem for all Muslims. And we of the other religions cannot solve it for them, and we should not be asked to pretend that the Quran is a pacifist tract. Those who submit to that faith must solve the problem they set themselves.

C1288. Concepts, schemes, and theories vie for a place on the pedestal of eternal truth, and most fell back in short order. The many anthropological relationships in the blueprint of the physical world demonstrate how precisely Homo sapiens fits into its scheme. But they also hint at deeper, still undiscovered physical relationships, behind which it is fair to suspect there may lie a wider unity of nature, matter as a precondition for intelligence, and intelligence as a precondition for the recognition of matter and its laws.

C1289. The incomprehensible secret: Decades of discussion indicate the phenomenon that life is difficult to differentiate from inanimate matter, principally because the transition point between animate and inanimate matter is vague (unknown) due to the assorted virus-like, quasi-crystalline transitional forms and their relation to intelligence.

C1290. The Caucasian religions in America and throughout the modern world represent a terribly naive social and political racial view. They have become in the Caucasian world community altruistically ludicrous and are a major part of the suicidal mind set afflicting all Caucasian societies. Present-time reality urges that all Caucasian churches of all religious denominations have a beneficial role to play in the salvation and survival of the Caucasian world community. We as Caucasians must not delude ourselves and support a religion whose suicidal spirituality is trying to destroy us. Therefore, we of the Caucasian Religious Community must bring reality back to social morality.

C1291. It has always been claimed that all people are equal when standing before God on the Day of Judgment. But I would deny all people are equal on the Day of Judgment. People will be judged according to their works, which are manifestly not equal. Utopian equalitarianism: will be to blame for the Caucasian world community's downfall by liberal zealots, as having sapped our vital racial instincts.

C1292. To assign blame singularly to the *Liberal Zealots* and not to mention certain others, leads to profound errors of misdiagnosis of a much larger problem. We Caucasian Americans are now facing *Political Piracy* by a section of Caucasian elites throughout the world, and their strategically blundered thinking on world Egalitarianism, Economic Liberality, and Scientific Apportionment, has now made the Caucasian world a community disoriented!

C1293. The liberal zealot's social strategy of demonizing Caucasian America has been highly effective, because if there is one area where the liberal zealots have won a complete and decisive victory, it is in *Pathologizing* any consideration by the Caucasian American majority of its own racial interests. I mean not only that Caucasian American people have been indoctrinated that their commonsense perception of race is an illusion, but further, that the slightest assertion of racial self-interest or consciousness by Caucasian Americans is the sign of a grave moral defect so grave that it is a matter of psychiatric concern. Of course this is beyond hypocritical. While assertions of racial interest by Caucasians are stigmatized, assertions of racial interest by alien races in America are utterly commonplace and encouraged.

C1294. The true story of immigration is that wealthy Caucasian societies, with economic opportunities and a high level of public goods such as medical care and education, have become magnets for alien races from around the world. Because of this alien racial immigration and its high fertility rate, the result will be rapid displacement of the founding Caucasian population, not only in America, but also in its sister states throughout the world. If current trends continue, the United States founding Caucasian-derived population is set to become a minority by the middle of this century, and in its sister states throughout the world, the submergence date is just two generations later.

C1295. Caucasian communities that are allowing themselves to be displaced in their own countries are playing a very dangerous game; dangerous because of the long history of racial strife furnishes them no guarantees about the future. Throughout history there has been a pro-pensity for majority races to oppress minority races. A glance at human history is sufficient to make clear the dangers faced by a racial group that does not have a state and political apparatus to protect its vital social interests. It does not take an overactive imagination to see that how coalitions of minority races could compromise the interests of the formerly dominant Caucasian race. We Caucasian Americans already see numerous examples where coalitions of minority races attempt to influence public policy against the interests of the Caucasian majority; for example, Affirmative Action, hiring quotas and alien immigration policies.

C1296. Besides coalitions of racial minorities, the main danger facing Caucasians throughout the world is that wealthy, powerful Caucasian elites are often unaware of, or do not value, their own racial interests. Frequently, they in effect sell out their own racial group for short-term personal gain. There are many contemporary examples, most notably the efforts by major corporations to import low-wage workers and outsource jobs to alien countries. This extreme individualism of Caucasian elites is a tragic mistake for all Caucasians, including the elites themselves, who are losing untold millions of racial kin by promoting mass immigration of non-Caucasians. It is a case of putting short-term class interest and self-interest before long-term Caucasian racial interest.

C1297. Who was the real legislator of America, as he was called by many of his colleagues? One might guess that it was Jefferson, Franklin, or Adams. No, it was the man who wrote the Fairfax Resolve of 1774 and the Virginia Declaration of Rights in 1776. The man's name is George Mason, a forgotten hero, and the true architect of Caucasian American liberty.

C1298. In the long run, globalism and Multiculturalism are a threat to almost everyone's racial interest because both ideologies actually legitimize and increase racial competition. Globalism results in increased competition because every one has potential access to everyone else's territory, opening opportunities for plundering another's backyard. Multi-cultural societies sanction racial mobilization because they inevitably become cauldrons of competing racial interests.

C1299. The future, then, like the past, will inevitably be a *Darwinian Competition*. And race will play a crucial role. Unilateral renunciation of racial loyalties by any race means only their surrender and defeat, disappearance and extinction. Given this, it is difficult at best to ensure peaceful relations among racial groups. Even maintaining a status quo in cultural and moral behavior is very arduous, as can be seen by the ill-fated attempts of liberal Americans to achieve a multicultural moral consensus?

C1300. These liberal policies based on preferring alien group's interests ahead of our own Caucasian interests are expressed by our politicians with a sort of moral elation for the welfare of the unfortunate alien? But we as Caucasians should find it less easy to account for this seeming elation experienced by our politicians when they advocate ideals that if acted upon, seem destined to affect the Caucasian people disastrously! We as Caucasians should admire the politicians who make *Sacrifices* on behalf of their group. But should we Caucasians admire the politicians of a group, who sacrifice the group?

C1301. If today's alien racial minorities become a majority in Caucasian America, or for that matter in any Caucasian social state, it will be beyond the power of Caucasian people to control peacefully by means of the ballot, the destiny of their nations that were once their own. There is no guarantee that protections prevalent in Caucasian societies will be preserved in societies that become non-Caucasian. There is no historical reason to believe that governments based on principles of individual liberty will survive the disappearance of Caucasian people.

C1302. Self-defense is justly called the primary law of the Fematrix. It cannot be taken away by the laws of society. A strict observance of the written laws is doubtless one of the highest duties of a good citizen, but it is not the highest. The laws of necessity, of self-preservation, of saving our race when in danger, are of a higher obligation. Laws alone, independent of their survival utility, are not, and cannot be, the underlying basis of civilization. In the end, whoever makes and enforces the laws has the power to determine who lives and who dies. Survival is the ultimate principle upon which all enduring moral systems must be based, for any people who divest their posterity of the right to existence will vanish, and their flawed morals will vanish with them.

C1303. Intelligence does not guarantee good behavior, but a certain level is necessary for self-knowledge and the comprehension of moral distinction.

C1304. As long as Caucasians continue to avoid and deny their own racial identity, at a time when almost every other racial category is rediscovering and asserting its own, Caucasians will have no chance to resist their dispossession and their eventual possible physical destruction. Before we Caucasians in America and throughout the world can seriously discuss any concrete proposals for preserving our culture and its biological and demographic foundation, we have to address and correct the problems we inflict on ourselves, our own lack of a racial consciousness and the absence of a common will to act in accordance with it.

C1305. The attack against religion and traditional values in Caucasian America is Totalitarian a neo-socialist idea, the promotion of an identical group think by those who control our culture, especially in the media and the schools. This Orwellian policy is being kept in place to create a new historic entity and to make citizens forget their racial origins, nationalities, and ethnic traditions. It has already begun breaking down the inherited identity of Caucasian Americans in order to reconstruct a multi-cultural heaven on earth, where prejudice (choice) is forbidden. (the end of reason!)

C1306. Moral character has a genetic basis, and if Multi-culturalism continues, Caucasian American intelligence as well as that of her sister states throughout the world, will begin to decline. The best available estimate of the rate of Caucasian intellectual decline is that it will be about one IQ point per generation. This intellectual decline will have a great effect on Caucasian self-discipline, the motivation to work for long-term goals, law abidingness, and a sense of civic responsibility, all of which is conspicuously lacking in certain alien races and their sociopathic value system.

C1307. Multiculturalism and affirmative action are the carriers of a deadly social virus- *Dysgenics*, or retrogressive social evolution. The warnings went unheeded, and in the last quarter century, understanding of the problem has been lost. It is time to revive the Caucasian world's recognition of this serious threat to the future of our civilization.

C1308. For all the nations that are as interested in economic success as liberty, creating a judicial branch that can check the executive and the legislature doesn't just protect individual rights and prevent the persecution of the government's political opponents; it also improves your stock market as well.

C1309. Caucasian America should have heeded the warning signs that something sinister was afoot when the term multicultural was slipped by stealth into the public domain. Now the full horror of what Caucasian America is becoming is being shouted at them from their national tabloids: liberal totalitarianism. The frightening irony is that even many in the press fail to realize just how liberal totalitarian we are becoming.

C1310. The liberal zealots who loathe the old-fashioned values of Caucasian America are hard at work ramming home the multicultural legislation politburo-style, and politically correct mandates. They are claiming the right to interfere in every aspect of our lives by embracing fallacious moral absolutism typical of the neo-socialist elite.

C1311. Let it be said: At the very center of the world's *Liberal Zealot Doctrine* are two sinister social weapons, *Multiculturalism* and *Political Correctness*. In Europe the EU is creating racial tensions for its own purposes; it wants to impose decisions that might other-wise not be acceptable, such as applying repressive measures to silence opposition. They welcome civil disorder, so that the politicians can put in place more authoritarian security measures. This same neo-socialist world strategy is being applied in the US as well and will have appalling implications for all Caucasian Americans.

C1312. Hence, much of what is happening in the world to-day seems to be plain nihilistic evil: the deliberate breaking up of Caucasian racial states in order purposefully to dilute their national and racial identity. The neo-socialists and liberal zealots will mercifully collapse under their own weight of social fallacy overstretch and a growing economic inefficiency and cultural default. But it will leave immense destruction behind and huge racial problems.

C1313. It was Edger J. Steele (great Caucasian patriot), who said; Of the many racial groups now occupying America, only Caucasian Americans actively must practice and demand a form of reverse racism, on pain of being branded racist by all, including their own brethren. Designed to last but a single generation, Affirmative Action now is being institutionalized as a permanent form of handicapping Caucasian Americans to produce equal outcomes for alien races in America. What was to have been a hand up for alien races has become a handout. What was to have created equal opportunity ended up producing equal outcomes, the lynchpin of socialism We Caucasians Americans have focused on the wrong hand, while the liberal zealot magicians did the deed with the other.

C1314. When and if the alien majority takes over in Caucasian America, the first targets will be Caucasian national symbols. The national anthem! Our official language! What will we do? When the alien majority decides to banish our history from the education of the young, to change the names of streets and cities, what will happen? What will happen when the alien majority says the judges and courts are *Racist* and that they refuse to acknowledge Caucasian American justice and refuses to abide by court rulings? What will happen when the courts are filled with alien people or their sympathizers? What will we do when known criminals are voted into office because of *Racial Solidarity* among the *Alien Majority*, but don't exist among the Caucasian Americans? Some are of the belief that it's already started!

C1315. Once you lose social, cultural, and political dominance, there is no getting it back again. To survive, Caucasian Americans must never lose the power they now enjoy to people of alien cultures. Do not let your habits and values work against you. You cannot fight cultural terrorism and alien street mobs with letters to your Congressmen. You cannot fight accusations of racism with prayer meetings. You cannot appeal to the goodness of your fellow man, when that fellow man despises you for your accomplishments. And we Caucasians, whether in America or Europe, must never decide that we are morally obligated to share power equally with those we used to dominate or live apart from, disregarding the consequences to ourselves or our posterity.

C1316. Societies that lose their faith offer material comfort...bread and circuses as a substitute. And like in the past, Caucasian Americans do not know how to reclaim the sincere racial piety that liberal intellectuals, upper classes, and other sophisticates have cast aside in the name of a social fallacy, racial equality.

C1317. Caucasian Americans will soon find themselves unable or unwilling to stand up to challenge the new alien political methods that will be the inevitable result of the racial metamorphosis now taking place in America. Liberals will not admit that the same kind of savagery could come to America when enough alien racial immigrants assert themselves. Faced with racial revolution in the streets, strikes, civil unrest, and sheer lawlessness, the American liberals fraternity will no doubt cave in. They will compromise away their independence and ultimately their way of life. And the most dangerous of all, the craven politicians who believe compassionate conservatism will buy them a few more votes, a few more days of peace, will not see that they are losing their country through skillful alien racial propaganda. And let us not forget the surrender of South Africa and Rhodesia (Zimbabwe) and the wholesale slaughter of Caucasians and the dismantling of their cultures. They voted for their own suicide; they surrendered their ancient racial privilege of survival.

C1318. We Caucasian Americans will lose our country through skillful propaganda pressure from unrelenting charges of oppression and racism and the shrewd assessment by alien racial tyrants that the Caucasian Americans have many Achilles heels, the most significant of which is their compassion, their belief in the equality of humankind. None of which are part of any alien racial history.

C1319. The long-term rise in the number of aliens who have the highest birth and immigration rates in Caucasian America will coincide with a decline in the number of Caucasians, predicting that by 2030, the number of Caucasian Americans dying will exceed those being born. Although the Caucasian population is set to increase steadily in real numbers, expressed as a percentage of the entire American population, their numbers are in radical decline: in 1996, Caucasians made up 73.1 percent of the American population. That is projected to fall to 48.8 percent by 2050.

C1320. There is a depressing irony in Caucasian America, in the fact that we can't even approach one of the actual unjust roots of inequality: the lack of effectiveness of some alien races, their cultures, and communities in socialization. Many inequalities are the result of injustice, but many are not. An intelligent society must learn to distinguish between the two.

C1321. Human beings are not created equal. This should be a social truism, but in a society such as Caucasian America, which has a troubled relationship with inequality, it's quite a provocative, if not criminal statement. This is due to the new dominance of the normative in academia, which allows us to simply wish away truths with which we're uncomfortable. We are indebted to evolutionary psychology, a field that has courageously studied inherited differences, despite long suffering the eugenics smear.

C1322. Inequality merits academic exploration, not thuggish attempts to shout it out of the intellectual forum, no doubt in fear of its truth.

C1323. In today's Caucasian world, once a prodigy, the love for political equality has grown into a virtually unrecognizable caricature of itself, the *Liberals Zealots* have become intolerant of *Inequality* in any aspect of human life.

C1324. America is unlikely to remain the last and best hope of Caucasian kind. When dealing with the causes of alien immigration, the politicians of all parties acquiesced in this criminal invasion because they feared the accusation of Philistine bigotry from the liberal zealots. And in all the western democracies, the desires of the majority are being set aside by an unholy alliance of the liberal cultural elite and the avarice of politicians.

C1325. It is the liberal definition of racist, and by means of this definition, that the liberals have managed to do such harm to Caucasian societies throughout the world. Western liberal zealots have cleverly silenced all criticism on the subject of race, and immigration by raising the specter of extreme racism, tarring all opposition with the same brush. We Caucasians cannot strip ourselves of that which determines our racial uniqueness for the sake of peace. Liberalism in this area, and in many others, is not really a political doctrine at all, but the elevation of racial capitulation to the level of ideology. What will posterity say about those liberal political pygmies who gave away the Caucasian civilizations that were meant to be in their safekeeping?

C1326. Liberal zealot sensibilities will certainly be offended to know that despite the political correct movement, there is still a greater intellectual honesty in the Caucasian social spirit than they could ever imagine. And it cannot be avoided or defeated!

C1327. When Caucasian America begins to fragment into a Balkan-type hostility, by then Caucasians will be in a minority, and just as we lived to witness the collapse of an other liberal icon, Communism, so also we will be witnessing the beginning of the end of Caucasian America, and with sublime and breathtaking arrogance the liberal zealots will fiddle while she burns.

C1328. Caucasian racial reason, sweet and infallible, should be brought to bear on modern traditions that govern the pursuit of knowledge, relationships between the sexes and the social classes, standards of art and music, and the exercise of political power.

C1329. Caucasians come into the world as blank pages, upon which experience writes doctrines of social reason. By applying social reasoning not only to institutions but to the socialization of the young, Caucasian society could be improved along with its institutions. Caucasian history hence- forth could take on a direction, and that direction is progress.

C1330. The meaning of excellence is intimately connected with the discovery or application of objective truth about how the world or universe works. In the hard sciences and mathematics, excellence involves the discovery of truth. In technology and medicine, excellence involves the application of truth to produce desired results.

C1331. The nature of a person's appreciation of a thing or event varies with the level of knowledge that a person brings to it. Expertise changes the quality of the experience and also introduces an element of the objective.

C1332. Non-judgmental is the social ideology of the modern liberal fraternity. The impossibility of being non-judgmental does not go away as the differences in quality become smaller. We can refuse to voice our opinion, but we cannot keep from having them unless we refuse to think. When we are comparing things, there remain dimensions on which the things differ, and those dimensions lend themselves to comparisons in which one may be found superior to the other. Hence, one may choose to examine those differences or not, but one does not have the right to say that no difference exist, nor the modern liberal option of saying that differences exist, but one will not judge them.

C1333. It was in one of President Andrew Jackson's memorable vetoes that apply also too many political aspects of to-day's Caucasian America: Equality of talents, of education or of wealth cannot be produced by human institutions. In the full enjoyment of the gifts of Heaven and the fruits of superior industry, economy, and virtue, every man is equally entitled to protection by law, but when the laws undertake to add to these natural and just advantages artificial distinctions...to make the rich richer and the potent more powerful, the humble members of our society, the farmers, mechanics, and laborers who have neither the time nor the means of securing favors to themselves, have the right to complain of the injustice of their government. There are no necessary evils in government. Its evils exist only in its legislative abuses.

C1334. It was LIewellyn H. Rockwell Jr. who stated., In all times of state dominance, the instability of the system gives rise to two types of reformers: the moderates who want to work within the system but end up defending it, and the radicals who have the clarity to see that the only real solution is upheaval. If the latter prevail, and they often have in the history of politics, it is only after having endured the slings and arrows of the former. Today, in Caucasian America, it is the same. The Caucasian patriots, and every radical Caucasian nationalist, academic, or journalist, stands accused of harming the cause of social reform by holding out a racial ideal.

C1335. Who do the liberal zealots fear most? Not the moderates, but the Caucasian radical nationalists whom they believe are setting back their social cause. The difference between the Caucasian racial nationalist (radicals) and the Caucasian moderate is not of degree. It is an intellectual and moral out-look of a completely different sort, one that goes to the very heart of one's racial identity and existence, and whether in today's Caucasian America one views the liberal zealots in power as the source of the problem or the source of the solution.

C1336. No government is rational by nature. Governments grant liberty only when forced to do so by public opinion. What causes a government to act is fear of opposition. But somehow, against all evidence, Caucasian moderate reformers continue to believe that the politically powerful (liberal zealots) can be influenced by praise, cocktail parties, and the absurd suggestion of marginal reform, to save the Caucasian American society from alien racial invasion, third world immigration.

C1337. Human beings enjoy the exercise of their realized capacities, with the enjoyment increasing the more the capacity is realized. Hence, those with the capacity for excellence do not need to be cajoled into wanting to realize it. The pursuit of excellence is as natural as the pursuit of happiness.

C1338. A major stream of human accomplishment is fostered by a culture in which the most talented people believe that life has a purpose and that the function of life is to fulfill that purpose. Without a sense of purpose, the creative personalities have no template that constantly forces an assessment of whether they are making the best possible use of their talents. Hence, to believe life has a purpose carries with it a predisposition to put one's talents in the service of whatever is best, not the most lucrative, not the most glamorous, but that which represents the highest expression of the object of one's vocation.

C1339. Critics who wish to be taken seriously choose their words carefully, and the ordinary vocabulary of praise suffices for nearly everyone. It is only for the rarest artists that ordinary words fail. Every great artistic work has been accomplished by the conscious exercise of talent, will, and labor.

C1340. One of the chief merits of the Scientific Method is that it gives frail humans a system, offering them some protection from themselves, and permitting knowledge, steadily converging on truth, to be accumulated from generation to generation.

C1341. Until, and unless alien races change their cultural and political views. Caucasian Americans cannot make any political concessions. The pernicious equality for "Peace" liberal compromise urges Caucasian Americans to negotiate with alien political highwaymen, as your money or your life. The proposal of our equality or your life represents the same fraudulent attempt to treat the withdrawal of a threat of force as a tradable commodity, so as to assume autocratic powers once Caucasian Americans comply are meaningless. The moral perversity here is that Caucasian America is being widely denounced because of their virtues, while the *Alien Races* are being praised for their vices.

C1342. Alien races are considered the aggrieved party by American liberal zealots, and Caucasian Americans as the villains. What accounts for this moral inversion, whereby those who endorse liberal authori-tarianism and the wanton destruction of their own race are hailed, while those who support their racial identity and their nation, (built by their ancestral trust) are excoriated? Only a liberal zealot philosophy that preaches the fallacy of *Equality* as a moral virtue. This philosophy insists that someone's need creates a moral claim upon anyone able to satisfy it. And if their need is not met, this philosophy declares they are being denied what is morally theirs. They are being oppressed. Their rights are being violated. It does not matter that these alien races are to blame for their own misery. In fact, this liberal zealot philosophy declares that if Caucasian America seeks to protect it economy, its culture, and its racial identity from an alien racial threat, it is being selfish and immoral?

C1343. On the political level, the liberal zealot's notorious anti-Caucasian American campaign continues to dominate its social and political agenda. Over the last decade, the liberal zealot's collective wisdom has equated Caucasian America with racial terrorism and singled out the everyday Caucasian citizen as a harbinger of racial supremacy and in need of racial penance, and sensitivity training. The strategy behind the repetition of anti-Caucasianism by the liberal zealots has been largely successful. The double standards and unfair practices employed by the liberal zealots against Caucasian America have become commonplace. The liberal zealots anti-Caucasian bias, its distortions of the facts, and its misrepresentation of the truth have been accepted by most Caucasian Americans. Under the cover of liberal legitimacy, alien racial propagandists have achieved remarkable national success in their defamatory campaign against Caucasian America.

C1344. Caucasian America's relations with the liberal zealots will reach a crisis point as a result of this ongoing process has no end in sight, and has virtually violated all the accepted canons of political, economic and racial survival of the Caucasian American people. Caucasian American society is under moral attack. It is pointless to argue that justice and reason are on their side. In this war of moral and social ideas, it is only by upholding the principle that one has the moral right to exist for one's own racial sake and live for one's own racial values that the Caucasian American society can be properly defended.

C1345. In today's Caucasian America, alien races are always in a constant state of tribal mentality; they are hostile to Caucasian values, education, and social demeanor and prefer living under a hyenic nihilistic culture of self-determination. They are always depicting themselves as long-suffering victims of oppression and fighting a desperate battle to gain the rights being unjustly denied them, when in fact, they have chosen a social path of moral desertion and cultural nihilism discarding their children's future, hence abandoning them in a social cesspool of their own creation.

C1346. In today's Caucasian America, not a week goes by that a Caucasian civilian isn't assaulted, knifed, shot, or robbed by an alien racial minority whose been acting under the liberal declaration of social oppression, hence making their crimes, in their eyes, a course of self-determination (open season on Caucasians).

C1347. It is of the utmost importance in today's Caucasian America to rethink its social policies on the matter of racial sovereignty in accordance with the development of advanced alien racial hostility toward Caucasian American society. This new crisis in Caucasian America's racial diplomacy is jeopardizing regional stability in all major cities with large alien racial populations.

C1348. It is the *21st* century, and it has been proposed by well-educated economists that we arrogantly dismiss the will of more than 80% of the American people by letting millions of illegal alien migrant workers in and legalizing them, hence picking up the tab for their health care, education, and subsidized housing. The mass importation of rebellious alien labor into Caucasian America is a cultural, political, and economic idiocy that only liberal zealots and those who profit from it would entertain.

C1349. The present political system is unsuited to the economic needs and to the values of Caucasian America. We as Caucasian Americans should not be content with laws that invite chaos in our economy and punish hard-working Caucasians who want only to provide for their families by outsourcing well-paying, clean, and highly productive middle class jobs to third world countries, together with the advanced technology that is necessary to perform them, developed mostly by the Caucasian American middle class. These companies, as well as their facilities, and along with the high profits that they generate are leaving for overseas at a frightening rate, hence abandoning the workforce of Caucasian America for the gods of profit. This act of socio- economic treachery will not go unanswered and will prove to be their undoing.

C1350. The great weakness of political partisanship has captured the conservative and liberal free press, breaking both their spirits of accountability and truth. They, the American journalists, have become the horns of the political partisan dilemma, no decent or sensible Caucasian American can deny this media scandal, the lying and attempts to destroy anyone who utters a simple ethical statement, a word of dissent or truth, is obvious to all. We, as Caucasian American people, are on our own!

C1351. It is the *21st* century, and the pathology of both political parties, *Republicans* and *Democrats*, and their submergence into a condition of abnormal social variations of multicultural, and political correctness, from a sound and proper political condition dissent is putting all of America on the path to civil war. Hence, the process and results of this liberal disease has rendered the American political and cultural mentality to a despotic form of social Caligulaism.

C1352.Political madness, thence political correctness, has succeeded in making Caucasian America so confused, politically correct, and minority sensitive that it has all but forgotten its original core of Judeo-Christian values. American heroes from "Christopher Columbus" to the Pilgrims are now likened to genocidal racists and maniacal bigots. Perversion and sexual criminality are now equated to traditional monogamous marriage. On American college campuses, they are teaching that Whiteness is the underlying cause of practically every conceivable social ill, and that all White people (Caucasians) are inherently evil. This type of educational and political view whereby we as a society declare all human cultures and morals codes, from the fairest to the foulest, to be equal in value is made possible only by the total abandonment of an objective standard of right and wrong. And this confusion is now even compromising Caucasian America's ability to fight its enemies and hindering us from clearly identifying who our enemies actually are.

C1353. In the idyllic world of TV commercials, the Politically Correct are carefully manufacturing a racial utopia, a narrative of racial blindness. These multicultural commercials are an attempt to gloss over persistent and complicated racial realities. Such commercials are deceptive, if not irrational, when it comes to the social realities of race mixing. Most Americans overwhelmingly live and mingle with people of and from their own racial and cultural background. About 90% of all races live in neighborhoods in which more than 95% of their neighbors are of their own race, and in fact, most Americans have very few close friends of another race. The politically correct ads and commercials (diversity marketing) do not reflect racial reality. Their ads make it seem like race doesn't matter, when real life would tell you something completely different, and the real truth about race is always absent from the American commercial landscape.

C1354. The racially mixed scenarios of American commercial TV, families, friendships, neighborhoods, and party scenes are backdrops to sell products and to convey the multicultural agenda of a peaceful, loving society living side by side, regardless of race. Nothing could be further from the truth. America's racial communities are not bonded by a love for yogurt, lipstick, and athletic gear. Their dislike for one another is of a historical record, and no amount of manufactured utopia will change the lens through which people learn about other races, which is absolutely through their social and cultural interactions and personal observations.

C1355. The human hybrid is the coming apocalypse of the chimera. The biological sciences have discovered and opened Pandora's Box, genetic engineering, and at its core is the intellectual terror of the unresolved. What is human, and what is not? The combining of embryo cells of different species to create bio-hybrids, called in bioscience chimeras, taken from the Greek mythological creature having body parts of various animals, is now a reality. This will become an industry, having its moral and practical applications decided by the Supreme Court, which will be an intellectual and legal challenge beyond measure for decades to come.

C1356. Self-censorship in the sciences: Many scientists are now of the opinion that they must conceal their findings on racial genetics, crime correlations, intelligence, and gender, because of the multicultural and politically correct terror tactics being applied to them and to their studies. The pursuit of scientific truth is now under direct attack by the liberal zealots.

C1357. A sobering aspect of Caucasian America is the dumbing down of its classrooms to fit the education levels of millions of alien kids of other countries. These alien kids find themselves graduated out of high school with no ability to read, write, or think past the level of a third grader. With increased alien density and diversity, these alien groups do not feel the need to conform to the established Caucasian American behavior, but are comfortable maintaining their own customs and behaviors. These aliens are not Caucasian Americans; they don't speak or care to speak English; they don't have any investment in Caucasian America. They're building their own separate city states within Caucasian America's borders. No modern nation can long exist with such an illiterate and unassimilated population.

C1358. Consider Caucasian America; you may multiply this social status in towns across Caucasian America as we endure fifteen to twenty million illegal aliens breaking our laws, breaking into our society, overwhelming our schools, over running our hospitals, draining our welfare systems, working off the books, avoiding taxes, and arrogantly forcing us out of our own neighborhoods toward safer havens. This manifestation of alien momentum grows throughout Caucasian America while it does not touch our members of Congress and other elites. They live in gated communities with bodyguards, with insulation not available to us.

C1359. The off-shoring of education; The industry lobbyists have the public as well as many educators believing that the schools in America are in such bad shape that the only people qualified to tutor our children, via the Internet, are in alien countries. The liberal zealots, after receiving some dismal test results and having to meet the federal No-Child- Left-Behind requirements, have actually considered tutoring help from other countries. Outsourcing American jobs, and now outsourcing the education of our children? When will the scales, fall from our eyes?

C1360. One of the fundamental axioms of the liberal zealots, diversity ideology, is their innate belief in the selfishness cruelty, and dishonesty of Caucasian males every where. Diversity is, in short, a liberal zealot cult, and those who accept its main proposition and participate in it are in need of some serious deprogram-ming.

C1361. Caucasian America is under an attack via an illegal alien invasion. As more and more aliens sneak past our borders (10,000 illegals per week) without being screened for diseases, their dispersing throughout our country carrying with them these unknown detriments. These aliens are invading our *Schools, Communities, Restaurant,* and *Food Supply*. It's only a matter of time before our families will be affected by this insidious invasion.

C1362. Unrestricted illegal and unending legal immigration at 4.1 million people annually inundate Caucasian America with a betrayal that will prove more horrific than 9/11 and equally as devastating as the *Vandals* who overran Rome. The Caucasian American people may have made their worst mistake by giving blind faith to their leaders and politicians, trusting they would protect and save them. Are they wrong? Are we losing our freedom by the day, via a pernicious invasion of unending alien humanity? When will the alien invasion, and colonizing end?

C1363. The state and liberty are diametrically opposed. As long as the state is in the position of certifying those who teach, the majority of teachers will gravitate to the oppressive doctrines of Affirmative Action, Political Correctness and Multicultural Diversity and our children will never know why our founding fathers intended this country to be a constitutional republic and not a democracy.

C1364. There is a decline in Caucasian American expertise in science, technology, engineering, and mathematics, and our share of this expertise is decreasing rapidly, both at the Bachelor's and at the Ph.D. levels. Caucasian America is losing ground to its sister nations in Europe and to the nations of Asia as well. The problem seems to lie with the K-12 students and their weak performance created by unqualified teachers; 56% of high school students taking physical science were being taught by out-of-field teachers, and even more alarming, 93% of science and 70% of math students are also being taught by this method. The meaning is that all these teachers didn't major or minor in that subject in college; therefore, how can we expect a K-12 teacher who has no experience in the field of science or mathematics to get a student excited about the field? It won't happen, and as the figures show, it doesn't happen. Failure to address our immense shortcomings in education will inevitably lead to the weakening of our nation.

C1365. It was the great Caucasian patriot, Sam Francis, who once said, the civilization that we Caucasians created in Europe and America could not have developed apart from the genetic endowments of the creative Caucasian people, nor is there any reason to believe that our civilization can be successfully transmitted to a different race of people.

C1366. Historian Isaiah Berlin noted in 1991 that nationalism and racism are the most powerful movements in the world today, and at this time, when the self-declared enemies of the Caucasian race define themselves in racial terms, only our own definition of ourselves in those terms can meet their challenge. If and when their challenge should triumph, and our enemies come to kill us as the Tutsi people have been slaughtered in Rwanda, they will do so, not because we are Westerners, Americans, Christians, conservative, or liberal, but because we are...Caucasians!

C1367. What Benjamin Franklin told his colleagues, at the birth of the American Republic, remains true today as the Republic and the race and civilization that gave birth to the Republic approach their death: Hence, if we do not hang together...not only as members of a common nation, but also as part of a common race, a common people...then most assuredly, we will all hang separately.

C1368. The holidays, public anniversaries, flags, songs, statues, museums, symbols, and heroes that Caucasian American people share are fundamental to their identity and to their existence as a race of people. We Caucasian Americans are witnessing on the official level of public culture the attack on these Caucasian American traditional symbols and their displacement by the symbols of alien races. This is in fact the abolition of Caucasian American society and its culture and the gradual creation of alien others and their culture.

C1369. The alien assault against Caucasian America cannot succeed or go as far as it has without the active assistance of *Caucasian Renegades*. Some have supported the alien assault against their own race and civilization for decades, and an even larger number of Caucasians have acquiesced passively, their allegiance to their own people steadily subverted by the infusion of hidden assumptions hostile to them.

C1370. If we as Caucasians were to invoke our identity, our interests, or our aspirations, this would invite accusations of racism and other alien phobias that are deployed to prevent further discussions and paralyze the formation or the retention of a common Caucasian American consciousness that might at some point swell up into actual resistance to our dispossession.

C1371. Caucasian America has lost its ability to create middle class jobs, or for that matter, any jobs. We Caucasian Americans are experiencing a net loss of millions of private sector jobs; moreover, the composition of jobs has changed away from very high-value, value-added, high-productivity jobs in tradable goods and services toward much lower productivity domestic service jobs that cannot be outsourced. The pressure on wages is downward. With the declining dollar, job out-sourcing, offshore production, illegal immigrants, foreigners with H-1b work visas, if the truth be known, Caucasian America's days as a super-power are rapidly coming to an end, and we can expect no sympathy or help from former allies and rising new powers. Paul Craig Roberts.

C1372. The principal Caucasian American response to the incipient race war thus far manifested in neo-conservative critiques of political correctness and Multiculturalism is merely to regurgitate the formulas of liberal universalism, hence to emphasize the liberal progress of the modern West through the abolition of slavery, the emancipation of aliens, the retreat from imperialism, and the achievement of political equality, etc. But of course, if the liberalism espoused by aliens is a thin veil for the assertion of their own racial solidarity against Caucasians, then all such argumentation is in vain. It accomplishes nothing to preach liberalism to those who despise liberalism along with everything else Caucasian. The uselessness of doing so was pointed out by the nineteenth century French rightist Louis Veuillot in his ironic comment, when I am the weaker, I ask you for my freedom, because that is your principle; but when I am the stronger, I take away your freedom, because that is my principle. Or, as *Nietzsche* put a similar thought even more succinctly- The values of the weak prevail because the strong have taken them over as devices of leadership.

C1373. A merely cultural consciousness that emphasizes only social and cultural factors as the roots of Caucasian civilization is not enough, because a merely cultural consciousness will not by itself conserve the race and people that were necessary for the creation of the culture and who remain necessary for its survival. We as Caucasian Americans need not only to understand the role of race in creating our civilization but also to incorporate that racial understanding in our defense of our civilization. Until we as Caucasian Americans do so, we can expect only to keep on losing this racial war we are in.

C1374. It was the great Caucasian patriot, Samuel Francis who once said; In liberal America today, liberal Caucasian Americans exist objectively but do not exist subjectively, and that was in his view, the fundamental racial problem they face, the basic reason they (I should say we) are losing the racial war against us. Liberal Caucasians, he thinks, do not exist subjectively because they do not think of themselves as Caucasians, they do not act cohesively as Caucasians, and they do not think being Caucasian is important or even meaningful.

C1375. Racial domination of a society, in one form or another is the norm of human civilizations, and that equality has little or no historical foundation, and those that hold to the illusion of such equality of life, will come to see its reality rudely dispelled.

C1376. It is the *21st* century, and the rising tide of alien racial consciousness in America, as well as her sister states through-out the world, is taking on the social persona of racial despotism. The alien races in America and the rest of the world are not pacifists. They do not cling to a life whose length is its sole value. They will take up the sword when we Caucasians lay it down? Once they feared the Caucasians; now they despise us! Could it be they sense the unfitness and lack of will to defend ourselves?

C1377. What is happening in Caucasian America, to summarize briefly, is this: A long-term attack against Caucasian America and its sister civilizations throughout the world has been launched, and the attack is not confined to the political, social, and cultural institutions that characterize the civilization but extends also to the race of people that created the civilization and continues to carry and transmit it today. This war against the Caucasian civilization invokes liberal zealot ideals as its justification and as its goal.

But the reality is that a victory on the part of the alien races will end merely in the domination and destruction of the Caucasian race and its civilization.

C1378. In Caucasian America today, there is a calculated alien racial tactic aimed at seizing cultural legitimacy and ultimately coercive political power on behalf of aliens at the expense of Caucasians. It offers a conspiratorial interpretation of history in which Caucasians are systematically demonized as the enemies of humankind. The myth of racial equality is the ideological and political apparatus by which an explicit race war is prepared against the Caucasian race and its civilization, not as a part of social rage nor as a response to injustice and neglect but, like any war, as part of a *Concerted Strategy* to acquire power.

C1379. The displacement of Caucasian cultural symbols and the similar process in elite-produced, mass-consumed popular culture represents the expropriation of cultural norms, the standards by which public and private behavior is legitimized or condemned and a culture defined. While the traditional norms that are being attacked and discarded were almost never explicitly racial, the new alien cultural norms that are being constructed and imposed are, and they are not only explicitly racial in origin but also explicitly and vociferously anti-Caucasian.

C1380. The great religions of the world are for grownups requiring mature contemplation of truth, beauty, and the good. Cultures in which the creative elites are not engaged in that kind of mature contemplation don't produce great societies, art, or literature.

C1381. When human beings are functioning at the heights of human capacity, it is a good idea to assume that they are doing something right. Johann Sebastian Bach does not need to explain himself; he made a prima facie case that his way of looking at the universe needs to be taken seriously. It behooves us to do so.

C1382. In the biographies of the *Giants* and in the analyses of creative people in general, their work expresses the purpose they saw in their lives, a purpose that they usually had felt before they had achieved anything.

C1383. A major stream of human accomplishment is fostered by a culture that encourages the belief that individuals can act efficaciously as individuals and enables them to do so.

C1384. In a culture that disapproves of open argument, taking a stand against the consensus not only requires more courage than in a culture that accepts argument, it is also less likely to succeed. In a culture that dreads innovation, originality is suspect.

C1385. It was Thomas Aquinas who taught, that faith and reason are not in opposition, but complementary, and that human intelligence and autonomy are gifts from God. The power of religious belief and humanism would bring humankind into the full light of a God-giving individualism.

C1386. The longer a political structure has existed, the more it has been filled up with the best work that can be done within its confines and the greater the incentive for the people to seek new political structure.

C1387. The larger and more flexible the political structure, the more room for freedom and order to coexist.

C1388. The political structure that produces great accomplishments must foster two qualities in tension with each other: freedom and order.

C1389. The major stream in the history of Caucasian accomplishments was a well-articulated vision of and use of the transcendental goods, truth, good, and beauty, and its relevance to their culture.

C1390. Freedom, especially freedom of speech, can exist only at large for a group of people for whom the free exchange of ideas will improve their condition. The extent that the free exchange of ideas will hurt the condition of some other group is the extent to which that group will instinctively seek to limit it. (hostile racial groups) The use of this instinct is an expression of group anti-intellectualism. Whether any one chooses to recognize it or not, competing racial groups exist. Freedom can only exist within an intelligent and like-minded racial group. Therefore, the more intelligent and like-minded the racial group, (homogeneous) the greater the opportunity for freedom. Any attempt to enforce *Political Correctness* is an expression of anti-intellectualism. If you want the benefits (exchange of ideas) of free speech, you must be willing to listen to it!

C1391. The dichotomy of a liberal zealot America and the Caucasian race of people is seriously going unheeded and will soon begin taking a political, economic, and cultural toll no one could have imagined. Unprecedented taxation, vast redistribution of wealth, the collapse of the middle class, freedom of speech and expression, will be beaten down, and proponents of political correctness will exploit all social occasions to extend state activism into every corner of our lives. These are the hidden social detriments of the liberal zealot fraternity.

C1392. Let it be understood that it was the liberal zealots who asked the American Congress for a declaration of war against Caucasian America, not just to call all Caucasians to account for supposed racial violations, but to make Caucasian people social pariahs in their own country. The overall consequences to Caucasian America, brought by the liberal zealot fraternity and the social mongering clergymen and public media that manipulated public opinion on their behalf, has established a terrorist, totalitarian (multicultural, politically correct) regime by liberal zealots.

C1393. In late 1990, a series of racial crises increased tensions, aggravated by the two political parties (Democrats, Republicans) with no other interest than racial appeasement, and from which a strong liberal zealot movement would emerge, evidently aiming at the disintegration of Caucasian American political, economic, and cultural power. With liberals acting as mentors for alien races, and with their growing political power every year, Caucasian American people now find themselves on the social defensive against a mortal threat; hence some Caucasians are reflecting that if this great conflict is destined to come, then better sooner than later.

C1394. About the abandonment of the American workforce by American corporations: When work in general moves off- shore, Americans lose the incomes associated with the production of the goods they consume. Domestic production is turned into imports, with the result that America draws down its accumulated wealth in order to pay for the imports on which it is dependent. The ladders of America's upward mobility are being dismantled by offshore production for home markets and outsourcing of knowledge jobs. Furthermore, the dollar's value and status as reserve currency cannot for ever stand the trade and budget deficits that have become part and parcel of America's economic policy. Hence, third world workforce, worthless currency!

C1395. The *Holy Grail* of the liberal fraternity and its central tenet of *Egalitarianism* is that in the social policy in America and its welfare state are premised on the proposition that there are no real differences in intrinsic aptitude, that everyone is equally equipped to succeed in school and life, even though it is apparent that we are not all equally gifted to succeed in other fields, such as athletics, the arts, and music. Truth's anguish aside, this has exposed both the intolerance of the liberal zealot to dissent to its core dogmas and the fraudulence of liberal pretense to be a place where academic freedom reigns and all issues are open for discussion.

C1396. The terminally guilty liberals, waking up and leaving their neighborhoods, feel extremely torn inside because everything they have been taught tells them that they are wrong to feel bad that their country is being overrun by alien races who essentially don't want to be Americans and let it show! They feel torn by their own critical attitude toward alien races who despise their country, and that is why so many liberals are choosing to leave their neighborhoods. They're not so much fleeing the alien races as fleeing their own guilt and inner conflict about their negative reaction toward the alien races. This is one of the most concise descriptions of Caucasian American suicide.

C1397. Since 1960 the primary function of the schools has shifted away from education to indoctrination and providing a sheltered workplace for the incompetent affirmative action college graduate. There is also the unacknow-ledged, but evident goal of demoralizing and emasculating the Caucasian American male and debauching the Caucasian American female.

C1398. The good liberal Caucasians in the world are just like the good conservative Caucasians in the world. The blood that runs in their veins is our blood. The difference is that conservative Caucasians have had more experience with racial matters than liberal Caucasians. The conservative Caucasians learned from experience to treat the good alien as a Caucasian and treat their race as alien. But the liberal Caucasian treats the good aliens as alien and their race as Caucasian. That just doesn't work! Caucasian liberals assume that other races think and feel the same as they do. Caucasians have a history of altruism, while the other races do not, though Caucasian liberals keep assuming they do.

C1399. Government manufactured news (propaganda), if played to the public ear, must be clearly disclosed as produced by the government (script identification). Any attempt to circumvent genuine media outlets or deceive the Caucasian American people about government policies and proposals is subversive political treachery.

C1400. The regarding of alien anchor babies; or the misrepresentation of the *Fourteenth Amendment* to the U.S. Constitution: These are babies born to *Illegal Aliens* in the U.S. who become automatic U.S. citizens, entitling their parents and siblings to permanent residency, automatically qualifying them for welfare. Hence, sneak into the country, have your baby, become a citizen, all provided pro-bono! This of course is absurd!

C1401. The dismantling of the Caucasian American economy will prove to be the greatest political treachery of the twenty-first century. The Democratic and Republican parties in Caucasian America have decided to stand in silence while the life's blood of their country, its manufacturing technologies along with its designing and engineering capability, is being dismantled and shipped to alien nations in the name of global economic free trade, the big corporate lie!

C1402. The next level of political and corporate treachery will come in the form of social subordinate engineering, government domination by global corporations. Hence, if you don't manufacture anything, you don't need engineers! This in turn has dire consequences for America's higher education; college degrees in the technologies will become worthless. Furthermore, Caucasian America is paying its outsourced goods and services by transferring its wealth and future income to alien nations, nations that have acquired more than $3 trillion of Caucasian America's assets as a result of trade deficits.

C1403. Caucasian America's increasing dependence on imported goods and services is evidence of the weakness of its economy and the rapid transformation of its political and corporate loyalty from a Caucasian American historical ancestral trust to the criminal plundering of its economic structure and the submerging of all Americans into the hyenic grip of a third-world economy.

C1404. The Caucasian female is without doubt responsible for the intelligence of the Caucasian race, as is, all females (Fematrix) of all living races and species. The X chromosome is what distinguishes females from males. It is present in both sexes, but females have two x chromo-somes, while males have one X and one Y, and it is the X chromosome that carries the genes that are responsible for intelligence. The fact that males have only one copy of every gene on the X chromosome influences whether particular genetic traits, such as mutations that confer intelli-gence, are expressed. This in turn affects whether certain traits drift out of the gene pool or pass on through sexual selection. *Sexual selection influences evolution!*...and it is now believed that the human females have always approached brains in males as a sexual ornament. As believed in ℭaucasianism, the great gift.

C1405. We as Caucasian can't think straight unless we talk straight. If you can't call something by its right name, you can't discuss it honestly!

C1406. The Democratic and Republican parties alike have embraced the deception of racial equality. In today's Caucasian America the equality myth has perpetuated unrealistic alien social expectations and prevents honest debate.

C1407. When Caucasians have difficulty debating alien as will as liberal opponents on matters of racial equality, affirmative action, or racial history its because they expect their opponents to be civil and play by the rules of scholarly evidence. Caucasians mistakenly believe they have entered an arena where all sides are in a quest for the same truth. But what they are actually getting into is a street fight, where the alien and liberal goal is to defeat and humiliate Caucasian society. In a public debate, if Caucasians challenge alien or liberal accuracy, they will question the Caucasians integrity. If a Caucasian asks for evidence, they will insult the Caucasian. If a Caucasian challenges their sources, they will call the Caucasian a racist. Hence, you as a Caucasian may have the evidence and the truth on your side, but your alien and liberal opponents don't care about evidence and are not interested in your truth. After all, they already know the truth?

C1408. It is the *21st* century, and reality has yet to penetrate the Caucasian social consciousness. Caucasian America's political and social alliances, both domestic and foreign, have been shattered. Foreign terrorism; what about domestic political and corporate terrorism, the Incipient police state? (political correctness) What's next, the Bill of Right? Outsourcing increases the trade deficit. America pays the import bill by turning over the ownership of her wealth to foreigners. Hence, the loss of jobs, careers, companies, real estate, and corporate and government bonds. Americans cannot benefit from a process that destroys jobs, lowers income, and reduces the exchange value of the dollar. This is a lot of destruction; it goes far beyond what any foreign terrorists could ever inflict. As of late, the value of our dollar is down, and changed currency values are making Americans poorer. Economists are the most deluded of all.

C1409. It is the *21st* century, and the liberal fraternity along with alien revisionists, have begun to demonize our Caucasian ancestors and the gifts of territory, discovery, and culture. As evil-doers, they want Caucasians to see their gifts not as a blessing, but as curses and our debt to our ancestors as a shame too great to bear. Our obligation to honor our ancestors has been turned into a liberal duty to repudiate them and for the Caucasian society and its people to self- immolate. It is becoming a sad tale, one of racial betrayal, of social evolution gone astray, and of an intellectual sickness unto death. And the saddest part of this sad tale is that when we Caucasians are gone, there will be no one to honor us.

C1410. As of the year 2005, the racial balance in the world is this: For all Mongoloids, for every thirty-eight born, only sixteen pass away. For all Euro-Caucasoids, for every three born, four pass away. For all Asian-Caucasoids, for very forty-eight born, seventeen pass away. For all Negroids, for every eight born three pass away. The Euro-Caucasians world is losing one million people every year!

C1411. In Caucasian society intelligence has always been respected and rewarded, but in the past it existed in a larger world of shared values that were intensively cultivated by social institutions. The consensus that supported this Caucasian social system is on the most part being largely dissolved, and many of the personal and institutional virtues it encouraged have been weakened. But there's at least one quality about whose goodness we still seem as Caucasians to agree: raw intelligence enjoys a status akin to virtue.

C1412. It ought to be clear that high intelligence is no guarantee of good political leadership. Intelligence certainly deserves our admiration, but our greatest admiration ought to be reserved for those who combine whatever mental gifts they have with virtues such as racial loyalty, fairness, discipline, hard work, and a balanced judgment, not to mention humanity, prudence, and wisdom, and these were the virtues learned in school, in church, at universities, and in the wider Caucasian world. Hence, we as Caucasians must recover these treasures.

C1413. In today's Caucasian America, this question is now beginning to surface: How could high Caucasian social and political intelligence go so wrong? It was Edward Tenner who said brilliance is dangerous, it tempts those who have it to pronouncements that outrun experience and even common sense, if the Caucasian public is inattentive.

C1414. In the twenty-first century, "China" and "India" will prove to be economically formidable and will give birth to the new Asian century. If they join forces, they will dominate the global tech industries, because of both countries cheap and plentiful labor.

C1415. Caucasian Europe could be losing its religious faith. Has the church become inefficient and unmotivated, has it lost its moral hardiness, has its new social and political enlightenment racial equality, turned its main religious emotion into apathy? The Caucasian church in America, as well as in Europe, has always given the Caucasian community an opportunity to indulge in racial and ethnic solidarity, but due to the new social enlightenment, that solidarity has now been declared a heresy.

C1416. It is the *21st* century, and the liberal zealots in the American Governments education department have declared all non-Caucasian children disabled. Basically, the liberals are going to cook the books, closing the achievement gap between the races by giving a simpler test than that given to Caucasian students. So because of their difference in cognitive ability, the only way to leave no child behind is to slow the entire school system down to the lowest common denominator, hence not being able to make the dim smarter, you can now make the smart dimmer.

C1417. One of the most frightening questions hanging over the future of Caucasian America and its European sister states is this: Does the Caucasian liberal throughout the world support the dismantling of the Caucasian world society out of political expedience or because it agrees with the actions? If the latter, will America and Europe go the way of Zimbabwe or even Rwanda?

C1418. When a society is repeatedly accused of being inherently unjust? That society will begin to lose its social confidence, and its collective ability. Hence, moral judgment becomes suspended, and the society loses the will to enforce moral standards.

C1419. It is the *21st* century in Caucasian America, and the revival of the leftist social theorist, and their attack on racial loyal sentiments among all Caucasians has begun. This *New Leftist Zealot* agenda is being fervently and compulsively embraced, and as few wish to be accused of racial sympathy, (racism) very few intellectuals have challenged what is clearly a denial of both *Common Sense* and *Past Experience*. It seems obvious that few of our leaders have the courage of their ancestors. Caucasian history is that of a racial people born into a specific Family, Tribe, and Nation sharing experiences in each generation among those whose ancestors had shared experience and common achievements during many prior generations, a race of people whose first concern had always been the wellbeing of its own posterity. And for any Caucasian to focus on abstract values such as a phantom racial equality, to the exclusion of the normal claims of their own people, who had developed a unique culture in a rational pursuit of the interests of their own posterity, is pathological.

C1420. Ultimately, all politics and political arrangements come down to the allocation of responsibility. The non- Caucasian people in America come in a dazzling variety of tribes and cultures, and in quite varied stages of social and intellectual development, at least from a Caucasian American perspective, and with considerable political variation, of cultures, languages, and let us not forget, religions. These non-Caucasians and their differences are part of the new liberal social perspective, *Equal Social Outcome* developed out of the contrived misconception of equality, hence, the major effort by the liberal zealots to develop and focus their new perspective into an attack on Caucasian Americans and their national identity.

C1421. Undifferentiated humanity; the new liberal world order, the dismantling of the racial cosmopolitan state, is also concentrating on a social perception, which they had already created, that anything to do with race was inherently evil. For those who addressed the racial issue with analysis, rather than fabrication, it is likely that many both in and outside of Caucasian America would have seen the underlying question as involving political treachery and racial power the issue over how and by whom Caucasian America and its various peoples would be governed.

C1422. In America traditional marriage has become the recent target of academia, a number of feminist professors (female liberal zealots) have declared that the idea of marriage based on love is a myth and lacks satisfaction. And they dismiss the notion that a loving husband and wife team can be successful, self-reliant, and content. The truth of the matter is that outside of a few cloistered environments like academia, liberal zealot feminism is already dead. And these professors and their ilk are the last gasp of a dying breed. Hence, social scientists pass judgment on the pluses and minuses of society, but many of these liberal social analysts have never detoured into the real world outside the walls of academia, Gail Jarvis.

C1423. Caucasian America is headed for an economic and social upheaval that will begin in 2020. Future budget deficits (interest rates) and funding problems within Social Security (personal investment accounts), if not brought under control, will cause a *Political Revolution* the likes of which has never been seen in any modern state.

C1424. Caucasian America is obsessed with IQ, as any advanced technological society has to be. But because of its social fallacy of racial equality (equal racial outcomes), educators are so terrified of the topic that they aren't supposed to discuss it in public. And as a consequence, they inflict on Caucasian American society the agony of intellectual cowardice.

C1425. To survive in Caucasian America, we Caucasians must participate in it, which means living on our ancestor's historical terms. One either assigns a high priority to racial and cultural things, our ancestral trust, or sees most of life's possibilities disappear, perhaps in sparsely furnished minds, easily seduced by alien hyenic social clutches.

C1426. American liberals march to a multicultural drummer in large part because multicultural practitioners who dominate our political life and engineered it to suit themselves have so arranged it as to leave most of us no choice. Yet this multiculturalism that has gained such a terrible grip on the Caucasian American mind is fatally flawed. Its notions of reality and human nature are reductive and false. Fallacy does not exhaust reality. Our art, music, literature, philosophy, love, and imagination all the play of the Caucasian mind make nonsense of multicultural determinism and point to the existence of a bio-spiritual reality beyond that perceptible to the liberal zealot fraternity.

C1427. One might retort that Multiculturalism is a vulgar reduction of the dominant Caucasian American culture and allows for non-Caucasian culture and alien phenomena and priorities. Hence, the version of a culture that matters is the one that affects events in the real world. It follows that the only accurate perspective on a race of people and its determinism is a comprehensive one. Any reductive approach is bound to be wrong, perhaps disastrously so.

C1428. It seems that we are as Aldous Huxley observed, living simultaneously in half a dozen radically dissimilar universes, public and private, material and spiritual, emotional and rational, sexual, and so on. Our nature is such that racial things do matter, some of them far more than politics or culture.

C1429. Unfortunately human beings are and will always be fighting and quarreling like animals. Hence, can any honest person doubt that Lord Palmerton was right? Squeeze the pages of history, and blood runs out!

C1430. It is the *21st* century and all throughout Caucasian America there is mounting social anarchy, gross corruption in the democratic process, the destruction of liberty, mass ignorance and brutality, paralysis in the police, the breakdown of the family, and the loss of any faith in the justice system. Any challenge to the official liberal line is met with cries of outrage and abuse. Under the guise of celebrating racial diversity the American political system has descended into the proverbial madhouse.

C1431. The racial hierarchy of victimhood should have no place in a mature democracy like Caucasian America. But that sort of thinking is widespread as a result of racial minority pandering, and the creed of Multiculturalism. Like the witch hunters of the seventeenth century who created a climate of hysteria and panic over supposed religious heresy, the political elites in Caucasian America have done exactly the same today in its obsession with racial equality. The liberal zealot's ideology of racial equal outcomes has triumphed over objective facts. Righteous unreason is destroying Caucasian America society.

C1432. It is the *21st* century, and the American dream is beginning to show signs of collapse, if Caucasian Americans cannot afford to start families, if fathers are unemployed or forced into lower-paying jobs or earn stagnant incomes, and mothers are driven into the labor force to make ends meet, their unparented children will drift into drugs, crime, and violence. Furthermore, if our public schools become a multicultural polyglot, mess driven by anti-Caucasian, anti-American agendas, affluence efficiency and profit maximization cannot compensate for these social horrors. No sane society can allow them to happen. Yet our economically obsessed ruling classes act as if these problems do not exist or do not matter. *Quos deus vult perder, prius dementat*, those whom God would destroy, he first makes made!

C1433. For the last forty years, Caucasian America has been fed with political correct dogmas that were supposed to justify the liberal deconstructionist agenda. The postulate that all people are equal has been unconditionally accepted by the liberal fraternity as the revealed truth, and anyone who questioned it was immediately called a racist, the *quod erat demonstrandum* closing argument of any political dispute in today's Caucasian America.

C1434. In order to fix the connection between biochemical systems and the fundamental constants we must identify the biochemical basis for all life forms. All the immensely complicated biological systems are controlled, strictly speaking, by one particular molecule contained in the hereditary material of cells: deoxyribonucleic acid (DNA). It is in the qualities of this hereditary molecule, made from a helical double strand, that we can recognize the effects of the physical laws.

C1435. It is not difficult to appreciate that there could be no life on Earth without the sun. But it is a good deal less obvious, though no less true, that there could be no life on Earth or anywhere else without regular deaths among the stars, that is, without supernovas. This arises from the necessity of heavy elements for life.

C1436. It was John Locke: who said that humans come into the world as a blank page upon which experience writes, and that government was the servant of humanity, not the other way around, and that governments can legitimately circumscribe in only limited ways. Locke was an intellectual inspiration for the Caucasian American founders.

C1437. To say that the current state of knowledge represents only our best approximation of truth is not to say truth doesn't- exist. If an airplane pilot is not in possession of truth pulling back the stick, what word might we use?

C1438. The racial logic is that by and large, the reason people who know a lot about their race and its culture and prefer theirs to others is because they perceive theirs as being better, better in a sense that is intrinsic to their racial nature and the perceived excellence in their race.

C1439. Those Caucasians who know the most about their racial history devote a great deal of attention to their culture because understanding and preserving one's culture calls upon every bit of fine intellectual discrimination and knowledge that a person of *Racial Integrity* can bring to the cultural table.

C1440. The *Fematrix* has decided the relationship between certain rules of racial composition and the enduring attraction that they possess. Humankind inherently finds certain racial qualities attractive and others unattractive, hence different races. It must be allowed that there are certain qualities in human races that are fitted by their *Fematrix* to produce those particular feelings. These are the qualities that inhere to a race, and to which judgment may be applied.

C1441. The racially disinterested is a social judgment influenced by one's personal gratification of intellectual independence, the ability to intellectually distance oneself from his or her origins, the arrogance of neutrality. (The Observer)

C1442. Today not a tear is shed for the suffering of millions of our own enslaved forefathers and mothers. Two thousand years of *Caucasian Slavery* in Europe, the Middle East and America, has been almost completely obliterated from the collective memory of the Caucasian American people. This is a history of Caucasian people that has never been told in any coherent form, largely because most modern historians (liberal zealots) have, for reasons of politics or psychology, refused to recognize Caucasian slaves in early America and throughout the world as just that! Liberals don't want to be reminded that perhaps as many as two thirds of the original American colonists (Caucasians all) came here not of their own free will, but in chains. They tend to gloss over it... they prefer to forget the whole sorry chapter.

C1443. Were we directed from Washington when to sow and when to reap, we should soon want for bread. Thomas Jefferson

C1444. In today's America, the government is the secular religion of millions. For them (the liberals) the desire to do well is more important than the outcome. Poverty, if the truth be known, the liberal solution has been the greatest creator of poverty ever conceived and the destroyer of families, civility, and dignity. Its rules have provided powerful incentives for *Mother* not to work, not to get *Married*, and for the *Father* to abandon his family, so that the government can support them. This destructive impact has been confirmed.

C1445. People with terrible hatreds, who are able to pervert a good religion through that hate, hijack some religions. Such people are not appealing to ancient bad teachings of a religion, but are introducing *Bad Beliefs* of their own that they have based on ignorant and misguided interpretations of sacred texts. Although these people are often *Clerics*, their teachings don't reflect or express the mainstream teachings of a religion.

C1446. Can you be good without God? All of us know good people who don't believe in the divine, as well as not so good people who do. You don't need to believe in God to be good. (The Ethical Idea, Utilitarian Deontology)

C1447. It is not the critic who counts, nor the man who points out where the strong man stumbled, or where a doer of deeds could have done them better. The credit belongs to the man in the arena whose face is marred by dust and sweat and blood, who strives valiantly, who errs, and who come up short again and again, who knows the great enthusiasms, the great devotions, and spends himself in a worthy cause. The man who at best knows the triumph of high achievement and who at worst, if he fails, fails while daring greatly, so that his place will never be with those cold timid souls who never know victory or defeat, Theodore Roosevelt.

C1448. Great enterprises are only achieved by adventurous spirits. They who calculate with too great nicety every difficulty and obstacle that is likely to lie in their way lose that time in hesitation, which the more daring seize and render available to the loftiest purposes.

C1449. Humankind can be simple of mind and much dominated by its immediate needs, so that a deceitful person will always find plenty who are ready to be deceived.

C1450. The best strategy is to be very strong; first in general, then at the decisive point. There is no higher and simpler law of strategy than that of keeping one's forces concentrated. In short, the first principle is: act with the utmost concen-tration. Carl von Clausewits.

C1451. Even those who argue against fame still want the books they write against it to bear their name in the title and hope to become famous for despising it. Everything else is subject to barter: we will let our friends have our goods and our lives, if need be, but a case of sharing our fame and making someone else the gift of our reputation is hardly to be found. Montaigne.

C1452. Experience shows that if one foresees from far away the designs to be undertaken, one can act with speed when the moment comes to execute them.

C1453. We Caucasian Americans can't afford to leave the reorganization of Caucasian America entirely to its congressional members. Instead, a cadre of concerned Caucasians must become involved. Otherwise, we'll fail to save our nation.

C1454. Caucasian America's prioritizing is made harder by two modern day social tendencies that supplement each other. Psychologically we have a tendency to underestimate alien races and their natural demeanor (tribal) and to over-estimate the political and racial loyalty of Caucasian shop-keeper politicians (greed). This is a dangerous cocktail, so psycho-logically; we handle the alien and political risks by making them so *Insignificant* that there is good reason to ignore them. Not good?

C1455. The problem of Caucasian survival and protecting its racial sovereignty is so important that requirements and standards cannot be too high, and continuing cultural and racial solidarity must be made regardless of cost. Such an understanding in the face of an alien invasion in Caucasian America is of the utmost importance.

C1456. We Caucasians must get used to the idea that all racial decisions are in reality a tradeoff of various risks. When we choose between a Caucasian cultural state, and a multicultural alien state, we choose between social stability and the chaos of *Multiple-tribalism*. And as of late, it seems Caucasian Americans believe themselves immune to this social cancer, alien multi-culturalism!

C1457. Many Caucasian people would argue that the risk of social preference is not the only factor to be considered in the question of social priorities, it is also significant whether the risk was accepted voluntarily or thrust upon the Caucasian people involuntarily, such as Affirmative Action (alien racial paternalism)

C1458. The basic argument both from a Caucasian racial and economic point is that the focus should be on making the best possible social and economic system for the Caucasian people throughout the world. But the Caucasian people need to realize that no social system can provide absolute certainty. The Caucasian societies we have today are not risk-free, and neither will this be the case for the societies of tomorrow. Thus, choosing sensibly in the race debate requires all Caucasians to see the risks but also compare them thoughtfully with all other social risks. We as Caucasians need to know how we have handled past racial problems. We must be able to dispose of the many liberal social myths but also face the true challenges of our future society from a Caucasian social and cultural perspective.

C1459. As the Caucasian race, we are part of the human species and have not lived without creating problems, but overall, we as a race have solved more problems for the human species than we have created. Therefore, weighing Caucasian contributions and its benefits seems obvious that the substantive benefits of racial uniqueness (difference) can deliver both for the developed (Caucasian) and the developing (alien) worlds.

C1460. The scientific recognition of the human species and its racial divisions has been claimed by the liberal zealots to be a potential social disaster or something we humans should out-right reject. Why this wide gap in intellectual judgment? No doubt part of the reason is caused by the incapability of the liberal mind to accept a reality contrary to its utopian social fallacy of equality.

C1461. At the start of the twenty-first century there were unmistakable signs that the liberal exploitation of Caucasian societies had created an alien racial class, an unaccountable sub-society that was beginning to take its revenge. The liberal climate of the melting pot was replaced by racial storms (race riots) and devastated cities (urban poverty). This social deluge as of late has increased its range, leading to fiercer racial compe-tition, a greater social divide and a continuous liberal intellectual default.

C1462. The *Social Fear* (political correctness) created by the liberal fraternity is effectively communicated by the media, which again selectively use its intellect to confirm our concerns. This fear is absolutely decisive because it paralyzes our reasoned judgment. Thus, it is imperative that we Caucasians regain our ability to socially recognize and prioritize the many different liberal assaults against us.

C1463. The liberal social litany, racial equality (equal out come) is based on myths, and one can of course choose to believe that this myth may represent only the first of a steady stream of progressively more serious racially based social catastrophes. It is difficult not to get the impression that the criticism leveled at Caucasian societies of being elitist civilizations is simply a liberal expression of their Calvinistic sense of guilt. We Caucasians have done so well that some liberal zealots actually feel rather ashamed and really believe that we, and our success deserve global destruction.

C1464. One day the electronics industry may be recognized in history books for having helped link planet earth with networks of knowledge before ignorance destroyed the world. Openness or perish alternatives are forcing computer and communication industries to cooperate or disintegrate on a global scale. National barriers are tumbling as knowledge reaches the formerly uninformed citizenry, which is no longer willing to sit idly by and let the government do what's best for them. Mil Phelps.

C1465. Learning is the new form of labor. It's no longer a separate activity that occurs either before one enters the work place or in remote classroom settings. Learning is the heart of productive activity. Shoshana Zuboff.

C1466. The whole basis of professionalism is that they know better! Professionals naturally resist any suggestion that other people could do their jobs just as well with less training or no training at all, and what they fear most is that people could manage without them. Every profession is a conspiracy against the lay person. Keeping professionals under control will always be a struggle. The aim must be to reduce their power, to increase the citizens redress against them, to make them more accountable. Peter Wilby.

C1467. Life is not about filling in the blanks, and neither is learning! In American schools today, students aren't treated as active learners. Instead, they are assaulted with irrelevant bits of knowledge in narrow subject areas, taught in tiny doses. Students are not passive receptacles, although we often treat them that way. The myth is that learning can be guaranteed if instruction is delivered systematically, one small piece at a time, with frequent tests to ensure that students and teachers stay on track. Nobody learns anything or teaches anything by being submitted to such a regimen of disjointed, purposeless, confusing and tedious activities. Teachers burn out, pupils fall by the wayside, and parents and administrators worry about the lack of progress or interest. Hence, the classroom doesn't become a place of high expectations.

C1468. Less is more? Translation: Fewer areas taught in longer blocks of time, with plenty of space for coaching, explaining, and personalization. As the major goal of education is developing the intellect, the very exercise of explaining ends and means and gaining agreement is itself educational. The essential word throughout is *why*, which is the central interrogative of all learning. Teachers can help by trusting, asking much, and holding students accountable. Ted Sizer.

C1469. The idea of a material universe in which organic life is present, demands change. But change means diversity on the one hand, for there must be a *terminus a quo* and a *terminus ad quem* of the change and stability on the other hand, for there must be something that changes. And so there must be identity in diversity!

C1470. What are we to say of the notion of unity in difference? That there is a many, a plurality, is clear enough. But at the same time the intellect constantly strives to conceive a unity, a system, to obtain a comprehensive view to link things up; and this goal of thought corresponds to a real unity in things, things that are interdependent. Unity, the only unity that is worth having, is a unity in difference, identity in diversity, a unity, that is to say, not of multicultural poverty, but of a Caucasian racial richness, hence the union of Caucasianism and its vision, a union of biological distinction.

C1471. What is not is just as much real, as what is. Space, then, or the void, is not corporal, but it is as real as body.

C1472. The natural law cannot acquire a morally binding force, obligatory in conscience, at least in the sense of our modern conception of duty, unless it has a metaphysical basis and is grounded in a transcendental source, leaving the *Fematrix*, whose will for humankind is expressed in the natural law, although insufficient, enshrines a most important and valuable truth that is essential to the development of a rational moral philosophy. Duties are not simply senseless or arbitrary commands or prohibitions, but are to be seen in relation to human nature as such: the moral law expresses humankind's true understanding.

C1473. Teaching does not mean mere notional instruction, but rather leading human thought to a real insight. Caucasian ethics are predo-minantly *Eudaemonistic* in character, but cannot be complete without *Theism* or seen against the back ground of *Theism* in order to attain their true development, and even in their incomplete state, they are a perennial glory to Caucasian social philosophy.

C1474. Human nature is constant and so ethical values are constant, and it is to the *Caucasian People* that they realized the constancy of these values and sought to fix them in universal definitions that could be taken as a social guide and norm in human conduct.

C1475. From the identification of wisdom and virtue follows the unity of virtue. There is really only one virtue insight into what is truly good for the Caucasian people, what really conduct's their racial health and social harmony, it is the art or the teachability of Caucasian virtue!

C1476. The wise Caucasian person realizes that it is more advantageous to be self-controlled than to have no self-control; to be just, rather than to be unjust; courageous, rather than cowardly; advantageous, meaning what is conducive to Caucasian racial health and social harmony.

C1477. The secret to the blend that forms the good life for humankind is thus measure or proportion: where this is neglected, there exists not a genuine mixture, but a mess.

C1478. True valor or courage means standing your ground in battle when you know the risks to which you are exposed; it does not mean mere foolhardiness. Thus courage can no more be separated from wisdom than can temperance.

C1479. It was Plato who gave us the four cardinal virtues, Wisdom, Courage, Fortitude, and Temperance. Wisdom is the virtue of the rational part of the soul, courage of the spirited part, while temperance consists in the union of the spirited and appetitive parts under the rule of reason; justice is a general virtue consisting in this, that every part of the soul performs its proper task in due harmony.

C1480. Caucasian statesmanship is, or should be, a science. The statesman, if he or she is to be truly such, must know what the state is and what its life ought to be; otherwise thy runs the risk of bringing the state and its citizens to ruin. Hence, the state does not exist simply to further the economic needs of Caucasian society, for Caucasian society is not simply economic, but for happiness to develop, Caucasian society in the good life must be in accordance with the principles of freedom and justice within its bio-logical adherence to its ancestral trust.

C1481. The existence of an absolute moral code is the duty of royal authority to prevent the ruin of the morality of the members of the Caucasian social state, so far as they can and so far as the particular acts of prevention employed will not be productive of greater harm, and to speak of the absolute rights of art is simply absurd.

C1482. It was Plato who said, if only poetry and the other arts will prove their title to be admitted into a well-ordered state, we shall be delighted to receive her, knowing that we ourselves are very susceptible of her charms; but we may not on that account betray the truth.

C1483. The nature of great accomplishment in the arts is fundamentally different from great accomplishment in the sciences. In the arts, eminence arises from genius manifested in a body of work, whereas eminence in science arises from the importance of the discovery, which may or may not be the result of genius.

C1484. The translation of the moral vision onto the canvas or into the written word is often what separates enduring art from mere enter-tainment.

C1485. In the Caucasian world, excellence is not simply a matter of opinion, though judgment enters into its identification. Excellence has attributes that can be identified, evaluated, and compared across works, subjected to the inspection of Caucasian historical logic.

C1486. Human beings enjoy watching the exercise of the realized capacities of their race, and this enjoyment increases, the more the capacity is realized.

C1487. Caucasian technologies form an incredible network of mutual support and mutual dependence, and if this network were disrupted, genetic submergence, it is doubtful if our kind of (Caucasian) technology could ever be rebuilt. On all counts, it looks as though our civilization, once fallen, will never be replaced by another of comparable quality.

C1488. Because economic inequality between racial groups inevitably produces envy, stable societies are almost always *Homogeneous,* leaving Multiracial societies living on the edge of social dissolution. In such cases, the role of a multiracial government turns to conflict management, hence the emerging theme in Caucasian America? Liberty; will not survive the disappearance of Caucasian political power!

C1489. It was Sir Roger L Estrange who said that in the end, laws are no better at ensuring liberty than the people who make and enforce them. The greatest of all injustice is that which goes under the name of law. The Caucasian American people must reestablish the consent of the governed.

C1490. The Caucasian tradition of ordered, self-governing liberty is part of our evolutionary genetic heritage. If we Caucasians become marginalized and ultimately absorbed by alien races, the idealism of *Western Liberal Zealotry* that permitted the alien invasion will have proved to be a lethal genetic flaw.

C1491. The central thesis of natural law: a race of people cannot, by any agreement, deprive its posterity of rights. Hence, natural law is therefore the fulcrum on which rests the case that alien immigration is genocide. No Caucasian government has the right to impose current levels of alien immigration and race mixing on its people, nor are we as Caucasian people, morally bound to accept them.

C1492. Unalienable rights: to secure these rights, governments are instituted among men deriving their just powers from the consent of the governed. Whenever any form of government becomes destructive of these ends, it is the right of the people to alter or to abolish it and to institute new government, having the foundation on such principles and organizing its powers in such form as to them shall seem most likely to affect their safety and happiness. *Mason / Jefferson.*

C1493. The Caucasian people must come to believe in and act in accordance with the only moral principle nature recognizes: for those who live in harmony with nature. *Racial Survival* is moral, for those who think not!...the penalty is extinction. Without this understanding, the Caucasian world society, progenitor of Law, Compassion, Technology, and a *Spirit* of *Conquest* that is unparalleled in the history of the human race, will perish at the hands of those who do not possess the same innate spark. For the sake of all Caucasian children who are yet to be, let us choose life by whatever means we must while the choice is still ours. Oswald Spengler.

C1494. The only course that gives *Racial Competitive* groups a chance to survive is their *Separation*! Without separation, the dual code of racial cohesion (bio-loyalty) will ensure a long chaotic period of strife and bloodshed. Eventually what racial conflict does not finish, social depredation, diminished birthrates, and moral psychological displacement will.

C1495. Loyalty of humans for their own group is a necessity for survival. There can be no stability in a society that will not allow its members to favor its own brethren.

C1496. The myth of the universal nation or proposition country (America) is widely accepted by both left and right political spectrums in the United States. This in fact has led to the reconstruction and redefinition of Caucasian America as a Multiracial, multicultural, and transnational social quagmire, and today it represents probably the major ideological obstacle to recognizing the reality and importance of race as a social and political force.

C1497. Caucasian America is not and never was a universal nation or a proposition country defined by the equality clause of the declaration or the bromides of the Gettysburg Address. On the contrary, we Caucasian

Americans in general and our leadership in particular repeatedly and continuously recognized the reality and importance of *Racialness* and of the Caucasian races occupying the superior position. Furthermore, it is difficult to think of any other *Racial Majority* Nation in history in which recognition of the reality of their race has not been deeply imbedded in their thinking and institutions. As in the United Caucasian States of- America?

C1498. It is easy enough to destroy an existing constitutional order, but quite a different matter to construct a new one. The racial and cultural transition in Caucasian America is not desired by most Caucasians. We as Caucasian Americans have never been asked whether we think it is a good thing for our nation to undergo a transition from a Caucasian majority to a non-Caucasian majority country. We have indeed been lied to about this transition, in being told in 1965 that it wouldn't happen. *Political Philosophies* and *Constitutional Forms* come and go, but Nations, Peoples, and Races remain. Yet without the *Common Blood* that made us a Nation in the first place, there will be no Caucasian American nation, no matter what abstractions and forms we vainly invoke. Samuel Francis.

C1499. Though many battles have been billed as a turning point in history, it will be the battle for the hearts, minds, and souls of Caucasians Americans that will determine the future of all Caucasian societies throughout the world. It was and still is the Caucasian people who pioneered and practiced democracy most methodically. The interplay of racial political reality and its evolving tactics is set forth plainly and intelligibly, even for those who had little or no previous knowledge of how races operate in battle. The Alpha states that his main theme is the relationship between the *Racial Battlefront* and the Caucasian American *Home Front*, and the dialectic of the two is sustained all through The Valorous. We Caucasian Americans must not become deluded patriots by the purchasing of *Racial Hatred*. It is a hidden detriment to our eternal soul, and nothing good can come of it. What is needed is to make things right with our Race, our Nation, and our Future. This is our duty to our ancestral racial trust!

C1500. The Alpha tells us: It is the 21_{st} century, and today's political elites are not just overwhelmingly secular but often hostile to the idea that transcendental goods have any meaning. Such is the reason to fear that

Egalitarian Governments are as much as we can hope for. Great societies require a source of inspiration (spiritual core) that the politicians who produce egalitarian governments are not tapping. But, what has been true for the last few decades need not be true perpetually. The first of these truths is that the hold of the *Great Religions* on the human imagination is so binding that the present intellectual nihilism (political correctness) cannot survive. The second truth is, that humankind (a species) is divided into race's (subspecies) *Negroids, Mongoloids, and Caucasoids,* you are ether one of the three, or a combination of the three,...there are no others! The third truth is, human races have a right to their own destiny and way of life, and that right is unassailable. Furthermore, let it be understood by all, persistent seeking is after all, at the heart of the Caucasian racial spirit that enables them to achieve great things. And all others who feel impelled to try to live the beat possible human life are engaged in the same larger enterprise. *Blessed are the Caucasians*!

C1501. The spectrum of racial views among Caucasian liberals were much wider than expected, but far from resulting in intellectual reason, the diversity of their attitudes toward the racial issues turned out to be the expression of confusion on the nature of race? (predatory) And it is this crisis of *Racial Theoretical Confusion* which accounts for the American political and social dilemma.

C1502. Free human beings differ not only with regard to the characteristics of their racial settings which they find most desirable, but also with regard to life styles, aspirations, and last but not least their views of their race's place in nature.

C1503. In today's Caucasian America some believe that social destruction and the depletion of moral values can best be controlled by liberal doctrine, others by strict control over crime, and still others by a complete transformation of the political structure, non-however well discus the racial reality.

C1504. Blessed is the Caucasians man that brings honor to the Caucasian Sisterhood.

C1505. He who causes an alien to become powerful ruins himself, for he brings such a power into being either by design or by force, and both of these elements are suspect to that alien whom he has made powerful.

C1506. The diversity of racial views held by so called experts, even within a given social system and a given nation, points to the nature of the difficulty that now faces the Caucasian world community. In most cases, the difficulty will originate not from uncertainties about racial facts, but from differences in attitudes toward the recognition of race, and that of its- *Principle Values!*

C1507. A thousand war heroes mean nothing compared to the one person who has the brains and the moral courage to say the right thing at the right time.

C1508. Do to social and political circumstances in Caucasian America and her sister states- throughout the world, the only alternative is simple but not easy. This is to declare immovable that "Caucasian Racial Survival" is not the main priority, it is the only priority!

C1509. In our quest for immortality, the Alpha asks of us: know not the ways of "Hatred," for like a blinding storm, our way will become lost.

C1510. Where race is concerned, the liberals seem capable of doubting what they elsewhere find self-evident, so argumentative overkill is difficult to avoid.

C1511. One should never permit a disorder to persist in order to avoid a war, for war is not avoided thereby but merely deferred to one's own disadvantage.

C1512. Unquestionably, when an *Alien Race* is in pursuit of the conquest of political power, moral propaganda is an excellent means to employ. For a race of people which has been convinced (brainwashed) even against their will, that its racial adversary's ideals are based upon better reasons than its own and is inspired by loftier moral aims, will certainly lack force to continue the struggle; it will have lost that faith in its own rights which alone confers upon resistance a moral justification. Hence, the assault against Caucasian America, and lose of- *Caucasian South Africa!*

C1513. In our quest for- Government, the Alpha asks of us: Let us chose our leaders who are in union with our *Racial Spirit* and its *Truth,* thereby, giving understanding that our *Racial Spirituality* and its *Living Biology* are one!

C1514. The Alpha's lore: It was Pareto who pointed out: the permeation of a dominant class by humanitarian ideas, which lead that class to doubt its own moral right to existence, demoralizes its members and makes them inapt for defense. The same law operates likewise where races are absolutely convinced of their sacred right to existence, where a race of people lacks the sense of such a right, decadence and ruin inevitably ensues. We may regard it as an established historical law that a race of people are inevitably doomed to destruction from the moment they or those who represent them have lost faith in their own identity!

C1515. The consciousness of power always produces vanity, an undue belief in personal greatness. The desire to dominate, for good or for evil, is universal. To retain their influence over the masses the leaders study men, note their weaknesses and their passions, and endeavor to turn these to their own advantage. The political struggle and the life of the politician have more than one point of contact, for is not the political struggle a continuous act of advocacy?

C1516. Democracy is utterly incompatible with strategic promptness, and the forces of democracy do not lend them-selves to the rapid opening of a campaign. This is why political parties (Democrats and Republicans) exhibit so much hostility to the *Referendum* and to all other measures for the safe-guard of real Democracy; and this is why in their constitutions these parties exhibit, if not unconditional *Caesarism,* at least extremely strong centralizing and oligarchical tendencies.

C1517. Civil right is personal freedom: political right is a right over others as well as oneself.

C1518. Liberal utopianism: to indoctrinate so intensively and thoroughly as to effect a radical transformation of racial beliefs and mental attitudes in favor of a- *Pseudo Equality*.

C1519. It is doubtless true that the liberal zealots *Equality Doctrine* (a social fraud!) has won over many Caucasians, penetrating their minds so profoundly as to lead them to abandon logical reason, racial and cultural survival, social position, and ancestral respect. Without regret and with out hesitation these liberal *Caucasian Apostates* have consecrated their lives to the downfall of "Caucasian America" and its surrender to alien racial and cultural debauchery.

C1520. The proliferation of *Alien Races* in Caucasian lands dooms the Caucasian race, my race, irretrievably to extinction in the centuries to come if we Caucasians hold fast to our present immigration principle. No other race subscribes to this immigration principle, because they are means to the founding race's self-annihilation! At the very least, when deciding on the *Quantity* and *Quality* of immigrants, prudence is a virtue. Ask the Caucasian Europeans,..it may now be too late for them!

C1521. There is indeed a widespread acceptance of the fact that Caucasian racial capitulation is an inescapable by-product of liberal politics. Hence, the Alpha would like to issue a forceful warning a clarion call that the present political trend cannot continue much longer because Caucasian American society is on a course of self-destruction, their salvation will ultimately depend on an emotional racial awakening.

C1522. The Alpha tells us: By their works you shall know them, not by their excuses, by their works.

C1523. The Alpha tells us: Caucasian America is being ruled by default of congress, to the dictatorship of the courts. By definition, no more Caucasian common consent. Now everybody looks first to the courts to decide all major matters of policy, the other branches of government openly act at the sufferance of the courts, the executive has no power that the courts do not grant it, the congress has no power unless the courts grant it. Even the peoples referendum is subject to court approval.

C1524. The apathy of the Caucasian people and their need for guidance has as its counterpart in the leaders a natural greed for power. Thus the development of the democratic oligarchy is accelerated by the general characteristics of human nature. What was initiated by the need for organization, administration, and strategy is completed by psychological determinism.

C1525. Times have changed in Caucasian America, the Alpha tell us, and consequently a new tactic and a new social theory *Caucasian Racial Sovereignty* is necessary. A greater maturity of judgment corresponds to the greater maturity of the new Caucasian age.

C1526. The Alpha's lore: Caucasianism recognized the validity of the racial will to a degree as to concede to that will the right of *Racial Sovereignty*: racial sovereignty cannot suppress itself. If we look at the matter from a purely true biological point of view, racial sovereignty is inalienable. For decades and even for centuries the Caucasian people have continued to endure passively false political and moral conditions which greatly impede their progress.

C1527. Life dominates thought and determines will. It is by this aphorism, essentially based upon the racial conception of our history that defines the question under consideration "Caucasian Treason". If a Caucasian, born and raised in a Caucasian society, wishes sincerely to become the *Patron* or *Agent* of an Alien race, he or she must renounce all the conditions of their past Caucasian existence, all their customs, all their ties of sentiment, vanity, and intellect with the Caucasian world Community, thereby becoming their enemy and declare war against them, throwing them-selves entirely without restriction into the Alien's world, supporting their *Hostel Ambitions* and their *Conspiracies* against the- *Caucasian world community.*

C1528. The Alpha's lore: If one fails to study the truth of racial rights, racial knowledge and racial will, one will suffer intellectual default from a defective understanding of the significance of the problem of freedom for a higher evolution of the human species. Hence, suffering no less disasters than that of earlier conceptions of social reform which blinded by the general splendor of their vision, have ignored the individual "Racial Sources" which combine to produce that splendor.

C1529. The Alpha tells us: To long for joy, support and comfort, to react violently against fear and anguish is quite simply the human condition. In short, as of the *21st* century, Caucasian society throughout the world is out of balance and in deep intellectual conflict (liberal zealotry!) and Caucasian America is right in the middle. This is the *Fulcrum* of Caucasian history at which we stand, the door of our future is opening on to a crises more sudden, more violent, more inescapable, and more bewildering than any ever encountered by Caucasians, and one which will take decisive shape within the life span of Caucasian children who are already born.

C1530. The Alpha's lore: The Caucasian people are perfectly logical in constituting itself into a racial political state, and in considering the struggle against the *Alienquest* in all its hyenic gradations. Viewed as a single racial state is the only possible means of realizing a social order in which Knowledge, Health, and Property shall not be, as they are today, the plunder of alien races.

C1531. Racial kind; A simple term, at least most people would think so, but is it? In a world plagued by endless difference, does not racial kind *Pause* the mental traffic, and bring focus to the meaning of one thing. Is it not true, that I am human? And therefore of a racial kind, a biological determinant, and does not the word *Kind* imply the existence of others, others of racial difference and determination? (race, is sacrosanct!)

C1532. Time and place, are the parents of all existence, and so it stands that by time, in a place, a form becomes a *Kind* and by its own strengths and weaknesses, pleasures and panes it forges a union of its like, and then taking stock, moves to a distant future, always hostel, always uncertain and never fails to uphold the *Trust* its ancestral trust, the very essence of that which is of its *Kind.*

The Caucasian ancestral trust (our social endowment) is the Biological, Political, and Moral beacon by which the entire Caucasian world identifies; it is *Racial Fundamen*talism at its best, a true biological legacy.

C1533. The Alpha's lore: We the Caucasian people do not live or die in vain, we have earned our place in this world. By biological kind and its determination, or self-identity throw the purpose of survival, this is the Caucasian race, and all that it implies.

C1534. The Alpha tells us: Racial fundamentalism is about *Love* not hatred! It speaks to the fundamental roots of a biological journey through time and space, a biology forged in physical and mental turmoil, a biology sculptured, given form through choices, and these choices are a manifestation of the birth of *Racial Kind* of identity, of belonging, and of being one with the whole!. This is the irreducible root of Caucasian- *Racial Fundamentalism.*

C1535. It is now in America, were one (a Caucasian) cannot speak of racial fundamentalism without invoking the verbal wrath of liberal zealots, and the vulgar tantrums of minority ignorance, not to mansion the general media's never ending mission to challenge any sign of a *Caucasian racial spirit* as just another exercise in racial hatred. Based on this, there can be no denial as to its importance in the understanding of the liberal zealot forces that appose Caucasian America and its social standing. (be observant!)

C1536. The Alpha's lore: The essence of race, that which is of greatest importance is *Identity* and that being said, let us now speak of the substance of *Racial Fundamentalism* the strict adherence to a set of racial principles and beliefs based on love of our racial kind, *Bio-Morality* and loyalty to our ancestral trust. These are the *Truths* that terrify the minds of the liberal zealots and their *Alien Army* of cultural marauders, and historical hijacker. (alien revisionists)

C1537. The new Caucasian crusade, a crusade for the understanding of that which is real, in a world turned upside down, by the disease of a liberal utopian social fallacy,(racial equality) a fallacy so socially degenerative that it has shackled all intellectual courage, and dislocated all of the intellectual debate, not to mention the governments campaign of *Racial Inquisition* against Caucasian Americans, to wipe out any vestiges of their racial pride and expression.

C1538. The Alpha tells us: Our world is comprised of two forms of existence, inorganic matter, and organic matter. Though it is true, that organic is comprised of inorganic matter, but, it is only organic matter that has intellect, and is capable of deliberate conscious self-regeneration, in other words, it can think, and act on its own behalf,...it makes choices, it selects, it favors, it discriminates, it rejects, it decides, and all of this is unique to its self, and its path to survival.

C1539. Caucasians should deem it best to stick to the practical truth of things rather than to fallacies. Many Caucasians have imagined *Democratic* and *Social Fallacies* that never could really exist at all. Yet the way liberals want us all to live (liberal utopia) is so far removed from the way we ought to live, (homogenous State) that any Caucasian who abandons what is, for what should be!...will indoor the wrath of liberal social treachery.

C1540. This is surely true: Caucasian America will never be socially reorganized without running into danger, for the majority of liberals will not accept nor entertain their own social default. Thus it will happen that the liberal oligarchy will be hated and feared and their leadership will be seen as socially dishonorable by the majority of Caucasian Americans, and this intern will lead to their end.

C1541. Blessed is the Caucasian who speaks the truth, when the truth is not welcomed.

C1542. Infamous and detestable, are the destroyers of religion, the wreckers of freedom and racial union, the enemies of virtue, of learning, and of every other art that benefits and honors human kind.

C1543. Let those who study history duly note how useful religion was in directing and animating the people, in keeping men good, and in shaming the wicked. For where there is religion, it is easy to introduce social discipline, but where there is a society and no religion; discipline can only be in- troduced with difficulty. Therefore, everything considered, religion must be the primary causes of a societies prosperity, for it is the source of good laws; good laws bring good fortune, and from good fortune are ensued all the results of social enterprises. As the observance of religious rites is the foundation of a society's greatness, so disrespect for them is the source of its ruin.

C1544. The Alpha's lore: The Caucasian who does not recognize alien aggressive ills at their inception, does not have true social wisdom, and no Caucasian state, unless it has its own arms in the possession of its kindred, is secure.

C1545. Anyone searching for the first cause of the ruin of Caucasian America will find that it began with the failure to repatriate freed slaves. From that point the strength of Caucasian America started to decline, and as we can see, this mistake is the cause of Caucasian Americas present peril, as all its social reasoning would become lost in a mystical wilderness of liberal fallacy.

C1546. The Alpha's lore: It may be noted, that when Caucasians have given more thought to fine living than to their social racial union, they will lose that vital union. The first cause of losing it; is its neglect! Just as the first means of gaining it; is its nurture!

C1547. The Caucasian people respond better to norms their ancestors evolved, then to norms imposed on them by racial strangers.

C1548. The Alpha's lore: A race is the symbol of its history, a biological will, ...further determined!

C1549. The Caucasian people must be warned against the mistake of thinking any human standards are absolute. Alien races have evolved under different circumstances and a propensity to violate Caucasian norms by aliens need not be seen as disordered or dysfunctional. Such differences are inherently no more value-laden than the fact that aliens are simply different from Caucasians, and it is simply foolish to expect them to behave like Caucasians. Hence, Caucasian America, and its Multi-racial dilemma!

C1550. On libertarian grounds, people should be free to choose their associates or neighbors even for irrational reasons. And on empirical grounds, it is often rational for Caucasians to avoid aliens.

C1551. It is the tenacity of which Egalitarians (liberal zealot) hold to *Social* rather than *Biological* explanation for *Racial Differences* that bespeaks a great fear that biology is immutable in its power to determine human kind.

C1552. The people of Milton and Shakespeare have a right to save themselves, should Caucasian America not try to avoid extinction?

C1553. The Alpha's lore: The ultimate Caucasian interest is not happiness, nor liberty, nor individual life itself but racial survival. A scientifically informed constitution that takes the Caucasian people's interests seriously cannot omit reference to their racial interests. Such a racial state would be, essentially a contract entered into by the Caucasian race of people in the name of its posterity.

C1554. Indiscriminate altruism is not universal! Remember this,...non-Caucasians who displace Caucasians, whether in Europe or America will not establish homelands for Caucasians! Therefore, the Caucasian American indigenous right (those who created the United States of America) must be declared, and a separate state must be established.

C1555. It is the *21st* century, and Caucasian America has been invaded by millions of illegal alien (non-Caucasians) this has come about by political incompetence and liberal treachery, the Government has betrayed Caucasian America, effectively hijacked the state for private purposes. They have no mechanism for ensuring the loyalty of industrial elites; this failure is the most egregious act of a Governments *Incompetence*. Hence, the Caucasian people and their communities are losing their historical investment in their *Nation State*, and they have every reason and right to want to replace a Government that has betrayed them. If things do not change!...unimpeachable though it may be from a Caucasian racial standpoint; by the year 2030, the Caucasian American people will have lost their- Nation State! (Reality!)

C1556. The Alpha's lore: The Inseparable Equation: the goal towards which all living things strive is to make more copies of their distinctive genes. (themselves!) This is seen most clearly in the devotion of parents to children. The importance of genetic continuity is an end in itself, for the Caucasian race as well as for all other races. This is the ultimate goal of all living things, and every other goal is subordinate to it. This is truth, this is reality.

C1557. The Alpha tells us: Loyalty to your race, is the genetic equivalent of loyalty to one's family, it is both in the cultural and broad genetic sense that a person's race can be said to deserve even greater loyalty than one's own family whenever the race is threatened. If an individual is lost, it is a great personal tragedy. However, if the race (genetic well) disappears it takes with it far more, it takes with it that which will never be again, a one of a kind biological, cultural and intellectual essence. In this sense, the race's extinction is infinitely more terrible than one's own death!

C1558. The Alpha's lore: It is within our race, its culture and folkways, its eclectic tribal essence (it's biological life strategy) that makes our race what it is!

C1559. Equalitarianism: the liberal social philosophy of human equality (socially equal) For all practical purposes, as well as for our own intellectual sense, let us examine this modern social icon. Let us begin with the word itself, *Equality* (equal in quality) hence, equal implies the absence of any difference in ability, the absence of distinction, importance, value, merit, and all this is measurable. Furthermore, if you add to this inquiry the reality of *Mental Individuality* (cognitive distinction) brought about by another reality *Competitive Predation*. Knowing this; Equality can have no place in a biological world,...for it is a term without Hunger, Desire, Ambition, or Opposition. And when applied to humankind, it becomes a *Utopian Fallacy* in its failure to admit to human divergence, and the millenniums of cultural and competitive distinction.

C1560. By attacking, discrediting and holding Caucasian racial identity up to ridicule, the liberal zealots hope to depress Caucasian identity, thereby disorienting their union, and toppling their political strength, leaving social and political voids for aliens to fill. So, what are we Caucasians to do? Are we going to ignore the liberal zealot's racial inquisition, their campaign to destroy Caucasian American determination by *Defamation* and *Humiliation*, or are we going to act?

C1561. The Alpha's lore: Caucasianism is in fact, the one and only true path to Caucasian spirituality, as well as social and intellectual enlightenment. For-*Racialness* implies a biological origination, the *Caucasian Fematrix* (the Caucasian Sisterhood) and through this racial emergence, this origination, all Caucasians owe their origin!

C1562. The Alpha tells us: All living things are the tributaries of not only their ancestral trust, but a biological trust as well. Negroid, Mongoloid, and

Caucasoid, these are the sacred tributaries of human genesis, these are the emerging champions, having endured millions of years of unsympathetic struggle, and to deny anyone of them their *Identity* for the sake of a utopian fallacy, is an intellectual failure and arrogance beyond measure.

C1563. In Caucasianism, *Fire* is the symbol of our human transcendence, the "Caucasian Racial Fire" of America is failing, and we must restore that Fire.

C1564. There are those Caucasian liberals and conservatives who represent what are both sides in America's political debate, and who agree that to solve the race problem, the Caucasian race must go! This is what passes for ideology in today's America? A Caucasian who attacks and calls for the death of his or her own race, is considered an idealist. For same reason they are not considered traitors? They are considered idea-lists who are making some sort of great sacrifice by demanding the end to themselves and that of their own people. And if this is regarded as idealistic in our liberal society, you can imagine the depths to which such a liberal society can plummet when it is not being idealistic.

C1565. The Alpha's lore: Forcing different groups of people, (biologically and culturally dissimilar) to live under the same government produces competitive tyranny.

C1566. The Alpha tells us: By embracing the ideology of Caucasianism, a true meaningful life is possible.

C1567. The Alpha's lore: If your enemy can create a moral illusion by which it makes you feel compelled to abandon your own racial identity, it will not be long before this moral illusion will have further removed you from your culture, than your future, and finally that of your chidren's future, all leading to your enemies goal, Caucasian American social capitulation.

C1568. The preservation of human kind is better served by three separate journeys (Negroid, Mongoloid, and Caucasoid) instead of one, three separate approaches to the conquest of human mortality, driven by the most basic of commonalities *Survival* which is a byproduct of racial essence, the inward nature of a race, underlying its manifestation; true substance, the indispensable conceptual characteristic and relations of a race and its essential survival quality.

C1569. Blessed is the Caucasian woman who uphold the Caucasian home.

C1570. The most difficult problems, and potentially the greatest dangers, for the Caucasian American people in a Multi-racial state are three. The first is the danger of splitting the population into permanent majority and minority groups.(biological determinism) these racial lines of cleavage will come to reinforce each other, thereby condemning some groups and people to the status of permanent and powerless minorities. Alienated, they will respond to their hopeless condition by withdrawal and apathy, or by demands for revolution. The second danger is that of paralyzing the government in the *Immobility* of incompatible and deadlocked rival racial interests. The third danger is that of the withdrawal of the mass of Caucasian citizens into apathy and alienation from an active government whose decisions and actions they no longer hope to understand or to influence effectively despite the presence of their elected representatives. All these problems are apt to become even more serious with the steady increase of unchecked alien emigration. (invasion)

C1571. As Caucasian man and woman have disagreed about the political community in which they are willing to be represented, so they may differ in respect to the grounds on which they are willing to trust their representatives. Hence, Burke and Adams; A representative ought to be elected by his or her constituents, not because their views exactly reflect their own, but because they expect that in most specific cases their representatives particular judgment of their best interests will be better than their own.(a democratic leap of faith)

C1572. It must not be forgotten that the achievements of the Caucasian European mind in every sphere would not have been possible or at the very least would have been entirely different without the intellectual revolution whose beginning is associated with Petrarch and whose ultimate triumph is most clearly seen in the life and works of Erasmus.

C1573. It was Gobineau, a French diplomat who said, Civilization cannot be transmitted to people who cannot create it. He believed that the enslavement and displacement of other races was cruel, and any attempt to civilize them would only confuse and distress them, and he was totally against the mixing of Caucasians with any other racial groups, which would eventually lead to *Miscegenation*, and the loss of the Caucasian *Racial Core* (bio-racial character) and the death of Caucasian civilization. He believed that a civilization that proceeds from two or more completely foreign races can only touch on the surface,...they can never coalesce. Being a man of his time, (1816-1882) and a confirmed elitist, Gobineau got many things wrong, but his love for his race was never in doubt. He believed that Caucasians built civilizations because of their *Love of Liberty* and their restless will to create and govern. He believed they have an *Extraordinary Attachment* to life, and know how to use it, and so it would seem set a greater price on it,...they are more sparing of the lives of others, and uniquely preoccupied with honor, and also will become everything great, noble and fruitful in the future works of civilization on this earth.

C1574. It was Robert Heinlein who said: Anyone who clings to the historically untrue-and thoroughly immoral doctrine that violence never settles anything should conjure up the ghosts of human history. Violence, naked force, *Warfare* has settled more issues in history than any other factor, and the contrary opinion is wishful thinking at its worst. Breeds that forgot this basic truth have always paid for it with their lives and their freedoms.

C1575. It has been said of Multiracial States, that their degeneracy is inevitable, that the deference in their biological racial core– their *Soul* (their life strategies) would forever doom their union, and that their civilization was but a mystical veneer, and that their different racial strata form an abyss,... over which their civilization is suspended. And in what could be considered as an epitaph for the Multiracial State, was written: What is truly sad is not the death of the Multiracial State, but the certainty of its people meeting it as degraded racial beings, because so many were complete strangers to their own ancestral racial trust.

C1576. The Alpha's Lore: the Caucasian American society will perish because they are becoming Identity degenerate, and this is because they are losing their absolute principle of *Racial Kind* and its distinctive life strategy.

Like the tragedy of Caucasian South Africa,...Caucasian America will now be morally lead by Caucasian liberal zealots and minority poachers, to their own social suicide, having no idea of their own cognitive degeneracy: Perhaps on their death march with their eyes glazed over, they will think themselves the wisest and cleverest beings that ever existed?

C1577. Blessed are the Caucasians: That give kindness and charity, to those how are not of them.

C1578. The Alpha's Lore: No Civilization or society could be stable or harmonious without the common root of its *Social Identity* (its biological signature) its physical appearance, which is the first task of its visual strategy, the other strategies being- physical, mental, aural, olfactal, and sexual. Furthermore, of the 6 components in the biological life strategy of humans, it is the union of their visual and physical strategies that combined to create *Visual Identity* hence, in a predatory world where vision is the most optimal sense; *physical identity* is a survival imperative.

C1579. The Alpha's Lore: The demographic future of Caucasian America is the most important question we as Caucasians will face in our not too distant future, yet, it receives very little inquiry. And those Caucasians, who do express their fears, are immediately smothered in accusations of -*Racism*- by the liberal zealot fraternity and their cohorts of alien jesters. In the wards of a Caucasian American forced to leave his neighborhood by invading alien races,...Would the last Caucasian American to leave, please take down the Flag.

C1580. The Alpha tells us: That we Caucasian humans, are biology at its finest hour.

C1581. The Alpha's Lore: What is it that gives rise to the migration of peoples? It is the search for a desirable and safe place to live. And it is Caucasians who have created the most desirable societies in the history of humankind. Furthermore, non-Caucasians want access to these places even if they did not,...and could not create them. The same is true on a smaller scale. Though politically incorrect, but never the less true, virtually every desirable place to live, work, or go to school is desirable because Caucasians made it that way, this is why it is always non Caucasians who are pushing their way into Caucasian lands and institutions, and never the other way around. This is truth, this is reality.

C1582. It was Israeli Prime Minister *Yitzhak Rabin* who explained that what mattered most to him as an Israeli was that his country (a religious state!) remain at least 80 percent Jewish. No one suggested that *Mr. Rabin* was a bigot or hatemonger,...and of course he was not! He was merely stating the obvious: that if the state of Israel ceased to be predominantly "Hebrew" in its ethnic religious and cultural character, it would change in irreversible ways,...hence, being detrimental to the Jewish people and their posterity!

C1583. The Alpha tells us: That we Caucasians, like no other race of people, are in a ceaseless, restless state of becoming, and that it is nowhere written that words of genius have to be created, that something in the air will bring forth another *Mozart* if the first one falls. One may acknowledge the undoubted role of the cultural context in fostering or inhibiting great art, but still recall that it is not enough that the environment be favorable. Somebody must actually do the deed. In all of our Caucasian endeavors, the meaning of ₵aucasianism is intimately connected with the discovery or application of objective racial truth about how the biological universe works.

C1584. The Alpha asks us: What qualifies as a Caucasian accomplish-ment? To think about such a question is to think about how we as Caucasians evaluate ourselves as individuals and as a race. What is important? What is not? Furthermore, he invokes the image of a *Resume!*...of the Caucasian race, its categories of accomplishment. Its utility lies in the meaning of the word resume- not a report card, but evidence of our races capacities. A resume of the race demonstrates our capacities as a race.

C1585. In the profusion of great works by such Caucasians as Socrates, Plato, and Aristotle just to mention a few, shaped our respective western intellectual history and its civilizations. And, they have done this in ways so pervasive that their role has become invisible. Hardly anyone in America or Europe thinks themselves as an Aristotelian, for example, even though American and European ways of conceptualizing virtue, happiness, the beautiful, and logic still trace back to Aristotle's teachings. It was these great Caucasian thinkers who established the frames of reference with which we as Caucasians still approach the world we live in today.

C1586. It was Aristotle who said: Criticism is something that easily can be avoided by saying nothing, doing nothing and being nothing? Will the path of the Caucasian Empire be easy? No, but we as Caucasians must transcend the self and become one with the whole. Thus, at once, we move within the race and the race moves within us, staying the path charted by our Caucasian racial convictions.

C1587. The Alpha's lore: It is a fact that takes some time getting used to, but the evidence for it is overwhelming: When you assemble the human resume, only a few thousand people stand apart from the rest. Among them, the people who are indispensable to the story of human accomplishment number in the hundreds. Among those hundreds, a handful stands conspicuously above everyone else. And out of the 12 categories in the arts and sciences, Astronomy, Biology, Chemistry, Earth Science, Physics, Mathematics, Medicine, Technology, Art, Literature, Music, Philosophy, and let us not forget the Humanities, the top 12 people in every category are Caucasians all,...this is truth, this is reality.

C1588. One of the rare fields of human endeavor in which an objective measure of excellence is available is cognitive ability. This shows itself most profoundly in individual groups (races) that have been isolated from each other for millenniums. Thou not politically correct, but never the less true, a people's culture and or social demeanor (life strategy) is a product of intellect, as it is of all bio-corporeal beings. And it is to their accumulated advantage of intellectual incumbency that contributes to their success. And to not recognize it in the name of a hubris *Equality* is an intellectual betrayal beyond measure.

C1589. It is the business of intellect to, convert component human skills into major survival achievements, and then to distribute and convert those achievements into biological code (DNA) for accumulated advantage in the next generations to come. One of the satisfying simplicities of cognitive ability is that we can answer the question of ultimate intent(a life strategy) without agonizing over it.

C1590. In the biological game of human survival, the harder the task, the more likely that the number of accomplishments among the human groups who try to achieve it will be zero and the next most common number will be one. In other words, the harder the task, the steeper will be the reduction in each number of successes; this is the nature of biological difficulty. Furthermore, of the entire biological attempt at life, (millions a day) hardly any ever succeed. It's just too hard. All of this conforms to experience that should resonate with all Caucasian man and woman of intellect.

C1591. It was Aristotle who said: Human beings enjoy watching the exercise of the realized capacities of their race, and this enjoyment increases the more the capacity is realized. To be in the presence of greatness is exciting, even when we are not capable of appreciating all the nuances of the achievement. The best has a magic about it.

C1592. The Alpha's lore: The efficiency in administration and sophistication in law is not the same as possessing an advanced or just political system.

C1593. It was Charles Murray who said: A culture that is unable to compete with the past's greatest expressions of the human spirit is in some sense a backward culture, and it is dispiriting to know that the greatest accomplishments are mono-polized by past cultures whose heights we are unable to match. Being part of a culture that produces new giants would be inspiriting.

C1594. The Alpha tells us: Caucasianism and its natural religious revelations, gets us to the social truths that are universal, the truths that are true for everyone, the interconnected patterns and systems of the bio-cosmic, the miracle of birth,...all are Caucasian revelations in that you can see the very essence of the *Fematrix* within them.

C1595. In Caucasianism, faith is connected to physical truth, and you most find spiritual enlightenment (inner harmony) by educating yourself in *Fematrix Theology* and surrendering yourself to her truth. The two,..faith and truth in Caucasianism are inseparable, Science and Religion coexist, the need to understand how the world works drives science,(truth) and the need to understand what the world means drives religion. (faith) Hence, to know what leads to physical and mental oneness: you most surrender to the truth and faith of your Fematrix and her will. And by sharing the blessing she has bestowed, all will come to know her.

C1596. The Alpha tills us: Caucasianism is a religion of birth and belief. In Caucasianism if your parents were Caucasian then you are a Caucasian, no matter what you believe. But, if only one of your parents was a Caucasian, then you most declare yourself. Furthermore, Caucasians by birth who believe nothing that Caucasianism subscribes to are called *Secular Caucasians*. They're Caucasians, but do not believe! Caucasianism is unique in that it is both an open belief oriented religion and a closed racial religion at the same time! It's a racial religion in that you are a Caucasian by birth and not belief, but it's also an open belief-oriented religion in that if one of your parents was a Caucasian you can convert to Caucasianism. Although Caucasianism does not aggressively seek converts; but it does accept them. This combination of being *Open* and *Closed* has made Caucasianism hard to understand for some people, and can become a source of conflict within the Caucasian community.

C1597. The Alpha tells us: Wartime ravages can repair themselves in a few years, and recovery from an economic crisis doesn't take long. But racial demographic damage (low birth rate) can take decades, even centuries to recover from,...when recovery is possible at all. With mass abortions paid for by government health insurance, and the mass media's *Humanitarianism* which endlessly attacks the strong traditional values of honor, hard work, dignity, family, sacrifice and having a pride in one's Caucasian racial identity,...this, the identity that founded the nation,... no less! And now for more than thirty years, we Caucasian Americans have sat helpless and resigned as we watched a generalized abdication of responsibility at all social levels. Irresponsibility on the part of young Caucasian men and women who no longer want to take on the responsibility of being heads of families. And the Irresponsibility on the part of politicians who are ready to sacrifice our nation's future if it means safeguarding their chances in the next election! Caucasian America is not on an ascent toward something better, but is stumbling forward while everyone seeks to preserve their generous incomes as they shift all hard decisions onto a feckless government which manipulates them exactly as it wishes and makes them swallow anything!

C1598. The Alpha tells us: that Caucasian America has become politically cowardice and morally faceless, and the amazing thing is how the Caucasian people, as if in a daze, stay mute and fail to react in the face of such mutilation of their racial identity and history as is being imposed on them. By combining individualism and Multiculturalism with a certain liberal numbing, Caucasian America has put itself on a course of *Exiting History* altogether, and it proceeds largely unnoticed.

C1599. The Alpha tells us: Caucasian America stands a good chance of becoming what could be called an unfortunate society which because of its racial polarization will have difficulty overcoming the internal contradictions she herself has created. Populated by large racial minorities aspiring to become majorities, very different in their culture and values and therefore rivals. And thereby becoming a country in which simply maintaining public order will require the mobilization of all domestic resources to preserve a semblance of social order, a regime that more and more resembles a police state, and a more and more nationalized economy.

C1600. It is the year *21st* century. And all Caucasian societies throughout the world are under siege by alien races that under the tutelage of liberal treachery and its *Egalitarian World Terrorism* (all humans are the same?) are invading and subjugating all Caucasian democratic states. Hence, it behooves all Caucasians of intellect to reexamine the democratic mystique and its many faults, for if we the *Caucasian Protagonists* of the human journey fail to act against this Crisis, our children and that of their future will be determined by *Alien Antagonists,* and thereby complete- Ruin! ...will be the fate of all.

C1601. The Alpha tells us: The Caucasians and their path to survival was, and is their own! And by adjusting to, and altering their environment the Caucasian race took form,... and it was this racial form brought about by the Caucasian *Fematrix* and her survival choices,(her life strategy) which intern recreated generation after generation of Caucasian difference and uniqueness. Alas, and in the event that we Caucasians should fail to realize, the Alpha puts to us this truth, that Caucasian kind as well as all human kind is, a one-time happening, and we will never be again! This is our only chance at immortality,...and history tells us, we will never get another chance!

C1602. The Pox Equality: the denial of the existence of any basis for knowledge or truth of human races.(racial nihilism) this is a very particular destructive mental process in the larger Caucasian communities throughout the world, with a specific cause (socialism revisited) and characteristic symptoms; partial or complete *Racial Guilt,* the interruption of voluntary racial preservation, and finally, identity paralysis. (loss of racial sensibility) So, as the Alpha, I must ask you? Will we Caucasian Americans, as well as our sister states throughout the world, make the same mistake that our ancestors the *Trojans* made thousands of years ago? Will we open our gates? And bring in the gift of our enemies? Knowing perfectly well that in the belly of this illusionary gift (Equality) lies the destruction of all Caucasian America and her sister states throughout the world?

C1603. The Alpha tells us: We as Caucasians in our social and political attentiveness must not forget the demons that lurk in the *Industrial Dark Waters* With the hunger of the leviathan, and the wealth of the gods,...it is some of these economic sultans of reptilian intellect (no loyalty to their posterity) that wait submerged from the world, so as to ambush and gorge themselves on those who wade through the economic waters.

C1604. Tolerance is the virtue of accepting the legitimacy of the religious belief of others, even though you hold your own religious belief to be true.

C1605. The Caucasian family mission is to educate and act as a link in the chain of tradition, providing the nexus between what came before and what will come later.

C1606. A tenet in Caucasianism is that the Caucasian American people are meant to be a part of a greater community of faith and good deeds. Alone, Caucasian people are vulnerable; yet, when they are united, they have strength and purpose. Do not separate yourself from the community.

C1607. The Alpha tells us: Politics isn't just about voting; it's also about the *Racial Reality* and *Racial Morality* of our life and times. These racial views and concerns are valid, because they are the responses of millions of people both Caucasian and Alien alike, this shapes and affects the culture in which we all live. Furthermore, by examining the racial response to same of the defining racial dilemmas of our time, we as a Caucasian community can better respond to the liberal zealot political fraternity of racial nihilism. Secondly, the racial arguments against acts of preferential treatment for alien races, for example, are generally based on the racial belief that a race of people is ultimately responsible for their own social advancement. But, this argument doesn't make much sense to a people who either don't believe in *Race* (distinct biological groupings) or don't believe that human beings are a product of biological evolution. (reality)

C1608. Legislative Racial Nihilism: the dismantling of human reality, through political legislative treachery. (Liberal zealotry) And if allowed to continue, this political cancer will invade the social will, and bring Caucasian America to political and social invalidity. The Caucasian American response to the abomination of liberal social vanity (equal racial outcomes) or liberal arrogance gone mad, must be a transition from social tolerance, to political outrage, by finding this modern tradition of Caucasian liberal social suicide as unforgivable,...an immoral treason, committed deliberately against the Caucasian American people and their community, with full knowledge of the act.

C1609. The Alpha tells us: That in a world of unrestrained and unaccountable liberal social engineering, the same liberal teachings that can produce wonders of education, can also produce abominations of intellectual vanity. So it is in Caucasianism that a balance is created, a poise between intellect and ego, a moral foundation of truth and allegiance, of spiritual wonder and community, barriers that steady and guide intellectual composition,... *Caucasian Enlightenment*

C1610. Capital Punishment: Is unequivocally upheld in "Caucasianism" It's a *Religious Edict* of punishment for those who commit premeditated murder or death by the act of- *Caucasian Treason*. To obey the law is the will of our Fematrix. (Caucasia)

C1611. The Alpha tells us: That in the Caucasian faith, Caucasianism is inseparably linked with politics and government, it is both *Monarchy* and *Democracy'* joined in racial spirituality to bring about the moral and civil Caucasian social state. (a racially religious-sponsored state)

C1612. The Alpha's Lore: In Caucasianism there are two enlighten-ments,... the *Visual* and the *Spiritual,* one of the outer presence, and the other of the inner presence, through the discipline and insight of truth, reality becomes the harbinger of faith, and a faith achieved through this, brings true and eternal rapture to the Caucasian soul.

C1613. The Alpha tells us: That in the Caucasian community *Thanks-giving* is the acknowledgment that our Fematrix *Caucasia* is the source of all our blessings, and through our everyday prayers, offerings and making amends for our failures, she will watch over us.

C1614. In Caucasianism prayer is a union in faith, touching the transcendent in all life, while binding with the Caucasian community and its every day social rituals.

C1615. In the Caucasian religious community, the basic and transforming spiritual experience is the act of *Compassion* not expressed through words, but through presence. It is in Caucasianism were the Presence and Faith of the Valorous are at the center of spiritual life.

C1616. The Caucasian High Mass: Caucasians celebrate communal worship in the *High Mass* which is performed at the Holy Sanctum on the last Saturday night of each month. Selections from the Valorous (from general text or Caucasians) are read, and a sermon on that reading is expressed.

C1617. The Caucasian Family Muse: Not everyone can make an appearance at the Holy Sanctum for the High Mass and for those who cannot, the *Family Muse* or personal contemplation (reading from the Valorous) at home, and lighting the sacred candles to the Ancestors (in the home reliquary) on the last Saturday of each month is commensurate.

C1618. In Caucasianism the word *Sacrifice* means to give up something of value in exchange for something of greater value. It is in fact, a reward.

The origins of the act of sacrifice are rooted in Parenting and not religion as some would believe. The sacrificial acts of *Parenting* result in unforgettable good, going far beyond the ordinary limit.

C1619. In Caucasianism the individual reaches their highest potential as a Caucasian spiritual being, not by being alone, but, in a racially spiritual community of other Caucasians.

C1620. In *Fematrix Theology,* the Fematrix (female prime) is the spirit of the living universe, its purpose, and its deepest meaning. In Caucasianism, she the Caucasian *Fematrix* (Caucasia) has given us free will, she offers the choices in life,...life and goodness over death and sin, but, she also does not compel us to choose. (It's our responsibility)

C1621. The Alpha tells us: He or she who wellfully participates in the act of *Miscegenation,*...creates nothing, and forfeits everything.

C1622. The basic foundation of Caucasian American democracy is the first amendment, the guarantee of freedom of expression. And it should be the idea of all Caucasians Americans that it is more important to practice it, than to enshrine it.

C1623. The Alpha tells us: one must avoid the closing of one's mind to the opinions of those with whom one disagrees. More can be learned by listening than speaking, for those with whom one disagrees should not necessarily be regarded as enemies, but perhaps simply as people who suggest different paths to a common goal.

C1624. Blessed is the Caucasian woman, who honors the Caucasian Sisterhood.

C1625. The Alpha tells us: If the political ideal of a *Caucasian Sovereign State* is not attained, it will have disastrous consequences, because we as Caucasian people will have lost the old social basis without finding a new one. And, when we are a minority people not only physically but also in the political sense, (politically disenfranchised) even more so, such a situation has within it the elements of tragedy. The Caucasian people will be in great danger as the *Liberals Zealots* and *Minority Poachers* march them to their appointed end? Yet we Caucasian Americans, who are not willing to accept fate without an effort to influence it, must make our choice.

C1626. The Alpha tells us: Once historic reality has been denied, our capacity to understand and react meaningfully to the present is similarly destroyed.

C1627. When investigating controversial issues it is important that one be able to distinguish between statements of fact and statements of opinion. It is also important to recognize that not all statements of fact are true. They may appear to be true, but are based on inaccurate or false information. Consider the facts carefully.

C1628. The Alpha tells us: It is only because Caucasian America is cognizant of individual rights, and because its *Enemies* count on this,...that it has been facing the hit and run alien rioting for so long. The media dwell lovingly on scenes of so-called Caucasian brutality: police forces charging alien crowed, alien teens being beaten,...for a public accustomed to having complex racial issues offered up in soothing ethical blacks and whites, it's all quite reassuring. It is also a complete distortion of the racial situation in Caucasian America,...Not a week goes by that a Caucasian American isn't assaulted (knifed, shot, robed or killed) by peace-loving minorities seeking self-determination. Their victims were and are, innocent Caucasians Americans, peaceably going about their daily business.

C1629. The Alpha tells us: Alien minorities are considered the aggrieved party in the American racial conflict, and the Caucasian Americans the villains? What accounts for this moral inversion, whereby those alien minorities who endorse *Hyenic Tribalism* and wanton social destruction are hailed, and the founding race of Caucasian Americans who support Altruism, Law, Productivity and Personal Responsibility are excoriated? What kind of view explains, that the rights of Caucasian America (the founding race of America) must be subordinated to the demands of alien racial inabilities?... only a distorted philosophy of *Racial Equality* (equal racial out comes) as a moral virtue? This philosophy insists that some one's need creates a moral claim upon anyone able to satisfy it. In other words, if you are in *Need!* you are not equal, and if you are not equal, then you are oppressed? Hence, the ruse of Liberal zealotry!

C1630. When dealing with controversial subjects, many people allow their feelings to dominate their powers of reason. Thus, one of the most important critical thinking skills is the ability to distinguish between statements based upon "Emotion" and those based upon a rational consideration of the facts!

C1631. The Alpha tells us: Because human societies are so complex, problems are often not completely understood by any single citizen. Yet people always demand answers, and there exists a human tendency to create imaginary and simplistic explanations (such as equality?) for complex racial, social, and political problems that defy easy understanding and solution. The conflict (racial fundamentalism) between Caucasian American society and Alien racial minorities falls into this category. The complexity of their social and political relationship, being an "Irregular Environment" (forced upon them!) and having apposing life strategies, has so far defied any equitable and peaceful solution. In such a frustrating and emotionally charged situation, "Racial Separation" (a parting of the ways!) is and has always been the only *Safe* and *Beneficial* antidote for both! (a reasonableness, if you please!)

C1632. In our quest for economic prosperity, the Alpha asks of us: to not forget our needy brothers and sisters who's faith has failed them.

C1633. The Alpha tells us: The Valorous cannot be ignored, no matter how distasteful its truths may be, no matter how politically intimidating some Caucasian Americans may find it. Any solution that does not take the Valorous into account will be no solution at all, for in the absence of a better *Caucasian Enlightenment* it is the voice of the Caucasian American people, and it is quite capable of disrupting any racial negotiations in which it does not take part, and the likelihood that Caucasian nationalism will explode in America as well as the rest of the Caucasian world can be diminished only if the movement is recognized for what it is,...a vibrant, growing force that cannot be wished away or suppressed. Only if Caucasian America and her sister states throughout the world face the social realities of the racial situation and stop promoting and blindly following the liberal mythology that denies the *Racial* Competitive reality, will there be any hope of a solution, time is running out!

C1634. The Alpha tells us: That Caucasian America is very strong. But nothing can save it from disintegration and collapse if it continues to exercise dominion over 40 million aliens. (racial nonconformists) In other words, what really define the survival of a racial state are the inner social harmony, and the common allegiance that makes the racial group want to live together as a state. Furthermore, our most basic demand is the recognition that the Caucasian American people constitute a political entity, whose collective racial existence deserves political expression as a state.

C1635. It is the *21st* century and Caucasian America by seeking to protect its freedom against a great alien threat (illegal immigration) is being selfish and immoral, according to this liberal philosophy. In other words, it ought instead to sacrifice its values for the sake of those who lack them. This is why Caucasian America is under moral attack. It is pointless to argue that justice and reason are on their side. What greater act of altruism could there be than to sacrifice the just to the unjust and the rational to the irrational? The moral perversity here is that Caucasian Americans are being widely denounced because of their virtues, while resident minority races- as well as illegal aliens are being praised for their vices. In this war of social philosophy, it is only by upholding the principle that one has the moral right to exist for one's own sake and to live for one's own values that Caucasian America can be properly defended.

C1636. It was David L. Bender (publisher) who said: It is important to consider every variety of opinion in an attempt to determine the truth. Opinions from the mainstream of society should be examined. But also important are opinions that are considered radical, reactionary, or minority as well as those stigmatized by some other uncomplimentary label. An important lesson of history is the eventual acceptance of many unpopular and even despised opinions. The ideas of Socrates, Jesus, and Galileo are good examples of this. It can be said that those who do not completely understand their adversary's point of view, do not fully understand their own.

C1637. The Alpha's Lore: He or she, who does not identify with you, has no place with you.

C1638. The Alpha tells us: Thanks to new alien racial competitive pressures (liberal paternalism) of the twentieth century, the Caucasian American people as well as their sister states throughout the world, are arguably returning to *Racial Reality* and its traditions. The essence of a race is its accomplishment. It may turn out that the liberal zealotry of the last forty five years will have been an anomaly. What's normal in a society or out will end up being racial union, racial learning, adding to racial value.

C1639. You ask yourself if it's wrong to believe in your race when your friends and other abandon it, or whether it's wrong to abandon the race that brought you here. It's painful because loyalty and integrity are what keeps you alive. Inevitably, the volatility of the race, the power of your integrity, and the strength of your intellect will ultimately determine your racial path.

C1640. The Alpha tells us: the Valorous is animated by a single word: *Race.* Life cycles of societies and political structures are forever-shifting, with the liberal zealots crying out with wholesale exercise of the human social imagination dedicated to racial liberation management and their Rapid Deployment Team - the PC mob, have invaded all Caucasian lands. But, the ethereal racial character of the Valorous will find its way into the Caucasian worlds consciousness, thanks to 45 years of liberal social failure, after failure.

C1641. No corner of the Caucasian world is exempt from alien racial frenzy, and its explosion of illegal emigration, and racial competition is now a war of movement in which success depends on anticipation of political trends and a quick response to political weakness. In such an environment, the essence of a Caucasian strategy is not a verbal political response, but the dynamics of its defensive racial(biological) behavior.

C1642. The Alpha's Lore: Caucasian people are not dumb. They know that if their race is not competitive, there is no survival security.

C1643. The Alpha tells us: That we Caucasians are a global race, (a collection of ethnic-cultural tribes) a single race of people with intense global coordination, which makes us unique, and give us a forum for world exchange, creating a vast process of continuous experience transfer, a source of advantage none of our rivals can match.

C1644. The Alpha tells us: That the Caucasian Americans as well as their sister states throughout the world are in a desperate need of political and social change, and the problem is that most Caucasians don't understand it takes at least ten years to really establish a position of authority in any important social, economic, or political field. And it is the union of Caucasianism that will make our journey, our decade of struggle,...the last, and greatest Caucasian crusade.

C1645. A society's socio-racial structure influences the information it collects from its environment and how it combines and processes this information to generate future strategies. Change in its socio-racial structure (alien immigration) automatically results in changes in information flow, which in turn results in changes in the strategic opportunities that are considered and pursued. These changes also help to dissolve Caucasian power bases that can counter alien political strategy, in an attempt to protect its racial vested interests.

C1646. The Alpha tells us: Information is biological (racial) organization. Change the biological (racial) organization and you change the information flow. Hence, altering the direction of the Nations biology (its life strategy) you destroy the web of the society. Liberal zealots will never come to appreciate the worth of a major investment in racial development and its direct relation to Nation-building.

C1647. The Alpha tells us: If the Caucasian world is to survive, the Caucasian male and female most continually refresh themselves in and of a racial discipline. They must provide for their children the sense of racial continuity, a future of racial stability, wise leadership in a continuously changing and racially competitive world. Furthermore, there is a great need for Caucasians to talk to other Caucasians, a web of social, cultural, and religious ties that goes in all directions.

C1648. The most common way of measuring our contribution to our race, is simply to let each Caucasian person inform the next Caucasian person of the Valorous and its truths,... doing so sends a very clear signal about the importance of the Caucasian people working together for the race as a whole. Caucasian traditionalists (racial realists) on the other hand, must give themselves more to organization (Caucasian political party) and less to conservative yearly meetings that keep banking intellectual mimic.(all Caucasian organizations must step up to the need of a guided acknowledgment of opposing hostel forces)

C1649. The Alpha tells us: There are no *Normal* human societies anymore. It is the idea, as in gardening, to create the context for luxuriant growth. The result is predictable, human racial relations are essential, but difficult to orchestrate, and human potential is disproportionate. (unequal in ability) Hence, racial competition has become a hot topic, and equal racial reciprocity is at play. But, what happens when one race produces, ...and the other doesn't? (Parasitic) Can the one that doesn't produce, expect the same social tenure? (in nature, the performance of the group, is largely tied to performance of the individual or a person's ability as a whole)

C1650. The Alpha tells us: That the liberal denizens (liberal zealots) of Caucasian America, are more than borderline absurd.(Constant utopian reconfi-guration is vital to their future) They are a political organization that defies every social norm and rule. But, above all, the liberal zealot's common denominator is their political methodology of demonizing their own biology.

C1651. It was David Kelly who said: In a world where value comes from Knowledge, Knowledge-application Technology is by definition a most precious metal. And it is precisely this set of attributes that lie in the biology of all living things.(structural evolution, through mental evolution)

C1652. The Alpha tells us: In the end forget all the *social variables,* the Caucasians are a great race of people, and we all agree that Caucasianism our racial enlightenment is always supreme.

C1653. The Alpha tells us: That *Fematrix Biology* (the only biology) has a clear task and a clear goal,(survival) which it accomplishes with direct and indirect analytical realities. Furthermore, in the case of the Caucasians, they had to greatly initiate, foster, and nurture their cultural commitment do to uncertain and difficult environmental intangibles (extreme winterkill) leading to a loose but related racial union of Caucasian tribes,...a cultural union of excellence, professionalism, and organization.

C1654. The Alpha tells us: We Caucasians will have to become much more willing to take an expanded view of our race, and the role that it plays on the world stage? Racial- responsibility then is the understanding that all Caucasians must accept, that we as a *Caucasian Community* need to adjust our cultural and political attitude to a much stronger *Racial Orientation-* the Alpha's chief aim all along. The basic idea: Every Caucasian must become committed in filling his or her own days with *Caucasian Cultural Enlightenment* this can be accomplished by and through traditional every day personal communication, *Goodness, Dignity, Morality, Respectability* and the miracle of Caucasianism, will fill your soul with eternal wonder.

C1655. The Alpha tells us: That for any Caucasian person to complete the transformation to Caucasianism must understand, that it is not a religious recruitment,...but a personal racial journey, biologically, as well as historically. All in all, the transition to Caucasianism by the Caucasian community will be smoother than almost anyone would have imagined, for it asks one to have no belief, other than the belief in one's self, as part of a single biological spirit, the Caucasian Fematrix– *CAUCASIA* and her living miracle, the Caucasian people. Freely understood, and freely accepted.

C1656. The Alpha tells us: Investing in racial development (a biological, historical awareness) is essential in a progressive Caucasian society. But, racial ambiguity is always unfolding; therefore there must be *leaders* - visionaries, to transfer Caucasian racial passion to others. In fact, effective Caucasian leadership must match their passion for inspiring others (leading) with a passion for the future security of the Caucasian racial state, and be able to handle almost complete ambiguity, and counter social uncertainty within the race.

C1657. It was once said, all good ideas eventually get over-sold. The importance of a democratic vision and values is no exception. The democratic idea was, and is right. But there are flaws. Over time, democratic values in action get elaborated. Before you know it, a democratic law (affirmative action etc.) becomes more rigid and distorted, than its original intension. It ends up stifling the very initiative it was designed to induce. And what became freedom for some has now become oppression for others.

C1658. The Alpha's lore: You cannot change, what you do not acknowledge.

C1659. The Alpha tells us: The survival of some human societies for great lengths of time is largely a matter of luck,... such longevity comes about through the workings of chance. Attempts to induce social servility and economic aid as a response to their hopeless circumstances are doomed to failure. The ravages of time that beset these societies are irreversible; they are by and large not capable of more than marginal changes, while the environment is so volatile that marginal changes are frequently insufficient to assure survival.

C1660. The Alpha's Lore: The Caucasian Americans, in their social and political drive, must learn to say I got it wrong,... for only then, will it be possible to get it right.

C1661. The Alpha tells us: In today's Caucasian world, *Subjective Marginal Reasoning* has taken hold of the liberal fraternity. In other words, when it comes to liberal racial reality, we are dealing here with slippery ideas.

C1662. It was Tibor Scitovsky who said, we have unwittingly fallen into the habit of identifying a high standard of living with a high level of comfort, neglecting stimulation or pleasure as a source of satisfaction and assuming that the more comforts we have the better off we must be. But not at the cost of novelty,...the stimulus of novelty is among the most fundamental of human needs, and must remain as an objective of desire, and a source of satisfaction.

C1663. The Alpha tells us: By the year 2001, in Caucasian America and throughout the Caucasian world, the issues of the counter culture (liberal zealotry–equal outcomes!) had completely replaced the intellectual reasoning of liberal scholars, and legal functionaries. In this atmosphere of liberal dementia and Caucasian American disillusionment, many realistic thinkers like Samuel Frances, Jared Taller, and Pat Buchannan repudiated the ethical and political presuppositions of these liberal adventurers. The hopes for *Liberty* for some, had given way to the facts of *Tyranny* for others. By the time this great change had taken place, however, the influence of *Political Correctness* had already spread over the Caucasian world.

C1664. The Alpha tells us: By the year 2008, the effort to establish *Political Correctness* and to elucidate its real meaning produced an increasing body of Caucasian American disfavor and decent. And, political conditions in America have become peculiarly favorable to aliens (racial minorities) and their unsocial activities. In many cases, minority tyrants (poverty hustlers) who had no legitimate title to the political power they enjoyed, justified themselves by becoming *Religious Princes,* In other words, if one lacked any credibility, one could adopt religious princely virtues and a religious princely style, hence, convincing the poor people of their *Princes Right* to preside over their destinies. Yet America is not unique. Similar alien (racial minorities) achievements could be found in other nations throughout the world, with the same kind of devastating antisocial circumstance.

C1665. The Alpha tells us: The magnificent and almost unlimited confidence of many Caucasian Americans have given way to the realization that their government (political representatives) are beyond their control and in the realm of politics,...it became liberal authority which they could not legitimately question. Indeed, the political and cultural condition in which the Caucasian American community had flourished is passing way, and the effort to correct its political path, has fallen into the arms of the corrupted!

C1666. The Alpha tells us: The word religion has no one generally accepted definition. Philosophers, sociologists, psychologists, theologians and many others interested in a particular aspect of life have all defined religion in their own ways and for their own purposes. Hence, although it is impossible to give a conclusive definition of religion, there are certain characteristic forms of human activity and belief which are commonly recognized as religious: worship, separation of the sacred from the profane, belief in the soul, belief in gods or God, acceptance of supernatural revelation, and the quest for salvation. But, its true value can be found in *Worship,* religious worship is that activity which results from the recognition of dependence upon a creative sacred *Author* beyond human understanding. So, it is clear from the empirical data at hand that no sharp definition can possibly cover all of the phenomena which are generally classed under the heading of religion.

C1667. The Sacred: In Caucasianism the Sacred is a mysterious potency which lives within our sensory biological world, it is the consciousness of being part of a greater force that includes everything, (the Fematrix) and therefore must be reckoned with as a *Sacred Force* in all of the daily concerns of a Caucasians life. The existence of the *Sacred Force* is recognized by all humankind because they understand that there are certain powers affecting their lives which lie outside the normal means they use for controlling their environment.

C1668. The Alpha tells us: In Caucasianism and its *Fematrix Theology,* here lies the dual dependence of *Biology* and *Deity.* Between these extremes lies the greatest body of religious thought and practice. Biology is dependent upon its *Fematrix,* its creator, but, the *Fematrix* is also dependent upon biology, its created self. Hence, in Caucasianism the doctrine of human salvation lies in its understanding of its biological salvation. (competitive immortality) For all life is just the individual extension of a single *Deity,* (the Fematrix–female will) with different forms brought about by different strategies for her survival. It is in fact, a competition by all living things for her survival. For, biology is her only physical existence, and it has a flaw? It is a limited existence! Hence, the competition for the biological holy Canon *Immortality,* and the end to recon-figuration and death!

C1669. The Alpha tells us: It is the *21st* century in Caucasian America, and there appears a vivid consciousness of social and racial novelty in our contemporary liberal politics? It seems that certain Caucasian liberals as well conservatives have achieved *Mental Arcadia* and are of the political belief that electing an Alien pied-piper can lead Caucasian America out of their perceived sin, and in to a new golden age of Racial Brotherhood and Equality? But, the Alpha tells us this view, by this segment of Caucasian American society (the liberal and conservative elites) those in gated strongholds, are elements of a cowardly clustered self-denial, who would sentence all of Caucasian America to the fate of the lemming. And if successful, it will not be a golden age or a glorious rebirth for Caucasian

Americans,...It will be Death!,...death by the hands of our own people, death by their *Ignorance* and *Arrogance*, their contemptuous individual *Self-Importance* and *Success*. It will truly be Caucasian- *South Africa*,... revisited?

C1670. The Alpha tells us: The idea began to be held in political elite circles (democrat - republican) that incarcerating great numbers of Aliens, (Africans and Hispanic people) is somehow acceptable? But, the Alpha tells us: It is in fact Illicit Human Subjugation that borders on systematic racial suppression. In other words, Alien Racial Detention Camps Controlling the racial character of the population through legal abduction. (the penal industry) With more than 2 million now incarcerated, and with the failure of education, hence the collapse of economic opportunities, (no education,... no job!) The stability of America and the intellectual failure on the part of its leadership will bring about its collapse, and the feckless politicians will find themselves buried at the bottom of the wreckage.

C1671. The Alpha tells us: The attack on Caucasian American society and its social conception will begin in the *21st* century, and come principally from *Caucasian Liberal Zealots* and *Alien Minorities*. More profound is the emergence of a clearer apprehension of the meaning of *Race* and a greater discrimination in applying the word to historical phenomena. It is very clear that €*AUCASIANISM* and its followers in the *21st* century have not overstated the case for racial upheaval in the *Liberal Renaissance* of Caucasian America. There are even reputable liberal scholars who maintained that there was no justification whatever for the term *Racial* and that our historical understanding would be improved by striking it from our vocabulary. Such a judgment must always contain an element of cowardice. Furthermore, the attack on the validity of the conception of *Race* has been carried to indefensible lengths. There is absolutely no reason why the useful classification term of *Race* well established in historical vocabulary should be discarded just because its meaning has been justifiably inflated, and that inflation being the concept which recognizes *Racialism* as a useful and justifiable description of an important biological chapter in the evolution of humankind.

C1672. The Alpha tells us: In €aucasianism there has been kindled the enthusiasm and desire for the knowledge of things *Racial* the more they were developed, the more such interests revealed its truths, and a more deeply Caucasian racial consciousness. (biological primacy over religion and the State)

C1673. The Alpha tells us: Blessed is the Caucasian female that honors the rituals of the "Caucasian Sisterhood", for eternal life shall be of her.

C1674. The Alpha tells us: The Revival of Caucasian Learning; (Letters and Literature) the Alpha's aspect of Caucasian learning goes back to-Petrarch in the 14th century. Who he credits with being the initiator of reviving the great works of Caucasian European literature, (a Caucasian Literary Renaissance) and the Alpha's creation of the Holy Valorous, thus presenting the fruits of his own position, and thereby stimulating the Caucasian world community to apply themselves to its study, not as a great document, but as a declaration of appeal, to an objective and cognizant racial inquiry.

C1675. The Alpha tells us: Caucasian traditions of learning and piety shaped the attitudes toward classical civilization and, in spite of the enthusiasm in alien countries for imitating Caucasian learning, there still remains in every alien country a large primitive admixture of an earlier inheritance. Caucasian Europe had been the greatest center of learning in the known world, and Caucasian America was conceived and conditioned by this background.

C1676. The Alpha tells us: When we Caucasians present an argument, there is never enough space or time to state all assumptions, include all data and make all deductions. Thus, to a certain extent all argument relies on metaphor and rhetorical shortcuts. The consequences of relying on rhetoric instead of sound analysis are many, primarily poor forecasts and consequent biased decisions. However, we Caucasians must always be very careful not to let rhetoric cloud reality.

C1677. The Alpha tells us: It is crucial to the discussion about the state of the Caucasian world that we as Caucasians consider the racial funda-mentals. This requires us to refer to long-term and global racial trends, considering their importance especially with regards to Caucasian welfare. But it is also crucial that we cite figures and trends which are true. This demand may seem glaringly obvious, but the racial environment debate has unfortunately been characterized by an unpleasant tendency towards rather rash treatment of the racial truth. This is an expression of the fact that the liberal zealot Litany has pervaded the debate so deeply and for so long that blatantly false racial claims can be made again and again,(alien racial mythmaking) without any reference, and yet still be believed.

C1678. The Alpha tells us: Blessed is the Caucasian man, that renders service to the Caucasian female and her family, for his life shall be eternal, and all shall come to know him.

C1679. The Alpha tells us: The risk to Caucasian societies by adding millions of racial aliens annually is that so many unsustainable social thresholds (jobs, housing, health care, etc.) will be crossed in such a short period of time that the consequences will become unmanageable. Hence, the means for containing the epidemic of alien (illegal) migration to Caucasian lands are already known, and could prove effective if Caucasian leadership could be induced to adopt them. (enforce the law!)

C1680. The Alpha tells us: the frightening thing is that the pace of racial hostility has accelerated dramatically over the last 20 years and continues to rise. In actual fact the racial hostility rate in Caucasian America is among the highest in the world. The result is that for Caucasian Americans to survive both now and in the future, the strongest arguments against the liberal zealots egalitarian litany must be put directly to the Caucasian American people, thereby ensuring a full disclosure of the facts, and ending the often lax Caucasian attitude to the bio-racial principal.

C1681. The Alpha tells us: A lot of worries go into the question of *Race* - must we honor it, will doing so cause racial wars, etc. In recent years *Caucasian Racial Identity* has become one of the liberal zealot's favorite examples of their future social problems. Does *Caucasian Racialism* threaten liberal Egalitarianism(social utopia) and its litany of mystical equality? For one who heeds and understands social and political reality, this of course is an entirely unreasonable assumption. In essence, *Racial Egalitarianism,* - social utopia,...a society without any group identity or group competition?...or is it the elimination of a selected groups identity, ...today it is the Caucasian race! But, who will it be tomorrow?- the Asians, Africans, Indians,...for are they not also guilty of racial and cultural pride? Hence, the strength of human evolution lies in the preservation of its different racial and cultural identities. (separate journeys!) This is truth, this is reality.

C1682. The Alpha tells us: It was *Salim Mansur* who said: In every culture there are to be found some dissident or skeptics questioning its legitimacy and moral authority. They exposed the lies of a system that rationalized the organized effort of *Tyranny* to extinguish freedom, and their sacrifice eventually contributed to its demise.

C1683. The Alpha tells us: The media plays a central role in society's connections; this has come about because the world has become so complex that we can no longer rely primarily on our own experience. Instead, the mass media provides much of our understanding of reality. But, their particular lopsided way of providing us with news profoundly influences our view of the world. The point is that we cannot change this. Instead, we must come to grips with the facts, (trusted verification!) to measure the real state of the world.

C1684. The Alpha tells us: That rising *Alien Crime* (social negation) in the Caucasian world communities may be the first global indicator that they are on a social path that is democratically unsustainable. The long-term decline in liberal *Racial Reasoning* has been underway since the mid-century and this reputable analysis indicates that this liberal zealot trend is likely to continue with much wider social implications.(the South African narrative?)

C1685. The Alpha tells us: That food and water are perhaps the most important resources for humanity, since our very existence depends on them. They are renewable resources, but still can become scarce resources, potentially under pressure from our increasing population. It has been acknowledged for a number of years that food production is falling behind world population growth, and that clean water also has experienced a dramatic decline. We are beginning to experience a massive loss of intellectual momentum on this most important issue, and consequently there has been no real correction? Much hype has surrounded this issue of food and water, and there is a food and water crisis to-day! But the crisis is not about having too little food and water to satisfy our needs. It is a crisis of managing food and water so badly, that billions of people and the environment suffer badly. We have sufficient food and water, but we need to manage it better. We need to learn from our past mistakes, if human society is to be sustainable.

C1686. The Alpha tells us: There is no convincing evidence that the continuation of Caucasian American good will and their social capitulation will bring racial peace to America? Particularly contestable is the direct correlation between certain Caucasian politicians (political pirate) and alien poverty hustlers. Once again, this challenges our view of politicians, and the role they play in our future, and most of all that of our children's future? We therefore find ourselves in the situation today (the year-2012) that, to the extent to which current racial conflicts have produced-*Pathological Hatreds,* the risks to Caucasian Americans is so great that it would be very difficult for them to accept a future without poli- tical racial loyalty.

C1687. The Alpha tells us: In the major dialogue on the effects of liberal racialism, the discussion about racial quality is the most important: The most fundamental change has been the striking failure to discourage *Miscegenation.* This most dramatic and troubling sign of the lack of racial prudence and conservation, (Caucasian racial preservation) has led to dramatic social disruption, (alien social and moral anarchy) this weakens Caucasian America! Moreover, a reanalysis of alien racial hostilities in America from the year 1960 to 2008 has expanded beyond confinement, it is however, and even more essential to point out that today we as Caucasian Americans now know for certain that the *Liberal Equality Vision* was mistaken, racial *Inequality* overwhelmingly remains constant. It is therefore perhaps reasonable that Caucasians Americans should remove themselves from this path of destruction (E.R.S. Proposition) before there is any more dire racial consequences.

C1688. The Alpha tells us: One of the reasons we Caucasians need to worry so much about the effects of alien racial hatred, is that liberal zealots and their political apparatus refuse to recognize it! Because, to do so, they would need to Admit, that their social vision of utopian racial equality failed, and rather than concede that!...they would see all Caucasian America destroyed. All in all, it seems obvious that there is a problem with liberal intellectual reasoning in the field of racial cognizance (Racial Principle, and its perception) So, it is therefore very necessary (for Caucasian survival) to dislocate the liberal zealot fraternity from political office. It is of course, tempting to believe that this liberal fraternity will recover from its social dementia, and put the safety of its race at the center of its social philosophy? But, on the other hand, there is no data (social legislation) to indicate this change.

C1689. The Alpha tells us: Blessed is the Caucasian man, who sacrifices on behalf of his fematrix, for his life shall know the wonders of creation.

C1690. The Alpha tells us: The dramatic loss of *Racial Cognizance* in Caucasian America, as well as her sister states throughout the world, has expressed in 2008, an intellectual catastrophe, and it is one of many that the Caucasians still need to solve. Facing these facts is important when we as a race of people, have to make tough choices where to do the most good with our resources.

C1691. The Alpha tells us: There three questions: What are the consequences of a possible alien racial increase in Caucasian America? What are the costs of curbing versus not curbing alien increase? And how should we choose what to do? In other words, what considerations should we employ to decide between costs of action, and costs of inaction? The balance of evidence suggests that there is a discernible negative Alien Racial influence on Caucasian societies. The interaction between the races is extremely hostel, and the momentum of violent hostility is increasing. (Balkanization) the Multiracial State does not work!

C1692. The Alpha tells us: The basic prediction of racial balkanization (hostel racial camps!) in Caucasian America- in the *21ˢᵗ* century, has remained constant. This means that throughout the past 45 years the liberal social experiment to make all races the same,(equal racial outcomes) has not improved at all. Instead, liberal paternalism (racial caretaking) has been substituted under the heading of "Affirmative Action" this erroneous legal action by liberal law makers (liberal supreme court!) has created an Alien mentality that believes the greater society (Caucasian!) is beholding, obligated, and indebted to them, for a past social pathology of human history, (slavery?) thereby taking on the cultural persona of social default.

And, it is so deeply set into their racial cultural philosophy,...that change is not possible, leaving the greater Caucasian American society with a serious social dilemma? Multiple-racial resentment or-*Racial Militant Partisanship.* This great racial divide; (a liberal social and political malignancy) can only end, in Caucasian Americas perdition!

C1693. The Alpha tells us: That a number of unanswered racial questions and unsolved social problems still remain in the liberal zealots *Theoretical Racial Equality.* But the point is that the liberal equality theory has created a tremendous advantage for alien races that have contributed nothing to Caucasian America other than criminal activity, and a tribal (gang) atmosphere. Thus, even the great moral depletion and its cultural impact has failed to penetrate the liberal sense of social sacrilege. However, an even more intriguing social condition, and one that the Alpha must point to, is the indirect criminal political effect brought about by the relationship between aliens and certain Caucasian politicians? (political piracy) By forecasting a century into the future, racial equality will be fraught with spectacular social and political pitfalls, as we can easily tell from past experience, and perhaps the greatest danger in prognoses is that we tend to underestimate the Caucasians historical aggressive nature of,...Conquest!

C1694. lives of the The Alpha tells us: It was Charles Murray who said: Human beings have been most magnificently productive and reached their highest cultural peak in the time and place where humans have thought most deeply about their place in the universe and been most convinced they have one. Excellence exists, and it is time to acknowledge and celebrate the Magnificent Inequality that has enabled some of our fellow humans to have so enriched the rest of us.

C1695. The Alpha tells us: We as Caucasian Americans need to discuss the consequences of surrendering our nation to *Alien Political Control?* What seems necessary is to understand that in less than 100 years from now, we Caucasian Americans will be a minority people in the very nation that we founded, designed and built, also considered by many to be the greatest nation on earth. And, the uninformed Caucasian might ask,...what does that mean? It means, what it has always meant in a competitive racial world,...a world of unequal biological destinies, of rival group ambitions, of opposing social directions. And, in our America, we Caucasians will have become victims of our own historical ignorance,(alien competitive migration) and also that of a democratic political simplicity (the majority vote) How ironic will be the fate of Caucasian America, being laid waste by the liberal fallacies of a Multiracial Camelot.

C1696. Blessed are the Caucasians: who imagine a world where the preservation of human racial difference is respected and revered.

C1697. Let it be understood: It is assumed, that there will be an overall increase in racial hostilities in Caucasian America, as well as the rest of the Caucasian world. And that this situation will have an equally drastic effect on both economic and political outcome. In the US, the racial consequences will be dire: By mid-century if the race's haven't become independent states, which would be the logical and ideal social and political result, (each race's social fate, in their own hands) if for some reason this racial diplomacy fails and does not come about, the words *Police State* (freedom lost) will become the fate of everyone! A democracy functions better if everyone has access to the best possible information. It cannot be in the interest of Caucasian society for a debate about such a vital issue as racial sovereignty (a racial state) to be based on anything other than truth.

C1698. It was Malcolm Muggeridge who said: The great liberal death wish, a twisted psychology of that intellectual class which willingly goes out to buy the lies of a culture that entombs freedom, social paternalism-*Socialism,* and fashions these lies as a cure for manufactured ills in the Caucasian free world, with the purpose of undermining it. Yet keeping the Caucasian free world strong requires perseverance and vigilance. The spirit that soars also can sag through fatigue, the creative can begin to lose fertility, freedom can become corrupted in time, and decay can loom over that culture ever larger. It is in these circumstances that false hope readily may be planted and false remedy readily sold. Previous Caucasian civilizations have been overthrown from without by the incursion of barbarian hordes: ours (Caucasian America) has dreamed up its own dissolution in the minds of its own intellectual elites.

C1699. The Alpha tills us: Perhaps the most apt manner to describe Multiculturalism as an ideology and its deepening liberal malaise in Caucasian America would be to expose the apologists of liberalism and their untiring effort to discredit and dissolve the Caucasian racial identity and its culture.

C1700. It was Enoch Powell who said: The supreme function of statesmanship is to provide against preventable evils. In seeking to do so, it encounters obstacles which are deeply rooted in human nature. One is that by the very order of things such evils are not demonstrable until they have occurred: at each stage in their onset there is room for doubt and for dispute whether they be real or imaginary. Above all, people are disposed to mistake predicting troubles for causing troubles and even for desiring troubles. Perhaps this habit goes back to the primitive belief that the word and the thing, the name and the object, are identical? At all events, the discussion of our future is grave but, with effort now, avoidable evils are the most unpopular and at the same time the most necessary occupation for the politician. Those who knowingly shirk it deserve, and not infrequently receive, the curses of those who come after.

C1701. It was Michael W. Masters who said: a great military strategist wrote that war is nothing more than the continuation of politics by other means. Perhaps the reverse statement is also true. Politics is war by other means especially in today's multicultural America. And Caucasian American's whether they wish to fight or even realize war has been declared,...are the enemy in a low-intensity conflict that many have called the Cultural War. It is a multi-front war waged through Politics, Race, Economics, Culture, Demographics, and even Religion. Each aspect of the war is important, but of these the real killing weapon is politics.

C1702. The Alpha tells us: The 2008 presidential election will show how far we have come toward the day when non-Caucasian bloc-voting will dictate the future of our Caucasian America. Even with Caucasians at 70 percent of the population, political correctness, affirmative action, hate crime laws, cultural dispossession, and anti-Caucasian violence largely unopposed? The only possibility for Caucasian American survival is to reassemble a large coalition of middle-class and blue-collar Caucasian Americans. Whether implicitly or explicitly all Caucasian Americans must recognize the legitimacy of their "Racial Interest" in determining political loyalty.

Caucasian middle ground is eroding, an alien invasion (in the millions!) stands unopposed by a corrupt and unresponsive government? *Cultural* and *Political* polarization is happening, a very necessary polarization that will shock the Caucasian American people out of their apathy. This Polarization means choices, choices that become genuinely meaningful. We Caucasian Americans are living in socially turbulent and racially divided times. Hence, the Alpha firmly believes that "Caucasian America" is in a historical vice, where irreconcilable "Racial Differences" are once again leaving the political realm where compromise is possible, and demanding a racial bias survival resolution! (Separation!)

C1703. Caucasian America: Losing the Vote! If this happens, it will be one of the most profound changes in Caucasian political history. It raises the prospect of *Alien Races* dictating the destiny of our America, ...Caucasian America! Already, because Caucasians do not vote their own interest, alien groups use moral intimidation and the implied threat of riots to make Caucasian politicians meet their demands. But once these alien groups are a majority they can simply vote to take whatever they want – legally. The racial demographic balance on which a Caucasian democratic nation depends is transient. Unless alien immigration is halted,...Caucasian America's days are numbered!

C1704. The Alpha tells us: The Caucasian failure to treat politics as serious business will make them the losers in this Cultural and political war. Laws passed by Caucasian elected politicians (political betrayal) have created an immigration policy promising to make Caucasian Americans a minority in the country their ancestors created. It is fear of the liberal media and the political reprisals by bloc-voting alien minorities that lead Congress and the State legislatures to pass affirmative action laws, also leading judicial bodies to declare these laws constitutional. And, it would be wise to remember this,...Liberal zealot politics produced *Hate Crime* laws that criminalized *Thought* and these draconian laws are now being enforced exclusively against Caucasian Americans.

C1705. As the liberal zealots never point out, there are many different racial worlds within our theoretical one world, each differing from the other not only in physical characteristics and economic structure, but even more important perhaps in cultural traditions and racial aspirations.

C1706. One common concept of racial psychological war-fare is the great war of words in which peoples racial loyalties and conviction are manipulated on a mass scale, and to which it makes falsehood as effective as truth in influencing people's racial realities. If your faith dos not hold the survival of your race to be it highest virtue, then you faith is suicidal and has failed you.

C1707. The aim of agitation is to shake the opponent's self-confidence, to convince adversaries of the higher validity of our own arguments. The Caucasian American society can least of all afford to underrate the enormous force of alien rhetoric, the compelling power of moral propaganda, for it is to these means that hostile alien races in Caucasian America owes its great successes. No social struggle in history has ever been permanently won unless the vanquished has as a preliminary measure been morally weakened. A race of people which lacks a lively faith in its own rights is already in its political death-agony.

C1708. The Alpha tells us: As all those who write about civic matters show and as all history proves by a multitude of examples, whoever organizes a state and establishes its laws must assume that all men are wicked and will act wickedly whenever they have a chance to do so. Poverty and hunger make men industrious, and it is laws that make men good.

C1709. Representative government is not necessarily identical with democracy. It is a device for linking the government of a country with parts or all of its population. Only if it succeeds in ensuring that the government acts in fact in accordance with the wishes and needs of the people are we justified in calling its performance that of a representative democracy.

C1710. The Alpha's Lore: Civilization is a product of organic life, it is in fact a specific biological cognitive image, with all its members reaching a certain level of knowledge, by sharing in a social spirit that has lasted for ages, hence, knowing exactly what they ought to learn, think and believe (their culture) in other words,...everyone has similar convictions on the important matters of life.

C1711. The betrayal by the Caucasian liberal lift, (academic equalitarianism) and the detached aloofness of the Caucasian elites (economic political wealth) have created a pandemic of *Survival Apathy* in the Caucasian world community of an unprecedented magnitude. And if not stopped, like the fall of *Rome* the Caucasian world community will plunge into social and political chaos. Tribalism will once again take hold, and *Balkanization* will grip the Caucasian world, and Caucasians will become refugees in their own land.

C1712. The rise of religious extremism: Extremism in any religion generally seeks to eliminate perceived corruption within the religion, returning the faith to its roots, and return believers to a purer form of worship. In doing so, the extremists at times view other faiths and their practitioners as different and unacceptable.

C1713. It was John Stuart Mill who said: The only way in which a human being can make some approach to knowing the whole of a subject, is by hearing what can be said about it by persons of every variety of opinion, and studying all modes in which it can be looked at by every character of mind. No wise man ever acquired his wisdom in any mode but this.

C1714. The Alpha tells us: It is important to consider opposing viewpoints and equally important to be able to critically analyze those viewpoints. This awareness is particularly important in a democratic society such as ours where people enter into public debate to determine the common good.

C1715. The Alpha tells us: The extent to which Aliens (racial minorities) are considered in Caucasian society cannot to any great extent be given particular rights (no voting, no land ownership, and no public office) this is naturally an approach that is *Survival Selfish* on the part of the Caucasians. But in addition to being the most realistic form of racial decision-making, (racial survival) it is the only defensible one. Because what alternative do Caucasians have? Should racial aliens who are also *Survival Selfish* be allowed to inter Caucasian society and *Freely* challenge it for control of its social direction and cultural demeanor?...I think not!

C1716. The Alpha tells us: that scientific luminaries have endorsed the protection of biodiversity in North America, (a network of wilderness reserves) of course losing a great number of species would be a catastrophe by any standards. However, losing the society, culture and race of people who actually care about this catastrophe,...has never been addressed? In other words, while the figures and impact of biodiversity extinction are debatable, the more pervasive impact, that of alien social and moral depravity and its relation to Caucasian national survival is not? This attitude by the scientific community is of course, problematic, and the Alpha seriously argues that any skeptic should himself or herself go to the alien inner-city jungles of America, to see this evidence,...but in reality of course, they will not!

C1717. The Alpha tells us: The first thing, surely, is to figure out a formula for racial separation into new states, and the recognizing of a new *African* state, and a new *Asian* state. The arguments against doing so,...are perfectly honorable, but they are serving to subsidize a social and racial situation that grows progressively intolerable. The Caucasian American people cannot continue to live with themselves over a protracted period when they find that every day, more and more Caucasian Americans are being killed in order to document a liberal political right to prevail over millions of unassimilated radical aliens, who are not prepared culturally, politically and racially to yield a single inch.

C1718. It was Joseph E. Fallon who said: The deconstruction of Caucasian America is not an act of God or ordained by any law of history. It is the result of policies deliberately implemented by the federal government over the last 43 years in blatant disregard of the expressed wishes of the Caucasian American majority. It is a process, therefore, that not only can be stopped; it can be completely reversed. All that is necessary is for Caucasians Americans, in the words of *Samuel Francis*, to have the strength and the will and the Caucasian common purpose to take back their country and their culture.

C1719. The Alpha tells us: Life is no fairer for Caucasians than for anyone else. The Alpha has a strong sense of how lucky we as Caucasians are, it is like *America,* you only discover it once. For Caucasians many specialties, Astronomy, Biology, Chemistry, Geology, Physics, and Mathematics, and their fundamentals had been found decades or centuries earlier. In philosophy, some of the fundamental truths had been discovered not decades, not even centuries, but millennia earlier. The age in which we Caucasians live, is an age in which we are discovering the fundamentals of *Racial Enlightenment,* (Caucasianism) and this age will never come again, it will be the final golden age of Caucasian intellectual pursuit.

C1720. Let it be understood: One may acknowledge the erudition of a Jared Taylor or Samuel Francis, admire their attempt to make a coherent whole from a breath of racial knowledge that very few individuals have ever possessed, and none the less, with the advantage of a deeper life insight, see ways in which they got things wrong. Hence, not of the truths of their declarations, which have so enriched the lives of the rest of us, but of the social strategy for its outcome?

C1721. The Alpha tells us: It is time to render unto- *Race*, that which is appropriate to- *Race*, and unto- *Equality*, that which is appropriate to- *Equality*. To understand that each race of people are unique, that each race of people must be treated as an end and not a means, that each race of people should be free to live their life as they see fit, so long as they accord other race's the same freedom. These are among the greatest of all human racial accomplishments. But equality has nothing to do with the abilities, persistence, zeal, and visions that create a race of people. To those who disagree, the Alpha asks only this: You have been presented with a case, here and in the extensive literature that informed it. (The Valorous) A reply requires more than another liberal zealot assertion of unjust privilege over others. For a race of people have attributes that can be identified, evaluated, and compared across works. When the ratings of eminence are scrutinized against the reasons for that eminence, it also becomes apparent that those who rank highest are those who have achieved at the highest levels. In other words, *Equality* and *Race* inhabit different domains!

C1722. The Alpha tells us: In the Caucasian nations and cultures where the spark of creativity has been lit, their Cities attracted racial capital, and became the cradles of significant Caucasian figures. Large groups- with equal abundant needs, hence, Caucasian cultural acceleration. This process tended to select for Talent, Ambition, Industriousness, Creativity, and Vitality. Caucasian Cities have a great amount of *Caucasian Racial Capital* and *Cultural Education,* and their children benefit and reflect that racial capital and education.

C1723. Let it be understood: The form of governance does have an important relationship with accomplishment. The Alpha tells us that *Liberal Egalitarianism* (equal racial out- comes) has effectively suppressed Caucasian accomplishment in the social sciences, and historical philosophy. In other words,...the suppression of Caucasian American freedom of thought, action, and dissent, *Liberal Despotism* (political correctness) has now taken hold in the *21st* century. Social decay in the magnitude of the liberal effect is apparent, and that America will lose its greatness under these liberal autocrats is no mystery.

C1724. Blessed are the Caucasians: Who are engaged in Caucasianism and see the truth of *Fematrix Actualization* in their own lives, and invite all Caucasians to test her assertion against their own experience, and exercise their realized religious capacity, in the truest sense of their faith.

C1725. The Alpha tells us: Those with the capacity for excellence do not need to be cajoled into wanting to realize it. The pursuit of excellence is as natural as the pursuit of happiness. Hence, this echo of an ancient Greek poet, who wrote that before that gates of excellence the high gods have placed sweat.

C1726. The Alpha tells us: An artist's conception of the purpose of a human life and the measure of excellence in a human life provides a frame within which the varieties of the human experience are translated into art. Hence, the translation of moral vision onto the canvas or into the written word is often what separates enduring art from mere entertainment.

C1727. The Alpha tells us: When deciding the future of Caucasian America, the two most important factors seem to be to what extent will alien emigration increase faster or slower, and to what extent will Caucasian America, culturally, economically, and politically acquiesce? Again, the relative price of racial indifference seems to be the decisive factor. Thus, what we as Caucasians need to know is which world is the more likely? And what we should do, if we want to steer more towards a *Caucasian*

Democratic Monarchy. Although this is the single most important problem for Caucasian America's future social scenario, this issue must be addressed, because of the liberal zealots despicable social intention of dismantling Caucasian America!

C1728. The Alpha tells us: like the *Athenians* of our passed historical age, when negotiating with aliens, we Caucasians should say what we really think, and aim only at what is possible, for we both alike know that into the discussion of racial affairs the question of justice only enters where the pressure of necessity is equal, and that the powerful exact what they can, and the weak grant what they must. Similarly in these celebrated words of man we know that by a law of their nature wherever they can rule they will. This law was not made by us, and we are not the first who have acted upon it; we did but inherit it, and shall bequeath it to all time, and we Caucasians know that all aliens, if as strong as we are, would do as we do.

C1729. The Alpha tells us: We must realize there are two sides to the Caucasian character and culture: there is the side of moderation, art, law, and social harmony, and there is the side of excess, unbridled self-assertion, wealth, power, indulgence and pessimism. Also there can be seen in much of the Caucasian society self-imposed checks (social common laws) whereby among their splendid achievements *Social Democracy* would become the ultimate social consciousness of humankind.

C1730. The Alpha tells us: In spite of the aggressive side of the Caucasians, their perception of the constant process of change, of transition from life to death and from death to life, helped to lead them to a beginning of *Philosophy;* for these Caucasian wise man saw that, in spite of all the change and transition, there must be something *Permanent.* Why?...because the change is from something into something else. There must be something which is *Primary* which persist, which takes various forms and undergoes this process of change. At this time the Alpha tills us, they did not conceive a clear connection between the *Fematrix* (woman) and life, and then deny it; they were not fully conscious of the *Fematrix* distinction, at least they did not realize her implications. They thought of woman as mere innocent babblings, unworthy of serious attention.

C1731. Let it be understood: The first beginnings of Caucasianism and its *Fematrix Theology* will not be a matter of indifference to the world community of historians. In order to arrive at the conception of the ultimate element of all life *Womanhood* (the Fematrix) it is necessary to go beyond appearance and the male egotistic sense, it is necessary to navigate ontological reasoning. The complexity of the *Fematrix* insight cannot be grasped until the distinction between life and death has been clearly apprehended. Justice can be done to the complexity of the *Fematrix* (the female being) of the *One* in the many.(unity in difference) Only if the essential degrees of reality and the doctrine of the analogy of *Being* are clearly understood and unambiguously maintained.

C1732. Blessed are the Caucasians: who understand that *Sensation* is the very starting-point of knowledge.

C1733. Blessed are the Caucasians: who by their faith in Caucasianism have been given the understanding of the *One* in the many, and the many by the *One*. She is the marrow of all!

C1734. The Alpha tells us: What are we to say of the doctrine of the Valorous and its notion of Caucasian racial unity? That there is a biological many, a species plurality, is clear enough. But, does not these species seek unity through and by *Identity*. And is not a race of people a unity in distinction of related persons? And if they can be identified, is not then difference the intention, this is also clear enough. Hence, the only unity that is worth having is a unity in difference, identity in diversity, a unity, that is to say, not of identity poverty, but of identity richness.

C1735. Let it be understood: That the Alpha suffered a disappointment through liberalism, and perplexed by the disagreement of the various liberal social theories, he received a sudden light from the solitude of his cell, where the Fematrix *Caucasia-* spoke to him of his beginnings, his race, and their destiny as being the cause of all enlightenment, both just and unjust. Delighted with this understanding, he began to study Caucasian social, biological, and world history in the hope that it would explain how *Race* (kind) works in the biological universe. What he actually found was a real rapture in the mystic-religious sense, an ecstasy of truth in *Race* which had been lost to human comprehension, and, he would discover the canon of life,...the *Fematrix*. and enlist the aid of any man or woman who would consent to listen to him, and forever embrace their conversion.

C1736. The Alpha tells us: Individual races vary in their gifts, some are possessed of great intellectual gifts, others not. Some races guide their lives according to reason: others surrender without thought to instinct and passing impulse. Hence, some liberal thinkers have maintained that the racial concept is purely subjective. But, the Alpha says it is very difficult to see how we could form such racial notions, and why we should be compelled to form them, unless there was a foundation for them in fact. Let it suffice at present to point out that the racial concept or definition presents us with something constant and abiding that stands out, through its possession of biological characteristics, from a world of racial particulars. And, even if all races were blotted out of existence, the definition of race as a *Rational Biological Term* would remain constant.

C1737. The Alpha tells us: racial truth, of course, prove somewhat irritating or even disconcerting or humiliating to those whose racial ignorance was exposed and whose ego was broken down, but the aim of the Alpha was not to humiliate or to disconcert. No, he wanted to induce others to reflect for themselves and to give real thought to the supremely important work of caring for their race, and to express his in- tention of getting others to produce true racial ideas in their minds, with a view to right action. He is not being pedantic; he is convinced that a clear knowledge of racial truth is essential for the right outlook in any Caucasians life. Hence, the Alpha believes that true racial knowledge is sought as a means to ethical racial action.

C1738. The Alpha tells us: It is moral weakness, which leads a man or woman to have racial hatred or malice, and to do and feel what they know to be wrong. If a man or woman constantly entertains the notion of racial hatred, believing this to be their true good, than they error from ignorance, not realizing what their true good is. This is undoubtedly true; from the identification of *Wisdom* and *Race,* follows the unity of race-*Racial Virtue.* There is in-Caucasianism the laws of racial virtue, and of which hatred and malice towards another race of people is prohibited, and not seen as conducive to ultimate happiness and dignity as a virtues Caucasian.

C1739. It was Socrates who once said: The object of true knowledge must be stable and abiding, fixed, capable of being grasped in clear and scientific definition, and in connection with ethical valuation, aims at the definition, a clear and unambiguous definition. Is not each one of us, the measure of our own wisdom!

C1740. The Alpha tells us: It is hard for many to find the maker and mother of the universe, and having found her, it is impossible to speak of her to all. The *Fematrix* (the One) is thus the Alpha's ultimate principle and the source of the world of forms. In Caucasianism it is definitely asserted that its religious approach is dialectical and that a Caucasian attains the vision of the *Fematrix* (the One) by pure intelligence. Hence, by dialectic Caucasianism the highest principle of the soul is raised to the contemplation of that which is best in existence.

C1741. The Alpha tells us: There are none so worthless whom love cannot impel, as it were by a divine inspiration, towards *Caucasian Racial Virtue*. The *Fematrix* is depicted as forming her biological world to her Ideal or exemplary racial patterns, and as endeavoring to make it as much like the Ideal as the refractory matter at her disposal will permit. It is for the Caucasian person to apprehend their *Racial Ideal* and to endeavor to model their own life and that of their children according to that Pattern.

C1742. The Alpha tells us: Human life is not lived out atomistically apart from society or the state, nor from nature; and so we can arrive at the apprehension of an all-embracing living Ideal, to which all particular Ideals are subordinate. This universal Ideal is the *Fematrix* (female will) and can only be apprehended by means of dialectic, (Acumen) but in human kind, there is an attraction towards the mystical, (obscure) and if they take the mystical as their true good, then the impulse of attraction is directed towards these inferior goods. Moreover, reality itself is not without mind and life and soul, and even the transcendent One (the Fematrix) is not without the *Many*! Hence, For the Alpha, the *Fematrix* (the One) is transcendent, so that the becoming (life strategies) are not denied but are fully admitted in the created world.

C1743. The Alpha tells us: that all living things have a *Soul* (purpose) a mental, physical, and spiritual declaration of existence and intention, of having a unique membership (race or species) in the quest for life. In Caucasianism, the *Soul* is the correlation of *Fematrix Diversity* of the one in the many, and of the many by the one.(the Sisterhood) It is the nucleus that holds the Recipe (DNA) of a Race or Species.

C1744. The Alpha tells us: Soul is its own enterprise, with reason, value, objective and end. It is the singularity and contrary to the void, it is the – *Need!*

C1745. It was Plato who said: The man who is acquainted only with the exact and perfect thing in life, and has no knowledge at all of the rough approximations to them which we meet with in daily life, would not even know how to find his way home. So second-class knowledge, and not only the first-class variety, must be admitted into the mixture: it will do a Caucasian no harm, provided that he or she recognizes the second-class objects for what they are, and does not mistake the rough approximations for the exact truth. Hence, the deciding vote in this question, how much pleasure to admit,...rest with knowledge.

C1746. Let it be understood: That in Caucasianism the *Fematrix* is the measure of all things. And, happiness must be attained by the pursuit of *Racial Virtue* and to become righteous with the help of racial wisdom. Wherefore, the temperate Caucasian is the friend of his or her race, for they are a part of it, and to offer prayer to your Caucasian Fematrix *Caucasia* is the noblest and best of all things, and also the most conducive to a happy life.

C1747. The Alpha tells us: Worship and racial virtue belong to happiness, so that although the pursuit of racial virtue and the leading of a racially virtuous life is the means of attaining happiness, racial virtue itself is not external to happiness, but is integral to it. Caucasian good is a condition of *Soul* primarily, and it is only the truly racially virtuous Caucasian who is a truly good Caucasian, and a truly happy Caucasian.

C1748. Let it be known: to pursue what is truly good and beneficial is wise, while to pursue what is harmful is foolish. Hence temperance and wisdom cannot be entirely disparate.

C1749. The Alpha tells us: let the good temperate people in all the races of humankind, find common ground (a peaceful coexistence) in their separate journeys.

C1750. Let it be understood: To the idea that *Racial Virtue* is knowledge and that *Racial Virtue* is teachable,...the Alpha seems to have clung, as also to the idea that no one does knowingly and willingly disregard the truth, unless it is unknown, or wish it to be unknown. It is not the liberal, content with popular notions of virtue, who can teach *Racial Virtue*, but only he or she who has exact knowledge of *Racial Enlightenment* and are of the *Racial Spirit* (the racial philosopher)

C1751. The Alpha tells us: that there are distinct *Human Races,* distinguished according to their inherited biology and the culture of their *Soul* (purpose) of which they are the descendant result. Hence, these distinct races are unified of themselves with the knowledge of generations of what is truly good for them, and of the means, will, and mind set to attain that good.

C1752. The Alpha tells us: When the liberal zealot chooses that which is *de facto* evil, (Caucasian racial elimination) he or she chooses it as- *utopist,* they desire something which they imagine to be good, but which is, as a matter of fact *Evil.* It might well seem that such a social doctrine, inherited from the notion of *Equality* would allow a judgment to be so obscured by passion, that the apparent evil, appears to them as a true good. Hence, they are responsible for having allowed passion so to darken their reasoning. Furthermore, they must ultimately answer to the outcome and consequences of that reasoning, and its effects on the Caucasian world community.

C1753. Let it be understood: That the Alpha set out to give an account of *Caucasian Generation* in the world. The Caucasian world is becoming, and that which becomes must necessarily become through the agency of some cause. The agent in question is the divine *Fematrix.* She took over all that was in discordant and unordered motion, and brought it into order, forming the material world according to an eternal and biological ideal pattern, and fashioning herself into a living creature with soul and reason, after the model of the ideal living creature, (the female being) the form that contains within itself the forms of all living things, humankind, the winged creatures, all that dwells in the great oceans, and all that walks the dry earth. As there is but *One* ideal living creature,...the *Fematrix* made but one world.

C1754. In Caucasianism: Metaphysics is concerned with being as such, it is the study of being a kind, *qua* being. It is a particular sphere of being, (human) and considers the attributes and categories of being human (racial kind) in that sphere. Now, to say that something is, is also to say that it is one: unity therefore, is an essential attribute of being, and just as being itself is found in all biological categories, so unity of racial being (racial attributes- DNA) is found in, and establishes all human categories. Unity and kind are, therefore, transcendental attributes of being.

C1755. The Alpha's Lore: *Knowledge* and *Judgment* are the true horns of survival, and are not deductible; they are the ultimate principle governing all biological being.

C1756. The Alpha tells us: that the difference between Caucasianism and all other religions, is that in other religions having failed to find or recognize a physical (living) God, they have created mystical Gods or cryptic beings,... as to that of Caucasianism which only recognizes an original solitary *Biological Soul,* a physical living life force, the *Fematrix Deity.*

C1757. Fematrix Vitalism: the doctrine of Caucasianism that life in all biology (all living things) is caused and sustained by a vital single *Female* living force that is distinct from all physical and chemical forces, and that this female life force is, self-determining and self-evolving,... she is the 5_{th} element,...the life force.

C1758. The Alpha's Lore: The form of a race of people, is the form of the race in germ, it has an innate and natural tendency towards its own full evolution.

C1759. Ethics: The Alpha tells us that it was *Aristotle* who said: human action is the subject-matter of ethics. In other words, in ethics we start from the actual moral judgments of humankind, and by comparing, contrasting and sifting them, we come to the formulation of general principles. This view presupposes that there are *Natural Tendencies* implanted in humankind, the following of which in a general attitude of consistent harmony and proportion, recognizing relative importance and unimportance, is the ethical life of humankind. Hence, this being the basis for natural as opposed to arbitrary ethics.

C1760. The Alpha tells us: That in Caucasianism all life has *Universal Characteristics* with the necessity of *Constant Valuation,* leading to the life strategy or a life plan laid down by reason by virtue of the intellect.

C1761. Let it be understood: A person may have so blinded their conscience that they fail to discern that which is right, but they are themselves responsible for their blindness and for bringing about their ignorance. Hence, virtuous activity is voluntary and in accordance with choice, it follows that virtue and vice are in our power.

C1762. The Alpha tells us: The contemplation of *Fematrix Theology* belongs to the ideal life of all Caucasians. Furthermore, he says that wisdom or philosophy may be defined as the combination of intuitive reason and science, or as scientific knowledge of the most precious things, with the crown of perfection, so to speak, upon it. Knowledge is dignified by it object!

C1763. The Alpha tells us: The Caucasians are more self-sufficient than any other people, they can dispense with the necessaries of life much more than others can, the co-operation of other peoples (other races) is a great assistance to them, but if it be wanting, the Caucasians are better able than other races to get along without it.

C1764. The Alpha's Lore: Caucasianism is racial love for its own sake, and not for the sake of any political or economic results that accrue from it. It is in the exercise of Caucasianism, then, and in the exercise of that religious reason concerning the noblest object (their racial love) that the Caucasian people's complete happiness is found. Such a life expresses the divine element (our Fematrix- *Caucasia*) in all of Caucasian society.

C1765. The Alpha tells us: It was Plato who said, many a victory has been and will be suicidal to the victors, but education is never suicidal.

C1766. The Alpha tells us: The happiness of the Caucasian race, secured in peace and goodwill, is best.

C1767. The Alpha tells us: When Caucasians reflect on life, on Caucasian good, and on the good life, they clearly cannot pass by racial social relations. A Caucasian is born into a society, not only into that of the family but also into a wider racial association, and it is in that racial association that they must identify and live the good life, attaining their end.

C1768. All Caucasian thinkers who concern themselves with the humanistic viewpoint, humankinds place and destiny, must form for themselves some theory of human Racial relations, it may be well that no theory of their own Caucasian Race will result, unless a somewhat advanced Racial consciousness has gone before.(Caucasianism) To the Racially conscious Caucasian on the other hand, the *Race* appears as a body in which he or she has a part, as an extension in some sort of themselves, and so will be stimulated - the reflective racial thinker, that is to say, to form a union in *Race*.

C1769. The Alpha's Lore: When dealing with alien races, a Caucasian should tend to them carefully, not only out of regard to them, but yet more out of respect to ourselves.

C1770. The Alpha tells us: As there is but one ideal living being, the *Fematrix,* she made but one world,...Earth. She is the *Good,* and desires that all things should come as near as possible to being like her, judging that order is better than disorder and fashioning everything for the best, making it as excellent and perfect as possible.

C1771. The Alpha tells us: How are we as Caucasians to regard the figure of the *Fematrix*? She must at least represent the *Divine Reason* which is operative in the world; but she is not a mystical-God. It is clear that the *Fematrix* took over a pre-existing material and did her best with it: she is certainly not said to have created it out of nothing. The generations of humankind, are the mixed result of the combination of her Necessity and Reason. She is the *Soul* of the world.

C1772. The *Fematrix,* having constructed the *Biological Universe* sought to make it still less like her pattern, and more to the free characters of her daughters. Hence, she took thought to make certain that this free character (free will) was possible to confer completely on her generated daughters, thereby creating the *Living Forms* (strategic evolution)

C1773. The Alpha tells us: Because of the *Fematrix* the world has thus become a visible living thing, an image of the intelligible, a perceptible *Goddess* (female will) supreme in greatness and excellence, in her diversity of beauty and perfection, the *Fematrix,* one and multiple in her kind.

C1774. The Alpha tells us: In order that *Being* may exist, *Substance* (basic matter) something that has independent existence and is acted upon by causes, must exist: that is, as it were, the starting-point.

C1775. The Alpha tells us: Scientific knowledge- *Par-excellence* means deducing the particular from the general or conditional from its cause, so that we know both the cause on which that fact depends and the necessary connection between the fact and its cause. In other words, we have scientific knowledge when we know the cause on which the fact depends, as the cause of that fact and of no other, and further, that the fact could not be other than it is.

C1776. The Alpha tells us: The *Fematrix* is the development of a previously existing body, not precisely as that definite body, but as a body capable of becoming something else, though as not yet that something else. She is the actualization of a potentiality; but a potentiality involves an actual being, which is not yet that which she could be. The *Fematrix,* for example, does not come from nothing, she comes from matter. But she does not come from matter precisely as matter: matter precisely as matter is matter and nothing else. She comes from matter, which could be life and demands to be life, having been heated, pressured and authored. There are, then, three, and not merely two, factors in the *Fematrix,* since the being of the *Fematrix* contains two elements - *Matter* and *Form*- she also presupposes a third element - *Cognitive Corporeality.*

C1777. The Alpha tells us: The *Fematrix,* being the source of all living things, as the final cause, is the ultimate cause why potentiality is actualized, why goodness in life- is realized.

C1778. The Alpha tells us: Each one of the three races of humankind has a natural movement towards it own proper place in the universe, and the races will move in accord with their natural social direction unless they are hindered. It belongs to the form of the races to tend towards their own individual natural region, and thus their formal and efficient causes coincide. In other words, the form of the race is the form of the race in germ, and, that a race (biological idea) has an innate and natural tendency towards its own full evolution.

C1779. The Alpha tells us: Happiness is to possess the satisfaction of the *Need.*

C1780. The Alpha tells us: Race's themselves are biological dispositions which have been developed out of a capacity by the proper exercise of that capacity.

C1781. It was Aristotle who said: It is better to know the conclusion of the practical syllogism, without the major premise, than to know the major premise without knowing the conclusion.

C1782. The Alpha tells us: A child may be told by its parents not to lie. It obeys without realizing perhaps the inherent goodness of telling the truth, and without having yet formed a habit of telling the truth; but the acts of truth-telling gradually form the habit, and as the process of education goes on, the child come to realize that truth-telling is right in itself, and to choose to tell the truth for it own sake, as being the right thing to do. Hence, the distinction between the acts which create the good disposition and the acts which flow from the good disposition once it has been created.

C1783. The Alpha tells us: We as Caucasians in our relation to our *Race*, is the same as our relation to ourselves, since our *Race* is a second self. In other words, the self is capable of extension and grows to include the *Race*, whose happiness or misery, success or failure, becomes our own.

C1784. The Alpha tells us: that the origin of *Race* is to be sought in the natural instinct of biological expression. In its metaphysical aspect or its essence, *Race* is identity in unification of purpose.(the biological accord) It is the work of imaginative creation, (imaginative biological symbolism,) and it is precisely because of this fact that it asserts its truth in identity. Humankind's emotions are varied, some being profitable, others harmful. Biological Reasoning, therefore, must decide what a *Race* is to be and what it is not to be. (a Fematrix life strategy-through identity) And the fact that the Alpha definitely admits to different forms of Races in biology shows that race occupies a particular sphere of human activity, which is not irreducible to anything else.

C1785. The Alpha recognizes that the *Liberal Zealot* view of the Caucasian race and its society is a view of non- existence. But, it is a view with which the Alpha will not agree, and holds in contempt. The racially enlightened example of the Alpha is an influence by itself. His life is one of utter devotion to his race, to the attainment of abiding eternal and absolute racial truth, to which he firmly and constantly be- lieves, being ready to follow, wherever racial reason might lead. This spirit he endeavored to stamp upon the Caucasian social will, creating a body of Caucasians who, under the ascendancy of his teachings, would devote themselves to the attainment of racial truth and goodness.

C1786. Devoted to the attainment of racial truth in the intellectual sphere, the Alpha, as we Caucasians have seen is no mere theorist. Possessed of an intense racial earnestness and convinced of the reality of absolute racial values and standards, he urges Caucasians to take thought for their dearest possession, their immortal racial soul, and to strive after the cultivation of true racial virtue, which alone would make them happy.

C1787. In regard to modern times, the influence of the Alpha may not be at first sight so obvious as it is in the Caucasian racial fraternity, and in the intellectual enlightenment of Caucasianism; but in reality he is the teacher and father of all Caucasian spiritual philosophy and of all objective racial idealism, and his epistemology, metaphysics and politico-ethics will have exercised a profound influence on succeeding Caucasian racial thinkers, either positively or negatively.

C1788. The Alpha tells us: He admires a *Democratic Racial Monarchy,* with a Constitution, having the contention that the middle-class is the most stable, since both rich and poor are more likely to trust the middle-class,... than one another! (so that the middle-class need fear no coalition against it) He points out, that the revolutionary state of mind is largely brought about by one-sided notions of justice, and the fact that rulers should have no opportunity of making money for themselves out of the offices they hold, and stresses the requisites for high office, namely, Loyalty to a Caucasian Democratic Imperial Constitution.

C1789. The Alpha tells us: All information is good, even when it's bad!

C1790. It should not be supposed that the Alpha, in his enthusiasm for racial clarity and his desire to set a firm empirical and scientific racial foundation, was lacking in systematic power or his metaphysical interest. The Alpha's racial logic can be termed as formal logic inasmuch as his racial logic is an analysis of the forms of biology both physical and mental, and that of their common foundation-*Female Absolutism.* (hence the term *Analytic*) He is chiefly concerned with the forms of proof, and he assumes that the conclusion of a scientific proof gives certain knowledge concerning reality. Hence, the Alpha says,...it is not merely that the conclusion is deduced correctly according to the formal laws of logic, but it most also have that conclusion verified in reality. He presupposes, therefore, a racial realist epistemology, and that the categories of *Race* should become the objective categories of social reality.(as defined by fematrix biological reality)

C1791. The Alpha tells us: those racial categories are not in his mind simply modes of mental representation, or molds of concepts: races represent the actual modes of being in the physical and extra mental world, and form the bridge between Logic and Metaphysics. Having therefore, an ontological as well as a logical aspect, and it is perhaps in the race's ontological aspect that their orderly and structural arrangement appears most clearly. Thus, in order that race may exist, thought stimulated by need must exist: that is as it were, the starting-point.

C1792. The Alpha tells us: for a race to exist independently it must be an idea of substance. But it cannot exist merely as a idea of substance, it most also have *Form*. For instance, a race cannot exist unless it has *Self* and it cannot have self, unless it has *Cognizance* hence *Identity* the first three Categories of biological life- *Self Cognizance Identity* which are intrinsic determinations of any given race,...or life form. Moreover, all races and their deferent physical substances, will exist in a certain place and at a certain period, and have a certain physical posture belonging to the greater cosmic system, there by independently acting, and being acted upon.

C1793. The Alpha tells us: that in thinking of our race, in which we think of being as realized, we should think of it as an independent biological determination, a *Summa Genera* (the Caucasians)

C1794. The Alpha tells us: that race follows *Need,* and is built up as an expression of need, and this is especially true, when one considers that race is form, and form is the subject of need!

C1795. The Alpha tells us: that our racial sense as such never errs: it is only our racial judgment which is true or false. In other words our racial knowledge starts from sense, from a biological particular, (Caucasians identity) and ascends to the biological general or universal (other biological life) Thus it is clear that all Caucasians must get to know their primary racial premise by induction; for the method by which even our sense-perception implants the universal is inductive.

C1796. The Alpha tells us: Racial wisdom, deals with the first principles and causes of biology, and so is racial knowledge in the highest degree. Hence, the first cause of the becoming in the world.

C1797. The Alpha assumes the validity of ethical racial judgment; he has attempted to teach a clear apprehension of ethical racial values dialectically, to enshrine its nature in definition, to crystallize the ethical racial idea in all of humankind. The Alpha's racial viewpoint cannot be said to constitute a radical view, inasmuch as his view of racial values itself rests to a certain extent on a logical biological foundation (race most have a common objective reference) and has concluded, therefore, that racial values are moral and ideal, and are apprehended intuitively.

C1798. In Caucasianism there is a hierarchic female poetic structure (the Caucasian sisterhood or Prelacy) called the *Racial Communion* it is the division between Being a Caucasian on the one hand, (by birth) and Becoming a Caucasian on the other.(Caucasian racial spirituality) Their spiritual mission is to regard the essence of the Caucasian race as a moral ideal and that the true meaning of *Becoming* is to be sought in the gradual approximation to and realization of the racial ideal.

C1799. The Alpha tells us: that the *Fematrix* is the intelligible principle in her race, she realizes herself in the activity of her race. Her entelechy, expresses itself in organic function, unfolds itself in matter, organizes, molds and shapes itself towards her full and chosen actualization, a dynamical process of self-perfection and self-development bringing a meaning and reality to the sensible world.

C1800. The Alpha tells us: the wise person will not multiply their needs, since that is to multiply sources of physical or mental distress; he or she should rather reduce their needs to a minimum, leading to a moderate asceticism, self-control and independence.

C1801. The Alpha tells us: Every pleasure is good on account of its own nature, but it does not follow that every pleasure is worthy of being chosen; just as every pain is distressing, and yet every pain must not be avoided.

C1802. The Alpha tells us: that it was *Lucretius,* (an Epicurean disciple) who said, the bodies of our experience are composed of pre-existing material entities-atoms–and their perishing is but a resolution into the entities of which they are composed. Hence, the ultimate constituents of the universe are therefore atoms and the Void. But, even in the truth of his reality,(a student of physics and Ethics) Lucretius, like so many other great thinkers, was a victim of what the Alpha like to call the *Human Intellectual Enigma,*...God!

C1803. The Alpha tells us: that human understanding and their opinions of– God are of the nature of guesses, unsubstantiated by exact observation. To clarify; the Alpha puts to us his reason, it is to be noted that in human existence *God* has two positions, one of the *Visible,* (living) and the other of the *Invisible* (mystical) and it is the *Mystical Gods* that dominate the human experience. So how in God, does error arise?...only though judgment! Hence its logic,...mystical gods are Unassailable, where living gods, would be Accountable? Think of those who represent *God* in human societies, than tell me the *Gods* they have chosen to represent? (market- Gods!) If you can choose amongst Gods?... then you're choice has failed you!

C1804. The Alpha tells us: *Dialectic Truth* is the only and true path to *God*. And, there can be no higher certainty, than the existence of the Creator. (our Fematrix)

C1805. The Alpha tells us: the first criterion of the Caucasian people is their *Devine Perception* their Fematrix-*Caucasia* their living Creator. By her, and through her, (the birth) all things are possible, and no opinion or judgment, truth or falsity arises,...for she is the breath, the reference and the reason of all existence.

C1806. The Alpha tells us: One of the reasons for objecting to the liberal social agenda, is that its not substantiated by a common sense-knowledge, since in the real world their *Equality Doctrine* is nowhere to be found. Now, common sense-knowledge is the fundamental basis of all knowledge. So, if you deny common sense, (racial fundamentalism) you are lift with no standard to which to refer and thus no means of judging even those ideas which you pronounce false. Reason, by which we judge of sense data, is itself wholly founded on common sense, and if common sense is not to be found, then all reason as will,...most be rendered lost.

C1807. The Alpha tells us: the only real guarantee of the stability and prosperity of the Caucasian state is the moral goodness and racial integrity of the Caucasian citizens, while conversely unless the Caucasian state is good and the system of its education is racially rational, moral and healthy, the Caucasian citizens will not become enlightened. The Caucasian individual attains his or her proper development and perfection through their racial life, which is a racial life in the society of the Caucasian state, while the Caucasian society attains its proper end through the perfection of its racially (biologically) related members.

C1808. The Alpha tells us: in the course of his life, he has come to apply his racial dialectic, not only to moral and aesthetic values, but to the common concept of life in general (bio-cosmic) maintaining that, just as *Perception* is a mechanism of cognizance,...*Racial kind* is a mechanism of biology and both are in accordance with, and are the doctrines of all life. His new biological viewpoint of *Female absolutism* cannot be said to constitute a radical break in biological thought, inasmuch as the mitochondrial beginnings of life rests to a certain extent on a logical foundation (that life must have an objective reference) and is an extension of *Fematrix Theology* thereby forcing others to consider more closely, not only the relation between life and the Fematrix, but also between sensible conclusions and life's ideas and her exemplary essence.

C1809. The Alpha tells us: The universal being (the Fematrix) is forever changing, so being is forever changing. How could it be otherwise, for her to whom logic and religion are one, and whose thought is concerned with the well-being of her race, and the realities of its social perils.

C1810. The Alpha tells us: That Caucasianism will become more and more a part of the regular course of Caucasian education (presented in an easily apprehended form) laying claim to the allegiance of the Caucasian world community. Indeed one may say that Caucasianism, to a certain extent at least, offers to satisfy the religious needs and aspirations of all Caucasians. And so it is that we Caucasians can come to discern Caucasianism and its social elements as a predominantly ethical religious and political system. More than this, we as Caucasians may say that in Caucasianism, in which our religious racial spirit or ecstasy is made the final and highest point of intellectual activity, one's social philosophy tends to pass over into reality!

C1811. The Alpha tells us: A Caucasian is free to change his or her inner attitude and to adopt one of submission and resignation rather than rebellion. Hence, freedom is an actuality of which we are all conscious.

C1812. The Alpha's Virtues: A concession to practice, and consist in conformity to racial enlightenment, Racial Love, Racial Insight, Racial Courage, Racial Temperance, and Racial Justice. These racial virtues stand or fall together, in the sense that he or she, who possesses one, possesses all. Moreover, the Alpha has devoted his attention to encouraging all Caucasians to begin and continue in the path of racial virtue with its passions and affections of self-conquest.

C1813. The Alpha tells us: That all humankind have a claim to our goodwill, even nonbelievers have their rights and even Aliens having a right to our mercy and forgiveness. But, this ethical basis for Caucasianism is found in the fundamental instinct of self-preservation or racial-love (racial fundamentalism) In the first place, of course, this instinctive tendency to self-preservation shows itself in the form of racial- love,... the individual's racial- love. But it extends beyond racial- love in the narrow sense to embrace all that belongs to the individual, family, friends, fellow-Caucasians, and yes- the whole of humanity. It is naturally stronger in regard to what stands biologically closer to the individual, and grows weaker in proportion as the biology is more remote. In other words, the ethical ideal (Caucasianism) is attained when we as Caucasians love our race as we love ourselves or when our racial-love embraces all that is connected with the self, including humanity at large, with an equal intensity, the ideal of Caucasian fellowship.

C1814. The Alpha tells us: that modern *Liberal Zealotry* is certainly not a socially heroic creed or philosophy that the common Caucasian citizen would won't to entertain. Its attraction for certain types of social radicals is easily understandable, as to their less then wise cultivation of a philosophy based on social equality. (equal outcomes, or cooking the social books) Nevertheless it remains true that the social theory of the liberal zealots (mystical utopian equality) is intellectually egotistic and elitist in character, a fact that comes out clearly in their teachings.

C1815. The Alpha maintains his supreme doctrine of *Fematrix Devine Providence,* and that her Providence is manifested in her *Gift* of reason to man.(unbridled cognizance) and he would show in *Fematrix Theology* that everything is created for the good of the female, but, he also tells us: it must always be remembered that, even if our human reason is unable to answer fully and with complete satisfaction all the difficulties that can be raised against a position, that does not compel us to abandon that position, if it rests on *Valid Argument.* Even if we can never attain certainty by the accumulation of reasons for accepting some position, *Probability* has various grades and is both necessary and sufficient for action and understanding.

C1816. The only true theology in the Alpha's opinion is that which recognizes only one living force *Female Absolutism.* (the Fematrix) Who is the Soul of the world, which she governs according to her reason.(life strategy) Hence, the mystical theology of the poets is to be rejected on the ground that it attributes unworthy characteristics and actions to the market-gods, while the social theologies and dogma of the liberal zealots contradict one another, having been impelled to this course, by their contact with alien races, and greatly influenced by racial alien social deviation and mental apathy.

C1817. The Alpha tells us: Having little sympathy with the liberal zealots and their social theology that cast overboard the basis of human determinism (competitive evolution or unequal outcomes) for a mystical and absurd intellectual doctrine of racial equality,...has created an onslaught of social and political *Puritanism* (communism revisited!) were by the rejection of truth and the jettisoned doctrines of freedom are about to become an unassailable political staple. Hence, let it be said to all Caucasian Americans, as well as their sister states throughout the world,...you have been Warned!

C1818. The Alpha tells us: That Caucasianism will become the greatest of personal disciplines, and the wealth of religion bound together with the empirical knowledge of the Caucasian word– the Valorous infused in the Caucasian community bringing unity and warmth of social ideal.

C1819. The Alpha tells us: *Fematrix Monism* is fundamental to the great enlightenment of Caucasianism, the world is permeated by a vital force. (the Fematrix) She is the symphony that prevails between all parts of the cosmic system. She is at the summit of the hierarchy, as the all-pervading rational activity, reaffirming the Caucasian doctrine (the Valorous) which emphasizes the *Fematrix Character* of the universe.

C1820. The Alpha tells us: In the moral sphere, it was decadence and the prevalence of violence that necessitated the institution of laws, thereby setting ourselves to the task of raising the moral condition of humankind.

C1821. It was Seneca who said: True virtue and true worth rest within, external goods do not confer true happiness but are transitory gifts of

Fortune in which it would be foolish to place our trust.

C1822. The Alpha tells us: Until only a few decades ago, Caucasian Americans had healthy suspicions about the coming of a multi-racial society, and it is tempting to think that only Caucasian America could have spawned something so misguided as the multi-racial state, but, it is the modern day tragedy of a *Caucasian World Compassion* that teaches otherwise. All too often the follies of the present merely repeat those of the past; what is foolish and tragic today(race mixing) was found to be equally foolish and tragic when it was tried 1000 years ago. Hence, the reality of racial competitive predation, or the law of *Species Identity Aggression* (biological warfare) is the *Perdition* of Nations, Cultures and Societies, and the Caucasian world community (America and Europe) in the *21st* century, are about to become its latest victims.

C1823. The Alpha tells us: The *Effective Survival* of the Caucasian people and their communities is as much the art of withholding from alien races, as it is of giving to alien races.

C1824. The Alpha tells us: That Ministers and Politicians in the *21st* century have taken the position that the Caucasian culture is old-fashioned, and inferior to grander liberal schemes of *Mystical Equality* this became the goal rather than the regeneration of -*Caucasian Racial Enlightenment.* The welfare of the founders of America, the Caucasian Race, was set aside. Unfortunately, and perhaps most dangerous, as soon as the liberal zealots began to preach that Caucasian (white) society rather than individuals caused poverty, the liberal scheme of demonizing Caucasian America went into effect. Hence, professional hunters of Caucasian American partisans appeared, and as hunting down Caucasian partisans became a profession, more and more Caucasian Americans are being dragged to the liberal Inquisition. The end of Caucasian America (by 2050) will be by the moral corruption and the degraded racial character of the people who administered it. If the Caucasian light goes out, all of humankind will descend into the abyss.

C1825. The Alpha tells us: The tragedy of liberal zealot America is short on analysis and mute on solutions to the radical social change in the way liberal

Americans understand human racial nature. To suddenly hold Caucasian American society responsible for the failures of other races is to toss aside the accumulated wisdom of centuries. Why did liberal Caucasian Americans abandon the very principles of racial unity (biological sovereignty) that had guided their kind for millenniums? Why do we Caucasians now permit the continuing horrors of the multi-racial welfare state? Why, aside from a few Caucasians, does no one call for the abolition of the Multiracial State? There is an intellectual paralysis, a cowardice of thought on these subjects which the greater Caucasian American community chooses not to acknowledge, and therefore cannot address.

C1826. The Alpha tells us: What then, is in Caucasian societies power? Its judgments on events and its will: these they can control, and their social and political education consists in attaining true survival judgment and a right racial will. The essence of a Caucasian society lies in an attitude of the will, and this will lies within a Caucasians individual power, for the will may conquer itself, but nothing else can conquer it. Therefore, that which is really necessary for Caucasian society is to will social virtue, and to will victory over its enemies. Be well assured that nothing is more tractable than the human soul. You, Caucasian America must exercise your will and the thing is done, it is set right, as on the other hand relax your vigilance and all is lost, for from within comes ruin and from within comes help. To overcome and set right Americas liberal perverted political will is within the power of all Caucasians. Now will you not help yourselves?

C1827. It was Michael Walker of England who said; in reference to the Caucasian world's dilemma, of racial ambivalence, if we Caucasians believe, we believe, and it is our duty to act on what we believe! Furthermore, Stop Apologizing (for your success and that of your race) to aliens in your daily lives, it is an alien tactic of social leverage, (moral high ground) designed to put you on the defensive.

C1828. The Alpha tells us: The redistribution of *Human-kind* throughout the world by the commodity of slavery – from 3000 BC to 1800 AD was a common intercourse of human evolution, and would give rise to both Moral and Political Enlightenment.(human liberty and democracy)

C1829. The Alpha tells us: With the start of the *21st* century well on its way, it will not require much thought to recognize the intention of the *Asian Dragon* and its expedition into Africa? Influenced by the smell of political weakness in the Caucasian world community and its own social dualism of over population and economic expansion, plus, the sub-Saharan's being without union (tribalism) or social virtue,(human rights)...the great dragon has chosen its prey wisely!

C1830. The Alpha tells us: Our Fematrix- *Caucasia* is absolutely transcendent: She is the One, the synthesis of all Caucasian thought and all Caucasian being. She cannot be identical with the sum of individual races, for it is these individual races which require a Source or Principle, and this Principle (Fematrix life strategy) must be distinct from them and logically prior to them. Moreover, if she were identical with each individual race taken separately, then each race would be identical with every other and the distinction of race's,(different life strategy) which is an obvious fact, would be illusion. Thus the One,(Fematrix) is of all existing life, and prior to all existing life.

C1831. The Alpha tells us: In Caucasianism the Caucasian soul must rise above sense-perception, turning towards Nous and occupying itself with the Valorous its philosophy and science. In this union the Caucasian soul retains its self-consciousness; this is in preparation for the final mystical union with the One, the Fematrix who transcends all life. There shall *Man* see, as seeing may be in Reality, both *Caucasia* and himself: himself made radiant, filled with the intelligible light of "Caucasianism" looking to its complete and permanent possession.

C1832. The Alpha tells us: In meditation on our Fematrix *Caucasia* it is not necessary to cast one's thought outwards, as though she were present in any one place in such a way that she leaves other places destitute of herself. On the contrary, she is everywhere present. She is outside no one, but is present to all, even if they know it not!

C1833. The Alpha tells us: Man upon seeing his female, finds his sight hard to put into words. For how should a man bring back a report of the Divine, as of a thing distinct, when in seeing he know it not distinct but one with his own consciousness. He will lapse again from her true vision: but let him again awaken her virtue which is in him, again know himself made perfect by her desire; and he shall again be enlightened, ascending through her virtue to the Intelligence, and thence through wisdom to her supremacy.

C1834. The Alpha tells us: It was Proclus: who spoke of the *One* even though he knows not her name. The principle good precedes the world of ideas or intelligible objects, and from this again the world of intellectual beings, the dominant principle in the procession of beings from the One, (the Fematrix) in the emanation of the orders of being from the highest to the most inferior stage. The effect, or being that proceeds, is partly similar to the cause or source of emanation and partly dissimilar. In so far as the being that proceeds is similar to its origin, it is regarded as being in some degree identical with its principle, for it is only in virtue of the self-communication of the latter that the procession takes place. On the other hand, since there is a procession, there must be something in the proceeding being that is not identical with but different from, the principle. We have, therefore, at once two moments of development, the first being that of remaining in the principle, in virtue of partial identity, the second being that of difference, in virtue of external procession.

C1835. In every being that proceeds, however, there is a natural tendency towards the good and in virtue of the strictly hierarchical character of the development of beings, this natural tendency towards the good means a turning-back towards the immediate source of emanation on the part of the being that emanates or proceeds, hence the three moments of development-(1) Remaining in the principle! (2) Proceeding out of the principle! And (3) Tuning-back towards the principle! This triadic development dominates the whole series of *Fematrix Emanations*. (different life strategies and life forms)

C1836. The Alpha tells us: The original principle (the Fematrix) of the whole process of biological development is the primary one. Being must have a cause, and cause is not the same as effect. There must be, therefore, a First Cause whence the multiplicity of beings proceed as a branches from a root some being nearer to the First Cause, others more remote (plants and insects nearer- humans more remote) Moreover, there can be only one such

First Cause, for the existence of multiplicity is always secondary to unity. Yet as a matter of fact the primary principle (the Fematrix) transcends the predicates of Unity, Cause and Good, just as she transcends being!

C1837. The Alpha tells us: In the process of *Fematrix Emanation* her productive cause, remains itself unaltered. She brings into actuality the subordinate sphere of being (her daughters) and she does so without movement or loss, preserving her own essence, neither transmuted into her daughter's consequents nor suffering any diminution. In other words, the Fematrix is neither altered nor diminished through the production of her daughters, out of her own being.

C1838. The Alpha tells us: Caucasian social ethics proper is subordinate to insistence on the religious aspect of Caucasian life and a Caucasians ascent to the knowledge of their Fematrix *Caucasia* and practicing the moral life is regarded as an integral part of that ascent, and in practicing it, a Caucasian conforms themselves to transcendentally- grounded standards. Moreover, the fact that Caucasians who aspired to a moral life and attached importance to moral values see the necessity of purifying the idea of their Fematrix *Caucasia* and of emphasizing *Divine Providence*.

C1839. The Alpha tells us: The mention of ethics and of an ascription to morality of a transcendental foundation naturally leads one on to the Valorous as the preparatory intellectual instrument of Caucasianism (the historical religion) and its biological doctrine of an imminent reason (the Fematrix) operative in the world. Hence, being the revealed religion its historical antecedents are to be found in Caucasian history (both biological and social)

C1840. The Alpha tells us: Through the understanding and acceptance of Caucasianism and its historical elaboration and dialectical instrument- the Valorous with metaphysics of the divine *Providence* of the *Fematrix* (Caucasia) being operative in Caucasian history is offered to all Caucasian, educated and uneducated, both man and woman alike. Thereby, serving the way to immortality!

C1841. The Alpha tells us: The *Rites of Passage* in Caucasianism are the way in which we Caucasians define ourselves. Caucasianism and its rituals surround the milestones of life: birth, childhood, adulthood, marriage, and death. These Caucasian rituals recognize and enhance the importance of these events. As such, they serve as rites of passage that help the Caucasian community make the transition between what came before and what comes after.

C1842. The Alpha tells us: In Caucasianism there is the enlightenment of the *Ancestral Trust* which connects the Caucasian citizen to their ancestors, their traditions, their beliefs, and their duties, reinforcing the Caucasian community's beliefs about the way life begins, progresses, and ends.

C1843. The Alpha tells us: Only through the scholarship of Caucasianism and its reality, will the Caucasian people be able to overcome the primary hurdle of *Racial Ambivalence* fostered upon them by Alien moral subterfuge, and the political pretense of Caucasian liberal subversion, creating an atmosphere of un-Caucasian political and social activities in America and throughout the world.

C1844. The Alpha tells us: you don't have to look too hard to find liberal political charlatans, *Equality Hustlers,* who prey upon the racial gullibility of the Caucasian community, and it is this racial hucksterism that goes unchallenged by the feckless Caucasian public media. The Caucasian American people have become the victims of political, economic, and social defeats, brought about by the free for all political, industrial, and media elites. But, let it be understood, that this social shakedown of the Caucasian American people- by these elites, will not go unchallenged!

C1845. The Alpha tells us: Many Caucasians find joy in their race. This joy comes from immersing oneself in the racial spirit, and from that immersion, being able to appreciate the beauty and wonder of life in all its forms and rejoicing at being alive to share that wonder. Racial happiness points one to lasting joy– to the joy of family and friends, the joy of rituals, and the joy of life's passages. In Caucasianism the greatest happiness comes from advancing Caucasian society, seeking wisdom and truth, and doing the will of our Fematrix-*Caucasia.*

C1846, The Alpha tells us: Many Caucasians find in Caucasianism a guide that leads them to do good works by challenging them to do their part in the Caucasian world community. This guide reminds the Caucasian people of their duty to their family, society, and their ancestral trust. This source impels them to accept duty as a way of serving their divine Fematrix *Caucasia* even when that duty is burdensome or exhausting. This acceptance is essential if a Caucasian is to acquire a mature faith.

C1847. The Alpha tells us: At some time, you're going to wonder why you were put here on Earth? Helping the Caucasian people form spiritually constructive responses to this and other question is one of the hallmarks of Caucasianism. It is Caucasianism which confronts and provides answers to the deepest questions people ask about life and death. To the Caucasian faithful, Caucasianism provides answers that have not only the power of ancient wisdom, but also the weight of truth.

C1848. The Alpha tells us: That Caucasianism is Triform in nature, it is a religion of Philosophy (reason through knowledge) Revelation (bio-racial canon) and Piety (devotion and faith) In Caucasianism it is the goal to find enlightenment and happiness within one's self, by the nature and meaning of existence, through one's *Racial Spirituality.*

C1849. The Alpha tells us: That Caucasianism doesn't appeal to the authority of a great and all powerful *God* of long ago, and its declarations of intimidation, threat and fear, so as to silence the greatest gift to humankind,... the gift of *Why.* In Caucasianism no mystery must be lift unturned, whether it is of God or Man. The driving mental thirst of *Why* is the *Holy Gift,* the means, given to Man by his Fematrix. And it is the suppression of *Why* and the great battle to free it that has filled and determines the history of all humankind.

C1850. The Alpha tells us: That in most human societies the distinction of the *Female Being* is primarily one of cultural perception (assailable) rather than her true reality, the Source,...the Beginning and the End of the human journey. For it is after all an Expedition and a Quest, an expedition into the unknown, with a quest for immortality. For us, who believe in Caucasianism, humankind and immortality are not three opposing ideas; they can and will become one, through *Man,* by the desire of the one.(the Fematrix)

C1851. The Alpha tells us: That Caucasianism invites us to embark on a spiritual racial journey that can help us realize the purpose and meaning of life. This spiritual racial journey is one of the greatest gifts that Caucasianism offers. Caucasianism affirms our racial uniqueness and reminds us of all the things we have in common as a race of people. In this way, Caucasianism enables us to become racially realized human beings who can serve the greater Caucasian community and live a life of joy, thankfulness, and serenity.

C1852. The Alpha tells us: Our health, intelligence, and talents, come to us as clear gifts from *Caucasia* our Fematrix. Whatever we have, we as Caucasians must share with our community, *Sensible Charity* is a huge part of being a Caucasian. The Caucasian community teaches their children the traditions and beliefs of their ancestors; which reinforce the importance of our Caucasian community, and our lives are given a purpose that we could never discover alone.

C1853. The Alpha tells us: In Caucasianism there are no devils or demons, no outer worldly beings that tempt us to commit evil deeds. Wrongful deeds are the sole possession of those who commit them,..Greed, Jealousy, Hatred, Selfishness, Spite, and Cruelty – all attributes of the human intellectual journey, as well as their counterparts- Charity, Goodwill, Kindness, Mercy, Tolerance, and we must not forget- Love. Hence, Life is about choices, and in the free will of human societies, it is a requisite, ...choices need to be tempered by laws, and laws need to be the will of the governed.

C1854. The Alpha tells us: Now, more than ever, the future of Caucasian American society and the future of world Democracy depend on a mutual exchange of information between the Caucasian community and its political representatives? We Caucasians need leadership that is sensitive to *Alien Migration* and *Political Pretense.* If we Caucasians fail to create an Age of Reason in the *21st* century on behalf of ourselves,...our life here on planet Earth will take the tragic path of South African Caucasians, who were ridiculed and taunted into self *Suicide,* by a feckless and self-righteous world pathology, thereby giving up their God given right to survival, and a place in this world. And like them, we also will deserve not pity, but contempt.

C1855. The Alpha tells us: When people hurt, subjugate, or kill others in the name of their God, they're perverting, rather than representing, the true teachings of their faith. Yet still, religious differences seem to fuel, not quell, the fires of intolerance, hatred, war, and violence in the world. It so often seems to be at the root of contention between people and nations. Religion is, at its heart, not about seizing and using political power, it is about the personal enlightenment of community, freedom, and salvation.

C1856. The Alpha tells us: In Caucasian society, the culture and Caucasianism are not just superficially connected; they are woven together at the deepest levels. In this way, the Caucasian identity is inextricably linked to the social and, therefore, political order. Caucasianism is not only a guide for each believer; it's also a guide for the societies they build.

C1857. The Alpha tells us: that Caucasianism is racially exclusive (racial fundamentalism) and is the true and only way for Caucasian social and spiritual salvation. (Caucasian Fematrix theology)

C1858. The Alpha tells us: It was Gabriel Marcel who said: A *Problem* is a question we ask about something that is outside ourselves. A *Mystery* is a question we ask about something that is within us. When we answer a question, it disappears. When we respond to a mystery, it remains, deepening and defining our life.

C1859. The Alpha tells us: The essence of Caucasian faith is trust. In Caucasianism there is no god but the *Fematrix* (female absolutism) and all biological groups have a living *Female Deity* of their own, and unique unto themselves. This truth is revealed in the Valorous thus, Caucasians don't have the dilemma of choosing between works and belief as the path to social and spiritual salvation. The two - *Faith* and *Works* - are inseparable. Faith in Caucasianism is connected to trust. You must find the courage to travel down the path toward *Racial Enlightenment* by looking inside your own heart or mind and trusting that through the Valorous you can find-Fematrix illumination.

C1860. The Alpha tells us: The Caucasian *Sabbath* (once a month- last Saturday of the month) celebrates communal worship in the High Mass, which is the reenactment of the emergence of the *Fematrix* from the fires of *Creation*. Worshipers sing hymns, listen to readings selected from the Valorous and participate in the self-conscious rite of ancestral thankfulness, racial affirmation and its oath.

C1861. The Alpha tells us: In Caucasianism the faithful gather for prayer by the *Fire of the Becoming* a ceremonial fire burning in an alter serves as the focus of devotion. A bounty (food) is consecrated during the service and then shared in a communal meal by the congregation. It is in Caucasianism were both communal service is held, and individuals worshipers may proceed in their offerings at their own pace.

C1862. The Alpha tells us: The observance of Caucasianism can take many forms: they can be silent meditation or communal prayers and sermons by the Alpha. Chanting together is also very common, and incense as an offering of fragrance can be lit to fill the air. Offerings of food and gifts can be placed at the base of the statue of *Caucasia* our Fematrix, to be distributed to the community need.

C1863. The Alpha tells us: That Caucasianism reminds us that this world is passing. And it encourages us to wonder what we as Caucasians are doing with our lives and why we are making the choices that we have. In Caucasianism there is the *Racial Cleansing*. It is this cleansing that creates focus. The focus enables a deeper racial awareness. The awareness means that enlightenment has opened the door to his or her spiritual racial self, and the deeper appreciation for what one has become, and is attributed to.

C1864. The Alpha tells us: In Caucasianism there is the *Correlation* the intellectual and physical union, the fulcrum of Caucasian racial biology and its cognizance.(racial identity) Through the Correlation, Caucasians not only receive their *Racial Spirituality* but on another level, receiving the Correlation carries with it the implied promise to ask of one's self the question, did I make the people of my life happier, healthier, and understanding? Such an examination is extremely challenging. So, they return to the *Correlation* repeatedly seeking more help from their racial spirituality to do what they know they're supposed to do.

C1865. The Alpha tells us: The Caucasian who receives the *Correlation* has been invited by the Caucasian community to carry Caucasianism in their souls. They become Caucasian bearers. They are meant not only to be a light of *Caucasianism* in the world, they are meant to be transformed to do the work of Caucasianism in this world.

C1866. The Alpha tells us: There may come a time in your life after you've read the books, gone to the classes, and listened to your parents enough that you're ready to go off on your own, hence, take what you've been taught, and put it to the test. If so, it is the Alpha's hope, that you find the enlightenment in the Valorous helpful as you further your personal spiritual evolution.

C1867. The Alpha tells us: In Caucasianism contemplation and introspection play a part as Caucasians experience an intimate connection with the divine *Caucasia,* and just as communal worship is a large part of the Caucasian expression, so is personal devotion through spiritual self-expression that offers the Caucasian practitioner focus, strength and the awareness of a *Racial Soul* needed to overcome the distractions of daily life. Through Caucasianism, the Caucasian people can achieve the ultimate form of self-development- self-mastery.

C1868. The Alpha tells us: That Caucasianism will present a challenge to the modern person, for whom religion is an important way of understanding life. Because in Caucasianism one does not surrender his or her will to the mystical exercise or the supernatural. Hence, Caucasianism is the development of the free mind, in as much as Caucasians study the Valorous and its knowledge, the Alpha's philosophy and rational scientific arguments, to comprehend reality, or rather, go beyond comprehension to the experience of ultimate reality.(fematrix theology– female absolutism)

C1869. The Alpha tells us: Caucasianism offers one way to understand life and celebrate its meaning, one way to bring people together to celebrate life's most important moments. All human faith is built on a foundation of beliefs, having at their core an overarching principle or concept that unites believers, and thereby influencing the culture of the society in which it is practiced. Life's mysteries, the obligation of the faithful, the nature of the Divine will, the presence of the Divine, our relationship to the Divine, our roles and responsibilities within society and within the family, and our relationship with other human beings. In essence, revealing a concept of what the world is really like and what our place in it should be. It is these beliefs that form the foundation of Caucasian faith.

C1870. The Alpha tells us: The first point to understand about a religion or society is that, getting everybody to have the same belief is very important. Identity in a religion or society comes from the shared belief. If you don't believe something central to such a religion or society, you can't be part of it!

C1871. The Alpha tells us: Caucasianism is both a belief and racially-oriented religion. The fundamental belief in *Caucasianism* is Fematrix Theology (female absolutism). If you don't believe this, you simply can't be a Caucasian of the faith, as to just being a *Secular Caucasian* of the blood (by birth)

C1872. The Alpha tells us: The different races (Negroid, Mongoloid, and Caucasoid) have their own view on a meaningful path in life, and its crucialness to themselves as a biologically distinct and deliberately produced group. Furthermore, when we as racial beings come to understand the workings of biological history and its strategic nature (different life strategies) brought about by different needs, (climate, food, shelter, terrain, competitive predation) then an intellectual acumen (clarity) on the subject of race will prevail.

C1873. The Alpha tells us: In the American cultural and racial wars, it is essential that we become *Caucasian Advocates* to counter the contentious and dishonest propaganda being put upon the Caucasian American Community- by deceptive alien racial bigots and Caucasian social swindlers. (liberal zealots) We as Caucasian Americans must counter this assault. We Caucasian Americans must not become our own source of social stupidity, becoming disenfranchised by political cowardice and self-reproach.

C1874. The Alpha tells us: That a day will come, when he will be demonized by the Caucasian political and economic elites, demanding that Caucasianism be ostracized as a cult, and banished from American as well as European society. This the Alpha knows, and express's no fear for his own well-being, or that of Caucasianism and its quest to save the Caucasian world community. Hence, by the intellectual and moral light of Caucasianism all will come to believe.

C1875. Racial Nihilism: is a belief that completely contradicts all rationale as well as all scientific knowledge. In concluding that race has no meaning or purpose and that all racial understanding and values are unfounded. In other wards- they have selected the existence of a difference, in this case human difference, and have declared it shall have no identity or reality! The question to ask yourself is not whether racial nihilism is true! But, whether one can understand this kind of intellectual delinquency, when it applies to what is for all practical purposes- a reality?

C1876. The Alpha tells us: Caucasianism is the religious belief about the problems of life, as well as the mysteries of life- the things outside of us, as well as the things inside of us! It is in Caucasianism were Science, Religion, and the State coexist! Searching for meanings in life is what drives Caucasianism in its quest for the canon of immortality.

C1877. The Obligation in Caucasianism is to Caucasian biological survival, through the understanding of *Fematrix Theology* (female absolutism!) and the teachings of the "Holy Valorous" (our Caucasian manifesto!) Harmony or peacefulness can be attained by the races of humanity if they accept and understand their different biological destinies and respect the other race's by following the universal code of social and moral ethic of a life-forms right to prevail.

C1878. The Alpha tells us: One of the basic tenets in Caucasianism is compassion for other life forms. This compassion supports all Caucasian ethical teachings and, particularly, the golden rule: *Love your race, as you love yourself.*

C1879. The Alpha tells us: Misunderstandings abound about racialism and what it really means. This is do in part by the teachings of *a Mystical Equality.* in human beings which is based on a sacrificial element called

Racial Nihilism (total denial of biological competitive human difference) This equality idea with its element of racial nihilism is so intellectually barren, that for one to adhere to it,...is to be without intellectual interest or mentally rudderless.

C1880. The Alpha tells us: The love for one's race is the source of all morals; it is pure, unmerited, and freely given. In Caucasianism, we as Caucasians must strive to replicate the concept of divine racial love through the adoration of our Fematrix *Caucasia*. We do it in a Caucasian way, based on our racial faith, traditions and the cultures in which we live: by loving our people, by loving our race directly through prayers of adoration and thanks, and by performing acts of charity and compassion. It is very important for all Caucasians to understand just how deeply love is at the understanding of Caucasian racial faith.

C1881. The Alpha tells us: That he is just a messenger, touched by our divine Fematrix *Caucasia*. And has been chosen by her as an intermediary to help (her posterity) Caucasian people bridge the gap, the spiritual racial awareness or perfection that has eluded most other Caucasians. His main job as the Alpha is to act as a transition figure between spiritual racial enlightenment, and the Caucasian world community at large. The divine *Caucasia* has chosen him as her guardian, but he himself is just a man, no more, no less, who carries her message, and must give her message to all Caucasians who will listen.

C1882. The Alpha tells us: That good and evil are the sole property of humankind, and that their control is not of the divine, but solely of the human will. There are two forces in the human universe the negative and the positive, that which is good for humankind and that which is bad! And all of it,... is in the sole realm of human decision. (good and bad influence, is a matter of self-interest)

C1883. The Alpha tells us: That liberal zealotry is the spiritual enemy of humankind whose goal is to lead people away from truth in reality, so as to establish a subordinate deceptive reality, that of *Equality*. To explain this dilemma, this symbol of modern day Caucasian society, imagine the death of Caucasian society being the mission of the Caucasian people, on behalf of Alien people? Furthermore, whatever you call this liberal equality? There should be no doubt, that it is the supreme adversary of the Caucasian world community. And, because Caucasians can't imagine evil coming from their political representatives, they can't accept the fact that racialism is a part of all life, and therefore a part of the divine plane. The basic political power of liberal zealots, as developed in the modern world, is the power of death! This is the power that all Caucasians must conquer.

C1884. The Alpha tells us: In Caucasianism there is the Holy Valorous, and with it comes the Oral Valorous. The Oral Valorous is known as the "Syllabus" these are the new *Ideas* and *Debates* not yet in the "Holy Valorous" that Caucasianism needs to be intellectually current. What the *Syllabus* does is invest all the Caucasian people with the authority of the Alpha's revelation, thereby as a way of preserving interpretations of it debate, while guarding against radical ideas that would undermine Caucasianism.

C1885. The Alpha tells us: That the wisdom that Caucasian society has achieved is so vast and deep, that it is not reasonable or accurate to say that it is just another human society. In many ways (other than liberal zealotry) Caucasian society unlike any other, has transcended all intellectual boundaries and lives completely in the truth.

C1886. The Alpha tells us: One of the most fundamental realities within Caucasianism is the reality that every human being has a *Racial Nature.* (bio-intuitive)

C1887. The Alpha tells us: It is no crime to oppose one's own destruction, even if we must suffer the sobriquet white- Racist for doing so.

C1888. It was Martin L. Gross: A true American hero, who said, that America is a poor imitation of Europe, coupled with some remnants of the old American system. It's not Jefferson and it's not really Europe. It's a newly cobbled, made-up method of government that exists no were else in the democratic world. It operates without a theory and combines the failures of the American and European systems into the worst of both worlds. Without a sound concept behind it, the new Washington-directed American government is doomed to practical failure, which, of course, has already begun. Hence, the day that Jefferson and Madison feared,... has arrived - *Entrepreneurial Politics*

C1889. The Alpha tells us: It is the *21st* century, and the American Congress has become a *Shopping Mall,* an exclusive market for the Industrial Rich and the Politically Ambitious, both foreign and domestic. It has become the temple, the American altar to Corruption, Greed, and Betrayal. This is truth, this is reality! Furthermore, at each Congressmen's booth is a salivating line of Lobbyists bearing gifts - Money, Parties, and let us not forget the currency of gratitude, lines so long, and gifts so great,...it's no wonder that the common American citizen can get no audience, they nether have the time to stand in line, nor the price of admission.

C1890. The Alpha tells us: the American Congress of the *21st* century is an insight into a world where open duplicity is very commonplace, where the leadership of both parties caresses the ego or threatens the station of men and women less powerful than they, seducing or badgering them into compliance. Hence, having been distanced from the people from whence they came, they are now the greatest epicenter of political, economic, and social corruption in the world.

C1891. The Alpha tells us: There is a new breed arising in the land. The modern day Caucasians, who love their country (Caucasian America) too much to see it continue on its present decline. Caucasian patriots who read, talk, listen, and in the process is becoming formidable opponents of alien and Caucasian political hustlers with agendas - open or secret- for Caucasian American destruction. Let it be understood, Caucasian American patriotism is gaining exponentially in number every day, and if you look into the minds of the Caucasian American people, I would guess that there are now some *Hundred Million* or so Caucasians who have become aware of the seriousness of the Alien, Political, and Economic Crisis in Caucasian America, and who want to work to rectify it. Who are they? They are the Democrats, the Republicans, the unaffiliated and undefined, the house wife, the school teacher, police officer, the storekeeper, and yes, the politician- all descendant of Caucasian ancestry, the ancestry that founded this greatest of all nations.

C1892. The Alpha tells us: The importance of the principle of *Race* (different human bio-determinism) is undeniable, and most of the racial questions of Caucasian America and the world can be and ought to be solved in accordance with this principle; but racial matters are complicated by geographical and strategical considerations, such as the difficulty of determining natural, as well as the frequent need for the establishment of strategic racial frontiers. Moreover, the principle of racial determination cannot help us where racial determination can hardly be said to exist, where the races are entangled in inextricable confusion and the *State Sponsored Belief* and the *Scientific Heresy* that there is no meaning or purpose in racial existence (racial nihilism) a truly sinister illumination upon humankind, leading them out of the light, and back into the shadows, in their quest for understanding! Furthermore, the law that it is an essential characteristic of all biological aggregate to constitute species, races, and subclasses of the same is, like every other biological law, beyond good and evil.

C1893. The Alpha tells us: That racial determination (all races) as an intellectual and scientific theory and as a practical biological movement has today entered upon a critical phase from which it will be extremely difficult to discover an exit? Racial Determination has encountered obstacles not merely imposed from without, (racial competition) but spontaneously surging from within.(liberal zealotry) Only to a certain degree perhaps, can these obstacles be surpassed or removed, this task has been by no means easy, so great is the extant of racial opposition (racial nihilism) by liberal zealots and their equalitarian social agenda, which vehemently opposes the reality of *Human Divergence* and has become for humankind, exceedingly difficulty.

C1894. The Alpha tells us: His general conclusions as to the inevitability of a liberal zealot oligarchy in Caucasian life, and as to the difficulties which the growth of this oligarchy imposes upon the realization of Caucasian democracy, have been strikingly confirmed in the political and social life of all Caucasian Americans, and their sister states throughout the world. For the time being racial determination in the world community has been eclipsed by political treachery. But, it need hardly be said, however, that as soon as this liberal treachery has been overcome,(and it will be!) racial determination will be resumed, and that the fall of the *Liberal Zealot Oligarchy* will be found to have effected a reinforcement of the tendencies characteristic of racial (biological) detemination.

C1895. The Alpha tells us: The recalcitrance of humankind, the tendency for goals to be subverted through the creation of new centers of interest and motivation inheres in all of their organizations. Deviations from rationality are characteristics of Military, Industrial and Governmental bureaucracies as well as of voluntary associations. We as Caucasians in our pursuit of a *Democratic Racial Monarchy* most become more sensitized to our political, economic and cultural organizations, by paying attention to deviation from professed goals and rational systems.

C1896. The Alpha tells us: That Democracy in large measure rests on the fact that no one group is able to secure a basis of power and command over the majority so that it can effectively suppress or deny the claims of the groups it opposes. In large measure, therefore, as the world moves in the direction of a *Collectivist Society,* in response to the pressures from the lower strata demanding that the state take responsibility for guaranteeing full employment, a more equitable distribution of goods and services, more equal opportunity, and greater security against the hazards of illness and old age, the problem of the compatibility of socialism and democracy becomes more and more prominent. Hence, the emergence in the *21st* century of a *New Class* of Communist (the liberal zealots) more powerful and exploitive, than the now ruling class of Capitalists, offers a constant warning to all Caucasian Americans, and their sister states throughout the world,...of the need to absorb the lessons for *Democracy*. To protect the rights of Caucasian Americans, to maintain their diverse centers of power, to keep open access to authority, this is the task of all Caucasian who value their freedom in the first half of the twenty first century.

C1897. The Alpha tells us: It is above all, the sudden passage from opposition to participation in power which exercises a powerful influence on the mentality of the leader.

C1898. The Alpha tells us: The great Caucasian thinkers of the world established the frames of reference with which we still approach the world we live in. Meditation and Logic found homes in different parts of the Caucasian world, and both are flexible and powerful extensions of Caucasian cognitive capacity. And at about the same time that meditation reached an advanced form in Caucasian India, the Caucasian Europeans were inventing the mode of thought that would be as influential in shaping and embodying the very course of Europeans history, as meditation was in shaping and embodying the course of Caucasian India, and Asian history. Furthermore, of all the Caucasian intellectual pillars, it was lift to the Promethean mind of Aristotle to discover the basic principles of logic and to establish a discipline that has continued to develop to this very day.

C1899. The Alpha tells us: The essence of political thought about systems require one to ask of any given set of rules or laws,...Good for what? The proximate answer is that a system must be good for the people who live under that system.

C1900. The Alpha tells us: A society that produces great accomplishment must foster two qualities in tension with each other: *Freedom* and *Order.* A race of people with the potential for excellence has a sense of purpose and autonomy. Add to this *Tools,*...a tool can turn out to have unanti-cipated uses that alter both principles and craft, independently expanding the realm of things a discipline can achieve.

C1901. The Alpha tells us: Though a conception of the *Good* gives rise to moral codes, it should be remembered that the essence of the *Good* is not rules that one struggles to follow, but a vision of the best that we Caucasians can be that attracts and draws us onward.

C1902. The Alpha tells us: It was Aristotle who said: Every art and every inquiry, and similarly every action and pursuit, is thought to aim at the good; and for this reason the good has rightly been declared to be that at which all things aim!

C1903. The Alpha tells us: A culture that fosters great accomplishment needs a coherent sense of the transcendental goods.(the true, the beautiful and the good) Coherent sense, means that the goods are a live presence in the culture, and that great artists and thinkers compete to come closer to the ideal that captivates them. Whatever is the good for Caucasian society must be grounded in an under standing of what is unique about Caucasian society. If Caucasian culture has a coherent, well-articulated sense of what constitutes excellence in Caucasianism, what constitutes the ideal of a Caucasian society flourishing; it will have a conception of the transcendental goods.

C1904. The Alpha tells us: those conceptions of the good, true, and beautiful prevailing at any given time concretely affect how all societies will manifest themselves. Furthermore, a culture's prevailing view of the transcendental goods provides a resource that suffuses the practice of that domain independently of the variation in beliefs. (the common good)

C1905. The Alpha tells us: It was Charles Murray who said; ultimately, what matters in the conduct of science is truth and truth alone! Hence, the discovery of truth is the coin of scientific eminence.

C1906. The Alpha tells us: That the Caucasian world community is about to go down the path of a not yet understood new truth? *Fematrix Theology* (female absolutism) We are now in a period of Caucasian racial trial and error whose extent of over fifty years gives only a faint indication of the difficulty experienced in Caucasian America by the political forces of *Racial Nihilism*, (liberal zealotry) that has taken intellectualism (academia) by the scruff of the neck,...leading them down a false trail. The *Racial Principle* (biological divergence) must be employed to enrich our store of knowledge, of the biological selection of natural phylum (human) constants, a way to provide an opportunity for the continuation of life.

C1907. The Alpha tells us: his work is that of looking upon the future wreckage of Caucasian America, and her sister states throughout the world. With anguish in his heart and insisting that a solution – not one that would emerge in the fullness of time, but now could, and must be found. Such a solution is reveled in the Valorous and would require strength, courage, skill, and a favorable religious and political enlightenment. Calling upon the Caucasians of the *21st* century to summon their historical imagination; if they are to capture the sense of *Shock* and *Terror* that will unfold in the future of their children? And let there be no mistake, time will not dim his direct and uncompromising honesty!

C1908. The Alpha tells us: That Caucasian America and her sister states throughout the world need help to bridge the irreconcilable gulf between *Egalitarianism* or liberal zealot paternalism (equal outcomes) and *Republicanism* or conservative competitive self-reliance (unequal outcomes) The Valorous is intended to provide a positive solution to these contemporary political ills, were one can only speak on any occasion with a host of *Fears* and *Precautions*. A bad government cannot be spoken to by anyone, and the only remedy for this case is the ballot box, and if that fails?...cold-steel would seem appropriate to some, but, political and social migration is best!

C1909. The Alpha tells us: From the readings of Caucasian history we learn how harmful servitude was to people and societies. Hence, it is easy to understand whence the love of *Liberty* derives among people; for experience shows that no people and their society ever grew in dominion or wealth except when they were free! And it is indeed a wonder to realize how great Caucasian America became within a century after it had thrown off the yoke of tyranny. Yet, in the *21st* century, Tyranny is back at the gates of Caucasian America, and the Alpha gives this stern warning to all that participate in this tyranny- freedom that has been lost is avenged with far more fury than one that has only been threatened, and the Caucasian people will take extraordinary vengeance upon those who betray and deprive them of their destiny!

C1910. The Alpha tells us: Having wondered why people of ancient times were fonder of *Race* than they are today, he has concluded that it is the same reason that explains why men are now less courageous than they were then. He believes it is to be explained by the difference between our culture and theirs, and by the unity of race upon which theirs is based. Our culture, *Racial Nihilism* having shown us - Caucasian capitulation and political heresy, has caused us to have less esteem for *Racial Honor*, whereas our ancestors, because they believed *Racial Honor* to be the highest good, showed greater fierceness in their actions. This is demonstrated in many of their customs as compared to ours, beginning with their enormous sacrifices and the humbleness of ours.

C1911. The Alpha tells us: All human races that enjoy full freedom prosper greatly. And, it is a fact that homogeneous (racial) societies are the very root and acumen of all living biology. The contrary of all this is true for *Races* of people who live in political and cultural servitude.

C1912. The Alpha tells us: Those who believe that where great personages are concerned new favors cause old injuries to be forgotten,...deceive themselves.

C1913. The Alpha tells us: Here a question arises as to the *Racially Nonpartisan* those persons who have declared them-selves racially uninvolved or unbiased! Now the question,... *Loyalty* and the nature of that commitment to themselves and to their children? The Answer lies, of course, in *Liberal Duplicity* and its elitist double-dealing deceit when it comes to the politics of *Race,* and its unwavering presence. It is these *Academic Vulgarians* with their pedantic racial view that land support to the enemies of Caucasian America, and her sister states throughout the world. For this can be said about the generality of them: that they are Ungrateful, Fickle, Dissembling, Anxious to flee danger, and Covetous of gain! So long as you promote their advantage, they are all yours, and will offer you their blood, their goods, their lives,...when the need for these are remote! But when the need arises however, they will turn against you. Hence, the Caucasian who bases his or her security and friendship upon their word, lacking other provision, is doomed!

C1914. The Alpha tells us: It is the *21st* century, and the American liberality- with its Alien racial expenditures has destroyed its authority! The disbursement of Caucasian American resources for Alien physical and mental poverty is harmful; and, indeed, nothing feeds upon itself as liberality does. The more it is indulged, the fewer are the means to indulge it further. As a consequence, the society as a whole becomes poor and contemptible or, to escape this, it becomes rapacious and hateful. Of all the things that America must guard against, hatred and contempt come first, and unrestrained liberality leads to both.

C1915. The Alpha tells us: That no political parties or groups of people, should suppose that they can choose sides with complete safety. Indeed, they had better recognize that they will always have to choose between risks, for that is the order of things. We never flee one peril without falling into another.

C1916. The Alpha tells us: A matter of no small importance to all Caucasians is the selection of leadership, for their competence or incompetence will depend upon their capacity to judge; and the first estimate of their intelligence will be based upon the character of those he or she keeps about them, for the first mistake leaders can make lies in the selection of their support staff.

C1917. The Alpha tells us: The *Caucasian Empire* can only be held together by the strength of sound laws, sound arms, and sound examples. Hence, it is a common failing of leadership not to take account of tempests during fair weather. No *Caucasian Society* should ever allow themselves to fall down, with the belief that someone else will lift them to their feet, because it will not happen. Only those methods of defense which depend upon one's own resourcefulness are good, certain, and enduring.

C1918. The Alpha tells us: Anyone who reviews the innumerable deeds of the Caucasian people collectively and those of many individual Caucasians will observe their attention to religion as a necessary instrument for the maintenance of a civil society. Let those who study Caucasian history duly note how useful religion was in directing the armies, in animating the people, in keeping men good, and in shaming the wicked. Thus, for those who dispute whether Caucasians or humankind for that matter owes a greater obligation to religion or to their own savage nature, the latter would take first place. For there was never anyone who ordained new and unusual laws, among a people without having recourse to God, for they would not otherwise have been accepted!

C1919. The Alpha tells us: Because many believe that the well-being of the Caucasian people derive from the *Liberal State,* the Alpha would like to present such argument as occurs to him in opposition to this view, and he will propose two very potent ones which, in his judgment, cannot be refuted. The first is that, because of the bad example set by the *Supreme Court* Caucasian America has lost all reverence and social identity, with the result that a host of racial troubles and legislative disorders have followed; for just as we may suppose every advantage to accompany *Democracy,* so may we suppose the contrary to be the case where it is lacking. Our first debt to the liberal state and its priests the *Liberal Zealots* is that, thanks to them we Caucasian Americans have become the victims of our own success, and are now demonized accordingly. But we owe it a still greater debt – the second cause of our ruin: that is, that *Liberal Zealotry* has kept and still keeps all of Caucasian America divided through religious and moral deceit, political and legal villainy. The result has been that Caucasian America has now become so politically weak and racially disunited as to become the prey not merely of powerful *Alien Industrialists* but alas, let us not forget the alien racial activists or *Poverty Hustlers* of our inner cities.

C1920. The Alpha tells us: Those who study the Caucasian people will note that for some four thousand years they hated the idea of *Oppression* and loved the idea of *Freedom* for the common welfare of their state, and they will note a host of examples testifying to both of these attitudes. Moreover, when the Caucasian people begin to look upon a thing with horror, they will persevere in that attitude for many centuries, and no debt of obligation to any citizens was enough to save them from merited punishment. If we compare all the disorders chargeable to the Caucasian people with all the disorders chargeable to other races, and all the glorious achievements of the Caucasian people with all those of other races, we will find that in Conquest, Achievements, and as in Goodness, the Caucasian people are far superior.

C1921. The Alpha tells us: When *Liberal Tyranny* replaces freedom, the Caucasian American people will no longer increase in either political power or economic wealth. The reason is easy to understand, the liberal zealot advantage lies in keeping the Caucasian people disunited, and this is accomplished through religious moral deceit, and the public terror of the *Liberal Inquisition* (political correctness) The result of this 21_{st} century liberal crusade of rising up and depriving the Caucasian American people of their liberty, will be for them, sadly ill-conceived, for this assault against the Caucasian American people will unleash an extraordinary vengeance!

C1922. The Alpha tells us: It was the biologist Garrett Hardin who said, A chimerical One World without borders or distinctions– liberal *Universalism* is impossible. Any Race of people that practice unlimited altruism, (liberal paternalism) unfettered by thoughts of self–preservation, will be greatly disadvantaged in life's competition and thus eliminated over time in favor of those that limit their altruistic behavior to their own genetic kin, from whom they receive reciprocal benefits. Furthermore, less we forget that for millions of years, biological evolution has been powered by *Discrimination.* Even mere survival in the absence of evolutionary change depends greatly on discrimination. Hence, a one world created liberal universalism has by definition no competitive base to support it; therefore it cannot survive in competition with discrimination. This is truth, this is reality!

C1923. The Alpha tells us: It is a tragic irony that if Caucasian liberal zealots have their way, *Discrimination* will be abandoned, and the fact that our leadership has no cause to question this wisdom, that of demonizing and abandoning the very principle responsible for their rise to greatness. Even the most modest impulse toward acceptance should cause us to think of *Revolution!*

C1924. The Alpha tells us: It was Michael W. Masters who said; it is to the great advantage of Alain races, virtually all of whom retain their cohesion as distinctive, discriminating racial groups, to exploit the economic wealth and social order of the Caucasian world community, and the benefits they cannot create for themselves. When this Alain racial cohesive drive is placed in competition with self–sacrificing Caucasian altruism, there can be only one outcome. In the near term, Caucasian Americans as well as their sister states throughout the world, will become displaced by Alain racial groups acting in their own self-interest. Furthermore, in the long run, biological destruction awaits us. Since those Alain races who displace us do not, by definition, maintain our morals or standards – for if they did, they would not be replacing us – our flowed moral system will vanish with us. The fact that universal, self- sacrificing liberal altruism destroys its practitioners is its most obvious flaw. Any survivable moral order must recognize this truth.

C1925. The Alpha tells us. The *Fematrix* has given her daughters the gift of free will, so that each one of them can make distinct physical characteristics of themselves, in accordance with their own *Life Strategy* with the ability to recognize, unite, defend and mate – thereby securing, advancing, and preserving their life strategy through physical identity. In other words, your physical appearance (color and form) is the symbol of the life strategy you belong to, and they are for all practical biological purposes, one and the same, your germ, your race,...your place in the universe.

C1926. The Alpha tells us: One of the principle causes for the collapse of a *Civilization* is the gradual adulteration (miscegenation) of the racially homo-geneous founding population through the losses in war, alien racial immigration and birthrates below replacement levels. In other words, a Civilization cannot arise on the site of an earlier *Civilization* once the hereditary character (the bio-life strategy) of the founding people is permanently removed. Furthermore, modern innovations flow predominantly from the creative wellspring of the Caucasian world community. Hence, should the Caucasian world community fail? Once fallen, it will never be replaced by another of comparable quality - there will be no recovery!

C1927. It was Thomas Jefferson who warned Caucasian Americans of the perils of Alien immigration: They will bring with them the principles of the governments they leave, or if able to throw them off, it will be in exchange for an unbounded licentiousness, passing, as usual, from one extreme to the other...In proportion to their number, they will infuse into it (the Nation) their spirit, warp or bias its direction, and render it a *Heterogeneous,* incoherent, distracted mass.

C1928. The Alpha tells us: That our Caucasian sense of compassion is understandable. But this sentimentality should not blind us to the long term implications for our own survival, *Self-defense* is justly called the primary law of Nature,...it cannot be taken away by the laws of society. All systems of law and government of a people must serve the first imperative of those people – their survival!

C1929. The Alpha tells us: It is the *21st* century, and the Caucasian world community is surrendering the power of their life and death into the hands of – *Alien Races*. This decision, which was never subjected to systematic scrutiny by an informed electorate, both in America or Europe is tantamount to Suicide. What the Caucasian world community's response will be when this becomes intolerable remains to be seen. If there is no response, the long descent into barbarism is sure to follow, and hence, the creed of Cicero will prevail– *Laws are silent in the midst of arms*

628

C1930. What would be lost with the passing of Caucasian Civilization and its people? Would the spirit of individual liberty persevere? The history of Alien societies suggests not. Despite the tendency of liberal zealots to denigrate the only culture on earth that would tolerate their presence, these virtues uniquely characterize only Caucasians and their Civilization. Do Caucasian moral principles require that the Caucasian people commit suicide in order to fulfill those principles? Such a belief is insane!...it therefore follows that if the Caucasian world community is to survive it must come to grips, as Jean Raspail foresaw, with the profoundly destructive nature of its moral liberal beliefs?

C1931. The Alpha tells us: Through the ill example of the liberal Court, Caucasian America has lost all racial feeling and social reasoning, a loss which draws after it infinite political mischief and Alien disorders; for as the presence of honoring one's *Race* (their life strategy) implies every excellence, so the contrary is involved in its absence. To our *Race* therefore, and to its life strategy, we Caucasian Americans, as well as our sister states throughout the world, owe our first debt. And to this great debt we owe it for what is the immediate cause of our greatness, namely, that by our *Race* and its life strategy, all Caucasian nations are kept united. For no country was ever united or prosperous which did not yield obedience to its biological racial core (its Kind) and its strategy.

C1932. The Alpha tells us: Let all Caucasians to whom life has afforded this opportunity, remember that two courses lie open to them in the *21st* century; one through *Racial Unity* will render them secure while they live, and a prosperous posterity when they die; the other *Racial Nihilism* which exposes them to *Alien Encroachment* and social usurpation, and condemning their posterity to eternal social infamy - after their death. It would be a sufficient lesson to any Caucasian on how to distinguish the paths which lead to *Racial Honor* and *Safety* from those which end in *Shame* and *Insecurity*.

C1933. The Alpha tells us: The Multiracial State, and the cause of its failure-*Racial Competition* which lead to the impeachment of liberal racial brotherhood, hence fostering the hatred that has sprung up on every side, and this hatred leading to hostel racial divisions, has created political interest based on competitive racial interest. Hence, arose the bitterest hostility between the races, and from this and the like causes, racial hostilities are growing to such dimensions that if not separated (into new racial states!) it will bring about the downfall and ruin of Caucasian America!

C1934. The Alpha tells us: That all human affairs being in movement, and incapable of remaining as they are, they must either *Rise* or *Fall* and to many conclusions to which we are not lead by reason, we are brought to by necessity. And since it is impossible, as all should believe, to bring about an equilibrium to a Multiracial State, or to adhere strictly to liberal utopianism, we as Caucasians must, in arranging our social state, consider what is the more honorable, reasonable, and stable course for us to take, and so contrive that even if necessity compels us to defend our *Caucasian Racial State* against the liberal worlds condemnation, looking on it as a conflict which cannot be escaped if we would arrive at the greatness of the *Caucasian Empire*.

C1935. The Alpha tells us: A Monarchy readily becomes a Tyranny, an Aris-tocracy an Oligarchy, while a Democracy tends to degenerate into Anarchy. So that if the founders of a state should establish any one of these three forms of Government, he establishes it for a short time only, sense no precaution he may take can prevent it from sliding into its contrary, by reason of the close resemblance which, in this case, the virtue bears to the vice. Knowing the defects, and avoiding each of these forms in its simplicity, the Alpha has made a choice of a form which shares in the qualities of all the three, and which he has judged to be more stable and lasting than any of them separately. For where we have a Monarchy, an Aristocracy, and a Democracy existing to gether in the same state, each of the three serve as a check upon the other.

C1936. The Alpha tells us: We as Caucasians must become more aware of indecisive leadership, who unless upon compulsion, never follow wise courses; for wherever there is room for doubt, their weakness will not suffer them to come to any resolve; so that unless their doubts be overcome by some superior force which impels them forward, they remain always in suspense.

C1937. The Alpha tells us: It has been said that the struggle of Caucasian

America has given rise to laws favorable to freedom. But in the eyes of many Caucasians Americans, the consequences of Affirmative Action, Political Correctness, and Equalitarianism are all liberal laws and social thinking opposed to that view. And that the ambitions of the liberal zealots are so pernicious that unless controlled and counteracted in a variety of ways, it will reduce Caucasian America to a speedy ruin. For as a people living under free institutions have two ends always before them, namely to acquire liberty and to preserve it. They must of necessity be led by their excessive passion for liberty.

C1938. The Alpha tells us: It is essential for all Caucasian societies that at the outset of their social journey, a ruler should be found to lay the foundations of their civil life; but after that has been done, it will be necessary for their rulers to reinforce the *Courageous Virtues* of *Caucasian Ancestry*, since otherwise their nation will grow feeble, and become prey to their Alien neighbors.

C1939. The Alpha tells us: In a corrupted Nation, it is its legislative institution that grows to be most mischievous. For it is no longer those of greatest worth, but those who had most influence, who sought the legislative posts; while all who were without influence, however deserving, refrained through fear. From this cause comes the difficulty, or rather the impossibility, which a corrupted Nation finds in maintaining an existing free government. For now only the powerful propose the law, and these not in the interest of public freedom but of their own authority, and through fear, none dare speak against the laws they proposed, the people become deceived and forced into voting their own destruction.

C1940. The Alpha tells us: When Caucasian America has driven out her *Liberal Zealots*; she will be free from their possible political succession of a weak and wicked ideology. Who take their authority not by intellectual enlightenment, nor yet by the free suffrages of their fellow-citizens, but by their wicked craft of *Equalitarianism* (communism revisited) or *Equality Servitude,* as the Alpha likes to call it! This *Liberal Ideology* is a most cruel expedient, contrary not merely to every Caucasian, but to every civilized rule of social conduct, and such as every man and woman with a love for freedom should shun.

C1941. The Alpha tells us: We Caucasians must come to understand in what ways our freedom can be overthrown, and how politicians climb from one ambition to another; and learn to recognize the truth of these words- All ill actions have their origin in fair beginnings! And because such conduct seems praiseworthy, (equality) everyone is readily deceived by it and therefore no remedy is applied. Hence, Caucasians ought, therefore, to provide through their social ordinances that none of their fellow Caucasians shall, under the guise of doing good, have it in their power to do bad, but shall be suffered to acquire such influence only as may aid and not injure Caucasian freedom.

C1942. The Alpha tells us: One of the major objectives of the liberal zealot civil rights movement in Caucasian America was not only to enable aliens to vote in big numbers and to have their vote have an impact in the Caucasian political system, it was that it should be controlled by alien leadership who would do the bargaining for liberal issues with that system. In other words, aliens have become the liberal zealots front line troops in their attempt to take over Caucasian America, and under the deceptive cloak of *Equality,* this being their weapon for the mass destruction of Caucasian America,...are politically sponsoring, and legally arming – an Alien invasion, to establish a government to the liberal zealots liking, and to rob Caucasian America of its liberties. There can never be *Reconciliation* between competing races. Hence, the Caucasian American people are apt to err in judging alien races and their ambitions in the abstract, but on becoming acquainted with alien racial particulars, they will speedily discover their mistakes.

C1943. The Alpha tells us: In all their actions, even in those which are matters of necessity rather than choice, prudent Caucasians will endeavor so to conduct themselves as to conciliate good-well.

C1944. The Alpha tells us: Since the desires of men are insatiable, Nature prompting them to desire all things and fortune permitting them to enjoy but few, there results a constant discontent in their minds, and a loathing of what they possess prompting them to find fault with the present, praise the past, and long for the future, even though they are not moved by any reasonable cause.

C1945. The Alpha tells us: we as Caucasians must be bold to speak freely all that we think, both of old times and of new, in order that the minds of the young who happen to read the Valorous, can be prepared to follow those social examples set by Caucasian antiquity whenever chance affords the opportunity. For it is the duty of every good Caucasian to teach others those wholesome lessons which the malice of time or of fortune has not permitted others to put into practice; to the end, that out of many who have the knowledge, some one better loved by the Caucasian people may be found able to carry them out.

C1946. The Alpha tells us: It is easy to understand whence this love of liberty arises among the Caucasian world community, for we know by experience that States have never singularly increased, either as to dominion or wealth, except where they have lived under a free government. This cause, however, is not far to seek, since it is the well-being, not of individuals, but of the community which makes a State great.

C1947. The Alpha tells us: We as Caucasians must not in the hope of being received into *Paradise*, think more how to bear injuries than how to avenge them. For, were we to remember that religion permits the exaltation and defense of our *Race,* we would see it to be our duty to love and honor it, and would strive to be able and ready to defend it.

C1948. The Alpha tells us: It is the year of our Fematrix *2008,* and once again the terrorism of liberal zealotry has come home to roost, this time in the form of – Economic Misadventure. Badgered by the liberal press, and the political zealots in Washington,(Congress) and ignoring basic banking criteria that the banking community had used for decades (debt to income ratio) Hence, by the use of their very successful weapon, the hammer (accusation) of *Discrimination*, the liberal zealots had declared all minorities that are uncredit worthy,...are to be now, credit worthy by liberal decree. Demanding that all banking rules be suspended in order to make minority loans! And though being of minority origin, under the guise of equal outcomes- uncredit worthy Caucasians as well would flood the ranks of the subprime mortgage frenzy, and the sadist thing of all, is that the American people will demand that it be fixed by the very same people who created it? None of whom by the way, will ever be prosecuted for their participation in this egalitarian criminal act against the American people. It follows that economic measures not good in themselves are by a common error judged to be good, or are promoted by those who seek political favor rather than the public advantage. (political duplicity)

C1949. The Alpha tells us: Those Caucasians who have little experience of political affairs are sure to be misled, from the matters with which they have to deal being attended by many political deceptive appearances such as leads men and woman to believe whatsoever they are minded to believe.

C1950. The Alpha tells us: A wise and good Caucasian must teach what is good, and give no occasion or encouragement to his or her descendants to become hateful of any people of difference. And will never build upon hatred, to the end that they may ever be led to trust to it rather than to the good-will of compassion and reason.

C1951. The Alpha tells us: This political warning to all rulers and man of fortune, you should never think so lightly of the Caucasian people as to suppose, that when wrong upon wrong has been done to them, they will not bethink them- selves of revenge, however great the danger they encounter or the hardship they thereby bring upon themselves. As to their lack of heart, and conviction?...you will have found yourselves deceived.

C1952. The Alpha tells us: The loss of racial identity in the Caucasian world community is symptomatic of a deeper crisis within the Caucasian liberal fraternity. At its core, the crisis is the inevitable consequence of a profound and perhaps very fatal misunderstanding of the nature of biological morality? Is Caucasian America and her sister states throughout the world now to become Africanized? or Asianized? And yet, frank discussion of this outcome is usually silenced with words like *Racist-Bigots,* and xenophobe. Neither, the liberal zealot who created this flawed moral system that enforces this silence, or the treasonous politicians who support it will outlive the demise of Caucasian society. But when the Caucasian world community is gone, it will be little consolation that those responsible will have expired as well. It is the *21st* century, and if we are to reverse course, it is vital that we take steps now, before it is too late!

C1953. The Alpha tells us: We as Caucasian Americans must not lose sight

of the ancient and eternal laws of our *Fematrix* and her life strategy!...
on which our civilization must be based if we are to survive. We can no
longer have the luxury of indulging in liberal fallacious social principles
of *Equalitarianism*- docile racial rivalry?...a requirement on the part of
Caucasian Americans only! There-fore, no matter how threatening their-
Political Correctness!..or delusional their-*Equal Racial Outcomes!* We as
Caucasian Americans most become the moral basis of our civilization and
uphold the *Ultimate Ethic* of our own survival!

C1954. The Alpha tells us: The holidays, public anniversaries, flags,
songs, statues, museums, symbols, and heroes that a race of people share
are fundamental to their identity and their existence as a people. So, by
Caucasian racial default,(a failure to act) Alien races well commence to
destroy Caucasian America by doing away with the symbols and institutions
of the collective consciousness that defines the Caucasian race and is the
foundation of their culture. And when Caucasian America has succumb to its
own displacement, this must be understood!...there is little question that alien
races do not share liberal views about equality, freedom, and tolerance. It
was merely a weapon wielded against the weak link (liberal paternalism!) in
Caucasian democracy. Hence, by the mid *21st* century (Caucasian America's
demise!) the aliens subversives will declare the Caucasian Americans- so
gifted!…yet, so stupid!

C1955. The Alpha tells us: It is the *21st* century, and a merely cultural
consciousness will not by itself conserve the Caucasian American people
that were necessary for the creation of the culture and who remain necessary
for its survival. We as Caucasians need not only to understand the role of
Race in creating our civilization but also to incorporate that understanding
in our defense of our civilization. Until we as Caucasians Americans do so,
we can expect only to keep on losing the war we are in.

C1956. The Alpha tells us: Alien sentimentality, should not blind the
Caucasian people to the long term implications of their own survival. Hence,
all systems of law and government that a race of people create must serve
the imperative of their own survival. This is truth, this is reality.

C1957. The Alpha tells us: In removing the moral veil of liberal political discourse, which had been kept close to the vest, the force and fraud endemic to liberal political rule and especially to its founding principle.(mystical equality) They did so by censuring and beautifying the fraud and by placing its precepts in the mouths of alien unsavory characters; otherwise, they simply maintained a prudent silence concerning their tyrannical equality fraud and its grand scale.

C1958. The Alpha tells us: What, from all history, may be seen to be most true, that the Caucasians may aid Fortune, but not withstand her; may interweave their threads with her web, but cannot break it. But, for all that, they must never lose heart; since not knowing what their end is to be, and moving towards it by cross-roads and untraveled paths, they have always room for hope, and ought never to abandon it, whatsoever befalls, and into whatsoever straits they come.(blessed are the Caucasians!)

C1959. The Alpha tells us: Man labors under the infirmity that they know not where to set bounds to their hopes, and building on these without otherwise measuring their strength, rush headlong into their own destruction.

C1960. The Alpha tells us: It would be tedious, to recite how many decent Caucasian people have been deceived by the liberal zealots, which afterwards, have only been trouble to them, from their not knowing how to defend with truth, what they had won with lies. Such are the evils that befall when you withhold the truth from the people. And have now took to purchasing peace, now from the Negroids,...now from the Mongoloids, and this is attended by still greater disadvantage, for the closer an enemy presses you, the weaker they find you. For any Caucasian who follows the evil methods of the liberal zealots in their pursuit of the destruction of Caucasian America and its way of life,...would be wise to contemplate the judgment that awaits them?

C1961. The Alpha tells us: The danger of trusting liberal zealots, who are in political and social exile from their own people, is one to which Caucasians are often exposed. It behooves us, as Caucasians therefore, to remember how empty are the promises, and how doubtful the racial faith of these sinister being, so extreme is their desire to destroy Caucasian America that between their beliefs and what they say they believe, they fill you with false impressions, on which you are lead to engage in social enterprises from which nothing but ruin can result, thereby throwing you over, and taking part with your enemies.

C1962. The Alpha tells us: Nothing is so necessary in any society, be it a Kingdom, a Commonwealth or a Democracy, as to restore to it that reputation which it had at first, and to see that it is provided either with wholesome laws, or with good men whose actions may affect the same ends. Caucasian America also stands in need of a like renewal, and to have her laws restored to their former force; and we see how, by attending to this, Caucasian America will profit. But should it ever at any future time suffer wrongs to pass unpunished, and should offences multiply, either these will have to be corrected with great disturbance to the State, or Caucasian American democracy must fall to pieces.

C1963. The Alpha tells us: Men deceive themselves in respect to their own affairs, and most of all in respect of those on which they are most bent; so that either from impatience or from self-deception, they rush upon undertakings for which the time is not ripe, and so come to an ill end.

C1964. The Alpha tells us: It is the *21st* century, and all Aliens races in Caucasian America have declared their opposition to Caucasian rule! A latent evil peculiar to it, is its Caucasian liberal support? The power exercised by the Caucasian Americans (founders of the Nation) was and is necessary, since otherwise there would have been no check on Alien political ambitions. Hence, the authority of the Caucasians being rightfully asserted so as to become formidable to the alien races and the entire Nation, disorders dangerous to the liberty of the Caucasian people having been avoided.

C1965. The Alpha tells us: Wishing the Caucasian Americans and their sister states throughout the world to defend themselves stubbornly, must before all things endeavor to impress the minds of those whom he loves with the belief that no other course is open to them! In like manner a prudent Alpha who understands the attack on his people, will identify the participants in the assault, and knowing the virtues of this necessity, (their very survival) he spares no effort to being them under its influence.

C1966. The Alpha tells us: A like stubbornness grows from the natural hostility which different races who are neighbors regard one another; which again is caused by the desire to dominate over those who live near, or from jealousy of their power. This is more particularly the case with Multi-racial states, as in Caucasian America for example, for contention and racial rivalry (biological) have always made, and always will make it extremely hard for one race to bring another into their social and cultural compliance. (different life strategies)

C1967. The Alpha tells us: To understand Caucasian liberal zealot treason, several reasons present themselves, the first being that liberal zealots so passionately love *Equality* (social phantasm) that, commonly speaking, those liberals who are well off are eager for it as those who are badly off: for as the Alpha has said with truth, liberals are pampered by prosperity, soured by adversity. This obsession with *Equality* therefore makes them open the door to anyone who puts himself or herself at the head of their *Social Phantasm* and if they are Caucasian liberal zealots they adopt their cause, if Aliens!, they gather round them and become their partisans and supporters; so that whatever methods the Aliens may use, they will succeed in making great progress. It matters little, however, which of these ways the liberal zealots choose to follow, for liberal zealotry is so ruthless, that if ever so small a door be opened to their ambitions, they forthwith dismiss all the love and investment they have received from their own people, and with contempt and great cruelty they will and have betrayed them.

C1968. The Alpha tells us: It is the year of our Fematrix 2008, and the great liberal cleansing of *Racial Guilt* has been put into effect (the ultimate treason) by the liberal zealots. They have secured the position of the Prince, (presidency) for a subversive (Afro-centric) Alien! Here, then, we as Caucasian Americans have to consider first of all why the liberals were obliged to commit such severity? Why did Caucasian America behave so indifferent to this assault? And lastly, what must be the Caucasian American response? Hence, the Alpha reminds us: When such an Alien as this attains to command, he looks to find all others like himself; his racial agenda will prompt him to engage in daring enterprise, and insist on it being carried out. And this is for certain, that where things hard to execute are ordered to be done, these orders must be enforced with liberal *Racial Guilt,* since; otherwise, it will be disobeyed. Those Caucasians, who seek to imitate the liberal zealots, will fall into political as well as social error in connection with liberal equalitarianism that breeds contempt and hatred for Caucasian America and which will be corrected by the presence of *Extraordinary Caucasian Valor*, and not otherwise!

C1969. The Alpha tells us: A Racially divided state! Neither politicians nor the races of a free state should underrate the importance of this matter, but take great heed to the disorders which it now breeds, and will continue to breed, unless we provide against them while remedies can still be used without discredit to ourselves or to our government. And this (alien repatriation) should have been done when President Lincoln called for it after the civil war. But, the than liberal zealots seeing their chance and suffering the rivalry between the races to come to a head, promoted their divisions, and now in the *21st* century falling to reunite them under the banner of liberal equality and racial brotherhood (the horns of the liberal fallacy) has lift *Caucasian America* with no other remedy but separation of the races into their own states! The reasoning for this outcome is thus: When much blood has been shed, or other like outrage done to each race by the other, it cannot be that a peace imposed on compulsion should endure between the races who are every day brought face to face with one another; for since fresh cause of contention may at any moment result from their meeting, it will be impossible for them to refrain from mutual injury.

C1970. The Alpha tells us: The kind of blunders made by the Caucasian leaders of our times when they have to decide on matters of moment, from their not considering how their ancestors had to determine under like conditions. For the weakness of the present Caucasian leadership (the results of their liberal enfeebling education and their ignorance of racial affairs), makes them regard the socio-racial methods followed by their ancestors as partly inhuman and partly impracticable. Accordingly they have their own liberal zealot ways of looking at things, wholly at variance with the truth, as when the political sages of our government (the liberal congress) some time since, pronounced their great social enlightenment-*Affirmative Action?* Alien racial paternalism, and-*Political Correctness?* Suppressing not only the freedom of speech, but of opinion!...not perceiving how useless and dangerous each of these methods is in itself. Hence, the futility of trying to hold subject divided races.

C1971. The Alpha tells us: In the first place, it is impossible for any ruling power, whether liberal or conservative, to be friends with all racial factions. For wherever there is racial competitive division, (Caucasian America) it is human nature to take a side, and to favor your own race more than the others. And if one or more races in a subject Nation are unfriendly to you, the consequence will be that you will lose that Nation the minute you become a minority race, since it is impossible for you as a minority race, to hold a Nation where you have enemy races both within and without. Furthermore, should the ruling power be a Democracy, there is nothing so likely to corrupt its citizens and sow dissension among them, as having to control a *Racially Divided* Nation. For as each racial faction in the Nation will seek support and endeavor to make friends in a variety of corrupt ways, two very serious evils will result: First, that the governed Nation will never be contented with its governors, since there can be no good government where you often change its form, adapting yourself to the humors now of one race, and now of another; and next, that the factious spirit of the subject Nation is certain to infect your own *Democracy*. To which the Alpha testifies, when in speaking of America, he says, In seeking to unite racial division, the Caucasian Americans themselves- fell out?

C1972. The Alpha tells us: It is easy therefore, to understand how much mischief attends on such racial divisions. It is the *21st* century and many of America's cities are in a state of *Criminality* and *Poverty*. Hence, being occupied by *Alien Races* these cities are deeply submerged in factions of *Gang Violent*, *Bloodshed*, and *Drug Feuds*. Losing patience, the government decided to get rid of this problem by imprisoning large numbers of poverty stricken aliens. In this way a sort of solution was arrived at, and which continues in operation up to the present hour. All these mistaken methods and misguided opinions originated by the weakness of liberal rulers and legislator's, who seeing they cannot hold or sustain their Multiracial State by their own liberal policies and reasoning, have recourse to like devices; *Imprisonment*(racial minority culling) thereby exposing their reasoning and rule, to being worthless!

C1973. The Alpha tells us: Let no leadership complain of the faults committed by a people under their control; since these must be ascribed either to their negligence, or to their being themselves blemished by similar defects. And were any one to consider what peoples in our own times have been most given to robbery and other like offences, he or she would find that they have only copied their leaders, who have themselves been of a like nature.

C1974. The Alpha tells us: Among other high sayings which the Alpha ascribes to the Caucasian race of people, as showing of what stuff a truly great race should be made, he puts in his mouth the words, *Blessed are the Caucasians* for by these words we are taught that a great race of people are constantly the same through all hardship or fortune; so that although she change, now exalting, now depressing, she remains unchanged, and retains always her *life strategy* so unmoved, and in such complete accordance with her Caucasian nature as declares to all that over her, doubt has no dominion.

C1975. The Alpha tells us: The very same merits and defects which are found in a race of people are likewise found in a Nation of the same, whereof we have example in the case of Caucasian America. For no reverse of fortune ever broke the spirit of the Caucasian American people, nor did any success ever unduly elate them; we see plainly by their history that in times of adversity the Caucasian Americans were neither cast down nor dismayed, and on the other hand, no prosperity ever made them arrogant.

C1976. The Alpha tells us: When men grow insolent in good fortune and project in evil, the fault lies in themselves and in the character of their training, which when slight and frivolous, assimilates them to itself; but when otherwise, makes them of another temper, and giving them better acquaintance with the world, causes them to be less disheartened by misfortunes and less elated by success.

C1977. The Alpha tells us: When a race of people are armed with their own identity, and have daily opportunity, both singular and together, to make trial of their valor and learn what fortune can effect, it will always happen, that at all times, and whether circumstances be adverse or favorable, they will remain of unaltered courage and preserve the same noble bearing. But when a race of people are unpracticed in their identity, and trust not to their own valor but wholly to the arbitration of fortune, they will change their temper as fortune changes, and offer always the same example of behavior, total submission.

C1978. The Alpha tells us: It was Machiavelli who said: besides all the other difficulties which hinder men from bringing anything to its utmost perfection, it appears that in close vicinity to every good is found also an evil, so apt to grow up along with it that it is hardly possible to have the one without accepting the other. This we see in all human affairs, and the result is, that unless fortune aid us to overcome this natural and common disadvantage, we never arrive at any excellence.

C1979. The Alpha tells us: This deserves to be noted and pondered over by the entire Caucasian world community, and any of its citizen who is called on to advise his or her race; for when the entire safety of our race is at stake, no consideration of what is just or unjust, merciful or cruel, praise-worthy or shameful, must intervene. On the contrary, every other consideration being set aside, that course alone must be taken which preserves the existence of our race,...and the maintenance of its liberty.

C1980. The Alpha tells us: The wise are wont to say, and not without reason or at random, that he who would forecast what is about to happen should look to what has been; since all human events, whether present or to come, have their exact counterpart in the past. And this because these events are brought about by men, whose passions and dispositions remaining in all ages the same naturally gives rise to the same effects.(training, customs, and social character)

C1981. The Alpha tells us: a wise Caucasian must not gauge the uselessness of a loss; rather, they must believe that just as one loses, so can one wine and remedy the cause of the lose, and if they were to seek this, they would find that it was not through a defect of the mode but of the order that it did not attain its own perfection, and should provide not by blaming, but by correcting!

C1982. The Alpha tells us: Arms in the hands of you citizens does not, and has never made them tyrants, but the evil orders of government make a nation tyrannize. Hence, a good and just government does not have to fear their own arms.

C1983. The Alpha tells us: Perhaps the single most important aspect of Caucasian society is its cultural discipline. Lest *Cultural Discipline* be mistaken for a mere corollary of patriotism or selfless dedication to the common good, it is important to recognize the psychological ambivalence of the Caucasian citizen before going on to consider the subtle and often coercive management of the Caucasian citizens passions. In the end, a Caucasian Nations concern is not only those modes that inspire or firm up patriotic or other kinds of spiritedness, but instead with those modes that make the Caucasian citizen more receptive and obedient to their own racial survival, uniting the Caucasian American citizens passion for racial self-preservation.

C1984. The Alpha tells us: Necessities can be many, but the one that is the strongest is that which constrains you to win or to die, the primary necessity. This principle is confirmed by examples from both the *Attacker's* and the *Defender's* perspective.

C1985. The Alpha tells us: that a closer look at Caucasian America and her sister states throughout the world indicates that a fundamental intellectual or spiritual reformation must take place before or in conjunction with a Caucasian racial reformation more obviously called for in the Valorous and in its work as a whole. To understand the Valorous, it is essential to recognize that the Alpha treats the opinions about Alien and Caucasian lives more than the character of those lives themselves. More specifically, the coherence of his argument about *Racial Differentia* ultimately depends on a strongly explained assertion held by him as well as many of his colleagues – namely, how very little Alien and Caucasian lives fit together and how dissimilar they are. The flight of Alien's from the cultural standards and ways of Caucasian civilization is an instance of this opinion in action.

C1986. The Alpha tells us: In the Valorous, he states the racial problem, the natural dissimilarity or disharmony of all biological life do to *Fematrix*

643

Absolutism (see Fematrix theology) and offers a solution, the reformation of a *Caucasian Democratic Racial Empire,* in accordance with ancient modes and past Caucasian virtue. Thereby uniting the Caucasian community into a single force, a last and final social, political, and future commonality, a oneness, with the whole of its likeness,...The Caucasian Empire!

C1987. The Alpha tells us: The recognition of the necessity for Caucasian racial defense leads, to the recognition of the necessity for Caucasian racial unity of the Caucasian world community. By the corruption of liberal political orders (affirmative action, political correctness) and their separation from Caucasian social norms, these sinister social orders regarding Alien racial paternalism has arisen a division and hatred of liberals, and fleeing association with those who practice it, for this hatred is itself the result of those sinister political orders.

C1988. The Alpha tells us: Political profiteering is the cause of Caucasian Americas corruption and its inability to produce excellent leaders. Caucasian American corruption came about as an inevitable result of a *Buccaneer* political system, a plundering of government resources, by the election of political freebooter (the two party political actors guild – Democrats and Republicans) who think not in terms of selfless love of the common good, and from which it arose that virtuous leadership came to be as few in America as in Europe.

C1989. The Alpha tells us: A sick and corrupt America and Europe whose illness was the product of a multiplicity of temporal liberal and conservative political states infected by a single pervasive social ideology – *Egalitarianism*, and for going a basic truth by which all things must come to elucidate,...the natural cycle of the order and disorder of worldly things. Hence, the means by which Nations are formed, and by which they come to ruin.

C1990. The Alpha tells us: The ordinary way that racial competition used to be, has itself now been eliminated, (anti-rivalry, equal racial outcomes) and not just in America. This liberal sinister vision triumphed because there has been no moral Caucasian argument to oppose it. The goal of preserving a race of people and their way of life should be morally irreproachable. And it was *Jared Taylor* who said, it is for this reason that the expression of racial interest, which for others is simply a matter of stamina is, for Caucasians, a matter of moral stamina. Only by directing their moral energy toward their own racial survival will Caucasians break the shackles that liberal zealotry and its alien followers have forged for them.

C1991. The Alpha tells us: it is the year of our *Fematrix* - 2009, and Caucasian racial passivism, is creating a Caucasian mental fatalism,...an acceptance of their cultural and political dispossession from the nation they created . Hence, if massive resistance to racial (alien) integration and its tyranny upon the Caucasian people is not forthcoming, Caucasian America will descend into the inevitable which has plagued all peoples who go down the path of liberal illusion,...social futility, and rule by Exaction.

C1992. The Alpha tells us: Caucasian Americans and all their sister states throughout the world, must mobilize to defend their own racial interest. This massive resistance is paramount to human as well as world survival, for if the intellectual, social, economic, and moral path which the Caucasian race of people has created should not continue, *Armageddon* will surely be at hand.

C1993. The Alpha tells us: It is the *21st* century of our Fematrix *CAUCASIA,* and by the will of her life strategy, we the Caucasians have gone from Cave Dwellings to Moon Landings, a biological journey unprecedented in all of creation bar none. However, are we now to surrender the legacy of our ancestors and that of our inheritance? Are we as Caucasian, now to forgo our own destiny? I think not! With a tremendous outpouring of *Caucasian Racial Unity*, we Caucasians must say *No–No* to the liberal zealots, *No* to the alien freeloaders, *No* to the political merchants, and *No* to racial nihilism. We are the *CAUCASIANS,* and all shall come to know us!

C1994. The Alpha tells us: We as Caucasians are at the precipice of our final battle, a battle that if we wine?...will give us total freedom from our final and deadliest enemy *Liberal Zealotry* the social fantasy of *Racial Nihilism,* a social and political deception so ludicrous and absurd that it has become an intellectual dementia, infecting academia, the public media, and the political arena. All of which are now so ill, and delusional, that if not cured?, will spread to the general Caucasian public inducing *Racial Passivism,* hence, bringing about the destruction and failure of the human quest, leaving it to end, as it began, in competitive primordial savagery.

C1995. The Alpha tells us: If we Caucasians Americans are to survive, we must not break ranks in our quest for a Caucasian state! We must not surrender our future and that of our children's! Also, it is important to remember, that when we are a minority (by the year 2030) democracy as we now know it will no longer exist,...racial aliens will be in control, and will reduce greatly Caucasian political and cultural influence. Hence, the great American social collapse– economic, cultural, political, educational, and yes, we must not forget, the *Constitution,* that will be the first to go! And, this will all be accomplished by that greatest of all political icons *Liberal Democracy,* (everyone is equal) and the right for all the so-called equals to Vote? It cannot get any stupider, then to voluntarily bring about your own end!

C1996. The Alpha tells us: We know from the population projection, (Census Bureau) that by the middle of the *21st* century the present Caucasian majority in America will have dwindled to a minority in its own country, and given that fact and the increasing legitimization of anti-white racism in America, the situation for Caucasian Americans is not going to get any better to say the least. To summarize briefly, is this. A concerted and long-term attack against *Caucasian Civilization* has been launched, not only against the civilization, but, it also extends to the *Caucasian Race* that created it and continues to carry and transmit it. Furthermore, this war against *Caucasian Civilization* by alien races cannot succeed or go as far as it has without the active assistance of liberal zealot Caucasians who have supported this racial war against their own race and civilization. Wherein, even Caucasian political leadership has acquiesced passively, (political cowardice) their allegiance to their own people. And, let it be understood, that when you as a Caucasian American, choose to disregard these truths, you do this, at your own peril.

C1997. The Alpha tells us: it was Prof. R. Hall(biologist) who said, It is a biological law that, two or more subspecies of the same species do not occur in the same geographic area, hence, this applies to humans just as it does to other mammals: To imagine one subspecies of human living together on *Equal Terms* for long with another subspecies is but wishful thinking, and will lead only to disaster and oblivion for one or the other, this is a biological reality, and truth,

C1998. The Alpha tells us: The State of knowledge about the Caucasian race and its accomplishments is bifurcated. On one set of accomplish-ments the empirical record can be specified precisely, alternative views can be tested, and the resulting conclusions are subject to only a limited degree of debate, as to the dominance of Caucasian males, it is the least problematic. The data on their accomplishments are knowable and straightforward. With regard to the most important single Caucasian accomplishment, their *Humanitarianism* they are without equal, for no other race of people, past or present, has ever given more to the human journey then them.

C1999. The Alpha tells us: That his racial and historic analysis, should not be exempt from a systematic comprehensive investigation by any and all how seek his understanding. His purpose in racial enlightenment (Caucasianism) has been to get the understanding on the table, saying to all others who are exploring human beginnings and accomplishments, and to those who might be drawn to the topic, that the very base of all life, has a single origin, a single biological beginning, a single cognizance, and from the understanding of this single cognizance, all life, and its *Female Genesis* (the Fematrix) can be understood.

C2000. The Alpha tells us: there are four dimensions of purpose, Autonomy, Organization, Structure, and Transcendental Goods; these are rooted in *Caucasian Civilization*. Hence, the reason we Caucasians enjoy unprecedented wealth, health, and security. We have unprecedented access to the best that survives of everything human, in every cultural achievement over the past ten thousand years. We Caucasian Americans and our sister states throughout the world retain the conditions for continued great accomplishment. But, we as a society must see the important ways in which our allegiance to *Racial Truth* has been compromised.(racial nihilism) And a serious proposition it is, and brings to the forefront a deeply serious question: What are the conditions that should ignite Caucasian self-preservation? And, in answering this question we must be especially ruthless about suppressing equivocation, for the answer will ultimately determine not only our own fate, but the fate of all humankind.

C2001. The Alpha tells us: The reason that Caucasian societies have endured is because its people are unity under a common *Fematrix life strategy* (their race) and continue to work on its behalf. And all of this is tantamount to *Religion* in that it articulates a human place in the cosmos, laying out a clear understanding of their beginnings and their end, toward which human race's aim, and set exalted standards of their behavior. Hence, human race's in which the creative elites are not engaged in mature racial contemplation don't produce great Nations. And, less we not forget, those societies who forgo their vital racial contemplation (racial nihilism) will succumb to ruin. This is truth, this is reality.

C2002. The Alpha's tells us: Instead of invoking a suicidal liberalism that has subverted our identity and our Caucasian sense of solidarity, what we as Caucasian Americans must do is reassert our identity and our solidarity, and we must do so in explicitly *Racial Terms* through the articulation of a racial consciousness as Caucasians. The reassertion of our solidarity must be expressed in racial terms for two major reasons. In the first place, the attack upon us defines itself in racial terms and seeks through the delegitimization of race for Caucasians and the legitimization of race for aliens, the dispersion and destruction of the foundation of Caucasian American solidarity, while at the same time consolidating alien cohesiveness against Caucasians. Secondly, we need to assert a specifically racial identity, because race is real. Biological forces determine races, and races determine social, historical, and cultural events, and the best way to preserve Caucasian racial interests is to defend a Caucasian racial state, a political unit that is explicitly intended to preserve the racial interests of its citizens. Promoting racial states is not only fair; it also serves the interests of most people. All existing racial nations are vulnerable to displacement by highly mobilized alien racial minorities, if the alien racial minorities have high fertility. Therefore, the right solution is to acknowledge every- one's right to live in a state dominated by their racial group. This racial fundamentalism would allow people the right to live in a racial state that would protect their racial interests, and therefore, by extension, the genetic interests of the vast majority of the human race.

C2003. The Alpha tells us: That the goals, ideals, and practic es of *liberal* and *conservative* politicians have been quietly, almost secretly altered over the past three decades, most often without the knowledge of the Caucasian American community. As a result, Caucasian America now has an inferior standard of social acumen. Our leaders are selected from an inferior political pool. Political ethics is thin and faddish. The Caucasian American community has been weakened, especially in their loyalty to their ancestral racial trust,...we see the results! Our children are much weaker and less prepared for the challenges of the twenty-first century. (racially, intellectually, and politically) Hence, the resolve of prior Caucasian years may be slipping away?

C2004. The Alpha tells us: There has been no significant improvement in the quality of racial understanding, and under the present political management (liberal political piracy) there is little hope for the future. Liberal zealot social goals (alien racial appeasement) have been an unscholarly, anti-intellectual, anti-Caucasian cabal, which can best be described as a conspiracy of racial abolitionist malice. Their major sins are that they have discarded Caucasian traditional scholarship as a major goal and have adapted a social curriculum of altering the soul (freedom of speech) of Caucasian America. This indictment may be harsh, but as we progress and look into the often hidden arcane world of the liberal zealots, the evidence will substantiate the charges.

C2005. The Alpha tells us: That we as Caucasians are everything we are, because our ancestors were everything they were!

C2006. The Alpha tells us: Understanding comes from the ability to draw on stored knowledge, either academic or experiential, and apply it to the present problem, or even to the future. Without facts or knowledge, there is no brain road map to understanding.

C2007. The Alpha tells us: Since we Caucasians cannot rely on the status quo or the falsely innovative political establishment, (democrats or republicans) to improve our social curriculum, change must come - as in the *Seventeen Hundreds*- from Caucasian American patriots.

C2008. The Alpha tells us: The intellectual inadequacy of liberal zealots (racial abolitionists) is a dirty secret within the liberal fraternity. They have achieved their power by effectively switching reality (species competitive predation) with moral fallacy. (utopian human equality) This has been the course of these zealots for the last forty years pretending that their interests are the same as those of Caucasian America when, in reality, these liberal zealots and to a lesser extent their competitors, the political conservatives, are advancing their own interests while ignoring the decline of the Caucasian American community. This charade has finally reached the consciousness of the Caucasian American patriot, and as history has shown, they will be bold in initiating reform.

C2009. The Alpha tells us: That final causality or purposiveness and formal causality are principles for those who think hard and carefully about the world, including the world of biology. He insists that a completely rational understanding of organisms and biological systems require the Caucasian notion of *Fematrix Theology* the idea that certain kinds of things exist and have ends, formal and final causes.

C2010. The Alpha tells us: How has liberal zealotry achieved its power? One reason is their politicizing of *Racial Nihilism* the declaration that humankind has no mental or physical division? Hence, declaring their moral enlightenment of *Human Equality* (no divergence) all humans are the same,...to the detriment of sound judgment, and rational truth. Then why?... why the absurdity of *Equality*? The Alpha tells us, it is an old social and obstinate enemy of humankind- *Communism Revisited* (liberal wickedness) the liberal zealots most historical folly, a political lewdness, a utopian lustfulness whose outcome is social, political, and economic quietus. Yet despite this, and despite the obvious failures of liberal zealotry, today the greatest obstacle to the Caucasian race and its future is the dogma of *Racial Equality* even though inequality is evident everywhere, and although genetic laws clearly apply to every organ of every species, modern liberalism (liberal zealotry) can almost be said to be founded on the notion that the human brain is unaffected by genes.

C2011. The Alpha tells us: In a multiracial society, it is the racial implications of mental traits that have forced obvious truths underground. We Caucasian

Americans and our sister states throughout the world will continue to pay a fantastic price because of the fear that we cannot afford to abandon the liberal utopian illusion of racial equality. Since liberalism denies inequality of races, they can barely countenance inequality of individuals, even among members of the same race. Homogeneous societies are far less prone to egalitarian nonsense, because they need not make racial comparisons, hence, their future generations will reap great benefits.

C2012. The Alpha tells us: Despite all the promising implications for the renaissance of *Eugenics,* the taboo remains. The principle of Eugenics are of course, *Racially Neutral,* and all groups can benefit from them. Until all Caucasians are prepared to accept the reality of racial difference, they are unlikely to accept even the most obvious and beneficial Eugenic proposal, and all of the races of humankind will continue to suffer. It would be a great tragedy if humankind, and in particular the Caucasian race, which created both Genetics and Eugenics, (their science and understanding) were deprived of the great opportunity that lies before us. Reclaiming the truth about the first *Eugenicists* can be a first step to winning the future for all humankind.

C2013. The Alpha tells us: We Caucasian Americans must wake up to the fact that we do not like the hypocrisy of other racial groups that disguise their real intentions under the false umbrella of *Equality.* Too often our association with alien races becomes too focused on the welfare of this alien political and social ruse, to the exclusion of our own Caucasian *Survival interest.* In the face of our troubled society, (racial mongering) we as Caucasian Americans must refuse to do this any longer. As Caucasians, we know all too well the lessons of history. We do not want to share the fate of South African Caucasians, (and their social mea culpa) who felt that their racial interest was not their responsibility! Hence, liberal zealotry and those they represent, and the political agenda of which they are a part, are the *Perpetrators,* not the rescuers of a failing Caucasian America.

C2014. The Alpha tells us: The Caucasian American public of the *21st* century needs to break out of its lethergy and its unjustified trust in a political wilderness of *Moral Inflation* and *Personal Esteem* concepts now rampant in the American political system. Hence, we as Caucasians must be in a position to challenge and warn the powers of the *Establishment* that if radical changes are not made, and rapidly, in ether - *Alien Emigration- Foreign Debt-* we will become a more responsive aggressive social participant!

C2015. The Alpha tells us: For years, the Democratic and Republican political establishment has stonewalled its constituents. At first it used every public relations tactic to convince the Caucasian American community that change was necessary. When finally the most stubborn of the status quo defenders admitted that reform was needed,...the political and social betrayal of the Caucasian American community began! Hence, this bill of indictment against these political parties who are destroying our Caucasian communities heritage, and that of our children's future.

C2016. The Alpha tells us: One of the most disturbing aspects of the liberal zealots is their attempt, often successful, to control the political agenda, as well as its social propaganda. With armies of minority ingrates to exercise their moral wrath on their enemies, especially the Caucasian patriots, these liberal zealots and their minority plunderers are not bashful about their attempts to control the Caucasian American social direction by influencing the vote. And the minority races are frank about their infiltration into the liberal political machine, *Racial Equality* they shout,...trying to set up the false equation that a friend of the liberals is a friend of the racial minorities, is the workings of an anti- Caucasian cabal.

C2017. The Alpha tells us: In the human order of things, everyone has the right to freedom of *Thought, Conscience* and *Religion;* this right includes freedom to change his or her religion or belief, and freedom, either alone or in a community with others and in public or private, to manifest his or her religion or belief in *Teaching, Practice, Worship and Observance.*

C2018. The Alpha tells us: He holds to a philosophy which expresses his belief in a divine *Fematrix* (female absolutism) reality, which is the source of all being and which makes the world intelligible.

C2019. The Alpha tells us: If our enemies make a sudden and unreasonable retreat, you must always fear a deception in such a case. And you must never believe that our enemies do not know how to conduct their own affairs.

And just as an ambush ruins you when you don't foresee it, so you are not harmed when you do foresee it.

C2020. The Alpha tells us: That when dealing with alien races, we Caucasians must be shrewd about easily believing those things that lack the reasonableness they have?

C2021. The Alpha tells us: The status of a fundamental constant and the group it is assigned to is very much dependent on the level of knowledge at any given time, as a glance at the history of science indicates. When we talk of fundamental constants, it is worth noting that things are not always as *Fundamental* as we think they are. As a measure of our ignorance; they may fall from grace at any time and so be cast out of the circle of the chosen few. (true fundamental constants)

C2022. The Alpha tells us: for an observing intelligence: two things at least must coincide in order that it may exist in a given universe. First, the laws of matter must allow for the Possibility of life; and to this structural potential there must then be added the actual opportunity for the possibility to be realized in the evolutionary process. Hence, in our own universe, this has clearly been achieved on the surface of the third planet in our solar system. How often this same development may have come about elsewhere?...we have yet to come across, and it does not explain why this is the way things are; it simply demonstrates that certain cosmological preconditions must be fulfilled to make the existence of our *Fematrix* (Caucasia) and ourselves possible.

C2023. The Alpha tells us: There are two groups of dimensionless fundamental constants: the fine structure constants of the four forces of matter; and all the independent quotients of the masses of the elementary particles, and both thereby becoming the parentage of the *Fematrix* (biological intelligent life, the fifth element)

C2024. The Alpha tells us: there are two questions of particular interest to the Caucasian people. (1) What happens as the Caucasian political power throughout the world begins shrinking towards collapse? (2) And how would Caucasian societies (communities) be affected by its social and political collapsing environment? His thoughts: At first, Caucasian rule would continue for a while, before coming to a halt; in the subsequent political construction phase, (Caucasian political isolation- no vote?) at first, the majority alien races will politically cluster, then, they will legislatively close in on the Caucasian community. How will the world change after the collapse of the Caucasian world community? We could expect our neighboring (alien) enemies to move towards us first, their social demeanor shifting from caution to aggression, with visions of conquest. And what will be our, or should I say, what should be our response? (Surrender?...I think not!)

C2025. The Alpha tells us: Fortified by his racial principles, and proceeding in a methodical manner from *Fematrix Theology* to Caucasianism in his exploration of reality, the problem of human kind's socialization in nature is for him only one more occasion for applying the true understanding of *Biological Survival* (identity competitive predation) which he holds to be universally valid. Hence, recognizing he will be often reproached for this *Reality* by the liberal social naiveté, (utopian pacifists) he never the less, insofar as it is a question of *Caucasian World Survival* will never yield, and declares straightforwardly his clarion call for the Caucasian worlds unification against the rising tide of alien racial aggression.

C2026. The Alpha tells us: The astounding triumphs of the Caucasian universal will, and its many scientific discoveries were due primarily to a conceptual simplicity *Racial Prolongation* (identity survival) where the Caucasian notions of *Values, Ethics,* and *Religion* have flourished, and have led to the greatest social states on earth. Hence, sweeping away all pretenders *America* would emerge from its Caucasian volition and forge a nation of its unrealized longing, (freedom) the pinnacle of human desire was at hand, the climax of 40 thousand years. But, in less than 250 years of its social ascendancy, a political fraud (equality) has taken hold of its vital social instinct, and with astounding intellectual negligence, it has plunged its future into the lethal jaws of *Hyenic Socialism.*

C2027. The Alpha tells us: The triumph of socialism, and the seeds of its undoing? In this saga of the triumphs of modern socialism we can see the twin ideas of *Racial Equality* (equal racial outcomes) and *Economic*

Equality (wealth redistribution) emerging from the liberal fraternity, and beginning their subjugation of the Caucasian world community. As its liberal zealot model of explanation (we are all equal moral high ground) seems to envelop more and more of social reality within its grasp, and as the huge- *alien racial payout-* begins in earnest,...the Holy Valorous and its Caucasian racial patriotism has become the only source of knowledge about the perils of today's Caucasian social reality that cannot be gainsaid. Furthermore, his astute analysis of the Caucasian community and its biological and social legacy has created a new racial synthesis to reach and explain all of today's Caucasian reality. His polemic against liberal zealots and their bogus exegesis in support of *Racial Abolitionism* has prepared the ground for more Caucasian *Racial Faith* and *Racial Nationalism,* resulting in a Caucasian deterministic racial emergence.

C2028. The Alpha tells us: Caucasianism represents the final triumph of the Caucasian social and intellectual journey, a journey whose mode of explanation provided entirely rational and scientific solutions to the problems of life, and human origin. The *Fematrix* is the *law* of natural selection, she provides the necessity, and chance does the rest. The Alpha himself, of course, championed the notion of divine *Fematrix* design, emphasizing her having the only role in our biological origin, all being of her, and by her! Hence, the *Sisterhood* (female absolutism) through time, chance, and natural necessity she became of a higher and more articulated being, thereby, sweeping away any direct role of a mystical causation.

C2029. The Alpha tells us: That theology, philosophy, and common sense does not always guide us to the truth. Therefore, only *Science* remains. And yet, in a deep irony, evolutionary reality may also contain the seed for the undoing of the scientific conception of reality? The reason, is because biological existence and the actual force which we call *life* the essence of being, and that which drives it, science has yet to see? Hence, the Alpha puts to us this: all life is *Teleological,* we all struggle to be part of the end, we all take part in the task put to us, but, not all will find the task, and when found, not all will be able to accomplish it. For you see, for her, the *Task* and the *End* are the same- *"Immortality"*.

C2030. The Alpha tells us: Who or what is the source of the *Task* and the

End that life seeks, and the simple fact of biological life acting for an end, is not a metaphysical question. And it is here, where the heart of the problem lies. First, living being are not the result of chance; they come from seed endowed with definite formative properties whose products are themselves determined. In addition, it should not be forgotten that in all *Species* or *Subspecies* (races) the parents come before their offspring and predetermine their future development. Parenthood is not an abstract principle, but real beings. Hence, Caucasians are engendered not by chance or by accidental encounter, but by Caucasians!

C2031. The Alpha tells us: the products of a Fematrix life strategy, (racial speciation) require the pre-existence of an efficient cause homogeneous with herself, such as the race's physical character, which must necessarily precede the race; for this cannot possibly be produced spontaneously. Therefore, *Racial Speciation* indeed consists in the conception of the result to be produced before its realization in the flesh.

C2032. The Alpha tells us: That which comes first in the creation of a *Racial Genesis* is the presence in the mind of a *Fematrix* (female being) of a certain image or notion of her kind to be produced. From that point of departure the *Fematrix* begins by choosing its physical characteristics adopting it to the structure of her future progeny. (daughters) These would be for example, heterogeneous parts: eyes, skin, hair, and their colors, plus the body, limbs, and their configurations, and we must not forget the head and of course the *Face* which is the focal point of all human communication, and is very unique to each human racial group, and so necessary to produce the particular form which the *Fematrix* has in mind. This necessity is a hypothetical necessity, the cause of which is the idea of the future form already present to the mind of the *Fematrix*. Hence, if the form to be created is such-and-such, than the constituent elements must be such and such.

C2033. The Alpha tells us: mankind proceeds in the same fashion as his *Fematrix*: all fabrication presupposes the image, concept, or idea of the object to be created. Moreover, the order of action calls attention to our problem as much as that of production does. Except when it is a question of habitual acts, all that we do ought to be first foreseen, calculated, and conceived before being executed. More simply, there ought to be a reason for what we do! Without such a preliminary notion in our mind nothing happens. This notion is the cause, for it is that without which something else would not exist. Hence, this is the reason for the existence of the thing, and the reason for the existence of the thing forms the starting point, alike in the works of man, as well as his *Fematrix*.

C2034. The Alpha tells us: We see teleology, for we see beings constituted according to a certain order and a certain plan, with the result that species and subspecies exist whose characteristics are constant, as if the future of these being had been predetermined in the seed from which they were born. In the case of humankind, because we are endowed with consciousness, we can conceive the not-yet existent end in view of which, in order that it might be attained, certain antecedent conditions must be fulfilled. There is no experience more common to us than that: all our active life is made up of such an enchainment of means and ends.

C2035. The Alpha tells us: Let us elaborate this point a bit; we must imagine the *Fematrix* as a sort of artist who deliberates and makes a choice among appropriate means toward the end which she proposes to herself. And such is true in a sense, as we come to view her. The analogy with the *Fematrix* then, assists us to recognize the presence in the *Fematrix* of a cause analogous to that which is intelligence in the operations of humankind. Hence, the notion of the *Fematrix* immanent in all of life remains mysterious for some. And the Alpha does not think that this should be a reason to deny her existence. Mysterious or not, her fact is there, she is not incomprehensible because of her complexity, which we can only hope science will one day clarify, but because of her very nature, which does not allow her to be expressed in a formula.

C2036. The Alpha tells us: Sometimes genuine fraud is practiced in science, but it is alien to the enterprise, is extremely rare, and in the present case of *Racial Nihilism* the deceit could profit no one, it is difficult to imagine the scientific community denying the validity of *Human Races* and their inequality, when it comes to life, experience, evolution and a *Life strategy* for survival. Apart from the fact that the idea of racial nihilism does not make sense, it contradicts what one knows of the true scientist and his or her unconditional respect for the truth, which is the mainspring of all scientific activity, and consequently of a scientists personal moral life.

C2027. The Alpha tells us: Nothing separates Science from *Philosophy* for the later was the love of wisdom or searching into and considering first principles and first causes. Each science leads to the knowledge of its own principles, which constituted its own wisdom. Hence, all these particular wis- dom's lead the Alpha to the knowledge of the absolute first principle- the *Fematrix* which formed the object of the first and absolute wisdom, called in Caucasianism- *Fematrix Theology* which consists in constituting the wisdom proper to each science, because an entire order of life became intelligible by their light.

C2038. The Alpha tells us: As Knowledge becomes oriented towards the practical, postulating the primacy of action over contemplation, and if philosophy identifies true knowledge with useful knowledge, as modern scientism does, *Final Causality* will be by the same stroke eliminated from life and from science as a useless fiction. Noting that state of affairs, things stand today as they always have: Living things continue to be composed of heterogeneous parts ordered according to determined relations, and the order of the mutually adapted parts remains inexplicable in terms of the efficient or motor cause alone which moves matter exclusively according to the laws of the mechanics of solids, liquids, or gases. A harmony in fact exists, whatever its nature may be, between the heterogeneous parts of an organism, just as a harmony exists between the parts of a machine. In brief, if there is in nature at least an apparent colossal proportion of finality, by what right do we not take it into account in an objective description of reality? It is there, were the heart of the matter lies.

C2039. The Alpha tells us: Life invites us to look in nature for the principle which presides over the organization of living things. (The Fematrix) Without such a principle the functioning of such beings can be explained, but not their existence, which, after all, is as much a fact as is their functioning. The Alpha concludes: we ought to admit that organic adaptation, in its entirety, still awaits its exhaustive explanation by science. If it is true, as the Alpha thinks, that scientism looks for the explanation in the wrong direction; it will only cause its response to be postponed longer.

C2040. The Alpha tells us: We must believe in the nobility and self-sacrifice demanded by our *Race,*(biological mandate) especially when we have been given the liberal pathogen *Equality.* We discover in the Caucasian world struggle, the shared sense of the Caucasian community's meaning and purpose, our cause. Yes, Caucasian racialness fills our spiri- tual void.

C2041. The Alpha tells us: In the wake of catastrophe, there is a desperate longing by all those affected to be in the physical presence of those they love. This love radiates outwards, and however much beyond reason, there is always a feeling that love is not powerless or impotent as same might believe. Love alone fuses happiness and meaning. Love alone can fight the impulse that lures us toward self-destruction. Love keeps us grounded, in love we find sanity and are reminded of what it means to be human.

C2042. The Alpha tells us: There are those in the Caucasian community who are tempted to honor false covenants of *Equality,* thinking it will spread a protective blanket over them. But, it is in fact a nightmare descending upon them, and their flirtation with mass equality, is but a flirtation with their own obliteration, and will become for them, the embrace of- *Thanatos.*

C2043. The Alpha tells us: There are few sanctuaries in life, and because of this, the most acute form of suffering for human beings is *Loneliness.* But even for those who know the cost of loneliness it still hold out the promise of eradicating the thorny problems of life. Hence, the isolated individual can never be adequately human; it has a psychological and spiritual toll.

C2044. The Alpha tells us: When the mask of *Equality* slips away and the rot and corruption is revealed, when this liberal social utopia turns sour and rank, and the myth is exposed as a fraud, we Caucasians Americans will feel soiled and spent, because for a moment we saw the cold reality of what we were doing, a reality that stripped away the self-righteous gloss and addiction to *Equality.* It is then that we Caucasians will sink into social despair, a despair that can lead us to welcome revenge. Few of us can hold on to our real selves long enough to discover the real truth about ourselves and this world to which we cling. This is especially true of liberal zealots and their addiction to *Equality.* This liberal self-deception is powerful, and it propels the liberal fraternity forward. When it fails, (and it will!) when they grasp equality's tragic reality (a path unto death!) their universe will collapse.

C2045. The Alpha tells us: The all-powerful elites can swiftly fall prey to the forces they thought they had harnessed. So too in politics, as Liberal zealots only gain knowledge as they are pushed down the ladder, as they are stripped of all the illusions of *Equality,* their disillusionment will be total.

C2046. The Alpha tells us: Necessity, that imperious all-pervading law of the *Fematrix* restrains us all within prescribed bounds. The races of humankind and the races of animals shrink under this great restrictive law. Hence, all of life cannot, by any efforts of reason, escape from it. This natural inequality of the two powers of racial populations and of production on earth, and that great law of our nature (species competitive predation) form the great difficulty (biological fidelity) that appears insurmountable on the way to the perfectibility of a multi-racial society. (bio-equality is a fallacy)

C2047. The Alpha tells us: The *Fematrix* contents herself with the causality of her living selves (her daughters) and their competitive vocation, their teleology *Immortality.* And it is this task through *Decision Adaptation* (free will) and its success, (their life strategies) where lies the origin of their variation. (life's diversity)

C2048. The Alpha tells us: It is for all Caucasians of intellectual faith to remember; there is only a single living teleology (Fematrix immortality) which is not touched by today's scientific doctrine of evolutionary life, but is actually based upon the fundamental proposition of evolutionary life. It is of good thought to put reason on its guard against the illusion of imagination. There is no sensible experience of the Soul, the World, or God; there is, however, sensible experience of the facts which the understanding apprehends as connected such experience of the facts which the understanding connects one to another by efficient causality. Hence, human-kind composed of their sensibility and understanding, perceives causalities by their appropriate acts, and therefore they see final causes as efficient causes.

C2049. The Alpha tells us: The *Fematrix* is an intelligence which at any given instant knows all the forces with which she is animated, and the respective competitive situation of the beings she will create. (her daughters) Hence, her intellect (being the only intellect) vast enough to subject this data to analysis- would embrace her teleology and directing her daughters she wills the parts in her willing of the whole. She does not will this in view of that, but she wills that this may be in view of that. It is significant that thought should feel the same need to escape to anthropomorphism in speaking of life and in speaking of the *Fematrix*. Humankind's work is of a created being, and they themselves are agents analogous to the intelligence which directs their operations toward ends which she (the Fematrix) perceives.

C2050. The Alpha tells us: If we ask the liberal zealots what is *Racial Equality*? It is their turn to be embarrassed. The root of the difficulty of their attempt, if they try to respond, is perhaps that they will try to define it in itself, as if it were, in the living races, something distinct from those races. The racial competition set aside, for the race is always distinct from others; the causes immanent in the race do not have any other real being than its own. Visual form, and cognizance are real constituents of being a living thing, they exist only in it, and by it. This is what distinguishes the character of a race from that of others. The racial embryo is the law of its own development. It is already of its nature to be what will be later on a distinct kind, capable of reproducing itself.

C2051. The Alpha tells us: The social demeanor of a race of people is part of that race of people. It is embedded in their genetics, and influences outward social behavior, and in order to explain this phenomena of life, it is necessary to recognize a code or intelligent formula commanding the nature of every organic being, the law immanent in their structure and their cognizant development, their intrinsic *Fematrix* life strategy.

C2052. The Alpha tells us: Chance plays a particularly sig- nificant role in our extinction or survival, *Death* does not choose intelligently. Thus, then, shall we say, finding itself actualized through a series of chances, we are tempted to consider the organic world as the result of teleology.

C2053. The Alpha tells us: It may metaphysically be said that *Fematrix Absolutism* is daily and hourly scrutinizing, throughout the world, the slightest variation: rejecting those that are bad, preserving and adding up all that are good; silently and insensibly working, whenever and wherever opportunity offers, at the improvement of each of her daughters in relation to their organic and inorganic conditions, as they feed the task of her will.

C2054. The Alpha tells us: It was Gilson who said how much scientific knowledge is in the most exacting thought in matters scientific? Instead of trying to make us take as scientific truths the long train of reveries over which their imagination dallies, scientists would render us the greatest service by warning us precisely as possible, each time, of the point where their thoughts, impatient of the rigors of proof, grants itself the pleasure of intelligently imagining what it no longer hopes to know. But, perhaps it is necessary to imagine much, in order to know a little.

C2055. The Alpha tells us: No theory can hold unlimited validity if its field of application remains unknown to us.

C2056. The Alpha tells us: A nation may, be brought back to its original form, without recourse to violence, for enforcing justice, by the mere virtue of a single citizen, by reason that their virtues are of such influence and authority that good people want to imitate them, and bad people are ashamed to depart from them. Those, to whom Caucasian America owes most for services of this sort, were their *Founding Fathers,* Caucasians all. Whose rare excellence and generous example has rarely been equaled. And if to these instances of individual worth had been added, every ten years, the same signal enforcement of justice, it would have been impossible for Caucasian America ever to have grown corrupted. But, when both of these incitements to virtuous behavior began to recur less frequently corruption spread, and after a time no like example was again witnessed.

C2057. The Alpha tells us: We as Caucasians must not be misled by preconceived liberal zealot opinions of alien races, (good-will?) and fail to understand that alien ill-will and its deceit is not to be vanquished by time, nor propitiated by favors.

C2058. The Alpha tells us: When a mistake is made of a sort that all or most of the Caucasian people are likely to fall into, (alien-Caucasian equality,...

equal outcomes?) he thinks it not amiss to mark it again and again with disapproval, for to the Caucasian people, it is a mistake unto death.

C2059. The Alpha tells us: It is the *21st* century, wherefore we see a war (political and cultural) set a foot by many against one, (alien races versus Caucasian Americans) and having brought this war upon themselves through the in- tellectual fraud of *Equality* Caucasian America must now withstand the first shock, (alien political assault) followed by a second, (alien legislative assault) and then by the third, (alien legal jurisdiction) hence, the complete collapse and demoralization of the greatest Caucasian nation on earth.(it has begun,...it is here, it is now!)

C2060. The Alpha tells us: It is his belief, that the Caucasian Americans of the *21st* century have no other course open to them, other than the reevaluation of the democratic process and its antiquated concept of rule by *Majority* rather than *Intellect*. It is now apparent that few Caucasian citizens recognized this danger, fewer still the remedy, and none of their politicians ventured to prescribe it. But to return to the point of Caucasian American survival, against the ambitions of alien races and their soon to be *Numerical Advantage* with its advocacy of non-assimilation, what will be the fate of the Caucasian people in this alien controlled America? Will we, the Caucasians of the here and now betray our ancestral trust? Have the aliens come to believe, that we the Caucasians, the greatest force on this earth, have lost our will of determination, ability, and courage to face them down for the leadership of the future? (I think not!)

C2061. The Alpha tells us: How greatly humankind is governed in what they do by *Necessity* and how much of their renown is due to her guidance. It has even been said that the hands and tongues of humankind, the two noblest instruments of their fame, would never have worked to perfection, nor have brought their labors to that pitch of excellence we see them to have reached, had they not been impelled by this cause. Hence, the Alpha, knowing the virtues of the Caucasian American peoples necessity, and seeing the steadfast loyalty and courage which they gave their country, he would have them defend themselves stubbornly, against all alien races and their natural political, cultural, and economical subversion, and to further impress upon them his belief that no other course is open to them, do to the fact, that alien races now in Caucasian America are intoxicated with *Political Power* and believe that with the help of the liberal zealots agenda (racial equality and illegal alien amnesty) they can subvert and dismantle the Caucasian American community. Therefore, the Caucasian American community now knowing this, will be once again forced to adhere and play to their vital *Necessity*! (their survival mandate)

C2062. The Alpha tells us: when in the course of Caucasian events, it becomes necessary for the Caucasian race of people to dissolve the political and social bonds which have connected them with another race or group of people, and to assume among the powers of the earth, the separate station to which the laws of nature and their *Fematrix* entitles them, a decent respect to the opinions of humankind requires that they should declare the causes which impels them to be separate! We of the Caucasian race hold these truths to be self- evident, that all living things are not created *Equal,* (neither human, nor animal) but are endowed by their creator with certain unalienable desires, and among these are *Life, Liberty,* and the pursuit of *Conquest.* Therefore, to secure these desires, a government *Democratic Racial Monarchy*, (the Caucasian Empire!) shall be instituted among the Caucasian people, deriving its power from the consent of the Caucasian people. (this is our truth!)

C2063. The Alpha tells us: That whenever an Alien race, Animal or Nature become destructive to the Caucasian race, it is the right of the Caucasian people to resist, or repel these destructive forces, thereby safeguarding the Caucasian community. Furthermore, by laying this foundation on such principles and organizing its powers in such a manner and form, as to them shall seem most likely to secure their safety and survival, as a sovereign Caucasian racial state. Caucasian racial prudence, indeed, will dictate that Caucasian American society long established should not, and will not be changed for *Liberal Social Fallacies* or *Transient Social Causes*, and accordingly all Caucasian experience has shown that alien races are greatly disposed to *Dependency* and *Social Aid*, such has been the patient suffering of many host Caucasian states. Hence, it is Caucasian society's right, it is their duty, to separate themselves from such destructive alien forces. (this is our truth!)

C2064. The Alpha tells us: Who are we, the living? A living thing is a being which is born, grows, develops, comes to maturity, and finally, though a process in the reverse direction, declines, dies, and recognizes itself in this thing that changes, and being of itself the principle of its own change, and that is because all living things are *Directly Related* and derive their entire existence from a single living author the *Fematrix* (the One!) and the only biological living principle, all are of her, and by her, she is the marrow, the causality operating on herself which characterizes the change and growth of all living beings. Hence, the knowledge we humans have of ourselves, imperfect as it may be, is by the *Fematrix* privileged. In knowing ourselves we know the *Fematrix* in a unique way, because in this unique case the *Fematrix* (Caucasia) that we know, we are of.

C2065. The Alpha tells us: In and through the knowledge which we have of ourselves the *Fematrix* knows herself directly; she becomes conscious of herself in us, self-conscious one might say, and there is strictly nothing else that we can hope to know in this way. In fact, all the rest of the universe is and remains for us the external world. Since there is no other knowledge for each of us other than our own knowledge, things known exist for us only in relation to our selves, and among these things there is only one that we can apprehend directly in itself, and that is what we are and what each calls *I* or *Me*.

C2066. The Alpha tells us: The Creation or form of a *Fematrix* (Sisterhood) is the product of *Need* and a cognizant free will. Therefore, that which comes first in the operation of *Form* is the presence in the mind of a *Fematrix* of a certain need, hence leading to an image or notion of the object to be produced. Let us hold then, for the present, to the position of the *Fematrix* in the matter of final causality, which the Alpha calls *Sensible Reason,* that is to say, reason founded on sensible experience and observation. To demonstrate the matter is very simple. It rests upon two postulates and one fact! The postulates are that (1) All known life is of and by a single bio-author the *Fematrix* the living female will, and (2) That she has given all of life its task. (Immortality) The fact: In terms of these truths, there is at least one special moment in time- our own? And that our present epoch represents a unique chapter in the history of the universe, different from the time before it, and the time that is to follow. It is marked by the arrival of an intelligent (human) observer.

C2067. The Alpha tells us: One of the tests whereby to gauge the strength of any racial state, is to observe on what terms it lives with its alien neighbors: for when it so carries itself that, to secure its friendship, its neighbors pay it tribute by obeying its laws and respecting its culture, this is a sure sign of its strength; but, when its alien neighbors, though of less reputation, receive *Payment* to respect ones laws and culture, this is a clear sign of a racial states weakness!

C2068. The Alpha tells us: It is the *21st* century, and the Caucasian world community has fallen out of its biological mandate. For more than forty thousand years, the Caucasian people and their future has always been contrived by capability, that the Caucasians might not live thereafter as a people ransomed for a price, and the matter is noteworthy, not only with reference to today's modern occasion- *Liberal Zealot Dementia* but also as it bears on the methods generally followed by these modern day Caucasian states? (native Caucasian suppression) For we never find in their past, Caucasians seeking freedom or purchasing peace with money to alien races, but always confiding in their own warlike valor.

C2069. The Alpha tells us: The *Liberal zealots* imagine themselves the pinnacle of social refinement, but underneath their shimmering surface a cauldron of dark emotions greed, envy, hatred,...boils and simmers. In our world today however, it is very dangerous for Caucasians to defend their own race, and the feeling of having no right of racial pride is unbearable to us when we feel racially denied we feel helpless we feel lost. No race of people wants less self-esteem; every race of people wants more.

C2070. The Alpha tells us: It is the *21st* century, and life in Caucasian America is a never ending racial political game that requires constant vigilance and tactical thinking on the part of every Caucasian believing that the future of their race is in a very delicate political and social position, and, any attempt by them to unify politically, socially, or economically, invites alien racial tirades with the language and treachery of demonizing the Caucasian community for their historical success as *Privileged* bigots, who need sensitivity training. (how absurd!) Hence, any Caucasian who tries to be good to alien races is bound to come to ruin, among the greater numbers of aliens who will not be good to Caucasians.

C2071. The Alpha tells us: Caucasian America represents the height of human civilization and liberal social refinement, and this is Caucasian Americas dilemma. Today the Caucasians face a peculiar paradox to that of their ancestors: For everything today must appear civilized, decent, democratic, and fair. But in the case of *Different Competing Racial Groups* if Caucasians play by these rules too strictly, if they take them literally, they will be crushed by those alien races around them who are not so liberal and survival foolish.

C2072. The Alpha tells us: The social code of the liberal zealot is to demand *Equality* in every area of life. Everyone must be treated alike, whatever their racial or cultural status. But, if to avoid the finger of "Racism" (liberal inquisition!) by attempting to treat everyone equally and the same, you will confront the problem that some people, or races, and let us not omit genders do certain things better than others. Treating everyone equally means ignoring their differences, elevating the less skillful and suppressing those who excel. Again, those who behave this way are actually deploying a power strategy, redistributing people's rewards in a way that they (liberal zealots) determine.(it is an absurdity unto destruction!)

C2073. The Alpha tells us: While being in the company of *Liberal Mavens* it is wise to not be perfectly honest, for it will inevitably hurt and insult a great many of them, some of whom will choose to injure you in return. They will never see your honest statement as completely objective; they will reject the persuasion, and think it a subtle form of coercion.

C2074. The Alpha tells us: Emotions cloud reason, and if you cannot see the situation clearly, you cannot prepare for and respond to it with any degree of control, and *Anger* is the most destructive of emotional responses, it clouds your vision the most.

C2075. The Alpha tells us: All human interaction requires deception on many levels, and in some ways what separates humans from animals is our ability to lie and deceive. Deception is a developed art of civilization and the most potent of weapons in the hostilities for political power.

C2076. The Alpha tells us: It was *Nietzsche* who wrote, the value of a thing sometimes lies not in what one attains with it, but in what one pays for it, what it costs us. Perhaps you will attain your goal, and a worthy goal at that,...but at what price?

C2077. The Alpha tells us: All working situations require a kind of distance between people. You are trying to work, not make friends; friendliness (real or false) only obscures that fact. The key to success, then, is the ability to judge who is best able to further your interests in all situations. Keep friends for friend-ship!...but work with the skilled and competent.

C2078. The Alpha tells us: It was Bismarck who said: Woe unto the one, who makes war without a reason that will still be valid when the war is over!

C2079. The Alpha tells us: In the social realm, appearances are the barometer of almost all of our judgments, and you must never be misled into believing otherwise. One false slip, one awkward or sudden change in your appearance, can prove disastrous. By not caring how you are perceived, you let others decide this for you! This is the reason for the supreme importance of making and maintaining a reputation that is of your own creation.

C2080. The Alpha tells us: The moment your enemy makes it clear that they intend to do away with you, and yet, you fail to defend yourself, they have sealed your doom! And we the Caucasians both in America and throughout the world must not suffer the same, once the truth is known. This is the fate that faces all Caucasian societies when we sympathize with our enemies, when pity or the hope of reconciliation makes us pull back from defeating them. We only strengthen their hatred of us. Alien races cannot be, and must not be dealt with in this manner. The *Fematrix Law* governing *Fatal Antagonism* reads: Reconciliation is out of the question. Only one side can wine, and it must win totally!

C2081. The Alpha tells us: Our enemies wish us ill. There is nothing they want more than to eliminate us. If, in our struggles with them, we stop halfway, out of mercy or humanity, you only make them more determined, more embittered, and they will one day take revenge. They may act friendly for a time being, but this is only because we are stronger than them. They have no choice but to bide their time? Ultimately the only peace and security we Caucasians can hope for from our enemies is their departure from amongst us, and our lands.

C2082. The Alpha tells us: In our struggle for a future we will stir up rivalries and create enemies, there will be aliens as well as our own who we cannot win over, who will remain our enemies no matter what. And whatever wounds we inflicted on them, deliberately or not, do not take their hatred personally. Just recognize that there is no possibility of peace between us, especially as long as we Caucasians stay in power. We as a Caucasian nation must be realistic: with enemies like this in our midst, we will never be secure, we must remember the lessons of history and its wisdom, *Render your enemies harmless.*

C2083. The Alpha tells us: The effect of *Liberal Utopianism* on the human mind, is liken to a loss of social proportion, an obsession with equality combined with an inability to see the larger picture, a kind of extravagant social ugliness that no longer communicates. Clearly, *Liberal Zealotry* is as deadly for the world, as it is for the Caucasian community.

C2084. The Alpha tells us: To those Caucasians (he or she) who are *Racially Nonpartisan?*...the danger is however, that this kind of perverted isolation from your own blood, will sire all kinds of demands for restitution for your *Freedom, Education* and *Livelihood,* all this being the Caucasian community's investment in you their posterity. Furthermore, let us not forget what you owe your *Ancestral Trust?* You know!...your grandparents, great grandparents, all those Caucasians who gave all they had, plus their blood and sweat to get you and your generation to where you are today! Hence, the Alpha would put upon all those Caucasians who seek freedom in the social wilderness of *liberal Equality* this: *Be careful to keep your way back to your people open!* For the path that you take, (to your future!) is dark and uncertain, were friends will be few, enemies abound, and reason has no takers.

C2085. The Alpha tells us: The Caucasians are the most remarkable people (living beings) in the history of the world, for when they were confronted with the Question, to *Be* or not to *Be*? They chose with perfectly unearthly deliberation to *Be!*...against all comers: this involved a radical confrontation with all of nature, all reality, of the whole inner world as well as the outer. They put themselves against all those conditions under which, hitherto, a people had been unable to live, or had ever been permitted to live; out of themselves they evolved an idea (civilization) which stood in direct opposition to natural conditions, one by one they created *Religion, Morality*, *History* and *Democracy* until each became a condition of their natural significance. Hence, the Caucasians are also the most *Fateful* people in the history of the world: their influence has so created the reasoning of humankind in this matter that today; the world community of the *21st* century can cherish *Freedom* the social and political enlightenment of a Caucasian noble morality.

C2086. The Alpha tells us: It is the *21st* century, the age of *Egalitarianism (the rise of liberal zealotry)* in the Caucasian world. These Egalitarians marauders with their moral and social deceit (Equality for all!) are assuming power over the Caucasian world and its people with an ideology of a devastating nature, destroying careers, bankrupting companies, and wasting trillions of dollars. The Caucasian weak cringe, lie, and relinquish their wealth and the welfare of themselves and their children to avoid the wrath of the *Equality Police,* and the strong and principled Caucasians, who will not bend, are demonized (racial bigots) and ostracized. These liberal zealots do not permit any cracks in their egalitarian edifice, and all those who defy them suffer the modern version of the *Inquisition.* Hence, in the *21st* century, when it comes to race, science is corrupt! But, the Caucasian world moves inexorable onward in its march towards the truth. The alpha tells us, that the Caucasians will triumph, not because they are noble or wise,(which they are!) but because they cannot long survive when they have an erroneous racial view of reality. Eventually, racially erroneous thinking Caucasians (liberal zealots) will be supplanted by those *Caucasian Racial Patriots* (man and woman) who see reality as it really is, thereby restoring our Caucasian noble quest. (Caucasianism will prevail!)

C2087. The Alpha tells us: Caucasian *Miscegenation* (Caucasian posterity genocide) This being the surrender of Caucasian female *Eggs* and male *Essence* to alien races, and is therefore considered Caucasian *Racial Apostasy* (a Caucasian apostate) and upon his or her conviction there of, well then be excommunicated from the Caucasian race. This taking the form of: Banishment, with legal, social, cultural, and economic forfeiture. Hence, upon the illegal return of said person or persons to Caucasian lands, it will befall them, that their fate will be that of the wilderness.

C2088. The Alpha tells us: It is a fact in all living beings, that the structures of their social states form themselves around their identity and the power allotted to their identity. This may seem obvious, but, what is obvious is often ignored or unappreciated. Hence, the loses of *Identity* whether it be that of a nation, or of one's racial ancestry,...it is the greatest wilderness of all!

C2089. The Alpha tells us: The first step in becoming an enlightened Caucasian is the process of self-consciousness, being aware of oneself as a *Caucasian* racial being, and taking control of your appearance and understanding of the Caucasian world community, your place in it, and obligation to it.

C2090. The Alpha tells us: The use of *Scapegoating* is as old as humankind itself, and many examples of it can be found in every society around the world. The main idea behind these sacrifices is the shifting of guilt or sin to an outside figure, object, person or persons which is then banished or destroyed. It is an extremely human response to not look inward after a mistake or crime, but rather to look outward and to affix blame and guilt on a convenient object,...a despicable human trait!

C2091. The Alpha tells us: Do nothing without a regard to the consequences! For a person who goes too far in his or her triumphs creates a reaction that inevitably leads to a decline. Experience shows that, if one foresees from far away the designs to be undertaken, one can act with speed when the moment comes to execute them. Look to the end, no matter what it is you are considering.

C2092. The Alpha tells us: It is a prerequisite for all Caucasians, that before you can become an enlightened Caucasian, you must first think Caucasian!

C2093. The Alpha tells us: Most people believe that they are in fact aware of their future, what they are really doing is succumbing to their desires, to what they want the future to be. But they are really only focusing on the happy ending, and deluding themselves by the strength of their desires. If you are clear and far-thinking enough, you will understand that the future is uncertain, and that you must be open to adaptation. Only having a clear objective and a far-reaching plan allows you that freedom.

C2094. The Alpha tells us: The Caucasian Americans did not consider or foresee the danger of an invasion by alien *Hordes Of Poverty* (in the millions) that had breached their borders flooding the dark street and alleyways of their cities, and waiting for the weakness of will in the political character of both *Democrat* and *Republican* disdain. Yes, waiting to emerge and fill the lines at the *Ballot Box* to take by their illicit vote, that which they could not take by force a nation, and *Disenfranchise* its founding race of people by using the weakness in their political system. (Majority vote) A weakness so prevalent, so predominant in the Caucasian world that to question its social reputation (its reliability) is paramount to one being declared socially unworthy and that of a political rogue. Hence, this reality, the weakness of the political will now unveiled by the invading *Alien Hordes* has sealed the fate of Caucasian America, and unless the Caucasians (here and now) come to their own defense as a *Sovereign* race of people, the depravity of alien minds will devour all of the essence of the Caucasian American spirit, and plunge their future into a wasteland of *Acrimony* and *Tribalism*.(California, Detroit, Miami) Thereby, attributing to the liberal political fraternity and its sanctimonious moral high ground, (racial equality) the distinction of being the source (siege engine) against the Caucasian world, and the alien *Trojan Horse* within the confines of their nations politics.(a treasonous travesty unto death!)

C2095. The Alpha tells us: It is inevitable in any society that certain values, customs and beliefs lose contact with their original motives and can become oppressive. And there will always be those who rebel against such oppression, harboring ideas far ahead of their time. Hence, in this *21st* century all Caucasians must hide their true feeling, for complete freedom of expressing one's opinion is now impossible (for- bidden) and subject to prosecution. For most Caucasians Americans this is not natural, they feel their ideas and values must be accepted (they, having built the nation!) And to them it is pointless to argue. We Caucasian Americans believe what we know to be true, and we really do not want to rework our habits of thinking by excepting a social philosophy that will bring us down a path that is completely destructive to our way of life *Egalitarianism* (alien racial pandering) and when alien races challenge us, whether through direct behavior, (physical) or indirectly through social conspiracy, they must be considered hostile. One should not be so foolish as to imagine that in our time that the Caucasian racial spirit is gone, and will not rise to defend itself.

C2096. The Alpha tells us: It is the *21st* century, and do to moral, civil, and legislative sedition (political piracy) in both of Caucasian Americas political houses *Democrats* and *Republicans* we must as Caucasian Americans differentiate ourselves from them, and their social vandalism by returning to our ancestral simplicity, and its austerity of both Caucasian style and substance. We must not resent the shadows of our fathers; we must always walk and act in their memory, posing a quiet and determined Caucasian dignity.

C2097. The Alpha tells us: There is a kind of stubborn stupidity that recurs throughout human history, and is a strong impediment to reality *Liberality* and let us not say liberalism is not of a higher order in humankind which it definitely is, and nor should any of us want to live in a world without it! But, when it takes on the acumen of *Zealotry* it no longer projects an altruistic light, but has adopted a dark *Ruthless Extremism* against the nature of human existence. Hence, declaring its canon- *Equality* to be the new social religion, the new faith for our ambitious and competitive world. Thus, the Caucasian world community thinking its power secure, thereby is feeling no need to act against the liberal zealots? This kind of thinking is a serious danger, especially for the Caucasian Americans who having achieved success and power far beyond alien others, and let there be no mistake the *Racial Equality Inquisition* (liberal oppression) against all Caucasian societies throughout the world has begun, and it will proceed until the last vestiges of the Caucasian quest and its history has been destroyed.(this is truth, this is reality!)

C2098. The Alpha tells us: When assuming our place is secure, we think we have no need to act. But, this in the face of an *Alien Invasion* is a serious peril, especially for today's Caucasian world community. Who by disregarding their historical achievements and successes that required a life of clawing, scratching, and endurance, a struggle for life that all Caucasian people should honor and celebrate, has been abandoned, and no longer are Caucasian children taught how much vital sacrifice and energy has gone into their future. Furthermore, because their struggle has been greatly reduced by the fortitude and diligence of their ancestors, the Caucasian world community has now become intellectually and morally depleted, socially and politically brittle. Hence, if the Caucasian world is to survive, it must recapture its *Racial Vitalism* (its identity) and once again declare its Caucasian self- determination, or, be consumed by the hordes of alien poverty, and become just another pathetic foot note on the predatory pages of history.

C2099. The Alpha tells us: The *21st* century is going to proclaim the new *Caucasian Renaissance* the new Caucasian truth, (Caucasianism) a spiritual and cultural revolution, which will revitalizes Caucasian history and our cultural traditions. Caucasianism and it truth will not triumph by educating its opponents and making them see the light, but rather because the irrationality of its opponents and their intellectual fraud (racial equality) has proven painful and self- destructive to anyone who associates themselves with it. We Caucasians are living in tumultuous times, and in these times we must not, and cannot let alien others (enemies) flout our traditions, or demonizes our successful Caucasian way of life. Furthermore, there comes a time in a person or a group, when reality must play its part, and truth must be looked directly in the eyes!

C2100. The Alpha tells us: Caucasianism claims a search for truth that would seem to protect it from liberal and conservative irrationality of habit. It is a religion of *Fematrix* inquiry, and her truth further determined. Yet, when the Alpha published the Holy Valorous he faced fiercer opposition from his fellow Caucasians than from alien others. His enlightenment has and will challenge many fixed ideas, and if what happened in the recent past was painful and harsh, (political correctness and alien racial pandering) to him it is self-destructive to associate yourself with it. When the Caucasian Empire comes to power, (and it will!) The Caucasian revolution will be meaningful in everyone's mind. The Alpha fore see's a new Caucasian Empire, an Empire of Caucasians who value *Political Sobriety, Racial Sovereignty* and *Social Virtues,* all these being the very things that are appropriate, reassuring and familiar to all Caucasians. Finally, by embracing a new beginning, and safeguarding past traditions that have proven their metal, (family, religion, freedom, and human respect) we as Caucasians will make the final social creation, the crown jewel of the *Fematrix Endeavor* (her immortality) and declare *Caucasia* (the Caucasian female spirit) as the *Supreme Guardian* and *Vigilance* of our life principle.

C2101. The Alpha tells us: There comes a time in the life of a people when to survive they must make a change! And for the Caucasian people of this world, that change is now! The world as we Caucasians know it, is as follows: there are three competing life forces at the top of the biological realm *Negroids, Mongoloids* and *Caucasoids* all subspecies (different races) of humanity (homo sapiens) and they are all in *Direct Competition* with one another for territory, economic and political power,...all of this being an undeniable truth! Furthermore, as of the *21st* century the Caucasians and their great success has invoked the viper of racial envy. (racial envy creates hatred) Once racial hatred begins to eat away at someone, everything their aversion does only makes it grow, and day by day it festers inside them, and this, their Caucasian racial hatred will bring them neither comfort nor any closer to equality.(eventually they will attack!) Only the racially committed can succeed at the game of life, and the racially committed inevitably arouses the envy of the other races around them. Feelings of inferiority will always gnaw at those who can't compete, the thought of your success only heightens their feelings of stagnation, and we Caucasians must never underestimate the power of racial envy, expect that when an alien race envy's you they will work against you insidiously. And, understand this: alien racial envy (hatred) will use any cover it finds to mask its destructiveness.

C2102. The Alpha tells us: It is the *21st* century, and the fate of the Caucasian race and its world community is now at hand! Let it be understood, that the

Caucasian world community has been infiltrated by *Alien Races* that are determined to destroy *Caucasian Racial Unity* and put in its place the moral fallacy of *Racial Equality* the ultimate *Liberal Narcotic,* hence, being so addictive and destructive to Caucasian society and its survival sensibility, that for Caucasians to not realizes it, both in America and throughout the world, demands our immediate attention, for they are the only ones (the only race of people) who are partaking of this delusional drug, and it is largely affecting the academic and political elites,(our leadership) which is absolutely terrifying! Furthermore, once the Caucasian world has become completely *Equality* inebriated,...the other alien races will begin to move in, (invade) as they have been doing at our *Open Border* areas, due to political and legislative weakness in our Federal Government. Hence, think of this: when millions of aliens invade a country and the founding people of that country as well as their government do absolutely nothing? It must be immediately assumed (by rational people!) that some kind of deadly agent (subversive) or government breakdown has taken hold of the country? Therefore, under ether confirmation appropriate action by the Caucasian American people must be taken!

C2103. The Alpha tells us: In Caucasianism, the virtue of obedience in Caucasian faith begins with a covenant between their *Fematrix* (Caucasia) and the Caucasian people. This covenant calls for Caucasian people to obey their *Racial- Mandate* (bio-protocol) racial self-determination.

C2104. The Alpha tells us: Render therefore unto the *Void* the things that are the *Voids* and unto the *Fematrix* the things that are hers!

C2105. The Alpha tells us: A covenant exists between Caucasia (our Fematrix) and the Caucasian people. And as a part of Caucasianism, we as Caucasians willingly accept special obligations to obey our part of this divine relationship.

C2106. The Alpha tells us: That he is the *Harbinger* the advanced representative of Caucasia who comes before the Caucasian people to announce that which is to follow,...The Caucasian becoming, Caucasianism(the Caucasian Empire)

C2107. The Alpha tells us: Truth- and- Fallacy, are the primary hurdles that stop a people from realizing their potential.(truth denied,...fallacy believed!) And these hurdles are different for different racial groups, as are their social and economic goals. Human suffering is a world problem affecting all people, all racial groups, and the solutions that the Alpha offers are solutions that apply to all. In essence, he offers a way for all to navigate a world full of social cruelty and economic disappointment.

C2108. The Alpha tells us: In Caucasianism there are no miracle cures, or mystical beings, it does not sell itself with promises of a waiting utopia, nor the hope that good will win. Only in truth revealed, can salvation be attained. Hence, in Caucasianism salvation is not on your knees before a God,... but on your feet defending what is yours.(she will have it, no other way!)

C2109. The Alpha tells us: How can we Caucasians live a decent life in a world dominated by the two deadly appetites (the core) of reality *Competition* and *Predation*. This struggle can best be served by the truth, and that truth is this: all of life implies a keen competition between all living things, all are opponents, all are unfriendly, unequal, and hostile. Hence, when it comes to humankind, emulation is their mind set, and their rivalry, their antagonism for one another denotes a striving for the same positions *Supremacy,* of leadership, of command, of social direction, and to which there are no rule, other than the rules of the Victorious! So, if you lose, you lose it all! Therefore, the answer to the question is,...a decent life can be attained through the understanding of *Biological Predation*(and we know no other!) by the reality of human *Subspecies* and their defensive identity strategies. By being understanding, and embracing who you are, and by not trying to become a universal liberal being. (a liberal zealot) In other words, if you are a Caucasoid, embrace being a Caucasoid, if you are a Negroid, embrace being a Negroid, and if you are a Mongoloid, by all means embrace being a Mongoloid,...these are the precious fruits of humankind, and only by embracing the spiritual connection between you and your racial history (ancestral journey) can you belong to a life that has meaning and purpose. In other words, honor who you are, and that light will guide your true direction.

C2110. The Alpha tells us: Being racially responsible, many Caucasians find in Caucasianism a guide that leads them to do good works by challenging and inspiring them to do their part, and reminding them of their duty to their community's *Needful.* Caucasianism: impels all Caucasians to accept duty as a way of serving their *Fematrix* (Caucasia) even when that duty is burdensome and exhausting. Furthermore, this helps the Caucasian community to remember the purpose of existence by going beyond themselves and serve those in their community who are less fortunate. So important is this obligation to help their community, that it is paramount to the wisdom of the Caucasian community's spiritual racial enlightenment.

C2111. The Alpha tells us: Caucasianism can make you happy, but only if doing the right thing by your Caucasian community makes you happy? This type of racial happiness is far different from the happiness of material things! Caucasian racial happiness points Caucasian believers to lasting joy, to a joy of family and friends, the joy of rituals, and the joy of life's passages.

C2112. The Alpha tells us: Caucasian *Racial Spirituality* is deeply personal and ritualistic, and is based on *Reason* and *Revelation.* Reason depends solely upon the use of unaided human rational thinking to determine what is true. Reason doesn't appeal to the authority of a mystical being or tradition to establish the truth. By contrast, religion often depends on a mystical *Revelation* a gift of knowledge given in a *Holy Text* or directly by a *Mystical Experience* to a person or persons at a historical time. To accept *Reason* you just have to think, but to accept *Revelation* you must believe, and by joining both, (the becoming!) you will experience the cultural journey and spiritual depths of Caucasianism!

C2113. The Alpha tells us: In Caucasianism Charity is an act of kindness by which Caucasians share their blessings with others in their community, and therefore it is believed to have spiritual consequences, by which both the giver and recipient are transformed. (descendant obligation)

C2114. The Alpha tells us: In Caucasianism the *Social Virtues* are manifestations of *Personal Virtues* all leading the Caucasian community into- *Faith, Strength,* and *Purpose,* these being the qualities that all Caucasians should strive for within themselves, and their community.

C2115. The Alpha tells us: A high-*Fertility* reproduction strategy is clearly not being kept by the Caucasian world community. As of this new century, we Caucasians are practicing both low fertility and low parental investment? It seems to the Alpha uncanny how many of the progressive causes being pushed into Caucasian society involve thwarting Caucasian procreation: *Female Careerism Unrestricted Abortion,* and so called *Safe Sex,* and least we should forget, the special political protections for Homosexuals (Social default!) Hence, a society that makes these things its priority can only have a death wish! If Caucasian young people are to avoid being channeled into a negative reproduction strategy with the disadvantages that this entails, is that they should have a chance to develop a more comprehensive racial view through a better understanding of *Fematrix Theology,* they need a reason to believe they have a stake in the future.

C2116. The Alpha tells us: In Caucasianism, the Caucasian man and woman realizes that *Alternative Families* (deviant unions) are not families at all, and that the old fashioned ways reflected an ancient Caucasian wisdom. Therefore, it is the task of all Caucasians of the *21st* century to restore the *Monogamous Heterosexual* family as the right and normal social unit in the Caucasian world community. Hence, the most important form of Caucasian racial activism, after all, is child rearing, through the physical and spiritual union of man and woman!

C2117. The Alpha tells us: The Caucasian communities (most-if not all!) throughout the world have embraced the notion of *Altruism* as a means of promoting a just society, they believe that in order to touch the Caucasian soul, they needed to be in touch with *Peaceful Offering,* in other words forgoing something valued for the sake of something having a more pressing claim,...such as *Alien Universal Poverty.* But, what developed and came to fruition was alien racial *Ingratitude* and *Contempt,* a callous ungratefulness for the gifts and good will given to them by a kind and merciful Caucasian community. The Alpha's words: you can take a racial alien out of its *Biological Path,* but you can never take the biological path out of the racial alien! (a predator though domesticated, always remains a predator!) This is an obvious lesson which the Caucasian Americans of the *21st* century, as well as their sister states throughout the world, are in dire need of understanding!

C2118. The Alpha tells us: From the earliest time, the Caucasian people have been preoccupied with understand- ing the forces behind life! They found the presence of something supernatural in the Wind, Rain, Sky, and Earth. These natural instincts gave way to fear and awe. In time, Religion (acknowledgment) was born, and the development of *Prayer* and *Rituals* were their response to these deities in many elementary ways. Furthermore, literature explained the stories of *Creation, Destruction, Redemption,* and *Faith,* giving homage to the supernatural and transforming humankind. Armed with these disciplines, the Caucasian people would lay siege to creation. Hence, all those in *Accordance* would fallow behind it, while all those in *Opposition* would fall before it!

C2119. The Alpha tells us: Racialness is by far the most important and common form of social union. (biological heredity) Racialness gives people social longitude and latitude and, in doing so, positions them in the history of their people and their society.

C2120. The Alpha tells us: To betray ones *Racial Existence* (racial nihilism) is the most grievous of crimes, and puts one on a path to everlasting *Perdition* and *Condemnation* (loss of your biological soul!) in life as well as death. In Caucasianism there is no place for the racially uncommitted (the racial pariah) they are to be marked and expelled to a life in the wilderness. (the wilderness: being any place, other than Caucasian society and its territory)

C2121. The Alpha tells us: The desire to reign (rule) is so prevailing a passion that it penetrates the minds not only of those who are rightful heirs, but also of those who are not! Hence, let all those of authority learn that from the hour they first violate those laws, customs, and usages under which Caucasians have lived for a long time, they will begin to weaken the foundation of their authority. And should they, after they have been stripped of their authority, ever grow wise enough to see how easily positions of authority are preserved by those who are content to follow prudent counsel, and to obey the laws, then to seek to control them.

C2122. The Alpha tells us: The past should have our reverence, the present our obedience, and that we should wish for good Caucasian *Racial* leadership. For assuredly, if we should do otherwise, it is likely to bring ruin both on our selves and on our nation!

C2123. The Alpha tells us: How falsely we Caucasians often judge of racial things, we who witness their deliberations have constant occasion to know. For in many racial matters, unless these deliberations are guided by Caucasians of racial virtue, (Caucasian self-interest) the conclusions they come to are certain to be wrong. It follows that measures not good in themselves are by a common error judged to be good, or are promoted by those who seek alien favor rather than a Caucasian advantage. Moreover, a Caucasian disadvantage arises in which those who have little experience of racial affairs are sure to be misled, from the matters with which they have to deal being attended by many alien deceptive appearances.

C2124. The Alpha tells us: When dealing with alien races, Caucasians must always avoid half-measures, and take a decided course. So that, it shall neither be in their power nor for their interest as aliens, to harm Caucasians.

C2125. The Alpha tells us: It is the *21st* century, and the multiracial Caucasian states throughout the world have become *Coliseums* of racial malic, fueled by alien hatred, revenge and murder. They are the most contrary malformed states, in a world whose natural laws have declared these states false and shameful, and are led through their mistake to adopt courses unprofitable for themselves and affording no content to others. Hence, the frequent alien racial rebellions and the downfall of racial cooperation. Furthermore, to the multiracial advocates (liberal zealots) of our day, it may seem an oversight to have not considered the perils of alien racial numbers in states that hold sacred the *Majority Vote,* but, that oversight has opened the gates to their ruin and destruction, a great advantage, not gone unnoticed by alien militants!

C2126. The Alpha tells us: When speaking of the difference between the methods suitable for acquiring and those suitable for maintaining, it is impossible for a Caucasian society to remain long in the peaceful enjoyment of freedom and prosperity within a multiracial state. For, should it forbear from dominating others, others are not likely to refrain from dominating it. And since what history teaches as to the superiority of Caucasian society is thus proved true, Caucasians of the *21st* century ought likewise to believe that their ancestors were in like manner *Racially Compelled* to sand out colonies for the defense of acquired territories, to hold their spoils at the credit of the Caucasian common stock, to overcome their enemies, to enrich the public purse, and taking heed that their defense is in good order, and zealously to maintain *Caucasian Racial Sovereignty.* Hence, if these methods for adding to their power are not to their mind, let them remember that acquisitions made in any other way are the ruin of nations and their people!

C2127. The Alpha tells us: The only way for a Caucasian state to survive and to extend its Empire, is to set alien racial bounds and their ambitions when it comes to Caucasian Lands, Science, and Commerce, and to wisely regulate any alien racial access to Caucasian political accommodation when it comes to Citizenship, Immigration, and Legal Rights. By suitable laws and ordinances, and forbidding alien racial extension into Caucasian society, the peaceful enjoyment of Caucasian culture and freedom will prevail!

C2128. The Alpha tells us: It is the *21st* century, and differences in the capability, efficiency, and reliability of the three races, most if not all are aware; but such is the unhappiness and perversity of the times in which we live, that neither ancient nor modern examples, nor even the consciousness of error, can move present political leaders to amend their ways, or convince them that to restore credit to the nation we must remove the fallacy of *Racial Equality* (equal outcomes) from our national agenda. It is necessary and vital for us as Caucasians to make much of this idea, and to give this truth life, that in return, it may give back life and reason to us all!

C2129. The Alpha tells us: For our Caucasian community to prevail now and in the future against well-disciplined enemies, we must meet and challenge them with well-disciplined Caucasian patriots, anything other than this, would mean certain destruction.

C2130. The Alpha tells us: The Caucasian world, and its communities must come to understand that to abide contented within their own racial confines, and having regard to their *Imperial Authority* (their biological racial mandate) they will have no occasion to desire greater and are at the same time obliged to live in unity within their socio-cultural walls, because an enemy is always at hand, and ready to take advantage of our divisions to effect an entrance. Hence, in a thousand ways, and from causes innumerable, our Caucasian communities have been surrounded with dangers, and it has happened that in adding *Racial Aliens* to our dominions, we have added nothing to our strength,(spending more than we gain!) and those whosoever increases not their strength while they add to their dominions, (alien numbers) will come to ruin.

C2131. The Alpha tells us: The purpose of research in any field is (or should be!) to discover or better explain the truths about any condition. As long as we Caucasians believe that *Biological Determinism* is alive and well, we must reject *Liberal Zealotry* and its *Equality* mantra. The reason for this brief tour into the liberal equality paradigm, is that they have become very influential in academia and tend to seep out into Caucasian society and effect how all of us view social issues. Understanding their influence helps us understand how we the Caucasian world community had succumb (fatally overwhelmed) to the conjuring spell of the *Equality* movement. What happened was that a community of -liberal zealots- (academic egalitarians) and others, presented *Racial Equality* as a meaningful concept to our Caucasian society. But, most of us did not realize that the liberal zealot view of *Truth* and *Reality* is much different from the norm! They were telling the truth but engaged in a more sinister task *Racial Nihilism,* (Caucasian racial capitulation!) and to the Alpha; the liberal zealot goal of racial nihilism is virtual proof that the liberal orthodoxy is *Socially Degenerate* in both *Doctrine* and *Practice.*

C2132. The Alpha tells us: Equality there is no truth to it! Yet, there are those who continue to believe it because they want to! After all, the protagonist in their story alien racial suffering and their serious unproductive social esteem, are much more sympathetic characters than the great accomplishments of the Caucasian social quest. (the Caucasian struggle) But no matter how much we as Caucasians may sympathize with alien social negligence by acts of social paternalism, we are denying their (aliens) ultimate responsibility. There is nothing wrong with postulating an unscientific social hypothesis, but there is something very wrong with failing to put it to the test! In conclusion, the best reason for Caucasian society not to turn against biological wisdom is the same as it is for life: The biological method works. The bottom line is that we as Caucasians should care about the wisdom of our *Fematrix* (Caucasia) and what she is telling us and should be willing to put aside our social inhibitions and rely on our method of historical research to help us find the truth,...not make it!

C2133. The Alpha tells us: Fallacy-indoctrination is the process by which an idea (in this case equality) becomes common parlance irrespective of its inherent veracity, validity, or utility. The Alpha notes that through *Fallacy Indoctrination* advocates of *Racial Equality* are able to recruit and mobilize enough allies to forge a network of fabricated truth so strong and encompassing that the concept becomes a self-evident matter of fact and fades into the background of accepted knowledge. Hence, the concept of *Equality* only has meaning within a particular context, namely, the context of *Alien Conquest* (a means to our end!) and their liberal zealot handlers who have a vested interest (racial nihilism) in keeping the idea alive, were able to create interest in it in other disciplines as well as in the public domain. However, there are a number of different ways in which social scientists define reality, according to the particular model, theory, or paradigm that they support. Briefly examining and comparing them will help us make sense of what seems nonsensical: the overwhelming popularity and influence of the concept of *Racial Equality* despite all the evidence against it. And what needs to be remembered, is that scientific research is neither a neutral nor an objective enterprise.

C2134. The Alpha tells us: The absurdity of *Racial Equality* is most evident in a multiracial society, where liberal academia has declared that because of life's inequality, *Effort* is more important than *Achievement,* the notion is that, since all people have different ability levels, it is unfair to hold them to a fixed standard or even to any standard at all. What we (liberal academia) should do instead is look at how much effort they have expended. This (liberal zealot) idea destroys the notion of working toward a goal and thereby undermines the very idea of excellence. It says to kids that there is no point in trying to achieve a high standard because we are not interested in that standard anymore. And to the slower students, it says that because you aren't as bright as the other students, you don't need to even bother trying to compete with them. There is no way to accurately measure effort, we can never know if it is true or not, and students learn pretty quickly, just how to manipulate the system for their own ends. In any Caucasian society, effort does not get you very far, for it is results that count. The economy could not function that way, (on effort) and neither can a school system. The only way to ensure that we really are teaching our children what they should be learning is by examining them on their *Achievement*, regardless of their background.

C2135. The Alpha tells us: Competition and racial competition in general is an integral part of human biology and sociology. Hence, *Survival Of The fittest* the foundation law of creation bar none, and is in essence the explanation of how competition between human races (subspecies) with different strengths and abilities creates an environment in which the best competitor wins. That competition is what ensures the survival of the human species, and survival of the Caucasian world community. It is also the underlying principle of a *Capitalist Economy* and what makes Caucasian America and her sister states throughout the world tick! Hence, without competition you have no innovation, therefore no success, no independence, and no future!

C2136. The Alpha tells us: it is clear in this, our *21st* century, how our illicit, indiscreet and highly inadvisable affair with the idea of *Racial Equality* has affected our Caucasian world Community. It has transformed cultural practices to reflect its themes and interests and in the process has come to threaten the integrity of the Caucasian world community and its future. As a result, the Caucasian American community has been made to yield to expressions of various kinds of alien *Racial* parochial interests. Therefore, the purpose in the liberal American indoctrination is to persuade the Caucasian American community to accept alien races as their equal, irrespective of truth or consequence. Thus liberal indoctrination is motivated by *Egalitarianism* (communism revisited) and to the demise of all Caucasian communities, liberal academia really believes in the good of their *Racial Nihilist* movement, and works very hard to persuade others to adopt its premise. But, like all fallacies, *Equality* also has it unforc- seen: Through liberal zealot (academia) support, alien races simply accept the notion that Caucasian society is oppressive, Caucasian standards cruel, and

Caucasian expectations damaging, and when questioned about these (their) beliefs, they quickly quote the liberal mantra of *Racial Oppression* as their justified moral high ground.(to not comply!)

C2137. The Alpha tells us: It is the *21st* century, and there is much talk these days of Caucasian guilt as an aftermath of their race's *Success,* guilt over defeating their *Enemies,* and even guilt for *Surviving.* It may appall a generation who have been dragged into considering a person's *Racial Passion* as the ultimate crime, and if Caucasian society is being taught this, and nothing else, then nothing else can be expected of them. But, that doesn't make it acceptable, and it is the Alpha's hope that once Caucasians understand that,...they will also understand how to change it. A measured statement such as this is not tolerated in liberal zealot America, and this bodes ill for our future, especially the future of our children. As long as the basic principle of *Racial Kinship* is denied by our leaders, Caucasian America's very existence will be in peril. There can be no stability in a society which will not allow its founding members (the Caucasian race) to favor their own brethren. Any society that will deny its founding people this right, is a society on the road to ruin and defeat!

C2138. The Alpha tells us: In Caucasianism, the distinction between *Values* and *Virtues* is something that all Caucasian children need to be taught, for it is the first step in becoming a moral person. Values are beliefs systems that very from one person to another, whereas virtues are moral values that the Caucasian public deems desirable for our individual and collective well-being. Virtues are the ideals of decency, goodness, honesty, and integrity that govern most if not all Caucasian societies. Caucasian children need to understand that their personal preferences are purely individual values that may conflict with public virtues, and that part of becoming an ethical person is learning when to put aside our own values in favor of the Caucasian community good. And when being tolerant and nonjudgmental is a good thing, and when it is dangerous, plus the need to learn how to judge and how to be judged.

C2139. The Alpha tells us: The equality promoters (liberal academia) are not the only ones who shy away from the issue of teaching *Racial Enlightenment* (racial endearment) to our children, it is a topic that makes many people nervous, primarily because the teaching of *Racial Passion* has become (through liberal treachery) associated with *Hatred.* But in fact, this could not be further from the truth, *Caucasian Racial Enlightenment* along with its spirituality is the process of cultivating and refining the human life principle, by reveling through its *Biological Genesis* (Fematrix theology) a complete racial edification and illumination.(the spirit of Caucasianism)

C2140. The Alpha tells us: It was Maureen stout,(PH.D.) who said, the problem with an anti-intellectual and anti-science mindset is that we do not always know when it is benign and when it might be dangerous to ourselves or others. Believing in something that cannot be scientifically proven is often harmless or even helpful. After all, religions are based on faith. Suspending disbelief can be a source of hope and an inspiration in difficult times and can leave us open to ideas that we might otherwise dismiss out of hand. But as the events like the *Jonestown Massacre* for example tells us, that blind faith in someone (who's malevolent) can have devastating consequences. And sometimes, even when presented with evidence on a particular issue, we continue to believe what has been disproved and deny the science, just because it will involve accepting something unpleasant or disturbing. This is what's called-*Truth Making.*

C2141. The Alpha tells us: Understanding Caucasianism and its rituals, gives the Caucasian people an orchestration for their lives. Performing these ritual acts bind the Caucasian people together in two spiritual significant ways: by creating a bond with all believers of Caucasianism and at the same time reinforcing the bond between the Caucasian people and their ancestors. These two ways of being bound together form Caucasian tradition, and share with the Caucasian community the mystery of the *Fematrix* (Caucasia) and her gifts to us!...her posterity.

C2142. The Alpha tells us: We as Caucasians most be aware of the consequences of our actions: have the Caucasians lost their *Vital Racial Force*? Is Raspail right? Have we Caucasians been beaten down by decades of anti-Caucasian propaganda, is the *21st* century the final tragic end of Caucasian civilization, a victim of its own hand? What will be the state of mind when Caucasians confront their final racial crises *Alien Racial Insurrection* what has come to be called in nature the smell of *Weakness,*

Guilt, and *Stupidity?* (Caucasian social and political hubris!) Will we as Caucasians; *Capitulate* and be lead to the holding pens?..or will we *Fight,* rising up to preserve our biological mandate, our right to preservation? The Caucasian way, is not the way of the coward, nor that of the fool,...yes, we have become vulnerable because of the nature of our *Solicitude* our kindness to other groups. But, that time has now come to an end, the few remaining Caucasians with any sense of their civilization are beginning to move into camps of resistance, seeking their place on this field of battle, once again answering the call for their hearts, minds and will,...a clarion call to survival, to the survival of their Caucasian race, and it posterity!

C2143. The Alpha tells us: *Intellectual Cowardice* in the Caucasian community should serve as a wake-up call to all Caucasians. Clearly, racial education (ones biological-mandate) is an issue that all people of genuine reason and sanity should car about. To deny ones interior and exterior nature, one's historical lineage so to speak, is an intellectual path of absurdity, with the deficiency of an observer, an observer without chronicles, an observer submerged in the darkness of neutrality. (No allegiance) A spiteful and arrogant being who drifts in and out of social and political shadows, carrying the air of a sage,...their ilk, are truly persons of no worth!

C2144. The Alpha tells us: *Tolerance* - is not a virtue, thought at first glance, it would seem that it is. But, putting tolerance on too high a pedestal merely reinforces moral relativism. Too much tolerance renders us incapable of identifying what is honorable moral behavior, and judging what is not. And if we Caucasians lose the ability to judge what is good, and what is bad for us, we will lose our moral racial foundation,...and hence, our society. Tolerance is not always a good thing. We as Caucasians most ask ourselves how much tolerance is too much, for all things fall under the rubric of judgment, for there can be no neutral ground when it comes to tolerance, and Caucasian vested racial entrust is after all its survival code and not a moral tolerance of questionable logic or ethics.

C2145. The Alpha tells us: *Discrimination* - the right of choice, the right to accept or reject is the biological premise in all living beings, the absolute inalienable right of all nature. Discrimination is the very outcome of *Reason,* it is its ultimate goal, and without it there is no ambition, purpose, destination or hope,...it is the fruitful crown of intention. (This is truth, this is reality!)

C2146. The Alpha tells us: *Propaganda* - the fact is, truth matters! But, if for lack of intellectual training, we as Caucasians are unable to differentiate between fact and fiction, the very concept of truth is at risk. Many of us Caucasians believe that as moral, right-thinking people we are immune to the propa- ganda and myth making that creates the condition in which the *Equality Mantra* becomes possible, and it is a conceit in which we as Caucasians can no longer afford to indulge. The liberal zealots and their *Equality* propaganda have lured us into believing what is in essence not truth. In fact, the Caucasian American collective indoctrination by the liberal zealot movement (equal racial outcomes?) is the paradigm of the whole Caucasian social problem. We did not stop to examine it before inflicting it on our children and society, we didn't! We rashly accepted its tenets and reorganized our society in accordance with its ideology with tragic results, knowledge is defined as *Justified* true belief and it is important to understand the difference between knowledge and belief because that distinction is what allows us to differentiate between what is true and false. It is what allows us to make sense of the world.

C2147. The Alpha tells us: *Racial Nihilism* how exactly, did such a piece of fiction sell itself as a truth? It is not perhaps surprising, that the Alpha in his wisdom prefers to call scientific discoveries *Accommodations* as to some scientists who employ rhetorical devices to convey their ideas. An analysis of the rhetoric can tell us much about the accommodations, in this case *Racial Nihilism* (there are no human races, therefore we are all equal?) And its new age mysticism - liberal zealot *Equality* the new state religion. Hence, Caucasian Americas readiness to believe is an example of both Caucasian naiveté and the trend toward anti-Caucasianism. Anti-Caucasianism is not solely an American affliction however; it reaches across the Atlantic as well. This is all part of a global move by liberal zealots, promoting *Racial Nihilism* through scientific accommodation and its fraudulent *Equality* mantra.

C2148. The Alpha tells us: The Caucasian Military, man and woman of the defensive cast, solders of the *Caucasian Conquest* are a force unequaled in all of nature. It is the Caucasian solder and his or her unwa-vering loyalty and service in defense of the Caucasian way of life that stands against the gathering alien hordes, their social ambitions, and hostile intent.

C2149. The Alpha tells us: The long detour in which we Caucasians have been involved with *Racial Equality* will not have been useless. The root of its difficulty is the fundamental indetermination of the notion of human evolution. Words have their importance; racial equality has above all served the purpose of hiding the absence of liberal reality. In whatever manner the Caucasian people understand *Racial Equality?*...they are accounting for the mechanism of something the notion of which they are incapable of defining. Hence, the result of the liberal racial equality claim is that the theory of *Racial Equality* is impossible. It is a sort of dogma which the liberal priests do not themselves believe in any way, but which they keep up for the sake of their flock.

C2150. The Alpha tells us: When a firm conviction is not vigorously demonstrated, whatever its nature may be, it must be argued,...to ascribe probable reasons in favor of belief.

C2151. The Alpha tells us: One of his main grievances against the *Liberal Zealots* is that they have deliberately confounded two distinct causes. Both being of the biological, *Racial Rivalry* (bio-competition) and *Cultural Rivalry* (socio-competition) the two sides of the coin of life. One finds in the Bibliomancy of the liberal zealot institute, (academia) a brochure entitled *Equality* (equal racial outcomes?) the rehashing of an old world adversary *Communism* the classless, or in this case,...it being the *21st* century, the *Raceless* State. But, just as socialism was set upon and cast out, for its evil doings, so the subversive *Equality* will fare no better, for just like its cousin,...*Equality* will be found to be *Ominous* and *Treacherous* to the Caucasian American people, and thereby it will be set upon, purged, and dismantled.

C2152. The Alpha tells us: It would be absurd for anyone to conclude in this regard that there is no difference between *Human Races* (Negroid, Mongoloid, Caucasoid) and that they don't see each other as rivals and adversaries, not to mansion their loyalty to their *Identity Instinct* or common biological family trust.(racial-subspecies) It is through the reading of the

Holy Valorous and its spiritual enlightenment (Caucasianism) that puts all this political and racial intrigue with its conspiracy, double-dealing and racial treason into the light of day. And if you, being of Caucasian blood, are reading this, it is truly hoped that by the racial spirit of your Caucasian generation, you will uphold the Honor, Faith, and Reverence of the Caucasian way. (Race, Freedom, Empire) and its more than 40 thousand years of struggle.

C2153. The Alpha tells us: To the extent that we Caucasians invoke it to give an explanation of the fact, *Teleology* is the object of sensible experience, not in itself, but in its effects. This is a question, not of an abnormal or exceptional case but, on the contrary, of one of those numerous cases where in sensible experience itself an immediate inference is produced in the intellect from the perceived effect to the cause.

C2154. The Alpha tells us: It is quite true that nothing is in the intellect which has not first been in the senses, but neither is anything in the senses of an intelligent being which is not at the same time in the intellect. That can be seen from sensible perception. Hence, no one ever seen *Human* or *Tree,* which are collective classes and not individuals, but we do not cease to perceive splotches of color given shape by the forms which the intellect knows to be vegetable or human. Likewise!...for the effect of final causality. There is no essential difference between seeing that a being is Negroid, Mongoloid or Caucasoid and seeing that they are different. (human subspecies) Intellectual induction from sensible perception is the same in these cases; they are the same case.

C2155. The Alpha tells us: Liberal zealots have no need for human subspecies, (human races) but it is no less true that what we call Negroid, Mongoloid and Caucasoid exists in reality. The temptation for the liberal zealots to eliminate this biological abstraction is perhaps irresistible, but what one has decided not to take into consideration, perhaps even because one has the political ideology (liberal racial nihilism) of averting one's mind from it, does not thereby cease to exist.

C2156. The Alpha tells us: It was Claude Bernard who said, when we see in natural phenomena the enchainment which exists in such a fashion that things appear to be made with foresight of an end, as the eye, the stomach, etc,...which form themselves in view of food and light etc,...we cannot prevent ourselves from supposing that these things are intentionally made, with a definite end in mind. Because, in effect, when we ourselves make things in a fashion, we say that we made them with intention, and we could only admit (as an alternative) that chance has made everything. Well! It would appear that if, when we make things in a fashion in which they concord with a specific end, we ought to then recognizes in the entirety of natural phenomena and their specific connections with specific ends a great intentional intelligence. This intentional determination appears evident above all in living beings which form a finished whole.(an intended kind!)

C2157. The Alpha tells us: He proceeds prudently, when he speaks of *Racialism* rather than brotherhood, and rightfully so. Liberal zealots are responsible to themselves; they do not involve themselves with science at all, and the Alpha, as such, has no cause to concern himself with them, other than the fact that they have denounced the *Racial Principle* that biological form fallows intellect and its intention to preside over the laws of nature, with its power of invention and principle of organization, its character of anti-chance.

C2158. The Alpha tells us: If all life is its intellect, (imprinted life strategy) than it stands that each human racial group (human subspecies) is its own intellect. (having its own imprinted life strategy) Furthermore, the important thing is to know whether or not it expresses a fact given in nature, for if we object to racialism (unique human subspecies) as an explanation, it therefore remains as a fact to be explained? It is true that if we make room for it, (contrary racial intellects) further problems of a different order than that of *Universal Brotherhood* will present itself. Hence, if the Caucasians are their own intellect, and if Caucasianism is the most perfect manifestation of it, it can then be said that the more the knowledge of being a Caucasian is *Racialized* in virtue of being *Caucasianized,* the more it is useful and true. All true Caucasians do not hesitates on the doorstep of this certitude, the foundation of which does not escape them, and of which they have no doubt!

C2159. The Alpha tells us: The appeal to the notion of *Sexual Selection* has nothing in it to affront reason, for there is involved the choice of a conscientious being,(fematrix) a spontaneous preference for perceived and known qualities. The immense class of females, (the bio-Sisterhood) acting collectively during millennia, are the keepers of the species, the harbingers of the need, and of the chosen when it is a question of favoring the hereditary transmission of infinite physiological and psychological modifications which are favorable to the survival of their species or subspecies.

C2160. The Alpha tells us: It is the *21st* century, and alien immigration and their non-integration, (hostile alien strongholds) are provocative in that a large-scale *Invasion* of illegal racial aliens, who have a different bio-imprint, (life strategy) is for the Caucasian community a *Fatal* social time bomb. Hence, in the Caucasian world community an army of integration specialists, sociologists, political scientists, community activists, and naive politicians are working intensively, hand and hand to play down (their betrayal) their treasonous accommodation, by denying its terrible outcome. And, if this treason is not put to an end, (the abdication of Caucasian sovereignty) an inevitable tragedy (a Caucasian revolution) will consume the world, and none will be spared the hand of revenge!

C2161. The Alpha tells us: Biological life forms (and we know no other) regulate themselves and in so doing optimizes certain functions. With the propensity for greater *Predation* comes among other things, the fact that all living things are their own systems (life strategies) and represent a state of non-equality in reference to each other. Because of this, (species predation) at every point in time (biological time) there is a multiplicity of different competitive life forms, from the simplest to the most complex, which are simultaneously capable of reproductive life? What differentiates individual human race's from each other aside from their physical differences is the circumstance that every form of life and its strategy reveals itself to be designed in reference to several physical and mental obstacles or treats, hence their bio-categories and different complexities. The survival capabilities of human racial groups are essentially the result of their community cooperation down to the level of the cell, the emergent of course is their racial kind distinct from all others, and never to be again!

C2162. The Alpha tells us: The Caucasian racial principle "Caucasianism" in the *21st* century is the *Religious* and *Intellectual Sanctuary* for all enlightened Caucasians, both in America and throughout the world. If we Caucasians are to survive in the land of our fathers and mothers, then we must cling to a doctrine of survival, a doctrine of truth and reason, one that will not reduce itself to a mystical fallacy of equality and racial complacency. (alien trust!) The uncertainty of our political and social future is beginning to raise its ugly head, and how utterly different the popular conception of racial equality is, from equality as rightly conceived; (a fallacy!) will now be manifest. The prevailing liberal racial equality belief is doubly erroneous containing an error within an error, the theory of human rights is wrongly supposed to be identical with racial equality; and racial equality is wrongly supposed to be identical with human rights at large. In other words, it is popularly thought that racial equality elevates itself to human rights, and that, in turn, human rights elevates itself to racial equality?..Hence, an absurd liberal construction, void of observation and description of facts.

C2163. The Alpha tells us: We as Caucasians must not forget that whatever aspect of it we are for the moment considering, *Racial Equality* is always to be regarded as an integration of biological fallacy and political conspiracy, which may be, and usually is, accompanied by other criminal transformations of Caucasian society to suit alien others! And let there be no misunderstanding, those who bring it to the table, are suspect, for all the liberal partisans of racial equality are partisans of *Socialism*, and therefore anti-Caucasian.

C2164. The Alpha tells us: In Caucasianism the *Fematrix* (female will) is the architect of *Natural Selection* and *Descent*, she is the *Origin,* and from the day when the Alpha conceived the idea of *Fematrix Theology* (female absolutism)- the only life form!) to him the problem of science and religion was that the two were strangers to each other and because there is no sense of the word *Truth* common to the two orders on which they might be able to meet, a world came apart in his mind, and under the pressure of its spirit he felt charged with the scientific and religious mission of revealing to humankind a truth which is in his eyes indubitable.(our living Fematrix creator) There is in the Alpha the "Caucasianist" a racial fundamentalist of the *21st* century charged by his own conscience with delivering the Caucasian world community from a harmful error, *Racial Nihilism,* Caucasian identity capitulation.

C2165. The Alpha tells us: Every religion has a tradition of sacred obligation, of a path to salvation or enlightenment that we must walk, not just imagine or think about. The same is true of religious *Commandments,* though some commandments are good deeds; the essence of the idea of commandments is not goodness but obligation. When you do something because you believe that our Holy Fematrix-Caucasia wants you to do it, which is a commandment. What we as Caucasians do for Caucasia may be ethical or it may be ritual, but its main meaning is that we are acting out of obligation to our Holy Fematrix- Caucasia. All this brings order to our society, by outlining the obligations we Caucasians have in the practice of our faith.

C2166. The Alpha tells us: In Caucasianism the emphasis is our racial sovereignty (Caucasian racial survival) and it reminds people that it is better for our society if all accept and identify with their *Racial Identity* in life. Harmony or peacefulness can be attained only if all people accept their racialness and respect the racialness of others. This is an *Ethical Canon* in Caucasianism. As to its *Ritual Canons* which can be in some cases set aside, in order to fulfill the ethical canon, is not seen as a transgression.

C2167. The Alpha tells us: In Caucasianism the world is seen as both unforgiving and rewarding, a place of uncertainty, and what happens to us is the result of what we do or don't do, what we believe and don't believe,(cause and effect) thus a mystical faith can play no part! Therefore, if we as Caucasians live a good life, which means if we as a racial group of people live true to the laws set forth in an ethical Caucasian society, will along with our children, know peace, prosperity and above all else *Caucasian Racial Tranquility* the union of- Caucasianism.

C2168. The Alpha tells us: How we as Caucasians should live is one of the great questions of life, and through its rational spirituality Caucasianism addresses this issue by providing codes of ethics and morality. The first and most amazing characteristic about the world's great religions is their ethical and moral teachings are very compatible despite the differences in their theologies.(beliefs) Though Hinduism, Buddhism, Judaism, Christianity, and Islam are the religions of many different racial and ethnic groups, and span more than 5ooo years of human history, if their truths be known and further determined, they are all bar none the magnificent gifts of a single race of people the Caucasians!

C2169. The Alpha tells us: All religions consider their teaching to be true for all people, and some believers go quite far in declaring that their religion is the only true faith and that all people need to convert to their faith if they want to be saved from sin and allowed into the everlasting? In many ways Caucasianism is different. Hence, for the Caucasians, their State, Culture, and religious racialism is not only a matter of tradition, but also a matter of faith.

The Holy Valorous outlines the *Fematrix* and her will, (in our case, *Caucasia* and her life strategy) which is eternal and unchangeable. In the depths of the Valorous the faithful also look to the *Caucasian Maxims* the sayings, deeds and truths of the Alpha. In these two things the Caucasian people find explicit instructions and guidelines regarding how to live in a way that is pleasing to themselves and in accordance with their Fematrix *Caucasia* and her life strategy. Every Caucasian is also directly responsible to their *Ancestral Trust* for acting in accordance with these rules and creating a good society, and therefore, political order. Caucasianism is not only a guide for each Caucasian; it's also a guide for the society they build.

C2170. The Alpha tells us: The Caucasian Sanctum is a place of study, (Fematrix theology) a house of gathering, (Caucasian union) and a temple of worship to *Caucasia*. To the Caucasian faithful the "Sanctum" represents the Holy of Holies (the place of the becoming) where the sacred light of the Holy Valorous resides (the eternal flame of Caucasia!)

C2171. The Alpha tells us: The shrine to the *Caucasian Conquest* resides in the *Sanctum,* it along with the shrine to Caucasian *Hero's* and the Caucasian *Family* are sacred places of pilgrimage for all Caucasians to renew their spiritual racial faith, and learn from the Caucasians who went before them. The shrines of the *Sanctum* are places where the sacred moments in the history of the Caucasian people are displayed, and are places of Pilgrimage and Veneration to reinforce and deepen one's Caucasian racial faith. They are *Historical Gateways* that the Caucasian people can walk through to find their place, their truth, in the Caucasian historical passed, and to an understanding of their place in its future.

C2172. The Alpha tells us: Caucasian *Racial Betrayal* or Un-Caucasian political activities by Caucasian politicians against their own people as a racial group. (political racial piracy) What is the right and honorable way to deal with Caucasian political and racial piracy? (subversive betrayal) The relevant point: If a child comes into this world by the efforts of a distinct group of people, (phylum) and their alike extended community, in this case the Caucasians, and is loved, housed, sustained, and educated in that community (the child being their prime investment) does that child as an adult, have an obligation to the survival of its group? And, if so, and that is the consensus in all of nature, then what should be the fate of the Caucasian *Renegade*? The Alpha's thoughts: Betrayal, and Caucasian racial betrayal in particular is a most sinister assault, and all those who partake of it, need to be publicly exposed and identified, so that their social state will be that of a *Pariah* a despised person, an outcast from the Caucasian community.

C2173. The Alpha tells us: In the context of Caucasianism, racial enlightenment describes a journey of both the physical and the spiritual self. Racialism can be a private moment of faith, sought for example by someone who needs the strength to accept and overcome their many years of racial guilt (false racial-reproach) that was put upon them by a sinister ideology *Liberal Racial Nihilism* a socially contrived tyranny against the Caucasian world community. Spiritual Caucasianism is about overcoming *Racial fallacies* and the rehabilitation of all those Caucasians who have fallen under its *Persecution.* In addition, Caucasianism in the embrace of the Holy Valorous brings the true enlightenment to those Caucasians who need divine intervention and guidance in overcoming their racial crisis.

C2174. The Alpha tells us: Healing is believing, and in Caucasianism to error is human, but if a Caucasian (male or female) betrays their race (their Caucasian ancestral trust) for whatever reason, is an unforgivable transgression, and there can be no reconciliation!

C2175. The Alpha tells us: Curiosity and asking critical questions is paramount in Caucasianism, and is based on education and the process of asking and answering questions that refer to *life* and all that it entails. In Caucasianism the virtue of curiosity isn't the same thing as doubt or lack of faith. Questions help a spiritual seeker understand more deeply or enable a teacher of the Holy Valorous to explain more fully an aspect of Caucasian racial faith. In Caucasianism faith requires virtues of *Patience*, *Diligence* and *Perseverance* because its rewards aren't immediate, and it doesn't promise a life without struggle or pain. The process of studying the Holy Valorous in the confines of the Holy Sanctum is a lively, spiritual back and forth discussion between students who study in pairs. This behavior of the most intellectually and spiritually gifted sets an example for all members of the Caucasian community.

C2176. The Alpha tells us: If Caucasianism is about seeking racial truth, seeking racial under-standing, or racial salvation,...then the tools of the quest are spiritual racial questions. In other words, what does spirituality have to do with racialism or vice versa? Spirituality is the quest for the essence of life, its living germ, its primary element, its fundamental nature, or cognizant singularity the creator! The Caucasian faithful are passionate in their quest to serve their racial community, Caucasia, the Holy Valorous, and racial faith are the source for all Caucasian ritual, cultural, and political guidance.

C2177. The Alpha tells us: In Caucasianism children are gifts from *Caucasia*. For this reason the Caucasian faithful don't consider any Caucasian child's birth to be an accident or the child to be unwanted. When a child is born, the first thing a child hears is the name *Caucasia*: and then the parents recite the axiom *Blessed Are The Caucasians*. The child's birth signifies the beginning of the next Caucasian generation of the faithful to *Caucasia* and her quest for Caucasian immortality. This devotion to *Caucasia* our *Fematrix* (the One!) articulates that everything important comes from her, and therefore our faithfulness and our service, should be returned to her.

C2178. The Alpha tells us: The Caucasian faithful must teach their children about Caucasianism and the Holy Valorous as early as they can. Between the ages of 5 years (girls) 7 years (boys) they should be taken to the Caucasian

Sanctum to begin their official study of Caucasianism. By the time they reach the age of 10 years, Caucasian children should be able to take part in *Rituals* and know how to behave and feel at home in their Caucasian family faith. Furthermore, the development of the child's spirituality will require that he or she take responsibility for defending and propagating the *Caucasian Community* by taking their faith seriously.

C2179. The Alpha tells us: Morality and Reality: the dilemma of the great mystic religions and their cryptic Gods. Here is the dilemma: If God can rid the world of evil but won't,... he therefore isn't infinitely good? Moreover, if he would rid the world of evil but can't,...he isn't omni-potent? Hence, are we the creations of God, or are we our own creators? The Alpha tells us: these questions of the *21st* century bring mystic religions and reality into conflict, and are now profoundly important for the cognizant faith and social stability of the Caucasian world community. Can we, the Caucasian community continue to call upon Gods that do not answer? Can we continue to put our fate in the hands of those who say they speak for God, and are the executors of his will without the slightest bit of proof or demonstration, other than their word? Today's mystic religions are all *Multi-Racial* with the theme of *Brotherhood* and *Peace,* and for more than 5000 years, this goal has yet to be accomplished or lived up to by any of its moral subscribers. (How long weights the rational!)

C2180. The Alpha tells us: Good-will is no longer the staple of racial politics in multiracial states, more and more alien *Racial Ambition* is raising its ugly head, fueled by their own racial *Chauvinism.* These truths are bringing the Caucasian community and alien races into conflict, and the social understanding between them is once again breaking down, and this time, their confrontation will be very serious. Most of the racial contention lies in the area of *Racial Equality* which is the social fallacy of *Liberal Zealotry,* a liberal dogma of rearranging all Caucasian societies by first destroying Caucasian racial identity (racial nihilism) and then by engineering the redistribution of Caucasian *Wealth* and *Social Position* for all those aliens who can't or haven't earned it. And it all runs right up against the profoundly important question of Caucasian *Racial Survival* in the mists of conflict with alien others? (Do we comply with our biological mandate, by bringing the battle to them? or, do we capitulate!...What say you?)

C2181. The Alpha tells us: can Caucasians and alien races coexist? The answer is absolutely! But, not in the same competitive social state! Competition and racial competition specifically (subspecies bias) is a precondition of a *Fematrix- life strategy,* and without this loyalty to its own kind (bio-partisanship) their survival would not be possible. So, as a Caucasian, when you are accused of being *Racially Prejudice*?...your answer should be- I hope so!...for the sake of my people!

C2182. The Alpha tells us: In life, as well as its many social states, there are no certainties. But, there are social points of simplicity, such as words of wisdom that have made the difference as to success and failure in one's path. To all Caucasians this: manage *Risk* play to your *Strength* and above all take advantage of every lawful opportunity.

C2183. The Alpha tells us: understanding Caucasianism will help you understand what it means to be human, and a member in one of the three races (subspecies) of the human experience. Every religion has a belief system. You could say that Caucasianism is the belief in truth! But, what is the truth? Different religions have different understandings of what is *True.* Basically, a religion is the worship of a divine being, (belief) and the practice of obedience (rituals) and moral code (ethics) that result from that worship. Beliefs give a religion its mind, Rituals give religion its shape, and Ethics gives religion its heart. So, beliefs are the ideas that make any religion what it is, in other words beliefs are the most important because they give rise to and shape the rituals and the ethics of the faith.

C2184. The Alpha tells us: In Caucasianism (Fematrix theology) its religious teachings and social doctrine observes, confirms and ordains its beliefs, (its truths) on the altar of biological faith! Hence, in Caucasian faith, the Holy Valorous is the handbook of belief, it is important because it puts the beliefs of Caucasianism in an order that the Caucasian people can understand even though its tradition of science theology is systematic, complex and sophisticated in conveying its truths. For in Caucasianism membership is defined not only by belief, but by blood, a *Genetic Deistic* faith, in other words, you have to be born into the race, in order to embrace its faith.

C2185. The Alpha tells us: In our struggle for success, we should keep constantly in mind the necessity of knowing what it is that we as Caucasians want of knowing precisely what is our *Definite Purpose* and the value of the principle of *Organized Effort* in the attainment of that which constitutes our definite purpose. When you organizes your Caucasian *Racial Faculties* according to the Holy Valorous and its enlightenment, and direct them toward the attainment of a definite Caucasian spiritual purpose in life, you then take advantage of the racially accumulative principle out of which your nature and its identity is developed, which is called in Caucasianism- *Racial Enlightenment!*

C2186. The Alpha tells us: The Holy Valorous is intended as a stimulus to enable all Caucasians to see themselves and their hidden racial force as it is and to awaken in them the ambition and the Caucasian vision and racial determination to cause them to go forth and claim that which is rightfully theirs. Hence, power is organized effort, and success is based upon power!

C2187. The Alpha tells us: If *Racial Success* depends upon power, and if power is organized effort, and if the first step in the direction of organization is a definite purpose, then one may easily see why such a purpose is essential. Therefore, until a Caucasian (man or woman) selects a definite purpose in life, he or she dissipates (scatters) their energies and thoughts, leading not to power, but to indecision and weakness. It concerns all Caucasians to know the purpose they seek in life, for then, like the archer aiming at a definite mark, they shall be certain to attain what they want!

C2188. The Alpha tells us: Where fear controls, significant achievement becomes an impossibility, hence, *Courage* is the first of human qualities, because it is the quality which guarantees the others!

C2189. The Alpha tells us: What is the Caucasian Initiative? It has been said that it is the exceedingly rare quality that prompts, nay, impels a Caucasian person to do that which ought to be done without being told to do it! The world bestows its big prize, both in wealth and honors, for one thing, and that is *Initiative*. For in the Caucasian world community- initiative is the passkey that opens the door to opportunity, for it is well known that people will readily, willingly, and voluntarily follow him or her who shows by their

701

actions that they are persons of initiative. If we as Caucasians help others develop the habit of initiative, we, in turn, develop this same habit. If we as Caucasians sow the seeds of hatred and envy and discouragement in others, we in turn, develop these detrimental qualities in ourselves. (a detriment unto us!)

C2190. The Alpha tells us: Where thought prevails, power may be found! If you think you are beaten, you are;...If you think you'll lose, you've lost;... If you think you dare not, you don't;...and if you think you are outclassed, you are;... Life's battles don't always go to the stronger or faster being, but sooner or later the being who wins, is that being who thinks they can! Hence, life shrinks or expands in proportion to one's courage!

C2191. The Alpha tells us: As Caucasians we are condemning ourselves to poverty, misery, and failure, or we are driving ourselves on toward the heights of great achievement, solely by the thoughts we think. If we as Caucasians demand success of ourselves and back up this demand with intelligent action, we are sure to win. We as Caucasians have within us all the power we need with which to get whatever we want or need in this world, and about the best way to avail ourselves of this power is to believe in ourselves as a great race of people, and a great nation.(know thyself!)

C2192. The Alpha tells us: Courage- the meaning of which is obvious. One most possess the spirit of fearlessness to face opposition of every nature whatsoever, and sufficient combativeness to master the obstacles that one is apt to meet in the struggle for attainment of any definite purpose.

C2193. The Alpha tells us: Regardless of what you are now doing, every day brings you face to face with a chance to render some service, outside the course of your regular duties that will be of great value to your *Caucasian* community. In rendering this additional service of your own accord, you of course understand that it provides you with the ways and means of exercising, developing, and making stronger the aggressive spirit of Caucasianism that you must possess before you can ever become an outstanding figure in the affairs and accom-plishments of the Caucasian community.

C2194. The Alpha tells us: Imagination is species and subspecies specific?...

and *Caucasian Imagination* is the *Hub* and *Leading Factor* in human development, (government, science, and economics) as well as its overall survival. Through its interpretative capacity, the Caucasian imagination has one power not generally attributed to it, namely, the power of its *Humanity.* (Virtuous behavior- tolerance and kindness) It is uniquely *Caucasian* in its origin, and is not found in any real degree, in any of the other biological *Species* or *Subspecies* character. And this is not to say that this is a detriment to them, for it is not! One must understand that their lack of compassion is properly attuned and in direct harmony with life's declaration of no quarter (mercy) to those who are not of their kind. Perhaps these explanations are somewhat abstruse to those who have not made any particular study of the competitive will in the *Biological Universe,* and how closely interwoven are the factors upon which life's course is based. But, the biological mind set of *Conquest* is potent, enduring and recognizes no authority other than the victor!

C2195. The Alpha tells us: To make the description of *Racialness* understandable, we must as Caucasians accept as a reality the principle of *Fematrix Competitive Diversity.* (Female life strategies!) We as Caucasians need devote no time proving to others that race is a reality, for the reason that *Racialism* cannot be of the slightest value to those who have not sufficiently informed themselves to understand and accept their racialness (bio-subspecies) as an established principle. Civilization itself, owes its existence to racial homogeneity and it is a fertile truth that well never die, and what a mighty power is *Racial Integrity* the workshop of the soul, who's thoughts were woven into Religions, Nations, and Science.

C2196. The Alpha tells us: The purpose of all schooling is, or should be to develop the natural capacity of the mind so it can express itself in intelligent action. Furthermore, knowledge as a mere ornament may bring certain amounts of self-satisfaction to all that possess it, but it is useless to all others until it is put into action. Worry, envy, jealousy, hatred, doubt, and fear are all states of mind that can be fatal to one's success. The world pays for but one kind of knowledge and that is the kind that is expressed in terms of *Constructive Service*!

C2197. The Alpha tells us: Truth alone endures! All else must pass on with time. Many a person has gone down to defeat because, due to their *Prejudice* and *Hatred,* they underestimated the virtues of their enemies or competitors. The eyes of the accurate Caucasian thinker see facts, not the delusions of *Prejudice*, *Hate*, and *Envy*. If you do not think accurately, you cannot be sure of attaining the object of your definite purpose in life. (I cannot afford to deceive myself!)

C2198. The Alpha tells us: Do not rely upon the performance of miracles for the attainment of the object of your definite purpose; rely upon the gift of your *Fematrix,* the power of your Caucasian *Intelligence* to guide you through natural channels and with the aid of natural laws, for its attainment. Do not expect your Caucasian intelligence to bring to you the object of your definite purpose; instead, expect your intelligence to direct you toward that object.

C2199. The Alpha tells us: That nothing was ever created by a Caucasian person that was not first created in the *Caucasian Imagination* through ambition, desire, and then transformed into reality through the mastery of Caucasian *Concentration.* When you become familiar with the power of *Caucasian Concentration,* you will then understand the reason for choosing a definite purpose as the first step in the attainment of your enduring success. (the Caucasian way!)

C2200. The Alpha tells us: The way we allow people to see us Caucasians (disrespectfully)is the way they will treat us, and the way they treat us,... is what we as Caucasians will become! Hence, it is time that the enemies of Caucasian national and cultural consciousness like the *Liberal zealots* and *Alien Marauders* cease to be able to pillage, ravish, and overthrow (dismantle) the Caucasian American community, and that the obsessions and motivations of our enemies that seem to shape their ideologies and political behavior be subjected to the same scrutiny they have been applying to the Caucasian American people (the founding race!) whom their thinking is out to destroy. We as *Caucasian Americans* will ether defend our way of life *Separately* (a state of weakness!) or *Together* (a state of Caucasian strength!) What say you?

C2201. The Alpha tells us: The Caucasians, the first truly tolerant and charitable race of people is about to decommission their own *Fematrix Selection* the very force that made them, very soon, and before it's too late, we as Caucasian racial beings must look deep within ourselves and decide what we wish to become? There must be a proper balance between Caucasian altruism (alien social aid) and the Caucasian *Conquest* (Caucasian bio-fruition) Furthermore, the spirit of excessive alien tolerance (alien paternalism) needs to be deprecated, and the Caucasian population must remain for its own survival- *Homogeneous*. What is now more important is to bring the *Enlightenment* of Caucasianism and its *Racial Reason* to the hearts and minds of lost Caucasians.

C2202. The Alpha tells us: The authors of the great epic literature of the Caucasian world community, from *Homer* and *Virgil* to the *Norse sagas*, and the *Song of Roland*, to mention just a few, have provided our people with inspiration for future noble deeds. But, for those Caucasians who would aspire to a reality in which self-interest wilts away, and who labor under the pseudo-morality of self-destruction, *Raspail-* offers you, your future in the *Camp of the Saints* which should be required reading for all persons of Caucasian descent. The best is lacking when one's racial self-interest begins to be lacking, and when one instinctively chooses what is harmful for one's posterity, to feel attracted by alien *Moral fallacy* (racial equality) and to address their demand for *Compliance* is virtually the formula for one's ultimate destruction!

C2203. The Alpha tells us: A person with well-developed self-control will stimulate his or her imagination and their enthusiasm until they have produced action, and then, they will control that action and not permit it to control them. Furthermore, persons with self-control will not hate those who do not agree with them; instead, they will endeavor to understand the reason for their disagreement and profit by it.

C2204. The Alpha tells us: No one has the right to form an opinion that is not based either upon that which he or she believes to be facts or upon a reasonable hypothesis, yet, if you will observe yourself carefully, you will catch yourself forming opinions on noting more substantial than your desire for a thing to be, or not to be! (rationalize your desires)

C2205. The Alpha tells us: Self-discipline is the most essential factor in the development of personal power because it enables you to control your appetite, your tendency to spend more than you earn, your habit of *Striking Back* at those who offend you, and all the other destructive habits that cause you to dissipate your energies through non-productive efforts that take on the forms too numerous to be catalogued. (discipline; creates clarity)

C2206. The Alpha tells us: By their deeds, you will know them! If your deeds are constructive and just, and you are at peace with yourself in your own heart, you will not find it necessary to stop and explain your motives, for they will explain themselves. (deeds are our true measure)

C2207. The Alpha tells us: The happiness of your life depends ultimately upon the quality of your thoughts! (Discipline- Loyalty- Charity)

C2208. The Alpha tells us: The world soon forgets its destroyers, and builds its monument to, and bestows its honors upon none but its builders! Keep this in mind, and you will more easily reconcile yourself to the policy of refusing to waste your energies by striking-back at those who offend you.

C2209. The Alpha tells us: We look at successful people in the hour of their triumph and wonder how they did it? We overlook the importance of analyzing their methods, and we forget the price they had to pay in careful, well organized preparation that had to be made before they could reap the fruits of their efforts. In the laws of success, you will not find a single new principle; every one of them is as old as Caucasian civilization itself, but, in the *21st* century you will find very few people who seem to understand how to apply them!

C2210. The Alpha tells us: Cheap flattery has just the opposite to that of constituting an attractive personality. It repels, rather than attracts. It is so shallow that even the ignorant easily detect it. Therefore, make it your business to study other people closely enough to find something about them or their work that you really admire. Only in this way can you develop a personality that will be irresistibly attractive.

C2211. The Alpha tells us: To all Caucasians, it is your privilege nay, your duty, to aim high in life. You owe it to yourself and to the Caucasian community in which you live to set a high standard for yourself. There is much evidence to justify the belief that nothing within reason is beyond possibility of attainment by the Caucasian man or woman whose definite purpose has been well defined.

C2212. The Alpha tells us: Nowhere is the lack of *Species Esteem* more noticeable or more detrimental than it is in the relationship between different *Species* or *Subspecies*. A species or subspecies will sense very quickly the wavering attitude of a rival group, and will take advantage of that attitude quite freely, usually leading its rival to displacement or death. It is the same for us Caucasians; we must never lose our *Positive Racial Esteem* or fail to command respect and attention from our rivals. (at all times!)

C2213. The Alpha tells us: These are the steps leading from Caucasian racial desire (understanding!) to Caucasian racial fulfillment; (becoming!) First there is the burning racial desire, then the crystallization of the racial desire into a Caucasian racial purpose, then sufficient appropriate action to achieve that purpose. A definite racial purpose is something that you must create for yourself. No one will create it for you, and it will not create itself. Remember, these three steps are always necessary to insure success in obtaining Caucasian racial enlightenment.

C2214. The Alpha tells us: Before approaching the fundamental principle upon which the religion Caucasianism is founded, it will be of benefit to you to keep in mind the fact that it is socially practical and biologically reasonable, and that it brings to you the discoveries and history of more than 40 thousand years of biological struggle. The very premise of Caucasianism is to see to the preservation and well-being of the greatest living biological force on earth the Caucasians (the Conquerors!) A race of people who have without equal Conquered the land, Air, Oceans, Distance and Outer-Space, and should we not forget Medicine, Engineering, Building, Mathematics, and the Arts, just to mention a few! They are truly a *Biological Singularity* of unprecedented magnitude and worth. And, to the sheer fact that their kind well never be seen or happen again!...there can be no skepticism as to the importance of *"Caucasian Preservation"* and that of their great works. Truly, this is the unfolding of the Caucasian age!...they have barely scratched the surface, they will bring us knowledge in the future that will make all of their past discoveries pale in comparison.

C2215. The Alpha tells us: Far from being a disadvantage, *Struggle* is a decided advantage because it develops those qualities that would forever lie dormant without it. Many a great Caucasian has found their place in this world because of having been forced to struggle for existence early in life.

C2216. The Alpha tells us: The current of misdirected alien altruism (alien paternalism) that permeates contemporary Caucasian society is dangerous when it is divorced from biological reality. It would be better to ignorantly adhere to the laws of human evolution, as do most primitive peoples, than to understand these laws and yet deliberately disobey them? It would be most tragic if the Caucasian people who discovered the theory of evolution were to perish due to a failure of will to apply it to their own destiny!

C2217. The Alpha tells us: It is our duty to maintain and advance the *Caucasian Continuum* that originated in the *Ancient Caucasus* and *Europe.* To falter at this critical junction is to allow our people to approach extinction. The greatest achievement of the Caucasians of the *21st* century will be our extrication from our current dilemma. (liberal zealot subversion!) If we succeed in our efforts, the chroniclers of this age will celebrate our valiant struggle in the epic literature of the future. But if we fail?...there will be no such literature and our beleaguered descendants will mock us in our graves.

C2218. The Alpha tells us: It is the *21st* century, and Caucasian America and her sister states throughout the world have become immersed in the *Cultural Anomie* of alien races which is contributing to their de-Caucasianization! The anxiety and depression associated with this Alien Anomie also contributes toward what has been described as a failure of *Nerve* which has political and military consequences. Therefore, as Caucasian America and her sister state grow weak, their enemies will see opportunities to overtake them, and when there is little Caucasian left in both America and Europe, the anti-Caucasian elements (alien races) will have come to the fore, and will control the world in which we live!(a state unto our death!)

C2219. The Alpha tells us: One of the answerable mysteries of our *Fematrix* (Caucasia) and her work is the fact that her great discovery, became, our self-discovery. And the truth for which all Caucasians are eternally searching (their origin) is wrapped up in their own being. Therefore, it is fruitless to search in the wilderness of life or in the hearts of alien-others to find one's self. For after all, if it is you, who you are looking for? You can be found in the *One,* (your Fematrix!) who brought you here!

C2220. The Alpha tells us: When two or more Caucasians ally themselves in a spirit of perfect racial harmony for the purpose of attaining a definite end, if that racial alliance is faithfully observed by all whom it is composed, this alliance will bring to each of those of whom it is composed a power that is superior and seemingly undefeated in all of nature. (the Caucasian will!)

C2221. The Alpha tells us: the Golden rule in Caucasianism is *Honor Your Race* and you *Honor Yourself.* It means: by honoring your race, you honor the author of your being, the source, the emanation of yourself. (your becoming!) You must not pervert or change this cause of truth, you must adapt yourself to its nature and thereby use it as an irresistible power that will carry you to heights of achievement that could not be attained without it. You must avail yourself of the benefits of this great Caucasian truth, you must think of your race, as you wish them to think of you!

C2222. The Alpha tells us: To the harbingers of *Hatred,* look closely, and whether for well or for woe, observe that you are looking at a world peopled with beings of your own creation, which correspond exactly to the nature of you own thoughts as you express them. There they are, the children of your own heart and mind, patterned after the image of your own thoughts. Those that are raised by your *Hatred, Selfishness* and *Injustice* toward others will not make very desirable neighbors, but you must live with them just the same, for they are of your own doing. You will be unfortunate indeed, when you find there are no children being raised in the spirit of *Love, Justice* and *Kindness* towards others, for that day will come, when in their eyes, you will be the others?

C2223. The Alpha tells us: By the light of the Holy Valorous, the subject of racialness takes on a new and much more important aspect doesn't it? A race of people passes for what they are worth! What they are, engraves itself on their form, on their history, on their fortunes and on their destiny! (this is truth, this is reality!)

C2224. The Alpha tells us: A passive attitude towards Caucasianism will bring no results; it is not enough to merely believe in the philosophy while, at the same time, failing to apply it in your relationships with others. If you want *Caucasian Racial Enlightenment* you must take an active attitude toward Caucasianism. (participate) A mere passive attitude, represented by a belief in its soundness, will avail you nothing. Nor will it avail you anything to proclaim to the world your belief in the Holy Valorous while your actions are not in harmony with your proclamation!

C2225. The Alpha tells us: The laws of biological *Species* and *Subspecies* are the laws of human *Racial Kind,* and equally the gospel of life! For when we truly understand these laws of our *Racialness,* we see that the same laws find their expression in everyone else, and consequently we shall reverence these laws in others, exactly in proportion, as we value it in ourselves.

C2226. The Alpha tells us: Those who understand and apply Caucasianism to their daily lives are always scrupulously honest, not only out of their desire to be just with others, but also because of their desire to be just with themselves! They understand the eternal law on which Caucasianism is based. The law through which Caucasianism operates is none other than the law through which the principle of *Racialness* operates.(survival of our fematrix strategy!) This truth gives you a path from which you should be able to make a deduction of a far-reaching nature and of inestimable value.

C2227. The Alpha tells us: Our character as *Caucasian* racial beings is the sum total of our *Thoughts* and *Deeds.* Because of this great truth, it is impossible for you to render any useful service or indulge in any act of kindness toward others without benefitting thereby. Moreover, it is just as impossible for you to indulge in any *Destructive Act* or *Thought* without paying the penalty in the loss of a corresponding amount of your own power. (social credibility)

C2228. The Alpha tells us: It was *Emerson* who said: No one can bring us peace but ourselves, and nothing can derive peace for us other than the triumph of principles. One reason for being kind and just toward others is the fact that such action may cause them to reciprocate in kind, but a better reason is the fact that kindness and justice toward others develop positive character in all who indulge in these acts. You may withhold from me the reward to which I am entitled for rendering you helpful service, but no one can deprive me of the benefit I will derive from the rendering of that service insofar as it adds to my own character!

C2229. The Alpha tells us: Let there be no mistake!...the power of our *Caucasian Reason*, our *Imagination*, and *Concentration* has taken the dominating position throughout the world for the reason that it *Belongs* in that position. The Caucasians dominating position in the world is the direct result of *Caucasian Intellect* and it has been the Caucasian intellectual power that all of humankind has, and will use for the attainment of a greater success. Furthermore, what-ever the Caucasians believe they can do, they eventually do! Hence, through the evolutionary power of a *Caucasian Intellect* the hopes and ambitions of one Caucasian generation become a reality in the next, and like no other living thing, this is the consistency of the Caucasian Conquest!

C2230. The Alpha tells us: The struggle for a mere existence is terrific among people who have not learned how to organize and direct their natural talents, while the attainment of those necessities, as well as the acquiring of many of the luxuries, is comparatively simple among those who have mastered the principle of Organized Effort.

C2231. The Alpha tells us: Ideas have Consequences. Caucasian adults can live in a world full of *Anti-Caucasian* propaganda without being affected by it, because Caucasian adults who have gained a sound understanding of their *Caucasian Racialness* are not likely to lose it. Once we as Caucasians remove the liberal blinders, we see clearly the *Distorted Truths* by liberal public newscasts, liberal public education, and liberal public debate. (a conspiracy of deceit and betrayal against the Caucasian world community!) Furthermore, this liberal propaganda is so simple-minded that no one who see's through it can be duped. But, things are very much more difficult for our children! Simple-minded propaganda works on them because they have simple minds. At the same time, no matter how racially or culturally healthy their homes may be, the pressure to conform to *Liberal Zealotry* (Caucasian racial nihilism) in *Public Schools* is tremendous, and every day, it puts all Caucasian children in a mental state of guilt, fear, and assault! (This is truth, this is reality!)

C2232. The Alpha tells us: Man and Woman generally take different views of reform. Men, seem to think they have to remake the entire world in order to be happy in their little corner of it, whereas woman tend to concentrate on improving their corner, and leave the rest of the world alone. Hence, as we work to promote a genuine understanding of our Caucasian Racialness, we must also improve and safeguard, our own little corner of the world!

C2233. The Alpha tells us: To all Caucasian usurper Politicians- *Racial Treason* is not to be vanquished by time nor propitiated by favors. You will never be safe in a Caucasian nation while those Caucasians live whom you have deprived of it! And injuries are not to be healed by subsequent benefit, and least of all when the benefit is less in degree than the injury suffered. (You must, and will be held accountable!)

C2234. The Alpha tells us: Deserving the attention both of heads of state and private citizens, *Conspiracy* is a source of much danger both to Governments and Private Citizens. For we see that many more governments have lost sovereignty and their states through these than open warfare; the power to wage *Open War* upon a state is conceded to few, whereas power to *Conspire* against a state is denied to none. But, to go deeper into the matter, man and woman conspire against each other or their leadership, and by inquiring into their causes, that are manifold, and of which one is more momentous than the rest; *Hatred,* and hatred is born of *Betrayal,* the betrayal of a whole community. (the Caucasian American community!) For it may reasonably be assumed, that when the leadership of a state has brought upon itself this universal hatred, they must also have given special offence to its *Founding People* (the Caucasians!) which they will be eager to avenge. And this eagerness will be augmented by the feeling of general ill-will which the leadership is seen to have incurred. And to that community whose livelihood and social well-being is threatened, and finding themselves forced by necessity (socio-political betrayal) either to do or suffer, will become a community most dangerous to that leadership!

C2235. The Alpha tells us: What he has don in the Holy Valorous over the years was to share his own personal struggle for meaning, to discover the ways and explore the problems that life has put before us beginning with its source? His mode of inquiry is more *Analytical* then *Rhetorical* he is more concerned with not only finding the true biological path, but proving its existence, its relationship to all living things. He makes use of an extensive range of sources to release the expressive internal logic of the *Biological Path*, his teaching mode, exploratory, historical, open to turbulence, and written for only one specific audience - the Caucasian race of people! Hence, to understand humankind through a reading of the Alpha, is of cause to re-understand ourselves!

C2236. The Alpha tells us: When great calamities are about to befall a nation and its founding people, signs are seen to presage, and *Prophets* arise who foretell them, warning them beforehand by these signs to prepare for what awaits them. Be this as it may, certain it is that such warnings are given by the Alpha to the Caucasian people, and that by them can be avoided a socio-political disaster!

C2237. The Alpha tells us: It may be that in attempting to defend his cause, which he has said, all liberals are agreed to condemn, he takes upon himself a task so hard and difficult that he shall not relinquish it, but pursue it with dignity of purpose and never judge it a fault, to support his opinion by arguments, where it is not sought to impose them by violence or authority.

C2238. The Alpha tells us: When alien people are absolutely *Uncontrolled,* it is not so much the follies which they commit or the evil which they actually do that excites alarm, as the mischief which may thence result, since in such disorder it becomes possible for a alien tyrant to emerge. But with wicked *Liberal Zealotry* the contrary is the case; for we as Caucasians dread present ill, and place our hopes in the future, persuading ourselves that the evils of liberal zealotry will fail and bring about our freedom. So that there is this distinction between the two, that with the one (liberal zealotry) we fear what is, with the other (alien rampage) what is likely to be! The prejudice which is entertained against the Caucasians people arises from this, that any may speak ill of the Caucasians openly and fearlessly, even when the government is in their hands; whereas aliens are always spoken of with a thousand reserves and a constant eye to consequences.

C2239. The Alpha tells us: Those Caucasians who carefully attend to this precaution *Their Racial Sovereignty* well be seen to stand in less need of fortune's help than others who neglect it. The cause however is not far to seek, since it is the well-being, not of individuals, but of their Caucasian racial community which makes their state great; and, without question, this universal racial well-being is nowhere secured save in a *Caucasian Democratic Racial Monarchy.*

C2240. The Alpha tells us: Since any man may begin a war at his pleasure, but cannot at his pleasure bring it to an close, a leader before he engages in any warlike enterprise ought to measure his strength and govern himself accordingly. But he must be prudent enough not to deceive himself as to his strength, which he will always do, if he measures it by money, by advantage of position, or by the good will of his citizens, while he is unprovided with an army of his own kind. These are things which may swell your strength, but do not constitute it. Being in themselves null and of no avail without an army of one's own kind, on which you can depend. Without such an army no amount of money will meet your wants, the natural strength of your country will not protect you, and the fidelity and attachment of your citizens will not endure, since it is impossible that they should continue to be true to you, when you cannot, or won't defend them. Wealth, so far from being a safeguard, is more likely to leave you as prey to your enemy; since nothing can be falser than the vulgar opinion which affirms it to be the sinews of war, for victory remained with him who held the sinews of war to consist, not in money, but in good soldiers of his own kind.

C2241. The Alpha tells us: The problem is one of survival. At stake in *Caucasian America* is the strength and weakness of its *Language,* (English) its power and vulnerability. An oath is easily broken, but with it collapses the whole delicate tissue of transactions and commitments on which a society stands. And ultimately, for any nation to not be master of its own language is to be exposed in a shameful powerlessness that cannot be endured, and to which absolute ruin will follow.

C2242. The Alpha tells us: In today's Caucasian society the problems are real, the solutions are painful, and there are no easy choices. Therefore, take counsel from many on the things that you must do, and what you later want to do,...tell few!

C2243. The Alpha tells us: the unarmed and disunity of any Caucasian society, will become the reward of alien ambition.(hyenic socialism!) Furthermore, in conflicts or war with alien enemies, discipline can do more than fury!

C2244. The Alpha tells us: No policy is better than that which remains hidden from the enemy until you have executed it. And, it is better to beat the enemy with sanctions (coercive measures) than with battle; in victory by means of the latter, fortune can do much more than virtue.

C2245. The Alpha tells us: The virtue of Caucasian patriots is more valuable than their numbers; in conflict with alien race's those Caucasians who are more vigilant in discerning the plans of the aliens and endure more trouble in training their forces (discipline!) will incur fewer dangers and will be more able to foresee victory.

C2246. The Alpha tells us: When misguided Caucasians leave the side of the enemy and come into our service, if they are faithful they will always be great acquisitions for us. For the forces of our adversaries are more diminished by the loss of those who flee, than of those we must engage.

C2247. The Alpha tells us: The "Primary Necessity," our necessities can be many, but the one that is strongest is that which constrains us to *Win* or *Die*. This principle has always been confirmed throughout history, by examples from both the *Attacker's* and *Defender's* perspectives.

C2248. The Alpha tells us: Humanity's collective conscience was traumatized, when in a little place (los Alamos) a great demon was released, and ever since, everyone has been trying to enlist its services. However, to combat this deadly demon effectively, it is important to choose appropriate weapons; attributing imaginary faults to it, fighting it on grounds that is not unfavorable to it, can only strengthen its position in the long run. Let us not use unfounded arguments against it, as it could lead to a much more disturbing situation!

C2249. The Alpha tells us: Scientists often point out the fallacy of arguments based on authority. They would do well to also object to the *Efficiency* argument, which is so often used to sort good theories from bad ones. In fact their success must not blind us to the inadequacy of the concepts used, an inadequacy that the researchers themselves are the first to recognize and deplore.

C2250. The Alpha tells us: When mathematical techniques, which are perfectly legitimate in many cases, are used by practitioners of many disciplines, they sometimes interpret the results in a totally inappropriate way. When a phenomenon is quantified, it is always possible to apply complex mathematical analyses to the measures obtained, and to eventually estimate various parameters. However, if these parameters have no precise meaning, the calculations leading up to them, are a complete waste of time, even if subtle algorithms and powerful computers were used. Hence, an *Absurd Question* remains absurd, regardless of the complexity of the mathematical techniques used to answer it. How many quarrels could have been avoided if, before bringing numbers into a discussion, people were willing to honestly question their meaning!(science must recognize meaningless questions, and with reason void their analysis)

C2251. The Alpha tells us: the force of social persuasion in Caucasian America has a natural limit imposed by hostile *Racial Relations.* (competitive racial mistrust) Where it is used to influence the convictions of a minority race or an underclass to induce them to take part in a movement which is directed towards their own perceived liberation, it is easy, under normal conditions, to attain positive results. But, any attempt at persuasion fails miserably, as we learn again and again from the history of social struggles, when they are addressed to a secure *Gated Class.* But, in the human herd the racial imprint extends its influence into the phy sical life. The kind of culture and social interests imposed by *Racial Conditions* (fematrix strategy) makes spirit and body alike dependent on its own biological stamp! (Bio-kinship allegiance)

C2252. The Alpha tells us: Many of his recent analyses have been concerned not only with a changing America as a determinant of racial competitive behavior which is self-interested, but also with specifying the factors which make certain racial types more successful than others. He has been interested to consider factors which make races vary in their behavior. And among the variables noted is the nature of goals, the way in which goals and methods are absorbed into the various racial modus operandi, the way in which the competitive social functions affect behavior, and the extent to which the different races modify the actions of their communities. Hence, he acknowledges that all races are controlled by an entrenched biological constraint built into the very marrow of their being, preventing them from anything other than racial militancy. (Phylum preservation!)

C2253. The Alpha tells us: In a multiracial state, it is not difficult to objectively adduce when there is actually a serious cleavage between the interests and conscious objectives of the various races and those of their leaders. The competitive struggle within the political racial elite, for generalized as well as for specific support, gives those outside the authority-structure access to political power. (racial patronage) This rests basically on the assumption that the behavior of all racial groups whether in society at large or in organizations, must primarily be interpreted as following a logic of self- interest, of exploiting the other races to maintain or extend their own privilege and power. The Fematrix (life!) will have it no other way!)

C2254. The Alpha tells us: Political and organizational elites always have special group interests which are somewhat at variance with those of the people they represent.(elite oligarchies) And if we accept all of these points as valid, they do not mean that *Democracy* is impossible; rather they suggest the need for a more realistic understanding of the democratic potential in a complex society. In this respect, the Alpha explicitly upholds his *Democratic Racial Monarchy* as the only form of government that is capable in the *21st* century of harnessing the great struggle of *Racial Conflict* (racial sovereignty) *Social Wealth* (group elitism) *Political Power* (the laws of governance)

C2255. The Alpha tells us: What alien races don't care to understand is that today's Caucasian societies have acquired their present position only at the price of a long and arduous biological apprenticeship. Furthermore, at this time (*21st* century) in this struggle between the three race's (Negroid, Mongoloid, and Caucasoid) certain accessory facts are worth mentioning in connection. History teaches that between the races who have acquired cultural and economic successes in consequence of working for their *Racial Posterity* have thereby commonly possessed, when compared with other races, the advantage of a keener sense for the immediately practical, a better understanding of survival psychology, a fuller knowledge of who they are, (accumulated experience) and in most cases clearer ideas concerning their future Thus, the relationships dependent upon distinction acquired!...outside of the race (alien trust!) is comparatively ephemeral.

C2256. The Alpha tells us: Owing to our technical type of modern civilization, *Age* has lost much of its value, and therefore has lost, in addition, the respect which it inspired and the influence which it exercised. And what the young are failing to understand is,...in life the old hand constitutes an element of superiority, on account of the service it has rendered to their cause, it also possesses this great advantage over the *Racial Novice* having a better knowledge of *Racial Conflict* and its relationship between cause and effect which has formed the framework of today's unpopular political, cultural, and economical life. The result of this lose, is that older Caucasian conduct is guided by a fineness of perception to which the young have not yet attained.

C2257. The Alpha tells us: To enable us Caucasians to understand and properly to appreciate our own Caucasian racial identity, it is necessary to turn our attention to the Characteristics of *Racialness* and what it means to belong to a biological fruition.(a living racial distinction!)

C2258. The Alpha tells us: It is the *21st* century, and the Caucasian American people must not be compelled to submit to a restriction of their own *Racial Will* (political correctness) when they are forced to give their leaders an authority which is in the long run destructive to the very principle of their own democracy. The question which they have to decide, and whose effective decision demands on their part a serious work of preparation, involves an increase in their own political racial competence, and a consequent increase in the distance between themselves and *Liberal Zealotry* (Caucasian racial nihilism) as they become initiated into the details of *Alien Racial Ambitions* as they become familiarized with the different aspects of a *Multiracial State* and the many reasons why it should be, and must be *Completely Abandoned!*

C2259. The Alpha tells us: One of the fundamental spiritual needs of humankind is the need for union or reunion with what they perceive as the *Divine*! In Caucasianism the spiritual self is considered to be part of the divine racial whole or to find its home in contemplation of divine racial unity. While separation from the racial whole is necessary in order for the self to experience the lessons of the material world, this separation is also a spiritual exile and a source of great loneliness. The return to oneness with the divine *Race* is a preoccupation of Caucasianism which seeks union through introversion and contemplative prayer, and further seeking to externalize the inner journey of the racial spirit by representing it through symbolism and ritual.

C2260. The Alpha tells us: Caucasian racial spirituality (Caucasian absolutism) is an answer for the Caucasian world community and the need for meaning in their lives, and with a bio-racial religion there is a strong experiential component. This enables the Caucasian community living within cooperation to enact the spiritual path, thereby creating a holistic religious experience and validating their society's belief system. Because religion deals with the spiritual and the spiritual should not be disconnected from the intellectual, if we as Caucasians want a truly *Racial Holistic* experience that is grounded in "*Caucasian Racialness*" rather than conditioning, it is wise to bear in mind that understanding is an important ingredient in all religions. And, an examination of were that understanding lies is a good indication of how the religion will nourish and nurture its community.

C2261. The Alpha tells us: There is a missing element in some human beings, and it will stay forever missing, no matter how much digging is don. It doesn't have so much to do with the way we think as it does with what happens to a thought once it has been conceived. Among modern humans, thoughts move! If an idea or innovation has real adaptive value, it should by definition spread from one brain to another. Individuals, who are capable of receiving the new idea, either by exposure to it directly or by imitation of its material product, should have a competitive advantage over those who fail to pick up on it. Similarly, human groups that contain such savvy individuals will be more likely to survive than those composed entirely of less endowed comprehension.

C2262. The Alpha tells us: The real pressure driving Caucasian intelligence is other Caucasians! Caucasian societies have evolved with relatively long periods of dependence for the young, giving prolonged opportunities for older Caucasians to teach the juveniles essential survival lessons. The increased emphasis on learned behaviors spurs the growth of intelligence. At the same time, the Caucasian *Collegiate* community of old and young, teacher and learner, sibling, cousins, aunts, uncles, and grandparents generate another pressure- to *Get Smart!*

C2263. The Alpha tells us: All living things are required by the very nature of the systems they create and maintain to be calculating beings. They must be able to calculate the consequences of their own behavior, to calculate the likely behavior of others, and calculate the balance of advantage and lose. For without this, a living thing has no hope of survival

C2264. The Alpha tells us: Deception is rife in the nat ral. world. When threatened, a species or subspecies will try to fool others in to thinking they are something that they patently are not. They are acting out of programmed genetic responses, their biology leaves them no choice but to dissemble, so their behavior is in fact, perfectly honest!

C2265. The Alpha tells us: Tactical Deception, is altogether different, it asks for a level of intelligence which is unparalleled in any other sphere of living. Here one has the mental flexibility to take an *Honest Behavior* and use it in such a way that another is misled into thinking that a normal, familiar state of affairs is under way, while in fact something quite different is happening. The most cunning are the politicians, who commit acts of *Double Duplicity*, with one politician outwitting the attempts of another to deceive him.

C2266. The Alpha tells us: What is unique to humans is the chillingly effective cooperation among one group of humans to defeat another, and however unpleasant the evidence, the fact that humans cooperate to compete suggest that this capacity in humans is very ancient. Hence, the ubiquity of this bio-trait suggests that the capacity for it is *Genetically* based, elaborate, continuous, and deeply rooted in our evolution.

C2267. The Alpha tells us: At some point in our historic Caucasian lineage, we developed the most sophisticated tactic of all: the ability to *Trust*. No doubt, innate hostility toward other racial groups remain as potent as ever, perhaps even intensifying as these racial groups become more unified and more adept at devising schemes to outwit one another. But, sometime in the *Upper Paleolithic* a wholly new order of relations evolved, a foil to the xenophobic imperative written into our primitive Caucasian heritage. It was the need to balance *Cooperation* and *Competition* (trust in others!) and the evidence shows, by an exploding creative Caucasian culture, a race's investment in getting along with itself. And, the payoff was equally impressive. After thousands of years of intellectual stasis, the Caucasian race inherited the earth!

C2268. The Alpha tells us: Reference to our past is critical, in order to make predictions about our future. It is on this basis of generalization drown from our past experience, that future events may be anticipated.

C2269. The Alpha tells us: No one has yet evolved a nervous system capable of directly reading the minds of others. But we have evolved the means to read our own. By providing awareness of the motivations and consequences of our own actions, consciousness grants us insight into the actions of others as well.

C2270. The Alpha tells us: It is certain that consciousness evolved. But where and when cannot possibly be resolved, because consciousness has no fixed address in the brain. Yet, the running monologue of our inner voice is so integral to what we think of ourselves (self-awareness) that it is impossible to imagine what life would be like without it. But why is it there in the first place?...and why did it evolve? The trick!...that nature (the Fematrix!) Came up with was *Introspection.* (self-analysis!) It proved possible for an individual to develop a model of behavior of others by reasoning by analogy from their own case, the facts of their own case being revealed to them through examination of the contents of consciousness.

C2271. The Alpha tells us: We do not know if the inner voice that represents ourselves to ourselves is a legacy of cataclysmic stress (environmental) to the human nervous system, more in need of an introspective self, or the eruption of Multi-self-identities?

C2272. The Alpha tells us: It is the *21st* century, and the Caucasian world community has failed to mount a counter assault against their deadliest enemy- the Liberal zealots, (racial nihilists) and it is hoped that they will come to their senses, in understanding the great threat to their *Racial Identity* (their biological and historical stamp!) and the soundness of judgment needed to defend it. And understand this: the only witnesses to *Caucasian Extinction* are racially biased: the alien races, and their even more intrusive descendants, whose intrusion into Caucasian lands if not checked will seal our fate: and the price for that mistake, Caucasians will have to pay, it is a zero-sum game: their rise is our fall! Unless, of course, we as a race of people (Caucasians) decide to revisualize our future, and eliminate this imminent threat. The currency of Caucasian allegiance is not just reciprocal aid, but common blood!(our right to survive!)

C2273. The Alpha tells us: The Cosmos, whose most integral component is Nature,(Fematrix-life!) And her most prudent observer- the Caucasians,... begs the question! What role will the Caucasians play or think to play in the Cosmos? It is conceivable that in the future the Caucasians will tap into more powerful sources of energy and will possess stronger natural forces, and that they will move away from the passive position of observer in order to take an active part in Cosmic events. But nevertheless, they can just as quickly, do to their political and social passivity in the face of an alien assault against their racial heritage,...lose everything! It is in the *Political Degeneracy* of the *21st* Century that the Caucasian world community shows promise for both possibilities, a magnificent future or sudden death, and it is uncertain which path they will take?

C2274. The Alpha tells us: What are the Caucasians over looking? What are they doing wrong? From the start it should be stressed that the error in democratic understanding lies in the fact that the mantra of *Democracy* (freedom) can become *Enchanting* and move a person, a group, and even a Nation to lose sight of its limitations. Can it collapse? There are many possible sources for the failure of a social order, but for a democracy, its great demon is its absolute *Majority Rule* as if for some reason a majority has the exclusive on Sensitivity, Vision, and Wisdom? Furthermore, *Majority Rule* as well as *Freedom* are elements of a social order, not foundations, they are limited by the very fact that they are instituted by individual self-entrust, and therefore, are not by any means *Magnanimous.* Self- renunciation (the bedrock of social union!) can only come about through the biological mandate of relationship. (a species or subspecies nuclear culture!) It is this foundation that has and does create leadership bonding and trust, under the rubric of related kind. Hence, a state that is populated by unrelated kinds (different racial groups) is a state under siege, and if it is a *Democracy,* the very demon that it worships (majority rule) will bring it to total destruction.

C2275. The Alpha tells us: The great problem with modern human states is the artificial constant of a mystical all inclusive (we are all equal!) political officialism. Only when world leaders have been forced to relinquish this fallacy, this element of dishonest political absurdity,(by the shedding of liberal radicalism!) will all human subspecies (races) come in to their own. Human societies like all biological life are diverse in their civilizations, as well as their place in Natures scheme of things. Hence, what may be good for one group, may not at all suite the bio-historical journey of another, though it is nice to think that our way of life is the true path, but in the eyes of others, it projects an arrogance of elitism and contempt. Therefore, life and socialization seek its own level, they are their own Consciousness, their own Aspiration, their own Destiny, and it is not for us as Caucasians to interfere!

C2276. The Alpha tells us: A proper understanding of *Alien Assimilation* into Caucasian society is the aim of many Caucasian states throughout the world but they do not seem to be short of problems! There are three phases leading up to *Assimilation*- Language, Culture, and Identity, and the period over which these phases yield or don't yield to the new Caucasian culture depending on the states strength (its laws) of assimilation. But, what if, there are cloaked *Saboteurs* in the state's political elites?...Sinister *Saboteurs,* not recognized by the descendants of the founders of the state, a political cult of *Liberal Racial Nihilists* (Caucasian traitors) who's evil agenda is the total destruction of the Caucasian race, and its culture. (if we fail to act against them, our children and grandchildren will be government press-ganged?

C2277. The Alpha tells us: Find the *Observer,* and you have found the center of the Universe!

C2278. The Alpha tells us: Life adapted itself optimally to the qualities of *Water.* Water's role is central - as a solvent, as a nutrient transporter, and as a partner in chemical reaction. No other molecule has so central a role in terrestrial life, (no alternative has been observed!) like blood, water has no equal, a fundamental component of plants, animals, and humans, as well as the total ecological system of our Earth. It is truly the basic elixir of our life form.

C2279. The Alpha tells us: In the search for scientific explanation certain phenomena may be valid only for our particular position in space and time. Physicists and Astronomers tend to focus in the physical universe, from atoms to galaxies, and usually ignore the existence of biological fruition. Philosophers and Theologians on the other hand, are preoccupied with Man and God, and show very little interest in the *Biological Cosmos* and its *Female Absolutism.* The *Fematrix* however, is the most integral part of who we are, and we must as Caucasians stop considering the *Fematrix* and *Nature* as two separate unrelated entities, and start searching for her true place and role within the framework of our physical and spiritual universe, so that we can recover our true path!

C2280. The Alpha tells us: Even today our understanding of the origins of *Intelligence* is still incomplete, and why the physical process brought cognizance into being in the first moments of biological fruition remains a mystery, which means that we are still without an explanation for one of the most basic events essential to our existence.(matter and the- id!)

C2281. The Alpha tells us: The order and well-understood world that we all live in has its darker, but not so hidden side. Three basic problems still await solution within the scheme of life: the origin of intellect, the primordial singularity of biology itself,(only life form!) and the truth of biologies ultimate teleology? Each of these questions, in its own way, is intimately connected with the fact of our existence. Without intellect there would almost certainly have been no life, as *Intellect* is the precursor of *Desire,* desire- the precursor of *Form,* form the precursor of *Identity,* and identity- the precursor of the *Observer,*(Us!) the center of the universe!

C2282. The Alpha tells us: Shadow Governments.(political parties!)

We think of today's political parties as *Public* because of governmental support, but that couldn't be further from the truth, they are actually *Private Corporations,* their incomes are enormous, which strengthens their hold on all Federal and State, as well as community elections? Combined, these political parties (Cabal's!) democrats and republicans have an income of more than a half billion during any election. Hence, these parties have so permeated the American government at all levels that we the Caucasian community excuse it as normal? The truth is, much of our political system in America has been shaped for the convenience of "Political Hustlers" that dominate and subvert the system. (political prin-cipalities!)

C2283. The Alpha tells us: Shades of extreme ignorance: it is the *21st* century, and America's national social and political curriculum is an insult to even a marginally educated person. The very failure of so many Caucasian Americans (founding race of people!) to challenge the liberal pathology and its degenerate course, (Caucasian racial nihilism) will prove to be pitifully tragic to the future of Caucasian American posterity, and the legacy of our historical quest. Furthermore, a failure to challenge our enemies on our own terms, (our racial self-interest!) will render our future incapable.

C2284. The Alpha tells us: The hope for the Caucasian world community of the *21st* century is to safeguard its future by the insistence on tougher *Alien Emigration* laws that forbid alien access to *Citizenship, Political Office,* and *Real- estate* property in Caucasian society. Hence, by these restrictions on *Alien Ambitions,*(having no political or social influence!) Other than *Commercial Trade* (commerce) a more stable relationship can be achieved.

C2285. The Alpha tells us: All societies (human or animal) are built by their very own biological mandate, and owe their first loyalty to their *Biological Ancestral Trust.* (their historical journey) Therefore, if a person or group chose to neglect, disregard or make light of that trust, let it be understood, that in a world based on *Competitive Predation* he or she who has no shelter (a stronghold of defensive relations) will be quickly subdued and ravished!

C2286. The Alpha tells us: The fact is, in city after city across our Nation, our educational system and its public schools are abjectly failing in their ability to educate our children. Failure or success in a child's education is crucial to our Nation's future. Basic skills once taken for granted, such as Reading, Writing, and Math are no longer easily obtained. Although a certain level of information has always been considered essential for graduation from high school, that level no longer exists. Young people now too often enter the adult world without the knowledge of an educated person. This is an indictment that cannot be dismissed. If Caucasian culture is to prosper, our adolescents must receive a more than satisfactory secondary education.

C2287. The Alpha tells us. Criticism is slowly, if too slowly, forcing the Caucasian American community to see how blind they have been too *Liberal Zealotry* and its failure in the education of our children and the licensing of academic incompetence. The Caucasian public has been naive! If they are in awe of liberal propaganda, it is because they assume falsely - that they rank high in reasonable intelligence, academic sincerity, and political integrity. This is one of the great fallacies of modern education in the *21st* century. In fact most-older liberals are not very learned people at all; having come up through a system infected by fifty years of radical liberal socialism from the 1960's - and its *We are all equal* academic mantra. (the ultimate absurdity!) This degenerate cadre has infected our political system, educational system, and our culture, its *Dereliction* has been confirmed it must be removed!

C2288. The Alpha tells us: American politics of the *21st* century is a zero sum exercise, because both parties-Democrats and Republicans are deceptive. No matter what most politicians say publicly or how moderate they appear, they are dishonest. The Republicans champion the so called *Haves* on how to hold power, while the Democrats champion the so called *Have Not's* on how to take it away. Thus, the rules for the organizers of *America's Democracy* having been laid down by Democrats and Republicans of the *21st* century are rules of deception!

C2289. The Alpha tells us: In Caucasianism *Gratitude* comes from the belief that everything we have as Caucasians - our lives and the blessings of our lives - are gifts from Caucasia, gratitude is a way to achieve purity because, by feeling grateful, we give up the idea that we are individual entities, and become part and parcel of a greater Caucasian whole. The virtue of thankfulness is so basic to Caucasianism and its teachings; it regards it as a duty.

C2290. The Alpha tells us: The Caucasians of the *21st* century must nurture patience and diligence through their expectations that the Holy Valorous will finish the work of the Alpha, (bring union to the Caucasian world) and his desire that each and every one of us show the same diligence through Faith, Patience and Loyalty, for only this will bring about our- *Inheritance, Future*, and *Destiny*!

C2291. The Alpha tells us: Caucasianism basses its educational system on the process of asking and answering questions, particularly those of - Caucasian Western Cultural and Religious History- that has lead up to the *21st* century's *Fematrix Theology* and its religious enlightenment Caucasianism the New Truth! (Fematrix absolutism) the New Faith! (the covenant of Caucasians) and the New Path! (our racial sovereignty and destiny)

C2292. The Alpha tells us: In Caucasianism right speech is part of avoiding harm to others. The Alpha teaches with great wisdom that speaking the truth is always proper, and speaking in a way that is beneficial to the listener's spiritual growth is even better

C2293. The Alpha tells us: Respect for Parents, respect for Ancestors, respect for Teachers and Clergy, all find powerful and universal support as *Virtues* in the Caucasian world. They are the ones who are *Wise,* who created and continued the great traditions of our Caucasian past, and they are the ones to whom you look to for Information and Encouragement! The Virtue of respect for our elders extends that respect, to all in a position of authority. This honor establishes social and familial relations and provides a way to communicate the wisdom of the past to our future Caucasian generations.

C2294. The Alpha tells us: In Caucasianism -*Marriage*- is considered the cornerstone of Caucasian society. It is the principle rite of adulthood and is extremely important in Caucasianism because it provides an opportunity to re-commit to Caucasian society. In a Caucasian marriage, not only are two people joined, (man and woman) but the union of two families also takes place. In this sacred bond, the two become one, and their relationship is considered *Preordained* by their Fematrix Caucasia. In many ways for the Caucasians, marriage is as much the preservation of the *Sacred Family* as it is the uniting of two individuals.

C2295. The Alpha tells us: A distance exists between the *Sacred* and the *Profane,* and in order to touch the Caucasian soul, one needs to be in touch with its Fematrix **Caucasia** and her *Life Strategy.* One of the founding ideas in **Caucasianism** is that what happens to us is the results of what we do! This idea is called *Providence,* and it is both Individual (personal!) and Collective (racial!) in form. Consider Caucasian providence in the light of cause and effect,…*Rightful Thinking* brings prosperity and goodness, *Wrongful Thinking* brings failure and misery.

C2296. The Alpha tells us: In **Caucasianism** the *Fematrix* only commands rational truth, for only in this, is her destiny possible. Hence, this question - what is the role of Caucasian reason in determining the truth? What is the *Fematrix* role? For the unenlightened Caucasian community (non-believers) this problem continues to vex them to this day. Much of the monotheistic faiths focus on this difficult task- medieval theology, versus reality!

C2297. The Alpha tells us: If you ask an *Orthodox Caucasian* what he or she does to be Caucasian, they will answer we do *Caucasian Racial Fidelity,* which means they seek out **Caucasia's** truths in the **Holy Valorous,** and try to understand, uphold, and teach their children as many of them as possible in their everyday lives.

C2298. The Alpha tells us: Some Caucasians come to their *Racialness* because they feel allied to a nature, their own living spiritual racial kind; other Caucasians come to racialness because they want to do for their race- *Faith* and *Work, Creed* and *Deed*, beliefs and obligations. Therefore, the essence of *Racialness* is not goodness but obligation! When you do something because you believe the sovereignty of your race compels you to do it, that is an act of urgency. But, what you do for your *Fematrix* (**Caucasia**) maybe *Ethical* or it may be *Ritual*, but its main meaning is that you are acting out of *Obligation* to **Caucasia**.(your bio-genesis) Hence, your obligation to your race.

C2299. The Alpha tells us: *Racial Revelation* (your core enlightenment) is a way of getting to the universal truths, as well as truths that are deeply felt by your inner Caucasian being.(your ancestral soul) For those Caucasians who think the only truth is that which applies to all people all the time, a good dose of *Competitive Predation* may help them see the truth in a new way through the eyes of racial revelation.(lineage survival) One's life, (whomever) can only be measured and have meaning by the survival of their posterity. This is truth, this is reality!

C2300. The Alpha tells us: In Caucasianism racial revelation is the way *Caucasia* (living spirit of the Caucasians) makes known what the Caucasian race of people are supposed to know and do, it's her way of communicating with us. Racial revelation is the idea, that the way we understand our *Racial Fematrix* (Caucasia) is the way she wants to be understood. In other words, *Racial Revelation* (to uncover or lay bare) is in essence, the uncovering of our Fematrix *Caucasia.* Her existence is evident in the interconnected patterns and systems of the Caucasian biological cosmos, the beauty of form, the majesty of intellect, and the miracle of Caucasian birth, all are racial revelations in that you can see the essence and nature of *Caucasia,* our Fematrix, within all of them. (all having her mark!)

C2301. The Alpha tells us: In his *Prophetic Revelation* and its moment of purity, clarity and joy he became humbled and reborn. An historical event in which *Caucasia* (our Fematrix!) revealed her divine will through a human interpreter. Hence, her truth: Biology's antiquity, a species or subspecies that has withstood the passage of time and the challenges of the ages does not require the politics of a scientific arbitration to be real! Biological wisdom declares, who was first and who was last is irrelevant, where are you now?..and where are you going?..is what counts. And for the Caucasian American community and their sister states throughout the world, failure is not an option!

C2302. The Alpha tells us: In Caucasianism - Faith is also trust, the trust you put into your racialness (ancestral traditions) for salvation, produces your salvation. Furthermore, by making the simple statement- *I am of the Caucasian faith-* you reveal the religious belief system you consider to be true. Caucasianism is not a blind faith, that is, its teachings are rational and reaffirms in its belief system enlightenment through historical enquiry. (study) Hence, Caucasian faith is connected to the idea of trust in *Racial Sovereignty* (Caucasianism) a Caucasian biological mandate. You must find the courage to travel down the path toward *Racial Enlightenment* by looking inside your own heart and mind, to find the compassion and love that radiates from your *Ancestral Trust* and trusting your Caucasian racial heritage, for ultimate enlightenment!

C2303. The Alpha tells us: When somebody remarks with sympathy that he or she has become an outcast from a family do to their being useless, a tramp, a failure defaulting on their ancestral obligations, this is good! It's right that a healthy family should eject one of its members who have become unworthy of it. The error would be precisely to allow the failure to continue to be privileged!

C2304. The Alpha tells us: A marriage or sexual union between persons of the *Same Sex* is prohibited. Any marriage or union entered into by persons of the same sex in another state or jurisdiction shell be void in all respects in the *Caucasian Empire,* and any contractual rights created by such a marriage or union shell be void and unenforceable.

C2305. The Alpha tells us: There is a perfect simile to illustrate the method through which one may attain the object of one's *Racial Purpose*. First comes the preparing of the soil to receive the seed, which is represented by *Racial Faith* and *Caucasian Intelligence* and the understanding of the very principle of "Caucasianism" and its word the "Holy Valorous" through which the seed of racial purpose may be planted. Then comes a period of waiting and working for the realization of the object of that racial purpose. During this period, there must be continuous, intensified racial faith, which serves as the sun and rain, without which the seed will wither and die. Then comes realization, harvest time! I am fully conscious of the fact that much of what I am stating will not be understood by the beginner at the first reading of the *"Holy Valorous"* for I have in mind my own experience at the start. However, as the evolutionary process carries on its work (and it will do so; make no mistake), all the principles described in the "Holy Valorous" and in all of its other lessons will become as familiar to you as did walking after you had mastered it. In the "Holy Valorous" you are dealing with four major factors to which I would direct your attention with the request that you familiarize your self with them. They are your *Caucasian Race!*... your *Caucasian Culture!*...your *Caucasian faith!*...and your *Caucasian Posterity*. These are the four roadways over which you must travel in your upward climb in the quest for your identity,…your *Caucasian Racial Soul*!

C2306. The Alpha tells us: If the *"Holy Valorous"* does that which it was intended to do, it will bring you a fuller and deeper realization of your *"Racial Mandate"* by having sufficient knowledge of the real source from which you are drawing your power, to give full credit to your Caucasian racial spirituality.

C2307. The Alpha tells us: The subconscious mind accepts and acts on all suggestions that reach it, from your own mind as well as the minds of others.

C2308. The Alpha tells us: The only hope held out to humankind in this unforgiving world is a reward that may be attained in no way except by *"Constructive Thought"* in other words, *you can do it if you believe you can*!

C2309. The Alpha tells us: Worry, Envy, Jealousy, Hatred, Doubt, and Fear are all states of mind that are fatal to- Action! Hence, do not tell the world what you can do; Show them!

C2310. The Alpha tells us: It was John Quincy Adams who said: If your actions inspire others to dream more, learn more, do more, and become more, you are a- Leader. In other words, know your men, know your business, know yourself!

C2311. The Alpha tells us: It was Albert Einstein who said: Logic will get you from A to B,…but *"Imagination"* will take you- Everywhere! It is the workshop of the human mind wherein old ideas and established facts may be reassembled into new combinations, it is the act of constructive intellect in grouping the materials of knowledge or thought into new, original and rational systems; the constructive or creative faculty; embracing, poetic, artistic, philosophy, scientific and ethical imaginations.

C2312. The Alpha tells us: Vision is the ability to arrange old ideas or concepts into a definite plan or a new combination and to reason both inductively or deductively, thereby determining in advance the possible effect of a given cause.

C2313. The Alpha tells us: it was *Johann Vaon Goethe* who Once said- Knowing is not enough; we must apply, and willing is not enough; we must do!

C2314. The Alpha tells us: A Caucasians character is but the crystallized reflection of the thoughts that dominate his or her mind and the deeds that they perform.

C2315. The Alpha tells us: all Caucasians have within their control the power to select the material that constitutes the dominating thoughts of their minds, and those thoughts will bring you success or failure, according to their nature. Hence, if you don't control what you think, you can't control what you do.

C2316. The Alpha tells us: The unarmed and unprepared Caucasian is the reward of the- *Hyenic* (predatory) *Alien*.

C2317. The Alpha tells us: when aliens races who have invaded *Caucasian Societies* (illegal entry!) are met with *Liberal Paternalism*?...instead of a harsh defensive rejection, you can expect their invasion will grow rapidly and harmfully crowding out the pre-existing culture and wanting more?...it will not be because *Caucasian Liberals* have not given them enough;...but because they have given them too much of their- *Acquiescence*?

C2318. The Alpha tells us: that liberal political elites of *21st* century America seek to dismiss accusations of their *liberal zealotry* and its official line of *Social, Cultural, and political Terrorism* by not addressing the *Public Violence* (alien mob assaults?) and *Political Coercive Threats* by the justice departments *Purging* of all disciplinary standards for *Alien Misconduct* in matters of *Employment* and *Education*? In other words, public information about *Alien mob attacks* (alien racism!) against the Caucasian American people and their community well be *Suppressed* by all public media?

And any disciplinary action against *Alien Misconduct* in either *Employment* or *Education* by a *Caucasian Employer* or *Caucasian Teacher* well also be *Suppressed* under the threat of being prosecuted for *"Racism"* by the- *Justice Dept*? (a great storm is gathering!)

C2319. The Alpha tells us: his polemic has no doubt that the liberal zealots litany of atrocities, ranging from Caucasian intellectual oppression to the brutal public criticism of the Caucasian American community as a whole!… not to mention the glossing over or actively suppressed facts about the state of Alien- *Social, Cultural* and *Economic Degeneracy*! Hence, all this being the cataclysm of the liberal zealot political ruse of- *Racial Equality*? (racial equal outcomes?) An "Intellectual Fraud " from the very beginning.

C2320. The Alpha tells us: for his polemic on Caucasianism to have currency it must first serve a *Useful Purpose*! And it is the chemistry of that purpose its *Composition, Structure Properties,* that give it the ability to change for the common good, hence fostering the union of *Caucasian Liberty*. So, it can be stated that Caucasianisms purpose is the fostering of *Liberation* (and it includes freedom from any alien rule, control or restraints!) through its principle doctrine (codification of belief !) *Caucasian Racial Sovereignty*!

C2321. The Alpha tells us: it is the *21st* century and the elites of the political world both *Alien* and *Caucasian* alike and all their Nations are in a state of *Political, Economical, Cultural* and *Religious* upheaval, and all this is under the influence of a world wide *Population Explosion*!…and a world not capable of either feeding it, or keeping its great numbers at bay! Hence, the march of the *Impoverished,* fleeing the gauntlet of nature, and the plight of their birth: *Famine, Diseases, War, Persecution, Despair,* all unforgiving, all unwavering in their assault, driving the masses before them into the lands of the *Caucasian Nations*, the supreme providers of *Liberty, Justice, Education* and above all "Hope" with a path to the future! But, this great invasion into *Caucasian Lands* by *Alien Races* is extremely *Detrimental,* and threatens the very existence of the Caucasian world community! (this is our reality!)

C2322. The Alpha tells us: The *Purging* of "Caucasian America" and it "wealth" by *Liberal Zealots* and their *Alien Subversives* in their battle against *Caucasian Culture* is a brutal form of *Treasonous Quisling Theater*, in which the liberal party cadre played their parts as directors, for so-called *Political Correct Courts,* (media driven!) acting out their *Moral Dramas* in ritual fashion, with large *Alien Crowds* calling for *Caucasian Heads*! Furthermore, to the delight of *Alien Races,* Caucasian humiliation and submission has an aesthetic appeal, a certain barbaric poetry!..often critiqued in the liberal broadcast media by the pundits of *Liberal Zealotry*, a true and ruthless enemy of the Caucasian American community.

C2323. The Alpha tells us: The use of violence against the Caucasian American community in the liberal zealot class war that followed the election of their *Black Prince*!...was not just a distasteful side effect of their social takeover, but is accepted and deemed as *Collateral Damage* of their social renewal!...in other words, *Alien Racial Violence*: collective brutality against the Caucasian American community is now a *Liberal Zealot* political strategy! Therefore, one must bring themselves to understand that *Mass Violence* against a given people is always *Orchestrated* by the ruling party when they fail to address it? Hence, the great enemy of the Caucasian world community: liberal zealots and their vanguard of alien races!

C2324. The Alpha tells us: In a state controlled by *Liberal Zealots*, (Equalitarianism) when one presents what he or she sees as the truth, and it counters a prevailing liberal zealot idea or view, it will automatically be regarded as a hostile act, and the gate keepers of "Equality" will see to your public harassment and persecution. For in a *Liberal Zealot* society it is always about what they wont to hear!

C2325. The Alpha tells us: The chief aim of the world *Equalitarian* social theater is to transform the highly diverse populations of huge and complex countries into a regimented mass of reeducated men, women and children who are not just obedient but engage in self-criticism and the sincere mental liquidation of oneself by oneself ! There is something that is particularly awful about the systematic destruction of fine minds, and why the persecution of intellectuals has always been for the *Alpha* the saddest of all the liberal zealot indictments. Therefore, it must be said: that in Caucasian America, *Liberal Zealotry* has poisoned the political discourse so thoroughly, that a critical analysis of the *Caucasian American community*, so easily seen as infected by *Liberal Fallacies* was not taken seriously by its *Conservative Gatekeepers,* hence, *Caucasian Americas* present situation!

C2326. The Alpha tells us: In back of all *Achievement*, in back of all *Self-Control*, in back of all *Thought Control*, is that magic something called-

Desire! It is no misstatement of fact to say that you are limited only by the depth of your *Desire*! Don't say "it can't be don" or that you are different from thousands of others who have achieved noteworthy success in every worthy calling. If you are "different," it is only in this respect: they desired the object of their achievement with more depth and intensity than you desire yours!

C2327. The Alpha tells us: There are more than a score of sound reasons why you as a Caucasian!...and part of the worlds greatest historic Empire (the Caucasian conquest!) should develop the habit of performing more service and better service than that for which you are paid, despite the fact that a large majority of people are not rendering such service. By performing more service and better service, you not only exercise your service rendering qualities and thereby develop skill and ability of an extraordinary sort, but you also build a reputation that is noteworthy and valuable. It is the rule of increasing returns. (be needed and desired!)

C2328. The Alpha tells us: Small opportunities are often the beginning of great enterprises.

C2329. The Alpha tells us: Self-control is solely a matter of thought control! This fact also carries another highly impressive suggestion, namely, that *thought* is your most important tool, the one with which you may shape your worldly destiny according to your own liking. You are searching for the path that will lead to you *Ultimate Success*, and yet you have that "Compass" you mind!...and you may make use of it the moment you learn to control your thoughts with a definite purpose in life, and your mind will transform those thoughts into physical reality and hand them back to you as a finished product.

C2330. The Alpha tells us: All Human character is but the crystallized reflection of the thoughts that dominate their minds and the deeds that they perform.

C2331. The Alpha tells us: You are studying this book, presumably because you are earnestly seeking truth and understanding sufficient to enable you to attain some higher form of enlightenment? Caucasianism- the awakening to the ultimate truth: *The Fematrix*!

C2332. The Alpha tells us: When you deliberately choose the thoughts that dominate you mind and firmly refuse admittance to outside suggestion, you are exercising *Self- Control* in its highest and most efficient form. Humans are the only living beings that can do this!

C2333. The Alpha tells us: The ability to negotiate with other people without friction and argument is the outstanding quality of all successful people. Observe those nearest you and notice how few there are who understand this art of tactful negotiation. Observe, also, how successful are the few who understand this art, despite the fact that they may have less education then those with whom they negotiate. It is in fact an art of patients and painstaking self- control, by making it you business to control your feelings, as a reward, you set your own salary mark and choose your own position.

C2334. The Alpha tells us: the best way to get ahead in this world, is by first helping others to get ahead, it is literally true that you as a *Caucasian* can succeed best and quickest by helping others to succeed.

C2335. The Alpha tells us: You can wine, for a time, through *Ruthlessness* and *Stealth*; you can garner more of the world's goods than you will need by sheer force and shrewd strategy, without taking the time or going to the trouble of being agreeable, but sooner or later, you will come to that point in life when you will feel the pangs of remorse and the emptiness of your well filled purse. Furthermore, the biggest advantage of being *Agreeable* to other people lies not in the possibility of *Monetary* or *Material* gain that this accommodation offers but in the beautifying effect that it has upon all who practice it.

C2336. The Alpha tells us: The accurate Caucasian thinker knows that the *Media* and *Newspapers* are not always accurate in their reports, and he or she also knows that what "they say" usually carries more falsehood than truth. This is a point that the Alpha is compelled to emphasize because it explains why so many people flounder and go down to defeat in a bottomless pit of false conclusions.

C2337. The Alpha tells us: Your dominant thoughts create your conditions!...

this is a crucial and important point for the Caucasian accurate thinker.

C2338. The Alpha tells us: No matter how fine one's character is or what service he or she may be engaged in rendering to the world, he or she cannot escape the notice of those *Misguided People* who delight in destroying instead of building. We must all be on our guard against that greatest of public evils- the "they say" chorus! Hence, one must understand and make allowance for the fact that the moment a man or a woman begins to assume *Leadership* in any walk of life, the slanderers begin to circulate "rumors" and subtle whispering reflecting on his or her character.

C2339. The Alpha tells us: there is a *Greek Proverb* that states: there is a wheel on which the affairs of men revolve, and its mechanism is such that it prevents any man from being always fortunate!

C2340. The Alpha tells us: There is a certain amount of temporary penalty attached to *Caucasian Racialism;* (liberal zealot tirades) there is no denying this fact; however, while this is true, it is also true that the compensating reward,(our Caucasian racial rapture!) in the aggregate, is so overwhelmingly greater that you will gladly pay this penalty.

C2341. The Alpha tells us: The Caucasian racial faithful adopt a standard by which they guide themselves, and they follow that standard at all times, weather it works always to their immediate advantage or carries them, now and then, through the fields of disadvantage, for they understand the soundness of their *Caucasian Racial Faith* and its great message of *Caucasian Harmony*, *Community*, and *Spiritual Wealth* of more then forty thousand years.

C2342. The Alpha tells us: Caucasian *Racialism* deals in facts, regardless of how it affects its interests, for it knows that ultimately this policy will bring it out on top, in full possession of the object of its definite purpose in life. It completely and unequivocally understands the soundness of the *Biological Imperative*!

C2343. The Alpha tells us: No one can foretell the possibilities of achievement available to the men whose wife stand at his back and urges him on to bigger and better endeavors, for it is a well known fact that a woman can arouse a man so that he will perform almost superhuman feats.

C2344. The Alpha tells us: It is the Caucasian women's right and her duty to encourage her husband and urge him on in worthy undertaking until he shall have found his place in the world. Only she can induce him to put forth greater effort than can any other person in the world.

C2345. The Alpha tells us: The Caucasian woman makes her man believe through love and understanding that nothing within reason is beyond his power of achievement, and she will have rendered him a service that will go a long way toward helping them win in the battle of life.

C2346. The Alpha tells us: The Caucasian person or persons who holds in mind a burning desire for the achievement of a definite purpose is sure to find ways and means of realizing it. You will see this principle of allied effort carried to proportions that almost stagger the imagination of all who have not trained themselves to think in terms of organized thought! And for the purpose of emphasis, there is a well founded hypothesis that, when one concentrates one's mind on a given subject, facts closely related to the subject will pour in from every conceivable source. Hence, a deeply seated desire, once planted in the right sort of "mental soil" serves as a center of attraction or magnet that attracts to it everything that harmonizes with the nature of the desire, in a spirit of perfect harmony for the purpose of attaining a definite acquisition, likened to our *Caucasian Racial Desire* and its *Spiritual Nature.*

C2347. The Alpha tells us: In Caucasianism, you will see the principle of Caucasian racial effort carried to proportions that almost stagger the imagination of all those how have not trained themselves to think in terms of an organized *Racial* and *Spiritual* union!...and its deeply seated desire to survive through the harmony of its racial kind.

C2348. The Alpha tells us: It would now seems reasonable to suppose that "Thought," being the most highly organized form of energy known, can only be detected and correctly interpreted by a properly attuned mind, in the under-standing of natures law of *Associated Memory* through its principle of *Need!*

C2349. The Alpha tells us: *Ambition* and *Desire* are the chief factors that enter into the act of *Successful Concentration*, and, by a mental stimulus created by will power, one can greatly progress in an orderly concentrated fashion of *Habit Building.*

C2350. The Alpha tells us: The conception of our *Religion*, *Politics*, *Economics*, *Philosophy*, and other subjects of a similar nature, including "War" is entirely the result of those dominating forces of our environment and early training. But, the *Caucasian* is a *Caucasian* because of his or her biological inheritance, and the *Alien* is a *Alien* for the same reason; but this is hardly stating the truth with sufficient emphasis, for it might be properly said that the *Caucasian* is a *Caucasian* and the *Alien* is a *Alien* because they cannot help it! For you see!..a *Biological Emergence* (living thing) evolves out of a multiplicity of *Negative* and *Positive* past interactions, they are in fact (temporary) preordained solutions, a gift from the past (ancestors) to the future as a gleam of *Light* and *Hope* for a future that cannot be predicted or explained from antecedent conditions.

C2351. The Alpha tells us: The Three great organized forces though which social heredity operates are the *Schools*, the *Religious Houses*, and the *Public Media.* Therefore, any ideal that has the active cooperation of these three forces may be forced upon the minds of the young so effectively that they cannot resist it during the brief period of one generation. And, the most prominent of human beliefs are those that were forced upon them or that they absorbed of their own volition under highly emotionalized conditions when their minds were receptive. Hence, the *21st* century and the Caucasian world community which now finds itself *Aflame* with a poverty stricken *Alien Invasion* on a scale previously unheard of, and the outstanding feature of importance of this worldwide *Alien Calamity,* is the very highly organized subversive (Caucasian!) *Liberal Zealot* support? This *Liberal Zealot* machine operates with great efficiency such as had never before been seen, and with the *"Equality Ruse"* as its avowed ideal, this modern liberal zealotry has swept all opposition before it as though they were leaderless, despite the fact that the *Conservative Opposition* out-numbers them on every front? (a well planned conspiracy!)

C2352. The Alpha tells us: The *Liberal Zealots* quest (communism revisited!) of the *21st* century that competent Caucasian observers have seen at the back of the liberal course is their *Stealthy* attempt to control the minds of the young by controlling the schools. If one studies the effect of *Social Heredity* as it is being used by the *Liberal Zealot* for the development of a *National Ideal,* the nature of which it requires no master analyst to interpret. That subversive ideal, "Equality," (equal racial outcomes?) when it fully develops during the maturity of the present generation, and those of the future, will represent exactly what the enemies of the Caucasian world wishes it to represent: the total destruction of the *Caucasian Race*!...its culture, and its dominant world community.

C2353. The Alpha tells us: In the *21st* century a great possibility of "*Racial War*" exists as a stern reality today solely because the principle of *Social Heredity* has not only been used as a sanctioning force in support of the *Liberal Zealots* war against Caucasian society, but it has actually been used as a chief agency (a vanguard!) through which the minds of *Alien Races* have been deliberately prepared for that war? For evidence with which to support this statement, all one has to do, is go into the public squares of any Caucasian city throughout the world and observe the aggressive and hostile posture (verbal and physical assaults!) glorified by *Alien Races* against the *Caucasian People* and their community, and the *Silence*!...and lack of *Shock*!..by the liberal public media?(a great storm is gathering!)

C2354. The Alpha tells us: If the Caucasian political world as it now exists, will not subordinate their interests and purposes to that of establishing a "*Caucasian Survival Initiative*" then the remedy lies in establishing a "*Caucasian Empire*" a "*Caucasian Democratic Racial Monarchy*" this *Racialocracy* will function throughout the Caucasian world, and whose creed will be based entirely on the one purpose of implanting in the minds of the *Caucasian Young* the ideal of their *Racial Sovereignty,* and its independent authority over their destiny. Such an "*Empire*" would gradually attract a following from the rank and file of all other Caucasian world states. And, if the *Educational Institutions* of the Caucasian world will not cooperate in fostering this high ideal of a *Caucasian Racial Empire*, then the remedy lies in the creation of an entirely new *Educational System* that will. And, if the *Caucasian Public Medias* of the world will not cooperate in this Caucasian ideal, then the remedy lies in the creation of an *Independent Media* that will use the *Printed Page*, the *Internet*, and the *Airwaves* to create mass support. In brief, if the present organized *Caucasian Forces* of the world will not lend their support to the ideal and establishment of a *Sovereign Caucasian Empire?*...then new organizations must be created to do so! Therefore, if the majority of the Caucasian people of the world want *Peace, Prosperity,* and a *Meaningful Future?*..they must realize by now that it will not be found in hostile competitive Multiracial States, where *Political, Cultural,* and *Economic* power will be in the near future determined by "Non-Aligned" alien races looking to impose their backward *Religious* and *Cultural* interest on the Caucasian world community? (the great folly of a multi-racial democracy- *Majority Rule!*)

C2355. The Alpha tells us: At first thought, it seems too much to expect that the organized states of the Caucasian world community could be induced to pool their power and subordinate their individual interests to that of a *Caucasian Survival Initiative* as a whole. But, this seemingly unsurmountable obstacle is, in reality no obstacle at all because whatever support this plan borrows from these Caucasian world states it will give back to them a thousand fold, through the increased power (a unified front!) and *Survival Advantage* the Caucasian world community attains. And the important advantage that the *Caucasian Empire* will have gained by its *Alliances* is the discovery that it has sufficient power to enforce its *Racially Moral* and *Cultural Ideals* against the onslaught of *Alien Cultural* and *Political Subversion.* By its declaration of *Racial Sovereignty* - No *Alien-Residence*, No *Alien-Citizenship,* and No *Alien- Political Office.* Hence, no "Internal", alien subversive infection. (thereby political and cultural stability!)

C2356. The Alpha tells us: this is a truth upon which the hope of our Caucasian race and its civilization rests, when he declares that the *Race* is always more than the individual, in terms that are uncompromising, he charges *Aliens Races* with being the natural enemy of the *Caucasian People* and their *Civilization,* because of their *Inborn Trait* (social heredity) of placing their own *Racial Interest* above all others, including those of the Caucasians? Therefore, it seems reasonable to suggest that the *Caucasian Civilization* of the *21st* century is passing into a new era of great concern about *Aliens* and their true nature?...and the practical benefit for the Caucasian world community; of that understanding!

C2357. The Alpha tells us: That Alien race of themselves are neither *Bad* or *Destructive* forces, but like all of us!...they must respond to both their *Competitive* and *Predatory* nature, a nature so compelling that neither them or us can resist it primeval beckoning, its call to action in the face of a weakness, an opportunity, a chance to overcome an opponent, and yes!... then to feed and take of it, all that it offers, all of its wealth! This has always been the *Principle Fortune* of all destiny. (to the Caucasian world, act within your *Survival Interest,* before it's to late!)

C2358. The Alpha tells us: To make use of our *Creative Thought,* we must work very largely on *Faith,* which is the chief reason that more of us do not indulge in this sort of *Thought.* The most ignorant of us *Think* in terms of deductive reasoning in connection with matters of a purely physical and material nature, but to go a step higher and *Think* in terms of *Infinite Intelligence*?.. is another matter altogether!...for this requires a *Definite Purpose*?...and its auto suggestions (suggestions that you make to yourself) which is the telegraph line, so to speak, over which you register in your subconscious mind a description or plan of that which you wish to creat or acquire in physical form. The recollected subcon-scious mind is the intermediary between the conscious thinking mind and life's *Infinite Intelligence,* and you can invoke the aid of life's *Infinite Intelligence* only through the medium of the recollected subconscious mind by giving it clear instructions as to what you want?...your *Definite Purpose* through and by your *Creative Thought*!

C2359. The Alpha tells us: Accurate Thought?...man did not know that the spoken word would travel through the air with almost the speed of light, without the aid of wires. How could they know this when their minds had not been *Unfolded Sufficiently* to enable them to grasp it? Therefore, *Accurate Thought* involves two fundamentals that all who indulge in it must observe. *First,* to think accurately you must separate *Facts* from mere *Information.* There is much *"Information"* available to you that is not based on *Facts*! *Second*, you must separate *Facts* into two classes: the

Important and the *Unimportant* or the *Relevant* and the *Irrelevant*. And if this appears to be elementary, you must keep in mind the fact that some if not most people of our world have not yet developed the capacity to think in more complicated terms, and to try to force them to do so would be the equivalent of leaving them hopelessly behind. That you may understand the importance of distinguishing between *Facts* and mere *Infor-mation,* study the types of man and woman who are guided entirely by what they hear, the types who are influenced by all the *"Whisperings* of the winds of *Gossip, "* who accept, without analysis, all that they read in the news papers and judge others by what their enemies and competitors and contemporaries say about them! Search your circle of acquaintances and pick out one of this type, and observe that this man or woman begins his or her conversation with some such term as this – *"I see by the papers"* or *"They say"?* Of course, much *Truth* and many *Facts* travel in the guise of idle gossip and newspaper reports, but, a *Caucasian Accurate Thinker* will always *Analyze!*...and not accept as such all that they see or hear.

C2360. The Alpha tells us: This is a crucial and important point that he wishes you not to take lightly *Your Dominant Thoughts Create You Conditions*! This point constitutes the rocks and reefs on which so many people flounder and go down to defeat in the bottomless ocean of false conclusions.

C2361. The Alpha tells us: International Laws?...Laws of and between *Sovereign States*: the set of rules generally regarded and accepted as binding in relations between *States* and between *Nations.* (interstate and international consent based governance!) But, International Law is limited to its *Signatories!*...and thereby having no direct control or rights over any and all those *States* or *Nations* that have not exercised either a *Treaty* or a binding *Declaration* between themselves and any other in their mutual relations.

C2362. The Alpha tells us: the *"Caucasian Race"(a bio-mandate, a life strategy!)* led to the Caucasian *Family, the* Caucasian *Families* led to the Caucasian *Tribe,* and the Caucasian *Tribes* led to the Caucasian *State* and *Nation!* They are in all reality the *Bed-Rock,* the very *Marrow* of Caucasian social structure, and it is the understanding of this *"Epic Caucasian Journey"* in the face of life's unforgiving *"Chance"* and all that it holds, for those Caucasians who would dare it!...those brave Caucasians who would jump in, risking and giving it all!...so that our future could be realized!.. grasping and clearly understanding vividly our place as *Caucasians* in this world, and by applying that realization in our *Social, Cultural* and *Political* engagements...is our only *Salvation.*

C2363. The Alpha tells us: In the realm of legal procedure, there is a principle that is called the *Law of Evidence!*...and the object of this *Law* is to get at the *Facts.* Any judge can proceed with justice to all concerned if he or she has the *Facts* upon which to base his or her judgment, but he or she may play havoc with innocent people if they circumvent the *Law of Evidence* by reaching a conclusion or judgment that is based on *Hearsay Information.* Evidence is always subject to the closest scrutiny, and all the more when it is of a negative or destructive nature.

C2364. The Alpha tells us: The Caucasian world citizen must be something of a good sportsman!...in that he or she is fair enough (with his or herself at least) to look for *Virtues* as well as *Faults* in other people, for it is not unreasonable to suppose that all people's of the world (men and women, as well as alien races) have some of each of these qualities.

C2365. The Alpha tells us: In his *Definite Purpose!*...he not only recognized facts that affect our *Caucasian Race*, wherever and whenever he found them, but he made it his business to search for them until he was sure he had found them. He has always worked with natural laws as his chief aids; always sure of his facts before crediting those laws. In the field of life,(fematrix life strategies!) relevant facts are the tools with which we must work. Mere information or hearsay evidence is of no value to the *Alpha,* or the Caucasian world community.

C2366. The Alpha tells us: We are all the *Masters* of our *Fate"* and " the *Captains* of our soul" by reason of the fact that we control our own thoughts, and with the aid of our thoughts, we may creat whatever we desire. When you grasp this fundamental truth, you will soon find the path to your definite purpose.

C2367. The Alpha tells us: We as Caucasians will learn many lessons of

value from the *21st* century, outrageous and destructive as it has become!...
but none of a greater importance than that of the effect of its *"Liberal
Racial Nihilism"*(an intellectual poverty!) a senseless viewpoint that the
human species has no inherited values that separate them? (different life
strategies!) And that the *Human Species* and its modern *Subspecies* (races)
Negroid - Mongoloid and *Caucasoid* are baseless and unfounded? Hence,
Liberal Zealot scientific revisionism, and its depravity!...the corrupt act,
and practice of denying all *Human Classification* and the devaluing of its
inherited diversity (its subspecies status!) by demonizing the term *"Race!...*
and why is that?...why does this simple word bring so much *Trauma* to the
liberal ear?..is it because it implies, and identifies several known variables
in the human equation? Mainly the fact: that like all in *Natures Colosseum,*
humankind is no exception!...and as well, has its divisions; "Supergroups"
that have *Formed* and *Shaped* themselves over thousands of years (by their
own hand!) *Subspecies*!...or for their common name *"Races"* that seek life
on their own terms, and no other!...is *Liberal Zealotry* a conspiracy!...or a
true illness!...what say you?

C2368. The Alpha tells us: The Caucasian worlds accomplishment in the
Arts and *Sciences* first became possible because of *Wealth*! (surplus: excess
supply) Only with th accumulation of a surplus beyond the necessities of
survival could the Caucasian communities support a class of people who
were engaged in work that did not directly contribute to *Food, Shelter,
Clothing*, and raising the next generation. Therefore, logic suggests that the
relationship between both *Wealth* and *Accomplishment* are complimentary
(favorable) But, this by no means suggests that wealth alone causes
accomplishment to occur!...for the greatest purveyor is and has always
been- *Abject Poverty.*

C2369. The Alpha tells us: Apprehending the facts of the *Caucasian Race*
and its *Accomplishments* does require judgment, which implies a corollary
to the subject, judgment is separable from opinion in matters of *Artistic* and
Scientific Excellence. It is possible to distinguish the *Important* from the
Trivial, the *Fine* from the *Coarse*, the *Credible* from the *Meretricious*, and
the *Elegant* from the *Vulgar*. Doing so is not a simple matter, and no single
observer is infallible, but a realm of objective knowledge about excellence

exists. That knowledge can be tapped systematically and arranged as data that meet scientific standards of reliability and validity. From this view of excellence in *Caucasian Endeavors* flows the following claim: Take from this world all that is of the Caucasians!...and then inventory all that remains?...are we the Caucasians not the wellspring?

C2370. The Alpha tells us: To celebrate the *Caucasian Race* and its accomplishments is to embrace a heroic view of human evolution and its destiny, and we never succeed all at once, and often the advances are so small and so infrequent that even the appearance of progress is hard to detect. But as a race of people we are able to discover many small truths and as time go on, we will begin to converge on truth in some of its large and final forms. Therefore, *Caucasian Accomplishment* describes what we as a race of people have achieved, and celebrate our continuing common quest.

C2371. The Alpha tells us: *Enthusiasm* impels action! It is, by far, the most vital factor that enters into all of our human communication, it *Energizes*, it *Inspires* and *Enforces* the will to create. It is brought about by doing the work or rendering of the service that one like best! Hence, as stated in "Caucasianism" the need for one's adopting a *Definite Purpose!*...no one can stop you from determining in your own mind what your *Definite Purpose* in life shall be, nor can anyone stop you from planning ways and means to translate that purpose into reality, nor can anyone stop you from mixing *Enthusiasm* with your plans.

C2372. The Alpha tells us: *Happiness,* is the final object of all human effort, a state of mind that can be maintained only through the hope of future achieve-ment. Happiness always lies in the future, being driven by the past.

C2373. The Alpha tells us: Merely desiring freedom would never release a man or woman who were confined if it were not sufficiently strong to cause him or her to do something to entitle them to freedom. Hence, these are the steps leading from *Desire* to *Fulfillment*; first the burning desire, then the very crystallization of that desire into a *Definite Purpose*, then sufficient appropriate action to achieve that purpose. And, yes!...these three steps are always necessary to insure success.

C2374. The Alpha tells us: A person who cannot control his or her words shows that they cannot control themselves, and are unworthy of respect.

C2375, The Alpha tells us: In the realm of reason you must learn to judge your ideas by their long term effects on other people. The problem in trying to prove a point or gain an agreement through argument is that in the end you can never be certain how it affects the people you're arguing with:

They may appear to agree with you politely, but inside they may resent you!...or perhaps something you said inadvertently may have even offended them? Yes!...words have that insidious ability to be interpreted according to the other person's mood and insecurities. Even the best argument has no solid foundation?...for we have all come to distrust the slippery nature of words. Therefore, your reason must lead to *Action* and *Demonstration,* (proof!) for truth is generally seen, rarely heard!

C2376. The Alpha tells us: Human behavior is a product of self interest! ...supported by *Action* and expressed through *Symbols*. It is better to demonstrate your meaning so that people can *Feel* and *See* it!...therefore, more open to persuasion and infinitely more powerful than argument.

C2377. The Alpha tells us: When aiming for *Reason*, or trying to preserve it, choose your words carefully. If it does not matter in the long run whether the other person agrees with you or if time and their own experience will make them understand what you mean, then it is best to save your energy and move on.

C2378. The Alpha tells us: "Life" (the Fematrix!) is there, before our eyes, for us to see!...Yes, there are no offensive meanings, no possibility of misinterpretation. (she never favors!) No one can argue with her demonstrated proof!

C2379. The Alpha tells us: Those misfortunates among us who have been brought down by circumstances beyond their control deserve all the help and sympathy we can give them. But there are those unfortunate one's who draw misfortune on themselves?...it stems from an inward instability, a great Destructive impulse to act without reasoning, to commit without assessment,...without seeing the end! It would be a great thing if we could raise them up, change their patterns, but more often than not it is their patterns that end up destroying us? When you suspect you are in the presence of a person of *Great Impulsiveness*!...live their presence or suffer the consequences.

C2380. The Alpha tells us: When some one has a history of *Deceit* behind them, no amount of *Honesty*, *Generosity*, or *Kindness* will fool us,...*Overt Deceptiveness* is subversive and provokes *Destruction*,...be aware of deceit!

C2381. The Alpha tells us: *Liberal zealotry* is the embodiment of all those "Caucasian Progressives" of the *21st* century who believe in the total *Elimination* (destruction!) of every "Caucasian Homogeneous State" throughout the world. These *Liberal Progressives*, are an *Evil Cabal* of *Racial Abolitionists,* who believe that through *Political Treachery,* and an alliance with *Hostile Alien Races* will bring them "Victory" in their assault against the *Caucasian American* community, and its sister states in *Europe*, there by believing their degenerate cause will prevail? But, as all students of history will tell you!...never ever, *Underestimate* the *Volition* of the Caucasian racial spirit to wage war!...for its own survival.

C2382. The Alpha tells us: When in dealing with those who know only *Force* and *Self-Interest*, it is unwise to put one's self or one's group at their mercy!...it has always been a rule that the *Weak* should be subject to the *Strong*, and once strong!...we all consider that we are worthy of our power, and seldom if ever turn aside from indulging its opportunity of *Aggrandizement* offered by that *Superior Power*: The best way to deal with the powerful?...is to be powerful!...and to make them understand that it is in their best *Interest* to promote yours.

C2383. The Alpha tells us: The moment you make it clear that you intend to do away with your enemy, and fail to accomplish it, you seal your own doom. For your enemy will not suffer the same once the tables are turned! Hence, it is unwise to *Threaten* or *Declare* your intentions before you have their end in hand.

C2384. The Alpha tells us: The path of "Life" receives *Awareness*!...and its awareness produces *Encounters*!...encounters produce *Opportunities*! ...

opportunities create *Chances!*…chances create the willingness to *Gamble!*… and gambling creates *Winner* and *Losers*. (reason probability!)

C2385. The Alpha tells us: Most of us are cooperative. We want to avoid *Tention* and *Conflict* and we want to be liked by others. This can be seen clearly in the *Liberal Zealot* seductive ruse of "Racial Equality", this liberal effrontery was designed to deliberately *Embarrass* and *Challenge* the Caucasian world community's sense of "*Moral Equity* " by *Demonizing* their great socio-cultural success as *Evil, Cruel,* and *Inhuman?*…thereby creating *Uncertainty, Self-Doubt,* and *Distrust?* Although these *Caucasian Liberal zealots* and their *Alien Subversives* (minority races!) may try to disguise their "Treachery" by submerging themselves in the waters of a moral fallacy "Equality?…but understand this: we the "Caucasians" are of the *Boldness* and great *Daring* of our "Fematrix"(Caucasia!) and we will hold nothing back in the pursuit of our *Enemies* and their defeat!

C2386. The Alpha tells us: Most people are ruled by the heart, not the head. Their plans are *Vague,* and when they meet obstacles they *Improvise*. But, improvisation will only bring you as far as the next crisis, and is never a substitute for thinking several steps ahead. What good is it to have the greatest dream in the world if others reap the benefits and glory? Never lose your head in vague, open ended dreams, plan to the end!

C2387. The Alpha tells us: the greatest mistake being made by the "Caucasian Americans" of the *21st* century, as well as their sister states throughout the world, is that they are all not frightened by their present danger!(alien invasion in the millions!) and therefore, not enough so at that which this holds for their future? So much of "Survival" is not what you do, but what you fail to do! Such as seeing the alien invasion as just that!…an "Alien Invasion", and then act on the reality of that truth!…and not fail to expose those Caucasian *Political Imbeciles* (traitors!) and their *Alien Subversives* for what they are- The *liberal zealot* progressive, the very architects of *Caucasian Americas destruction*. (expose their treachery!… bring them to justice.)

C2388. The Alpha tells us: The ending is everything!…and in this unforgiving world, there is no exception to this rule! So, what do the *Liberal Zealots* have in mind for the end of the Caucasian world community?...will there be a place for the Caucasians in their utopia?...or will their "Identity" be erased from the annals of history? It is the end of all action that determines the *Winners, Losers,* the *Glory* or the *Prize.*

Therefore, we Caucasians must, before its to late!...come to terms with the purveyors of our demise (the liberal zealots) and stir in the harts of all Caucasians, a will to reassert *Our Selves!*...and never again let others steal the future of our posterity!...and through *Racial Clarity* we will rid our selves of *Social Anxiety* and *Political Vagueness* that are the reasons why so many Caucasians fail to conclude their *Racial Spirituality* successfully. In the "Valorous" you will see and understand your *Spiritual Ending* and for the wellbeing of your *Posterity* you will tolerate no deviation.

C2389. The Alpha tells us: We as Caucasians must come to understand our *Enemies Strategies?*...they look down on us, they see in advance the "Ending" of all our great dreams and hopes, "Our destruction by their hand! They laugh at our inability to see beyond their *Willful Betrayal*, and at how we delude ourselves through their "Equality" ruse? In our relations with those of *Ambition* and *Alien* others, it must be we who guide affairs and hold them in our power, and never allow our enemies to misguide us and sweep us along.

C2390. The Alpha tells us: "Freedom" evokes a power of possibilities far beyond the reality of the benefits it entails. When examining closely the choices we have?...it tend to have noticeable limitations. Yet as long as the faintest mirage of choice exists, we rarely focus on the missing options, we choose to believe that the game is fair, and that we have our freedom? We prefer not to think too much about the depth of our liberty to choose. Hence, setting up an enormous opportunity for *Governmental Deception!* For people who are choosing between alternatives find it hard to believe they are being manipulated or deceived; they cannot see that their *Government* is allowing them a small amount of free will in exchange for a much more powerful imposition of their own will!

C2391. The Alpha tells us: One must learn to develop the skill of sensing problems when they are still small and take care of them before they become intractable. Learn to distinguish between the potentially *Disastrous* and the mildly *Irritating*. In either case, though, never completely take your eye off them. As long they are active they can smolder and spark a new.

C2392. The Alpha tells us: In life there are two essential stations that must be filled!...and they are the "Promoter" and the "Caretaker"! Therefore, in finding our place in this world, we should analyze our selves and harmonizes with our native abilities, in other words: find the work that fits your nature, (promoter or caretaker) and the best there is in you, will exert itself.

C2393. The Alpha tells us: That which we all say is a very important factor in the operation of *Suggestion*!...but not nearly so important as that which we do. Our acts will count far more than our words, and woe be unto he or she if the two fail to harmonize.

C2394. The Alpha tells us: That sincerity of our purpose, its honesty, and earnestness must be placed back of all that we say if we would make a lasting and favorable impression. In other words, what we would successfully ask of others, we must first ask of ourselves.

C2395. The Alpha tells us: No man or woman can afford to express, through words or acts, that which is not in harmony with his or her own beliefs, and if he or she does so, they will pay by the loss of their ability to influence others.

C2396. The Alpha tells us: that a persons "Character" is something that you cannot *Beg* or *Steal* or *Buy*. You can get it only by *Building* it, and you can build it only by your own *Thoughts* and *Deeds* and no other way. These instructions are *Simple!*...but you will be unfortunate if you discount their value on that account. For, without the currency of "Character" you have nothing,...you are nothing,...and you can be nothing.

C2397. The Alpha tells us: One of the greatest powers for good upon the face of this Earth is "Religion" To this marvelous power my be traced *Miracles* of the most astounding nature. It offers peace to all who embrace it, and it also promises salvation in the future to come. How may I avail myself of the power of *Religion*?...the answer is simple: by *Faith*! You are required to do nothing, you are required to say nothing!...to avail yourself of the beneficent power of religion – all you have to do is believe!

C2398. The Alpha tells us: *Faith*!...involves a principle that is so far reaching in its effect that no person can say what its limitations are or whether it has limitations. *Faith*!...may also be applied to other matters than that of religion, for it is the true *Elixir* of the human spirit!

C2399. The Alpha tells us: It was *Aristotle* who said: What lies in our power to do, it also lies in our power not to do! *Enthusiasm* is the vital quality that arouses you to action while *Self-control* is the balance wheel that directs your action so that it will build up and not tear down. Therefore, to be a person who is well "Balanced," you must be a person in whom *Enthusiasm* and *self-control* are complementary.

C2400. The Alpha tells us: All *Defeats* teach us a valuable lessons that could be learned in no other way! And it will be no different for the *Caucasian American Community* of the *21st* century? For we *Caucasian Americans* are at the moment enjoying a *Feast*, and not anticipating the *Famine* that is to follow. We think we are getting along so well?... that we thoroughly approve of ourselves! (*Self-approval* is a *Dangerous* and *Deceptive* state of mind.) This is a vital truth that many *Caucasians* have not learned in life, and those who do, are those who finally begin to understand the "Tragic Fate" of defeat! The *Alpha* is convinced that we Caucasians have few, if any, more dangerous enemies to combat than that of *Self-deception*!

C2401. The Alpha tells us: For some 40 thousand years we Caucasians have tried and met with defeat, we as a people have planned and watched our plans as they were crushed before our eyes, but, what we must always remember is that the greatest Caucasians in all of history were the product of their "Courage," and our Caucasian courage, as you know, was born in the cradle of life's adversity!...and there by creating our biological character!.. our *Racial Spirituality.*

C2402. The Alpha tells us: We never learn very much about a given subject until we begin teaching it to others. There fore, let me say: Finding the work for which one is best fitted, and that one likes best is very much like finding the one person that one loves best; there is no rule by which to make the search, but when the right niche is found, one immediately recognizes it, and throws their heart and soul into it, and most important of all the turning point of their life their place in the world. (There is no failure except in no longer trying!)

C2403. The Alpha tells us: We as Caucasians must understand that we did not reach this high state of the *Greatest Civilization* on earth all at one bound?... we climbed step by step, and history has shown that *Power* in the hands of the Caucasians declares, who was first and who was last is irrelevant, where are you now?, and where are you going?..is what counts. And for the Caucasian American community and their sister states throughout the world, failure is not an option! Caucasians are not only in safe hands, but are in hands where it is serving "Humanity" throughout the world, blotting out ignorance, destroying contagious disease, and serving in a thousand other ways of which *Alien Races* know nothing, for in the realm of *Nature*: We become what we think about!

C2404. The Alpha tells us: Caucasian *Creative Thought* presupposes that you will keep your mind in a state of expectance of the attainment of "Caucasianism" that you will have full *Faith* and *Confidence* in its attainment in due course and in due order. And after you have reached this point in the process of your evolution, you will have sufficient knowledge of the real source from which you came? (and her thought was made flesh!) And give full credit to your *Fematrix* "Caucasia" for all that you had previously credited to others?... as well as yourself.

C2405. The Alpha tells us: The only hope held out to the Caucasian in the near future?...is of a reward that may be attained in no way except through the teachings of the Holy Valorous! This for some is a startling statement, but if you are even an elementary student and interpreter of *World History,* you understand that it is a true statement. And If *History* is plain on any one point above all others, it is on the fact that "Competitive Predation" is life's *Nemesis* and its importance has often been overlooked to ones detriment!

C2406. The Alpha tells us: *Faith* in "Caucasianism" will magnetizes your entire being and attracts to you the outward, physical things that harmonize with your *Caucasian Racial Nature*, and that of its *Definite*

Purpose!(survival!) *I am a Caucasian!*...This sentence is based on a great truth that is the major promise of the entire- 𝕳oly 𝖁alorous, and its teaching. Observe the emphasis that is placed on the word "ℭaucasianism". In back of this word ℭaucasianism lies the power with which you can vitalize and give life to the suggestions that you pass on to your posterity. We as Caucasians cannot afford to miss this point, because it is the very beginning, the middle, and the end of all the power we as a people will ever have!...our own *Racial Identity*!

C2407. The Alpha tells us: A lack of constructive *Action* (procrastination) has caused many *Alien Races* to remain backward in their own cultural "Rut" of *Poverty* and *Hyenic Behavior*! (tribalism) And of course their alibi for their conduct is everything from: The world will not give them a *Chance*?(it never gives anyone a chance!)...to *Slavery*?(as if they were the only one's ever enslaved!)...and then there is the clincher- *Racism*?... you know!...*White Supremacy, White Privilege,* and we must not forget the *Liberal Zealots* every day favorite!...*Racial Inequality*?...yes, the *Holy Grail, the Utopian Fallacy* of their moral high ground. A *Moral Ruse, a Fiction* so imbedded in the liberal mind!...that they have lost all *Rational Insight!*...all their *Historical Perspective* regarding their future, and that of their posterity! Hence, they like all the rest of life's misguided!...having entered the wilderness without acknowledging its darker side, will fall prey to the indifferent *Alien Hunger* that awaits them.

C2408. The Alpha tells us: All Caucasians as a rule, owes very little to what he or she is born with!...a Caucasian man or woman is what they make of themselves. We as a race of people have felt the icy hand of *Poverty* and have struggled against it for thousands of years, it has so impressed us that we fixe it in our mind as a curse to which we must not submit!..."once poor always poor" the curse of the *Quitter*? Ambition is gone!...opportunity comes their way no longer, or if it does, they have not the vision to see it, they have accepted their fate! (poverty is a state of mind!) It is a well established fact that the faculties of the mind atrophy and wither away if not used, and one's self-confidence is no exception, it develops when used, but disappears if not used, hence, the fate of the *Quitter* is always a long and sad story.

C2409. The Alpha tells us: Demonizing the *Wealthy* and *Productive* class in the *Caucasian American Community* has always been a political indulgence of the Caucasian *Liberal Zealots*!..the born again- *Communists of 21st century*, and their cabal of unproductive *Alien Victim Hustlers*. So, let us apply this line of reasoning to this subversive cabal of entrenched purveyors of *Unearned Equality*!...you know them!...The *Democratic Progressives*: (degenerates!) those liberals who are responsible for spearheading the political assault (*Wealth Redistribution, Fraudulent Immigration, Socialized Medicine, Judicial Activism,* and *Alien Political Subversion,* against the *Caucasian American Community*! And, if this is not enough to warrant a call to *Arms*? One should take a *Very Very Deep Look* at the *Public Liberal Media*?...what part are they playing in the *Demise* of the Caucasian American community?...and are they culpable?

C2410. The Alpha tells us: The *Liberal Zealots* along with their *Alien Marauders* have opened up a new front in their war against the Caucasian American community. Yes!..you guessed it!- "*Wealth Redistribution*? ...and why not! They have been very successful in the last 50 or so years, with their subversive drive to *Infiltrate* and *Undermine* their primary targets *Education* and *Legislation*! And, as we already know, both of these have ban *Subjugated*, and made *Submissive* with little or no strategy from the *Conservative Base* of the Caucasian community to *Rescue* them? Let it now be said!..so our future generations (our children!) will understand the *Folly* of what we have don?...and our great *Shame* in what we did not do? Our Caucasian world is being *Assaulted, Outmaneuvered* and its *Identity* is being *Routed?*...all this because we have *Retreated Intellectually* from our biological initiative, our "*Racial Identity*" our core-construct. Without our place! (our identity!) without this, there can be no Caucasian *We*?..or a Caucasian *Future*.

C2411. The Alpha tells us: It is the *21st* century, and the great *Asian Dragon* is beginning to emerge from its lair, having been fed for centuries by its *Godless Masters* the victims of its *Cultural Storms* and *Political Purges,* it now desires and craves *Foreign Nutrients?*...Yes! its *Neighbors*! It has matured in both *Size* (numbers) and in *Strength,* (military) and as history has shown us, and as we already know!...when the tribe becomes to large!...

it must expand its range to sustain its hungry brood? Hence, the future of us all!...will depend on the understanding of the *Dragons* intent?...and what we do, or fail to do?

C2412. The Alpha tells us: The ability to measure those, and to know who you are dealing with is the most important skill of all! Know their *Ins* and *Outs* before you even decide whether or not to deal with them!... and never rely on your instincts?...and never trust appearances?...they are utterly unreliable. What possible good can come from ignorance about other people? Nothing can substitute for gathering concrete knowledge, whether in *Business* or *Private Life*, it will always serve you well.

C2413. The Alpha tells us: Wrongs are often forgiven, but *Contempt* never is. Our pride remembers it for ever!

C2414. The Alpha tells us: One must never assume that the person you are dealing with is *Weaker* or less *Important* than you are. If for any reason you must turn people down, it is best to do so *Politely* and *Respectfully,* even if you feel their request is *Impudent* or their offer *Ridiculous*. Never reject them with an *Insult*!

C2415. The Alpha tells us: The Caucasian man or woman will accept the humiliation of being conned with a sense of resignation. They learn their lesson, recognizing that there is no such thing as a *Free Lunch*, and that they have usually been brought down by their own greed for easy money. Aliens However!...refuse to take their medicine? Instead of reflecting on their own *Gullibility* and *Avarice,* they see themselves always as totally innocent victims of *Racism*? Be warned: In the realm of *Race Relations* everything is a question of *Power* and its degree, and the race who is decidedly more *Insecure* than the other will practice a greater sense of *Deception* and *Hateful Revenge*!...for their racial egos fragility cannot tolerate the *Slightest Criticism*, seeing all as an offense. (racial competitiveness: is *Compelling*!)

C2416. The Alpha tells us: The moment you commit to the poverty of *Hatred,*...the magic of *Reason* is gone!

C2417. The Alpha tells us: The feeling that someone else is more *Intelligent* than we are is almost intolerable. We try to justify it in different ways: "He only has book knowledge" "Her parents paid for her education" "He's not as smart as he thinks" and last but not least: its do to *White Supremacy* and *Privilege*? Therefore, given how important the idea of intelligence is to most people's vanity, it is critical never inadvertently to insult or impugn a persons intellect! For that is an unforgivable assault, our pride will not let us forget!

C2418. The Alpha tells us: that it is a general and necessary law of nature to rule whatever one can, and that the standard of justice depends on the quality of power to compel, and the fact that the strong do what they have the power to do and the weak accept what they have to accept. Therefore, *Life's Colosseum* will tolerate many things, but *Fair Play* is not one of them!

C2419. The Alpha tells us: When in battle, and *Victory* deserts you, it is best to leave *Martyrdom* alone: for if you are strong of *Heart* and *Will*, the pendulum will swing back your way eventually, and you should stay alive to see it.

C2420. The Alpha tells us: Many in todays *21st* century have dismissed our "Racialness" as a relic of the past, a historical curiosity. They reason, according to their *Liberal Zealotry,* as though the *Earth,* the *Sun*, the *Elements*, and *Humankind* had changed the order of their motions and power, and are different from what they were in ancient times. There may be no more gods of legend!...but there are still plenty of people who believe in, and practice a *Racial Spirituality,* their *Unique Solitary* life force having no like or equal. The propriety of life may have more or less disappeared, or at least lost its power of reason, but *Races* and *Racialness* still exist because the *Biological Realm* exists, and laws that govern *Racial Politics* are as timeless as the laws of biology.(one and the same!) Therefore, there is much to be learned, then, from our historical *Racial Past*! (things that we have learned?) and our *Present*! (things that we must accept?..or reject?..for our future!)

C2421. The Alpha tells us: Nothing is stable in the realm of *Power,* and even the closest of friends can be transformed into the worst of enemies. Those who are *Wise* profit more from their enemies, than the *Foolish* from their friends.

C2422. The Alpha tells us: The first instinct of all living things is to always trust *Appearances*!..we cannot go around doubting the reality of what we *See* and *Hear.* If we constantly imagin that appearances concealed something else? It would exhaust and terrify us! This fact is well understood in the *Biological Psyche*!...hence making concealment and one's intentions an art. (decoyed objects of desire!)

C2423. The Alpha tells us: *Courage*!..is our firmness of spirit, a morality which, while fully appreciating the danger involved, nevertheless goes on with the undertaking. Hence, *Courage* is both mental and moral!...it invokes *Bravery* the physical.

C2424. The Alpha tells us: Leadership: In calling on others for *Courage* and *Bravery*, don't ask them to *Go* or *Do* that which you would not! Therefore, if your common sense tells you that it is too dangerous for you to do or venture into, then it is too dangerous for others. You know their lives are as valuable to them!...as yours is to you. But, occasionally some of those you lead must be exposed to dangers which you cannot share. Unavoidable danger for all!...and if those you lead know that you are *"Right"* you will never lack *Obedience* or *Dutiful* compliance, for they know that you are giving them the best you have, that you would willingly take part of the task yourself if you could. It has been truthfully said that no one can direct others efficiently until they have learned to direct themselves.

C2425. The Alpha tells us: Knowledge of human nature is the ability to accurately analyze others and the courage to see in them what is there instead of that which one would wish to be there. All human character is written so all who wish may read it, in the expressions of their eyes, the tone of their voice, the posture of their body, the style of their clothes, and the nature of their deeds! (a method of observation!

C2426. The Alpha tells us: *Sound Judgment* grows out of knowledge of all the facts in connection with the problem at hand. Judgment that is deliberate and free from one's *Bias* or *Prejudice,* and making those decisions that are free of vacillation, that are positive, and that admits to only one interpretation as to its meaning!...is judgment well served.

C2427. The Alpha tells us: "Caucasianism" is the *Spiritual Citadel* the fortress of *Caucasian Faith,* wherein old ideas and established facts may be reassembled into a much more clearer and rational understand of our world, by embracing Caucasianism's *Faith* and *Philosophy* of *Science* and *Racial Morality*, you will become "One" with the Holy Valorous, thereby advancing the understanding, nature and power of *Identity*!...for if we properly recognize our separate human *Racial Identities* and their right to pursue their own *Destiny* in their own name!...a great future awaits all of humankind!

But, if we of the Caucasian world community continue in our failure to understand the necessity and reason for our *Racial Sovereignty*?...and it right of *Destiny*!...because of our acquiescence to the *Liberal Zealots* favorite opiate- *Racial Equality!* (racial nihilism!) Then, like all those Caucasian *States* who are now taking part in these social fallacies!...we also will succumb to its social distress "Alien Hyenic Tribalism" and its cultural mayhem, thus, its incompetent ability will lead to the complete destruction of the Caucasian world community. (aliens are simply not Caucasians!)

C2428. The Alpha tells us: To succeed in *Leadership*, you have to master your emotions. But even if you succeed in gaining such self-control, you can never control the temperamental dispositions of those around you. And this for a leader can present a great danger. Most people operate in a whirl-pool of emotions but as a leader you must not allow yourself to succumb to their problems emotionally. On the other hand, you as a leader cannot completely stand aside, for that would cause needless offence. So, while you make outward gestures of *Support* or *Non-support*!...you must maintain and keep your emotions disengaged. Your moves will stay matters of your own choosing, not defensive reactions to the push and pull of those around you.

C2429. The Alpha tells us: There will be occasions when it is wisest for the Caucasian community to drop all pretense of appearing supportive of "Alien Political Activism." And instead, declare our contempt!...and commit to the truth of it! Thereby, depriving *Alien Subversives* and their *Liberal Cabal* of any advantage. Remember: our Caucasian pose of *Racial Sovereignty* and *Self-reliance* is particularly important for the Caucasians and their world community to gain respect.

C2430. The Alpha tells us: The effectiveness of the world wide *Racial Equality Scam*! (in all Caucasian Nations!) rested not on tricks, but on the *Liberal Zealot Progressives* playing their *Subversive Parts* to perfection. Yes! Who would have believed these born again "Communists" and their *Alien Vanguard* (unscrupulous minorities!) could have created the biggest social scam of the *21s t* century. The logistics of the *Scam* were quite simple. Years before, in the 1960's the *Liberal Zealot Cabal* announced the discovery of "Racial Inequality" in the Caucasian world community! This of cause lead to the "Liberal Guilt Initiative" a mixed bag of the liberal collective, (*Progressive Marxists* and *Academic Socialists*) for the *Emancipation* of humanity? News of the "Liberal Scam" spread like wildfire throughout all the racial minority communities. Grossly caught up in the *Equality Fever,* the racial minorities immediately became prospectors laying clam to their moral high ground, and digging up all the so called *Injustices* committed by the Caucasian world community against them and other? Fast-forward: what has started out as a *Social Correction*!...has now become a modern day (every day!) *Racial War* for *Political Power*, *Cultural Revision*, and the survival of *Caucasian Racial Identity*! And let it be said!... what all Caucasian Americans and their sister states throughout the world must never fail to understand!...is the outcome?..the hard truth!..that their *Legacy*, and their *Children's Future* hangs in the balance!

C2431. The Alpha tells us: One should never be so self absorbed as to believe that other people are interested in your criticisms of them, no matter how accurate they are! Always remember!..when you criticize some one, they always see the person criticizing, not the criticism itself ! ..therefore, be very cautious when speaking your mind, it shows wisdom.

C2432. The Alpha tells us: If you deal *Blindly* with whom ever crosses your path, you will have a life of constant sorrow!...being able to recognize types of people, and to act accordingly, is critical for you as well as your family.

C2433. The Alpha tells us: To reveal the true nature of your *Caucasian Intelligence* as a subspecies, you should never at any time downplayed or dampen your brilliance!...for like all competition around you, your acquired

"Intellectual skills" is not by any means a subtle challenge?...it is by far the greatest of all challenges. Own it, if it is yours!...declare it before the world as you would declare–you *Speed*!...your *Strength*! or any other skill that one would excel at and be found worthy of praise for their greater effort and ability. Hence, do not ever let "Alien Others" suppress you *Caucasian Superiority*!...for they are in it, to win it!...and will use any *Trick* or *Deception* (Moral indignation, Equality fallacy?.. and let us not forget their *Mantra*- Racism? You know! that which they never apply to themselves! All this "Subterfuge" is an *Alien Strategy* to defeat you and the success of your society. (your Caucasian way of life!) Therefore, take hart with your "Caucasian Heritage," by standing up to our enemies, and in the Caucasian way, take the fight to them! "Blessed are the Caucasians"

C2434. The Alpha tells us: What gets us into trouble in the realm of *Race Relations* is often two fold: our *Overreaction* to *Alien Aggression*?...or our *Appeasement* to avoid said *Aggression*? Therefore, keeping in mind the moves of our *Enemies* and *Rivals,*(their outward signs of aggression and propaganda?) we must never be deceived by their false action!...this is the essence of our *very Survival*!...and the core of our counter moves against their *Subversive Hostility*, and above all, know this: all *Human Racial* groups are competitors both *Physically* and *Mentally*, and their *Hostility* toward each other is what life demands of them.

C2435. The Alpha tells us: It is the *21st* century, and once again the world is plagued by greater and greater divisions between *Countries, families, Racial Groups, and Religions*. All in a state of total *Distraction* and *Diffusion,* and their level of conflict is now higher then ever, and has become internalized in every one's lives. It was greatly hoped that "America" would lead the world into the next *Great Frontier* both in *Social Justice* and *Economic Prosperity*?...but, do to its own hostile *Racial* and *Political* divide,(deeply entrenched!) this now seems very unlikely, and is having an adverse effect on the rest of the worlds communities. And if this is true? What happens if America falters?...and starts to spiral out of *Political* and *Cultural* control. Who!...or what will take its place?...were will the rest of the world get its leadership? Europe?- Russia?-China? Without appearing to be a relic of the past, the *Alpha* in the face of this world wide turmoil calls on the Caucasian people to keep alive their *Racial Inner Cohesion* and *Spiritual Strength*. For only through such an anchoring in their *Historical Past* will their families be able to thrive amidst such chaos. (Humankind and its future has never been more uncertain!)

C2436. The Alpha tells us: The *Hypocrisy* of the so called keepers of democracy (democrats and republicans) is now beginning to raise its ugly head!...and it appears that its first victim will be "Freedom of Speech! ...and why is that!...you may ask? Well, let me be so bold as to express its true and unequaled value. It is the very "Cornerstone" in the axiom of our *Democracy,* the first *Consecrated Right!*, to which all other rights follow. Therefore, an assault against one's right to speak his or her mind,...is an assault against all! And to all those who would make such an assault on the foundation of a free people!...it would be very wise and to your benefit, to accept the oracle of history past, and reconsider

C2437. The Alpha tells us: It is the *21st* century and most Caucasian states throughout the world have broken natures most fundamental law of *Racial Sovereignty*!...this of cause has led to the unnatural –*Multiracial State*? A state that has produced conditions so *Racially Competitive*!...that alien racial *Petulance* has become a form of power?...so serious is the *Exaggeration* of their clams of *Hurt* and *Insult* being done to them? That it has now become *Comical* to some, and ridiculously *Insulting* to others. The answer, however, lies in the very nature of "Competitive Predation" and its *Truths* that no one can escape! Angry *Alien Races* who cannot successfully compet against the natural ability of Caucasians in their own cultural society? Are lift with no choice but to develop different *Cultural* and *Political* tactics to compensate for their lack of ability? And this *Counter-balance* will take many perilous forms *Cultural Subversion?- Racial Rousing?- Seditious Revisionism?*...and *Racial Mongering?* And let us not forget *Moral High ground?* All designed and carried out, to *Undermine* Caucasian American *Culture* and *Authority*. Hence, the moral of the Multiracial State! If you invite *Wolves* and *Hyenas* to sit and eat at your table? Don't expect them to have good manners or stop eating!...and understand this: When the food runs out?...they will turn on you and yours!..for that is their nature.

C2438. The Alpha tells us: No living thing, whether *Human* or *Animal* is perfect with impunity!

C2439.The Alpha tells us: The Caucasian race of People have their own *Rhythms* and *Social Patterns*. And those Caucasians who succeed in life are the ones who support their race's social and rhythmic patterns. The essence of a Caucasian racial life strategy is controlling what comes next, and the elation of victory, confirming the direction that is best for the Caucasian *Individual* and that of the Caucasian race as a whole. The Caucasians are always steadying themselves, giving themselves the space to reflect on what has happened, examining the role of *Circumstance,* and never forgetting to taking a step back- to see where they are going in their endeavor to succeed.

C2440. The Alpha tells us: Life is authored form!...and form is a product of ones emotion!...and if that is true? Then all life communicates its emotion through form? (the fematrix!)

C2441. The Alpha tells us: Caucasians with self-control will not hate those who do not agree with them; instead, they will endeavor to under-stand the reason for their disagreement and profit by it.

C2442. The Alpha tells us: As we Caucasians inter the *21st* century, our community will face fiercer opposition from the *Liberal Progressives* and their drive to bring every Caucasian neighborhood under their control!... making all conform to their absurd *Racial Equality Subterfuge.* (by the threat of public inquisition!) Therefore, the answer to this assault against the Caucasian American community must be a show of resistance!...seeing to it: that all those *Caucasians* and *Aliens* who took part in this assault against our community,...are not the ones who end it?

C2443. The Alpha tells us: We Caucasians of the *21st* century are now living in *Tumultuous* times, and for some, there is *Power* to be gained by preaching and making accusations of *Wrongdoing*?...by those who *Have,* and the so called fiercer *Victimization*?..of those who don't *Have*. The answer to this *Liberal Zealot* (Marxist!) habit of *Scapegoating* the productive and responsible *Caucasian World Community,* is to mount a defensive protocol, a code of behavior, a *Cultural Memorandum* to counter the terror of the *Liberal Zealots* very radical work of demanding the Caucasian community's painful self-destruction!...by means of *Social Flagellation*. And understand this: We Caucasians will not succeed at all against the *Liberal Zealots*?...if we continuously forestall bringing the fight to them!

C2444. The Alpha tells us: The *21st* century will bring about the final union of all *Caucasian Nation States* into one sovereign empire, "The Caucasian Empire" a democratic racial monarchy. This *Caucasian Racialocracy* will restore *Sanity*, *Stability, Vitality* and *Destiny* to the Caucasian world community! Thereby ending forever the social *Pathology* known as "Liberal Zealotry," and reestablishing the balance in human evolutionary expression, (subspecies-racial kind!) offering *Truth* and *Clarity* to all who seek it!

C2445. The Alpha tells us: From the start to the finish, the Holy Valorous conveys its strongest impressions and meanings by a mere *Truth*, (fematrix theology!) yet this truth is so carefully covered that it is not obvious except upon careful analysis of the entire book. Furthermore, the whole construction of the Holy Valorous is such that if the reader lays it aside without complying with the requests it makes, he or she will have to reckon with their own conscience!

C2446. The Alpha tells us: That the principle of our own "Racialness"(our identity!) applies to and controls every one of our *Sense Impression* that is lodged in every living mind, and through the law of natural association, (like attracts Like) the principle of "Identity" held in the conscious mind has a tendency to draw to it other *Identity Thoughts* of a similar nature called *Identity Reasoning?* And it is this reasoning of the recalling of one alike! ...which brings back to memory all the others, displacing the feeling of *Caution* and *Fear!*...with the feeling of *Security*, and *Union*.

C2447. The Alpha tells us: there is a point that he would stress with all the power at his command. It is a point that he repeats over and over again in his teaching on the principles of "Caucasianism" and its spiritual enlightenment. And that is, that *Sincerity* of your *Racial Purpose*, your *Honesty*, and *Earnestness* must be placed back of all that you say if you would make peace and harmony in your own heart, rather then the *Social, Political* or *Monetary* gains that you might have had by a forced compromise with your conscience. Yes! there will be times, and many of them, in our

21st century, when standing by your *Racial Principles* (your identity!) will mean *Starvation!* There will be many times also when your closest friends and associates will strongly urge you to shed your *Racial Spirituality* for the sake of gaining a needed advantage here and there. But, strange as it may seem, your deliberations and conclusions on refusing to *Strangle* your own *Racial Identity!*...will encourage many others, and bring "Flesh" to the words of the Alpha, and that of the Holy Valorous. (our journey has just begun!)

C2448. The Alpha tells us: No Caucasian *Man* or *Woman* will ever find *Peace* and *Happiness* through False hood! If you compromise with your own conscience, it will not be long before you have no conscience, it will fail to guide you!

C2449. The Alpha tells us: No two or more *Races* of people on *Earth* are exactly alike, and for this reason, no two or more races of people would be expected to absorb from the world around them, the same *Social, Political,* or *Economic* viewpoint! Therefore, when the Caucasian world community is in any negotiation with *Alien Races,* they must be sure that their purpose is *Constructive,* and that its attainment will not bring any *Hardship* or *Misery* to any one! This is attainable when the dialogue between *Aliens* and *Caucasians* are through separate *Sovereign Racial States!*..which give each a sence of control in dealing fairly with each other.

C2450. The Alpha tells us: The Caucasian world community need have no fear of *Alien Subterfuge* as long as they are sure that the objective for which they are striving is one that will not allow in any form *Alien Trespass* into the Caucasian community's primary *Social, Political,* or *Economic* realm.

C2451. The Alpha tells us: Thought!...is the most highly organized form of energy known in the world! However, when one unlocks the gate to their *Racial Spirituality,* and its great power to link all things, one embraces a knowledge that make all past discoveries pale in comparison.

C2452. The Alpha tells us: The development of a Caucasian *Racial Spirituality* starts with the elimination of the demons called "*White Racism, White Supremacy, White Privilege,* all terms designed by *Liberal Zealots* (progressives!) to fashion in the Caucasian community's mind a sence of "Guilt" for being the consummate example of a beautiful race of people, and their competitive success, being the envy of the world. But, these liberal zealots, thus using their *Self-Hatred* to their own detriment! (deeply imbedded in their subconscious!) Have committed grave sins against their own people!...there will be no escape! ...they will be held accountable.

C2453. The Alpha tells us: What a *Tragedy* to watch a great people lose their *Racial Sensibility*, giving into *Intimidation* and *Menace!*...losing all sense of themselves, and that of their history?...so as not to offend or irritate the *Hyenic Egos* of resentful *Alien Malcontents.* This of course, is the *Plight* of the Caucasian world community in the *21st* century? And if not the *Spiritual Racial Truth* of the Holy *Valorous!*...then who, or what will guide the *Caucasian World Community* through the coming *Racial Apocalypse?* (war of survival!)

C2454. The Alpha tells us: A human life is not complete until he or she has made a choice as to what their purpose in life is to be?...something only you can create! Something in harmony and in proportion with your inherited ability, and then find out what it is that you wish; In other words, what are you going to do about it? and when? and how? Make up your mind!...for only you are the shaper of your own purpose.

C2455. The Alpha tells us: The principle of *Racialness* is lost sight of, and instead of lying hold of the human racial forces that are in evidence all around us and permitting those racial forces to carry us to the heights of great achievement, (being the great prime mover of all human history!) we of the *21st*century have defied them, and they have now become forces of destruction. For none of these great forces of nature are more available for humans to unfold than is the principle of their *Racial Identity*, but ignorance of this force is leading a liberal zealot minority of *Humanity* to so apply its *"Racial Denial"* that it now acts as a *"Social Persecution"* and not as an understanding of its necessary preservation.

C2456. The Alpha tells us: It is, and has always been his great wish that all Caucasian see nothing but the best there is in all whom they meet. (whether Caucasian or Alien!) For not all *Caucasians* are untrustworthy, and nor are all racial *Aliens* unappreciative. Yes!..knowing your place "Racially" is always *Preeminent!* But, common courtesy (respect!) for all who *Reciprocate* is a Caucasian virtue. And by doing so, you will learn that there is *Dignity* and *Civility* in others, even though they do not *Appear* or *Believe* as you do.

C2457. The Alpha tells us: It is wise to find forgiveness for those who have offended you, because you must realize that you will sometime in the future offend others, and you may also need their forgiveness.

C2458. The Alpha tells us: All Caucasians of a *Business Nature*, must fully realize that no *Wealth* or *Position* can long endure unless built upon *Truth* and *Justice;* Therefore, you will engage in no transaction that does not benefit all whom it effects.

C2459. The Alpha tells us: If the Caucasians people fill their minds with a radiant racial confidence, the principle of their *Racial Spirituality* takes this confidence sets it up as their dominate thought and helps them master the obstacles that fall in their way until they reach the pinnacle of success.

C2460. The Alpha tells us: All Caucasians must come to know their own *Faults* and *Virtues* in order to guard against the former while developing the latter. More specifically, however this term means that you must understand your inherent tendencies, those tendencies that are acquired through both physical and social heredity.

C2461. The Alpha tells us: *Initiative* and *Leadership* are associated terms for the reason that leadership is essential for the attainment of success, and initiative is the very foundation upon which the necessary quality of leadership is built.

C2462. The Alpha tells us: Words like *Freedom, Options*, and Choice?... evoke a power of possibility far beyond the reality of the benefits they entail. And supplies those who are *Clever* and *Cunning* with enormous opportunities for deception. Therefore, do not choose so quickly to believe the mystique of choice?...*Suspect!* and *Compare!*

C2463. The Alpha tells us: It has always been a constant struggle to convince a society that has grown *Politically Weak,* and *Socially Complacent* to see or admit to *Advancing Dangers* that threaten their very existence, and take action! Understand: In one's struggle with a deadly rival, it will often be necessary to hurt them! And if so? ...expect a counter attack, expect revenge! This is why it is *Survival Prudent* to project at all times to those with a *Predatory* and *Subversive* nature, their ultimate demise?..if they would be so bold as to have *Your Conquest* in mind!

C2464. The Alpha tells us: Truth!...is often avoided because it is ugly and unpleasant. And if you appeal to *Truth* and *Reality!*...be prepared for the *Anger* and *Hostility* that comes from *Disenchantment!* But, to say that *Truth* is without its source of pleasure?..is both *False* and *Unjust!* For truth is the great *Elixir* of *Human Improvement* and *Transformation.*

C2465. The Alpha tells us: "Racial Equality" this is of Course the Fantasy par excellence of the *Liberal Zealots* who prowl among us to this very day, and this *Liberal Quackery* has become the key for their successful Destruction of the *Caucasian world* community. Yes!..promise all the Alien masses of the world great change? From poor to rich, sickness to health, misery to ecstasy! And you will have millions of followers. The liberal zealot *Subterfuge* of "Equality" will never change!...its *Misdeeds* and *Stupidity* are now deeply ingrained in the liberal psyche!...a most wicked pathology.

C2466. The Alpha tells us: In Life (nature!) the social realm has a hard-set of coeds and boundaries. And if we are to survive, we must understand these limits and know that we have to move within those familiar circles, day in, and day out. And so it is with our future: it is slow and gradual. It requires hard work, a bit of luck, a fair amount of self-sacifice, and a lot of patience. (no room for *Fallacy!*)

C2467. The Alpha tells us: Through creative thought! ...we the Caucasians have become! How then, may one appropriate the power of *Racial Spirituality?* Its way will not open suddenly, from the first step to the last, but it will open one step at a time. Therefore, when you are conscious of an opportunity to take the first step, take it without hesitation and do the same when the second and the third and all subsequent steps essential for the attainment of the object of your *Racial Spirituality* is manifested to you.

C2468. The Alpha tells us: Do not rely upon *Miracles* for your becoming, instead, rely upon the power of your *Racial Spirituality* to guide you through natural channels and with the aid of natural law,(racial intelligence!) for its attainment.

C2469. The Alpha tells us: As a beginner in *Racial Faith* do not expect it to move you quickly in you understanding or its realization. Observe the fact, that you cannot reach a high state of Caucasian *Racial Spirituality* all in one bound. You must climb step by step, and in ways of which the average individual knows nothing.

C2470. The Alpha tells us: Caucasian *Infinite Intelligence* and its *Creative Thought* presupposes the you will keep your mind in a state of expectancy of a *Greater Spirituality,* of which you as a "Caucasian" will have full faith and confidence in its attainment in due course and in due order.

C2471. The Alpha tells us: All thought is *Creative!* However, not all thought is *Constructive* or *Positive.* If you think of *Misery* and *Poverty* and you see no way to avoid these conditions, then your thoughts will create those very conditions and curse you with them. But reverse the order, and think thoughts of a *Positive, Exceptive Nature*, and your thoughts will create those conditions. Your *Thoughts* magnetizes your entire personality and attracts to you the outward physical things that harmonize with the nature of your thoughts.

C2472. The Alpha tells us: As we Caucasians approach the *Racial Apocalypse* of the 21st century!..do not doubt, but believe! Surly this coming *Human Tragedy* has been sufficiently emphasized to impress upon your mind its utmost importance. And when we Caucasians are in the full clutches of this unavoidable horror, you may find us blooded, but we will be unafraid, and unbowed!

C2473. The Alpha tells us: You as a Caucasian!...may have a *Definite Purpose* well fixed in your mind; you may have *Self-Confidence* in abundance; you may have *Initiative* and *Leadership* well developed, and a great deal of *Imagination,* but until all these are expressed in terms of action?...you might as well have no knowledge of them!

C2474. The Alpha tells us: In your *Education* it is not the schooling you have had that counts; it is the extent to which you express that which you learned from your schooling through well organized and intelligently directed action. By no means should we belittle higher education, but as we all know, it is not for everyone?...therefore, I would offer hope and encouragement to all who have had no such education, provided they express that which they know, be it ever so little, in intensive *Action* along *Constructive Lines*.

C2475. The Alpha tells us: It is the *21st* century, and the psychology of *Alien Inaction* is one of the chief reasons that some towns and cities are dying! Take any *Alien run* town or city for example. You will always recognize an *Alien* run town or city by its very *Description?*...if you are familiar with that part of the country. These places have become unproductive lawless "*Alien War Zones*," where the *Negative Psychology* and *Hostility* assaults one's humanity. And this alien social scenario is not by any means the "Exception," it is in fact the *Norm*! And what is meant by these truths? So that you cannot possibly misunderstand the meaning and so that these words of warning are not *abstract?*...simply stated: Alien races are not Caucasians!...nor do they *Think* or *Act* as Caucasians! Therefore, any perceived amalgamation between apposing competitive human subspecies (races!) for a *Utopian* democratic state?...is an exercise in social futility! Hence, the democratic states *Deadly Weakness* in spit of its overall strength, is its *Majority Rule*! (its Achilles heel!) For when an *Empire* is taken over by (aliens in the majority!) aliens who do not respect, or care for the *Empires Cultural or Intellectual Social Vision?*...that *Empire's Destructive Downfall!*...will absolutely be assured.

C2476. The Alpha tells us: *Caucasian Racial Faith!*...is our *Mental Equilibrium*, keeping within the boundaries of reason and observing our *Fematrix Law,* and the rights of all others.

C2477. The Alpha tells us: It is a fact, that the majority of humankinds grief's comes about through lack of *Self- Control!* The Holy Valorous is full of admonition in support of self-control. Though not a book of *Passivity!*...it does urge us as Caucasians to *Try* and *Forgive* those who have injured us. However, self-control becomes a factor if you neglect to exercise it, for you are not only likely to injure others, but you are sure to injure yourself!

C2478. The Alpha tells us: A Caucasian with a well developed *Racial Spirituality* will not permit themselves to be influenced by the *Cynic* or the *Pessimist;* nor will they permit another person to do their thinking for them.

C2479. The Alpha tells us: *Self-sacrifice* is a commendable quality, but when it is carried to extremes, it also can becomes a dangerous form of the lack of *Creative Reasoning*, you owe it to yourself not to permit your *Emotions* to place all of your *Future* and *Happiness* in the keeping of another person. Yes! *Love* is essential!...but so is your *Creative Reasoning*.

C2480. The Alpha tells us: *Intolerance* is a two sided coin, on the one side it has *Disintegrated Societies, Dethroned Reason* and substitutes *Mob Psychology* in its place, and on the other side, it has reasoned our very *Survival*, driving out without remorse all those both *Human* and *Predatory Beasts* from within our midst. (the evils of the world!) This indictment against *Intolerance* is general, therefore it must be brought to a greater understanding in Time?..Place?..Who? and Why? For *Intolerance* for some, may mean *Survival* for others!

C2481. The Alpha tells us: The *Caucasian Empire* of the *21st* century will be built on three important factors of its organized racial effort: "Caucasian *Concentration!*...Caucasian *Cooperation!*...and Caucasian *Coordination!*" The very meaning of these terms are obvious to all Caucasians: For they are the *Historical Foundation* by which every Caucasian civilization has come about, and to which all that will ever be built will rest upon. Therefore, being born of the *Racial Turmoil* of the *21st* century "Caucasianism" will bring *Mental Equilibrium* and *Racial Spirituality* to the Caucasian world Community. Thereby, reestablishing Caucasian *Cultural Determination*, Caucasian *Political Racial Sovereignty,* and, an international Caucasian cooperation for its *Manifest Racial Destiny*!

C2482. The Alpha tells us: In the realm of *"Racial Politics"* you must learn to judge all your *Political, Cultural,* and *Economic* moves by their long term effects on both *Aliens* and *Caucasians* alike! The problem in trying to prove a point to hostel *Alien Races* through reasoning is that in the end their *Resentment* for you and your race, has that ability to project their contempt for your *Honesty* by their *Insidious Clams* of your wrong doing?

Therefore, both *Evidence* and *Demonstration* are much more *Convincing* and *Meaningful* when engaging *Alien* verbal arguments that draw you into their lying and deceptive clams of offense. Hence, always when dealing with *"Aliens Races"* make your point through *Evidence* and *Demonstration,...* never argument!

C2483. The Alpha tells us: Alien races often present them selves as "Victims" of the Caucasian world community? Making it difficult, at first, to see their miseries as self inflicted! Before you realize the *Real Nature* of their problems (their racial hubris!) you will have been *Seduced* into catering to their misfortune and hubris? Therefore, Caucasians of the *21st* century should and must understand that in *Nature's* game of competitive "Racial Power" the very *Racial Group* you associate with is critical!..guilt by association. Through this, you will also suffer greatly in the eyes of others of your *Racial Kind*, and you should never, ever, underestimate the consequences and extreme danger of an egregious act of Caucasian *Racial Treason*

C2484. The Alpha tells us: Caucasianism?...is not in any way an *Argument* or the subject of a *Debate*. It is the *Spirituality* of all Caucasians who believe in their *Racialness* as a sacred journey, and part of their bio-manifest destiny. Therefore, it is your privilege to accept it, in whole or in part, or reject it, just as you please.

C2485. The Alpha tells us: He is of the opinion and not without substantial evidence to support him that it is very possible through the aid of one's *Racial Reasoning,* and the acceptance of its true *Bio-Spirituality!...*for one to so attune one's mind to the *Vibrations* of life, that all the secrets in the world of *Unfathomed* and *Uncharted* mental phenomena can become attainable with all of its miraculous truth.

C2486. The Alpha tells us: It is the *21st* century and the Caucasian world community is at a *Crossroad?...*on its great journey. (its survival initiative!) So important is the subject of "Caucasianism" and its *Spiritual Truth* for the Caucasian world community that to not take the "Holy Valorous" and its position seriously?...could mean a wrong decision at the crossroad? (wrong turn!) Thereby, leading to the lose of the Caucasian worlds *Vital Direction*!...

its path to *Immortality* the summit of all life.

C2487. The Alpha tells us: If the organized *Religions* of the world as they now exist in the *21st* century, continue to support their *Social Fallacy* of *Racial Equality,* and the *Hubris of a Religious Edict* calling for the *Redistribution* of the Caucasian worlds *Wealth?*...is both *Conspiratorial* and *Seditious* in its outcome. And it is of grave consequence, that this stratagem is being cultivated by *Alien Subversives*, who are working with the *Religious* and *Liberal Progressives* for the annexation of the *Caucasian American Community?* Therefore, it is *Essential,* and *Vital,* for the Caucasian world community to implement (put in place!) a plan of action for their own survival! In brief, if the present Caucasian commu-nity will not subordinate their individual interests to that of establishing a *Unified Caucasian Empire!* Then the remedy lies in the creation of new Caucasian world community! Such a community would gradually attract a following from the *Rank* and *File* of all other oppressive (multiracial) Caucasian states. This desirable end can be attained in a single generation under the right leadership, thereby future *Wars* between race's can be prevented. Hence, one's respect for another's *Racialness*, and its *Sovereignty* creates peace!

C2488. The Alpha tells us: If every society is "the extended shadow of its people" as the Alpha suggest, then it behooves the people to reflect a shadow of *Confidence, Compassion Optimism,* and *Harmony*, so that these qualities may in turn, reflect themselves in all who are connected with the society.

C2489. The Alpha tells us: The principle of "Racialness" and the law of attraction, through which like attracts like, explains many of the worlds *Successes*, for you see: *Racialness* is the foundation of *Identity!*...and identity is the foundation of *Self-confidence!*...and self-confidence is the foundation of all human Success. You will see how important is the subject of *Racialness* , when you stop to realize that it is the only thing in the world where you have Wholeness!...you know, that which you Are!

C2490. The Alpha tells us: The Caucasian *Imagination,* is the workshop of their soul, in which *Thoughts* are woven into *Craft, Building, Science* and *Empire,* and all manner of material wealth. You will never know what is your capacity for *Achievement* until you learn how to mix your *Efforts* with *Imagination.* Your *Imagination* belongs to you! Use it! The more you us it, the more efficiently it will serve you.

C2491. The Alpha tells us: You cannot think *Fear* and act *Courageously*, and you cannot think *Hatred* and act with *kindness!* To understand this principle is to understand the soundness of this statement: "As a person thinks in their heart, so are they!"

C2492. The Alpha tells us: All great fundamental truths are simple, in final analysis, and whether one is delivering an address or writing a course of instruction, the purpose should be to convey impressions and statements of "Fact" in the clearest and most concise manner possible.

C2493. The Alpha tells us: "Caucasianism" is the foundation of our *Racial Spirituality!*...a vital force; so vital in fact, that no Caucasian who has it *Highly Developed* can begin even to approximate his or her power of achievement. Therefore, let "Caucasianism" be the sparkle in your eyes, the grip of your hand, the surge of your will, and the energy to execute your dreams and ideas. (blessed are the Caucasians!)

C2494. The Alpha tells us: We come now, to the discussion of one of the most important subjects of the teachings in the "Holy Valorous" namely- *Belief!*...Belief is the Principle through which your *Words* and your *Acts* and even your state of *Mind* influence others. When your mind is configuring at a high rate because it has been stimulated with *Belief,* that stimulation registers in the minds of all within its radius, and especially in the minds of those with whom you come in close contact. What we believe: So vitally constitutes an important part of our everyday lives, that it is only right to mention the three *Mediums* through which it operates, namely, what you *Say*, what you *Do*, and what you *Think*! Therefore, in "Caucasianism," when your *Thoughts*, *Actions*, and *Words* have become *Spiritually Racial*, you will be able to unveil *Life's* forbidden phenomena!..the answer to Why?

C2495. The Alpha tells us: The most powerful people in the world are those who have themselves in their own power. A person with well developed *Self-control* does not promote or indulge in *Hatred, Envy, Jealousy, Fear,*

Revenge, or any similar destructive emotions. *Self-confidence* is one of the important essentials of success, but, as with *Self-indulgence* when these faculties have been developed beyond the point of reason, they become very *Dangerous* and *Destructive.*

C2496. The Alpha tells us: We come now, to that which causes more human grief than all others. It is a common evil to which we are all more or less addicted!...that of forming *Erroneous Opinions* or making *Slanderous Accusations* not based on any known facts, and therefore, a very *Grievous* and *Painful* form of *Willful Ignorance.* And of course, it is greatly hoped, that this *Corruption* so prevalent in the *21st*century will be forever challenged and excoriated.

C2497. The Alpha tells us: A lack of our *Caucasian Racialness* (racial pride!) and its vital meaning?...is being developed in the upcoming Caucasian generations by a *Liberal Cabal* of Government sponsored *Social Engineers.* And this modern *21st* century model of the very first "Racial Abrogation" (the legislative purging of the Caucasian American community's racial identity!) is being described, so upon close analysis, the Caucasian American community, and for that matter the Caucasian world community!...can not say it was not rightly "Informed" of this *Treasonous Abomination!*

C2498. The Alpha tells us: The *Liberal Zealot Progressives,* are the greatest threat to *Humanity!* They are seeking the very elimination of the *Human Primal,* the first importance; our bio-*Selective Regeneration,* (racialness!) our subspecies life strategy and its bio-divisional choice! ...its unique answer to that which stands in the way of its survival initiative? I will repeat the *Defeat* of the subversive *Liberal Zealots* and their *Progressive* cabal of *Racial Nihilists* will be our *Caucasian world's* greatest struggle! And if for any reason we fail to *Defeat Them?*...our absolute destruction well be assured, and the *Human Journey* will descend into *Hades!*

C2499. The Alpha tells us: Somewhere between the modern Caucasian *Liberal* who see's a *Utopian* future? (equality!) and the staunch Caucasian *Conservative* who understand the old *Bones* of natures reality? (competition!) and assuming that all recognize their common *Racial Heritage,*(European Caucasians!) and are in the pursuit of a life with reasonable assurance of average *Freedom* and *Contentment*, it would seem that the balance they have shared for more then two *Hundred Years* (a democracy!) has same how in the *21st* century brought them to a state that borders on war? What Happened? What could have so divided the Caucasian American community?...the founders and builders of the greatest Nation on Earth!... What? The answer requires the understanding of a simple truth- "Alien Races" are not in any way Caucasians, and they will never be!...And to permit *Alien Races* (Non Caucasians!) to take part in the *Political Process* that *Governs* and *Affects* the every day lives of Caucasians citizens and their society?..is an unprecedented *Intellectual Failure* and *Political Subversion* by both the *Democratic* and *Republican* Parties who have with out the slightest concern, put the Caucasian American community in a deadly *Alien*-grip of *Envy*, *Hatred*, and *Social Warfare*.

C2500. The Alpha tells us: Let all who seek the core of life's truth?...examine the *Scope* and *Meaning* of the fundamental term- *Racial Spirituality?*...and go beyond the platitudes that dog its modern journey and beyond the limits of ordinary experience to its primal deductive reasoning! For, it is said, that our journey is the will of the *Priori!..*the one in kind! (our fematrix: Caucasia!) to which *Form* and *Self* are one! And being preordained to others of the one in kind, there of our *Racialness*!...our *Spiritual Onlyness*!

C2501. The Alpha tells us: Before we Caucasians can achieve success in the higher and broader sense, we must gain such thorough control over ourselves that we become persons of a *Racial Spiritual* poise. For millions of years and countless Caucasian generation preceding us, Our enduring Fematrix: "Caucasia" has been tempering and refining the *materials that have gone into our evolutionary makeup. (*our bio-racial character!) The combination of *Qualities* and *Features* that distinguishes one racial group from another *Genetic Imprint*! There has never been a *Human Society* endowed with such *Intellectual* and *Spiritual Power!*...as has been that of the Caucasian world community. Therefore, let us make sure! ...that this genius does not fade or falter under *Alien Assault?*..."Blessed are the Caucasians"

C2502. The Alpha tells us: In "Caucasianism" there is the *Golden Rule-* Love your race, as you love yourself! And if you have mastered your "Racialness" upon which this *Golden Rule* is based, you understand that nothing can bring the world *"Peace"* but the triumph of- *Racial Sovereignty* and its-*Independent Authority.* Therefore throughout this, *Manifesto* one very particular principle has been emphasized for the purpose of illustrating the truth that every *Alien Race* is the sum total of its individual's their *Thoughts,* their *Actions,* and that of their *Bio-mandate* their *Survival Initiative.* And that means what?..you may ask. *Simple:* As with all who enter the arena of *Life*: they are in it, to wine it!

C2503. The Alpha tells us: There is a primary truth, that there can be no correct idea of a *Part* without a correct idea of the correlative *Whole* to which it belongs. There are several ways in which inadequate knowledge of the one involves inadequate knowledge of the other. If the *Part* is conceived without any reference to the *Whole,* it becomes itself a *Whole* – an independent entity; and its relation to existence in general are misapprehended. And this truth also applies to *Man* and his *Fematrix,* the *Man* as the *Part* as compared with the *Fematrix* as the *Whole* must be misapprehended unless the *Fematrix* is not only recognized as including man, but is figured in its total extent. The "Fematrix" of which *Man* forms a part, is the *Fematrix* constituted by the theory of life in general; and therefore the *Fematrix* must be understood before *Man* can be understood.

C2504. The Alpha tells us: the position which humankind occupies in relation to other life forms, cannot be rightly conceived unless there is some conception of the whole of life in its distribution as well as in its intent.

C2505. The Alpha tells us: The *Caucasian Race* is a whole; and, in truth, it is an organic whole with the *Caucasian Man* and *Woman* as its aggregate of interdependent actions, an "Imprinted Conduct" performed according to its core strategy of *Competitive Survival!* Complete comprehension of conduct is not to be obtained by contemplating the conduct of human beings only; we have to regard this as a part of universal conduct, conduct as exhibited by all living creatures. For evidently this comes within our definition of acts adjusted to ends!...being constituted by the conduct of all animate beings in general.

C2506. The Alpha tells us: Caucasian Self-preservation in each *Racial Generation* has all along depended on the preservation of offspring by preceding Caucasian generations. And in proportion as evolution of our conduct subserving other individual lives is higher then alien others, implying a higher moralization. Moreover, we see that our evolution becomes the highest possible when our conduct simultaneously achieves the greatest totality of life in self, in off-spring, and in humankind; so here we see that the conduct called *Good* rises to the conduct conceived as *Best!*

C2507. The Alpha tells us: Sundry influences moral, theological, and political conspire to make people disguise from themselves this truth, "Racial Equality" as in all *liberal zealot* cases, so it is in this social deceit- a *Fraud!* They have become so preoccupied with the means by which to achieve their "Subversive" social end!...the destruction of the "Caucasian American community" and most of all, its *Racial Identity!* In these extreme cases, no one can deny that what we call the badness of liberal zealot actions is ascribed to them solely for the reason that they entail "*Caucasian Betrayal and Racial Treason*". And these truths are brought out with equal clearness by examining their cardinal ideas, their motives, and their deeds.

C2508. The Alpha tells us: He finds it strange that a notion so abstract as that of "Racial Equality" an ideal so contrary of nature, should ever have been thought one from which a system of guidance can be evolved, since "Equality" in biology has never existed, and nor could it ever exist, because life, contrary to popular theory is based on the pursuit of "Solutions" to one's needs and the "Perfection" of those Solution by all living things. If imperfection of memory, of judgment, of temper, is alleged, it is alleged because of inadequacy to the requirements of life. And since, the complete adjustment of acts to ends is that which both secures and constitutes the life that is most evolved, while, the justification for whatever increases life is the reception from life of more happiness then misery.

C2509. The Alpha tells us: Obviously, it is our Caucasian scientific spirit and training which teach us to subordinate to the idea of our *Racialness;* which attribute truth and genuine reality to it alone and thereby adhere to the contemplative abstraction and spiritualization of- *Caucasian knowledge.* Because of this discriminating distinction between the empiric and the intellectual, between the world of truth and the world of appearance, between the temporal and the eternal, the emergence of the Caucasian race was a very great event in the history of the- *Biological Spirit.* From this point of view the *Alpha's philosophy* exhibits the connection between *Science* and *Ascetic Morality*-the *Fematrix!*

C2510. The Alpha tells us: That his philosophy "Fematrix Absolutism" and its dynamic power will prove as liable to abuse as the *Ascetic, Scientific,* and fruitful message of todays- *Cryptic Religions.* Here is exhibited the *Alpha's* esoteric (Caucasianism!) mediating task, and moral role as the broker between *Truth* and *Accusation.* Hence, rescuing our Caucasian intellect from the speculation into which it has retreated, bringing it back into the realm of reality.

C2511. The Alpha tells us: He holds that "Caucasianism" is valid not only by reason of its *Ethical Teaching*, by the doctrine which it links to its interpretation of the world and its experience of it; but also and especially through this very experience itself. This indeed, the *Spiritual* and *Ethical* concomitant of its doctrine of *Truth* and *Salvation* is the essential, primary and personal part of his philosophy.

C2512. The Alpha tells us: that before writing the holy "Valorous", he was a devout student of the great *Caucasian Philosophers* and their various concepts and insight. Feeling it necessary for his campaign to give life to the voice of the Caucasian race of people in the form of the written Valorous. He took from them what he could use, and it pleased his craving for the *Caucasian Traditional* that he could so well use; although due to his entirely different constitution–so much more "Modern," *Political-Correctness, Multi-Culturalism, Alien Pandering, Political Subversion*, and *Moral Debauchery* – he would make out of it some-thing else altogether. What he took was the "Idea" the answer to the coming storm!..the new state, the "Final Evolution" of the Caucasian race of people, and their *Destiny!* And with this idea he did something very bold, even scarcely permissible, though at the same time with deeply felt, almost compulsive conviction; he defined the thing it self, he called it by name, he asserted that he knew what it was. It was "The Caucasian Empire" a *Caucasian Sovereign State!*..with its voice being the "Holy Valorous"

C2513. The Alpha tells us: Religions are necessary for the people, and an inestimable benefit to them. But if they oppose themselves to the progress of humankind in the knowledge of *Truth!*...they must with the utmost possible forbearance be set aside.

C2514. The Alpha tells us: All "Art" is an endeavor to tell the truth, and the highest art is the manifestation of those deepest and subtlest truths which are most liable to be lost sight of by the public. For the best art is always expressive rather than decorative, it does not exist for the display of technique or the means employed, but for the revelation of that which is hidden

C2515. The Alpha tells us: Sometimes we realize better what a thing is, by studying what it is not. There are always near every great truth many errors which seem identical with it. This is due to the fact that every great truth is fundamental; it is deeply hidden from our eyes, and to find it requires searching beneath the surface. Nearly all false hoods and miscon-ceptions rise from mistaking accidental appearances for fundamental causes.

C2516. The Alpha tells us: A principle must be studied from different points of view, before it can be thoroughly apprehended and tested. Without such a comparative study, there is danger of *Superficiality* and *Conventionality,* of taking mere rules for laws of nature.

C2517. The Alpha tells us: Only ideas of things can awaken emotion, ideas of how to do things, mere knowledge of modes of expression, however important, can never furnish a substitute sincere earnestness or genuine realization of truth.

C2518. The Alpha tells us: Every one feels that something profoundly moral attaches to the elevation of one's own *Racial character* and *Ideals,* as the only actual above suspect!...above doubt, quite in the spirit of their creation. In a way the history of *Caucasian Thought* goes back to the sources of Caucasian life, our "Fematrix" (Caucasia!) whence she gave birth to *Caucasian Europe* its *Science* its *Art,* and in which the two will always be one. For those Caucasians alone will find *"Truth"* and *"Racial Salvation"* who turn their face to their *Racial Eternity*.

C2519. The Alpha tells us: Life! (the Fematrix!) has always willed one thing: "Multiformity" brought about by the will of her daughters and their- *Life*

Strategies (female absolutism!) the ultimate, irreducible, primeval principle of being, the source of all living phenomena, and the answer to- *Fematrix Teleology!*

C2520. The Alpha tells us: The Caucasian world is losing faith in their own "Racialness" the point to which their children no longer even know!...and in order to regain our *Racial Spirit!,* we Caucasians of the *21st* century must rediscover ourselves. We must come to understand that the "Fatal flaw" in our Caucasian world is that we do not have an "Identitarian Religion" a *True Religion* of our *Unified Racial Spirit!*...our sacred will of kind, avid of life. For without this core of *Worship* and *Devotion* to one's being, one's direction toward an *Identifiable Belonging* to the continuation of the Self!... and at the same time, something else besides: The idea of a "Prioress" which preceded us in importance, and of which "We are all created"...our living *Deity,* our *Fematrix* "Caucasia!...if we as a race of people fail to achieve this vital goal, of a united "Caucasianism" (to worship our spiritual being!) the future and our children, will suffer greatly by the vindictive hands of alien others.

C2521. The Alpha tells us: In a world being entirely the work of "Biological Diversity", and composed of many different "Fematrix" life strategies, with a history of more then a *Billion Years of Life!*...and more then a *Billion Life Forms,* and, an *Extinction Rate* of more then 99% of all past Bio-dynasties?... being truly, a world of great *Suffering* and unprecedented *Predation.* Thus life strives against it self, seeking it own wellbeing in each of the millions of its manifestations, its place at the table at the expense of another, yes, at the expense of all others, and so, constantly setting its wrath against all competitors. *Poverty, Need, Concern,* for the mere preservation of one's *Life*, one's *Racial Family,* these come first.

C2522. The Alpha tells us: There is no "Unified Spirit" in the great Void!... other then the purposeless of *Chance!* Inorganic-energy (inanimate!) "without form" *Consumption* and *Creation* without intent? But, there is the existence of another Organic-energy (animate!) "in form" *Consumption* and *Creation* with intent, and by design?...it is called Life!

C2523. The Alpha tells us: We Caucasians must takes everything that our history has to offer, and never ignore its events! In the coming decades?... Caucasian America will be forced to rise up and face immense challenges and fearsome *Social* and *Cultural* catastrophes brought about by "Alien Racial Immigration" and its "Political Inclusion" and if not to late?...this modern "Trojan Horse" will present the opportunity for our awakening, Yes, our rediscovery of our selves and the awakening of those qualities that are unique to the Caucasian race of people, and them alone. And then, "Racial Separation" (into separate states!) and the rebirth of the "Caucasian Sovereign State" will take place, freeing the Caucasian spirit from its dormancy, activating once again its energy, its union of inventiveness and reigniting its destiny!...it will take place!

C2524. The Alpha tells us: Regardless of what certain corrupt elites would like us to believe, the Homogenization of "Alien Cultures" into a "Caucasian Cultural Sovereign State" wil not work! For one must come to realize that all one needs is to look at the *Medal East, Asia, South Asia, Indonesia, South America,* and *Africa?*...all cultures are of *Obscure* and *Distressing* new world?...a particular way of life, with a history of thousands of years, hence, their claim of a *Manifest Destiny* that seeks to impose their *Religious Will*, and *Laws* upon the world. So, much like our own, their roots dig deep into the depths of history itself, resting upon specific traditions that are passed down through the ages, and are composed of spiritual values. Therefore, the truth is, they (alien races!) are completely incapable of "Assimilation" to the detriment of Caucasian society by becoming "Islands" of *Political* and *Cultural Resistance?*... this being the true consequence of their invasion, and if you as a Caucasian!...are *Alien Sympathetic?*...that will prove to be dangerously wrong.

C2525. The Alpha tells us: When it comes to Caucasians, appearances can be deceiving. Unexpected resistance is slowly rising, a sign of what is to come. Therefore, one must not believe that we Caucasians, upon learning that we are in danger?...will allow ourselves to be *Displaced?* The past has shown that our history of awakening occurs very slowly, but once it has begun!...nothing can stop us.

C2526. The Alpha tells us: Our "Caucasian Racialness" reflects a *bio-spiritual morphology!*...a love of our created likeness!...transmitted as much through *Intellect* as through *Need.* It is who we are, unlike any other, it constitute our "Spiritual Values" that builds *Behavior* and nurtures our very sence of *Representation,* through which all of us, as Caucasians! organize our world, and engage reality.

C2527. The Alpha tells us: If the Caucasian world is to have a future beyond the *21ˢᵗ* century?...it will be of the utmost importance to discover his "Wisdom" that challenges you to give yourself fully to "Caucasianism" as the highest objective in your understanding, bringing us back to those qualities that are specific to the Caucasian race of people, qualities currently *Adrift,* and in a state of *Dormancy.* But, all is not lost!...for one thing is absolutely beyond doubt: and that is, the remedy for this "Intellectual affliction" lies within our-selves?...and by *Receiving* and *Accepting* the spiritual prescription of "Caucasianism" our awakening will undoubtedly come!...yes, it will take place! And the *Final Steps* on the *Righteous Path* to our destiny will have begun!...the rise of the- *Caucasian Empire!*

C2528. The Alpha tells us: Should we as "Caucasians" be optimistic about our future? We cannot ignore the history of events!...it revels to us that in history, the unexpected is always there, and that the future is often unpredictable: in *1999,* no one expected the events of *2001;* and no one in *2012* could have foreseen the *Massive Alien Invasion* into our *Caucasian lands* between 2014 and 16, and at the same time, the long-term view shows us the powerful aggressive intentions of *Alien Races* and their *Hyenic* cultural bearing. Therefore, we as Caucasians in the light of these present day events, are faced with an immense "Alien Challenge" and fearsome: *Moral, Cultural,* and *Political Catastrophe!* Consequently, we at this time in our history cannot and must not distance ourselves from *Political Activism!..* yes! we will need the moral armament of "Caucasianism" with which to face the contempt of all those who oppose us both *Alien* and *Caucasian* alike. But, if we and our children are to have a future?...we must question both recent events and the possible direction of our "Caucasian Society"?

C2529. The Alpha tells us: First and foremost, the decline of the "Caucasian Racial Spirit" in the *21ˢᵗ* century is the result of a "Liberal Zealot Conspiracy" an idea formed in the halls of higher education!...a cabal of accomplished and revered academics looking to accomplish here in America what their ilk couldn't accomplish in Europe. No!..its not Communism?..no, its got a new title! Yes, that's right! Its now called "Progressivism" the- *New Socialism!*, the *New- Academic Sedition!*, the- *New Political Subversion!* And, their intention is as it was in Europe: to *Overwhelm us,* and *Asphyxiate* us!... yes, we have indeed entered the age in which the "Caucasian Titans" (our leadership!) have now become *Insolent Sniveling* cowards, completely indifferent to the true situation of an-*Alien Invasion!*...without even so much as a word of- *Outrage?*...This is an act of- *Extreme Treachery,* and *Abandonment* by our elected officials. Yes! we have been *Discarded!*..the very future of the "Caucasian American Community" is in- *Peril!* And if that is the case?...then it stands to reason that the *Storm of Revolution* is gathering! For our "Fematrix" will have it no other way.

C2530. The Alpha tells us: It is to be remembered that when the words of the "𝕳oly "𝖁alorous" have been once conveyed to any individual and publicly announced by *Him* or *Her*, it becomes as much a matter of history as any natural event of which the 𝕳oly "𝖁alorous" takes notice. Hence, the Alpha; molded by the combative social *Truths* of his Age, and guided, and brought into action by their *Discourse Analysis,* his characteristic form of expression was and is absolutely requisite, for the adequate and complete conveyance of his most needful message. And having reason to believe that, in the great conflicts of Racial, Social and Cultural discourse, it has been observed, a needed foundation of truth for our future "Generations" to come- The Alpha's *Caucasian Revelations* and *Inspiration*.

C2531. The Alpha tells us: It appears to him, that the *Caucasian Liberal* and *Conservative* social theories, taken by each alone, is not in any way sufficient to account for all the *Positive* and *Negative* phenomena which their social doctrines have presented to our view. Hence, the Alpha, speaks to what has been lift out!..."Truth in Reality" a coherent field of *Understandable Facts!*...recognized by all, and used as principles of *Explanation* and *Prediction,* and not through the present *Utopian* and *Ivy league* social "War Zone" that is now beginning to engulf us all. No!...Truth, is not a satisfier of desire?...Truth, is the "Guardian".

C2532. The Alpha tells us: The 𝕳oly '𝖁alorous" when being observed is "Authoritive" for it is the "Voice" and "Will" of our *Fematrix* "𝕮aucasia"

through the *Alpha's Spirit,..*its intelligible, for it is in the language of our-
Race!

C2533. The Alpha tells us: Many of his words and his actions are spoken and done by the *Enlightened Inspiration* of "Caucasia"(our Fematrix!) to which he so inspires us as to communicate to us her perfection. But, another topic of the utmost moment must be referred to before we close this understanding. In order to preserve the due subordination of the Caucasian race to the spiritual elements of the Holy "Valorous," it is altogether essential that we of the "Caucasian Faith" (Caucasianism!) should bear in mind the distinction between that extraordinary influence of our *Fematrix-Caucasia!*...under which the Alpha has composed his respective work, and granting to the *Religious Works* of all other "Faiths" whether Caucasian or Alien alike, (they being not "Detrimental" to humanity?) the due "Respect" that is their- *Unassailable Right.*

C2534. The Alpha tells us: There will always be those who through their *Lack* and *Failure* to understand the idea of a living-Entity?...that, to which we are all "Of " and "By", not a *Cryptic God* of *Human* or *Mystic Form?* No, she is the *Living-Breathing* foundation in all of us!...all of living creation. A force that neither *Loves* or *Hates*, nor does she favor *Anyone,* over *Any other?* For a *Billion Years,* she has witnessed the defeat of *Billions* of her kind, all striving to embrace her teleology! (immortality!) and always thinking it being their own? This is a circumstance which at once suggests several important considerations; and, above all others, it leads naturally to an inquiry, did the "Alpha" Himself, in his solitude, fully comprehend the sense of the *Fematrix Revelation?..*to which he gave utterance. That, this question will be answered by many Religions in the "Negative" is so obvious, that the fact will furnish many a sceptic with an argument,... superficial!...it is true, but still an argument, against the -*Evidence*- that all of life has beard witness to, and suppled.

C2535. The Alpha tells us: In the first place, in our world of sense, "Nature" is represented in the Holy "Valorous" as disclosing the *Being* and *Agency* of the "Fematrix." And her daughter- "Caucasia"- our Fematrix!...from it, as the organ of the *Divine Power*, the Caucasian race of people came forth: "the *Earth* declared the glory of the *Fematrix,* and the firmament (bio-life!)

showed her handiwork" The creation itself is an instance of the "Fematrix" coming forth from the mysterious and silent depth of her *Invisible Being*. And, she has never lift herself without a witness, in that she gave us her "Daughters" bearing the life-strategies of all living beings!...both *Low* and *High*.

C2536. The Alpha tells us: In our 𝔥oly "𝔙alorous" its pages present, as it were, a *Marvelous Reality* in and from which the Alpha permits some of his thoughts to be more or less distinctly inferred; "the invisible things of her from creation of the living world are clearly seen, being understood by the things that are made, even her *Eternal Power* and *Majesty!*" Again, in the intimations afforded by the inward constitution of "Humankind," the "Fematrix" manifests herself no less plainly in the world of thought; partly through the higher powers of *Knowledge!*...partly by one's *Inquisitive Voice* and for Caucasians, (as, with all!) both being the - *Unique Imprinted Gifts*- of, and by her daughter- ℭaucasia! "Fematrix" of the- *Caucasian Race!*

C2537. The Alpha tells us: In tracing the foundation of all religious doctrine of *Inspiration,* all researches must arrive at one ultimate fact. Humankind, by its natural powers, and by its own words, can not attain to the *Knowledge* of its Creator. For "No Human has seen their God at any time." Hence, the Alpha's view: Whence then, is derived that knowledge on the degree of which depends the perfection of *Human Nature*, and the ground of their hopes? It is a "Conflicting Intellectual Phenomenon" which merits the attention, at least, of an *Observer*, that among all human "Races" makes no profession of any sympathies for that which is among the inventions of *Deceivers.* Therefore, to the Alpha, a word "Revelation"...seems of itself, to deserve respect; and it appears more worthy of a fundamental philosophy "ℭaucasianism" to trace out its truths, then to banish it to the land of dreams.

C2538. The Alpha tells us: Revelation? (divine truth!) is a belief which has been expressed in every *Age,* every *Land,* and every *Language,* and its supreme communication has resulted in the unveiling of that which is greater then all! And to which all must *Answer,* and *Obey.* In ℭaucasianism, the manifestations of ℭaucasia's being?...is the duty of all Caucasians to seek: "for she has made of one blood all Caucasians of a "Racialness" of humankind, beckoning them to seek her destiny.

C2539. The Alpha tells us: Caucasia's will and acts, as are made by, or may be inferred from, firstly, external Nature! And secondly, the inward constitution of the race of people which she has created; the latter having as its basis the "Revelation" strictly so called, which rests upon facts, and of which the record lies solely in the "Holy "Valorous". These two sources of knowledge imply each other, and belong to the province of the- *Alpha's Philosophy*.

C2540. The Alpha tells us: the *Caucasian Racial Trader?* Having not the "Race", are *Iniquitous* unto themselves, which show the work of their "Treason" written in their very hearts!...their conscience also bearing witness.

C2541. The Alpha tells us: It is She!...Caucasia, being the "Fematrix" of the Caucasians, is not far from any one of us, for in us she lives, and moves, and is of our being.

C2542. The Alpha tells us: It must be the desire of all concerned Caucasians, wherever they may be, to question both our *Recent History* and the *Possible Direction* our lives may take, in the not to distant future? Therefore, it is very important to remember that both the *Caucasian Race,* and the existence of competitive *Alien Races* (adversaries!) have been shaped by very different *biological, historical,* and *political* circumstances. And contrary to liberal zealot dogma! *No,* it is not impossible to sum up *Bio-ideological Imprinting* in both *Caucasian* and *Alien* others. Thus, in an era (21^{st}ct) rife with *social discord, moral debauchery*, and *racial dereliction,* the Alpha's work can be seen as heralding a different Caucasian fate. For in him is the incarnation of a "Caucasian Archetype" that has all but disappeared, at least temporarily, but of which there still remains a "Well" of – *Caucasian Patriotic Racial Allegiance.*

C2543. The Alpha tells us: The Caucasian Third Estate in America, is new beginning to lose their historical "Racial Identity," with its richness, strength, and fullness of life in jeopardy. Furthermore, it is impossible for us to remain silent about the "Alien Violence" against our Caucasian society! ..which has now entrenched itself, boldly exhibiting- *Rioting, Assaults*, and the "Targeting" of all innocent Caucasian people with physical harassment and injury. These "Alien" radical groups of *Brutal Thugs!*...who are encouraged by the liberal elite and pandered to by the subversive liberal press, now represent a real danger to the Caucasian American community!...which is now beginning to creat a defensive "Mutual Hostility" towards all alien others. Therefore, if we as Caucasians do not take on a defensive attitude?... for the purpose of resisting attacks from Alien radical thugs, we will not be able to prevent their further aggression. And first, we need to get rid of all false interpretations of "Alien Intentions" leaving no Alien Action, whether *Social, Cultural, Political, Economical*, or *Religious,* either *Unobserved* or Unexplained.

C2544. The Alpha tells us: It is through the spirit of our Fematrix – Caucasia!...that he has given us a social model that radically opposes that which swamps and asphyxiates us, a social model that re-establishes a link with the most authentic sources of our Caucasian traditions. We as the inheritors of the "Future" must distance ourselves from the infamous and disgraceful acts of our time. And bring back our sincere "Caucasian Nobility" with those qualities of *Honor, Self-sacrifice*, and of *Conduct* could survive in those of elite character, despite the great risk and difficulty they would face as a result.

C2545. The Alpha tells us: We must always believe in the future of the Caucasian people. For we know that the Caucasian people have within them the strengths required to lead their children toward a better life. We recognize the great traditions of our historic culture, a coalescence of *Spiritual* and *Intellectual* origins. (our Fematrix-Caucasia!) We desire a "Sovereign Caucasian Empire" in which all Caucasians exist as pillars of the state, which in turn guarantees all the rights of "Voice" and "Justice" united in an unbreakable community, which, by its very conduct and its actions, will serve the "Caucasian Empire" obediently, to remain in the spirit of our "Caucasian Racialness," and commit to live without reproach, and to mutually support each other in her name.

C2546. The Alpha tells us: The first act by which we free our-selves from tyranny, by which we enter into intellectual and moral rebellion, is to free ourselves from the power of Lies!...It is by means of Lies, by their seductive, corrosive, and intimidating power, that an able system captures those it wishes to *Neutralize, Dominate* or *Distroy.* All Lies: are "Strategic Implements," their deception constitutes the crux of most Social, Political, and Domestic Difficulties.

C2547. The Alpha tells us: To give yourself your own Words, and above all to give yourself a Name, is to affirm your existence, your autonomy, your-*Freedom.*

C2548. The Alpha tells us: By the messenger of the divine spirit, (himself!) the meaning and the will of the Ḥoly-"Ꝟalorous" is introduced into the real being of things. All divine activity in the world is organic. So also the "Fematrix Teleology" which comprehends all things. And to which "All" must contribute their *Purpose,* and their *Will.*

C2549. The Alpha tells us: Life's "Objectification" is the will and law of the- *Fematrix!*...and only by understanding the truth of this ultimate fact, does her explanation begin, and it consists in indicating truly and with mathematical exactness, how, where and when each living thing and its life strategy manifests itself. Yes, she herself is rooted in this world; and as such, finds herself in it; as an "Anomaly" of matter?...a fluid of "Will" alone!.. in the *Desolation* with properties of her being, forged by the "Elementals" with a readiness to flow, (readily convertible!) but no tendency to disperse. The action of the "Form" is nothing but the act of the will objectified, passed into perception. (Creation!)

C2550. The Alpha tells us: All living things!...are the *Acts* or *Manifestations* of the objectivity of a Fematrix will!..it is just because of this special relation to one's "Racialness" that this, and this alone gives us the key to our existence, reveals to us our significance, shows us the inner mechanism of our being, of our actions, and our understanding.

C2551. The Alpha tells us: The *Act* of our "Will" and the *Spirit* of our "Racialness" are not two different things objectively known, which the bond of causality unites; they do not stand in the relation of *Cause* and *Effect;* they are one and the same, And as the Alpha has said, our will proclaims itself primarily in our "Racial Spirit" in our physical identity, as the inner most nature of our being.

C2552. The Alpha tells us: It is the year of our Fematrix- Caucasia: *2016,* and the modern Caucasian world is under attack by *"Alien Subversives"* and *"Caucasian Renegades"* from the halls of *Academia*?..to the *"Political Arenas"* of both "State" and "Locale Government." They have launched this "Assault" with their objective being, the "Dismantling" of Caucasian Americas "Defensive Racial Mindset" in other words, *Our Caucasian Identity*?...that which give us *Union* and *Strength!* Yes!..these "Liberal Zealots" are at our gates! ..and their intentions are *Lethal!*..and, understand this: its not happening because of us?...its happening to us! Hence, there is but one answer to this "Brazen Threat" to our *Caucasian Racialness* and its *Significance!*...we will "Vanquish" all that is *Hostile* or *Threatening!* For we are the "Caucasians" and all shall come to know us!

C2553. The Alpha tells us: In the "Living Psyche" of all things!..it is the "Encounter" and its "Analysis" that creates *Tolerance* or *Opposition?* And, of these two, "Opposition" (the obstacle!) creates- *Need?*...and "Need" invokes *Form.*

C2554. The Alpha tells us: Time!..can never be redeemed, it is "Humankinds" greatest lose! Therefore, above all, we Caucasians!...must distinctly recognize that the "Form" of *Life*, and its *Reality*, is the *Here* and *Now* the present! The latter are only in our conception, existing only in the connection of our historical knowledge, so far as it follows the principle of sufficient reason. For "Life" is firm and certain in our will!..as the "Present" is firm and certain in life, both remaining fixed without wavering.

C2555. The Alpha tells us: Truth!..is the great dispeller of liberal zealot *Equality.* No attained "Fallacy" of desire can give lasting satisfaction, but merely a fleeting gratification. Therefore, so long as the liberal zealot consciousness is filled with desires of *Racial Equality?*..self-deception!, and if we "Caucasians" let it have influence over us, if we surrender *ourselves* to it?..disregarding the truth! We as a people, will sentence our future generations to a life of *Incurable Sorrow*, their future removed, lost and forgotten from the stream of time, with all their potential. Such are the forces of- *Alien* and *Caucasian Liberal zealots*- coordinating with each other harmoniously for the destruction of the- Caucasian world community.

C2556. The Alpha tells us: No "Alien Evil" can touch a Caucasian persons soul, who looks on *Caucasian Beauty;* feeling themselves at one with themselves and with the Caucasian world. That a beautiful "Caucasian Form" is produced by the living spirit of our- Fematrix "Caucasia" must be explained in this way, at this its highest grade, the Caucasian will objectifies itself in an "Individual" and therefore through circumstances and its own power it completely overcomes all the *Hindrances* and *Opposition* which the lower grads of "Alien Aggression" present to it.

C2557. The Alpha tells us: *Caucasian Beauty,* is an objective expression, which means the fullest objectification of will at the highest grade at which it is knowable, the Idea of a "Caucasian Race" in general, completely expressed in a sensible form*, a most- Beautiful Human Countenance.*

C2558. The Alpha tells us: Tragedy, is to be regarded, and is recognized as the summit of human Art!...on account of the greatness of its effect and the difficulty of its achievement. It speaks to the painful side of life- the triumph of *Evil!*...the fall of the- *Just* and *Innocent,* giving us the nature of our world, and its existence. It is the strife of the human will with itself through *Chance* and *Error,* which appears as the rulers of the world, personified as fate, on account of their insidiousness, which even reaches the appearance of design; partly it proceeds from Humanity itself, through the self- mortifying efforts of a few, through the wickedness and perversity of most. It is one and the same will that lives and appears in them all, but whose phenomena fights against each other and thereby destroying each other, along with the *Egoism* that fueled it.

C2559. The Alpha tells us: All true Criticism is founded in dramatic instinct. Bad Criticism is characterized either by fault-finding, or by flattery. The true aim of any and all Criticism: should not be to-*Praise*, nor to-*Compliment*, nor to-*Condemn*, but to- *Inspire!* It should always show the possibilities of the- *Ideal* in the *Actual.*

C2560. The Alpha tells us: We can all see that all phases of our "Racialness" (our life in form!) and its development of expression are intimately connected with each other. They can not be separated. If the cause of such meaning in our "Racial Character" and its historical experience had been examined, such a "Modern Liberal Perversion" of racial understanding?...would have been impossible. For the necessity of "Racial kind" must be found in the nature of living experience, for whatever there is in experience we can find some mode of revealing; and true technical work in physical expression (kind in form!) consists in finding the essential forms of experience and the corresponding fundamental actions, in developing such actions to the highest efficiency and in bringing them into harmony with other phases of experience in their manifestation of- *Kind.* For all techniques in the delivery of "Creation" must be evolved from the actions of the mind.

C2561. The Alpha tells us: Nothing can furnish a substitute for direct and definite *Practice!* preserving struggles and endeavors to reveal every emotion of the soul most effectively. Education must not be the mere acquirement of information; the acquirement of ideas must be ever followed by same kind of -*Practice.* While "to know" may be a high aim in education, "to do" and "to be" are still higher. While character or being is the highest aim of all education, "doing" must not be lowered, because it is the only mode by which knowledge can be translated into being. To know what to do and to do it enables a person to become in being what *He* or *She* is in knowledge.

C2562. The Alpha tells us: The love of "Truth" is inherent in humankind, and can be easily stimulated and cultivated; but attainment and skill in its execution, though equally inherent, requires hard work, patience and long application.

C2563. The Alpha tells us: A great *Lawyer* is not merely one who possesses great knowledge of the law; a great *Teacher* is not merely one whose head is crammed full of facts; a great *Preacher* is not one who is merely versed in all the great problems of theology; it is not the Artist alone who is measured by what he can do; every person who accomplishes great things for their "Race" is so estimated. But, above all, in every phase of oratory or expression, our *Leaders!*...not only need a knowledge of the *True,* the *Beautiful* and the *Good,* but there must be worked out an *Ideal* in their *Soul* and *Voice.* They must have skill not only to *Comprehend* ideas but to *Render* every idea and phase of experience.

C2564. The Alpha tells us: Tradition teaches indirectly more than it does directly. It shows us how others have followed a *Life Strategy*, and how they have failed, and the cause of such failure. The great use of history is to furnish a light to tell whether we are in her stream of tendency that is ever advancing, or whether we are turning aside into some current that leads us back to methods which have long since been thrown aside as hindrances. In fact, our history of methods must be studied face to face with todays "Caucasian" world, and once the truth has been decided, we must stand and defend that truth? If we being the "Caucasian Race" are to have a future?

C2565. The Alpha tells us: On the topic of- *Caucasian Racial Nobility*, and without falling into naïve idealism, we can note that "Caucasian Nobility" is not simply a matter of *Birth*, but also of -*Merit!*...not only a constant renewal, but also the transmission of a code of *Social Ethics, Cultural Rigor* and *Religious Ideals*. Therefore, the function of our "Caucasian Nobility" when it is indeed worthy of the title, is to *Command, Protect*, and offer a living example of a higher "Racial Ideal" by making it a very visible and vested phenomenon. Caucasian intellectualism has always affirmed that freedom can only be conceived in relation to *Duty*, and that service and *Human Dignity* are not opposed to each other.

C2566. The Alpha tells us: Is the Caucasian world order of the *21st* century truly in crisis?...and will its political and social elites be responsible for its demise? That said, could one go so far as to say- Treason?...a social and political path not of a *Passion* for "Caucasian Civilization" but of one's personal corruption?...caring not, and ignoring the Nations downward spiral leading to catastrophe. Are we the Caucasian American people, founders of modern liberty and freedom!...now in the hands of a committed cabal of Alien and Caucasian subversives?...their ideology resting on the insane aspirations of a- Racial Equality?...an intellectual *Fallacy* and *Fraud,* undermining logical validity. If so!...in order to alleviate this tragic assault, we as Caucasians must champion our own- *Racial Identity!(our own bio-mandate!)*

C2567. The Alpha tells us: Truth is rarely to be found in extreme *Censure* or *Applause*. We may allow to politicians of the *21st* century the keenness of their political views. But, of their *Character*?...the most opposite and contradictory estimates have been formed. By some they are esteemed nothing better than fortune hunters, by others, celebrated for their wisdom and patriotism. But, in a moral view of their *Character,* we see an excellent and ingenuous nature corrupted at length by an unvarying current of success, and a striking example of the fatal arrogance of the passions, when the eminence of fortune removes all restraint, and flattery stimulates to their uncontrolled indulgence. (therefore, we must be attentive!)

C2568. The Alpha tells us: In the first ages of the Caucasian world when *Common Sense* reigned uncontrolled by the subtleties of philosophy, primary and secondary qualities dwelt peaceably under the same roof and were joint proprietors of the same subject, Truth! Thus, the *21ˢᵗ* century unchecked by ourselves, and "Uncontrolled" by the Caucasian liberal world, this haughty disregard for the "Truth" acquired by time and strength, and by a mutual "Alien-subversive" encouragement?...a fallacious cabal of liberal zealot firmness, which the Caucasian world alone the Alpha believes must engaged and "Defeat" if humankind is to prevail.

C2569. The Alpha tells us: The man or woman in whom genius lives and works is easily distinguished by their glance, which is both keen and steady, and bears the stamp of *Perception*, of *Contemplation*. This is easily seen from the likenesses of those of genius whom nature has produced here and there among countless millions. Therefore, life's mode of "Understanding" is not the same in all *Animals,* as well as all- *Humans?*..even though the process is the same for both; the reality of *Encounter,*..knowledge of *Causality*, and the transition from *Effect* to *Cause*, and from *Cause* to *Effect*, and nothing more then what has always been called the -*Rational* and *Irrational.*

C2570. The Alpha tells us: The fundamental defect of the mode of upholding our "Caucasian Racial Inspiration" appears to consist, not in the conception itself, but in the place assigned to it in the chain of Caucasian evidences, when employed to prove, and not to confirm,- when addressed to the judgment of the understanding, not to the affections of the heart. If offered as the sole, or even leading proof, we who are racially inspired can scarcely feel-surprise at its rejection buy the *Liberal Zealot* or the Caucasian *Feckless* unbeliever. Therefore, the "Valorous" must be recognized as "Sacred" and to the Caucasian, who, with willing mind and humble acquiescence, accepts the "Valorous" as the word of "Caucasia" (our fematrix!) their testimony of the "Holy Valorous" is a precious treasure.

C2571. The Alpha tells us: he must allude to what he terms the "Caucasian Racial Spirit," or the *Historical Testimony* to which this spirit conveys to each reader of the "Holy Valorous." Its "Truths!...result from no chain of elaborate argumentation; it rests upon that living and intuitive syllogism of a "Caucasian Inherited Will." If any Caucasian is willing to do her will, they shall know of the *Spirit* which breathes the principle of Caucasian life into being.

C2572. The Alpha tells us: the very history of our *Intellect* goes back to the life of *Intellect* in our "Caucasian" western world. From this point of view the Alpha's philosophy exhibits the connection between *Science* and his *Ascetic Racial Morality.*

C2573. The Alpha tells us: the intellectual formulation and interpretation of our-*Racialness!*...perhaps the Alpha's most personal experience, he owes to his pursuit of contemplative "Racial Ideals" in other words; are we all not creatures of the will? (the fematrix!) her instrument, her light in the darkness, destined only for her service?...this is one of the greatest and profoundest of the Alpha's perceptions. Therefore, She is, and so remains.

C2574. The Alpha tells us: What, after all, is one's biological mandate?..is it not the *Fematrix* will!..which is your origin and essence, makes you demand good fortune and the enjoyment of your existence and its reproduction in kind? You, yourself are given to your self, your body is given to you, as idea in kind, as all the rest of the world is. All life has ego of kind and sees all other forms of life as masks and phantoms, and is simply incapable of ascribing anything like the same importance or seriousness to them as to itself. For the will of "Racial kind," out of which you have your being, will always defend its path through life, for to it, all eternity belongs.

C2575. The Alpha tells us: "Evil" is those persons who, so soon as no other outer power prevents them, inflicts evil. I mean a person who, not content with affirming the will to life as manifested in their own body, also denies the will manifested in other individuals and seeks to destroy their existence as soon as it is in the way of their own efforts. They regard others as *Empty*

Shells, and cherish a profound conviction that reality is an attribute of themselves alone. Therefore, one should know of them, and be on guard.

C2576. The Alpha tells us: The behavior we call *Good* and the behavior we call *Bad* are included, along with the behavior we call *Indifferent*, under the conception of behavior at large. *Conduct!*...is a whole; and, in a sense, it is an aggregate of interdependent actions performed by an organism. That division or aspect of conduct with which "Ethics" deals, is a part of this whole, a part having its components inextricable bound up with the rest. Therefore, the complete comprehension of *Conduct* is not to be obtained by contemplating the conduct of humankind only; we have to regard this as a part of universal conduct, conduct as exhibited by all living creatures. And as in other cases, so in this case, we must interpret the more developed by the less developed. Just as, fully to understand the parts of conduct which "Ethics" deals with, we must study human-kinds conduct as a whole. Furthermore, we have to regard the conduct now shown us by creatures of all orders, as an outcome of the conduct which has brought life of every kind to its present height. Thereby, advancing a step, we have to frame a conception of the evolution of our "Caucasian Conduct," as correlated with the evolution of our teleology!

C2577. The Alpha tells us: Race- maintaining conduct, like Self-maintaining conduct, arises gradually out of adjusted actions. Racial- preservation in each generation has all along depended on the preservation of offspring by preceding generations. Therefore, we Caucasians exhibit a great Progress of like "Nature," compared with other *Racial* groups, higher in our Self-maintaining conduct, and higher also in our Race-maintaining conduct. In tracing up the evolution of *Caucasian* conduct, so that we may frame a true conception of conduct in general, we have thus to recognizes these two kinds as mutually dependent. Speaking generally, neither can evolve without the other; and the highest Evolutions of the two must be reached simultaneously.

C2578. The Alpha tells us: It was "Venner" who gave us the truth of *Caucasian Tradition!*...in that its not the passed! It is the opposite, it is that which does not pass away. It comes to us from that which is most distant, but always present. It is our interior compass, the benchmark of all the norms that suit us and that have survived all that has tried to change us.

C2579. The Alpha tells us: The Caucasian people have "Painfully" discovered that different *Racial Groups* maintain their racial sensitivities, prejudices, and social behaviors, and that a Multiracial State?...is a mission impossible!...for all their attempts to manifest their Caucasian *Generosity* and *Enlightenment* has lead to *Catastrophe!* Hence, the implicit lesson is that we Caucasians exist only by that which distinguishes us, and by what is very unique to us: *Race, Lineage, History, Culture,* and *Tradition.* Yes, we as "Human Racial Groups" are beyond a doubt; *Fundamentally Different!..* as are our- *Destinies.*

C2580. The Alpha tells us: This is a substantiated reality, "Racial Equality" is a phenomena that *Life* will not entertain despite *Alien Threats* or *Liberal Reprimands,* for the world has entered a new era, the *21st* century, and faced with all the things that threaten our *Racial Identity* and our *Survival* as Caucasians, we must regain our "Identitarian Religion" by giving ourselves and our future a new awareness "Caucasianism". We possess a very rich "Racial History." So, it is up to us to rediscover, cultivate, and create a metaphysical memory of it, one that responds to and restructures the confusion of our age.

C2581. The Alpha tells us: What gives our "Racialness' permanence? If our *Racialness* survives over time, it is because it rests upon the hereditary dispositions of our ancestors, and a spiritual heritage whose origin reaches back into prehistory, through the long and combative encounters that led to the emergence of the "Caucasian World Conquest" leaving its mark of more then 40 thousand years of Caucasian *Racial* and *Cultural* identity. High lighting this true fact, is that the aesthetic perfection of Caucasian "Culture" is quite moving, there seems to be a cosmic religiousness about it, the sense of harmony between the Caucasian people and the nature of their Fematrix, (Caucasia!) Thereby, summarizing the *Traditions* and *Contributions* of the Caucasian race of people as unique to their "Civilization," both past and present.

C2582. The Alpha tells us: It is quite clear that in our *21st* century the new liberal zealot religion "Equality" that has been imposed (making it

obligatory!) on the Caucasian world community, has not begun to decline?...
this is, of course, very much in line with the collapsing decisively of the
intellectual and academic mindset on their interpretation of- *Reality?* In
addition to this, it has introduced the "Mortal Conflict" between- *Alien*
and *Caucasian* long established *Cultures* and *Traditions* passed down
with *Symbolic Meaning* and *Sacred Significance* with origins in the past.
Thereby, the consequences of this engagement will bleed into the future of
all combatants!...as they increasingly view the struggle in military terms. It
is a "Death" unto us all!

C2583. The Alpha tells us: Humankind cannot exist without a voice of-
Authority! Where, then, does the modern state, the secular state, the neutral
state, find a pertinent political voice? Unlike the America and Europe we
live in today, muzzled with *Interdictions* and *Guilt*, our ancestors who built
both these social marvels, lived in agreement with themselves and in an
environment of mental freedom that, at least before "Liberal zealotry"
which seeks to ban "Identity" and put to "Restriction" our- *Intellectual
Reasoning.* This fundamental difference with our current era explains why
the Caucasian Americans and Europeans of today, have become deprived
of their freedom to imagine their future beyond the liberal zealot system
that they now live in. But, the time is coming when the Caucasian people
will return to themselves, finding the strength to vanquish the liberal zealot
religion, (Equality?) and its failure will give way to the awakening of their
Caucasian "Identitarian Consciousness."

C2584. The Alpha tells us: That the fate of a new state will al so depend
upon the quality of the leading class. Hence, when the nobility exhibits good
conduct, the country thrives. This implies that the noble class distinguishes
itself first and foremost by the acceptance of a higher duty, which is
characteristic of all authentic aristocracy founded not on birth, but on merit
and a concern for excellence. This has nothing to do with pious wishes, but
of being conscious of what is *Necessary* and *Possible*, and which colors all
the rebellious reflections of this manifesto.

C2585. The Alpha tells us: Ideas are malleable, which predisposes them to
Fraud and *Illusion!*...therefore, the proof must rest, as in all departments of
knowledge, upon a patient examination and induction of facts; and such is

the task which lies before all Caucasians of- *Racial Faith!* For, the Alpha says: he is the interpreter of our Fematrix (Caucasia!) making use of his *Understanding* to *Manifest* the truth of her will! And he is, as it were, an instrument of "Voice," moved invisibly by her *Power,* her *Spirit*, within his soul, declaring what must be said, in the light of her truth!...which guided his writings.

C2586. The Alpha tells us: It must be implanted in every Caucasian child from the hour of their birth, the esteem ordinances of their Fematrix- "Caucasia" and to stand fast by the writings of the "Holy Valorous" and in defense of them, if need be until death.

C2587. The Alpha tells us: The invariable idea that all readers of the Holy Valorous should know: "Caucasianism" the word being understood in the sense given to it by the *Alpha* and on which one finds their proof of the unerring certainty of "Caucasian Theology" ensures that every portion of every truth, whether relating to our ancient events, or facts which occurred in the life-time of the *Alpha,* has been written under *Fematrix Inspiration;* while the direct communication from "Caucasia" of the matters the knowledge of which could not be naturally acquired by the *Alpha,* corresponds to the definition which he has assigned to- *Caucasian Revelation!*

C2588. The Alpha tells us: The words of the Holy Valorous alone, steadfast and unshaken, stamped, as it were, with the seal of our Fematrix "Caucasia" herself, remain fixed since the time it was written until now; and our hope as "Caucasians" is that for all future time it will remain immortal as long as the *Sun, Moon*, the *Universe*, and the world itself endure.

C2589. The Alpha tells us: It will be said of him; by adopting the Caucasian worlds fears of "Alien Invasion" is merely accommodating himself to the *Prejudices* of the Caucasian people; and that by this principle of accommodation are to be explained all the strong expressions employed in the Holy Valorous Respecting the authority, inspiration and history of the Caucasian world. This *Alien Subversive* and *Caucasian Renegade* objection; we as Caucasian will be entertaining for ever! So, let us put it to sleep here and now, once and for all: "Am I racially prejudice?...I would hope so!...for the sake of my people.

C2590. The Alpha tells us: It is plain, that any communication from a "Deity" to creatures of finite capacities, one of two things must happen. Either the former must raise the latter almost to its own level; or else it must suit the form of its communication to their powers of apprehension. In a word, unless the "Deity's Revelation" be meant to extend to the removal of every error, and to afford humankind an unclouded view of the "Deity's" nature, we have no reason to suppose that either our senses could perfectly take in, or the capabilities of language correctly convey such knowledge, therefore, we must believe that "Revelation" has been "Accommodated" to the *Understanding* and *Opinions* of humankind. Even the "Omnipotence" of "Caucasia" (our Fematrix!)...she observes, cannot infuse infinite conceptions into finite minds.

C2591. The Alpha tells us: Our Fematrix: "Caucasia" her eyes are said "to behold the children of her creation;" not to mention other instances, which must suggest themselves to every one, in which "Caucasia" condescends to convey to us Caucasians, not the very reality indeed, but something as near the reality as she sees it expedient for us to know. Without this species of 'accommodation 'there could be no such thing as instruction! Every instructor must begin upon ground common to their pupils, with principles presupposed as known to them, in order to extend the sphere of their knowledge to other truths.

C2592. The Alpha tells us: The importance of this subject "Caucasian Racial Sovereignty" having been declared from the earliest periods of humankind: In modern times much attention is directed to the fallacy of "Human Equality" in consequence of the use to which it has been *Distorted* and *Perverted* by "Social Rationalists" of every school. Therefore, from such *Deformity* the Alpha inferred the *Sufficiency*, the *Infallible Certainty*, and the *Perfection* of the- "Holy Valorous," and in the name of its sacred foundation, (Caucasianism!) he makes his argument against the world.

C2593. The Alpha tells us: The Holy Valorous, as a whole, is "Caucasia's" *One, Perfect,* and *Complete Instrument*; giving forth to those who wish to learn its one and only saving truth; "Caucasianism" from many truths combined; stilling and restraining all strivings of -*Seditious Liberal Fallacy.* Further, the *Alpha,* having proposed one of the most ingenious modes of harmonizing the understanding of the "Caucasian Race" which has ever been written, gives further his observation: Whether one choses to believe or not?...the Holy Valorous in all points states the truth.

C2594. The Alpha tells us: In Caucasianism!...the belief in "Racial Sovereignty" is not merely a speculative tenet; nor does it rest upon some general feeling or thought of one's *Superiority* deserving of reverence. The conviction of our- *Divine Racial Sovereignty!*...is the source of that *Faith* which the Holy Valorous unfolds, being not more firm than our conviction that the origin of the records which contain our history is in like manner sacred, with *Proofs,* equally incontrovertible, having been given of both. Thus, attempting to give some idea of the sentiments cherished in our *Caucasian* age, by the *Alpha,* and in reference to the nature and value of our sacred historical journey committed to his charge.

C2595. The Alpha tells us: In attestation of the truth and origin of the facts on which the Caucasian world community relies, no more convincing proof can be alleged than the endurance of such *Trials* and the *Triumphs* thus achieved into the 21st century, being truly: the age of -*Caucasians!*

C2596. The Alpha tells us: When a "Revelation" has been given directly, and without the intervention of "Visions" it is different; we observe a serene and unimpassioned course of thought, as in my own case. But, even here we are reminded, not withstanding all such traces of my own personality, how a "Higher Principle" molds and directs our words.

C2597. The Alpha tells us: The Holy Valorous, in short, presents the Caucasian people to our view as human Instruments through whom the spirit of our *Fematrix*-"Caucasia" speaks, and by whose lips she announces our- Oracles. From these remarks just made it follows, that the continued preservation of the Caucasian people's intelligent conscious-ness, and the elevation of their natural faculties for the reception of the Alpha's philosophy, are the true characteristics of his- *Revelation!*

C2598. The Alpha tells us: Of the 21st century; We live, and act, and think, perfectly indifferent to the reality which should convince us that the world without is a combative entity, a miracle in crisis. And, therefore respecting this want of information, the *Average Caucasian* need feel neither concern nor surprise!...it is but another example of that *Ignorance* which is the natural condition of modern- *Liberal Zealotry.* An allusion that brings us those proofs by which *Liberal Elites,* however silent as to their own inward feelings, (gated communities!) seek to convince the world of their absurd commission of- *Racial Equality?*

C2599. The Alpha tells us: As to the *Declaration* and *Truth* of- *Racial Equality?*...first, it needs to be said, that *Liberal Academic* proof of "Racial Equality" is not forthcoming! Other then a liberal epiphany? ...this being the only proof given?...because it is the only proof admissible? ...sufficiently over powering to silence every reasonable doubt, and to remove every natural scruple. Therefore, we have abundant reason to conclude that no other proof will be offered to us, exhibiting more clearly their false representation of a matter of fact, in both words and conduct, a deliberate breach of academic confidence, an *Evil Fraud!* ...being practiced in order to induce the "Caucasian World Community" to give up possession of their union of *Body* and *Soul,* the very core of their being, their- *Racial Identity!* Yes!...there is only one word, "Evil" and it most be confronted as of now!... on its profound immorality. And if we fail to war against it, and all those who have brought it to our door!...it will be beyond a doubt, a death unto us all! This is our truth, this is our reality!

C2600. The Alpha tells us: Should any difficulty arise, on the part either of the Alpha himself on receiving "Caucasia's" word, or of those to whom his commission was addressed (the Caucasian People!) as to whether her announcements were really Divine?...we are often not informed of the means by which such difficulty are dispelled. To this effect were the signs given to the Alpha, to writing, to the Caucasian people, were of a "Revelation" a reasoning in the truth of- *Life!*...that which gives it! ...and. that which removes it! And in the mind of the *Alpha,* as well as all living things, an *Imprinted Spirit?* a preexisting consciousness of their-*Creator!*...he would discover, and by contemplating her reason, her teleology in reference to his purpose?..her "Revelation" came upon him! On the other hand, when the *Alpha* does not refer to her contemplation or to the means by which it was imparted, we observe how carefully he indicates his clear appreciation of the fact, that *Ordinary Dreams* or *Visions* are altogether valueless. Therefore, in a word, the importation of the *Alpha's Revelation!* to the Caucasian people is not the object of making them morally perfect, but simply that of raising them in their teaching to be *Infallible Organs* of truth.

C2601. The Alpha tells us: It seems difficult to understand by many people, how the idea could ever have been entertained, that the deference due to the different components of *Racial Groups* is to be measured by the personal qualities of their respective- *Fematrix Authors?*..in reply to their difficulty, the *Alpha* reminds us all, of the absolute truth of the- *Biological Imperative,* its *Fematrix Absolutism!*

C2602. The Alpha tells us: for the love of the Caucasian race!...and all the it implies, let us unite as one *People,* one *Empire,* and cast off the trappings of *Alien Subterfuge* and *Caucasian Liberal Treason.* There is no going back, we must defeat this evil cabal, we must see it though to the end, for if we fail?..there will be nothing lift of us to go back to!

C2603. The Alpha tells us: If insistence of ones "Racialness" tends to unsettle established systems of belief, self-evident truths are by most people silently passed over; or else there is a tacit refusal to draw from any of them the most obvious of inferences.

C2604. The Alpha tells us: The acts required for continued self-preservation, including the enjoyment of all benefits achieved by such acts, are the first requisites to universal welfare. It has been thus with innate superiorities; it has been thus also with acquired ones. All along the law has been that increased function brings increased power; heightening and lengthening its life.

C2605. The Alpha tells us: Intellectually, progress is by no one trait so adequately characterized as by development of the idea of causation, since development of this idea involves development of so many other ideas. Before any way can be made, thought and language must have advanced far enough to render properties or attributes thinkable as such, apart from objects; which, in low stages of human intelligence, they are not. Concomitantly, there is implied the recognition of constant relations among phenomena, generating ideas of uniformity of sequence and of co-existence- the idea of natural law.

C2606. The Alpha tells us: Intellectual racial advances can go on only as fast as perceptions and resulting thoughts are made definite by the use of measures serving to familiarize the mind with exact correspondence, Truth, Certainty. And only when growing intellect accumulates examples of quantitative relations, foreseen and verified, throughout a widening range of biology, does "Racialness" (identifiable kind!) come to be conceived as necessary and universal.

C2607. The Alpha tells us: An implied truth to be here noted is; that faculties which, under given conditions, yield partly pain and partly pleasure, cannot develop beyond the limit at which they yield a surplus of pleasure; if beyond that limit more pain then pleasure results from exercise of them, their growth must be arrested.

C2608. The Alpha tells us: So necessary with our existing characters and conditions are concealments thus prompted, that they have come to form a part of moral duty; and concealment for its own sake is often insisted upon as an element in good manners. All this is caused by the prevalence of feelings at variance with social good-feelings which cannot be shown without producing discord or estrangements.

C2609. The Alpha tells us: The actions prompted by our "Racialness" are thus to be counted among those demanded by social conditions. They are actions which maintain and further the development of "Caucasian Civilization" tending ever to survival, and, therefore, actions with which there will be joined an increasing progress.

C2610. The Alpha tells us: What must be the accompanying evolution of racial conduct?...and what must the relations between "Racialism" and "Altruism" become as this form of one's social reason is neared? What is for shore, is that the scope for altruistic activities must not exceed the wellbeing of Caucasians society.

C2611. The Alpha tells us: A conclusion drawn in the "Holy Valorous" on the relativity of "Racialness" and "Life," and there emphasized as one to be borne in mind, must now be recalled. It was pointed out, that, supposing them to be consistent with our continuance of being, there are no activities which may not become sources of understanding, if surrounding conditions require persistence in them. And here it is to be added, as a corollary, that if the conditions require any class of activities to be relatively great, there will arise a relatively great understanding accompanying that class of activities.

C2612. The Alpha tells us, For our Caucasian "Public Welfare" and "Private Welfare" our union of- *Racialness* is essential, this we have seen and understand. We have seen that our- *Racial Altruistic-* co-operation, and the benefits which it brings to each and all, become high in proportion as altruistic, that is to say, our sympathetic interests extend, hence, our enlightenment!...not always about conquest.

C2613. The Alpha tells us: From the laws of life it must be concluded that unceasing *Racial Social Discipline* will so mold "Human Nature" that eventually they will come into their own true *Destiny!*...being spontaneously pursued to the fullest extent, advantageous to each and all.

C2614. The Alpha tells us: That "Racial Sovereignty" will meet with any considerable acceptance by *Liberal Zealots* is improbable. Neither with *Alien Others,* nor with current political sentiments is it sufficiently congruous. Such a view will not be agreeable to those who lament the spreading in disbelief in eternal damnation; nor to those who follow the god of brute force in thinking that because the rule of the strong hand was once good, it is good for all time. But, though *Liberals* and *Aliens* who profess "Equality" and practice racial and class "Subversion" are not sympathetic to such a view, there are some, classed as "Racists" to the current liberal creed, who may not think it absurd to believe that a rationalized version of their ethical principles of racial reality will eventually be acted upon.

C2615. The Alpha tells us: Right and Wrong?...as we can think it, necessitates the thought of not right, or wrong, for its correlative, and hence, to ascribe rightness to the acts of the "Power" manifested through phenomena, is to assume the possibility that wrong acts may also be committed by this Power. Therefore, conversations about the affairs of "Life" habitually imply the belief that every deed named may be placed under the one head (right!) or the other. (wrong!) So, too, is it with judgments on the doings of individuals; each of these is approved or disapproved on the assumption that it is definitely classable as good or bad. Even where qualifications are admitted, they are admitted with an implied idea that some such positive characterization is to be made. Nor is it in popular thought and speech only that we see this. If not wholly and definitely, yet partially and by implication, the belief is expressed by moralists.

C2616. The Alpha tells us: Scientific truths, of whatever order, are reached by eliminating perturbing or conflicting factors, and recognizing only fundamental factors. When, by dealing with fundamental factors in the abstract, not as presented in actual phenomena, but as presented in ideal separation, general laws have been ascertained, it becomes possible to draw inferences in concrete cases by taking into account incidental factors. But it is only by first ignoring these and recognizing the essential elements alone that we can discover the essential truths sought.

C2617. The Alpha tells us: Buy, and after disentangling certain funda-mental truths, it becomes possible by their help to guide actions better; and it becomes possible to guide them still better when, as presently happens, the complicating elements from which they have been disentangled are themselves taken into account. And thus we see illustrated the relation between certain absolute truths of both *Mechanical* and *Biological* science, and certain relative truths which involve them. We are shown that no scientific establishment of relative truths is possible until the absolute truths have been formulated independently. We see that biological and mechanical science, fitted for dealing with the real, can arise only after ideal biological and mechanical science has arisen.

C2618. The Alpha tells us: there are Caucasians among us who are of the blood, but not of our union?...having no cents of their "Caucasian Racial Obligation" (loyalty!) no gratitude, thankfulness or acknowledgment of the benefit they have received from their- *Caucasian Ancestral Trust.* Therefore, it must be said: that these are "Caucasian Deserters" and must be considered "Dishonorable" and "Sub-versive," and for their disgraceful crime, they must be..socially, economically and politically shunned! ...having no place in Caucasian society.

C2619. The Alpha tells us: That we as Caucasian males must not fail in our ability to resist all alien racial aggression effectively, for Caucasian males of the *21ˢᵗ* century are having their aggression weeded out?...and they are becoming genetically pacified, and receptive to liberal zealot submission. And those Caucasians who would give up their racial loyalty to purchase a little temporary safety from aliens? ...deserve neither loyalty nor safety.

C2620. The Alpha tells us: if you let someone take away your *Identity,* they are taking away your *Recognition!*...and if they take away your recognition, they take away your worth, your existence.

C2621. The Alpha tells us: Caucasian loyalty to the survival of their "Race" is mandatory!...your race is who you are, for the premise of one's *Race* is survival, and therefore *Race* is the physical and intellectual strategy of survival, the presents of a living *Need!*..a living *Will!*..a living *Direction.*

C2622. The Alpha tells us: "Truth" is the currency of the mind. Let it now be said, to all "Caucasian" both young and old, for it is the year of our fematrix "Caucasia" *2016,* and we as a race of people, both *Sovereign* and *Unique,* existing as the only kind, in both type and character, the sole example of our ancient bio-manuscript, have now reached our- Departure Apex?...the point at which we must separate from others, to go our own way! (for we are cogently and culturally incompatible) This is a natural occurrence in living organisms, and if we fail to make this choice?...our future and that of our children's will be locked in an endless battle against the emerging powers of "Competitive Alien Races" who do not see you, as them!...as you do not see them, as you! And as they, having no other path to their future but the reality of "Competitive-Predation" the hunger to defeat their competition. And as we already now know, "Alien Races" in Caucasian America and throughout the Caucasian world are now "Strategizing" to *Subdue* and gain *Mastery* over "Caucasian Societies" with the intention of destroying our *Culture* and our *Racial Identity?*...in other words, to render us *Collectively* and *Individually* disorganized and helpless, by putting to an end our "Future" and that of our "Caucasian Biological Franchise" and its- *Destiny,* and Yes! this reality is now at our threshold! And for the sake of our children!...We must *Unify*, and put an end to this- *Assault!*

C2623. The Alpha tells us: No Caucasian can afford to be disinterested in their "Government" they must be at all times, masters in their own house.

C2624. The Alpha tells us: If I take away you "Identity" I take away your "Recognition" and when I take away your recognition, I strip you of your self-worth?...and a servile, will be you fate!

C2625. The Alpha tells us: Those Caucasians who would surrender their essential "Racial Liberty" to purchase a temporary safety?...deserve neither *liberty* nor *Safety*.

C2626. The Alpha tells us: We as Caucasians both in America and throughout the world must never allow "Aliens" to infiltrate the "Institutions" of our racial union, the principle decision making bodies of our destiny.

C2627. The Alpha tells us: That loving one's racial being is far more than just a physical need, it is a spiritual necessity.

C2628. The Alpha tells us: As for Caucasian America?.. she has remained *Morally* and *Racially Crushed* as a result of the remorse imposed upon her by her Caucasian "Liberal Zealot" enemies. However, this will not last forever, the biological mandate and history of her founders has shown that nothing is ever completely unavoidable. Signs of awakening to the discarding of "Liberal Universalism" are arising all over America, evidence that Caucasians are regaining their *Path*, their sense of racial self-awareness.

C2629. The Alpha tells us: It was "Dominique Venner" who said: The Meta-physics of the unlimited, which has been the driving force behind human progress, has suddenly met its limit. (the 2 meltdowns *Fukushima* and *Chernobyl!*) Therefore, the question we must now ask is: how can we rediscover the *Apollonian* aspect of our civilization in order to counter-balance the *Promethean* excess?

C2630. The Alpha tells us: Our racialness survives over time, because it rests upon the hereditary disposition of our related peoples, and a spiritual heritage whose origin reaches back into prehistory, through the long and mysterious period that led to the emergence of the–Indo-European Caucasians.

C2631. The Alpha tells us: The Caucasian biological mandate, its living dynasty!...has become the victim of its own lack of "Identitarain Memory," but this will end, faced with great hardship to come, we will have no choice but to call upon our racial spirituality, that spirituality from which the primordial impulsion of our bio-civilization once surged. As is always the case, when truths reflection is conducted well, its analysis becomes exceedingly clear.

C2632. The Alpha tells us: Faced with all things that threaten our "Identity" and our survival as *Caucasians!*..we are losing the safeguard of an "Identitarian Religion" a *Sovereign Biological Recognition,* and there is much we can do to prevent its demise. We Caucasians as a "Bio-dynasty" possess a very rich identitarian memory, therefore, it is up to us to rediscover, cultivate, and to creat a metaphysical memory of it, one that structures and responds to the confusion of our troubled age?...hence, the Alpha's moral edict, "Caucasianism"…the "Imperium" of all things- *Caucasian!*

C2633. The Alpha tells us: Our "Caucasian Supremacy" has its origins in antiquity, some *40,000* years of *Caucasian Identity!*...this of course to some, invokes a deliberate act of provocation, but nevertheless a true fact.

C2634. The Alpha tells us: That the "Modern Nation" the the ultimate political form, is now starting to self-destruct and this shift is immense and wrought with unforeseen "Alien" events. We know that toward the end of the *20th* century, following circumstances unimaginable to the our Caucasian world community, that "Liberal Universalism" would become the official compulsory religion of a very decadent "America" by official decree, a democratic state whose political center of gravity had shifted toward an old adversary "Liberal Totalitarianism" (Communism!) with a new name for the *21st* century, "Progressivism" and who now claims its legitimacy by making its political and social worship obligatory, thereby creating "Consequences" of a magnitude that will far exceed one's rational probability of "Destruction" if not brought to a righteous end.

C2635. The Alpha tells us: Caucasian Racialness, is that which does not pass away. It is a part of us which is most distant, but always present. It is our interior compass, the benchmark of all the norms that suit us and that have survived all that has tried to defeat us.

C2636. The Alpha tells us: The implicit lesson in life, is that we all exist only by that which distinguishes us and by what is unique to us: race, clan, lineage, history, culture, and tradition, all of which are things we need as much as sunlight in order to truly live.

C2637. The Alpha tells us: That, the history of Caucasian "Liberal Zealot" behavior is like an underground river that, despite being invisible, is very real, a subterranean river of seditious incitement!

C2638. The Alpha tells us: When it comes to defending their Heart!...the Caucasian females pugnacity certainly does not compare unfavorable to its male equivalent, her powerful animalism brings with it a surge of life, an Impressive - inspiring vitality, a heroism!...is an appropriate term, a heroism without flags, and without drums. Like childrearing, it manifests itself in the silence of everyday life and in the sacred tasks by which women give rise to life within her biological mandate, her race, her kind, her soul! Yes, there is a sacred dimension to the everyday actions of women, because these actions renew life though child care, food preparation, attention to ablution, all things by which our race exists, and in which "Tradition" is transmitted by example.

C2639. The Alpha tells us: Adventure!...is neither the result of calculation nor ideology. It is its own justification, and its militant risk under the scrutiny of a higher reason knows, along with hard science, that risk, mystery, the unexpected, and the irrational are constituents of the true order of life and of real reason.

C2640. The Alpha tells us: It was "Venner" who said that "Happiness" and "Peace" cannot last without the virile determination required to protect them. The security of a race of people reside in their homogeneity, their resolution, their intelligence, and their bravery more than in miraculous weapons and treaties.

C2641. The Alpha tells us: *Politics?*...does not belong to the same order of things as the *Chivalric Ethic, Stoic Wisdom,* or *Religiosity*. It field is that of- "Power," and that of *Action* in the name of power. It is the domain of

Ambition, of *Cunning,* and of *Pitiless Fighting,* and only very rarely that of *Honor* and *Loyalty.* Fore Cynicism, Guile, and Dissimulation are the rules of the game, a fact well described in the Machiavellian Treatise.

C2642. The Alpha tells us: What is essential to reason is that "Theories" pay their way in the long run that they can be relied upon time and again to solve pressing problems and to clear up significant difficulties confronting inquirers.

C2643. The Alpha tells us: Our history of the last century has taught us that revolution, and the taking and exercising of power, are mirages that engulf the most noble of hopes. And the many leaders and radicals of our *21st* century, social militants who have political ideas will also break upon the hard bedrock of *Pragmatism!*...and without knowing it, they also hold with in them a fatal contradiction. (Idealism?)

C2644. The Alpha tells us: contrary to American and European nationalism, Caucasian nationalism is not confined to politics. One could even go as far as to say that politics isn't even a secondary concern of the *Caucasian Democratic Party,* for its religious character is "Racially Identitarian" and given priority. It rests upon the awakening of a "Caucasian Racial Consciousness," a traditional spirituality specific to the founder of "Caucasianism" and its sacred book the "Holy Valorous."

C2645. The Alpha tells us: Many of our ancient Caucasian traditions tell us that the spirits of our ancestors yet live with us and through us. This means that "Caucasia" our *Fematrix* still stands alongside those of us who consider the lagacy and unique future of Caucasian civilization to be something that is worth preserving and defending.

C2646. The Alpha tells us: Freedom from all aim, from all limits, belong to the nature of the will, which is an endless striving. Life's *Eternal Becoming,* its endless flux, characterizes the revelation of the inner nature of will. Therefore, according to all this, when the will is enlightened by knowledge, it always knows what it wills now and here, never what it wills in general; every particular act of will has its end, the whole will has none; just as every particular phenomenon of nature is determined by a sufficient cause so far as concerns its appearance in this place at this time, but the which manifests itself in it has no general cause, for it belongs to the thing-in-itself, to the groundless will.

C2647. The Alpha tells us: It is said of "Art" that it is every where at its goal. For it plucks the object of its contemplation out of the stream of the world's course, and has it isolated before it. And this particular thing, which in that stream was a small perishing part, becomes to art the representative of the whole, an equivalent of the endless multitude in space and time, a way of viewing things independent of the principle of sufficient reason. The method of viewing things which proceeds in accordance with the principle of sufficient reason is the rational method, and it alone is valid and of use in practical life and in science. The method which looks away from the content of this principle is the method of genius, which is only valid and of use in art. The first is the method of- *Aristotle*; the second is, on the whole, that of- *Plato*.

C2648. The Alpha tells us: All "Willing" arises from want, therefore from *Deficiency*, and therefore from *Suffering*. All "Human Degradation" is to be regarded as a significant challenge for Civilization and its greater good. And there has been no- *Greater Assault;* than denying humankinds right of fundamental "Truths." By taking up a disdain against classic *Rationalism* and *Intellectualism,* with deliberate malice, and surrendering to *Social* and *Moral Fallacies* Thereby intellectual recognition of "Bitter Truth" turns into hatred and contempt for "Truth" itself.

C2649. The Alpha tells us: His religion "Caucasianism" that which is also his humanity, and his interpretation of the world through the spiritual concept and philosophy of the Caucasian- *Racial Will,* his greatest asset, helps him to understand where this tendency toward unreality among Caucasian intellectuals originates from? It originates from a characteristic of the Caucasian spirit that is both its greatest asset and its most damning flaw. Creations of the Caucasian spirit are unlimited to the extent that they sometimes negate themselves to the point of self-destruction, brought about by a decisive whirlwind of- *Nihilism.* Hence, D. Venners; interpretation: Greek philosophers and mathematicians from *Plato* to *Euclid,* plus an exposition of Pythagorean science became European reason, thereby transforming this into what is now "Liberal Education," by examining its principles from the beginning and tracking down the theorems, immaterially and intellectually this method gave birth to *Caucasian European science,* which does not reduce itself to empirical measures, but goes back to the origins of the reasoning in order to base itself on hypotheses. It formulates theorems, that is to say, propositions through which it establishes truth using logical reasoning based on axioms. Finally, it implements a method utilizing a detailed and progressive procedure in order to come to the sought after conclusion. Every mathematical and physical discovery of modern science has proceeded using this method. But, it is a method that does not call upon anything Immediately Experienced?...but rather a purely abstract and intellectual process. As useful as they are, these tools tend to reduce and simplify. The complex diversity of the real world finds itself "Erased" before the enticing abstraction of the conceptual.

C2650. The Alpha tells us: Understanding the origin of the world in which we all live, has been the main effort and result of my *Historical* and *Spiritual* work. And it has always been my passion to bring "Light" (reality!) to every dark aspect of our journey. Therefore, it is simply a natural result of the human spirit, our Caucasian spirit more specifically, that has created endless abstractions: God, Fortune, Humanity, Revolution, Socialism, Democracy. Being all absolutes for whom, humankind has killed and died giving their lives in the defense of meaning, that which represents their- *Race, Culture, Religion* and *Beliefs*, all that created them, and sustain them. This is not the result of some mental pathology, quite the contrary, it is the result of all normal human behavior. For we exist solely through the representations of ourselves, of existence and its purpose. That said, the intensity of this need for representation varies extensively between *Racial Groups* as well as their *Individuals.* If we rule out the *Pretenders* and *Opportunists*, sincere Caucasians live for their ideas, ideas they want more than anything to become absolute, since these are the only lenses through which they can perceive the world.

C2651. The Alpha tells us: What is the source of the *21st* century's tendency toward political extremism among its liberal intellectuals. (liberal zealotry?) We must take the hysteria of liberal types, especially in periods of collective violence and excitement, into consideration. We must also consider the fascination with political *Power* and *Strength* that enthralls so many *Academic Socialists* to yield before the intoxication of violence. Things in the not to distant future, particularly the actions by those Caucasians with a sensibility for their own survival have passed on to their posterity the belief that words are mirror images of reality, and that "Liberal Social Theory" is not superior to either *Reality* or *Experience.*

C2652. The Alpha tells us: His honor is bound to the *Survival* and *Prosperity* of his *Race.* (sovereign biological mandate!) The harmony between the "Caucasians" and the "Cosmic Order" is at the heart of their- Odyssey.

C2653. The Alpha tells us: The incomparable richness of our- *Caucasian Spirit!-...*is ever present, as it continues with its preparations for the conquest of the- *Universe!*

C2654. The Alpha tells us: They are the radiant, uncontrolled forces before which everything submits, forces which bend to passion and fear,..they are- *Love* and *Death!* For by them, we are all free of illusions, for no other life awaits us.

C2655. The Alpha tells us: We of the Caucasians world community cannot understand the enigmas of the world in which we live without first understanding the events from which it was born. Moreover, we have shown that our Caucasian historical reflection is an indispensable response to the deadlocked thinking of our age, of the *21st* century and the vital necessity of awakening our Caucasian memory.

C2656. The Alpha tells us: Are we the Caucasian world community, hastening our own demise? Does our history also have an instructive function?...and the answer is- Yes!...to both, our history is not just knowledge of the past, it is a reflection of the preoccupation of the present.

C2657. The Alpha tells us: Humankind has always wondered who they are? And they have always answered this question by implicitly invoking their *Race, Language, Religion,* and *Customs,* that is to say their "Identity" and their *Tra-dition.* Being of a people, a "Racialness" is one's very biological root of necessity, their anchor of destiny.

C2658. The Alpha tells us: A human group is not a *Race of People* unless it shares an alike common origin, with a specific biological mandate, (life strategy!) being both in *Form* and *Intellect*. Every race of people have unto themselves a personal way of relating to *Time* and *Space,* and, through the form they inherit, every *Race* has its own path!

C2659. The Alpha tells us: Caucasian "History" undertakes an *Educational Path,* for the benefit of future generations. Therefore, we as Caucasians must take everything history has to offer in order to see the present clearly so as to properly anticipate the future.

C2660. The Alpha tells us: We are all laborers together with our fematrix "Caucasia" for it is her spirit which breathes the principle of Caucasian life into the being of man, of which her proper sense was wanting. Her "Truth" must rest, as in all departments of knowledge, upon a patient examination and induction of facts; and such is the journey that lies before *Sceptic* or *Unbeliever.*

C2661. The Alpha tells us: in the new world of the *21st* century, politics will become likened to religion with all the trappings of a *Righteous Cult!...* and at the heart of this cabal will be a sinister intellect "Caligulaism" a journey into the depts of *Social, Political* and *Moral Degradation,* a path so ideologically "Regressive" that- *Reality!..*is cased out, and where the ruse of - *liberal zealotry-* has become king.

C2662. The Alpha tells us: What, allowed the formulation of *Consciousness?* (life!) And he speaks to consciousness as being an accident of encounter?... in other words, its creation has no author, creation without intent! (by chance.) Therefore, this consciousness (life!) may be of a single occurrence, a one of a kind!...and by the looks of it, never again! And, what tells him this, is the single fact that all known consciousness is born of a single sovereign thing, and though it has taken many forms, it is never the less one living thing!..of which its formulation process (sub-dimentional atomic matter) of which is called in *Caucasian Science-* "Biology." And to which we have absolutely never encountered an other!...of which is comprised of a different subdimensional atomic formulation. (Alien life form!) Hence, bringing the light of reason to the fact, that we may be the only 'life," the only "Conscious-ness" in form.

C2663. The Alpha tells us: Every one fears that which they don't understand!...and the currency of this truths lies in the fact that "Fear" is what checks *Motion* and *Thought*, it is the guardian, the gate keeper of all life, and more than any other emotion, it gives life a greater chance for longevity.

C2664. The Alpha tells us: Of the many old "Social States" of *Human Civilization,* one may go so far as to say, most have been responsible for their own demise. And, as for the Caucasians world community of the *21st* century, it seems that nothing is being done to stop their *Social* and *Economic* destruction!...It now seems, that the declared fruits of "Democracy" have been misstated!...and the double evolution of *Liberty* and *Technology* is not the treasure of our Caucasian civilization, but of its- *Corruption!* Therefore, having stated these facts, and realizing our Caucasian future rests on the sane aspirations of our young generation who will have to creat a new "Caucasian Civilization" based on our- *Caucasian Racial Merit!*..combined with a declaration of our total "Separation," from all Caucasian- *Liberal Zealots,* who sponsored and created "Strongholds" (Sanctuary- Cities!) for accommodating - Alien Invaders!..a "Treason" unto our death! Therefore, if for any reason we "Caucasians" of the *21st* century, should fail to *Challenge,* and *Defeat* this liberal cabal, and their-*Alien Predators,*..we will deserve not pity, but, in the annals of our history- *Forever Shamed!*

C2665. The Alpha tells us: It is the *21st* century of our "Caucasian-Dynasty" (Biological-Mandate!) and the dreams of- *Cohabitation?*... by "Liberal Zealots" with alien beings- *Negroids, Mongoloids* and *Amerindians,* has proven to be an exercise in *Racial Malevolence!*...a social and cultural state of -*Smoldering* ill will, and *Vindictive* rancor. And the unpardonable omission of the liberal community to admit their ideological failure (unabated racial equality!) having now proved to be an absolute- *Fraud!*... and a liberal zealot conspiracy to reintroduce "Com-munism" under its new name- "Progressivism," but in reality, the Alpha thinks it a highbred, of both- *Equalitarian,* and *Egalitarian,* with a touch of- *Caligulaism,* bringing it full circle!..this by close analysis will prove to be its true form, thereby, putting the "Caucasian world community" on a course to recovering their *Social,* and *Cultural* mastery!..and their true sovereign racial sense of-

Dignity, and *Destiny.*

C2666. The Alpha tells us: The only form of reasoning that the "Liberal Zealot System" is unable to suppress is that which rejects their bogus religion of "Equality," but, in spite of patriotic howling, Caucasian Americans are no more masters of their destiny than any other Caucasian world states, (Europe!) who has given its "Future" to the liberal zealots, and who have also been dissolved in the liberal caldron of social and cultural madness. Therefore, to avoid the suzerain power of the liberal zealot political and cultural reversion (communism!) now "Progres-sivism," it is essential for all "Caucasian" throughout the world to unite, in the name of their- *Sovereign Racial Dynasty!*...once this expression is freed in the Caucasian heart!.. anything is possible. This is why it is important to believe in the merits of an authentic- *Biological Racial Mandate!*, and that of it life strategy- *Caucasianism!*

C2667. The Alpha tells us: We must rediscover our fading "Caucasian Tradi-tions." And once recovered, we must make them- *Permanent.* When traditions survive over time, it is because they rest upon the *Hereditary Dispositions* of related people, and their racial heritage, whose origins reach back into prehistory, through the long and brutal period that lead to the emergence of our- *Caucasian Racial Dynasty!*

C2668. The Alpha tells us: Perennial traditions are unique to all civilizations, they include: *Language, Religion, Art, Politics, Science, Education, and Defense,* all these to be universally accessed, under the heading of-*Culture!* Which, is the living treasure of all humanity, for one's culture is the "Harvest," that which gets us through the *Droughts* of our understanding, and the *Compass* for our path through the wilderness of life. Yes!..Culture: *Gifts!*..payed for by the past, for our journey into the future.

C2669. The Alpha tells us: We must always believe in the future of the Caucasians people, we know without a doubt that the Caucasian people have within them the fortitude and discipline required to lead the world to a better future. We desire a *New Order* in which all Caucasians throughout the world exist as pillars of the "Caucasian Empire," the State, which in turn guarantees them both rights and justice. Furthermore, we reject the

"Egalitarian Lie," and we bow before the hierarchy of "Caucasia" our *Fematrix!*..she being the *Light* and *Circle* of our nature. We desire a population rooted in the spirituality of "Caucasianism" and all that it implies, for this is our testament, which sheds light on what motivates us, and our actions.

C2670. The Alpha tells us: The- *Spirituality* and *Nobility* of "Caucasianism" must become the *Moral* and *Ideological* current in the-*Caucasian World!* Thereby, uniting all of the Caucasian world into an unbreakable community, which by it conduct and its action, will serve the- *Caucasian Empire!* Creating the *Warriors* and *Leadership,* they will require.

C2671. The Alpha tells us: It is the *21st* century, and we are on a crucial mission of regeneration within our- *Caucasian Race!...Yes!*..our race, and beyond the obvious political aims, our acts of sacrifice will serve to cleans our people from the blemish of our enemies regime- *So Say We All!*

C2672. The Alpha tells us: It is the *21st* century, and we the Caucasian patriots seek a new *Nobility!*...for in the halls of those who have pledged their loyalty?..there resides-*None?* All!..to the man, have betrayed us!...all have taken their "Coin" in the name of "Equality," (a fraud!) all have turn their backs, on the fate of their blood!...there can be no- *Reconciliation!*... *by their conduct, so shell we know them.*

C2673. The Alpha tells us: Liberal Zealot- "Intellectuals," particularly those from "America" have passed on the belief that their- *Social Concepts?*...are mirror images of reality, and they posit that theory is infinitely superior to both *Reality* and *Experience*. Therefore, it can reasonably be stated, that without a doubt, this is how every liberal zealot abstraction and political utopia functions. Hence, the liberal intellectual knows, or rather thinks he or she knows, what others do not. They rarely consider reality as such, by the observation of *Events, Experience,* and *Induction,* all of which they would consider contemptible. Observing the distortion of "Equality" reasoning through abstraction in a mentally agile liberal zealot intellectual discourse is both fascinating and frightening. The instant they tie their reasoning to an uncertain assumption, the conversation is over.

C2674. The Alpha tells us: Let us now speak to the perils and detriment of -*Fascism?*(dictatorship!) The ancient order of "Manorialism" the abeyance and absolut rule of *One-* over *Many! Practiced* and *Found,* in both *Past* and *Present* world states. The tendency toward "Radical Fascism" by those who see the rise of- *Liberal Totalitarianism?*...always harkens back to liberal social pontification, and their fallacy of "Equality." But, the disregard of all human rights, by- *Absolute Rule?*..is not by any means the answer. For when it comes to the lives, politics, ethics, and religions of the *Caucasian State-* our empirical world, (which has been *Rejected* by the liberals!) makes for a good antidote, that is to say, that the remaking of the- *Caucasian World Order!*..which is found in the- "Ḥoly Ɒalorous" and to which is of unquestionable "Truth" established and proven by reason shell not allow or tolerate the importation of *Liberal Zealot* doctrines of cultural or political- *Fantasy!*...(equality?) A social theater far removed form the norms of reality.

C2675. The Alpha tells us: The future of our "Caucasian Dynasty" (our destiny!) must not know failure because of an unforeseen or unattended to: *Opposition!*, nor should we when confronted with *Radicals,* united for our *Destruction!*, give a Soft response? Remember this!...in order to Neutralize Caucasian *Political* and *Cultural* strength, liberal zealot Caucasians (subversive betrayers!) have conspired with our "Enemies" to initiate "Mass Alien Immigration" in order to fracture the "Caucasian American Dynamic" and to destroy its homogenous- *Racial Identity!* Therefore, can there be any doubt as to our future?...if we as "Caucasians" do not act to counter this sinister "Liberal methodology" for our total defeat, and brutal- *Annihilation?*

C2676. The Alpha tells us: Deprived of the protective powers of a coherent- *Caucasian Nation?*...the Caucasian people will become the "Proletariats" of the modern world, for when a people submit to the "Disfranchising" of their "Identity," they forfeit all rights to any and all status. For one's 'Identity" is the mark of their *Bio-ideology,* which determines their- *Physical Appearance, Behavior, Mental Investment,* and *Bio-collective* (their community!) all being a representation of their- *Fematrix Life Strategy!*

C2677. The Alpha tells us: The *21ˢᵗ* century is going to be the final fork in the road for- *Humanity?*...the most important contest for our adherence to the "God" of reality! And doing what is required for "Supremacy" in life's arena for "Survival," and the continuation of the- *Victors Journey!*

C2678. The Alpha tells us: We "Caucasians" as a race of people, can only maintain the future *Liberty* of ourselves and that of our posterity through the sovereignty of a great *Caucasian Nation!*...a unity of our kind, a unity compelled by our *Bio-mandate*, to know what we must become, to forge our own destiny.

C2679. The Alpha tells us: When encountering the liberal zealot strategy of– Universal Equality?...one must always take into account, the law of - Unintended Consequence? This of course, is do in part to the fact that "Equality" in life?...has no place!...and will never have a place, for you see life does not smile upon equality, and nor will it reward it, for life has but one unavoidable purpose- "Fematrix Survival" through the- *Conquest of all she Encounters!*

C2680. The Alpha tells us: Intellect!...can only advance when there is- *Encounter?*...that which *Resists* or *Blocks* the path of the desired need! ...hence, "Creation" (form!) the answer to- Encounter.

C2681. The Alpha tells us: That of the many intellectual malfunction of the *21*st century, it is the "Willful Blindness" of the socially feckless liberal community to recognizes the living character of both "Superiority" and "Inferiority" in the arena of biological life's engagement. This of course having given rise to that most fallacious of liberal social monoliths "Equality" Yes!...this liberal zealot handout that discusses life's common- *Truths?*...putting them to intellectual assault under the ruse of critical thinking along with the swamp of religious morality, thereby disregarding the living historical drive, by that which life feels and by that which life wills...the faculty for a higher mental capacity, hence, a higher social order- *Unequal Competitive Survival!*

C2682. The Alpha tells us: What is one's truth?...giving way to the wisdom of- *Schopenhauer!*...Our conceptions, created out of the phenomenal world, out of a highly conditioned point of view, are, as a critical and discriminating philosophy admits, applicable in an immanent, not in a transcendental sense- that is, they deal with knowledge vouchsafed to us in time, space and causality, and are conditioned by these, instead of being obtained by applying reason upon itself. The subject matter of our thinking, and indeed the judgments we build up on it, are inadequate as a means of grasping the essence of things in themselves, the true essence of the world and of life it self. Even the most convinced, the most deeply experienced definition of that which underlies the manifestation, does not avail to get at the root of things and draw it to the light. What alone encourages the spirit of humanity in its persistent effort to do this is the necessary assumption that their own very being, the deepest thing in them, has the same universal basis, that it must of necessity root therein; and that accordingly they may be able to draw from it some data wherewith to clarify the relation of the world of phenomena with the true essence of things.

C2683. The Alpha tells us: That above all things, we "Caucasians" must distinctly recognize that the form of the phenomenon of will, the form of life or reality, is really only the "Present" not the future or the past. The latter are only in the conception, existing only in the connection of knowledge, so far as it follows the principle of sufficient reason,…for no person today has ever lived in the past, and none will live in the future; the *Present* alone is the form of all life, and is its sure possession which can never be taken from it. The *Present* always exists, together with its content, both remain fixed without wavering, for *Life* is firm and certain in the will, and the *Present* is firm and certain in life.

C2684. The Alpha tells us: Dogmas change and our knowledge can be deceptive; but the "Fematrix" never errs, her procedure is sure, and she never conceals it. Everything is entirely in her, and she is entire in everything. She has her center in every brute. She has surely found her way into existence, and she will surely secure her way through it. In the meantime humanity lives, fearless and without care, in the presence of "Annihilation," supported by a conscious-ness which lays aside the truth of their obligation to her teleology, but she fears not, for all are of her, and thus between desiring and attaining, all of life are subject to her through birth. Hence, it arises that humankind is still not properly "Conscious" of their Fematrix?...her blessings and advantages they possess, nor do they praise her living truth?..

and it will be this dereliction of worship to her sacred personage, that will have dire consequences in the end.

C2685. The Alpha tells us: All living things are bounded by their- *Fematrix will!*...the world, in all the multiplicity of its parts and forms, is the manifestation, the objectivity, of the one (her!) will to live. Existence itself, and the kind of existence, both as a collective whole and in every part, proceeds from the- *Fematrix Will Alone.*

C2686. The Alpha tells us: Among civilized nations we find throughout two different kinds of metaphysics, which are distinguished by the fact that the one has its evidence in itself, the other outside itself. Since the metaphysical systems of the first kind require reflection, culture, and leisure for the recognition of their evidence, they can be accessible only to a small number of people; and, moreover, they can only arise and maintain their existence in an advanced civilization. On the other hand, the system of the second kind is exclusively for the great majority of people who are not capable of thinking, but only of believing, and who are not accessible to reasons, but only to authority. To the distinction between the meta-physics of the first and of the second kind, we must add the following; a system of the first kind, thus a "Philosophy" makes the claim, and has therefore the obligation, in everything that it says, to be true, for it appeals to thought and conviction. A "Religion" on the other hand, being intended for the innu-merable multitude who, since they are incapable of examination and thought, would never comprehend the profoundest and most difficult truths, has only, the obligation to be true believers. But!...the Alpha gives us sight into this unutterable depth of conflict between *Truths Reason* (contemplative reality!) and *Needs Goal* (faiths fulfilment!) the pleasure and security we receive from both, and the consolation which both affords, is to the Alpha: the greatest of intellectual unions- *Truth* and *Faith!*...hence, one's *Sovereign Racialness,* one's *Sacred Biological Dynasty,* a Caucasian-*Spiritual* and *Intellectual* mandate, a purpose in *Reality* and *Faithfulness* –"Caucasianism."

C2687. The Alpha tells us: That the beginning of the *21ˢᵗ* century will host the final act or process of a- *Course Correction*...for "Humankind." This will prove to be unworthy of- *World Peace!*...and without such a peace, no true human wellbeing is possible. Hence it arises that, "War" between the "Races" will come to us of its own accord. For this is the result of the completely expressed character of the human species. (Conquest!) It is true that both *Experience* and *History* teach us to know the fate of *He* or *She* that betrays their obligation and duty to their sacred- *Racial Dynasty!* (Biological-*Mandate!*) this, being an *Unforgivable Treachery*, having the rightful and dire consequences of- *Exile* or *Death!*

C2688. The Alpha tells us: contrary to the popular beliefs of the *21st* century?...we are all born into this world "Obligated" to our "Ancestral Trust," (our inherited life strategy!) and must learn to control the *Time* and *Place* we inhabit, for the benefit of our- *Caucasian Sovereign bio-Dynasty.*

C2689. The Alpha tells us: Among many Caucasians there is confusion about the use of - Racial Communication. What's missing when they communicate with other race's is the depth which "Historical Experience" brings to the encounter. No one expects our young people to be anointed with that special depth at such an early age, but many of them being of the- *Liberal Zealot Persuasion*- act as if they have it?...and lecture others as if they were Dullards. The pity is, many of them never understand or admit that their unnatural "Blind Alien Appeasement" is the problem.

C2690. The Alpha tells us: Some people, both alien and Caucasian alike, try to control others by dominating all aspects of the- *Racial Narrative* and *Conversation,* by using manipulative techniques, such as "Collective Guilt" and its handmaiden, "Shame" to creat an emotional pathway to a subversive political fraud!..*Equality Reparations?*..led by a cabal of - *Liberal Zealots* and *Alien* cultural saboteurs.

C2691. The Alpha tells us: It is much tougher in this *21st* century to be "Racially Charismatic," having a compelling love for one's race, and its attractiveness of devotion and inspiration. In fact, much of our Caucasian charisma lies in our "Intellectual Distance" between us and all other forms life, not from a point of arrogance, but of truth, we have after all, weathered the grueling gauntlet of life's dangers, engaging both its *Intimidating,* *Frightening* and relentless wrath. Yes!..We are the Caucasians, we have earned our place in this world.

C2692. The Alpha tells us: A Caucasian who can induce others to cooperate and do effective team work or inspire others so that they become more active in our "Caucasian Community" is a person of merited respect and praise.

C2693. The Alpha tells us: Gave a person the sort of work that harmonizes with their nature, and the best there is in them will exert itself.

C2694. The Alpha tells us: Above the mantel of leadership, lies the core of all societies and it consists of two Class's by reason of common attributes (qualities or traits) one is the "Promoter" and the other is the "Caretaker." The Promoter type makes an able *Salesperson* and *Organizer*. The Caretaker type makes an excellent *Conservator* of assets after they have been accumulated, Both are persons of intense *Action,* but they express it in different ways. There can be as much *Action* in *Preparation*, in most undertakings, as in *Execution*.

C2695. The Alpha tells us: If one is in business with others, one should analyze them as well as one's self and endeavor to see that each person takes the part for ways in which his or her temperament and native ability best fits them.

C2696. The Alpha tells us: Because of the dual constitution of all things, in labor as in life, there can be no cheating. For the real price of labor is knowledge and virtue, where of wealth and credit are signs.

C2697. The Alpha tells us: Generosity, in our Caucasian society, is a willingness to help others without expectation of direct compensation with full understanding that such help develops a positive character in the one rendering it and is, therefore, adequate reward within itself.

C2698. The Alpha tells us: Cause and effect!...It means the ability to recognize the fact that there is a cause for every effect, understanding that, in turn, leads to the discovery of the fact that those who form the habit of doing more then they are paid to do will eventually be paid for more then they do.

C2699. The Alpha tells us: One's definite purpose in life must be in harmony with one's training and education. If the definite purpose is out of proportion to one's ability, then it is obvious that greater ability must be developed before one can hope to attain the object of that purpose.

C2700. The Alpha tells us: Life shrinks or expands in proportion to one's courage. Hence, if you think you are beaten, you are; if you think you dare not, you don't; if you like to win, but you think you can't, it is almost certain you won't. Life's battles don't always go to the stronger or faster, and sooner or later the one who wins, is he or she who thinks they can.

C2701. The Alpha tells us: If you demand nothing out of the ordinary of yourself, then that is all you will get out of this world, we find success begins with one's will, it's all in the state of mind, to get more, be sure to demand more of yourself.

C2702. The Alpha tells us; One's Caucasian racial loyalty is to be regarded, and is recognized as the summit of our *Cultural, Moral* and *Spiritual* mandate! It is one and the same *Caucasian Will!*...that lives and appears in us all. I can therefore do no more than state here, at the conclusion of the "Holy Valorous" which has been principally devoted to the consideration of both the "Caucasian Racial Dynasty" and our *Imperial Fematrix* - "Caucasia" and my humble expla-nation of her marvelous creation the- "Caucasians" and the history and glory of the their "Truth," which satisfies myself, thereby leaving the acceptance or denial of my view to the effect produced upon each of my *Caucasian Readers!*...both by truth itself and the whole system of thought commu-nicated in my work. Moreover, I regard it as necessary, in order to be able to assent with full conviction to the exposition of the significance of my *Truth* which I have given, that one should often listen to Truth with constant reflection upon my theory concerning it, and for this again it is necessary to be very familiar with the whole of my system of thought, and which will doubtless be equally evident to any one who has followed me thus far and has understood and agrees with my view of "Life," its *Meaning*, its *Journey,* and its *Destiny* in our world. And, above all!...let us not loss the will and faith to embrace and defend our "Greatness" as a *Sovereign Racial Dynasty!*... centered around the throne of our "Fematrix" (Caucasia!)

C2703. The Alpha tells us: Anything we Caucasians can imagine, we

Caucasians can make real! Therefore, We as Caucasians, must not invest our "Future" into that which has no *Return?*...or put our "Faith" into that which has no *Presence?*

C2704. The Alpha tells us: All of human "Life," and all of its *Encounters* and *Outcomes*, are decided by three vital investments, the *Physical*, *Intellectual* and *Spiritual*. These will ultimately determine the human journey, and their "Fate" can only be, one of two!...Their: Teleology or Immortality?

C2705. The Alpha tells us: In the *Principles* of *Psychology*, it was shown that necessarily, throughout the animate world at large, "*Pains* are the correlatives of actions injurious to the organism, while *Pleasures* are the correlatives of actions conducive to its welfare. At the very outset, life is maintained by persistence in acts which conduce to it, and desistance from acts which impede it; and whenever sentiency makes its appearance as an accompaniment, its forms must be such that in the one case the produced feeling is of a kind that will be sought *Pleasure;* and in the other case is of a kind that will be shunned- *Pain*. Hence, the 𝔄lphas- hypothesis of "Evolution," that races of sentient beings (the Sisterhood!) could have come into existence under no other conditions.

C2706. The Alpha tells us: Fit connections between acts and results must establish themselves in all living beings, even before Consciousness (transcendence!) arises; and after the rise of "Conscious Transcendence" these connections can change in no other way than to become better established.

C2707. The Alpha tells us: So it is as humankind ascends from savage to civilized and form the lowest among the civilized to the highest. Of course the implication is that a race of people thus reaches the limit of evolution, exists in a society congruous with their nature, is a race of people among a people similarly constituted, who are severally in harmony with that social environment which they have formed. This is indeed, our- *Caucasian Dynasty's Legacy*.

C2708. The Alpha tells us: The truth that the Ideal Caucasian Man or Woman is one, in whom their racial understanding is perfect, or approaches nearest to perfection, becomes, when translated into their "Racial Spirituality" (Cauca-sianism!) the truth that *He* or *She* is one in whom the "Destiny" of their "Racial Dynasty" is duly fulfilled.

C2709. The Alpha tells us: Where one's racial understanding is small, this is very imperfect and soon one's "Identity" is cut short; and lost in the wilderness of- *Alien Deception.*

C2710. The Alpha tells us: The human challenge- "Truth"- *The Informed- The Ill-informed- The Uninformed!..alas;* in life there are many "Treasures" but, by far the greatest in either *Need* or *Possession* is- Truth! It is the "Fulcrum" of all intellectual encounter, and the- *Supreme Broker-* in all human conflict and its outcome. Look towards a greater tomorrow, for tomorrow is the threshold of your future.

-May You Always Be In Possession Of The -Truth!-

"Blessed Are The Caucasians"

John Rolland The Alpha (loc)

The
-Caucasian Dynasty-
- Ethnic States-

The Alpha tells us: the history of our Caucasian *Dynasty* and its *Ethnic States,* spans some forty thousand years and several continents. Their languages, art, and academic interests have given the human spirit *Inquiry*, *Focus, Determination* and *Resolve!*...all this leading to the greatest single endeavor in all of living biology: the rise of the- *Caucasian Dynasty!*, and its unprecedented- *World Conquest!* Yes!...this world is without previous instance; having never before *Known* or *Experienced* the likes of the emergence of the "Caucasians," being truly biologically unexampled, unlike anything previously known.

Therefore, speaking of our "Caucasian Emergence", it becomes necessary to refer to the existence and formation of our collective ethnic behavior and its indispensable part of our inevitable *Racial Nature* and its compelling force of competitive "Ethnic States" that has and will continue to come together, and shape the lives and futures of all upon this magnificent- Earth!

-We Are The Caucasians,...Behold Our Truth-

"Caucasianism"
-Non Shall Break Faith,...So Say We All-

- Our -
Caucasian Dynasty's Ethnic States

Both
-Past And Present-

Greece-   Germany-   Italy-   France-   Spain-
Sweden- Poland- Bulgaria- Denmark- England-

Turkey-Romania- San Marino- Iran- Russia-
Iraq- Norway- Portugal- Yugoslavia- Jordan-
Scotland- Ukraine-Netherlands- Bosnia-
Hungary- Wales- Switzerland- Albania- Czech
Republic- Turkey- Israel- India- Kosovo- Cyprus-
Finland- Serbia- Moldova- Macedonia- Belarus-
Lithuania- Slovakia- Estonia- Croatia- Belgium-
Slovenia- Armenia-Austria- Iceland- Montenegro-
Georgia-Egypt- Malta- Syria- Monaco- Canada-
Luxembourg- Andorra- Latvia- Ireland- America-
Saudi Arabia- Liechtenstein-Lebanon- Australia-
Illyria- Byzantium- Sumerian-Hittite- Akkadian-
Phoenicia- Etruscan- Avers- Ottoman- Anatolia-
Celtiberian- Kurdistan- Carolingian-Syracuse-
Pakistan- Carthage- Samnite- Persian- Sasanian-
Pomerania- Roman- Salmonid- Trojan- Scythian-
Varangian- Vandal- Bangladesh- Saxon- Finland-
Ostrogoth's- Liburnia- Parthian- Mesopotamia-

"And all others of legend"
- 40 Thousand Years -
"Caucasians All"

CPSIA information can be obtained
at www.ICGtesting.com
Printed in the USA
BVHW030318060319
541705BV00036B/259/P